TODAY'S SPECIAL

TODAY'S SPECIAL

20

LEADING CHEFS
CHOOSE

100

EMERGING CHEFS

CONTENTS

INTRODUCTION

Today's Special has been an incredibly inspiring project to develop and put together. We selected twenty culinary icons and leading voices in kitchens around the world—ten women and ten men. We asked each of them to choose five emerging chefs from among those they felt were the most exciting rising stars paving the future of the industry.

The resulting emerging chef list here is quite diverse, with contributors from many different backgrounds. From America to Africa, Sweden to Slovenia, Chile to China, the book represents the brightest talents from all over the globe. There are chefs with exclusive tasting menus, chefs with local bistros, and even some who are admired for their pop-ups or rolling dinner series.

In 2009, Phaidon published an unprecedented guide to the most exceptional talent in the international restaurant world. This was the bestselling *Coco*, and in fact, some of those nominated chefs are nominators in *Today's Special*. For that enticing and enduring volume, then lesser-known promising chefs, including Skye Gyngell, Hugh Acheson, Alex Atala, April Bloomfield, and David Chang, were nominated years before they became the culinary superstars they are today. Phaidon created a true classic. We hope we have achieved the same goals with our new book, on an even bigger scale, providing fascinating insights into the dazzling range of culinary creatives working today. Like the chefs themselves, the recipes are not uniform in style. To preserve the voices and personalities of the chefs, we have presented them much in the form in which they were submitted.

This book came together before our world changed. The restaurant industry has been hit very hard, and now these pages contain an extraordinary source of hope in the innovative and determined spirit of those sustaining our culinary future. *Today's Special* is a who's who of who's next in the global dining world—men and women making their distinctive marks across continents, techniques, and styles. They will continue their stories by reopening their restaurants, reimagining them, or paving new courses forward; they are indeed leaders among the exciting ones to watch. Even if these chefs were going through very difficult times, they still provided us with the last recipes and images to complete the book, proving once again how resilient and passionate chefs are and what a powerful community they compose.

The publication of *Today's Special* is a celebration of an endlessly dynamic industry that has, most recently, shown courage and solidarity in the face of great challenges. With it I hope we lift up both the people in the industry and their fans as we join in paying tribute to the young creators who remain eminently influential in their generation's future.

Emily Takoudes
Executive Commissioning Editor

20 LEADING CHEFS/ 100 EMERGING CHEFS

HUGH ACHESON

ALEX CHEN
MATT HARPER
MEI LIN
FLYNN MCGARRY
RYAN SMITH

PALISA ANDERSON

BEN DEVLIN
THOMAS FREBEL
MAT LINDSAY
NATALIE PAULL
JASON SAXBY

JOSÉ ANDRÉS

CARLOTA CLAVER
DULCE MARTÍNEZ
VICTOR MORENO
JOHNNY SPERO
AITOR ZABALA

SELASSIE ATADIKA

SUZANNE BARR
MICHAEL ELÉGBÈDÉ
MONIQUE FISO
DIEUVEIL MALONGA
OMAR TATE

DANIEL BOULUD

DAVE BERAN
GAVIN KAYSEN
JAMES KENT
PATRICK KRISS
MELISSA RODRIGUEZ

RAQUEL CARENA

NATALIA CROZON
JUAN JOSÉ
    MARQUÉS GARRIDO
AMAIUR MARTÍNEZ
    ORTUZAR
TOYOMITSU NAKAYAMA
CAROLE PEYRICHOU

MAY CHOW

DANIEL CALVERT
ROSETTA LIN
DIEGO ROSSI
PRATEEK SADHU
KWANG UH

DOMINIQUE CRENN

BÉRANGÈRE BOUCHER
MANOELLA BUFFARA
MARTINA CARUSO
MACARENA DE CASTRO
ANTONIA KLUGMANN

SKYE GYNGELL

DANIELLE ALVAREZ
CLARE DE BOER &
    JESS SHADBOLT
JAMES HENRY
MERLIN LABRON-JOHNSON
JOSH NILAND

MARGOT HENDERSON

NEIL BORTHWICK
PAMELA BRUNTON
JEREMY CHAN
MIA CHRISTIANSEN
JAMES FERGUSON

DAVID KINCH

MATTHEW KAMMERER
CHIHO KANZAKI &
    MARCELO DI GIACOMO
PIM TECHAMUANVIVIT
BRADY WILLIAMS
JUSTIN WOODWARD

JESSICA KOSLOW

EVAN FUNKE
THI LE
NORMA LISTMAN &
    SAQIB KEVAL
JAMIE MALONE
ANNA POSEY &
    DAVID POSEY

DAVID MCMILLAN

ANNIE BRACE-LAVOIE
FANNY DUCHARME
ZACH KOLOMEIR
JESSICA NOËL
CARLA PEREZ-GALLARDO &
    HANNAH BLACK

VIRGILIO MARTÍNEZ

JORDAN KAHN
PÍA LEÓN
JUAN LUIS MARTÍNEZ &
    JOSÉ LUIS SAUME
OSWALDO OLIVA
SEBASTIÁN PINZÓN
    GIRALDO & JAIME
    RODRÍGUEZ CAMACHO

YOSHIHIRO NARISAWA

KUNIHIKO KATO
IZUMI KIMURA
KEITA KITAMURA
TAKAYUKI NAKATSUKA
TAKAYOSHI WATANABE

YOTAM OTTOLENGHI

WILLIAM GLEAVE &
    GIUSEPPE BELVEDERE
TOMOS PARRY
RAMAEL SCULLY
COŞKUN UYSAL
DAVE VERHEUL

ANA ROŠ

BERNARD KORAK
LUKA KOŠIR
LISA LOV
JAKOB PINTAR
PHILIP RACHINGER

MARCUS SAMUELSSON

PAUL CARMICHAEL
DIANA DÁVILA
JONATHAN "JONNY"
    RHODES
LENA SAREINI
AARON VERZOSA

EYAL SHANI

TAKASHI ENDO
YUVAL LESHEM
ELDAD SHMUELI
FRANCESCO VINCENZI
DYLAN WATSON-BRAWN

DANIELA SOTO-INNES

LUIS ARELLANO
ELENA REYGADAS
JEREMIAH STONE &
    FABIÁN VON HAUSKE
    VALTIERRA
JONATHAN TAM
SILVANA VILLEGAS &
    MARIANA VILLEGAS

DANIELLE ALVAREZ

FRED'S
Sydney, Australia

SKYE GYNGELL

MENU

OYSTERS WITH CILANTRO AND WHITE PEPPER MIGNONETTE

CHILLED BEET AND TOMATO SOUP WITH WILD FENNEL AND CRÈME FRAÎCHE

LAMB LEG "À LA FICELLE" WITH ANCHOVY BUTTER, WARM TAPENADE, AND ZUCCHINI GRATIN

BLACK CURRANT JELLY AND VANILLA PANNA COTTA WITH PISTACHIO TUILLES

American Danielle Alvarez is executive chef at Fred's in Sydney, Australia, where she creates produce-driven menus that change daily, always with a focus on bold flavors. Dishes such as *stracciatella cappelletti*, with sweet corn, honey butter, and Aleppo pepper or grilled quail with pancetta, squash, and jus, highlight her cooking style: Let the seasonal ingredients shine. Alvarez has built her restaurant and reputation around principles of mutual esteem and inspiration: She believes that creating a beautiful work environment in which trust and respect are paramount stimulates her kitchen team and improves each individual's self-worth.

Alvarez grew up in Florida in a large family of Cuban immigrants, and a passion for food and cooking were constants in their household. Still, it was a desire for a creative career, rather than a clear vision for herself of becoming a chef, that led her to culinary school. Right after completing the program, Alvarez landed an internship at Thomas Keller's Napa Valley icon, the French Laundry. Next, Alvarez spent two years working for Chef Amaryll Schwertner at her elegant, ingredient-driven San Francisco restaurant, Boulettes Larder; there, Alvarez continued to learn a tremendous amount—including that she didn't want to pursue traditional fine dining.

So, Alvarez next set her ambitious sights on cooking at Alice Waters's seminal farm-to-table stronghold, Chez Panisse, in Berkeley, California. After a trial, she landed a job, and soon found that she relished the quality of life, the camaraderie, and, of course, the food principles unique to that restaurant.

After four productive years at Chez Panisse, Alvarez decided she needed a new adventure, and set off to explore Australia. She felt an immediate kinship to the country and culture. A chance introduction to restaurateur Justin Hemmes of the Merivale hospitality group led Alvarez to her current post.

Alvarez describes the impact of her Cuban heritage on her as a chef as less about her cooking style and more about a deeply ingrained spirit of hospitality and community, which she brings to her classical Old World culinary approach. Alvarez has received international attention for her work at Fred's, including *Gourmet Traveller*'s New Restaurant of the Year award in 2018.

OYSTERS WITH CILANTRO AND WHITE PEPPER MIGNONETTE
Serves 4

3 tablespoons agrodolce-style Chardonnay vinegar • 1 tablespoon sherry vinegar • 1 small shallot, finely diced • 1 teaspoon minced cilantro (coriander) stems • ½ teaspoon grated lime zest • ⅛ teaspoon freshly ground white pepper • 1 dozen oysters, freshly shucked, on the half shell • 3–4 lemon wedges

In a bowl, mix together the vinegars, shallot, cilantro (coriander) stems, lime zest, and white pepper. Serve the oysters on a bed of crushed ice (or rock salt if you don't like them cold) along with the lemon wedges and the white pepper mignonette.

CHILLED BEET AND TOMATO SOUP WITH WILD FENNEL AND CRÈME FRAÎCHE
Serves 4–6

2–3 large red beets • Salt • 2 tablespoons olive oil, plus more for roasting and garnishing • 1 medium onion, thinly sliced •
1 large carrot, thinly sliced • 2–3 large heirloom tomatoes, peeled, seeded, and roughly chopped • 3⅓ cups (800 ml) vegetable stock or water • 2 tablespoons Chardonnay vinegar, plus more to taste • 1 bulb fennel, diced • 4 tablespoons crème fraîche, for serving • Fresh wild fennel, for garnish

Preheat the oven to 390°F (200°C).
Place the beets in a baking pan, sprinkle with salt, a splash of water, and a good glug of olive oil. Cover the pan with foil and roast until tender, about 1 hour. Once cooled, peel and roughly chop.
In a medium soup pot, heat the olive oil over medium-low heat. Add the sliced onion, carrot, and 1 teaspoon salt and cook until completely soft and translucent, about 10 minutes. Add the beets and the roughly chopped tomatoes and another 1 teaspoon salt. Sauté everything together for 15 minutes.

Add the stock and bring everything to a simmer. You are aiming to cover the vegetables by about 1 inch (2–3 cm), so add a bit more water if needed. Simmer together for 20–30 minutes.
Blend everything in a high-powered blender until completely smooth, then pass through a chinois. Check for seasoning, then stir in the vinegar to taste (consider tasting again when its chilled as the flavor will change). Refrigerate until completely cold.
In a pan of boiling salted water, blanch the diced fennel. Drain and refrigerate until ready to serve.
Serve the soup in small bowls and add a spoonful of crème fraîche to the top of each bowl. Drizzle with olive oil and then spoon over the diced fennel. Garnish with wild fennel and serve.

CHILLED BEET AND TOMATO SOUP WITH
WILD FENNEL AND CRÈME FRAÎCHE

DANIELLE'S COOKING IS PRODUCE-DRIVEN AND TRULY DELICIOUS IN A VERY NATURAL WAY! IT IS REFRESHINGLY UNPRETENTIOUS. — Skye Gyngell

DANIELLE ALVAREZ

LUIS ARELLANO

DANIELA SOTO-INNES

Luis Arellano's career thus far has been an ode to his home country of Mexico. Born and raised in the Cañada region of Oaxaca, Arellano's parents owned a bakery, where his love for the culinary arts began at a young age, leading him to some of Mexico's greatest kitchens.

In 2006, Arellano landed at Alejandro Ruiz's esteemed Casa Oaxaca. Ruiz, according to many, is perhaps one of the most prolific mentors in the area. Having heavily influenced modern Oaxacan cuisine and those behind it, Casa Oaxaca fostered growth for those who applied themselves. Arellano worked his way up the ladder and ultimately became Ruiz's sous chef, also spearheading the restaurant's creative efforts.

After six years, Arellano ventured to Mexico City to work for another revered Mexican chef, who would forever alter the course of his culinary career as he knew it. Arellano joined the team at Enrique Olvera's Pujol in 2012, bringing with him his passion for, and extensive knowledge of, native Oaxacan ingredients. Pastry was a strong suit, as was his other familiar territory, from mole, chocolate, and *tlayudas* (Oaxacan quesadillas) to working with clay as a means of cooking.

During his time at Pujol, Arellano began to solidify his place in the global culinary scene, making various appearances at prestigious events in New York, Berlin, Spain, France, and throughout his home country. He again rose up the restaurant's ranks to become sous chef and "Head of Creativity." By 2015, Arellano was ready to launch his own concept— Olvera gave him his blessing and joined him as a partner to open Criollo in Oaxaca.

A colonial mansion flanking Oaxaca's old city center is where Arellano now calls his culinary home. Criollo has become one of the greats, strikingly modern in design and with one common cause: to preserve the integrity of Mexican gastronomy while making everyone who experiences it feel at home. This is truly Arellano's place, and while the tasting menu is ever-changing with the seasons, he is committed to staying connected to the roots of his land's storied past.

MENU

COCTEL DE CIRUELA FERMENTADA Y MEZCAL (FERMENTED RED PLUM COCKTAIL)

SALSA ROJA MOLCAJETEADA (RED MOLCAJETE SALSA), TOSTADAS

TLAYUDA, CHORIZO, QUELITES

HUACHINANGO EMPAPELADO (BANANA LEAF–STEAMED RED SNAPPER)

GRANITAS DE NARANJA Y MARACUYÁ (ORANGE AND PASSION FRUIT GRANITAS)

TAMAL DE CHOCOLATE Y PLÁTANO

COCTEL DE CIRUELA FERMENTADA Y MEZCAL (FERMENTED RED PLUM COCKTAIL)
Serves 1

Ice • 60 ml juice from Red Plum Ferment *(recipe follows)* • 15 ml bicuishe mezcal (or espadín if necessary) • 90 ml sparkling white wine • 6 corn husks, for garnish

In an ice-filled mixing glass, combine the plum juice, mezcal, and wine. Stir. Strain into an ice-filled rocks glass. Garnish with a piece of husk.

RED PLUM FERMENT
500 g pitted red plums • 500 g sugar • 500 ml water

In a medium pot, combine the red plums, sugar, and water. Bring to a simmer over high heat and cook for 5 minutes without letting it break a boil.

Pour the plums with their liquid into a clean jar, cover, and tie a piece of cheesecloth (muslin) over the mouth and place in a dry place for 3 days.

SALSA ROJA MOLCAJETEADA (RED MOLCAJETE SALSA), TOASTADAS
Makes about 1 liter

12 heirloom (heritage) or plum tomatoes • ½ white onion • 2 fresh chiles de agua or other fresh chilies • 2 cloves garlic, peeled • 1 teaspoon coarse sea salt, plus more to taste • Tostadas or totopos, for serving

In a comal or frying pan, combine the tomatoes, onion, and chilies and cook over high heat until tender and charred on all sides. The tomatoes and onion will take about 30 minutes. The chilies will take about 15 minutes.

Clean off the charred skin and pull out the stems. (Don't do this under running water or you will wash away the flavor.) Depending on the desired level of heat, leave (hotter) or remove (milder) the seeds and ribs from the chilies.
In a molcajete, combine the chilies, raw garlic, and salt and crush to a paste. Add the onions and crush. Add the tomatoes one by one and crush until you reach your desired level of chunkiness.
Serve with tostadas or totopos as a snack or use it as a topping on tacos.

HUACHINANGO EMPAPELADO (BANANA LEAF–STEAMED RED SNAPPER)
Serves 2

For the ginger mojo:
2 large cloves garlic, peeled • 1 teaspoon chopped fresh ginger • 120 ml olive oil

BANANA LEAF-STEAMED RED SNAPPER

For the snapper:
1 whole red snapper (about 600 g), cleaned and skinned • Ginger Mojo (above) • 1 orange, sliced • ½ white onion, sliced • 1 lemongrass leaf (substitute for root if unavailable) • 1 tablespoon coarse sea salt • 3 or 4 large banana leaves

Make the ginger mojo:
In a molcajete or spice grinder, grind the garlic and ginger to a paste. Add the olive oil and mix well.

Prepare the snapper:
Cover the red snapper inside and out with the ginger mojo. Stuff the red snapper with the sliced orange, onion, lemongrass, and sea salt. Wrap the red snapper in banana leaves and set aside to marinate. While the fish marinates, prepare a steamer.
Once the water in the steamer boils, add the fish to the steamer rack, cover, and cook until the fish just flakes with a fork, about 35 minutes.

GRANITAS DE NARANJA Y MARACUYÁ (ORANGE AND PASSION FRUIT GRANITAS)
Serves 4

For the orange granita:
650 ml fresh orange juice • 140 g water • 2 sheets gelatin • 90 ml corn syrup • 200 g sugar

For the passion fruit granita:
400 g fresh passion fruit pulp • 270 g water • 2 sheets gelatin • 90 ml corn syrup • 200 g sugar

For serving:
Lime zest • Ground chilies • A couple of orange supremes, for garnish

Make the orange granita:
In a small bowl, combine 60 ml of the orange juice and 60 g of the water and hydrate the gelatin in the mixture.
In a small pot, combine the remaining 590 ml orange juice, remaining water, and the corn syrup. Bring to a simmer and cook for 5 minutes. Once simmering, add the gelatin and the juice you hydrated it in. Pour into a small container. Let cool, then transfer to the freezer.

Make the passion fruit granita:
In a small bowl, combine 60 g of the passion fruit juice and 60 g of the water and hydrate the gelatin in the mixture.
In a small pot, combine the remaining 340 g passion fruit juice, the remaining 210 g water, and the corn syrup. Bring to a simmer and cook for 5 minutes. Once simmering, add the gelatin and the juice you hydrated it in. Pour into a small container. Let cool, then transfer to the freezer.
Once both granitas are fully frozen, take them out and scrape with a fork. Spoon a bit of each granita into a bowl, layering one over the other, and garnish with lime zest, ground chilies, and orange supremes.

FERMENTED RED PLUM COCKTAIL

ORANGE AND PASSIONFRUIT GRANITAS

16

LUIS IS AN OPEN BOOK—
BY LOOKING AT HIS HANDS
YOU CAN TELL HE IS A
REAL COOK.
— Daniela Soto-Innes

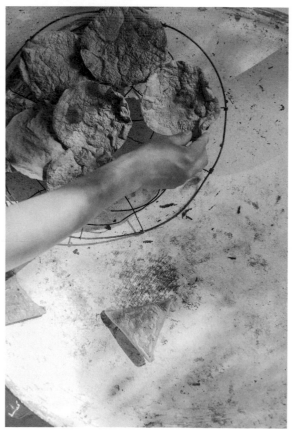

LUIS ARELLANO

SUZANNE BARR

SELASSIE ATADIKA

Chef, restaurateur, author, advocate, and public speaker are just a few words that can be used to describe Suzanne Barr. Although her identity in the food world is largely associated with Toronto, where she has established her family and restaurant career, her past takes us elsewhere on the map.

Born in Toronto but raised mostly in Florida, Barr spent the first phase of her professional life in New York City, where she spent about fifteen years as a producer for MTV before she took a step back to rethink her path, particularly on a spiritual level. This brought her to an ashram in upstate New York, where she volunteered in the kitchen. Upon her return to the city, she enrolled in a course at the Natural Gourmet Institute, leaving MTV to focus on cooking. After completing her schooling, she moved to Kauai, Hawaii, for an externship, after which she began working as a private chef for a family. With them, Barr split her time for the next four years between New York City, the Hamptons on New York's Long Island, Miami, and France. She then spent some time on her own living in Miami and France, before meeting her husband and settling in Toronto.

When it comes to her cooking, Barr is inspired by many things: music, her travels, and her Caribbean roots (her mother was born in Jamaica, though raised in England, which has also influenced Barr's culinary style). But it is emotion and personal experience that have been the dominant influences on her cuisine throughout her various chef roles in Toronto at the Gladstone Hotel and Avling Kitchen and Brewery, as well as Sand and Pearl Oyster Bar on Prince Edward Island. Barr's second venture was True True Diner, where she served comfort food in a modern diner setting. The menu was an homage to Barr's travels and life experiences. The diner closed in the summer of 2020 following hardships due to the Covid-19 pandemic.

Barr, a frequent speaker, writer, and advocate for marginalized communities, is still doing important work in the wake of her restaurant's closure. She works for her community as a board member for two nonprofits championing mental health for service industry workers, and food security, respectively. At the 2018 Women In Hospitality United symposium in New York City, she presented The Dinette's Program, which provides training and support to a new generation of women leaders in the restaurant industry.

MENU

SWEET-AND-SOUR BEEF BACK RIBS AND OXTAIL

PLANTAIN MASH AND COLLARD GREENS

PEPPA SHRIMP WITH SESAME GOCHUJANG SLAW

Pour over the seared ribs and oxtail. Place a sheet of parchment paper on top and then cover with foil. Transfer to the oven and cook until fork-tender, about 2 hours. Remove the meat from the braising liquid and place on a cooling rack until ready to portion and serve.

Strain the braising liquid into a soup pot and cook until reduced to 2 cups. Measure out ½ cup (120 ml) and reserve for Plantain Mash *(below)*.

Make the sweet and sour sauce:
In a saucepan, combine 1½ cups (355 ml) reduced braising liquid, the carrots, onion, and tomato paste (puree). Cook until the onions and carrots are soft. Taste and add the maple syrup if needed to attain that sweet-and-sour flavor.

Serve with Plantain Mash and Collard Greens.

PLANTAIN MASH
Serves 4

2 green plantains, cut into thirds (do not peel) • ½ cup (120 ml) braising liquid (from Sweet-and-Sour Ribs, above) • 1–2 cups (190–380 g) packed light brown sugar • 2 sticks (8 oz/225 g) cold unsalted butter, cubed • Salt

SWEET-AND-SOUR BEEF BACK RIBS AND OXTAIL
Serves 4

For the ribs and oxtail:
1 rack beef back ribs • 1 oxtail • Salt and freshly ground black pepper • 1 tablespoon grapeseed oil

For the braising liquid:
2⅓ cups (19 fl oz/568 ml) hard cider • 2 cups (475 ml) rice vinegar • 1 cup (240 ml) red wine vinegar • 1 cup (190 g) packed light brown sugar • 4–6 cups (950 ml to 1.4 liters) water • 5 cloves garlic, smashed • ½ bunch fresh thyme

For the sweet-and-sour sauce:
1 cup (130 g) finely diced carrots • 1 cup (160 g) finely diced white onion

• 3 tablespoons tomato paste (puree) • 1 tablespoon maple syrup (optional)

Prepare the ribs and oxtail:
Place the ribs and oxtail on butcher's paper and liberally salt and pepper. Wrap in them in the butcher paper and allow them to come to room temperature.

In a large frying pan, heat the oil over high heat until smoking. Place the ribs carefully in the pan and sear on all sides. Repeat with the oxtail. Place seared ribs and oxtail in a deep roasting pan.

Preheat a convection (fan-assisted) oven to 300°F (150°C).

Make the braising liquid:
In a bowl, stir together the cider, vinegars, brown sugar, and water until the sugar is dissolved. Add the garlic and thyme.

Place the green plantains in a pot of cold water and cook over medium-high heat until fork-tender.

Meanwhile, reheat the braising liquid. When cool enough to handle, peel the plantains and place in a food processor with the warm braising liquid and brown sugar to taste. With the machine running, add the butter a few tablespoons at a time and puree until the consistency of glutinous plantain mash. Re-season with salt.

COLLARD GREENS
Serves 4

½ bunch collard greens, stems and midribs removed • Oil • Garlic • Crushed chili flakes • Salt

Set up a large bowl of ice and water. Bring a pot of salted water to a boil. Add the collard greens and cook for 2 minutes. Scoop out of the pot and transfer to the ice water bath. Let sit for about 5 minutes to halt the cooking. Squeeze out any excess water and cut the collards lengthwise.

In a frying pan, sauté with fresh garlic, chili flakes, and salt.

Serve on plate with plantain mash and sweet- and-sour ribs and oxtail. Garnish the plate with crispy leeks and enjoy with a glass of red wine! Now that's True True style!

PEPPA SHRIMP
Serves 4

For the shrimp:
1 box tiger prawns with head-on (20–22 pcs per box) • ½ gallon water • 1 liter white wine • 2 cups of orange juice • 3 bay leaves • 4 stalks celery, cut into medium dice • 2 oranges sliced 1½ inch thick • 1 leek, sliced into 2-inch rounds • 4 head fennel, cut into medium dice • 2 sprigs tarragon • 2 carrots, cut into medium dice • 1 table-spoon salt

For the peppa sauce:
2 pcs pickled scotch bonnet (quick pickle scotch bonnets reserve liquid for hot sauce) • 1½ cup court bouillon liquid • ½ cup peeled garlic • ⅓ cup smoked paprika • ¼ cup garlic powder • ¼ cup onion powder • 1 teaspoon celery salt • ¼ cup orange juice • ¼ cup lemon juice • 3 tablespoons lime juice • 1 cup chopped parsley

Make the shrimp:
Fill large bowl with ice and water place aside. Prepare all ingredients except prawns and place in large stock pot and bring to boil over medium high heat. Add prawns to pot and cook for 5–9 minutes or until shrimp turns pink be sure to check heads as they sometimes need additional time. Remove prawns and place in ice bath until ready to mix with sauce.

Make the peppa sauce:
Place all ingredients into blender until combined into rich, red, saucy consistency. Remove prawns from ice bath and place in bowl be sure there is no excess water.

To serve, pour peppa sauce onto prawns and using gloves mix well until prawns or covered in sauce. Garnish with curly scallions and chopped parsley and serve with Sesame Gochujang Slaw *(below)*. Be sure to suck the head ... Enjoy!

SESAME GOCHUJANG SLAW
Serves 4–6

For the dressing:
½ cup red wine vinegar • ½ cup lime juice • 3 tablespoons honey • 1 tablespoon Gochujang paste • 1 cup toasted sesame oil • 3 teaspoons kosher salt • 1 teaspoon fresh ground peppercorns

1 head napa cabbage, cored and thinly sliced • ½ medium red onion, julienned • 2 scallions thinly sliced bias cut • 2 julienned carrots bias cut • ½ cup sunflower seeds • 2 tablespoons white sesame seeds

Make the dressing:
Place all ingredients in a small bowl except oil, salt, and pepper. Slowly drizzle oil into the bowl until vinaigrette consistency is achieved. Season to taste with salt and pepper.

In a bowl, mix the dressing with the cabbage, red onion, scallions, and carrots. Add the sunflower seeds and sesame seeds. Mix well, until vegetables are fully coated. Serve with Peppa Shrimp and a Caipirinha! Enjoy!

KOFTE

PHILLY CHICKEN SANDWICH

GEM SALAD

SUZANNE HAS RECEIVED
PRAISE FROM OTHER
CHEFS FOR BEING A
CHAMPION AND ADVOCATE
FOR DIVERSITY AND
ISSUES RANGING FROM
LOCAL COMMUNITY, TO
FOOD SECURITY, TO
MENTORING OF YOUTH,
TO ADVOCACY FOR PEOPLE
OF COLOR AND LGBTQ
COMMUNITIES.
— Selassie Atadika

SUZANNE BARR

DAVE BERAN

DIALOGUE, PASJOLI
Los Angeles, California,
United States

DANIEL BOULUD

Dave Beran is a sotryteller at heart, and his restaurants, Dialogue and Pasjoli, are meticulous works of art that have earned him much-deserved prestige. After a decade with the Alinea Group, it comes as no surprise that Beran is making waves, this time in the Los Angeles food scene.

Beran was born in Ashland, Wisconsin. After graduating from Lake Forest College, outside of Chicago, in 2003 with a business degree, Beran pivoted to the culinary arts. There were many steps in between—he first fell in love with food while working at a restaurant in Michigan one summer. Back in Chicago, stints at MK Restaurant and Tru led to a position at Alinea in 2006. Beran was promoted to chef de cuisine just two years later, and in 2011 transitioned to executive chef at Next, where he spearheaded fifteen highly lauded menus that transcended borders, drawing inspiration from all over the world. Two James Beard Foundation awards later, he decided to pursue his dream of opening his own restaurant, which brought him to Los Angeles. Dialogue opened in 2017 in Santa Monica, and today, Beran's affinity for refined simplicity and kaiseki-inspired course cadence have earned him a place among the city's culinary elite.

Beran brought to Santa Monica a tasting menu in a league of its own, a poetic experience leading guests on an ethereal, three-season journey based on Southern California's seasonal ingredients. It is as much about the experience as it is the cuisine, with a subtly theatrical setting serving as a stage for fine dining stripped of any pretentiousness. Dialogue has earned a Michelin star, a spot on GQ's Best New Restaurants in America list, and five stars in the *Forbes Travel Guide*. Beran's second LA restaurant, Pasjoli, opened in 2019 to much acclaim—the restaurant is an à la carte ode to the markets and bistros of Paris, again putting hyperlocal ingredients to use in the process. No matter the format, season, or city, Beran's thoughtful cooking is a living, breathing dining experience to remember.

MENU

BROCCOLINI AND PASSION-FRUIT BÉARNAISE

MONTEREY BAY RED DULSE SEAWEED

FOIE GRAS, PASSION FRUIT, RUTABAGA

SMOKED MAITAKE, FRIED LEEK, BURNT ONION JUS

CORN, HAZELNUT, TRUFFLE

COFFEE, CAVIAR, LAPSANG

BROCCOLINI AND PASSION-FRUIT BÉARNAISE
Serves 4

For the béarnaise reduction:
200 g white wine • 200 g white wine vinegar • 50 g shallots • 20 g tarragon leaves • 5 g black peppercorns

For the nori/passion-fruit/mustard béarnaise:
55 g Béarnaise Reduction *(above)* • 3 egg yolks • 225 g unsalted butter, melted • 75 g passion-fruit juice • 8 g salt • 20 g Dijon mustard • 2 g nori powder

For the mint oil:
500 g grapeseed oil • 250 g mint • 50 g spinach

For the charred broccolini:
500 g broccolini (Tenderstem broccoli) • 50 g neutral oil • 5 g salt

For the garnish:
Frilly mustard greens • Ogo • Powdered nori

Make the béarnaise reduction:
In a pan, combine all the ingredients. Reduce by two-thirds and strain.

Make the nori/passion-fruit/mustard béarnaise:
In a double boiler, combine the béarnaise reduction and egg yolks and slowly cook until the eggs are cooked and frothy. Emulsify in the melted butter. Add the passion-fruit juice. Adjust the seasoning with more reduction and salt. Strain and place in the canister of a whipper siphon. Charge twice.

Make the mint oil:
In a blender, puree the oil, mint, and spinach. Transfer to a saucepan and bring to simmer. Strain, return to a saucepan, and cook to 225°F (107°C). Hold there until all the moisture has evaporated. Pass through a coffee filter, refrigerate, and reserve.

Make the charred broccolini:
Toss the broccolini with the oil and salt. In a cast-iron pan over high heat, sear the broccolini until well charred.

To plate:
Place roughly 75 g of charred broccolini in the center of the plate and season with about 10 g of mint oil. Express whipped béarnaise over the top of the broccolini, hiding it completely. Using the mustard greens, create a spiral nest around the broccolini. Top with ogo and a light dusting of nori.

CORN, HAZELNUT, TRUFFLE
Serves 6

For the malted milk/smoke seasoning:
100 g malted milk powder • 2 g smoked salt • 1 g freshly ground black pepper

For the cooked FD corn:
100 g FD corn • 150 g browned butter, melted and warm • 0.5 g smoked salt • 5 g truffle oil • 1 g salt

For the fried hazelnuts:
100 g peeled hazelnuts • neutral oil, for frying • salt and freshly ground black pepper

For the crispy corn/hazelnut mix:
100 g cooked FD Corn *(above)* • 100 g Fried Hazelnuts *(above)*, crushed • 0.3 g freshly ground black pepper • 2 g picked thyme leaves • salt

CORN, HAZELNUT, TRUFFLE

DAVE IS A WIZARD IN THE KITCHEN AND HAS MASTERFULLY COMBINED CLASSIC FRENCH CUISINE WITH A CALIFORNIAN EDGE. — Daniel Boulud

COFFEE, CAVIAR, LAPSANG

For the bourbon reduction:
250 g bourbon • 150 g brown sugar
• 50 g sherry vinegar

For the brown butter emulsion:
3 egg yolks • 100 g Bourbon Reduction
(above) • 225 g brown butter • 3 g salt
• Sherry vinegar

Make the malted milk/smoke seasoning:
Combine all the ingredients.

Cook the FD corn:
Stir all the ingredients together and vacuum-seal (lay the bag flat before compressing). Simmer for 15 minutes, then transfer to an ice bath. Crumble.

Fry the hazelnuts:
Heat the oil to 300°F (149°C). Fry the hazelnuts, drain, and season with salt and pepper.

Make the crispy corn/hazelnut mix:
Combine all the ingredients. Adjust seasoning to taste with salt.

Make the bourbon reduction:
In a saucepan, bring the bourbon to a simmer and flame off the alcohol. Add the brown sugar and vinegar and cook until reduced to 200 g.

Make the brown butter emulsion:
In a double boiler, combine the egg yolks and bourbon reduction. Cook until the yolks are thick and frothy. Slowly emulsify the brown butter into the cooked egg. Finish with the salt and adjust seasoning with sherry vinegar.

Components:
Crispy corn/hazelnut mix, 15 g • Black truffle, 5 g per plate • Malted milk/smoke seasoning, light dusting on top to finish • Brown butter emulsion, 5 g as base • Golden Osetra

COFFEE, CAVIAR, LAPSANG
Serves 25

For the coffee cream:
25 g ground coffee • 150 g whole milk • 150 g heavy cream

For the coffee anglaise:
4 egg yolks • 5 g cornstarch (corn flour) • 35 g sugar • 250 g Coffee Cream *(above)* • 5 g salt • 1 vanilla bean, scraped • 0.5 g black peppercorns

For the hazelnuts:
75 g hazelnuts

For the lapsang oil:
50 g lapsang souchong tea • 25 g water • 100 g grapeseed oil

For serving:
Freshly cracked black pepper • Osetra caviar (10 g per portion) • Alyssum flowers (10 per portion)

Make the coffee cream:
Combine the ingredients and cold infuse for 48 hours. Strain out the solids.

Make the coffee anglaise:
In a bowl, whisk together the egg yolks, cornstarch, and sugar.
In a saucepan, combine the coffee cream, salt, vanilla seeds, and pod and bring to simmer. Temper the hot cream into the egg mixture, then return all to the pan and bring to a simmer.
Strain into a bowl over an ice bath and whisk until cool. (If necessary, balance with salt and sugar. If too thick, add a minimal amount of milk.)

Roast the hazelnuts:
Preheat the oven to 325°F (160°C). Roast the hazelnuts until golden brown. Let cool, then crush to small pieces.

Make the lapsang oil:
In a saucepan, combine all the ingredients and bring to simmer. Cook until all the water has evaporated. Strain and reserve.

To plate:
For each bowl, place 3 g hazelnuts on the bottom. Add a crack of black pepper. Add 1.5 g lapsang oil, 10 g coffee anglaise, the caviar, and alyssum flowers.

DAVE BERAN

NEIL BORTHWICK

MARGOT HENDERSON

THE FRENCH HOUSE
London, England

MENU

LAMB NAVARIN

PUMPKIN, BEET, BITTER LEAF AND PICKLED WALNUT SALAD

PARIS-BREST WITH CHOCOLATE SAUCE

The French House, a second-floor pocket-size restaurant in London's Soho, has been in operation for over one hundred years, and has long been known as one of the city's best dining rooms. (It is also known as the site where Charles de Gaulle wrote his "To all Frenchmen" speech, which fueled the French resistance during World War II.) A lineage of notable chefs have helmed the kitchen, including Fergus and Margot Henderson in the 1990s and Florence Knight in the 2000s. And the food emerging from this small kitchen continues to invoke great praise, thanks to the prowess of its current chef, Neil Borthwick.

Borthwick met the challenges of walking into a storied restaurant by both hewing to its history and adding his own touches; his cuisine is based on a classic French bistro style, while his dexterity with finding new or updated joys within its framework makes his skills shine. In a culinary world that tirelessly seeks innovation, his deftness for coaxing the historical into charming contemporary sensibilities could be his most daring achievement.

Borthwick grew up in Falkirk, Scotland, and attended catering school in Glasgow, where he later secured a post at Gordon Ramsay's Amaryllis—his first Michelin-starred stint. Soon after, he set off for France. He worked for several formative years at Maison Bras, in Laguiole, ascending to sous-chef and mastering the restaurant's rigorously creative cuisine, and pioneering vegetable-centered menus. Upon his return to the UK, he found work at the Square in London, where Philip Howard schooled him in flavor profiles. Borthwick then opened, with Angela Hartnett, Merchants Tavern, where he became known for his modern yet simple pan-European menus with a Bras-influenced attentiveness to vegetables.

At the French House, Borthwick's menus harken to another time and place, and constantly evolve to showcase classic French and British cooking using London's best produce. His dish of brains cooked in brown butter impresses with the contrast between its crisp exterior and silky interior and is punctuated by the salty tang of capers. He serves leeks cooked perfectly in the classic French style: melting beneath a *sauce gribiche*. Potatoes are featured in a rustic aligot—whipped and combined with garlic and enough cheese to make the whole dish stretchy like melted mozzarella. Borthwick's vanilla custard tart—which has been described as hailing from the heavens—lingers long in diners' memories.

LAMB NAVARIN
Serves 4

4 lamb neck fillets, cut into 4 pieces • Salt • Mirepoix: 1 onion, 2 carrots • 1 garlic bulb, halved • 3 tablespoons tomato paste (puree) • 1 bouquet garni: thyme, bay leaf, rosemary • 1 liter chicken stock • 500 ml veal stock • 6 organic carrots, peeled and cut into chunks • 2 turnips, peeled and cut into chunks • 2 stalks celery, cut into lozenges • Olive oil • Chopped fresh parsley • Fresh mint

Season the lamb well. In a sauté pan, sear the lamb until golden brown all over and set aside.
Add the mirepoix to the pan along with the garlic and cook until caramelized.
Add the tomato paste (puree) and cook for

4–5 minutes. Return the lamb to the pan along with the bouquet garni and both the stocks. Bring to a gentle simmer, skim well, reduce the heat, and cook until the lamb is tender when pressed with a finger, 1–1½ hours. Set aside and allow to cool for 1 hour. In a large pot of boiling salted water, cook the carrots, turnips, and celery until just tender. Shock in an ice bath. Drain and set aside.
Remove the lamb from the braise and pass the sauce through a sieve, pressing as much of the vegetables through as well, which will help to thicken the sauce and give you lots of flavor.
Return the lamb, along with the cooked vegetables, to the sauce and finish with chopped parsley and a touch of mint. Serve with buttery mashed potato.

PUMPKIN, BEET, BITTER LEAF, AND PICKLED WALNUT SALAD
Serves 4

For the salad:
100 g beets • 100 g pumpkin, peeled and chopped • Olive oil • Salt and freshly ground black pepper • 2 banana shallots, finely sliced • 100 g pickled walnuts, chopped • 1 head Tardivo radicchio • 1 Belgian endive • 1 bunch of arugula (rocket)

For the classic dressing:
50 g white wine vinegar • 50 g Dijon mustard • Salt • 250 ml olive oil

To finish:
Salt and freshly cracked black pepper • Parmesan cheese • Chopped fresh parsley

Prepare the salad:
Wrap the beet tightly in foil with 200 ml water and steam-roast in the oven for 1–1½ hours.
Toss the pumpkin with some olive oil and season with salt and pepper. Spread on a sheet pan and roast until just tender and set aside.
In a bowl, toss the shallots and pickled walnuts with some olive oil to loosen. Prepare and wash the salad greens, leaving them in their natural shapes and spin dry. Peel the cooked beets and dress in the red wine vinegar, sea salt, and olive oil.

Make the classic dressing:
In a bowl, whisk together the white wine vinegar, mustard, a touch of salt, and the olive oil.

To finish:
Place all the ingredients in a large bowl and dress with the classic dressing and salt and pepper to taste, making sure all the leaves are dressed and delicious. Divide onto four plates and finish with grated Parmesan and some chopped parsley.

PARIS-BREST WITH CHOCO-LATE SAUCE
Serves 8

For the choux pastry:
250 ml water • 100 g unsalted butter • Good pinch of sugar • Pinch of salt • 140 g all-purpose (plain) flour • 5 eggs • Egg wash • Sliced (flaked) almonds

For the caramelized hazelnuts:
25 blanched hazelnuts • 100 g superfine (caster) sugar

For the praline Chantilly:
250 ml double cream • 10 g praline paste

For the chocolate sauce:
50 g sugar • 200 ml water • 160 g dark chocolate, chopped

For assembly:
Praline paste • Powdered (icing) sugar

Make the choux pastry:
Preheat the oven to 350°F (180°C). Line a sheet pan with parchment paper.
In a saucepan, combine the water, butter, sugar, and salt and bring to a boil. Whisk in the flour and cook over medium heat until the paste comes away from the sides of the pan.
Transfer to a stand mixer with the paddle attachment and beat until it's cool enough to add the eggs. Add the eggs one at a time, beating well after each addition.
Transfer the dough to a piping bag and pipe into rings (to represent a bicycle-wheel shape) onto the lined pan. Brush with egg wash and top with the almonds.
Bake for 20 minutes. Rotate each pan front to back and bake until cooked, 20–30 minutes longer.

Meanwhile, caramelize the hazelnuts:
Spread the hazelnuts on a sheet pan and roast in the oven for 10–12 minutes.
In a saucepan, cook the sugar to a golden caramel, add the hazelnuts, coat well, and spread on a tray to cool.

Make the praline Chantilly:
Lightly whip the cream and praline paste together and place in a piping bar with a star tip (nozzle).

Make the chocolate sauce:
In a saucepan, bring the sugar and water to a boil. Whisk in the chocolate and cook over gentle heat to thicken slightly.

To assemble:
Halve the Paris-Brest horizontally. Pipe the Chantilly cream on the bottom half, then drizzle a little more praline paste on top, and add some caramelized hazelnuts. Place the other half on top, pour the chocolate sauce in the middle, and dust with powdered (icing) sugar.

LAMB NAVARIN

NEIL'S FOOD IS MEMORABLE AND DELICIOUS, LEAVING YOU ALWAYS WANTING MORE. HIS COOKING CENTERS AROUND THE PILLARS OF THE PLEASURE OF FOOD, FRIENDS, AND WINE ALL COMING TOGETHER.

— Margot Henderson

PARIS-BREST WITH CHOCOLATE SAUCE

PUMPKIN, BEET, BITTER LEAF AND
PICKLED WALNUT SALAD

NEIL BORTHWICK

BÉRANGÈRE BOUCHER

NOMIKAÏ
Paris, France

DOMINIQUE CRENN

There is classic Parisian, and then there is classic Parisian as imagined and interpreted by Nomikaï's Bérangère Boucher. A perpetual student of the craft, Boucher has never stopped inquiring, learning, or applying—at heart, it is the hallmark of a publisher, a nod to Boucher's previous career before finding her way into a chef's coat.

Boucher spent about a decade in Paris's publishing houses before the art of bento piqued her interest, drawing her into the world of cooking. She then signed up for an evening CAP Cuisine course in 2012, putting her practice into action by quietly launching a supper club for her friends, hosted in her own home. After securing her diploma, she landed in Chef Brice Morvent's kitchen at Le Comptoir de Brice, and in 2013 decided it was time to venture off to explore the landscape on her own.

Upon launching The Kitchen Lab, a private chef project, Boucher took on special catering projects ranging in size from intimate to larger than life, an endeavor that lasted four years before she found herself wanting to return to restaurant life. So in 2018, she opened Nomikaï in the 12th arrondissement. The Paris food scene has not quite been the same since. Boucher's serving style is inspired by *izakaya*, and each local ingredient is carefully selected for its quality and ecological soundness. Seafood is brought in from her fishmonger neighbor, Le Poisson d'Aligre, while meat is sourced only from small, ethical breeders. Boucher's team also strives to minimize waste in the kitchen.

Complemented by an equally thoughtful natural wine list, with bottles sourced from beloved wine shop La Cave d'Ivry, Boucher's menu changes on a daily basis, but strikes a consistent balance between classic bistro fare and her affinity for global flavors, with nods to Asian culture. She also contributes to the brunch movement in Paris, drawing locals and visitors alike with her signature gravlax and *onsen tamago* dish and the restaurant's quaint terrace, drenched in sun on a good day. It is a place full of goodness in more ways than one, and that's what Boucher is all about.

MENU

SEA BREAM CARPACCIO X VODKA LEMON ICE CUBE

RAZOR CLAMS X MORTEAU CREAM

HAMPE X GOCHUJANG

SHELLS X BLACK GARLIC CREAM

SALAD X PICKLES X TSUKEMONO

YUZU CRÉMEUX

SEA BREAM CARPACCIO × VODKA LEMON ICE CUBE
Serves 6

2 skinless sea bream fillets

For the ice cubes:
30 ml vodka • 30 ml still mineral water • 30 ml lemon juice

For the dressing:
100 ml olive oil • 10 ml lemon juice • Drizzle of yuzu juice • Salt

For assembly:
1 lemon • Fleur de sel • Freshly ground Kampot pepper

Lay the sea bream fillets flat in a blast freezer or regular freezer. Freezing them quickly eliminates parasites and makes them easier to cut.

Make the ice cubes:
Spread a sheet of plastic wrap (cling film) on your work surface. Position six 3-inch (8 cm) ring molds on the plastic at regular intervals. With scissors, cut a square of plastic wrap under each round. Pull the plastic up around the mold and secure to the mold with a rubber band. Transfer the molds to a baking sheet.
In a saucepan, combine the vodka, mineral water, and lemon juice and bring to a boil. Pour a thin layer of this mixture into each ring mold. Put into the blast freezer or regular freezer to freeze.

Make the dressing:
Emulsify all the elements of the dressing well and transfer it to a pipette.

To assemble:
Place an 8-inch (20 cm) diameter ring mold on each of 6 plates. Cut the fish into very thin even strips and arrange them attractively in the molds.
Spread the dressing on each carpaccio, spreading it evenly with a brush.
Grate lemon zest over each plate and add a little fleur de sel and ground pepper. Unmold an ice cube onto each plate. Serve immediately.

RAZOR CLAMS × MORTEAU CREAM
Serves 6

For the carrot-infused vinegar:
300 g organic carrot peels • 1 liter artisanal vinegar

For the vinegar gel:
2 g agar powder • 500 ml Carrot-Infused Vinegar *(above)*

For the clams:
About 1 kg clams (6 to 8 per person, depending on size) • Kosher (flaked) salt

For the Morteau cream:
500 ml heavy (whipping) cream • 200 g Morteau sausage, diced • 1 clove garlic, smashed • Salt

SEA BREAM CARPACCIO

For assembly:
Olive oil • Freshly ground Kampot rouge pepper • Fleur de sel • Chives

Make the carrot-infused vinegar:
Combine the carrot peels and vinegar in a glass jar. Let sit in the refrigerator for at least 10 days to infuse.

Make the vinegar gel:
In a saucepan, stir the agar powder into the vinegar. Bring to a boil and cook for 1 minute. Remove from the heat and let cool. The mixture will gel.

Prepare the clams:
Wash the clams in at least three changes of water, adding kosher salt to the first two changes of water to disgorge them well. Drain and set aside in a cool place.

Make the Morteau cream:
In a saucepan, combine the cream, sausage, and garlic. Infuse over low heat for 20 minutes. Season with salt, strain, and set aside.

To assemble:
Return the strained Morteau cream to a pan and gently warm. Emulsify with a hand blender.

In a sauté pan, heat a drizzle of olive oil. Fry the clams over medium heat—they should remain slightly translucent. Season well with pepper.
Arrange the clams on the plates, aligning them. Season with fleur de sel. Pour on 2 tablespoons of emulsified cream. Carefully add 5 dots of vinegar gel. Add some chives and serve hot.

31

SALAD X PICKLES X TSUKEMONO

YUZU CRÉMEUX

BÉRANGÈRE
APPROACHES FOOD
WITH THE EAGERNESS
AND APPLICATION OF
A STUDENT.
— Dominique Crenn

BÉRANGÈRE BOUCHER

ANNIE BRACE-LAVOIE

DAVID MCMILLAN

BAR KISMET
Halifax, Nova Scotia,
Canada

MENU

RAW SCALLOP, LEMONGRASS, AND DAIKON

CHICKEN LIVER MOUSSE, VINCOTTO, AND PISTACHIO

CORN FAGOTTINI AND SIDE STRIPE SHRIMP

CHARRED OCTOPUS AND GREEN LENTILS

GRILLED BRANZINO AND SALSA VERDE

PARIS-BREST

Ask any chef to describe Annie Brace-Lavoie, and chances are they'll tell you about her extraordinary work ethic. This—coupled with sincerity and humility—is what has propelled her on a dynamic career path, culminating in a place to call her own, along with her husband, award-winning bartender Jenner Cormier. Together, at Bar Kismet, the duo constantly proves to the Halifax, Nova Scotia, dining scene that a sense of home in cooking goes a long way.

Brace-Lavoie, a native of Montreal, began her career as a makeup artist before switching gears at age twenty-two to study at Leiths School of Food and Wine in London. After graduating in 2009, she landed at Gallery Mess at the esteemed Saatchi Gallery, where she worked before returning to Canada to study at the Institut de Tourisme et d'Hôtellerie du Québec. A string of stints at some of the country's best kitchens followed: Buca, Liverpool House, Nora Gray, and Bar Isabel. Her time at Liverpool House was pivotal—there she worked alongside Emma Cardarelli, whom she followed to Nora Gray. In 2014, Brace-Lavoie made another key move to Toronto's Bar Raval, where she met Cormier.

The decision to open Bar Kismet was a thoughtful and carefully planned one inspired by a trip to the lesser-traveled pockets of Nova Scotia, during which Cormier was tasked with showing Brace-Lavoie the area's best seafood. The space took more than a year to find, then the restaurant opened to much acclaim. Brace-Lavoie's comfort cuisine style is unfussy yet refined and free of pretentiousness, influenced by Mediterranean and French techniques and her love of watching videos of Italian grandmothers making pasta. Bar Kismet earned its spot on Canada's 100 Best list at number 15. Though the space itself is designed to make the guests feel at home, Brace-Lavoie has a personal knack for doing that just about anywhere.

RAW SCALLOP, LEMONGRASS, AND DAIKON
Serves 4

3 stalks fresh lemongrass, peeled and finely chopped • ½ cup (120 ml) olive oil • 4 tablespoons black sesame seeds • 8 large Atlantic scallops, side muscles removed • 2 tablespoons fresh lime juice • Large pinch of kosher (flaked) salt • ¼ bunch cilantro (fresh coriander), leaves picked • ½ cup (60 g) brunoised purple daikon • 1 serrano chili, finely sliced • Maldon sea salt

In a small saucepan, combine the lemongrass and olive oil. Bring to a simmer and remove from the heat once the lemongrass starts to turn golden. Let cool, strain, and bottle. Set aside until ready to serve.
In a small frying pan, toast the sesame seeds over low heat. Tip out of the pan and let cool, then blitz in a coffee grinder or mortar and pestle until it is a fine powder.
Slice each scallop horizontally into 2 or 3 equal slices and place them in a small bowl. Add the lime juice and kosher salt and stir to coat.

In each of 4 shallow serving bowls, arrange 5 or 6 pieces of scallop and distribute any leftover lime juice into the bowls. Drizzle each scallop with a generous amount of lemongrass oil. Garnish with the cilantro (coriander), daikon, and serrano chili. Finish with toasted black sesame powder and a pinch of Maldon salt.

CHICKEN LIVER MOUSSE, VINCOTTO, AND PISTACHIO
Serves 4–6

280 g chicken livers (cleaned) • 4 eggs • 1 egg yolk • 3 teaspoons salt • ½ teaspoon pink curing salt • 3 tablespoons Vincotto *(recipe follows)* • 1½ sticks (170 g) unsalted butter, cubed, at room temperature • 1 cup (240 ml) heavy (whipping) cream

For serving:
Sliced baguette or sourdough bread • Roughly chopped toasted pistachios • Finely sliced candied orange zest (from Oleo-Saccharum, *below*) • Vincotto *(recipe follows)* • Finely sliced chives

Position a rack in the center of the oven and preheat to 350°F (180°C). Set aside a deep baking dish and a nonstick loaf pan that can easily fit inside the dish.
Bring a medium pot of water to a boil.
In a blender, combine the chicken livers, whole eggs, egg yolk, salt, pink salt, vincotto, and butter and mix until completely smooth. Add the cream just to combine—do not overmix.
Strain the mixture through a fine-mesh sieve into the loaf pan and cover the surface with a piece of plastic wrap (cling film), trying to eliminate any air. Stretch another piece of plastic wrap over the top of the loaf pan to seal it. Then cover with a piece of foil. Place the loaf pan in the baking dish and fill with boiling water until it reaches three-quarters of the way up the sides of the loaf pan. Transfer the pans to the oven and reduce the temperature to 275°F (140°C/Gas Mark 1). Cook until the center feels slightly firm to the touch, about 1 hour 30 minutes. Remove the foil and plastic wrap and let cool for 10 minutes at room temperature before refrigerating to cool completely and set (ideally 4–5 hours or overnight).

Once cooled, scrape off the top layer of the mousse and discard. (It will taste fine but will be brownish in color.)

Push the mixture through a fine-mesh sieve into a bowl. Use a spatula to put it into a piping bag with the tip (nozzle) of your choice. You can now pipe into any vessel or directly onto toasted bread if you choose. Garnish and serve.

VINCOTTO
1 (750 ml) bottle Sangiovese red wine • 1 sprig rosemary • 2 sprigs thyme • 1 clove garlic, peeled and smashed • 15 black peppercorns • Zest strips from 1 orange • ½ cup (120 ml) Oleo-Saccharum *(recipe follows)* or sugar

In a medium saucepan, combine the wine, rosemary, thyme, garlic, peppercorns, orange zest, and oleo-saccharum and bring to a boil. Reduce the heat to a simmer and cook until the wine has reduced to one-quarter of the original volume. (Take care not to overcook or it will be bitter and unusable.) It should appear syrupy and like it could coat the back of a spoon.

Strain through a fine-mesh sieve and allow to cool. Transfer to a squeeze bottle for use.

OLEO-SACCHARUM
150 g orange zest strips • 150 g sugar

Place orange zest and sugar in a medium vacuum pack bag and seal. Leave in a room temp/warm place for 4–5 days until the sugar is almost fully liquified.

Transfer the sugar/zest mixture to a medium saucepan and bring to a simmer while gently stirring to dissolve any remaining sugar. Strain out the candied orange zests and reserve for garnish.

CORN FAGOTTINI AND SIDE STRIPE SHRIMP
Serves 4

For the pasta dough:
1 cup (130 g) all-purpose (plain) flour • 7 tablespoons (75 g) semolina • 9 egg yolks • 1 tablespoon olive oil

For the corn filling:
2 tablespoons olive oil • 1 medium onion, diced • 1 teaspoon salt • 1 clove garlic, grated • 3 cups (435 g) fresh corn kernels (save the cobs for the corn stock) • ½ cup (125 g) ricotta cheese • ½ cup (115 g) mascarpone • ½ cup (45 g) grated Parmesan cheese

For the corn stock:
6 corncobs • 1 medium onion, roughly chopped • 1 bay leaf • 10 black peppercorns

For the barely poached side stripe shrimp:
1 large carrot, roughly chopped • 2 stalks celery, roughly chopped • 1 large onion, roughly chopped • 10 black peppercorns • 1 bay leaf • 1 pound (455 g) side stripe shrimp (prawns)

CORN FAGOTTINI AND SIDE STRIPE SHRIMP

For assembly:
Salt • ½ cup (120 ml) Corn Stock *(above)* • Butter, cubed and cold • Smoked paprika • Finely sliced chives • Grilled corn, cut off the cob

Make the pasta dough:
In a stand mixer fitted with the dough hook, mix the flour and semolina on low for 1 minute. Stop the mixer. Pour the egg yolks and olive oil in the center of the bowl and start the machine again on low. As the dough starts to come together, add water 1 tablespoon at a time if the dough seems dry. Once the dough has completely come together, continue to mix for 2 minutes. Remove the dough from the mixer and knead by hand for at least 10 minutes until it bounces back to the touch. Cover with plastic wrap (cling film) and let rest at room temperature for 30 minutes to 1 hour.

Make the corn filling:
In a large pot, heat the olive oil. Add the onion and salt and cook until translucent and any liquid has evaporated. Add the garlic and cook for 1 minute until fragrant. Add corn and cook until softened, and any possible liquid has evaporated.

Remove the pot from the heat and mix in the ricotta and mascarpone until combined. Stir in the Parmesan. Transfer to a blender and mix until very smooth. Check the seasoning and set aside in a bowl in the fridge with plastic wrap directly on the surface until completely cool.

Place the filling in a piping bag.

Roll out the dough using a pasta machine until it is thin enough to see your hand through. Cut the pasta into 2 lines of squares that are about 2½–3 inches (6.5–7.5 cm) per side. Or whatever size you choose, really.

To make the fagottini, pipe a teaspoon-size dollop of filling on each square of pasta. Grab two opposite points and press together, then grab the remaining points and fold in to meet the others. Press down along the seams to ensure they are sealed. Store the fagottini in the fridge on a baking sheet on parchment paper with a light dusting of semolina underneath and a thin tea towel gently placed over them until ready to serve.

Make the corn stock:
In a medium pot, combine the corncobs, onion, bay leaf, peppercorns, and water to cover. Bring to a boil, then reduce to a simmer and simmer for 45 minutes. Strain through a fine-mesh sieve and let cool.

Poach the shrimp:
In a medium pot, combine the carrot, celery, onion, peppercorns, bay leaf, and 2 liters water and simmer for 30 minutes. Let the poaching liquid cool to 175°F (80°C). Place the shrimp (prawns) in a large bowl and strain the poaching liquid over them. Start a timer for 1 minute and stir the shrimp constantly. Strain off the poaching liquid and shock the shrimp in an ice bath. Once completely cooled, peel the shrimp. You are looking for them to be plump and set on the outside and almost translucent on the inside.

To assemble:
Bring a medium pot of heavily salted water to a boil for the pasta.
In a saucepan, bring the corn stock to a boil over high heat and slowly whisk in cubes of butter until a slightly thicker, smooth, and emulsified sauce has formed. Season with salt and a dash of smoked paprika and remove from the heat.
Drop the fagottini into the boiling water and cook for about 2 minutes. Remove them gently with a small mesh sieve and place in the saucepan, being careful to not bring any

additional pasta water along with them. Return the saucepan to medium heat and toss in 1 shrimp for every piece of stuffed pasta and use a spoon to cover the shrimp and pasta with your sauce. You're just looking to warm the shrimp through, not cook them any further.
Plate the pasta first, then the shrimp, and spoon the sauce to coat the pasta and lightly pool in the plate. Garnish with chives, grilled corn kernels, and smoked paprika.

GRILLED BRANZINO AND SALSA VERDE
Serves 2

2 whole branzino (about 400–600 g each), butterflied • Kosher (flaked) salt • Vegetable oil • Good-quality olive oil • 1 large clove garlic, grated • ½ cup Campo Real olives, smashed and pitted • Salsa Verde (recipe follows) • 1 bunch dandelion leaves, washed and tough stems removed • Lemon juice • Maldon sea salt

Preheat a barbecue grill to high. Meanwhile, set the branzino out for 15 minutes to warm up.
Season both flesh and skin with kosher salt and rub a small drop of vegetable oil onto each side to avoid sticking—but you want to avoid overoiling and causing flare-ups.
In a small saucepan, combine ¼ cup (60 ml) olive oil, the garlic, and olives and heat until the garlic is fragrant. Season with salt and keep warm
Place the branzino skin-side down on the grill and cook for 1 minute until you have a nice char mark, then rotate the fish to create your crosshatch grill marks and cook for another minute. At this point the skin should be crispy and the flesh should be halfway cooked.
Flip the fish to just kiss the grill and cook for 30 seconds. Your goal is to have the

branzino be just cooked. This beautiful fish can be served raw so it would be a huge mistake to overcook it.

To plate, spread a generous amount of salsa verde on the bottom of the plates and place the grilled fish flesh-side down on the plates. Pour the warm olive mixture evenly over both fish. Dress the dandelion leaves heavily with lemon juice and Maldon salt and place on top.

SALSA VERDE
2 shallots, finely chopped • 6 cloves garlic, grated • 1 cup (50 g) roughly chopped fresh parsley • 1 cup (50 g) roughly chopped fresh mint • 1 cup (40 g) roughly chopped fresh basil • 1 cup (40 g) roughly chopped fresh cilantro (coriander) • 1 cup (240 ml) olive oil • 2 tablespoons red wine vinegar, more to taste if needed (you want it to be quite punchy) • Kosher (flaked) salt and freshly ground black pepper

In a food processor, pulse the shallots and garlic until fine. Add the herbs and half the oil and pulse until the herbs have broken down to half their size. Add the remaining oil and process until the herbs are quite fine and still bright green and you have a smooth yet chunky sauce. Stir in the red wine vinegar and salt and pepper to taste.

ANNIE IS THE EXAMPLE OF WHAT HARD WORK LOOKS LIKE, AND HOW GREATLY IT CAN PAY OFF IF YOU TAKE THE TIME. HER COOKING IS PERFECT AND ACCURATE AND TIMELY. — David McMillan

CHICKEN LIVER MOUSSE

RAW SCALLOP, LEMONGRASS, AND DAIKON

GRILLED BRANZINO AND SALSA VERDE

ANNIE BRACE-LAVOIE

PAMELA BRUNTON

INVER
Cairndow, Scotland

MARGOT HENDERSON

In the kitchen of a white cottage overlooking Scotland's longest sea loch, Pamela Brunton transforms the larder of the landscape into dishes she describes as "modern Scottish." This cozy establishment, called Inver, is tucked away on a bay just outside the nearest hamlet, Strathlachlan. Brunton's menus nod to the regional cuisine while incorporating elements from the surrounding landscape with rigor and playfulness. Brunton imbues her menus with both the historic and geographic influences of her milieu. Oysters, mussels, and langoustines come from the lochs; samphire, sorrel, and mustard are harvested from the adjacent marshes and forests. In June, a walk down the road or in a meadow can yield thousands of coral-hued salmonberries. Innovative dishes with traditional touches include duck served in a fragrant bowl of baked-potato-skin broth, draped with Scottish truffles, or mackerel garnished with fermented coffee, oil of voatsiperifery, and cultured cream. Her take on fish and chips: raw and pickled.

In 2015, Brunton opened Inver with her partner, Rob Latimer, after about a decade of working her way through Michelin-starred restaurants and beacons of New Nordic cuisine. Her roots are grounded in French technique learned at places in London, including the Tom Aikens Restaurant, the Greenhouse, and the restaurants of Marco Pierre White, and in France, at Le Moulin de l'Abbaye. Stints at Noma, Fäviken, and In De Wulf also influenced her passion for translating the landscape to the plate. While Brunton's time at such establishments gave her the skills, experience, and determination to realize her vision for Inver, she remembers that her palate developed at an early age, awakened and then fine-tuned by the steady supply of vegetables from her mother's garden. But she never considered a career as a chef until she abandoned university, where she had been studying philosophy. She tried bartending, then got work at a seafood joint near the Isle of Skye in Scotland. In that kitchen, she formed, for the first time, a true identity: she was a chef. At Inver, Brunton's connection to a sense of place and time, both present and past, is felt immediately by anyone who comes to eat in her kitchen.

MENU

POTATO ICE CREAM, PEPPER DULSE AND CAVIAR

PUMPKIN, SEA BUCKTHORN AND MARIGOLD

WHOLE STEAMED CRAB AND HOT BROWN BUTTER

GIGHA HALIBUT, COASTAL GREENS AND SMOKY MUSSEL BUTTER

AUCHENTULLICH FARM BEEF, FIGS AND FARM MILK

DARK CHOCOLATE, BARLEY AND BEER BUBBLES

POTATO ICE CREAM, PEPPER DULSE, AND CAVIAR
Serves 6

For the potato crisps:
1 large potato • Oil, for deep-frying • Powdered dulse, for dusting

For the baked potato milk:
150 g baked potato skins*, very well colored all over • 250 g cold whole milk

For the potato ice cream:
20 g sugar • 2 g sorbet stabilizer • 200 g Baked Potato Milk (above), well chilled • 100 g baked potato flesh* • 200 g crème fraîche • 2 g salt

For assembly:
Hazelnut oil • Exmoor caviar • Fresh pepper dulse

*After baking potatoes to make the baked potato milk, scoop out and save the baked potato flesh for the potato ice cream.

Make the potato crisps:
Wash the potato, dice it, and boil it in unsalted water until soft. Set a sieve over a bowl and pour in the potato and cooking liquid. Reserve the cooking liquid and transfer the potato to a blender. Blend the potato to a thin smooth puree, adding enough cooking liquid to the blender to achieve a consistency just thicker than soup.
Spread this puree thinly on a silicone mat and dehydrate, either in a dehydrator or in a 160°F (70°C) oven until dry and crisp. Break into pieces and deep-fry for 1 second in 350°F (180°C) oil. Drain on paper towels and dust with powdered seaweed.

Make the baked potato milk:
Make sure the potato skins are cold after baking. In a bowl, cover the skins with the milk and leave for 24 hours, or longer. Freezing the milk with the skins also helps intensify flavor, just allow enough time then for the block of frozen milk ice to thaw before using it! Strain the milk through a sieve set over a bowl, pushing down on the skins to extract all the milk and all the potato flavor. Refrigerate until well chilled.

Make the potato ice cream:
In a small saucepan, stir together the sugar and stabilizer powder. Add the cold potato milk and let sit for 15 minutes to hydrate. Bring the milk to a boil, whisking to thicken the stabilizer. Chill the mixture again.
In a Thermomix or other powerful blender, combine the milk mixture and the potato flesh and blend until smooth. Add the crème fraîche and salt and blend again briefly to combine.
Pass the mixture though a fine-mesh sieve. Freeze in Pacojet beakers and spin when frozen. (Alternatively, churn in an ice cream machine and freeze.)

38

To assemble:
Put a small scoop of ice cream in each chilled bowl and, with the back of a spoon, indent the ice cream and drop in some hazelnut oil. Add a spoonful of caviar (you can choose the size of the spoon) and add a few sprigs of pepper dulse and the potato crisps. Serve immediately, lest the ice cream lose its ice.

PUMPKIN, SEA BUCKTHORN, AND MARIGOLD
Serves 10

For the sheep cheese and beremeal shortbread:
100 g cold unsalted butter, cut into chunks • 100 g beremeal (whole-grain barley flour), plus more for rolling out • Pinch of salt • Pinch of cayenne pepper • 3 g mustard powder • 100 g finely grated pecorino cheese, plus a little extra • 1 egg, beaten

For the pumpkin seed cream:
500 g organic hulled pumpkin seeds • 625 g roast squash juice* or apple cider (cloudy apple juice) • Salt

For the pumpkin seed mousse:
300 g Pumpkin Seed Cream *(above)* • 125 g pumpkin seed miso or shiro (white) miso • 200 g plus 25 g roast squash juice* • 3 g salt • 3 leaves gelatin, bloomed in cold water until soft • 200 g double cream

For the sea buckthorn gel:
100 g sea buckthorn juice • 100 g freshly squeezed orange juice • 20 g sugar, or more to taste • 2 g agar-agar powder

For assembly:
1 wedge baked pumpkin (such as Crown Prince) per person • Sprouted pumpkin seeds • Apple marigold leaves • Marigold petals

> *To get roast squash juice, bake some butternut squash until collapsing— the squash, not you—and squeeze through cheesecloth (muslin).*

Make the shortbread:
Preheat the oven to 320°F (160°C). Line a sheet pan with parchment paper.
In a food processor, combine the butter, flour, salt, cayenne, mustard powder, and cheese. Pulse to get everything together, then finely pulse the mixture in short spurts as you notice the mixture coming together—it will eventually bind. Wrap in parchment paper and refrigerate for at least 30 minutes. Lightly flour a work surface. Cut off one-quarter of the dough and gently roll out to a scant ¼-inch (6 mm) thickness. Transfer the pastry to the lined pan. It will spread a little. (Refrigerate or freeze the rest of the dough and bake when needed, either as a sheet or cut into little rounds, egg washed and sprinkled with more cheese, for a tasty snack.)
Bake for 15 minutes, rotate the pan front to back, and bake until the shortbread is

a gentle golden-brown color and baked through in the middle, another 4–6 minutes. Allow to cool on the pan.
Crumble the shortbread roughly, leaving larger lumps for pleasing texture. Store in an airtight container and use within a day or two.

Make the pumpkin seed cream:
Warm a wok. Put the seeds in the wok and allow them to heat. DO NOT leave the wok. In a couple of minutes, the first seeds will start to pop. Immediately start vigorously and constantly stirring them or tossing them. The seeds should turn a more vibrant green in a couple of minutes. Do not allow the seeds to brown, even in patches. This will change the flavor and color of the sauce. Keep the seeds moving! And do not leave the wok!
Remove the wok from the heat and tip the seeds onto a baking sheet to cool for 5 minutes.
Transfer the seeds to a Thermomix or powerful blender and start to blend. The seeds will first turn to a powder, then start to clump. This is the oils starting to come out of the seeds. Stop the blender and scrape the seeds back from the sides. Resume the blending. Keep blending for 25–30 minutes on a medium speed, scraping down the sides every few minutes. For the last few minutes, turn to high speed. The paste is ready when it is creamy and pourable. To check, switch off the blender and allow to settle: The oil should begin to accumulate on the surface. If this does not happen, keep blending.
When the seeds have reached the creamy stage, in a small saucepan warm the squash juice. Add the hot juice to the pumpkin seed paste and blend until smooth, another 1 minute. Add a few grains of salt.

Immediately cool the sauce in a metal bowl set over ice (this preserves the green color). Stir the pumpkin seed cream until cool, then cover the surface with parchment paper to avoid a thin skin forming.

Make the pumpkin seed mousse:
Blend together the pumpkin seed cream, miso, 200 g squash juice and salt until very smooth. Pass through a fine sieve.
In a small saucepan, warm the 25 g squash juice and melt the bloomed gelatin in it. Chill over an ice bath, stirring occasionally until the gelatin starts to set. Whip the double cream to soft peaks and fold evenly into the partially set pumpkin seed cream. Refrigerate until completely set.

Make the sea buckthorn gel:
In a saucepan, combine the juices and sugar and heat to dissolve the sugar. Sprinkle the agar-agar over the surface of the juices and whisk immediately, then bring the juice to the boil, still whisking, and simmer for a few seconds to gel the agar-agar. Pour into a shallow container and refrigerate until it sets. Blitz the brittle gel into a smooth paste, using a spice grinder or blender.

To assemble:
Warm a wedge of baked pumpkin and place on a plate. In the hollow of the pumpkin, pile some shortbread crumbles and dot with some of the sea buckthorn gel. Using a large serving spoon or a piping bag, cover the crumble with a dome of the pumpkin seed mousse and strew with the sprouted pumpkin seeds, a few small leaves of apple marigold, and the petals pulled off the marigold flowers. Serve immediately, so the warm pumpkin melts the mousse into a creamy sauce at the table.

POTATO ICE CREAM, PEPPER DULSE AND CAVIAR

WHOLE STEAMED CRAB AND HOT BROWN BUTTER
Serves 1

1 live brown cock crab (about 1 kg) • Salt • Brown butter • Lemon juice, plus lemons for serving • Flaky sea salt • Good bread and fresh butter

To prepare a crab (limiting injury to the crab, and maximizing delight for the diner):
Wrap the crab in a damp towel or seaweed and put it in the freezer for 1 hour—the cold will render it sleepy. Meanwhile, bring a large pan of heavily salted water to the boil. Lift the flap on the underside of the chilled crab and insert a skewer into its nerve center. YouTube videos will show you the details. It will kill the crab immediately. Cook the crab in the boiling salted water for 10–12 minutes. Remove from the pot. Cool in ice water or in a bowl under a cold running tap, until it's possible to handle the warm crab without pain.
Remove the large legs, crack the claws with a heavy object, and cleaver the end joint off to allow access to the bottom sections of the large legs. The smaller legs need only have the bottom joint trimmed off.
Remove the "dead men's fingers" from the body of the crab and discard them. These are the gray gills, and must not be eaten. Sever the body in two with a cleaver or heavy knife down the natural division, to allow access to the meaty channels therein. Scoop all the brown meat from the head into a blender (or into a deep cup or jug if you're using a hand blender). Blend until smooth. If in doing so you detect the rhythmic crunch of flying shell fragments, pass this goop through a sieve to remove the injurious and unsavory splinters. Transfer to a saucepan.

When ready to serve, warm the crab limbs and head through in the oven, covered so they don't dry out. Warm the saucepan of brown meat—it will thicken a little. Whisk or blend in (using the hand blender) as much brown butter as you can, and season with lemon juice. It shouldn't need much salt. Pour the cold wine, have the bread sliced, and the butter, flaky salt, and lemons, plus shellfish crackers and pickers, already on the table. Assemble the crab pieces on a large plate and pour the buttery brown meat into the handy bowl created by the crab's head. Pick, smear, and eat.

GIGHA HALIBUT, COASTAL GREENS, AND SMOKY MUSSEL BUTTER
Serves 10–12

For the smoked mussel stock:
1 kg mussels, scrubbed • 1 shallot, sliced • 75 ml white wine • 75 ml water

For the smoky mussel butter:
200 ml hot Smoked Mussel Stock *(above)* • 275 g cold unsalted butter, diced • 30 ml fresh lemon juice • Pinch of sea salt

For assembly:
1 (150 g) piece Gigha halibut fillet per person (from a whole fish that weighed 4–5 kg) • Fine sea salt • Neutral oil, for cooking the halibut • Flaky sea salt • Lemons, for squeezing • Various seashore greens, like samphire, sea blite, sandwort, sea aster, sea plantain, and arrowgrass, and seaweeds like sea spaghetti and dulse* • 1 piece of halibut "skirt" per person, bread crumbed and deep-fried • A few mussels per person • Crispy fried dulse • Seaweed "tartar sauce": ground pepper dulse, capers, finely diced shallots, and lots of lemon juice

*Clean the sea greens of any clay, shingle, and sand, and wash well.

Make the smoked mussel stock:
In a deep pan, about twice the height of the level of the unopened mussels, combine the mussels, shallot, wine, water, and shallot. Cover and bring to a boil, then reduce the heat and simmer for 45 minutes. Remove from the heat. Let the mussels infuse in their liquor for 45 minutes. Tip the lot into a large colander set over a bowl, mixing the mussels around to allow all the juice to drain out the shells into the bowl.
Strain the stock through a fine-mesh sieve lined with cheesecloth (muslin).
Reserve half of the spent mussels (scatter the remaining mussels on your nearest sea shore for the seagulls to enjoy). Pick the mussel meat from the shells. Smoke the mussels over hay for 20 minutes, stirring the mussels and relighting the hay after 10 minutes.
Bring the stock to a simmer, then remove from the heat. Add the smoked mussels to the hot stock and infuse the stock for 30 minutes. Strain again into a saucepan. Reduce the mussel liquor by around one-third to 200 ml.

Make the smoky mussel butter:
Using a hand blender, add the diced butter to the hot stock one piece at a time, blending until emulsified after each addition. Season with the lemon juice and salt. (This is enough for around 10–12 servings. It's hard to make a smaller quantity, but it freezes well.)

To assemble:
Warm the mussel butter.
Lightly season the halibut with fine sea salt. In a frying pan, heat a little oil over high heat until hot. Add the halibut skin-side down and cook without moving for 1 minute, then reduce the heat and continue to cook for another 2 minutes. Add a little butter to the pan and when it melts and foams, spoon the hot butter over the fish to finish the cooking. It should take no longer than 4 minutes to cook through sufficiently. Remove from the pan and season with flaky sea salt and a squeeze of lemon juice. Meanwhile, lightly blanch the greens in boiling water, fry the halibut skirt, and steam open the mussels.
Transfer the cooked fish to a shallow bowl or plate, add the greens, mussels, crispy seaweed, and puffed skin to the side of the fish, so it all looks a little like a tide line after a storm, and spoon over the smoky mussel butter sauce. Serve the crispy crumbed halibut skirt on the side, with the seaweed tartar sauce.

PAM IS ONE OF THOSE
EXCEPTIONAL CHEFS WHO
UNDERSTANDS WHERE SHE
IS IN PLACE AND TIME. SHE
BRINGS TO THE PLATE HER
HISTORY OF SCOTLAND AND
BRINGS TOGETHER HER
TALENT, EXPERIENCE, AND
LOVE OF FOOD.
— Margot Henderson

PUMPKIN, SEA BUCKTHORN, AND MARIGOLD

PAMELA BRUNTON

MANOELLA BUFFARA

DOMINIQUE CRENN

For Manoella "Manu" Buffara, the role of chef goes far beyond its traditional parameters and meanings—the act of cooking is not just about her guests or herself, but about the entire ecosystem that makes serving food possible. A champion of climate awareness and sustainability, Buffara brings an extraordinary culinary experience to the guests of her restaurant Manu, but also aims to leave the environment a better place than when she found it. Through her work, she strives to imprint her passion and know-how on those around her along the way.

Born in 1983 to a farming family in the city of Maringa in southern Brazil, Buffara's inspiration as a conservationist comes largely from her father, who managed an ecosystem of goats, cows, corn, and other crops. Growing up on a farm taught her the importance of honoring the land around her. And her grandmother solidified young Manu's future as a chef by showing her the ropes in the kitchen and, through her recipes, how to use the fruits of the family's labor. Buffara worked in restaurants outside of Seattle as a teenager, then on a fishing boat and at a cannery in Alaska, ultimately returning to Brazil to attend hotel school and study journalism. She found herself gravitating back to the world of food, and she moved to Italy for cooking school, where she ended up in the kitchens of Noma and Alinea prior to venturing out on her own.

With Manu's 2011 debut in the Brazilian city of Curitiba, Buffara did much more than just open a restaurant: The modest ten-seat space belies what she and her team have set out to achieve both within and beyond its walls. To source products for the restaurant, she gathered an army of local producers from around the state of Paraná and literally pollinated Curitiba by establishing thousands of beehives and planting nearly one hundred community gardens in otherwise abandoned areas. Beyond the plate, she concentrates her efforts on the kitchen's sustainability and waste minimization. And with her tasting menu of locally influenced bites inspired by her grandfather, she put an area primarily known for its urban development and industrialism on the global fine-dining scene's radar, all while sharing her passion for gardening and waste minimization with thousands of families in the area. And now, with multiple awards under her belt and an imminent New York City opening, Buffara is poised to be a leader for fine-dining chefs worldwide who aim to make a lasting impact on the world through sustainability efforts.

MENU

OCTOPUS, SHISO, AND AVOCADO

CURED BEEF IN YERBA MATÉ, SUGAR APPLE, AND COCONUT BACON

OYSTER, PALM HEART, AND MARROW

MACKEREL, FENNEL

PORK, BLACK GARLIC

TUCUPI, COCONUT

Bring the oil up to 390°F (200°C). Break the fish skin into snall pieces, then fry until puffed and crispy. Remove from the oil and lightly salt.

On a fried shiso leaf, spread a bit of the octopus reduction. Top with three dots of avocado sauce, and place a piece of fried fish skin on each dot.

SEAWEED, MUSHROOM, AND DILL
Serves 8

500 g fior di latte gelato • 100 g organic homemade granola

For the seaweed sauce:
20 g nori • 150 g water • 70 g soy sauce • 25 g lemon juice • 2 g xanthan gum

For the dill oil:
200 g dill leaves • 200 g grapeseed oil

For the mushroom powder:
200 g shimeji mushrooms • 200 g shiitake mushrooms

Make the seaweed sauce:
In a blender, blend the nori, water, soy sauce, and lemon juice. Shear in the xanthan gum and blend for 5 minutes.

OCTOPUS, SHISO, AND AVOCADO
Serves 8

For the octopus reduction:
1 octopus (5 kg) • Lemon thyme • 20 g garlic • 1.5 liters water • Manioc starch

For the avocado sauce:
2 avocados • Juice of 1 lemon • Pinch of salt • 1 clove garlic • Olive oil

For assembly:
Oil for frying • 8 shiso leaves • scaled fish skin

Make the octopus reduction:
In a pot, place the octopus, lemon thyme, and garlic and add the water to cover. Cook for 2 hours. Strain the broth and return the broth to a pan. Cook until reduced by half, then thicken it with a little bit of tapioca flour until the texture becomes a gel.

Make the avocado sauce:
In a blender, mix the avocados, lemon juice, salt, and garlic. With the machine running, emulsify in the olive oil.

To assemble:
Heat a small pot of oil to 355°F (180°C). Fry ths shiso leaves until crispy, then remove from the oil and reserve in a warm place.

Make the dill oil:
In a blender, puree the dill and oil together. Filter through a paper bag overnight.

Make the mushroom powder:
Preheat the oven to 250°F (120°C). Arrange the mushrooms on a silicone baking mat and bake until completely dried, 3 to 4 hours. Let cool, then blend the dried mushrooms to a powder and pass through a sieve.

To assemble:
Place a teaspoon of seaweed sauce in the bottom of a bowl. Sprinkle a bit of granola over the sauce, then place a quenelle of gelato on top of the granola. Garnish with mushroom powder and serve immediately.

CURED BEEF IN YERBA MATÉ, SUGAR APPLE, AND COCONUT BACON
Serves 8

For the beef tartare:
30 g yerba maté • 30 g oolong tea • 100 g sugar • 45 g salt • 500 g trimmed beef tenderloin • Olive oil • Sea salt • Black Pepper

For the sugar apple:
150 g sugar-apple (sweetsop) pulp • 50 g onion pickle • Finely chopped cilantro (coriander) • Salt

For the coconut bacon:
180 g thinly sliced coconut meat (or large unsweetened coconut flakes) • 50 ml soy sauce • 5 ml liquid smoke • 15 g brown sugar

For plating:
Oxalis

Make the beef tartare:
In a small bowl, combine the two teas, the sugar, and salt. Cover the beef with the mixture, vacuum-seal, and let it cure for 2 days. Wash the cure off the beef and pat the beef dry. Finely mince the beef like a tartare. Season it with olive oil, salt, and a grind of black pepper.

Make the sugarbapple:
Chop the sugar-apple pulp and season with the onion pickle, cilantro, and a bit of salt.

Make the coconut bacon:
Preheat the oven to 338°F (170°C). Line a large baking sheet with a silicone mat. In a bowl, drizzle the coconut with the soy sauce, liquid smoke, and brown sugar. Mix well. Spread the flakes into an even layer on the lined pan.
Bake until the flakes are mostly dry and turning golden on the edges, 12 to 14 minutes. As they cool, they are going to turn crispy.

To plate:
Put a little of the sugar apple on a plate. (You also may plate on a crispy base, for eating in one bite, like a potato chip or similar.) Cover with beef tartare. Put some slices of coconut bacon on the top. Garnish with oxalis.

OYSTER, PALM HEART, AND MARROW
Serves 12

For the palm heart sauce:
1 kg cleaned fresh hearts of palm • 40 g bacon, chopped • 20 g cassava starch • 100 ml coconut milk

For the bone marrow:
100 g bone marrow • 20 g fresh herbs, finely chopped

For plating:
12 fresh oysters, shucked, shells reserved • Sunweed oil, for grilling

Make the palm heart sauce:
Pass the hearts of palm through a juicer. Combine the juice and pulp and bring to a simmer slowly in a warm temperature (50°–60°C) for 1 day, until reduced to 400 ml. Ferment it. Strain out the pulp and reserve the juice.
In a saucepan, fry the bacon and add the fermented palm heart juice. Let it cook for a few minutes. Meanwhile, stir the tapioca flour into the coconut milk. Add the mixture to the pan and cook until the mixture has thickened.

Prepare the bone marrow:
In a sauté pan, fry the bone marrow until it melts. Add the fresh herbs while it's warm.

To plate:
Grill the oysters quickly with a little oil, as fast as you can, just to warm them. Put each oyster in a shell, cover with the palm heart sauce (warm), and put a few drops of bone marrow on the top.

OCTOPUS, SHISO, AND AVOCADO

COOKING WITH HER OR EATING HER FOOD IS LIKE ATTENDING A PARTY ALONGSIDE HER. SHE GUIDES YOU WITH HER FLAVORS; SHE SHOWS YOU HOW MUCH FUN YOU COULD BE HAVING.

— Dominique Crenn

SEAWEED, MUSHROOM, AND DILL

MANOELLA BUFFARA

DANIEL CALVERT

MAY CHOW

BELON
Hong Kong

With the work ethic and integrity of a chef's chef, and the laser precision to back it up, Daniel Calvert cooks spectacular, refined modern French food. A shining example of Thomas Keller class, he first left his native UK to become sous chef at Per Se in New York, and the lessons he learned there play out in his dovetailing of French and Asian cuisines at Belon in Hong Kong. As the sourdough loaves and Breton butter on the tables signal, Calvert strives to remind diners of the iconic foods and dynamic scene around the 11th arrondissement of Paris. Meanwhile, well traveled and open to influences from diverse cultures, he has the confidence to create menus that comprise dishes like foie gras *au torchon* and Hokkaido scallops with kombu and pomelo.

Calvert was sixteen years old and fresh out of school when he joined the brigade at the Ivy in London's West End. Following that stint, three years at Shane Osborn's Pied à Terre, in central London, set him on the road to classical savoir faire. A leap over the Atlantic to Per Se established Calvert as a perfectionist and kick-started his absorption of global cuisines. His next move took him to Epicure at Le Bristol Paris hotel, a star in the French classical firmament. Exploring the *néo-bistrots* of the 11th arrondissement inspired Calvert to develop his own style of elevated bistro food.

Since Calvert took the helm at Belon in 2017, he has been creating, with his eight-member kitchen staff, sincere, thrilling dishes using ingredients from a wide range of French regions—Racan pigeon from the Loire Valley, Menton lemons, girolles from Provence—along with seafood and produce from Hong Kong and Japan. Now only served off-menu, his pigeon *pithivier* with figs and amaretto exemplifies Calvert's craftsmanlike approach. The sheer variety of produce and his open-mindedness give Belon's menus an innovative and refreshing quality, but far from gratuitous iconoclasm. Calvert pays confident homage to his roots with classics like his chocolate tart Bernard Pacaud. Dishes such as salade Niçoise made with *shima-aji* (striped jack) whitefish or John Dory with clams and green olives, not to mention perfect mille-feuille, showcase Calvert's talent for fusion and skills that are more 8th arrondissement than gritty 11th.

MENU

PIEDMONT HAZELNUT AND BLACK TRUFFLE MILLECRÊPE

DRUNKEN PIGEON

VEAL SWEETBREAD "EN BRIOCHE" WITH MOREL MUSHROOMS AND YELLOW WINE

PIEDMONT HAZELNUT AND BLACK TRUFFLE MILLECRÊPE
Serves 8

For the crêpes:
1 vanilla bean • 500 g whole milk • 4 eggs • 20 g unsalted butter, melted • 20 g sugar • 5 g salt • 60 g Frangelico • 60 g hazelnut flour • 100 g all-purpose (plain) flour

For the hazelnut crème diplomat:
2 sheets silver leaf gelatin, bloomed • 560 g pastry cream • 90 g hazelnut paste • 200 g heavy (whipping) cream

For assembly:
15 Crêpes *(above)* • 420 g Hazelnut Crème Diplomat *(above)* • Black truffle

Make the crêpes:
Scrape the vanilla pod and to a blender add the seeds. Add the rest of the ingredients and blend until smooth. Allow to rest overnight.

Make the hazelnut crème diplomat:
Melt the bloomed gelatin into the pastry cream. In a stand mixer with the paddle attachment, beat together the pastry cream and the hazelnut paste.
In a separate bowl, whip the cream to soft peaks.
Fold the whipped cream into the pastry cream mixture gently.

To assemble:
Build a cake with the crepes, layering 30 g of crème diplomat in each layer. Every three layers, shave 5 g of black truffle. Allow to rest overnight before serving.

DRUNKEN PIGEON
Serves 6

4.5 liters water • 175 g kosher (flaked) salt • 100 g sugar • Thyme • Garlic • Black peppercorns • Dried mushrooms • 500 g vin jaune • 3 pigeons (500 g each)

In a rondeau, combine the water, salt, sugar, thyme, garlic, black peppercorns, and dried mushrooms and bring to a boil. Remove from the heat and let cool. When cold, stir in the vin jaune.
In a separate rondeau, make a well-seasoned blanching liquid of water, thyme, garlic, salt, and sugar. Bring to a boil. When boiling, dunk the pigeons in and out of the boiling stock and finally leave in the pan. Remove from the heat and leave to cook in the residual heat for 30 minutes.
Remove the pigeons from the blanching pot and submerge in the brine. Leave in the brine for a minimum of 3 days.
To serve, carve the pigeon breast off the bone and remove the legs. Split the legs through the thigh bone and serve on a plate with a salad of celtuce and sorrel and dress with the sauce.

DRUNKEN PIGEON

VEAL SWEETBREAD "EN BRIOCHE"

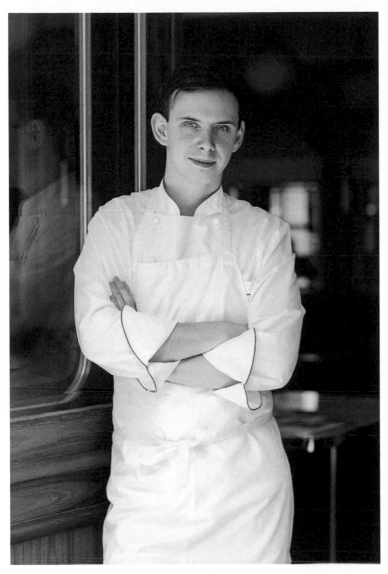

DANIEL CALVERT IS A
MODERN REINCARNATION
OF THE BEST OF FRENCH
CULINARY EXCELLENCE.
— May Chow

DANIEL CALVERT

PAUL CARMICHAEL

MARCUS SAMUELSSON

A source of boundless positive energy, Paul Carmichael is the best kind of leader: one who motivates people by empowering them. His high standards are bolstered by his sincere appreciation and empathy for every member of his team, from top-ranking cooks to hardworking porters. At Sydney's Momofuku Seiōbo, Carmichael has created an environment that inspires his staff and delights his diners.

Raised in Barbados, Carmichael represents the fourth generation of a family deeply connected to food. As a child, he learned Bajan cooking alongside his mother, uncle, grandmother, and great-grandmother. Barbecued pig tails, blood pudding, and fish cakes were among his most cherished childhood favorites. The family closest to him made a living selling their specialties to eager customers. Decades later, Carmichael carries on the tradition, just in a slightly different setting.

After cooking in island restaurants as a teen, Carmichael left home to train at the Culinary Institute of America. He then logged time in a succession of New York City kitchens, including Aquavit, wd~50, and Má Pêche, the latter bringing his initial introduction to David Chang. Carmichael was hesitant when Chang asked him if he would move to Australia to run Seiōbo, but he took the plunge. He initially operated the new venture in a manner familiar to fans of Momofuku restaurants, but gradually worked more of both his culinary roots and personality into the menu, a transition Chang encouraged.

Taking advantage of his adopted country's peerless meat, seafood, and produce, Carmichael now reinterprets the flavors of home in exhilarating tastings. His influence is recognizable throughout the Seiōbo experience, from the vibe-setting soundtrack to the salt cod, plantains, and escabeche scattered across the menu. Sofrito-drizzled marron, a lobster-like crustacean, and jerked Kurobuta pork chops are just two examples of his ability to close the distance between where he's from, where he trained, and where he lives. But a chef is nothing without a dedicated team, and the respectful, supportive, inspiring spirit Carmichael exudes is another key to his success, eveident in his teamwork with manager Kylie Javier-Ashton. As a result, Australians now have, more than ten thousand miles from Carmichael's native waters, a world-class Caribbean restaurant.

MENU

SEA URCHIN, CASSAVA, BAJAN PEPPER SAUCE, BUTTER

COU-COU, CAVIAR, CORN

AVOCADO, SALT COD, CREOLE

PERMIL, CHOKO, SHADOW BENNIE

YOGURT AND BANANA LEAF

Bring the pot of water to a boil and add the polenta. Cook, stirring, until smooth, about 15 minutes, then stir in the reserved okra/shallot mixture and the butter and season to taste with salt.

Make the white wine base:
In a saucepan, combine the wine, shallots, thyme, bay leaves, peppercorns, and coriander seeds. Cook until reduced to 180g. Strain

Make the corn puree:
Cut the kernels off the cobs. In a saucepan, melt the butter over medium-low heat, add the corn, scallions (spring onions), and bay leaf and cook until softened but not browned, 7–8 minutes. Discard the bay leaf. Transfer mixture to a blender and puree, then pass through a fine-mesh sieve.

Make the corn sauce:
In a saucepan, combine the corn puree, wine base, and cream and bring to a simmer. Whisk in the butter. Adjust the seasoning with salt and lemon juice

To assemble:
Add a scoop of the cou-cou to a bowl, add a nice dollop of caviar on top of the cou-cou. Add a generous amount of corn sauce (it should be saucy). Serve hot.

YOGURT AND BANANA LEAF
Serves 6

For the sorbet syrup:
238 g glucose • 190 g sugar • 575 g water

COU-COU, CAVIAR, CORN
Serves 6

For the cou-cou:
180 g polenta • 10 ml grapeseed oil • ½ banana shallot, diced • 50 g okra, diced • 1 sprig thyme • 150 g butter • Salt

For the white wine base:
1 (750 ml) bottle white wine • 20 g banana shallots, sliced • 3 sprigs thyme • 3 bay leaves • 6 black peppercorns • 6 coriander seeds • 1 clove garlic, smashed

For the corn puree:
5 ears of corn, husked • 40 g butter • 2 scallions (spring onions), root end trimmed • 1 bay leaf

For the corn sauce:
200 g Corn Puree *(above)* • 60 g White Wine Base *(above)* • 50 g heavy (whipping) cream • 200 g butter • Salt • Lemon juice

For assembly:
Caviar (Choose one that can stand up to bold flavors.)

Make the cou-cou:
In a bowl, combine the polenta and 300 g water and let soak for 30 minutes. In a frying pan, heat the oil, add the shallot, okra, and thyme and cook until softened but not browned, 3–5 minutes. Add 800 g water and simmer until the items are cooked. Set a sieve over a clean pot and pour the okra mixture into it. Set the okra/shallot mixture aside.

For the yogurt sorbet:
950 g yogurt • 50 g lemon juice • 75 g malto-dextrin • 10 g gelatin • 4 g sorbet stabilizer • Sorbet Syrup *(above)*, as needed

For the banana leaf oil:
200 g banana leaves • 1 liter grapeseed oil

Make the sorbet syrup:
In a saucepan, combine the glucose, sugar, and water. Bring to a boil and let cool.

Make the yogurt sorbet:
In a blender, combine the yogurt, lemon juice, maltodextrin, gelatin, and stabilizer and blend. Add enough sorbet syrup to bring the sorbet base to 28 Brix. Cool and make into sorbet with your given equipment.

Make the banana leaf oil:
Dehydrate the banana leaves overnight at 158°F (70°C).
Blend with the oil until warm and strain.

To assemble:
In a bowl, place a quenelle of sorbet and drizzle a healthy amount of banana leaf oil. Finish with a few grains of fleur de sel.

HIS SPIRIT AND ENERGY
IN THE KITCHEN ARE TWO
TRAITS THAT ARE LOVED
MOST ABOUT PAUL.
— Marcus Samuelsson

PERNIL, CHOKO, SHADOW BENNIE

SEA URCHIN, CASSAVA, BAJAN PEPPER SAUCE, BUTTER

PAUL CARMICHAEL

MARTINA CARUSO

DOMINIQUE CRENN

MENU

BAGNA CAUDA WITH
SEA URCHIN

CONFIT MACKEREL WITH
GREEN OLIVE SOUP, BUFFALO
MOZZARELLA, AND
CANDIED CAPERS

SPAGHETTI WITH GARLIC,
OLIVE OIL, AND CHILI IN A
FISH BROTH WITH PARSLEY

RED MULLET STUFFED WITH
ITS OFFAL, CACCIUCCO SAUCE,
SAMPHIRE WITH OIL
AND LEMON

CAPER ICE CREAM

MILK SOUP WITH CHOCOLATE,
COFFEE, AND CAROB

It is a family affair at Hotel Signum, a coastal resort tucked away in Malfa, on the island of Salina, one of seven in Sicily's Aeolian archipelago. It is there that decorated chef Martina Caruso helms the esteemed kitchen of the world-class hotel alongside her father, Michele, while brother Luca is the restaurant's manager. Clara Rametta, their mother, doubles as Malfa's mayor while also running the hotel.

Caruso was born in 1989—one year after Signum's opening—and raised on the small volcanic island, where a life in the kitchen quickly became second nature to her through generational tradition. Michele was taught by his own mother to cook, and Martina took after her father, learning both the basics and the nuances of regional cuisine from him as she grew, pursuing a career as a chef at quite an early age (one might call her a prodigy).

Caruso left Malfa as a teenager to begin her studies in Cefalù on Palermo's Tyrrhenian coast, first attending accounting and hotel courses before enrolling in courses at the Gambero Rosso cooking school in 2008. A string of prestigious stints followed, bringing her to Trattoria la Rosetta in Rome with chef-owner Massimo Riccioli; at Jamie Oliver's London restaurant, Jamie's Italian, under the guiding hand of Gennaro Contaldo; and at Malabar in Lima, Peru. She worked with Gennaro Esposito at La Torre del Saracino on the Amalfi Coast, and in Rome at Open Colonna and Pipero al Rex. During the summers, Caruso returned to her roots, working at Signum with her family. The flavors of Caruso's hometown—hot pepper, octopus, garlic, oil, lemon, and capers, to name a few—have defined her style of cooking, and some can even be found tattooed on her arm.

Signum is now Caruso's permanent home, bringing her career full circle, and she has already garnered several awards, including the Michelin Female Chef Award 2019, and the youngest Italian to earn a Michelin star. Her key to early success is inspired simplicity fueled by the small producers who shape Sicily's dynamic agricultural landscape, accented by her own creativity and boundless love of her surroundings.

Finish the dish with toasted bread crumbs and the parsley concentrate obtained by mixing of parsley and water.

SPAGHETTI WITH GARLIC, OLIVE OIL, AND CHILI IN A FISH BROTH WITH PARSLEY
Serves 4

50 g garlic • 1 teaspoon crushed chili flakes • 60 g olive oil • 10 g white wine • 200 ml fish broth • 500 g spaghetti • 100 g Parmesan cheese • 200 g toasted bread crumbs • 100 g chopped parsley • 20 g water • 5 g salt

In a sauté pan, fry the garlic and chili flakes in the olive oil. Add the wine and let evaporate. Add the fish broth and reduce a little. In the meantime, cook the spaghetti in abundant salted water, drain "al dente". Dress the spaghetti in the sauce and add some grated Parmesan cheese.

RED MULLET STUFFED WITH ITS OFFAL, CACCIUCCO SAUCE, SAMPHIRE WITH OIL AND LEMON
Serves 4

For the cacciucco sauce:
500 g octopus • 500 g mussels • 500 g shrimp (prawn) heads • 500 g red mullet bones • 40 g extra-virgin olive oil • ½ carrot • 1 onion • ½ stalk celery • Basil • Parsley • Wild fennel fronds • 250 g tomatoes • 100 g white wine

4 red mullets • 1 shallot, peeled and chopped • 50 g unsalted butter • White wine vinegar • Honey • 400 g samphire • Extra-virgin olive oil • Lemon • Sage leaves

Make the cacciucco sauce:
Clean all the fish well and chop it. Dice the vegetables. In a saucepan, heat the oil, then cook the carrot, onion, celery, basil, parsley, and fennel. Add the tomato and the chopped fish. Add the wine and reduce, then the water and ice and filter.

Clean, descale, and gut the red mullets, then rinse under running water and allow to dry. Reserve the fish scales and the liver. Filet the fish, leaving the tails on. In a pan, cook the reserved livers, shallots, butter, vinegar and honey. Stuff the mullets with this paté, then cook in a steam oven. Clean and blanche the samphire, then grill and dress with olive oil and lemon. Fry the reserved fish scales and the sage leaves.

To serve, plate the fish and finish with flaky salt and extra virgin olive oil. Add the Caciucco sauce and the samphire, then garnish with the fried fish scales and sage.

CONFIT MACKEREL

SALINA RED PRAWN, BLOODY MARY, SALTED LEMON

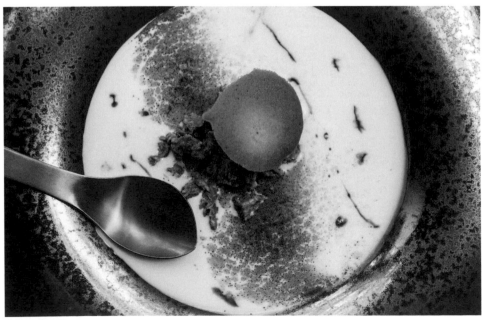

MILK SOUP

DESPITE HER STAR RISING, DESPITE HER BEING CONSIDERED PART OF A NEW GENERATION OF TRENDY CHEFS, SHE IS ALSO AN OLD SOUL.
— Dominique Crenn

BAGNA CAUDA

MARTINA CARUSO

JEREMY CHAN

IKOYI LONDON
London, England

MARGOT HENDERSON

MENU

PLANTAIN, SMOKED SCOTCH BONNET, AND RASPBERRY

SORGHUM TART, SMOKED EEL CREAM, AGED BEEF, AND MUSTARD SALT

LINE-CAUGHT RED MULLET, SAFFRON DAIKON VELOUTÉ, GARLIC PEPPERCORN BUTTER

NATIVE BEEF AND PEPPERCORN BLEND

BLACK-EYED PEA, DARK CHOCOLATE, AND CÈPES

Chef Jeremy Chan opened his London restaurant, Ikoyi, in 2017, with his best friend and ultimately the business arm of the enterprise, Iré Hassan-Odukale. Originally, Hassan-Odukale had decided to start a restaurant, and invited Chan to join. Chan eagerly jumped on board, welcoming an opportunity to explore and expand his interest in traditional West African ingredients, which have ongoingly shaped the modern, creative lexicon of his cuisine. Just one deliciously notable example of this synthesis is Chan's plantain fritters dusted with raspberry powder and served with a smoked Scotch bonnet chile sauce.

Chan is Chinese Canadian, but the fact that he has no West African roots nor had had any experience cooking that region's food didn't prevent him from finding great inspiration in the cuisine. His perpetual search for challenge, his aversion to the easy way, and his passion for research propelled him while he was developing Ikoyi's menus.

Those same impulses led Chan to cooking in the first place. As a teenager, he would research and recipe-test days ahead of family meals, which were infrequent, to make sure their time together was satisfying and well spent. Later, he obsessed over cookbooks, absorbing the contents of hundreds of volumes. When he starting working in top-ranked kitchens (including Claude Bosi's Hibiscus, René Redzepi's Noma, and Dinner by Heston Blumenthal), even though he was green, the contents of the library in his head and his ability to recall it all offered substantial material to draw upon.

Although he doesn't have a direct cultural relationship to Nigerian food, Chan's approach to cooking at Ikoyi is connected through affinity and research. He scoured the archives at the British Library to inform his knowledge of West African cuisine and history, and he has cited everything from science-fiction movies, such as *Blade Runner*, to Mark Rothko canvases as aesthetic inspiration. These influences animate his wild, unexpected dishes, while his days working under exceptional chefs instilled in him the confidence to serve them.

For Chan, dining is art—it can be complex and challenging, yet should always be rewarding. He is young among his peers but has already earned accolades, earning a Michelin star at Ikoyi just one year after opening.

SORGHUM TART, SMOKED EEL CREAM, AGED BEEF, AND MUSTARD SALT
Serves 50–60

For the tart shells:
500 g flour • 350 g sorghum flour • 20 g sugar • 15 g salt • 10 eggs • 2 kg milk • 150 g beef fat, rendered • 250 g butter, melted

For the smoked eel cream:
300 g smoked eel (prepped weight) • 300 g crème fraîche • Smoked salt

For the aged beef:
500 g rib trim of 3-month aged Warren's beef • 150 g peeled shallots, finely brunoised • 35 g walnut oil • 10 g squid garum • 10 g Worcestershire sauce • 10 g Minus 8 Maple Brix verjus • 5 g Tabasco sauce • 10 g Dijon mustard • 2 g lemon juice • 15 g kumquat kosho

For the mustard salt:
2 kg collard greens (unprepped weight) • 20 g salt (4%) • 25 g mustard seeds (5%)

For the honey pickle citrus:
1 kg buddha's hand citron • 120 g honey • 150 g Minus 8 Maple Brix verjus • 20 g salt • 180 g water

To finish:
1 black truffle

Make the tart shells:
Preheat the oven to 280°F (140°C). In a large bowl, blend all the ingredients together. It will be like a pancake batter. Cook the base in a nonstick pan and then cut out rounds with a 2.5-inch (6.5 cm) ring cutter. Fit the rounds into 2-inch plastic molds (the edges will overlap the mould and then shrink during baking) and bake for 30 minutes.

Make the smoked eel cream:
Fillet and pin bone the eel. Chop gently and fold into the crème fraîche. Season to taste with smoked salt.

Prepare the aged beef:
In a bowl, mix everything together and season well with salt.

Make the mustard salt:
Dehydrate the collard greens at 167°F (75°C) for 1 to 2 hours. Weigh out 500 g of the dried collards and blend with the salt and mustard seeds for 2 to 3 minutes to create a very green and well seasoned powder.

Make the honey pickle citrus:
Slice the citron thinly on a mandoline. In a saucepan, combine the honey, verjus, salt, and 180 g water. Bring the pickling liquid to a boil, then take off the heat. Vacuum-seal the sliced citron with the brine.

To finish:
Place a piece of citron in the base of the tart shell, followed by a generous teaspoon of the beef. Spread the eel cream over the top until flat. Dust with the mustard salt and then the truffle.

NATIVE BEEF AND PEPPERCORN BLEND
Serves 50–60

For the fermented daikon greens:
1 kg organic daikon greens (freshly harvested) • 20 g salt • Smoked salt • Apple cider vinegar

For the peppercorn sauce:
15 kg aged beef trim and rib bones • 2 kg peeled Jerusalem artichokes • 100 g butter • 100 g aged beef fat • 100 g peeled garlic, sliced • 25 g black peppercorns • 20 g Malabar peppercorns • 20 g Penja peppercorns • 15 g uziza peppercorns • 15 g white Penja peppercorns • 10 g Gola peppercorns • 10 g grains of paradise • 10 g Sichuan peppercorns • 40 g smoked paprika • 700 g brandy • 25 g uda pods • 1 kg light (single) cream • 200 g Minus 8 Maple Brix verjus • Smoked salt

For the pickled peppercorns:
200 g sugar • 250 g apple cider vinegar • 150 g water • 20 g urfa biber • 150 g green peppercorns • 150 g pink peppercorns

For the beef fat and beef:
4 kg fat from 3-month aged Warren's beef native beef • 1 whole untrimmed native 2- to 3-month aged beef rib • Smoked butter

To finish:
Irú XO Sauce *(recipe follows)* • Smoked salt

Make the fermented daikon greens:
Wash the greens very lightly to maintain the wild bacteria. Place in a vacuum bag with salt and shake well before sealing on full pressure. Ferment for 2 weeks in a 68°F (20°C) environment. Chop well and season further with the smoked salt and vinegar if required.

Make the peppercorn sauce:
In a large stockpot, place the bones and trim and cover with water. Simmer for 12 hours, then strain out the solids and strain the stock through cheesecloth (muslin). Return to the pot and reduce to 4.5 kg to achieve an intense aged beef stock.
In a food processor, blend the Jerusalem artichokes. In a large pot, caramelize the Jerusalem artichokes in the butter and beef fat until very golden brown. Add the garlic and continue to cook but make sure the garlic doesn't burn, staying a nice golden color. In a dry pan, toast all the different peppers and then blend with the smoked paprika. Add the spices to the artichokes, then

add the brandy. Reduce by half, then add the beef stock, the uda pods, and cream. Reduce until the sauce coats the back of a spoon. Strain out the uda pods. Working in batches, blitz the sauce in a blender to a fine consistency for 8 minutes at a time. Season with the verjus and smoked salt.

Make the pickled peppercorns:
Dissolve the sugar into the vinegar and water. Add the urfa biber and the peppercorns and store vacuum-sealed.

Render the beef fat:
Bake the fat overnight at 240°F (115°C) to fully render. The next day, pass it through a chinois.

Prepare and cook the beef:
Remove the fat and rib cap of the beef. Clean the rib caps and trim well, reserve for other use. Separate the deckle muscle from the rib eye. Trim and portion the eye into 130–140 g pieces.
Warm the beef fat to 122°F (50°C). Gently poach the beef in the fat until the internal temperature reaches 118°F (48°C). Remove and rest before grilling.
Prepare a charcoal fire and grill the beef quickly while brushing with smoked butter. It is important to not overgrill the outside of the beef to maintain the pure taste of the fat and meat flavor.

To finish:
Warm the peppercorn sauce and finish with a spoonful of the pickled peppercorns and chopped fermented daikon tops.
Let the beef rest then carve in half. Brush the face with irú XO sauce and season with smoked salt.

IRÚ XO SAUCE
Boiling water • 50 g irú • 400 g dried porcini mushrooms • 400 g dried shiitake mushrooms • 300 g dried crayfish • 1.6 kg vegetable oil • 300 g aged beef rib trim, minced • 600 g aged beef fat, minced • 400 g shallots, finely minced • 75 g ginger, finely minced • 30 cloves garlic, finely minced • 6 Scotch bonnet chilies, finely minced • 100 g rum • 50 g Maple8 vinegar • 75 g light brown sugar • 3 whole star anise • 20 g chipotle chili powder • 20 g red hot chili powder • Smoked salt

Place the irú and dried mushrooms together in a heatproof bowl. Place the crayfish in a separate heatproof bowl. Pour boiling water over the mushrooms and irú and soak for at least 3 hours or overnight. Pour boiling water over the crayfish and infuse for 1 hour. Set a sieve over a bowl and drain the mushrooms, reserving the soaking liquid. Measure out 500 g of mushroom stock and set aside. Drain the crayfish. Mince everything separately until fine but not pureed. In a deep heavy-bottomed pot, heat the vegetable oil over low heat. Add the beef and beef fat and cook until crisp and golden. Add the crayfish and continue to cook until the meat/fish is a deep rich golden color. Add the mushrooms, shallots, ginger, garlic, and chilies and cook for 10 to 15 minutes until everything is golden, caramelized, and bubbling with the oil. Move everything to a large hotel pan (gastronorm). Deglaze the pot with the rum and the reserved mushroom stock and then scrape, adding everything to the hotel pan with the other ingredients.
Cook on full dehydration in the oven at 293°F (145°C) with a 30-minute timer, turning every 30 minutes. Continue to cook for 1 hour, then add the tamari, maple verjus, brown sugar, star anise, and chili powders. Cook for a further 3 to 4 hours until a really dark caramelized consistency forms.
Blitz everything in batches in a Thermomix and season well.

BLACK-EYED PEA, DARK CHOCOLATE, AND CÈPES
Serves 50–60

For the black-eyed pea ice cream:
1.85 kg soy milk • 50 g tapioca starch • 300 g cooked black-eyed peas • 300 g honey • 100 g dextrose • 100 g ice cream stabilizer • 50 g light brown sugar • 15 g smoked salt

For the cèpe/shiitake oil:
1.5 kg grapeseed oil • 250 g dried cèpes (porcini) • 250 g dried shiitake mushrooms

For the sorghum beef fat crumb:
300 g sorghum tart trim • 140 g light brown sugar • 90 g rendered aged beef fat

For the dark chocolate shards:
500 g dark chocolate (65% cacao) • 200 g light brown sugar • Smoked salt

Make the black-eyed pea ice cream:
In a saucepan, combine 1 kg of the soy milk and 40 g of the tapioca starch, bring to a boil, and quickly whisk. Set aside to cool slightly. Working in batches, blitz the black-eyed peas with the tapioca soy milk, the remaining 850 g soy milk, the honey, dextrose, stabilizer, brown sugar, and smoked salt. Blend each batch for 6 minutes to make sure the peas are fully broken into the milk and as smooth as possible.
Pass through a chinois and then freeze in Pacojet beakers overnight.

Make the cèpe/shiitake oil:
In saucepan, heat the oil to 185°F (85°C) and pour over the dried mushrooms. Cover well with plastic wrap (cling film) and

cook in a 185°F (85°C) oven for 12 hours. Allow to cool, then vacuum-seal with the mushrooms for 48 hours. Strain the oil and reserve the mushrooms for another use.

Make the sorghum beef fat crumb:
In a food processor, blitz the tart trim, brown sugar, and beef fat together. Spread on a sheet pan and bake at 250°F (120°C) until golden, about 45 minutes. Keep frozen.

Make the dark chocolate chards:
Melt the chocolate in a bain-marie until just melted. Add the brown sugar and whisk well. Line a large hotel pan (gastronorm) with parchment paper. Pour the melted chocolate into a very thin layer in the pan. Freeze overnight, then carefully break into shards (using gloves so as to not leave any fingerprints on the chocolate).

To finish:
Place a spoonful of the sorghum crumb into a bowl followed by a large quenelle of the ice cream. Make an indentation and fill with the cèpe/shiitake oil. Place a shard of chocolate alongside the ice cream.

JEREMY'S FOOD IS EXACTING, PRECISE BUT ALSO OFF-PISTE—HE'S ALMOST LIKE A RESEARCHER IN THE WAY HE TAKES TRADITIONAL RECIPES FROM THE HISTORY BOOKS AND COURAGEOUSLY TRANSFORMS THEM INTO SOMETHING QUITE DIFFERENT.
— Margot Henderson

SORGHUM TART, SMOKED EEL CREAM, AGED BEEF

JEREMY CHAN

ALEX CHEN

HUGH ACHESON

BOULEVARD KITCHEN &
OYSTER BAR
Vancouver, British Columbia,
Canada

MENU

GREAT BEAR SCALLOP CRUDO

TERRINE OF HAMACHI

SLOW ROASTED SALMON

DUCK FAT POACHED HALIBUT

KING CRAB EN CROUTE DE SEL, CAVIAR BUTTER

DRY AGED SQUAB, PORCINI, JAMON IBERICO

SUGAR "CRUST" SLOW-COOKED PINEAPPLE

Though his achievements are countless, Alex Chen is not a flashy chef. He did captain Team Canada at Lyon's esteemed Bocuse d'Or, and has won other culinary competitions, but you are much more likely to find him working service at Boulevard, his Vancouver restaurant. Precision is the first quality that comes to mind when assessing Chen's cooking, built on an old-school French foundation, but with zero pomp. Instead, he melds wild and fresh West Coast sensibilities with an atlas full of flavors to make an elegant declaration all his own.

Originally from Malaysia, Chen and his family arrived in Vancouver when he was thirteen years old. He got serious about cooking during high school, then completed a culinary degree and started his career, training under revered Canadian chefs Robert Sulatycky and Bruno Marti. Sulatycky was a mentor at the Four Seasons Hotel in Toronto who then later recruited Chen to join his team at the Beverly Hills Hotel in Southern California, where Chen would rise to become the property's executive chef.

Sophisticated fine dining was clearly a natural fit for Chen, as were high-stakes situations such as the culinary competitions. As much as he relishes those arenas, however, the older, wiser Chen now values collaboration above all else—with partners and colleagues, but especially with the unparalleled ingredients of British Columbia.

Chen has a knack for applying his deft, thoughtful eye and hand to the bounty of western Canada, always doing just enough to leave an impression without compromising any natural splendor. This touch is exemplified in his seafood towers, overflowing with wild British Columbia shrimp, Read Island mussels escabeche, and Dungeness crab Louie—all pristine seafood, elevated by the gentlest of preparations. The chef's deep understanding of Asian cookery comes into play with dishes such as Balinese chicken curry or gorgeously roasted sable glazed with soy and sake and served with baby hakurei turnips. With his ability and leadership skills alike, Chen is truly a chef's chef, understanding what it takes and instilling that fire in everyone around him.

DUCK FAT POACHED HALIBUT
Serves 6

For the cured halibut:
Grated zest of 1 lemon • 6 tablespoons sea salt • 6 halibut fillets (4 oz/120 g each)

For the geoduck clam:
1 lb (455 g) live baby geoduck clam (preferably from Taylor's Shellfish)

For the Manila clams:
15 g grapeseed oil • 1 medium shallot, thinly sliced • ½ clove garlic, thinly sliced • ¼ small bulb fennel, thinly sliced • 1 lb (455 g) Manila clams, rinsed, cleaned, and free of sand • 200 g Noilly Prat • 1 bay leaf

For the BC razor clams:
1 lb (455 g) live razor clams (3–4, depending on size)

For the tapioca pearls:
2 tablespoons tapioca pearls • Kosher (flaked) salt

For the clam velouté:
15 g grapeseed oil • 2 small shallots, thinly sliced • ¼ bulb fennel, thinly sliced • ½ stalk celery, thinly sliced • ½ cup (120 ml) Errázuriz late-harvest Sauvignon Blanc • 2 cups (475 ml) halibut stock • ¼ teaspoon fennel pollen • 1 sprig tarragon • 1 sprig dill • ¼ cup (60 ml) heavy (whipping) cream • Sea salt • Juice of ¼ lemon

For the poached halibut:
4 cups (950 ml) duck fat • 4 portions Cured Halibut *(above)* • Pinch of fennel pollen • Small pinch of Espelette pepper • Sea salt • 1 lemon, halved

To finish:
1 tablespoon (15 g) unsalted butter • 1 teaspoon finely chopped chives • ½ teaspoon chopped fresh dill • ¼ teaspoon chopped fresh tarragon • 3 tablespoons small squares (scant ¼ inch/5 mm) fresh BC bull kelp • Grated zest of ⅙ lemon • 1 tablespoon Northern Divine caviar

Cure the halibut:
In a small bowl, mix the zest with the sea salt. Season the halibut aggressively with the lemon salt. Set a timer and cure for 6 minutes. Rinse the salt off the halibut in a stainless steel bowl full of cold water, gently washing off the salt for 10 seconds. Pat dry with paper towels and reserve the cured halibut in the fridge.

KING CRAB EN CROUTE DE SEL, CAVIAR BUTTER

GRASS-FED BUTTERED CUCUMBER BLOSSOMS

DUNGENESS CRAB, PERSIMMON, WHITE SOY, CRAB-LIVER DASHI

Prepare the geoduck:
Bring a pot of water to a boil. Submerge the clam in the boiling water for 10 seconds. Remove the clam from boiling water and plunge into a bowl full of ice water to chill it down for 3 minutes. The outer skin of the geoduck should now come off easily. Using a small, flexible offset spatula, follow the shape of the clam to shuck and cut the adductor muscle of the clam shell to expose the inside of the clam. Remove the round ball shape part of the clam and discard. Split the siphon of the clam in half and thinly slice the meat. Save the bottom part of the clam and all the liquor for the velouté *(below)*. Reserve the thinly sliced clam in the fridge.

Prepare the Manila clams:
Heat a pot over medium-high heat and add the oil. Add the shallot, garlic, and fennel and sweat for 30 seconds. Add the clams and deglaze with Noilly Prat. Add the bay leaf. Cover and steam until the clams fully open, about 2 minutes. Strain the broth right away. Let the clams cool down at room temperature until cool enough to handle. Remove the clams from the shells and using a paring knife cut the "cockscomb" part away from the stomach of the clam. Save the cockscomb in the fridge along with the sliced geoduck. Keep the broth and the other part of the clams for the velouté *(below)*.

Prepare the razor clams:
Bring a pot of water to a boil. Submerge the razor clams into the boiling water for 10 seconds, then chill in a big bowl of ice water for 3 minutes. Using a flexible offset spatula, remove the meat from the shell. Save the siphon part of the clam and set the remainder aside for the velouté *(below)*. Collect any liquor when processing the clams.
Cut the clam meat into small bite-size slices, about ⅜ inch (1 cm) wide.

Cook the tapioca:
Bring a pot of water to a boil. Add the tapioca pearls and ½ tablespoon of kosher salt per 1 liter of water. Cook, stirring often with a whisk, until the tapioca is translucent and tender when chewed. Drain and rinse under cold water until cool. Keep in the fridge.

Make the clam velouté:
Heat a pot over medium heat and add the oil. Add the shallots, fennel, and celery and sweat for 1 minute. Deglaze with the wine and reduce by two-thirds. Add the halibut stock, reserved clam trimmings, clam juice, clam liquor, fennel pollen, tarragon, and dill. Reduce slowly and turn the heat down to low. Skim often to remove the scum from the stock. Reduce to one-quarter of the original volume. Stir in the cream and reduce the liquid by half. Adjust the seasoning, balance with the lemon juice. Strain through a fine chinois. Reserve the sauce until the last minute.

Poach the halibut:
Warm the duck fat to 140°F (60°C). Season the halibut with a small amount of fennel pollen and Espelette. Submerge in the duck fat and cook to an internal temperature of 125°F (52°C).
Remove the halibut from the duck fat and season lightly with sea salt and a small squeeze of lemon juice

To finish:
In a pot, bring the clam velouté to a boil. Taste and adjust seasoning. Mount the sauce with the butter. Stir in the chives, dill, tarragon, and kelp. Add the tapioca and all the clams. Bring the sauce back to a low simmer. Add the lemon zest and the caviar. To plate, divide the sauce into 4 equal portions and serve the halibut on top of the sauce.

TERRINE OF HAMACHI, FOIS GRAS, LOCAL SIDE STRIPE
Serves 12

For the terrine:
½ cup (67 g) kosher (flaked) salt • Grated zest of ½ lemon • 1 lb (455 g) fresh hamachi loin, 12 inches (30.5 cm) long, 3 inches (7.5 cm) wide, and ½ inch (1.25 cm) thick • 6 pucks Rougié foie gras • Salt and freshly ground black pepper • 1 lb (455 g) shell-on side stripe shrimp (prawns), heads off • 2 tablespoons chopped chives • 1 oz (28 g) Périgord truffles, thinly sliced

For the sunchoke consommé:
2 lbs sunchokes (Jerusalem artichokes) • 2 tablespoons oil • 2 sprigs tarragon • ¼ lb (115 g) white fish fillet • ½ lb (225 g) peeled side stripe shrimp • ½ head fennel, finely diced • Small leeks, thinly sliced • ½ stalk celery, diced • 4 egg whites • Salt and freshly ground black pepper • 2 tablespoons white shoyu • ¼ cup (60 ml) dry white wine

Make the terrine:
Mix the kosher (flaked) salt and lemon zest together. Sprinkle over the hamachi and cure for 6 minutes. Rinse and pat dry.
Season the foie gras with salt and pepper. Sear in a pan over medium-high heat for 30 seconds on each side. Remove the foie gras from the pan and chill in the fridge.
In a pot, bring 3 liters water to a boil and add 2 tablespoon kosher salt. Add the shrimp (prawns) and cook for 30 seconds. Drain and let the shrimp cool at room temperature for 10 minutes. Peel the shrimp and reserve the shells for the consommé.
Line the inside of a terrine mold with plastic wrap (cling film). Line the bottom of the mold with the cured hamachi, trimming as needed depending on the shape and dimension of your terrine mold. Make a middle layer with peeled shrimp and sprinkle with the chives. Arrange the black truffle slices to cover the shrimp. Make a final layer with the foie gras.

Wrap the terrine tightly with plastic wrap. Set a steamer at 125°F (52°C) and steam for 1 hour.
Let the terrine cool at room temperature for 20 minutes. Then refrigerate overnight to chill.

Make the consommé:
In a pan, roast the sunchokes (Jerusalem artichokes) with oil with medium heat for 5 minutes. Turn the heat down to low and slowly roast for 20 minutes.
In a small pressure cooker, combine the sunchokes and just enough water to cover. Add the tarragon and reserved shrimp shells and pressure cook for 20 minutes. Strain the stock through a chinois and let cool over an ice bath for 30 minutes.
In a food processor, combine the white fish fillet, peeled shrimp, fennel, leeks, celery, and egg whites and process for 30 seconds. In a soup pot, combine the sunchoke stock and processed fish. Stir with a whisk and slowly bring the stock to a simmer. Stop whisking and slow simmer for 45 minutes to clarify. Strain the consommé through a coffee filter.
Adjust the seasoning with salt and pepper and add the white shoyu.
To plate, use a hot long slicing knife to evenly cut the terrine, then let sliced terrine sit at room temperature for 10 minutes. Brush a slice of terrine with a small amount of olive oil and season with small amount of cracked black pepper and fine sea salt. In a bowl, add 3 fl oz of sunchoke consommé and place a slice of terrine on top. Garnish with sliced truffles, trimmed fennel, fennel flowers, and coriander blossom.

ALEX CHEN IS PROBABLY THE MOST PRECISE CHEF I HAVE EVER SEEN WORK. THERE IS NOT MUCH IN FOOD THAT HE IS INCAPABLE OF.
— Hugh Acheson

KING CRAB EN CROUTE DE SEL, CAVIAR BUTTER

ALEX CHEN

MIA CHRISTIANSEN

MARGOT HENDERSON

BARR
Copenhagen, Denmark

Mia Christiansen's menu at Barr, in Copenhagen, could be called a paean to Northern Europe—in particular, Scandinavia, the British Isles, and the Benelux countries—though some may fondly just call it "beer food." But while she does indeed embrace the classics of what the Barr team calls "Northern Sea cuisine," her dishes are fresh and creative. Occupying the space of the original Noma, Barr opened as a collaboration between René Redzepi and Chef Thorsten Schmidt, with Christiansen helming the kitchen. She makes use of New Nordic techniques, but the menu is more fine dining meets comfort food: in dishes like Schnitzel Weiner Art, a tender schnitzel of pork with horseradish and anchovies; herring with plums, salted rhubarb, and rosehip; and a dessert sourdough pancake served with cloudberries, caramelized whey, and soft-serve ice cream.

Christiansen grew up on the mainland of Denmark, and began cooking when she was about fifteen years old. She credits her childhood for her own culinary inspirations and style: her constant surroundings of plants, flowers, and nature; hunting for wild game with her father and grandfather; enjoying the masterful home cooking of her mother and grandmother. While working as a dishwasher at Belli, in Århus, she fell in love with the restaurant business, and eventually pursued a culinary degree after starting university studies in Middle Eastern cultures. She has since worked in food venues from bakeries and pastry shops in Austria to street-food stalls in Thailand and Malaysia to the two-Michelin-starred Maaemo in Oslo. Before opening Barr, she worked at the café-cum-nightclub Castenskiold in Århus and the Brøndums Hotel, a historic inn located in Skagen, a northern port town in Denmark.

Christiansen's personal history provides hints to the sources of an intangible magic that infuses her dishes. At Barr, the same care and warmth pervades the whole restaurant, yielding an all-compassing conviviality unique to the restaurant's vision—and to its chef's philosophy.

MENU

BEET SALAD WITH GREEN STRAWBERRIES AND HORSERADISH CREAM

SOURDOUGH PANCAKES WITH MUSSELS, ELDERFLOWER, AND CAVIAR

HOT-SMOKED MACKEREL WITH TOMATOES AND HIPBERRIES

SMOKED FRESH CHEESE, PRESERVES, AND A VEGETABLE PLATTER

SMOKED BONE MARROW WITH GREEN GOOSEBERRY SALSA, TOASTED RYE, AND ARUGULA FLOWERS

CRISPY CHOUX PASTRY, RED CURRANTS, AND WHIPPED CREAM

SOURDOUGH PANCAKES WITH MUSSELS, ELDERFLOWER, AND CAVIAR

For the sourdough pancakes:
300 g milk • 100 g sourdough • 50 g dark beer • 130 g wheat flour • 8 g salt • 10 g Microplaned lemon zest • Butter

For the mussel stock:
10 kg blue mussels, scrubbed and rinsed • 1 kg white wine • Butter • Elderflower vinegar

To finish:
Brown butter • Fresh elderflowers • White sturgeon caviar • Wood ants

Make the sourdough pancakes:
In a bowl, stick blend the milk, sourdough, beer, flour, and salt. Pass through a chinois and stir in the lemon zest.
Pan-fry pancakes in butter.

Make the mussel stock:
Heat up a large pot, add the mussels, then the white wine. Cover tightly and simmer for 25 minutes.
Strain and reduce. Add butter and elderflower vinegar to taste.
Broil (grill) the pancake and brush it with brown butter. Fold it and sprinkle fresh elderflowers on the top. Make a quenelle of caviar on the side and top it off with a generous amount of wood ants.
Foam the sauce with a stick blender and place it in the middle of the pancake and the caviar.

HOT-SMOKED MACKEREL WITH TOMATOES AND HIPBERRIES

For the hot smoked mackerel:
1 mackerel • Brown butter • Hay and nettles (for cold-smoking)

For the tomato vinaigrette:
220 g cherry tomatoes • 200 g neutral oil • 75 g rose vinegar • 0.5 g Xantana

For the confit tomatoes and rose hips:
Sweet cherry tomatoes, halved • Rose hips (hipberries), halved • Neutral oil

Smoke the mackerel:
Butterfly the mackerel, brush with brown butter, and cold-smoke with hay and nettles for 30 minutes.
Run the mackerel under a salamander and replace with brown butter.

Make the tomato vinaigrette:
Blitz everything in the Thermomix, then pass through a chinois.

Confit the tomatoes and rose hips:
Dehydrate the tomatoes and rose hips at 140°F (60°C) overnight. Rehydrate in rose oil.

SMOKED BONE MARROW WITH GREEN GOOSEBERRY SALSA, TOASTED RYE, AND ARUGULA FLOWERS

For the gooseberry salsa:
100 g fermented green gooseberries • 100 g parsley, with stem, chopped • 100 g shallots, chopped • 100 g parsley oil

For the rye crumble:
300 g dark rye bread

To finish:
1 marrow bone, split • Rose salt • Arugula (rocket) flowers

Make the gooseberry salsa:
Blend all ingredients until smooth.

Make the rye crumble:
Preheat the oven to 350°F (180°C). Blend the rye bread to a fine crumble. Spread on a pan and toast in the oven until crispy.

To finish:
Broil the marrow and season it well with rose salt.
Plate the marrow on a hay-lined plate with the toasted rye bread crumble, gooseberry salsa, and finish with arugula flowers on the top.

SMOKED BONE MARROW

MIA IS AN INCREDIBLE CHEF, AND HER MODERN TAKE ON CLASSIC NORDIC FOOD IS SUBLIME.
I LOVE THAT IN COPENHAGEN BARR'S FOOD IS CALLED CASUAL EATING—IT'S ASTOUNDING, AS NOTHING FEELS CASUAL ABOUT THIS EXCEPTIONAL LEVEL OF COOKERY!

— Margot Henderson

MIA CHRISTIANSEN

CARLOTA CLAVER

LA GORMANDA
Barcelona, Spain

JOSÉ ANDRÉS

MENU

CALABAZA A LA BRASA CON PAPADA IBÉRICA, SETAS DE TEMPORADA Y CARBONARA DE PIÑONES

BOMBA DE PULPO

PERDIZ EN DOS COCCIONES, NABO NEGRO, BIZCOCHO DE ACEITUNA Y AJO BLANCO DE CASTAÑA

ARROZ DE BACALAO, CON GUISANTE LAGRIMA, ALCACHOFAS Y BUTIFARRA NEGRA

Carlota Claver is the chef-proprietor of La Gormanda, a restaurant in Barcelona's Eixample neighborhood. At La Gormanda, Claver serves up contemporary Catalan cuisine—an internationally inspired medley with traditional roots.

This credo makes sense given Claver's heritage: She is the daughter of the restaurateurs behind two successful Barcelona spots, Alba Granados and Alba Paris. After graduating from the Hofmann Culinary School, Claver spent years working in the family business before striking out on her own to open La Gormanda in 2017. There, she created an outlet for expressing her personal culinary vision, in ways more contemporary and nuanced than those of the traditional Catalan restaurants she grew up in.

Playfulness is prevalent at La Gormanda, where Claver's innovations include stuffing traditional *carne d'olla* into gyozas; pumpkin in pine-nut carbonara; and lobster chickpeas. In other words, she marches to the beat of her own culinary drum. Her food is at once referential to and reverential of her Catalan roots and yet utterly free of the constraints associated with them.

For La Gormanda, Claver renovated an old grocery shop to accommodate the tables. Not surprisingly, in addition to her Catalan heritage, seasonality and local produce are central to Claver's vision. Together, the dishes are comforting and familiar, contemporary and original. Despite cooking in one of the most revered and competitive gastronomic cities in the world, Claver's technique and spirit are setting La Gormanda apart. Together with her husband, Ignasi Céspedes, who runs the front of house, Claver is redefining Catalan cuisine.

BOMBA DE PULPO (OCTOPUS BOMBA)
Serves 4

For the potato puree:
400 g Mona Lisa potatoes • 2 g salt • 2 g freshly ground black pepper • 10 ml extra-virgin olive oil

For the bomba filling:
150 g octopus tentacles • Salt and freshly ground black pepper • 5 g hot pimentón de la Vera • 5 g sweet pimentón de la Vera • 10 ml extra-virgin olive oil • 200 g onion, brunoised • 50 g plum tomatoes, finely diced • 2 dried ñora chilies • 1 clove garlic

For the black garlic aioli:
2 organic eggs • 3 cloves black garlic • 150 ml extra-virgin olive oil

For the rocoto pepper cremoso:
50 g mascarpone • 10 g rocoto chili (seeded) • 2 g salt • 2 g freshly ground black pepper

For assembly:
80 g Potato Purée *(above)* • 35 g Bomba Filling *(above)* • 1 egg, beaten • 100 g panko bread crumbs • Olive oil, for frying

For plating:
Flake salt • Chili threads

Make the potato puree:
In a pot of boiling water, cook the unpeeled potatoes until fork-tender. Cool slightly and pass through a food mill. Season with the salt and pepper while still warm. Set aside.

Make the bomba filling:
Season the octopus tentacles with salt and pepper. Vacuum-seal the octopus, both pimentóns, and the oil. Set a circulating water bath to 85°C and cook for 90 minutes. In a pot, brown the onion. Add the tomatoes and the flesh of the peeled ñora chilies. Cook down until the mixture thickens into a compote.
Add the cooked and brunoised octopus and set the sofrito aside to cool.

Make the black garlic aioli:
In a blender, blend the eggs, black garlic, and olive oil until emulsified and thick. Transfer to a piping bag.

Make the rocoto pepper cremoso:
In a bowl, whisk together the mascarpone, rocoto, salt, and pepper. Transfer to a piping bag.

Assemble the dish:
Spread the potato purée into a round and place the bomba filling in the center. Pull the potato puree around the filling and pat into a homogenous ball. Coat with egg and roll in the panko. Refrigerate for 1 hour to firm up.
Bring a pot of oil to 320°F (160ºC). Fry the bomba until golden brown, about 3 minutes. Drain on on paper towels.

To plate:
Place the bomba on a serving plate, then add the aioli and rocoto pepper cremoso on top. Finish with flake salt and a few chile threads.

OCTOPUS BOMBA

PERDIZ EN DOS COCCIONES, NABO NEGRO, BIZCOCHO DE ACEITUNA Y AJO BLANCO DE CASTAÑA (PARTRIDGE COOKED TWO WAYS WITH CHESTNUT AJO BLANCO)
Serves 4

For the partridges and partridge stock:
4 red partridges • 100 g onion, brunoised • 50 g celery, brunoised • 50 g plum tomato, diced • 30 g carrot, brunoised • 30 g parsnip, brunoised • 10 g black turnip, brunoised • 100 ml red wine • 2 sprigs thyme • 1 bay leaf • 2 sprigs rosemary

For the pâté:
Partridge livers • 10 ml extra-virgin olive oil • 30 ml Cognac • 20 ml cream • 2 g salt • 2 g freshly ground black pepper

For the black turnips:
1 black turnip • 2 g salt • 2 g freshly ground black pepper • 5 ml extra-virgin olive oil

For the black olive cake:
50 g black olives • 2 eggs • 1 tablespoon sugar • 60 g all-purpose (plain) flour • 5 g yeast • 1 teaspoon extra-virgin olive oil

For the chestnut ajo blanco:
1 clove garlic • 150 g chestnuts • 50 ml Partridge Stock *(above)* • 20 ml cream • 2 g salt • 2 g freshly ground black pepper

For assembly:
8 partridge breasts (reserved from Partridge Stock, *above*) • 20 g unsalted butter • 5 g rosemary • 5 g salt • 5 g freshly ground black pepper • Flake salt • Olive powder

Prepare the partridges:
Bone the partridges, separate the breasts and thighs, and set aside.
In a large pot, sear the carcasses. Remove them from the pot and add the vegetables to make a mirepoix. Deglaze with the red wine, add the aromatic herbs, and cook for about 1 hour.
For the thighs, brown the thighs and baste with the partridge broth, repeat this process for 1 hour until the thighs are tender and separate easily from the bone.

Make the pâté:
In a sauté pan, sauté the livers and flambé with the Cognac. Transfer to a bowl and mash the livers with the nata to thicken. Set aside until ready to plate.

Prepare the black turnips:
Clean and peel the turnip and vacuum-seal with the salt, pepper, and oil. Set a circulating water bath to 85°C and cook for 1 hour.

Make the black olive cake:
Preheat the oven to 320°F (160°C).
Drain the olives and mash. In a bowl, beat together the eggs, sugar, flour, and yeast. Place the mixture in a silicone mold and bake for 20 minutes.

Make the chestnut ajo blanco:
In a sauté pan, brown the garlic and toast the chestnuts. Moisten with the partridge stock and cook for 20 minutes.
Strain and add the nata, salt, and pepper.

To assemble:
Cook the breasts à la française to the desired doneness.
On each plate, arrange the breasts and thighs harmoniously, leaving enough space to add the other preparations: olive cake, chestnut ajo blanco, black turnip, and pâté. Finish the dish with flake salt, shredded chestnut, and olive powder.

BARCELONA IS ONE OF THE WORLD'S MOST COMPETITIVE CITIES FOR GASTRONOMY. ON THE OTHER HAND, THERE'S UNLIMITED OPPORTUNITY TO CREATE, EXPLORE, AND TAKE RISKS, AND CARLOTA IS DOING ALL OF THOSE THINGS WITH A MATURITY UNLIKE ANY YOUNG CHEF I'VE SEEN.
— José Andrés

BALFEGÓ TUNA BELLY, SEA URCHIN, SALMON ROE AND CRISPY SKIN

CARLOTA CLAVER

NATALIA CROZON

RAQUEL CARENA

LA COURTILLE
Tavel, France

MENU

PORK EAR SALAD

TRIPE GRATIN PARMESAN

CHERRY CLAFOUTIS

Since 2018, Natalia Crozon has been making the atmosphere of La Courtille—located in the sunny courtyard of a historic building that formerly housed a silkworm farm—vibrate with a cuisine that thrives on the goodness of the country: simple recipes that showcase sun-drenched vegetables, vibrant herbs, and aromatic flowers from nearby gardens. The restaurant is a jewel for Tavel, a commune and AOC in the southern Rhône wine region of France, about 10 miles (15 km) from Avignon. Officially designated for rosé wines only, this is also the homeland of Crozon's life partner, Thibault Pfifferling of the revered family of winegrowers and makers behind Domaine L'Anglore. The two met while working at Argentinian chef Raquel Carena's Le Baratin in Paris, an influential purveyor of natural wines.

In fact, it all started with wine. After graduating from high school, Crozon worked at La Carte des Vins, a large and conventional but open-minded Parisian winery. While there, she trained in the dining room at Le Baratin, where she first encountered natural wine and learned about its unique production and qualities. After Crozon eventually settled in the south of France, she found Carena's food had cast its spell on her; she wanted to learn and share the language of her magical way of cooking. Over the course of many trips between Tavel and Paris, Crozon tenaciously taught herself, experimented, cultivated a vegetable garden—and found the perfect site for Courtille. With no more hesitation, she rolled up her sleeves and took the plunge as a proprietor and chef.

Every day, Crozon prepares dishes that celebrate the good life, often flavored with the prized wines of Anglore and other labels from Tavel. Offal meats are a definitive part of her menu, with the influence of her Argentinean mentor deliciously evident in the lemon-buttered brains, fried sweetbreads, and roasted ribs or lamb shoulder. There is an appealing sincerity and intimacy behind the large open space at La Courtille—the front-of-house is run with a small team, hosting less than forty covers a service. The menu is handwritten on a chalkboard. And in the shade of the central hundred-year-old cedar tree, Crozon takes care of some of her prep work, perhaps shelling navy beans for her pistou soup, sharing with her customers the traditional hands-on cooking she represents.

PORK EAR SALAD

2–3 pork ears, well washed • 1 red onion, finely chopped • Carrots • Sprigs of parsley • Salt and freshly ground black pepper • A few chopped cornichons, to taste • Chopped chives or parsley, to taste • Vinaigrette • Salad greens

In a saucepan, combine the pork ears, onion, carrots, parsley sprigs, and water to cover. Season with salt and pepper. Bring to a simmer and cook until tender, about 50 minutes.
Drain and set the ears aside to cool for a bit, then refrigerate.
Once the ears have cooled down, cut them into small pieces and mix them together with the cornichons and chopped herbs. Season with salt and pepper, dress with vinaigrette, and toss to mix. Accompany the ear salad with salad greens.

TRIPE GRATIN PARMESAN (TRIPE GRATIN À LA PARMIGIANA)
Serves 6 to 8

For the tripe:
500 g tripe • Celery, parsley, or thyme, depending on the season and your preference • Beef stock • 5 onions, coarsely chopped • Olive oil • Salt and freshly ground black pepper

For the eggplant:
10 medium eggplants • Frying oil • Fine salt

For the tomato sauce:
5 onions, coarsely chopped • Olive oil • 10 tomatoes, quartered • 1 clove garlic, smashed • Salt and freshly ground black pepper

For assembly:
Grated Parmesan cheese • Chopped basil • Olive oil

Prepare the tripe:
Since tripe is usually sold cleaned and blanched, all that remains to do is to stew it in a pot or saucepan. Add the aromatics, and beef stock to cover. Bring to a low simmer and cook for about 3 hours, or more. Drain the tripe, reserving the cooking liquid, and cut into small squares.
In a rondeau, sauté the onions in some olive oil until they are translucent. Add the tripe, season with salt and pepper, and add some of the cooking liquid so that the tripe completely absorbs it.

Prepare the eggplant:
Cut the eggplant lengthwise into slabs about ⅓ inch (1 cm) thick. In a pot of hot oil, fry the eggplant and drain on paper towels. Season with fine salt and set aside.

LAMB NECK WITH BULGUR AND SWEET SPICES

LA COURTILLE HAS EVERYTHING I LOVE: IT'S LIVELY, THE PANS ARE STEAMING, THE PLATES ARE BOISTEROUS. NATALIA EMBUES EVERYTHING WITH FRESHNESS, WITHOUT A BUSINESS PLAN BUT WITH THE DESIRE TO SHARE A WAY OF LIFE AND A KITCHEN THAT NOURISHES.
— Raquel Carena

Make the tomato sauce:
Preheat the oven to 355°F (180°C).
In an ovenproof saucepan, sauté the onions in some olive oil until they are just translucent. Add the tomatoes and garlic. Season with salt and pepper to taste. Cover the pan, bring to a simmer, and then transfer to the oven to cook for 2 hours.
Discard the clove of garlic and pass the mixture through a food mill to make a fine puree. Set aside.

To assemble:
Preheat the oven to 355°F (180°C).
Once all three elements—the tripe, eggplant, and tomato sauce—have been prepared, arrange in layers in a baking dish, adding the Parmesan and chopped basil as you go. Once fully layered, cover everything with more Parmesan and basil, and drizzle with olive oil. Bake gently in the oven just until the top of the dish is well browned.

CHERRY CLAFOUTIS
Serves 6

100 g unsalted butter • 150 g powdered (icing) sugar • 75 g all-purpose (plain) flour, sifted • Pinch of salt • 150 g almond flour • 2 eggs • 150 ml milk • 600 g cherries

Preheat the oven to 395°F (200°C).
In a small saucepan, melt and brown the butter. When the butter stops foaming—when it no longer "sings"—it is ready.

Generously butter the bottom and sides of a baking dish with some of the browned butter. Add the sugar, shaking it around so that it covers all the interior surfaces. Empty the excess sugar into a bowl.

To the bowl, add the all-purpose (plain) flour, salt, and almond flour and mix together. Whisk in the eggs, milk, and remaining browned butter.
Arrange the cherries (pitted, or not, according to your preference) in the baking dish. Pour the batter over top.
Bake until cooked through (check with a knife), about 40 minutes. Serve while still lightly warm.

GARDEN TOMATOES WITH RICOTTA AND PESTO

TARAMA WITH RED CABBAGE AND CILANTRO SALAD

VEAL KIDNEYS WITH SMASHED POTATOES

NATALIA CROZON

DIANA DÁVILA

MI TOCAYA ANTOJERÍA
Chicago, Illinois, United States

MARCUS SAMUELSSON

"Rethink your understanding of mexican cuisine." That is the message displayed front and center on the homepage of the website for Diana Dávila's Chicago restaurant. It is not quite a mandate, but she makes her point of view clear—to eat at Mi Tocaya Antojería is to amend your most ingrained assumptions, the lofty goal of a chef in full command of her vision. Though Dávila was born and raised in Illinois, her family hails from San Luis Potosí, and she traveled throughout Mexico frequently as a child. Her grandmother, aunts, and uncles shaped her culinary worldview from an early age, as did her parents, who owned and operated Mexican restaurants in the Chicago suburbs. Dávila was in fifth grade when she began working for them; by the age of twenty-one, she had become the head chef of their Hacienda Jalapeños in Oak Forest, where her edgy, unconventional cooking stood out in an otherwise traditional setting.

Formative stints alongside well-regarded Chicago chefs, including Ryan Poli and Giuseppe Tentori, as well as training in Oaxaca and a successful run in Washington, DC, built Dávila's resume, but returning to Chicago and opening a place of her own was always the goal. In 2017, she realized the dream with Mi Tocaya—a term of endearment meaning "my namesake"—in Logan Square. There, the small plates typical of an antojería explode with big ideas, subtle musings, and audacious risks that honor her heritage while challenging the often myopic view of Mexican cuisine outside Mexico.

Dávila's restaurant is unequivocally hers, a canvas for a school of culinary expression she defines as "Midwest Mexican." She plates decadent croquettes of pig's-tail carnitas with cauliflower and lentils, and blankets fish in a complex green mole just as rich and vibrant as the more common dark-hued rendition. Stalwarts of the Mexican pantry, like hoja santa, tomatillos, pumpkin seeds, and dried chiles, come together with unexpected ingredients, like arugula, sweetbreads, or romanesco. Dávila is truly fearless when it comes to pushing boundaries—and this boldness has put her on the map, in Chicago and beyond.

MENU

GUACAMOLE

LECHUGA ASADA WITH CAULIFLOWER AND SIKIL PAK

ENSALADA DE NOPALES WITH BURRATA AND CHILTOMATE

MUSHROOM FLAUTAS WITH PARSNIP CREMA

ENCHILADAS POTOSINAS WITH ENSALADA FRESCA, SALSA CRUDA

GUACAMOLE
Serves 8–10

1 ounce (28 g) garlic • 2 ounces (56 g) serrano chilies, sliced • 4 avocados, halved and pitted • Grated zest and juice of 3 limes • Salt

In a blender, puree the garlic and serranos (or muddle with a molcajete). Scoop the avocado flesh into a large stainless steel bowl and mash with a large masher.
Add the garlic/chili mixture to the smashed avocado in stages, slowly folding it in and tasting as you go (to make sure the guacamole is not too garlicky or spicy). Do not overmash the avocados. Add lime zest and more lime juice. Salt if needed.

ENSALADA DE NOPALES WITH BURRATA AND CHILTOMATE
Serves 4–6

2 red onions, thinly sliced • 2 pounds (910 g) Salted Nopales (recipe follows) • ¼ cup (60 ml) Lime Vinaigrette (recipe follows) • Salt and freshly ground black pepper • 4 ounces (115 g) burrata • 1 cup (240 ml) Tomato Aderezo (recipe follows) • ½ head cauliflower, shaved • 1 bunch cilantro (fresh coriander), picked

In a large bowl, toss the red onions and nopales with the lime vinaigrette. Lightly season with salt and black pepper.
To plate, place in a low bowl with burrata in the center. Top the burrata with the tomato aderezo. Top with shaved cauliflower and garnish with cilantro (coriander).

SALTED NOPALES
Makes 8 quarts (8 liters)

15 pounds (6.8 kg) nopales, cleaned and julienned • 10 ounces (283 g) sea salt

Place the nopales in a large plastic tub and add the salt. Start working salt into the nopales to extract water content. Rinse with cold water and pat dry.

TOMATO ADEREZO
Makes 3 quarts (3 liters)

24 tomatoes, diced and salted for 30 minutes • 8 serrano chilies, charred • 10 ounces (283 g) lime juice • 10 ounces (283 g) roasted garlic oil

In a pot, bring the tomatoes to a boil, then reduce the heat and simmer 20–30 minutes. Add the serranos.
Transfer to a blender and puree super fine. Blend in the lime juice, then the roasted garlic oil.

LIME VINAIGRETTE
Makes 1 quart (1 liter)

6 ounces (170 g) Lime Reduction (recipe follows) • 1 cup (240 ml) sunflower oil • 1 cup (240 ml) vegetable oil • 1 cup (240 ml) extra-virgin olive oil • ¼ cup (60 ml) lime juice • Sea salt

Place the lime reduction in a stainless steel bowl. Whisk the oils in slowly. Finish with the lime juice and check for salt.

ENSALADA DE NOPALES

LIME REDUCTION
Makes 12 ounces (340 g)

4 cups (975 g) lime juice • 8 ounces (225 g) sugar

In a saucepan, combine the lime juice and bring to a boil. Reduce to a simmer and cook until reduced by one-quarter.

ENCHILADAS POTOSINAS WITH ENSALADA FRESCA, SALSA CRUDA
Makes 54 enchiladas

For the enchilado:
½ ounce (15 g) crushed guajillo chili (no stems/seeds) • ½ ounce (15 g) crushed ancho chili (no stems/seeds) • 3 g pimentón • 1 g dried Mexican oregano • 9 g granulated onion • 7 g salt • 2 ounces (55 g) vegetable oil • 3 ounces (85 g) water

For the salsa for queso:
8 ounces (225 g) charred tomatillos • 1 charred plum tomato • 7 g charred, smashed garlic • 2 charred, stemmed serrano chilies • ¼ cup (60 ml) sunflower oil • Salt (optional)

For the queso salsero:
7 ounces (200 g) grated queso Sincho • 7 ounces (200 g) grated queso fresco • 5 ounces (140 g) Salsa for Queso (above)

For the enchiladas Potosinas:
1 pound (455 g) masa • 1¼ pounds (565 g) Queso Salsero (above)

For the salsa cruda:
4 tomatillos, quartered • 1 serrano chili, sliced • 1 avocado, pitted and halved • ½ bunch cilantro (fresh coriander), chopped • 1 ounce (28 g) lime juice • Salt

For the ensalada fresca:
Thinly sliced red cabbage • Finely sliced white onion • Finely julienned black radish • Diagonally thinly sliced scallion (spring onion) • Avocado oil • Lime juice • Salt • Salsa Cruda (above) • Micro cilantro, for garnish

Make the enchilado:
In a stainless steel bowl, combine the chilies, pimentón, granulated onion, and salt. Mix by hand.
In a medium saucepan, heat the oil and to 350°F (177°C). Add the chili mixture and cook, stirring constantly so the paste fries evenly but does not burn. Add a touch of salt. Add the water. Set to 210°F (99°C), occasionally stirring, for 10 minutes, until the chilies reconstitute and turn into a paste. Let the enchilada (chili paste) completely cool before using.

Make the salsa for queso:
Muddle the ingredients in a lava rock molcajete or coarsely blend, adding salt if needed. Transfer to a pan and bring up to a boil, then reduce the heat and simmer for 10 minutes. Set aside to cool.

Make the queso salsero:
In a stainless steel bowl, hand mix the cheeses and the salsa. Set aside for stuffing.

Make the enchiladas Potosinas:
In a bowl, work the cooled chili paste (enchilada) into the masa with your hands until it's evenly incorporated into the masa.
Hand-press a ball of masa (about 15 g) into a thin tortilla round (use a plastic bag as a liner so it doesn't stick). Cook the tortilla on a hot flattop. Only cook the tortilla on one side—it should be raw on the other side (making it adhesive). Remove from the heat and place about 1 teaspoon of the queso salsero mixture in the center. Fold the tortilla in half, enclosing the stuffing and pinching the seams. Return to the flattop to dry the masa on both sides and bind the ingredients. Let cool.
To finish, lightly panfry or sear on the flattop until both sides are crisp. Do not deep fry!

Make the salsa cruda:
In a blender, puree all the ingredients until silky smooth. Taste for salt.

Make the ensalada fresca:
In a large bowl, toss together the cabbage, onion, radish, and scallion (green onion). Toss with avocado oil, lime juice, and salt to taste. Dress with salsa cruda.
Serve the enchiladas with salsa and ensalada on the side.

WHEN EATING DIANA'S FOOD, THERE IS NO DOUBT ABOUT HER FEARLESSNESS WHEN IT COMES TO LAYERING FLAVORS. IT'S ALWAYS A PLEASURE TO SEE A CHEF WHO IS FULLY IN COMMAND OF HER VISION.
— Marcus Samuelsson

ENCHILADAS POTOSINAS

DIANA DÁVILA

CLARE DE BOER &
JESS SHADBOLT

SKYE GYNGELL

KING
New York, New York,
United States

Clare de Boer and Jess Shadbolt are the British co–head chefs of King, a neighborhood restaurant in New York City that the pair opened in 2016 with Annie Shi, who oversees the front of house and wine program.

Shadbolt and de Boer's food at King is inspired by seasonal ingredients and the elegant simplicity of French and Italian cuisines, which they incorporate into succinct daily menus that express both their moods and the best and freshest foods available that day. Their signature *carta di musica* starters, rustic polenta, and grilled meat and fish dishes evolve and revolve around each service but are all beloved among their regulars for their comfort and deceptive simplicity.

The two chefs met while cooking together under Ruth Rogers at the River Café, the famed restaurant in London, before setting their sights on New York as the home of their first business together. In the *New York Times*, the pair modestly resisted the notion that they are really trained chefs and contended that they merely love to cook and eat—that for them King is akin to cooking at home for friends. And indeed, no matter what their path, with King, they created a restaurant that feels like a home. In a highly competitive dining city, their approach is refreshing and disarming, and they have won accolades and a loyal following for their seemingly effortless but astute cooking.

Under de Boer and Shadbolt's direction, King received a glowing two-star review from the *New York Times* restaurant critic Pete Wells, who additionally named King one of the Top New York Restaurants of 2017. The pair were named *Food & Wine*'s Best New Chefs of 2018.

MENU

ARTICHOKE VINAIGRETTE

WILD STRIPED BASS POACHED WITH SUN GOLDS, FENNEL, AND WHIPPED BOTTARGA

PEACH AND POLENTA CAKE

COLONEL

ARTICHOKE VINAIGRETTE
Serves 2

2 globe artichokes • Kosher (flaked) salt • 4 tablespoons Dijon mustard • 2 tablespoons red wine vinegar • ½ cup (120 ml) extra-virgin olive oil, plus more for serving • Maldon salt

Place the artichokes, whole, in a pot of heavily salted cold water and bring to a gentle simmer. When the stem can be pierced (without pressure) with a knife, turn the heat off and let the artichoke sit in the liquid until ready to serve.
In a food processor, combine the mustard and red wine vinegar. With the machine running, add the olive oil in a steady stream until the result is thick and emulsified. Salt to taste and let down with a splash of water for a looser consistency.

To serve, drain the artichoke. Slice the stem off and peel away any woody strings. Place the peeled stem in the bowl. Gently open up the bud of the artichoke without detaching any leaves. Sprinkle it with Maldon sea salt and ladle the vinaigrette over the artichokes. Finish with a drizzle of olive oil.

PEACH AND POLENTA CAKE
Serves 10–12

2¼ cups (470 g) sugar • 2 sticks plus 6 tablespoons (305 g) unsalted butter, at room temperature • 6 to 8 peaches, nectarines, or plums (or use a mix), peeled, pitted, and halved • 1½ cups (230 g) slivered almonds • 1 scant cup (230 g) polenta or cornmeal *(see Note)* • ½ cup plus 1 tablespoon (70 g) all-purpose (plain) flour • ½ teaspoon kosher (flaked) salt • 1 teaspoon baking powder • Grated zest of 1 lemon • 4 eggs • Crème fraîche, for serving

Preheat the oven to 300°F (150°C). Generously butter the bottom and sides of a 9-inch (23 cm) round cake pan and line the bottom with a round of parchment paper. Cut one long strip of parchment paper to line the sides of the pan so that the paper reaches all the way around the pan, with no gap at the seam, and stands about 3 inches (7.5 cm) high.
In a saucepan, combine 1 cup (200 g) of the sugar with just enough water to cover. Stir well and set over medium heat. When the sugar turns the color of maple syrup, remove from the heat and add 2 tablespoons (35 g) of the butter. Swirl to incorporate and pour into the cake pan.
Place the fruit flesh-side down in a single layer all over the caramel, cutting a few pieces smaller if necessary to make it all fit. You can cram the fruit in as it will shrink as it cooks.

ARTICHOKE VINAIGRETTE

In a food processor, combine the almonds and polenta and process until fine. Transfer to a large bowl and stir in the flour, salt, baking powder, and lemon zest.

In the same food processor, cream the remaining 270 g butter and 270 g sugar. Add the eggs one at a time, making sure each is incorporated before adding the next. Scrape the mixture into the bowl with the flour mixture and fold into the ingredients until smooth.

Spoon the batter on top of the fruit and even out the top. Bake until the top is golden in color, crackled, and firm to the touch, about 2 hours. Set the cake pan on a rack to cool.

Once the cake has completely cooled, loosen the sides with the tip of a knife and flip it over in one quick motion, directly onto a serving platter. Holding onto the upside-down cake pan and the platter at the same time, shake and bump the pan a

little, if necessary, to release the cake, before lifting the pan away. Gently peel away any parchment paper.

Slice and serve as is, or with a little crème fraîche on the side.

PEACH AND POLENTA CAKE

KING IS JUST A REALLY GORGEOUS NEIGHBORHOOD RESTAURANT. IT'S A REFLECTION OF LOCAL COMMUNITY AND HOW PEOPLE WANT TO COME TOGETHER AND EAT NOW! — Skye Gyngell

CLARE DE BOER & JESS SHADBOLT

MACARENA DE CASTRO

DOMINIQUE CRENN

MENU

FAVA BEAN LEAF, SEA CUCUMBER, BONE MARROW

CIDRA SQUASH, ANGEL HAIR, RUCOLA, CUTTLEFISH

ALCUDIA SAFFRON, ARTICHOKE, DUCK EGG

SPRING ONION, RED SHRIMP, WOODSORREL

BEETROOT, PIG'S TROTTERS, RADISH

PINE CONE, PINE ICE CREAM, PINE SEED HORCHATA

Macarena "Maca" de Castro is a modern pioneer of Balearic cuisine, her career an ode to Mallorcan tradition and terroir. Her restaurant, Maca de Castro (formerly Jardín), is among the finest this side of Spain, decorated with one Michelin star and several Suns awarded by Repsol. The restaurant's journey, like her own, is a storied and meticulous one.

De Castro was born in Mallorca in 1981 to an already gastronomically inclined family. In 1996, the de Castros opened Jardín in Port d'Alcúdia (and a burger place in the same area), and Maca thus began her career as a server. In 2000, she transitioned to back of house, as a kitchen assistant, and in 2003 was promoted to chef. The family business grew robustly over the next few years, expanding its spaces and branching into catering, and in 2012 Jardín was awarded its Michelin star. This was an important time for the de Castros—Maca was named Chef of the Year 2012 by the Associació de Periodistes i Escriptors Gastronòmics de Balears, and her family's reputation gained even more traction. Global awards followed as well as expansion to Uruguay and Düsseldorf, Germany, and in 2018, Jardín transformed into what we know it as today: Maca de Castro.

With the flagship restaurant's new name, de Castro is putting her own spin on things while maintaining close ties to her family's traditions and culinary identity—embodying Mallorcan culture through the bounty of local purveyors and producers remains a tenet, serving as a foundation for a dynamic cuisine style, a reflection of de Castro's own personal and professional evolution. She is pursuing her own legacy and honoring and building that of her family's at the same time, creating jobs and contributing to the agricultural enrichment of her island in the process. With such a rich history of growth and expansion, it is safe to say that Maca de Castro (both person and place) won't be slowing down any time soon.

BEETROOT, PIG'S TROTTERS, RADISH
Serves 10

For the roasted beets:
2 kg beets • 2 liters water • 60 g lime juice

For the beet juice:
2 kg beets

For the beef jus:
8 kg beef ribs • 2 onions, cut into thick julienne • 2 leeks, cut into thick julienne • 5 carrots, cut into thick julienne

For the pig's foot jus:
2 onions, julienned • 1 leek, julienned • 3 carrots • olive oil, for browning • 10 kg pig's feet (trotters)

For the beef nose jus:
Beef nose, enough quantity • water, enough quantity

For the meat and beet sauce:
250 g Pig's Foot Jus *(above)* • 200 g Beef Jus *(above)* • 50 g Beef Nose Jus *(above)* • 20 g Beet Juice *(above)*

For plating:
Beans of radish seeds • Radish flowers (optional)

Prepare the beets:
Preheat the oven to 320°F (160°C). Peel and chop the beets. Keep in a bowl of lime juice and water for 3 hours, stirring every 20 minutes.
Drain, spread on a sheet pan, and bake for 1 hour 15 minutes. Put it to rest and get moist.

Make the beet jus:
In a large pot of boiling water, boil the beets until tender. Put through the liquidizer. Measure out 600 ml of juice.

Make the beef jus:
Preheat the oven to 425°F (220°C). Roast the ribs for 20 minutes. Add the vegetables and arrange so the vegetables get browned with the fat of the ribs. Bake for another 10–15 minutes.

Make the pig's foot jus:
In a large pot, brown the vegetables in olive oil until caramelized.
Clean the pig's feet (trotters) and burn off any remaining hair. Clean off all the singed hair. In a large pot of boiling water, blanch the trotters to remove the waste.
Transfer the pig's feet to the pot with the browned vegetables and cover with water. Bring to a boil and cook until the collagen in the pig's feet starts to melt. Strain the stock, return to the pan, and cook until reduced to 1.5 liters.

Make the beef nose jus:
Clean the nose removing any hair and dirt.
In a large pot of boiling water, blanch the
nose. Repeat once or twice until the smell
is gone.
Boil in fresh water for 3 hours, until the
nose gets white.
Remove the nose and reserve for further
preparations. Reduce the stock and reserve.

Make the meat and beet sauce:
Combine the 3 meat jus and add the beet
juice just before the service. Have it ready
in a pot.

To plate:
Heat the pot with the meat and beetroot
sauce with 5 chunks of roasted beet per
person. Place the chunks in the middle of
the plate with a touch of sauce. Top with
3 beans of radish seeds and, if available,
1 radish flower.

ALCUDIA SAFFRON, ARTICHOKE, DUCK EGG
Serves 10

For the artichoke:
Artichoke • Ascorbic acid • Olive oil
(0.4° acidity) • Salt • Garlic • Bay leaves

For the saffron broth:
John Dory bones • fish bones • saffron
threads

For the hollandaise sauce:
Duck's egg yolk • Clarified butter • Saffron
threads • Salt • Saffron Broth *(above)*

Prepare the artichoke:
Preheat the oven to 350°F (180°C).
Trim the artichokes down to the stem and
heart. (Reserve the artichoke leaves in
acidulated water: 10 g ascorbic acid for every
1 liter of water.) Arrange the artichoke

heart/stem pieces in a baking pan and add
the olive oil. Add salt, garlic and bay leaves.
Confit in the oven for 22 minutes.

Make the saffron broth:
In a stockpot, cover the fish bones in water
and boil for 1 hour 30 minutes. Strain the
stock, return to the pot, and cook until
reduced to 500 ml. Infuse the stock with the
saffron threads. Set aside.

Make the hollandaise sauce:
Whisk together the duck's egg yolk and
clarified butter. Add saffron threads and
a pinch of salt. Add the saffron broth and
keep whisking, adding more clarified butter
until the desired texture is achieved.

To plate:
Drain the artichokes thoroughly of excess
oil and heat under the salamander. Place
the artichoke upside down in the center of
a dinner plate and add a pinch of salt. Coat
with the hollandaise sauce whipped à la
minute. Garnish with artichoke leaves and
3 of the saffron threads used to infuse the
saffron broth.

PINE CONE, PINE ICE CREAM, PINE SEED HORCHATA
Serves 10

For the pine nut milk:
300 g pine nuts • 400 ml water • 45 g sugar •
½ teaspoon ground cinnamon • lemon zest
(enough quantity)

For the pine cones:
40 baby pine cones • 200 g sugar • 200 ml
water • 1 strip of lemon zest • 1 strip of
orange zest • Sherry vinegar

For the pine tree ice cream:
520 g whole milk • 20 g fresh pine sprouts
• 220 g double cream • 35 g 1% powdered

milk • 145 g glucose • 75 g sugar • 5 g ice
cream stabilizer

For plating:
Finely chopped pine sprouts • Pine seeds

Make the pine nut milk:
Moisten the pine nuts for an easier shred.
In a Thermomix, combine the pine nuts,
water, sugar, cinnamon, and lemon zest.
Process at speed 10 and 140°F (60°C) for
6 minutes. Strain and transfer to the freezer
to freeze.

Make the pine cones:
In a large pot of boiling water, blanch the
baby pine cones for 5 minutes. Do this
3 times, changing the water every time.
In a pot, combine the sugar, water, and
zests. Bring to a boil, and the pine cones,
and cook for at least 8 hours in syrup.
Change the syrup as often as needed.
Drain and keep in the fridge.

Make the pine tree ice cream:
In a Thermomix, bring the whole milk to
a boil, add the pine sprouts, and turn off the
heat to infuse. Grind and let sit for 1 hour.
Strain and return to the Thermomix.
Add the double cream, powdered milk, and
glucose and set to 113°F (45°C). Add the
sugar with the stabilizer and stop heating
when it starts to boil.
Pour in Pacojet beakers and freeze. Spin up
in the Pacojet before the service.

To plate:
Have small bowls ready in the freezer.
Spread a spoonful of ice cream in the bowl's
wall, add some finely chopped pine sprouts
and grate one pine nut.
Place 2 pine cones, one in the upper part
and the other in the bottom. Add a spoonful of grated frozen pine nut milk.

ALCUDIA SAFFRON, ARTICHOKE, DUCK EGG

THIS IS A PERSON WHO HAS TAKEN HER PASSION AND MOVED IT BEYOND HERSELF, SHE HAS CREATED A LIVING LEGACY.

— Dominique Crenn

MACARENA DE CASTRO

BEN DEVLIN

PIPIT RESTAURANT
Pottsville, Australia

PALISA ANDERSON

In the New South Wales town of Pottsville, a lively restaurant called Pipit sits nearly seaside, but Chef Ben Devlin won't serve just any fish from the nearby waters: He made an oath to serve only fish identified as sustainable. And so, some days there is no fish featured on his almost entirely "hoof-free" menu. Devlin can get away with this move. When he launched Pipit in 2019 with his wife, Yen Trinh, he already had fifteen years of experience during which he acquired the creativity and aplomb needed to navigate the challenges of running a high-end restaurant driven by sustainability. The result is an engaging experience that reflects his deep respect for the region's produce and producers, from the ingredients and preparation to the materials used to construct the restaurant.

In the years prior to opening Pipit, Devlin ran the show at Paper Daisy, also in the NSW Northern Rivers region, where he built a Rolodex of its products and producers and became known for his sophisticated menus studded with star local ingredients. Before Paper Daisy, Devlin crafted some of Brisbane's most inventive tasting menus under Chef Ryan Squires at Esquire; and before that, he honed his foraging skills during two years at Noma. At Pipit, Devlin designs dishes with ingredients like wattleseed (native acacia seeds used for everything from grain to spice to thickener), wing beans (a tropical legume), and pipis (a small saltwater mollusk)—staples of traditional Aboriginal diets rarely seen in restaurants. You may see fried chips made from the shells of local soft-shell lobsters, cobia marinated in house-made kelp oil and vinegar, or spatchcocked chicken with local bunya nuts (from a local conifer, with a flavor like chestnuts). Ample bar space invites diners to watch Devlin and his team ply their skills around the open kitchen's charcoal pit. While Devlin's high-end culinary training is unabashedly evident, he strives to create a space that welcomes the entire community. And he has more than succeeded—Pipit has already been marked as one of Australia's best restaurants.

MENU

ALBACORE WITH SOUR TOMATO AND YELLOW PEA KOJI
Serves 4

For the sour tomato juice:
200 g tomatoes • 4 g salt

For the smoked tomatoes:
Canola oil, for frying • 16 mixed cherry tomatoes

For the tomato skin oil:
Tomato skins (reserved from Smoked Tomatoes, *above*) • 200 g canola oil • 50 g skins of peeled fresh horseradish

For the yellow pea koji:
100 g dried yellow peas • Koji spores • Canola oil • Chardonnay vinegar • Salt

For the albacore:
About 250 g albacore loin • 25 g roasted kelp powder

For plating:
Fresh horseradish • Lucid Gem tomato, sliced • Purslane • Holy basil

Make the sour tomato juice:
Blend the tomatoes and salt, pour into a jar, and ferment at room temperature for 2 days, then refrigerate for 2 weeks. When the tomato smells nice and sour, strain the pulp through cheesecloth (muslin) or a coffee filter. Cook to reduce by two-thirds.

Make the smoked tomatoes:
Pour several inches oil into a pot and heat to 350°F (180°C). Blanch the tomatoes until the skin just splits, then chill in iced water. Peel off the skins (reserve them for the tomato skin oil, next step). Place the tomatoes high above a wood-burning grill for 1–3 days depending on the size: The result you are looking for is soft and a little chewy.

Make the tomato skin oil:
Toast the tomato skins over a charcoal grill until they are caramelized. Transfer to a blender and add the canola oil and horseradish peelings. Blend the mixture until it heats up and becomes aromatic, cool the mixture down and allow it to infuse for at least 8 hours, then pass the mixture through an oil filter.

Make the yellow pea koji:
Wash the yellow peas and then soak them well. Steam the peas until tender. Once they are soft, weigh the peas and keep them covered as they cool down. For every 250 g of cooked peas, weigh out 0.5 g koji spores. Preset a climate control chamber or water circulator to 98°F (37°C). Monitor the temperature of the cooked yellow peas as they cool down and once they hit 102°F (39°C), add the koji spores and mix well. Straight away, put the inoculated grain into a covered container that will fit into your water circulator or climate control chamber. Allow the koji mold to grow, ideally for 40 hours or so. When the peas have sufficient mold growth they can be blended.
Blend the peas with equal parts water and season with olive oil, Chardonnay vinegar, and salt.

Prepare the albacore:
Clean excess sinew from the albacore loin. If the piece is too wide, cut it in half to make the pieces a suitable size for serving. Dust the exterior of the pieces with the roasted kelp powder, then store the pieces on a plastic draining tray, set on a sheet pan,

covered loosely with a piece of parchment paper. Age the tuna in the fridge overnight.

To plate:
Thinly slice the albacore across the grain, about 50 g per person. Spread a large tablespoon of yellow pea koji across each plate, lay out the slices of albacore and season each with salt and horseradish. Arrange 5 or 6 small smoked tomatoes and 2 or 3 slices of fresh Lucid Gem tomatoes over each. Dress the plates with a spoon of the sour tomato juice and the tomato skin oil, then finish with a few leaves of purslane and holy basil.

SUGARLOAF CABBAGE WITH SPANNER CRAB, FINGER LIME, AND MACADAMIA MISO
Serves 4

For the macadamia miso:
250 g macadamia nut, ground to a rough crumble • 250 g koji rice • 115 g water • 45 g salt • 5 g miso

For the egg yolk vinegar:
3 egg yolks • Chardonnay vinegar • Shrimp garum or fish sauce

For the crab:
About 1 kg whole spanner crab (swimmer crab or mud crab also work)

For the crab sauce base:
About 500 g crab shells • 100 g shallots, finely sliced • 100 g fennel, finely sliced •

50 g garlic, finely sliced • 10 g peppercorns • 100 g sherry • 100 g port • 3 liters fish stock

For the crab farce:
75 g macadamia nuts • 75 g water • Crab-head juice • 150 g crabmeat (as much as possible from the bod, not claws) • 3 egg yolks • Salt

For the stuffed cabbage:
1 small sugarloaf cabbage • Crab Farce (above)

For plating:
60 g unsalted butter • 30 ml macadamia oil • Lemon juice • Salt • Crab coral • 150 g crabmeat (preferably from the claws) • Canola oil and butter for grilling • 1 finger lime, halved • 50 g fresh horseradish • 50 g macadamia nuts, toasted • Bronze fennel sprigs

Make the macadamia miso:
Combine all of the ingredients and pack them into a jar or crock. Place a ceramic or stone weight on top. Allow this to age at room temperature for a minimum of 2 months. When ready it will smell savory and round. Blend to a smooth paste, adjusting with a little water if needed.

Make the egg yolk vinegar:
Weigh the egg yolks, mix in an equal weight of vinegar, season with a little shrimp garum.

Prepare the crabs:
Place the live crabs in a freezer or an ice slurry to put them to sleep, then kill them by inserting a knife between the eyes. Separate the meat from the shell. Keep the body meat separate from the claw meat (the total meat weight should be about 300g). Reserve the head juice (for the Crab Farce) and the coral (for plating).

Make the crab sauce base:
In a hot pot, heat the crab shells until well caramelized. Remove and set aside. Add the vegetables and peppercorns and allow the vegetables to caramelize well, then return the crab shells to the pot. Once the pot is hot again, add the sherry and port and burn them off. Reduce the liquid to a glaze, add the fish stock, and reduce the heat to medium. When the stock starts to simmer, skim off the foam, then cook slowly until the stock starts to reduce lower than the shells. At that point, strain the stock through a fine-mesh sieve into a clean pot. Reduce the stock slowly to a strong glaze, then strain the glaze through a coffee filter.

Make the crab farce:
Soak the macadamia nuts in the water for at least 2 hours, preferably in the fridge. Place a Thermomix bowl or blender jar in the fridge and keep all of the ingredients as cold as possible. Blend the macadamia and water into a smooth paste, then add the crab-head juice and meat, blend until smooth, and season with salt. Cool the farce.

BEN BUILT THE MAJORITY OF HIS RESTAURANT USING MATERIALS AND ARTISANS LOCAL TO THE REGION, AND HIS MENU IS REFLECTIVE OF THIS CONTINUED ETHOS AND RESPECT FOR PRODUCE. — *Palisa Anderson*

Make the stuffed cabbage:
Trim the tougher outer leaves from the cabbage and quarter the cabbage length-wise. Use a palette knife to spread the farce in between the layers of the cabbage, try to fill them completely. Lay the filled cabbage on a tray lined with parchment paper. Steam the cabbages at (212°F (100°C) for about 12 minutes or the farce in the center reads above 176°F (80°C) on an instant-read thermometer.

To plate:
Warm up the crab base, emulsify in the butter and macadamia oil, adjust the seasoning with a little lemon juice and salt. Add the crab coral and blend the sauce with a hand blender. Add the crabmeat and cook gently. Grill or panfry the stuffed cabbage with a little oil and butter, caramelizing on both cut sides, ensuring that the cabbage is golden brown and warmed through. Remove the cabbage from the heat, brush it with the egg yolk vinegar.
Place the glazed cabbage on the plate, cover it with the crab sauce, then squeeze finger lime on top, and grate horseradish and toasted macadamia all over the top. Place sprigs of bronze fennel on the cabbage and a spoon of macadamia miso off to the side.

BLACK SAPOTE SORBET WITH CARAMELIZED COCONUT AND PASSION FRUIT
Serves 4

For the black sapote sorbet:
200 g black sapote fruit pulp • 200 g water • 20 g dextrose powder • 2 g sorbet stabilizer • Salt to taste

For the banana crisp:
3 ripe bananas

For the coconut crisp:
250 ml coconut milk • 25 g coconut sugar • 0.5 g xanthan gum • 1 g iota-carrageenan • 25 g freeze-dried coconut milk powder

For the caramelized coconut milk:
500 ml coconut milk • 50 ml coconut cream • 35 g coconut sugar • 35 g brown sugar • ¼ teaspoon baking soda (bicarbonate of soda)

For the coconut custard:
250 g coconut milk • 50 g coconut sugar • 10 g cornstarch (corn flour) • 3.5 g agar-agar

For the sapote "ganache":
200 g sapote pulp • 20 g molasses • 50 g water • 1.5 g agar-agar

For plating:
1 passion fruit • Salt

Make the black sapote sorbet:
Blend all the ingredients. Strain and check the level of seasoning. Freeze in a Pacojet beaker or batch ice cream maker.

Make the banana crisp:
Preheat the oven to 158°F (70°C). Line a sheet pan with a silicone baking mat. Peel and blend the banana. Spread it thinly on the baking mat. Roast the banana until it is well caramelized. Break into large pieces and store in an airtight container until needed.

Make the coconut crisp:
In a Thermomix, combine the coconut milk and coconut sugar and blend on medium speed. With the machine running, add the xanthan gum and carrageenan powders. Set the Thermomix to 194°F (90°C), blend in the coconut milk powder, and cook out for 2 minutes. Pour the liquid into the bowl of a stand mixer and whisk until it is cool and fluffy. Spread the mixture evenly on silicone mats and then dehydrate until crisp.

Make the caramelized coconut milk:
In a saucepan, combine the coconut milk, coconut cream, coconut sugar, and brown sugar and bring to a simmer. Whisk in the baking soda (bicarb). Allow to simmer gently until the mixture has reduced to a caramel—whisk frequently and do not let the mixture catch and burn on the bottom. Once it has caramelized, strain it and allow the mixture to cool to room temperature.

Make the coconut custard:
In a small bowl, combine 20 g of the coconut milk with the cornstarch (corn flour) and combine to create a slurry. In a pot, combine the remaining 230 g coconut milk with the coconut sugar in a pot. Start to cook the coconut milk over low heat and as it is heating up, blend in the agar-agar using a hand blender. When the mixture comes to a simmer, add the cornstarch slurry and whisk well. Bring the mixture to a boil for 30 seconds. Pour the mixture out into a sheet pan and cool in the fridge. When the mixture is set firm, use a blender to blend the mixture to a smooth paste and transfer it to a piping bag.

Make the sapote "ganache:"
In a Thermomix, combine all of the ingredients and blend on slow speed. Increase the speed to medium and set to 194°F (90°C). Blend for 1 minute and then spread on a sheet pan to cool. Once it has set firm, blend in a blender and transfer to a piping bag.

To plate:
Break the banana crisp and coconut crisp into manageable-size pieces. Place a dot of random size of each of the sapote "ganache," coconut custard, and caramelized coconut milk at the back of the plate. Rest one of the coconut crisps on it at a 45-degree angle. Repeat that process with alternating banana and coconut crisps down one side of the plate, then dress lightly with fresh passion fruit pulp and place a scoop of sapote sorbet to the side, with a small pinch of salt on top.

ALBACORE WITH SOUR TOMATO

SUGARLOAF CABBAGE

BEN DEVLIN

FANNY DUCHARME

RESTAURANT L'ÉPICURIEUX
Val David, Quebec, Canada

DAVID MCMILLAN

Nestled in the heart of the Laurentian Mountains of Québec, the village of Val-David is home to Fanny Ducharme's L'Épicurieux. Ducharme opened the small, vegetable-forward restaurant with friends Dominic Tougas and Maxime Laverdure in 2016. Its bright, airy interior and creative menu of shareable dishes have drawn locals and tourists alike, the latter in droves, in spite of the trek required to get to the relatively remote locale.

Ducharme, who is originally from Sainte-Adèle, studied at the École Hôtelière des Laurentides and found her identity as a chef in the kitchen at Chef Martin Picard's Cabane à Sucre au Pied de Cochon in Mirabel, Québec. Throughout her culinary career, among her greatest sources of inspiration has been her parents' comfort-food cooking, and her delivery (particularly now that she's in a space of her own) is the product of keeping a close eye on modern aesthetics. She has long been a fan of combining unexpected elements, both ingredients and visual cues, and her ambitions are all the more impressive given the constraints of running a restaurant in a small, somewhat isolated locale.

For the level of execution in Ducharme's kitchen, L'Épicurieux is incredibly unpretentious. Ducharme and Tougas, who are now the owners, maintain a personal rapport with guests during service—a regular occurrence and one of the benefits of operating in an intimate space. When it comes to sourcing, Ducharme's kitchen is stocked by local producers and purveyors, each ingredient carefully selected with peak freshness in mind. Traditional proteins play a supporting role, with vegetables typically the star. It can be a challenge, but one that Ducharme enjoys. And though she is still young (she was twenty-five when the restaurant opened), she sees the value in mentorship, and has already put it into practice with her sous chef, Arianne Faucher—a point of pride for Ducharme is her female-led kitchen. Together, they are creating magic in a quiet, unexpected place, and the world has heard it and is taking note.

MENU

DAIKON: ONION, CASHEW, DARK BEER, CHIVE

CARROT: RICOTTA, PUMPKIN SEEDS, BALSAM FIR

AUTUMN: CARROT, SEA BUCKTHORN, SESAME

POACHED: PEAR, CREAM, MISO, FIR SPROUTS

ICE CREAM: BURNT BREAD

CARROT: RICOTTA, PUMPKIN SEEDS, BALSAM FIR
Serves 4

For the roasted carrots:
25 Nantes carrots • 50 ml olive oil

For the balsam fir powder:
3–4 branches of balsam fir*

For the homemade ricotta:
4 liters whole milk (3.25%) • 1 liter buttermilk • Salt • 100 ml heavy (whipping) cream (35%)

For the pumpkin seed salsa:
300 g hulled pumpkin seeds • 500 ml olive oil • 2 cloves garlic, finely chopped

If you're lucky, like us in Québec, you may find some right in your yard! If not, you can place an order in a supermarket.

Roast the carrots:
Preheat the oven to 400°F (200°C).
Place the carrots on a baking sheet and coat with the oil. Roast until browned (we want them a little darkened), about 30 minutes.

Make the balsam fir powder:
Dry in the oven at low temperature for about 1 hour (the balsam simply has to be dry). Grind in a spice mill to a smooth powder.

Make the ricotta:
In a large pot, heat the milk and buttermilk over medium heat to 140°F (60°C).
Line a fine-mesh sieve with dampened cheesecloth (muslin) and spoon the mixture into the sieve. Let drain for about 15 minutes, until the ricotta is well drained.
In a bowl, mix the ricotta with the cream and season with salt to taste.

Make the pumpkin seed salsa:
Preheat the oven to 400°F (200°C).
Roast the seeds for about 8 minutes. Meanwhile, in a bowl, combine the oil and garlic.
Pour the hot seeds on the oil and the garlic. When hot seeds come out of the oven, add them to the bowl.

To plate:
Make a round of ricotta in the center of the plate. Place the carrots on top. Pour some pumpkin seed salsa over the carrots and sprinkle with some balsam fir powder.

AUTUMN: CARROT, SEA BUCKTHORN, SESAME
Serves 6

For the sea buckthorn cream:
500 ml sea buckthorn juice • 4 egg yolks
125 g sugar • 45 g cornstarch (corn flour) •
185 g unsalted butter, at room temperature

CARROT: RICOTTA, PUMPKIN SEEDS, BALSAM FIR

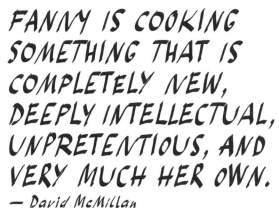

FANNY IS COOKING SOMETHING THAT IS COMPLETELY NEW, DEEPLY INTELLECTUAL, UNPRETENTIOUS, AND VERY MUCH HER OWN.
— David McMillan

ICE CREAM: BURNT BREAD

POACHED: PEAR, CREAM, MISO, FIR SPROUTS

DAIKON: ONION, CASHEW, DARK BEER, CHIVE

96

For the carrot sorbet:
3 g sorbet stabilizer (optional) • 250 g sugar
• 250 ml water • 35 g glucose or corn syrup •
500 ml carrot juice

For the sesame tuiles:
125 g salted butter • 125 g brown sugar •
60 ml honey • 60 ml maple syrup • 125 g all-
purpose (plain) flour • Sesame seeds, toasted

For the sesame malto powder:
30 g maltodextrin • 30 g sesame oil

Make the sea buckthorn cream:
In a saucepan, heat 450 ml of the sea buckthorn juice.
In a bowl, blend the egg yolks with the sugar,
cornstarch (corn flour), and the remaining
50 ml sea buckthorn juice. Pour the hot sea
buckthorn juice over the egg yolk mixture.
Return the whole mixture to the saucepan,
whisking constantly, and bring to a boil.
Spread the preparation on a plate lined with
plastic wrap and refrigerate until it cools to
room temperature, about 30 minutes. (The
next step will be longer if it was left more
than 30 minutes in the refrigerator.)
In a stand mixer fitted with the whisk,
whisk the butter. Beat in one-quarter of
the sea buckthorn preparation. Add the sea
buckthorn mixture in 3 more additions,
until everything is incorporated.
Transfer the mixture to a plain piping bag
and store in the refrigerator.

Make the carrot sorbet:
In a saucepan, mix the stabilizer with the
sugar. Whisk in the water, then add the
glucose. Bring the mixture to a boil, then
remove from the heat. Stir in the carrot juice.
Refrigerate until well chilled, about 4 hours.
Make the sorbet in an ice cream maker.
Transfer the sorbet to an airtight container
and put in the freezer. Wait at least 4 hours
before serving.

Make the sesame tuiles:
In a food processor fitted with the paddle,
cream the butter and brown sugar. Beat
in the honey and maple syrup. When the
mixture is well blended, beat in the flour.
Refrigerate for 1 hour.
Preheat the oven to 400°F (200°C). Line
a baking sheet with a silicone baking mat.
Spread small amounts of batter and make
rounds using a cookie cutter and a small
offset spatula or the back of a spoon. The
tuiles should be 1/16 inch (1–2 mm) thick.
Garnish each tuile generously with toasted
sesame seeds.
Bake for about 5 minutes, then rotate the
baking sheet front to back and bake for
another 2–4 minutes to make sure it all
cooks evenly. Make sure to keep an eye on
them—they should be golden caramel color.
Remove from the oven and let the tuiles
cool completely before delicately peeling
them off.

Make the sesame malto powder:
Gently mix the two ingredients with
a whisk until a homogeneous powder is
obtained.

To assemble:
To serve, pipe some sea buckthorn cream
into the middle of a bowl. Sprinkle the
sesame malto powder around the cream.
Put in a nice scoop of the carrot sorbet and
top with a sesame tuile.

POACHED: PEAR, CREAM, MISO, FIR SPROUTS
Serves 5

For the poached pear:
5 pears • 750 ml sugar • 750 ml water
• 500 ml white wine • ½ vanilla bean •
2 whole star anise • ½ cinnamon stick

For the smoked cream:
500 ml heavy (whipping) cream (35%) •
Liquid smoke (optional)

For the miso butter:
227 g unsalted butter • 100 g miso

For plating:
Fir sprouts • Celery sprouts • Heavy (whipping) cream (35%)

Poach the pears:
Peel the pears and place them in a large
wide pot filled with the sugar, water, white
wine, vanilla, star anise, and cinnamon.
Bring to a boil, then reduce the heat to
medium and cook until the tip of a knife
can easily go through the pear. Cool the
pears in a container in the fridge.

Make the smoked cream:
If you have a smoker, put the cream in a
receptacle and smoke for about 1 hour.
If you do not have a smoker, add a few drops
of liquid smoke to the cream.

Make the miso butter:
In a saucepan, heat the butter until it
browns, then stir in the miso.

To plate:
To serve, pour the poached pear into a bowl,
scoop the miso butter on top, and drizzle with
the smoked cream. Garnish with the sprouts.

ICE CREAM: BURNT BREAD
Makes 2 quarts (2 liters)

For the burnt bread:
1 French baguette, thinly sliced

For the ice cream:
1.5 liters heavy (whipping) cream (35%) •
150 g Burnt Bread *(above)* • 6 egg yolks •
180 g sugar

Make the burnt bread:
Preheat the oven to 400°F (200°C).
Spread the baguette on a baking sheet and
bake for 30 minutes (Don't worry, the bread
has to be burnt!)

Make the ice cream:
In a bowl, infuse 1 liter of the cream with
the burnt bread for 20 minutes. Strain the
cream (discard the bread) and add enough
plain cream to come up to 750 ml. Transfer
to a saucepan.
Fill a large bowl with ice and set an empty
bowl on top.
In a separate bowl, whip the egg yolks with
the sugar.
Heat up the cream and when hot, slowly
whisk into the egg yolks to temper. Return
everything to the saucepan and gently heat
while stirring with a heatproof spatula
(scrape the bottom of the pan at all times)
until you reach 185°F (85°C).
Immediately pour the hot custard into the
empty bowl sitting in the ice bath. Cool until
there is no more vapor from the custard.
Transfer to an airtight container and let the
cream cool completely in the refrigerator,
about 4 hours.
Churn in an ice cream maker, then transfer
to an airtight container and put in the
freezer. Wait at least 4 hours before serving.

FANNY DUCHARME

MICHAEL ELÉGBÈDÉ

SELASSIE ATADIKA

MENU

BOLI ATI EPA: ROASTED PLANTAIN, ORANGE SEGMENTS, PEANUT CRUMBLE, PEANUT VINAIGRETTE

PRAWN BANGA: POACHED PRAWN WITH BANGA SOUP

EWA AGANYIN: HONEY BEANS WITH EWA AGANYIN SAUCE AND PLANTAIN CHIPS

EBA: EBA CRISPS WITH SMOKED MACKEREL, ATA DINDIN COULIS, EFO, AND EGUSI

OFADA: DWARF GOAT SHANK SLOW COOKED IN AYAMASE

The future of Nigerian cuisine lies in the hands of young, passionate chefs like Michael Elégbèdé. In the heart of bustling Lagos, Elégbèdé's test kitchen ÌTÀN is a place of experimentation, an ode to Nigeria's traditional methods and ingredients and the reimagination thereof.

Born in 1989, Elégbèdé comes from a family of Nigerian cooks, his mother and grandmother both restaurateurs and chefs who actively taught their craft to young local women. Elégbèdé's family eventually emigrated to the United States, where his mother opened a new restaurant, and at age thirteen, Elégbèdé found himself helping out with the family business. When it came time to attend college, he initially enrolled in a biology program at the University of Illinois at Chicago, though his calling to become a third-generation chef inevitably took hold. Elégbèdé went on to learn the ins and outs of classic French baking and pastry at Chicago's Alliance Bakery, then to complete the Culinary Arts program at The Culinary Institute of America at Greystone in St. Helena, California. After graduating, Elégbèdé planted roots in New York to work as chef de partie under Daniel Humm at his iconic Eleven Madison Park and the NoMad restaurants. Then in 2016, after thirteen years of life in the United States, Elégbèdé returned to Nigeria to pursue a dream of owning his own place, following in the footsteps of his foremothers.

As ÌTÀN's owner and executive chef, Elégbèdé is bringing a kind of cuisine to the table that the country has not quite seen before. His training in fine dining and his hunger for pushing the boundaries of tradition are redefining Nigeria's modern culinary landscape, and his efforts have not gone unnoticed. In 2018, he was inducted into the SDG2 Advocacy Hub's Chefs' Manifesto and also hosted the James Beard Foundation's "This Is Nigeria" dinner, during which he showcased his team's inventive cuisine.

In 2019, Elégbèdé opened a second branch of ÌTÀN in the city's affluent Ikoyi neighborhood, and he launched ABÓRI, a summit around sustainability in the food industry. In Elégbèdé's quest to honor Nigerian cuisine's past (*ìtàn* literally means "story" or "history" in Yoruba), he is also helping to fortify its future.

BOLI ATI EPA
Serves 4

For the peanut-citrus vinaigrette:
¼ cup (35 g) peanuts, roasted • ½ cup (120 ml) orange juice • ½ cup (120 ml) peanut (groundnut) oil • Pinch of cayenne pepper • Pinch of salt

For the boli:
1 ripe plantain, peeled • 6–8 orange segments • 4–8 basil sprigs with buds • 2–4 teaspoons Peanut-Citrus • Vinaigrette (*above*) • Sea salt

Make the peanut-citrus vinaigrette:
In a blender, combine all the ingredients and blend until completely smooth. Keep refrigerated. Can hold for 3 days.

Make the boli:
On a grill, cook the plantain, turning as necessary, to caramelize on all sides. Cut into 3-inch (7.5 cm) segments.
Place a piece of plantain on a plate. Garnish with 3 orange segments and 2 sprigs basil. Dress with 1 teaspoon peanut-citrus vinaigrette. Finish with sea salt. Serve immediately.

PRAWN BANGA
Serves 10

For the prawns:
10 prawns (150 g each) with roe, roe reserved

For the banga soup:
2 liters fish stock • 3 cups palm butter (reduced) • ¼ cup crayfish • 2 onions • 1 small Scotch bonnet chili • 10 prawn roe (from prawns, *above*) • 1 oburunbebe (licorice)

stick • ¼ teaspoon ogiri • ¼ teaspoon otiako • Pinch of rohojie • Salt • 1 stalk lemongrass • 2 lime leaves • 2 scent leaves

Cook the prawns:
In a large pot of boiling water, blanch prawns for 4 minutes. Shock in an ice bath. Peel and set aside. Reserve the shells for the soup.

Make the banga soup:
In a heavy-bottomed soup pot, bring the fish stock and reserved prawn shells to a boil, then simmer for 20 minutes to extract flavor from the shells. Strain the liquid (and compost the shells).
Return the fortified stock to the pot and add the palm butter, crayfish, onions, Scotch bonnet, and reserved roe and cook at a high simmer for 35 minutes.
Transfer the soup to a blender and blend until smooth.
Return the soup to the pot and add the oburunbebe, ogiri, otiako, and rohojie and cook at a low simmer for another 15 minutes to completely infuse the flavors.
Remove from the heat and add a bouquet of lemongrass, lime leaves, and scent leaves. Let steep for 5 minutes.
To serve, place prawns in a bowl and pour hot soup over them. This can be eaten alone or with a starch.

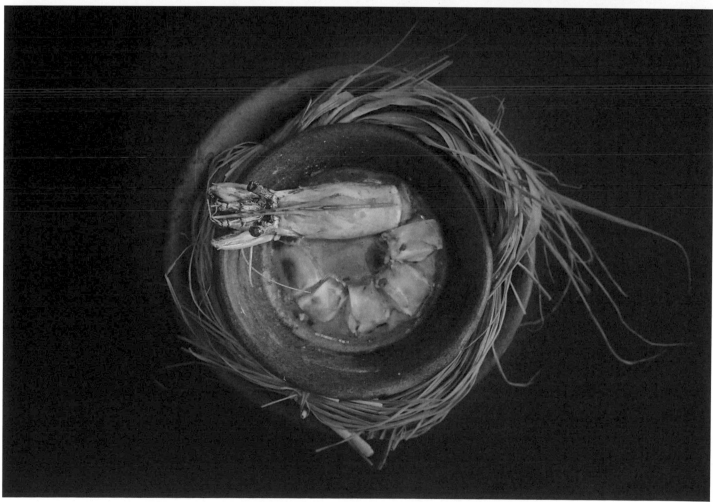

PRAWN BANGA

CHEF MICHAEL ELÉGBÈDÉ EMBODIES THE FUTURE OF AFRICA IN HIS CUISINE.
— Selassie Atadika

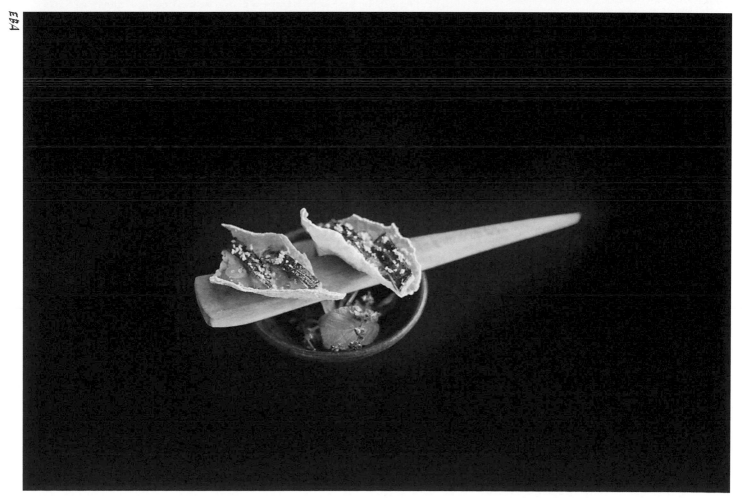

MICHAEL ELÉGBÈDÉ

TAKASHI ENDO

EYAL SHANI

RESTAURANT SAN
Kanazawa, Japan

MENU

KYOTO SUMMER APPETIZER

HANDMADE WINTER SOBA WITH VEGETABLES AND DUCK

BROILED CONGER EEL (HAMO) WITH SEASONAL VEGETABLES

CHARCOAL-GRILLED SWEETFISH (AYU) WITH CUCUMBER COOKED IN DASHI

Seasonality is a given for many chefs, but Takashi Endo's careful attention to detail is what takes his cooking style to the next level. Coming from a family of civil servants, Endo's interest in becoming a chef was not inherited, instead arising independently—from the time he was very young, Endo was inspired by the discipline, art, and tradition behind Japanese cuisine, and above all by a love for food. Upon completing his studies, Endo dove headfirst into pursuing mastery of the craft in Tokyo, then continued on to further refine his skills in kitchens around Kyoto, Kanazawa, and Nagoya. Ultimately, Endo planted his roots in Kyoto, where he connected with the owner of Washoku Restaurant San, Shintaro Yabe—interestingly, through a shared love of antique porcelain dishes.

Because of this bond, it seems, a visual perspective drives and shapes Endo's Washoku tasting menu at San today. Inside the former teahouse that overlooks the cherry trees along the Takase River, the porcelain is a strong focus—arguably as much as the food itself. Modern dishes such as handmade seasonal soba noodles, "phantom" crab from northern Kyoto, and tsubaki mochi are served atop antique platters from the Edo period, an era associated with some of the country's first porcelain. Some of Endo's porcelain collection also comes from contemporary local artists. As such, old and new meet harmoniously in a dining experience that's as visual as it is tactile and gustatory. This is how Endo converses with his guests.

Endo is perhaps best known for his affinity for soba, a traditional buckwheat noodle he makes by hand—a dish that has become known as San's specialty. Using seasonal ingredients, such as root vegetables and duck roasted with sake in the wintertime, he puts an updated spin on the classic and widely beloved dish. It's no surprise that Endo's soba noodles are consistently among his guests' favorite orders.

BROILED CONGER EEL (HAMO) WITH SEASONAL VEGETABLES

Conger eel (hamo) • Tomato, thinly sliced • Broad beans • Onions, thinly sliced • Microleaf • Shiso flowers • Sudachi

Conger eel is a fish with innumerable bones, and a special knife is used to remove them. The unique sound of the knife deboning the eels is also a summer feature in Kyoto.

The eel is best raw, but the skin is good cooked. Season the eel with salt and roast only the skin over hot charcoal. Transfer the eel to a freezer at -4°F (-20°C) for about 30 seconds to prevent the heat from burning the fish—the flesh is best at room temperature allowing the true taste of the fish to come through. To serve the eel, plate slices of the flesh alternated with slices of cooked skin. Garnish with tomato, broad beans, onion, microleaf, shiso flowers, and sudachi.

RED BOWL

300 ml dashi • 600 ml crab broth • Asparagus • Leek • Japanese beef • Green onion • Microleaf

In a pot, combine the dashi and crab broth and season with soy sauce, salt, and sugar to taste. Keep the salt concentration at 2.5–3%. Bring the stock up to a boil and quickly blanch the asparagus and leek. Remove the vegetables and return the stock to a boil. Quickly cook the beef to rare temperature in the stock. Finish with the soup stock that was used last and garnish with the green onion and microleaf.

HANDMADE WINTER SOBA WITH VEGETABLES AND DUCK

30 g bonito flakes • 15 g kombu • Winter vegetables such as radish, lotus root, lily bulb, etc. • 60 g buckwheat flour • 300 g duck breast • 750 ml sake • 15 g sugar • 15 ml soy sauce, plus more for seasoning

Make a dashi with the bonito, kombu, and 1 liter of water. Remove the bonito and kombu and season the dashi with salt and soy sauce to taste.

Cook the vegetables in the dashi, then remove from the heat. Let the vegetables steep in the dashi for a day or so in order to soak up a lot of flavor.

Make the soba by mixing the buckwheat flour with about 30 g water. Form a dough then roll and cut noodles with a soba knife. Trim the duck of any unneccessary fat or tendon. Grill over over a charcoal fire to cook and render the skin. In a small pot, combine the sake, sugar and soy sauce, and bring up to 133°F (56°C). Place the duck into the hot sauce and cook for about an hour. Remove and slice.

Cook the soba and serve with the duck and vegetables on the side.

HANDMADE WINTER SOBA WITH VEGETABLES AND DUCK

THE DELICACY OF HIS
HAND MOVEMENT
REFLECTS THE
DELICACY OF HIS
CREATIONS, WHICH IS IN
TURN COMPLEMENTED
BY THE DELICACY
OF THE PORCELAIN
VESSELS THAT HOLDS
THE FOOD. ONE OF MY
MOST MEMORABLE
EXPERIENCES.
— Eyal Shani

CHARCOAL-GRILLED SWEETFISH (AYU) WITH CUCUMBER COOKED IN DASHI

105

TAKASHI ENDO

MARGOT HENDERSON

MENU

PIG'S HEAD CROQUETTES, SMOKED COD'S ROE, AND PICKLED RADISHES

ROMANESCO CAULIFLOWER, LEEKS, CHICKPEAS, CORRA LINN

CURED BEEF, GOAT CURD, FENNEL, AND BLOOD ORANGE

SKATE, COCKLES, SEA PURSLANE, CRISP POTATOES

GRILLED VENISON, CELERIAC, SUTHERLAND KALE, SMOKED BACON

MARMALADE TREACLE TART AND CRÈME FRAÎCHE

In the historic county of Fife, along Scotland's wind- and sea-battered coast, stands a seventeenth-century inn at the heart of the village of Kilconquhar, population two hundred. On many a cold, dark night, warm flickering light beckons from its square windows to passersby. Once inside, they can settle down for a drink at the pub or, if there's space, a hearty meal in the dining room. Here at the Kinneuchar Inn, James Ferguson is responsible for the provisions of this 32-cover restaurant, and his partner, Alethea Palmer, makes the warm welcomes. Ferguson concocts simple, straightforward dishes—traditional British food with Mediterranean underpinnings, elevated by the local seafood, native breeds of meat and game, and produce sourced from the neighboring Balcaskie Estate. The honest, unpretentious food rests on the foundation of Ferguson's classical training and years of experience.

Growing up at his parents' Greek restaurant in Yorkshire, Ferguson was washing dishes by age eight and cooking by fourteen. Yet it was after he had finished studying music in college that he realized he wanted to pursue cooking as a career. He enrolled in a catering school, and then worked under Chef Angela Hartnett at Gordon Ramsay's London restaurant the Connaught. Finding himself unsuited to true fine dining, James caught wind of Chef Margot Henderson and the nose-to-tail ethos she was applying to her style of British comfort food at Rochelle Canteen. He landed the position of head chef there, where he resonated with the more casual culture. His next post as head chef was at Beagle, in East London, where he shifted to modern British cooking.

A recurring theme for Ferguson has been his adherence to food that is simple, accessible, and, by broad consensus, delicious. He happily works outside the race toward Michelin stars, likely thanks to his Greek grandmother, whose simplicity of kitchen techniques Ferguson credits as his most significant influence. Sometimes her imprint shows up on his menus, for example in his recreation of her lemon potatoes. At the Kinneuchar Inn, Ferguson's food is similarly both gentle and firm in its philosophy. His menus show off his butchery skills, his love of cooking with fire, and his classical training. One might choose from deep-fried pig's head served with plumlike damson ketchup; local Shetland squid served with *skordalia* (a Greek potato and garlic spread); or a tender slow-braised hare. And for dessert? A classic milk ice cream alongside marmalade treacle tart.

ROMANESCO CAULIFLOWER, LEEKS, CHICKPEAS, CORRA LINN
Serves 4

200 g dried chickpeas • 2 bay leaves • 2 cloves garlic, peeled • 2 medium leeks, halved lengthwise and very thinly sliced • 150 ml extra-virgin olive oil • A good glug of sherry vinegar • 1 head Romanesco cauliflower, cut into florets • 100 g Corra Linn cheese (or Manchego or pecorino), shaved with a peeler • 1 bunch flat-leaf parsley • Salt and freshly ground black pepper

Soak the chickpeas overnight.
Drain the chickpeas and place in a saucepan with cold water to cover. Bring to a simmer, skimming any foam, and add the bay leaves and 1 of the garlic cloves. Cook until soft and cloudlike.

In a sauté pan, sweat the leeks in the olive oil until soft. Paste the remaining garlic clove and add it to the pan along with the sherry vinegar.
In a pot of boiling salted water, cook the Romanesco for about 1 minute. Drain and add to the leek mixture.
Transfer to a bowl and add the chickpeas, Corra Linn cheese, and parsley. Season to taste.

CURED BEEF, GOAT CURD, FENNEL, AND BLOOD ORANGE
Serves 4

For the cured beef:
60 g coarse sea salt • 30 g superfine (caster) sugar • Grated zest of 2 oranges • 8 g chopped fresh rosemary • 6 g fresh thyme leaves • 5 g freshly ground black pepper • 5 g ground allspice • 5 whole cloves, ground • 5 juniper berries, crushed with a mortar and pestle • 1.5 kg beef eye cut from the top round (top side) or bottom round (silver side), no bigger than 3 inches (8 cm) in diameter

For the blood orange and fennel salad:
1 Tarocco blood orange, peeled and segmented • 1 bulb fennel, finely sliced on a mandoline • 10 mint leaves, finely sliced 10 lilliput capers • Pinch of salt • 2 tablespoons Moscatel vinegar • 2 tablespoons Arbequina olive oil

For plating:
200 g fresh goat curd • 16 thin slices Cured Beef *(above)* • Arbequina olive oil • Freshly ground black pepper

GRILLED FISH, TOMATO SALAD

ROMANESCO CAULIFLOWER

Cure the beef:

In a blender, combine the salt, sugar, orange zest, rosemary, thyme, pepper, and all the spices and grind to a fine powder. Weigh the resulting powder and split the mixture into two parts. Rub half of it over the meat, making sure it's evenly covered. Tightly wrap in plastic wrap (cling film) and put in a plastic container. Refrigerate for 7 days, turning the meat every couple of days. Remove the beef, discard the liquid, and rub in the remaining spice cure. Refrigerate for another 7 days.

Rinse the beef off thoroughly, removing any spices, and pat dry with paper towels. Place on a rack and allow to dry at room temperature for 3 hours.

Wrap in cheesecloth (muslin) and tie with butcher's twine. Hang in a well-ventilated space at about 57°F (14°C) for about 3 weeks. The meat will be firm and dark on the outside but soft and buttery in the center when sliced

Make the blood orange and fennel salad:

In a bowl, combine the blood orange, fennel, mint, and capers and season with salt. Dress with the vinegar and olive oil.

To plate:

Place 50 g of fresh curd on each of four plates. Top it with 4 thin slices of the cured beef. Place the salad on the side. Drizzle some Arbequina olive oil over the whole plate. Finish with a nice grind of black pepper

SKATE, COCKLES, SEA PURSLANE, CRISP POTATOES
Serves 4

4 medium Yukon Gold potatoes, peeled and cut into 1¼-inch (3 cm) chunks • Salt • 4 tablespoons olive oil, plus more for the skate wings • Freshly ground black pepper • 2 shallots, finely diced • 1 clove garlic, smooshed to a paste • 250 ml white wine • 1 kg live cockles, cleaned • 4 skate wings (250 g each) • 150 g cold unsalted butter, diced • 100 g sea purslane • Juice of ½ lemon • Handful of chopped flat-leaf parsley.

In a pot, combine the potatoes with cold water to cover and salt the water. Bring to a boil and simmer until they are soft. Meanwhile, preheat the oven to 392°F (200°C) and put a roasting pan in the oven to preheat.

Drain the potatoes, return to the pan, and rough them up. Put 2 tablespoons of the olive oil into the now hot roasting pan, add the potatoes, and toss to coat them. Season with salt and pepper and return the pan to the oven to roast until the potatoes are crisp and golden, shuffling them every 20 minutes. Keep warm.

In a saucepan large enough to comfortably hold the cockles, sweat the shallots in the remaining 2 tablespoons olive oil until really soft and opaque. Add the garlic and cook

for a minute, then tip in the white wine. Increase the heat, and once the wine is nicely steaming, add the cockles, give them a stir around, cover, and steam for about 1 minute, then take a look. If the cockles have opened, take the pan off the heat, otherwise give them a little bit longer (discard any that have not opened). Set a sieve over a bowl to catch the juices and drain the cockles in the sieve. Pick the cockles from their shells, keeping a few still in their shells for garnish.

If the oven isn't still on to 392°F (200°C), preheat again.

Heat an ovenproof skillet that's large enough to hold all the skate wings until it's very hot. Add a good drizzle of olive oil and place the seasoned skate wings thick-side down in the pan. Reduce the heat and allow the fish to relax. Transfer the pan to the oven and roast for 7 minutes. Remove from the oven and using metal spatula (fish slice), turn the skate. Give it 1 minute and then remove the skate to a warm baking sheet.

Add the reserved cockle cooking liquid to the skillet along with the cold butter. Once the butter has melted and starts to form an emulsion, add the cockles and sea purslane. Give the mixture a moment to get to know itself and warm the cockles through. Remove from the heat and add the lemon juice. Finish the potatoes with the parsley and divide onto four plates. Place the skate on top and then pour over the cockle mixture. Garnish with a few of the cockles in the shell.

MARMALADE TREACLE TART AND CRÈME FRAÎCHE
Makes one 11-inch (28 cm) tart

For the sweet pastry:
450 g all-purpose (plain) flour • 150 g superfine (caster) sugar • Pinch of salt • 250 g cold unsalted butter, diced • 2 eggs • 1 egg yolk • Cold water (if necessary)

For the beurre noisette:
250 g butter

For the filling:
170 g Beurre Noisette *(above)* • 450 g golden syrup • 450 g marmalade • 3 eggs • 75 ml double cream • 2 teaspoons table salt • Juice of 2 lemons • 180 g brown bread crumbs • Grated zest of 3 lemons

Make the sweet pastry:
This makes enough for two tarts.
In a food processor, blend the flour, sugar, and salt. Add the butter and process until it resembles fine bread crumbs. Add the whole eggs and egg yolk and pulse until it all combines (you may need a little cold water). Tip out and form into a uniform dough. Divide into 2 equal parts, wrap in plastic wrap (cling film), and refrigerate one portion until ready to use. (Freeze the second one for later use.)

Make the beurre noisette:
In a saucepan, heat the butter over high heat until it becomes a dark, nutty brown. Pass through a fine-mesh sieve. This should yield about 170 g beurre noisette.

Make the filling:
In a bowl, combine the beurre noisette, golden syrup, and marmalade. In a separate bowl, whisk together the eggs, cream, salt, and lemon juice. Combine the two mixtures and stir in the bread crumbs and lemon zest.

Assemble the tart:
Preheat the oven to 320°F (160°C).
Roll out the pastry to ⅛ inch (3 mm) thick and fit it into a pre-prepared tart case. Prick the dough with a fork and line the tart shell with parchment paper and pie weights (baking beans).
Blind bake for about 30 minutes. Take out the paper and weights, return to the oven, and bake for another 10 minutes to brown the bottom.
Pour in the filling and bake for about 45 minutes, at which point a skin should have formed.
Allow to cool for at least 30 minutes before slicing.

JAMES COOKS WITH BEAUTIFUL EFFORTLESSNESS, BRINGING TOGETHER THE FOOD OF HIS CHILDHOOD WITH HIS LOVE OF HEARTY FLAVORS AND HIS BRILLIANCE WHEN IT COMES TO FINE DINING.
— Margot Henderson

MARMALADE TREACLE TART

JAMES FERGUSON

MONIQUE FISO

HIAKAI
Wellington, New Zealand

SELASSIE ATADIKA

Giving a voice to Māori and Polynesian cultures through food is a big undertaking, one that Monique Fiso has not only pioneered, but that has made her a modern icon in the process. Born in New Zealand in 1987, Fiso, who is of Samoan and Māori descent, graduated first in her class from Wellington Institute of Technology's cookery and patisserie program. After nearly two years working under esteemed New Zealand chef Martin Bosley, Fiso set out for New York, where she would make the next phase of her culinary career a dynamic one. Fiso's time in New York led her to cook in some of the city's most revered and decorated kitchens. From PUBLIC Kitchen, Saxon + Parole, and A Voce to baking at Black Seed Bagels and serving as sous chef at The Musket Room, an icon for fine New Zealand cuisine in the United States. Fiso also spent some time as a pastry chef at The Surf Lodge in Montauk on Long Island.

The year 2016 was a big one for Fiso, bringing her back to New Zealand, where she began writing for a national magazine and for a Māori television network, while gearing up for the launch of her pop-up dining series, Hiakai. The series was created with the intention of creating awareness of Māori cuisine on an exploratory level and of honoring the history of the Māori people in the process. Fiso's efforts brought to light the traditional *hāngi* method of cooking—which involves using heated stones inside a pit dug into the earth—in a way the country had not yet seen before. Hiakai's success was undeniable—the following year, Fiso and her team were recognized by the New Zealand Innovation Council. Unsurprisingly (but to the delight of many), Hiakai ultimately became a permanent fixture in the Wellington dining scene.

In tandem with Hiakai's rise, Fiso is quickly becoming a household name in New Zealand and beyond. Locally, she has appeared on radio and television, including on National Geographic's *Gordon Ramsay: Uncharted* and competing on Netflix's *The Final Table* series. Hiakai was named one of *Time*'s World's 100 Greatest Places of 2019.

MENU

AVOCADO, MAMAKU ASK, KARAMU TEA, SNAP PEAS

KAMOKAMO, YOGURT TAHINI, WILD RICE

TUNA CARPACCIO, ANCHOVY ICE CREAM, ROMAINE, BLACK OLIVE DUST

VENISON, SUNCHOKE, MUSHROOM ESSENCE, CHLOROPHYLL

PEACH, KAWAKAWA BERRY, LIME CURD, MERINGUE

TUNA CARPACCIO, ANCHOVY ICE CREAM, ROMAINE, BLACK OLIVE DUST

For the tuna carpaccio:
300 g albacore tuna loin • Lemon-infused olive oil • Sea salt • Lemon juice

For the anchovy ice cream:
50 g heavy (whipping) cream • 30 g glucose syrup • 60 g salted anchovies • 30 g sugar • 10 g low-fat milk powder • 5 g sea salt • 330 ml cold milk • 500 ml to 1 liter liquid nitrogen

For the black olive dust:
100 g Kalamata olives

For the charred baby romaine:
1 head baby romaine • Olive oil • Sea salt • Lemon juice

For the herb aioli:
2 egg yolks • 2 cloves garlic, peeled • 50 g parsley, leaves only • 20 g chives, finely sliced • 1 teaspoon Dijon mustard • 1 teaspoon white wine vinegar • 250 ml neutral vegetable oil • Flaky sea salt • Juice of ½ lemon

For the pickled pikopiko:
100 g white wine vinegar • 40 g sugar • 5 g salt • 50 g fiddleheads

For plating:
9 small warrigal leaves • 9 sea celery/sea parsley leaves

Make the tuna carpaccio:
Portion the tuna into 3 × 20 g cubes. Line a work surface with two layers of plastic wrap (cling film) about 11 × 6 inches (30 × 15 cm). Make it as smooth as possible with no any air bubbles in the plastic. Evenly space the tuna on the plastic wrap. Lay another layer of plastic wrap over the top. Use a mallet or a small heavy-bottomed saucepan to flatten the tuna evenly until it is a scant 1/16 inch (1 mm) thick. Place in the fridge until required.

Closer to service, remove the tuna from the plastic wrap and rub each slice with a little lemon-infused olive oil. Season with salt and a little lemon juice just before it gets plated. Do not do this too far ahead of time or you will cure/cook the fish with the salt and acid.

Make the anchovy ice cream:
In a small saucepan, combine the cream, glucose, and anchovies. Bring to a simmer and stir well to melt the glucose into the cream.
In a small container or bowl, whisk together the sugar, milk powder, and sea salt until well combined.
Place the cold milk in a separate bowl and whisk in the heated anchovy cream, followed by the milk powder mix. Transfer the ice cream base to a high-powered blender and blend on high for 30 seconds until it's very smooth. Adjust the seasoning with salt if necessary. Transfer the ice cream base to two 250 ml squeeze bottles and place in the fridge until required.

Make the black olive dust:
Rinse, pit, and quarter the olives. Dehydrate at 140°F (60°C) for 12 hours.

110

this stage, try and keep the romaine intact. Once the pieces are portioned, trim as much of the core from the leaves as you can. Ideally you want to be left with portions that are 2 inches (5–6 cm) in length.

Combine every portion of charred romaine with 1 teaspoon herb aioli. Mix well and adjust the seasoning with salt and/or lemon juice if necessary.

Fill a ⅙-size hotel pan one-third of the way with liquid nitrogen. Using a steady hand, place droplets of the ice cream base into the nitrogen. They should be individual "pearls." Strain the ice cream pearls from the liquid nitrogen using a mesh sieve. Keep in the freezer until ready to plate.

Serve the ice cream immediately over the tuna and top with pickled piko piko, warrigal leaves, and sea celery/sea parsley leaves.

VENISON, SUNCHOKE, MUSHROOM ESSENCE, CHLOROPHYLL

For the jus:
10 kg chicken bones • 2 onions, mirepoix • 2 carrots, mirepoix • ½ celery head, mirepoix • ½ garlic bulb • 4 sprigs rosemary • 2 bunches thyme • Cabernet sauvignon vinegar • Flaky sea salt

For the mushroom essence:
2.5 kg portobello mushrooms • 2.5 kg white button mushrooms

For the venison:
14 kg venison, Denver leg cut

For the sunchoke puree:
1 onion, thinly sliced • 4 cloves garlic, sliced • 1 kg sunchokes, cut into small pieces • 500 ml heavy (whipping) cream • Xanthan gum • Salt

For the sunchoke chips:
Oil, for deep-frying • 10 large sunchokes • Salt

For the chlorophyll:
500 g spinach • 200 g parsley • 200 g watercress • Ice water • 100 ml neutral vegetable oil • 2 g xanthan gum • Flaky sea salt

For the honeyed kale:
50 g honey • 50 g water • 15 large lacinato kale (cavolo nero) leaves • Salt

For the pickled mushrooms:
500 g cremini (chestnut) mushrooms, stemmed • 50 g dried wild mushrooms • Cabernet sauvignon vinegar • Salt

For the oyster mushrooms:
400 g oyster mushrooms • Thyme • Butter • Flaky sea salt

For finishing:
Oil • Salt • 2 tablespoons butter • 1 clove garlic, peeled • 1 sprig thyme

Using a spice grinder, blend the dehydrated olives to a rough crumb. Transfer to a container.

Make the charred baby romaine:
Heat a charbroiler (chargrill) or woodfire oven until it is very hot.

Cut the romaine in half lengthwise, then drizzle both halves with olive oil and season with sea salt.

Place the romaine halves on the grill and cook until it is wilted and cooked to crisp-tender. The outer leaves should have a good amount of char. Once they're cooked, place on a small tray and drizzle with a little more olive oil and a small squeeze of lemon juice.

Store in the fridge until required, but serve at room temperature.

Make the herb aioli:
In a blender, combine the egg yolks, garlic, parsley, chives, mustard, and vinegar. Turn the blender to high and mix for 30 seconds. With the machine running, start slowly emulsifying in the oil. Season with salt and lemon juice.

Make the pickled pikopiko:
In a saucepan, combine the vinegar, sugar, and salt and bring to a simmer to dissolve the sugar and salt completely. Let it cool. Clean and trim the fiddleheads. Vacuum-seal the fiddleheads with the pickling liquid and tightly compress. Leave them in the bag overnight.

Slice the ferns a generous 1/16 inch (2 mm) on a bias.

To plate:
Portion the romaine lengthwise. You should get 4 portions from each romaine half. At

BADASS! THAT'S THE WORD THAT COMES TO MIND WHEN I THINK OF CHEF MONIQUE FISO.
— Selassie Atadika

Make the jus:
Preheat the oven to 392°F (200°C).
Roast the bones until evenly colored and a dark golden brown.
Place the bones in a stockpot and add water to cover, the vegetables, and herbs. Bring to a simmer and cook gently for 24 hours. Strain the stock, return to a pot, and cook until the stock reaches jus consistency. Pass the jus through a fine chinois, then season with vinegar and salt.

Make the mushroom essence:
Break the mushrooms into small chunks and cook in a saucepan to give them color, then add water to cover and simmer for 12 hours.
Strain the stock, return to the pan, and reduce the stock until a thick umami liquid remains.

Cook the venison:
Set a circulating water bath to 48°C.
Trim the venison by removing any silver skin or cartilage. Roll tightly into a torchon using plastic wrap (cling film). Tie the ends off so that no water can enter the packet during the cooking process. Cook sous vide for 1 hour.
Remove from the water bath and place in an ice bath to stop the venison from cooking any further.
Once cool, unwrap the venison and set on a cooling rack for 30 minutes to air-dry.

Make the sunchoke puree:
In a heavy-bottomed pan, start to cook the onion and garlic, then add the sunchokes and cook over a low heat so the mixture doesn't stick to the pan. Once cooked out and nicely caramelized, add just enough cream to cover the bottom of the pan. Cook out for 10 minutes. Transfer to a blender and with the machine running, shear in the xanthan gum. Season with salt. Pass through a chinois and cool.

Make the sunchoke chips:
Fill a deep fryer with oil and heat to 347°F (175°C).
Thinly slice the sunchokes on a mandoline. You want the sunchokes to be a scant 1/16 inch (1 mm) thick.
Fry the sunchokes until golden brown. Transfer to paper towels to drain. Season with salt and keep in an airtight container until needed.

Make the chlorophyll:
Line a perforated hotel pan (gastronorm) with fine-mesh cheesecloth (muslin) and set in the freezer.
In a blender, combine the spinach, parsley, watercress, and ice water and blend to create the herb water.
Pass through a fine chinois into a heavy-bottomed pot. Set the pot over heat and gently bring the herb water to 136°F (58°C). It will begin to coagulate. Scoop out

the coagulated particles and place on the frozen perforated pan that you prepared earlier. Return to the freezer to cool as rapidly as possible to keep color.
Remove from the freezer, transfer to a blender, and, with the machine running, emulsify in the oil and xanthan.

Make the honeyed kale:
Preheat the oven to 320°F (160°C), low fan. Line sheet pans with nonstick baking mats and lightly coat them with oil spray.
In a small pan, combine the honey and water and melt over heat to form a syrup. Remove from the heat.
Lightly and evenly brush the kale leaves with the honey syrup. Place the kale on the lined pans and bake until golden and crispy, checking every 5 minutes.

Make the pickled mushrooms:
In a rondeau, sauté the cremini. Add the dried wild mushrooms and water to cover. Simmer for 20 minutes. Pass the stock through a chinois.

In the same rondeau used for the stock, sauté the mushrooms. Add the mushroom stock to cover, add a cartouche, and let simmer until two-thirds of the liquid has evaporated. Finish with cabernet sauvignon vinegar and salt.

Make the oyster mushrooms:
Remove the bottoms of the oyster mushrooms and tear each mushroom individually in half. Allow to semidry for service to allow a golden crispy mushroom.

To finish:
Heat a cast-iron skillet until very hot. Oil the pan, season the venison, and sear all the sides of the venison very quickly. In the final moments of searing, add the butter, garlic, and thyme and use those ingredients to baste the venison.
Remove from the pan and let rest for 5 minutes before carving.

MONIQUE FISO

THOMAS FREBEL

INUA
Tokyo, Japan

PALISA ANDERSON

MENU

AERATED MONKFISH LIVER TERRINE, ASPARAGUS, AND BEECHNUTS

SEASONAL CITRUS, ROASTED KELP OIL

AGED AND SMOKED MAITAKE BRAISED IN PINE-NEEDLE DASHI

PLUM LEATHER WITH FRESH AROMATIC FLOWERS

PUMPKIN AND "PUMPKIN-BUSHI"

SEAWEED MILLE-FEUILLE

In a building in Tokyo's Iidabashi neighborhood, through the windows of a dining room on the ninth floor, one can drink in the sprawling Tokyo skyline. Then, from the kitchen, comes a picture frame poised on a plate. Inside the frame lies a small, golden sheet of beeswax, a burgundy layer of plum leather atop it, meticulously decorated with tiny aromatic flowers and herbs. This is just one scene from Inua's tasting menu, a carefully considered drama that tells the story of how Thomas Frebel's Nordic culinary roots mingle with Japanese ingredients. As the courses unfold, dishes may include new-season rice adorned with beechnuts, sansho tips, forest herbs, and a crisp lid of duck fat; a dessert of pine cones foraged from Ibaraki preserved in syrup, and Hokkaido spruce shoots; or ten types of seaweed in a Nordic-Japanese fusion that involves uni, pickled white asparagus, and an oil combining notes of black currant wood and rice.

Frebel's life in Japan, he says, matches almost unbelievably the one he envisioned for himself as a teenager in Germany. As a child he grew up in the kitchen, snagging cookie dough from his grandmother's countertops. He began to cook in earnest in his teens, and not long after, Frebel stumbled upon a book by the chef Eckart Witzigmann, whose descriptions of encountering the world through cultures and foods transfixed him. Frebel began his training in fine-dining establishments around Germany, including under chefs Gohren Mahas, Heinz Weman, Klaus-Peter Lund, and Joachim Wissler. During this time, Frebel traveled to Copenhagen to dine at Noma, and was captivated by the purity of ingredients. He sought a trail, and ended up spending the next ten years at Noma, first as chef de partie, and ultimately as the head of research and development.

With Noma, Frebel created pop-up restaurants in Japan, Mexico, and Australia, searching every corner for the best ingredients and producers in those places. Having been deeply affected by Japan's landscape and culture, when he heard that Noma had an opportunity to open a permanent restaurant there, Frebel volunteered to head the project. Since opening Inua in 2018, Frebel has garnered numerous recognitions, including two Michelin stars and recognition at the World Restaurant Awards as the Arrival of the Year.

SEASONAL CITRUS, ROASTED KELP OIL
Serves 5

For the pickled black currant leaves/shoots:
50 g fresh black currant shoots (on stem) • 150 g apple cider vinegar (5%)

For the pickled sage flowers:
50 g fresh sage flowers (on stem) • 150 g apple cider vinegar (5%)

For the pickled dill flowers:
50 g fresh dill flowers (on stem) 150 g apple cider vinegar (5%)

For the lactic-fermented barley koji water:
500 g pearl barley koji • 1 kg filtered water • 20 g sea salt • 1 g lactic acid bacteria

For the kanzuri water:
500 g aged kanzuri • 1 kg filtered water

For the roasted kelp oil:
300 g Rausu kombu • 600 g rice bran oil

For the Kaffir lime leaf oil:
200 g fresh Kaffir lime leaves • 400 g rice bran oil

For the lemongrass oil:
200 g fresh lemongrass • 400 g rice bran oil

To finish:
1 Hassaku orange • 1 buntan (pomelo) • 500 g Kanzuri Water *(above)*

For plating:
1 fresh kihada berry, halved and seeded • 1 fresh green juniper berry, halved and seeded • 4 Pickled Dill Flowers *(above)* • 2 Pickled Black Currant Leaves *(above)* • 2 Pickled Black Currant Shoots *(above)* • 4 Pickled Sage Flowers *(above)* • 2 fresh black currant buds, halved • INUA Shichimi Spice Mix *(recipe follows)*

Pickle the black currant shoots:
Vacuum-seal the black currant shoots and vinegar to 100%. Pickle for a minimum of 3 weeks before use. Once adequately

pickled, pick the young leaves from the shoots and reserve both.

Pickle the sage flowers:
Vacuum-seal the sage flowers and vinegar to 100%. Pickle for a minimum of 3 weeks before use.

Pickle the dill flowers:
Vacuum-seal the dill flowers and vinegar to 100%. Pickle for a minimum of 3 weeks before use.

Make the lactic-fermented barley koji water:
Combine all the ingredients and blitz in a blender for 30 seconds, transfer to a vacuum bag, and vacuum-seal to 100%. Ferment at 90°F (32°C) for 3 days. During the course of the 3 days, the bag with gradually inflate. Open the bag, taste, and if a stronger fermented flavor is desired, reseal the bag and ferment for a further 1–2 days.
When ready, open the bag into a container or hotel pan (gastro), freeze, then ice-clarify in the fridge. Reserve the liquid until use.

The liquid will still continue to ferment slowly even at fridge temperature, so if not making use of it immediately, return to the freezer until use. When ready to use, transfer to a spray bottle.

Make the kanzuri water:
Blend the kanzuri with the water. Freeze the liquid in a single solid block. Once completely frozen, turn out the frozen block onto a fine cheesecloth (muslin). Refrigerate and ice-clarify the melting liquid. Once fully melted, discard the sediment and reserve the liquid.

Make the roasted kelp oil:
Dry the kombu in a dehydrator for 8 hours at 104°F (40°C).
Blend the dried kombu with the oil on full speed for 7 minutes. Pour the contents into a heavy-bottomed rondeau and bring the temperature up until the oil starts to bubble. Reduce the heat to a bare simmer and stir constantly for 6 hours. Cool everything down, then return to a blender and blend for another 7 minutes. Refrigerate for 12 hours to infuse, then pass through a fine cheesecloth.

Make the Kaffir lime leaf oil:
Blend the leaves and oil together for 7 minutes. Vacuum-seal and infuse for 24 hours, then hang through a fine cheesecloth.

Make the lemongrass oil:
Blend the lemongrass and oil together for 7 minutes. Vacuum-seal and infuse in the fridge for 24 hours, then hang through a fine cheesecloth.

To finish:
Peel a segment of each variety of citrus without the use of a knife to preserve as much of its textural integrity. Submerge in the kanzuri water and cure for 2 hours.

To plate:
Take the segments out of the kanzuri water and arrange on the plate. Garnish each citrus with fresh berries and the pickles. Place 3 drops of lemongrass oil and Kaffir lime leaf oil on each segment, and carefully pool 8 g roasted kelp oil in the center of the plate, between the two segments of citrus. Spray each segment twice with the barley koji water. Finish with a generous amount of "shichimi" spice mix.

INUA SHICHIMI SPICE MIX
Makes 57 grams

24 g dehydrated tomato • 12 g dehydrated bergamot skin • 12 g dehydrated hibiscus flower • 3.6 g dehydrated curry leaves • 3 g dehydrated red sanshō pepper • 2.4 g dehydrated kihada berry • 0.1 g dehydrated smoked habanero

Blend all the ingredients together in a spice grinder. Store in a cool, dry place.

PLUM LEATHER WITH FRESH AROMATIC FLOWERS
Serves 6

For the pickled long peppers:
50 g fresh ripe long peppers • 150 g apple cider vinegar (5%)

For the plum juice:
4 kg Early River plums (must be ripe and dark-skinned)

For the plum leather:
Oil • 300 g Plum Juice *(above)* **• 20 g rose oil**

For the kelp salt:
1 liter filtered water • 60 g rishiri kombu

For plating:
1 portion Plum Leather *(above)* **• 5 g rose oil • Beeswax • 3 coriander flowers • 3 dill flowers • 4 sprigs lemon thyme flowers • 7 lemon thyme leaves • 1 beach rose petal, torn into 5 pieces • 0.1 g Kelp Salt** *(above)* **• 0.1 g Pickled Long Peppers** *(above)*

Make the pickled long peppers:
Vacuum-seal the whole long pepper and vinegar to 100%. Pickle for a minimum of 3 weeks before use. When preparing for the dish, slice cross sections as thin as possible and store in the pickling liquid.

Make the plum juice:
Halve all the plums and freeze in a flat layer in a large hotel pan (gastro). Take out of the freezer and thaw at room temperature for 1 hour.
Wrap the pan tightly in plastic wrap (cling film) to ensure zero escape of steam. Steam the trays in the combi oven at 80°C for 2 hours. Remove from the oven and let infuse for another 2 hours, then hang the plums in a fine cheesecloth (muslin) to extract and catch the juice.

Make the plum leather:
In a saucepan, heat the plum juice until it starts to steam. Blowtorch the surface of the juice to remove bubbles, and skim any impurities that rise to the top. Pass through a fish net and let cool to room temperature. Heavily oil a two-thirds sheet pan. Apply the oil with paper towel as if polishing the pan, ensuring an equally thin spread, especially the sides and corners. The amount of oil left on the tray should be generous, but not nearly enough for the oil to drip or run. Place the tray in the blast freezer to chill to roughly 32°F (0°C).
Pour the cooled plum juice onto the chilled sheet pan and place on a dehydrator rack. Ensure the dehydrator itself is on a perfectly flat surface. Set the dehydrator to 149°F (65°C). Dehydrate for 1 hour, then carefully rotate the tray. Dehydrate for 3 hours longer. Remove the tray from the dehydrator and let come to room temperature naturally. Lightly oil the surface of the plum leather with the rose oil, then cut into desired portions. Carefully pull each portion off the tray and store between parchment paper.

Make the kelp salt:
Vacuum-seal the water and kombu together and infuse in the fridge for at least 9 hours. Strain the dashi through fine cheesecloth.

In a nonstick pan, bring the dashi to a gentle simmer and reduce by one-quarter, skimming regularly. Transfer the reduced dashi to a plastic container and place uncovered in a dehydrator set at 140°F (60°C). Dehydrate the dashi until salt crystals form.

To plate:
Oil both sides of the plum leather portion with rose oil, place on a portioned sheet of beeswax and arrange the fresh coriander and dill flowers on top. Vacuum-seal for 30 seconds, opening the bag immediately after. Dress the plum leather with the remaining condiments, ensuring each component is spaced out evenly, but avoiding symmetry. Serve in a picture frame from which guests will peel the plum leather from the beeswax as they eat.

AGED AND SMOKED MAITAKE BRAISED IN PINE-NEEDLE DASHI
Serves 7

For the rice koji oil:
500 g dehydrated rice koji • 1 kg rice bran oil

For the smoked maitake:
One 750 g maitake mushroom, aged 5 days, uncovered, in a refrigerated environment with good airflow • 300 g Rice Koji Oil *(above)*

For the miso water:
500 g hagoromo miso • 2 kg filtered water

For the pine dashi:
1 liter filtered water • 60 g rishiri kombu • 60 g dried pine needles

For the baked maitake mushroom:
Smoked Maitake *(above)* • Miso Water *(above)*, ratio dependent • Pine Dashi *(above)*, ratio dependent

Make the rice koji oil:
In a food processor, blend the dried rice koji and oil together for 7 minutes. Let infuse for 24 hours, then strain the oil through a fine cheesecloth.

Smoke the maitake:
Vacuum-seal the aged maitake mushrooms with the rice koji oil. Rest for 1 hour, then open the bag and place on a grill grate or oven rack with a flat tray underneath to catch the oil that drips off during the smoking process. Smoke the maitake mushroom over a gentle smoke (free-flowing and uncontained) for 3 days in a warm area (above a wood-fire barbecue, for example).

Make the miso water:
Blend the miso and water together and freeze completely. Ice-clarify through a fine cheesecloth, reserving the liquid.

Make the pine dashi:
Vacuum-seal the water and kombu and infuse in the fridge for at least 9 hours. Strain through fine cheesecloth. Vacuum-seal the kombu dashi with the pine needles and steam in a combi oven at 140°F (60°C) for 1 hour. Pass through a fine cheesecloth and reserve the liquid in the fridge until use.

Bake the maitake:
Preheat the oven to 572°F (300°C). Get the final weight of the smoked maitake and place in a clay pot. Weigh out 1:1:2 of maitake:miso water:pine dashi for each serving and add to the pot. Tightly wrap the lidded clay pot with two layers of foil, then bake for 30 minutes. Take the pot out of the oven and rest the maitake in the pot for 15 minutes longer before removing.

To Plate:
Pass the smoked maitake broth through a fine cheesecloth. Slice the baked mushroom into generous portions, ensuring each portion has a fair share of caps and a thick section of stalk for maximum texture. Warm up the portions in some of the broth, but be careful not to boil. Plate the portion of mushroom in a bowl and pour the broth tableside.

SEAWEED MILLE-FEUILLE
Serves 4

For the black currant wood oil:
100 g young (green) black currant wood • 150 g rice bran oil

For the cold-infused kombu dashi:
1 liter filtered water • 60 g rishiri kombu

For the pine dashi:
1 liter Cold-Infused Kombu Dashi *(above)* • 60 g dried pine needles

For the caramelized hirome sheets:
1 kg Pine Dashi *(above)* • 45 g chestnut honey • 100 g superfine (caster) sugar • 500 g fresh hirome seaweed • Clarified butter • Powdered (icing) sugar

For the pine salt:
10 g fresh momi fir pine needles • 10 g Maldon sea salt

For plating:
1 green yuzu • 20 g whipped double cream (48%), soft peaks

Make the black currant wood oil:
Pound the wood with a hammer until it shatters and splits. Vacuum-seal with the oil and steam in a combi oven at 140°F (60°C) for 6 hours. Cool down the bag in an ice slurry and allow the oil to infuse overnight. Open the bags over a fine cheesecloth (muslin) and hang to extract the oil. Discard the wood.

Make the kombu dashi:
Vacuum-seal the water and kombu and infuse in fridge for at least 9 hours. Strain through fine cheesecloth.

Make the pine dashi:
Vacuum-seal the kombu dashi and pine needles and steam in a combi oven at 140°F (60°C) for 1 hour. Pass through a fine cheesecloth and reserve the liquid in the fridge until use.

Make the caramelized hirome sheets:
In a large pan, combine the pine dashi, honey, and sugar and bring to a boil. Take half out of the pan and cool down in a blast freezer, stirring occasionally to achieve an ice slurry to be used as the refreshing liquid after blanching.
Trim away the main stem of the seaweed so all that is left is the thin "leaves" on either side. Blanch the trimmed seaweed in the sweetened pine dashi for 30 seconds, then refresh in the ice slurry. Once fully chilled, drain the seaweed well and lay flat on trays lined with paper towels to remove all excess moisture.
Preheat a combi oven to 347°F (175°C) at 50% steam. Line a sheet pan with parchment paper and brush generously with melted clarified butter. Give the entire tray a light dusting of powdered (icing) sugar over the clarified butter.
Lay the seaweed down as flat as possible on the pan. Brush the seaweed with clarified butter and dust with a generous amount of powdered sugar. Place in the oven and bake for 5 minutes.
After 5 minutes, remove the pan and fold each piece of seaweed over itself, and bake for 4 minutes longer. Remove from the oven again and cut into 2-inch (5 cm) squares. Return to the oven and bake for another 5 minutes.
Transfer the caramelized seaweed squares to a clean tray lined with paper towels to cool down and absorb excess fat. Transfer to a dehydrator set to 122°F (50°C) until use.

Make the pine salt:
Freeze the pine needles with liquid nitrogen, using as much as needed to pound to a powder with a mortar and pestle. Add the salt, pound again, and keep frozen until use.

To plate:
Line up 9 squares of caramelized seaweed. Place 3 drops of black currant wood oil on each square. Zest the green yuzu using a Japanese citrus zester and brush lightly over the seaweed. Sprinkle a small amount of pine salt on each square. Place ½ teaspoon whipped double cream on 8 of the 9 squares. Carefully stack the seasoned squares. Serve immediately.

SEASONAL CITRUS, ROASTED KELP OIL

THOMAS IS ENTIRELY DEVOTED TO THE CRAFT AND LEADS WITH HIS PASSION, PUTTING IN THE HARD WORK AND TIME THAT INSPIRES HIS TEAM TO FOLLOW HIS EXAMPLE. HE IS WITHOUT A DOUBT ONE OF THE GREATS OF OUR TIME. — Palisa Anderson

SEAWEED MILLE-FEUILLE

THOMAS FREBEL

EVAN FUNKE

FELIX TRATTORIA
Los Angeles, California,
United States

JESSICA KOSLOW

MENU

FOCACCIA

FIORI DI ZUCCA CON MOZZARELLA DI BUFALA E ALICI

STRANGOLAPRETI DI SPINACI CON BURRO FUSO E SALVIA

Chefs are often lauded for reaching the pinnacles of their field, but Evan Funke stands out because he never will. Anyone who has lost themselves in his Old World and otherworldly pastas at Felix Trattoria in Venice Beach might disagree, but the *sfoglino* himself will tell you that his quest for flour-dusted transcendence will never be complete.

The son of an Oscar-winning special effects cinematographer, Funke grew up immersed in the world of film, but it was the drama of the kitchen that ended up capturing his imagination. After logging six years under Wolfgang Puck at Spago in Beverly Hills, Funke moved on to other chef jobs, but found himself unfulfilled. He had long been enthralled by the beauty, tradition, and precision of pasta, but he was uneducated in the nuances of the artform, so in 2007, he took a bold leap and went to northern Italy to train under legendary *maestra di cucina* Alessandra Spisni at La Vecchia Scuola Bolognese.

In Emilia-Romagna, the ancestral home of the *sfoglia* school of hand-wrought pasta craft, Funke threw out everything he thought he knew about cooking. He spent up to twelve hours a day coaxing double-zero flour, tepid water, and eggs into silky dough and working it into *sfoglia*, or sheets, with a *mattarello*, the traditional one-meter-long wooden rolling pin. He labored to master the most fundamental steps before moving onto flashier work—pinching, crimping, and cutting dough into shapes that Italians have been making for centuries.

At Felix, Funke shares every morsel of knowledge he has absorbed during his years of study, and his passion is rivaled only by his unwavering preparation. His attention to detail guides him in all aspects of leadership, from the care he pays to his arsenal of artisanal tools to the warm, demonstrative manner in which he mentors his staff. Confident and credible, his voice carries much weight as a teacher—but he will always see himself as a student, and that might be the greatest lesson of all.

FIORI DI ZUCCA CON MOZZARELLA DI BUFALA E ALICI
Serves 6

Vegetable or seed oil, for deep-frying • 12 squash blossoms • 250 g mozzarella di bufala • 250 g fine rice flour • 250 g cornstarch (corn flour) • 120 g all-purpose (plain) flour, plus more for dredging • 20 g kosher (flaked) salt • 15 g baking powder • Sparkling water, as needed • 12 oil-packed anchovy fillets • Fine sea salt

Pour 2 inches (5 cm) oil into a wide heavy-bottomed pot or sautoir and bring to 360°F (182°C).
Meanwhile, open each blossom and remove and discard the stamen. Be careful not to rip the petals. Set the blossoms aside on a tray.
Slice the mozzarella into sticks about 1½ inches (4 cm) long and ¼ inch (6 mm) thick. Set aside.
In a bowl, whisk together the rice flour, cornstarch, all-purpose (plain) flour, kosher salt, and baking powder. With your hand make a well in the flour and begin adding the carbonated water while incorporating the flour mixture until you achieve a smooth runny batter. The batter should coat the back of a spoon and run easily away. Refrigerate.
To stuff the blossoms, place a stick of mozzarella inside the blossom and lay an anchovy fillet directly on top of the mozzarella. Close the blossom by gently twisting the tips of the petals together.
Spread all-purpose flour in a wide flat vessel and dredge the blossoms to coat thoroughly. Working in batches or 3 to 4 at a time, dip each blossom into the batter, allowing it to run off, leaving a thin veneer. In a "paint brush" movement, drag the tips of the blossom in the oil toward you and release away from you. Fry each batch for 45–60 seconds. Remove from the oil with a spider and season immediately with fine sea salt. Serve immediately.

STRANGOLAPRETI DI SPINACI CON BURRO FUSO E SALVIA
Serves 6
Makes about 46 strangolapreti

Salt, for the blanching water • 500 g spinach • 104 g eggs • 285 g cow's milk ricotta • 100 g Parmigiano-Reggiano cheese, grated • 10 g salt • 60 g toasted bread crumbs • 10 grates nutmeg • 25 g tipo "00" flour • 350 g semola rimacinata, for coating

To finish:
25 g unsalted butter • 4 or 5 sage leaves • Parmigiano-Reggiano cheese

Bring a large pot of water to a rapid boil and season with salt.
Blanch the spinach for about 1 minute, then drain and shock in an ice bath.
Remove the spinach from ice bath and wring out in an absorbent terry cloth towel until very dry. Measure out 200 g (which is about what you should have after wringing it dry).
In a blender, combine 100 g of the spinach and the eggs and puree until very smooth. Finely chop the remaining 100 g spinach and set aside.
In a bowl, combine the ricotta, Parmigiano, salt, bread crumbs, and spinach puree.

Grate in the nutmeg and one-quarter of the flour and mix thoroughly with a whisk until smooth.

Fold the remaining flour into the mixture with a rubber spatula until combined. Cover the bowl with plastic wrap (cling film) and refrigerate for 1 hour.

Spread the semola rimacinata on a sheet pan or a flat wide baking pan. With a small ice cream scoop or spoon, portion 17 g of the mixture and place in the semola to coat. Form round or oval shapes and then place on a new pan lined with parchment paper. Refrigerate until use.

To finish:
When ready to serve, in a sauté pan, lightly brown the butter over medium heat. Add the sage leaves and fry in the butter. Meanwhile, bring a pot of water to a boil and season well. Working in batches of 7, cook the strangolapreti for 1 minute 45 seconds. Remove the strangolapreti and drain all water.

Gently add the strangolapreti to the browned butter and swirl, do not toss. Spoon the strangolapreti onto the service vessel, finish with the browned butter, sage, and generous amount of Parmigiano-Reggiano.

POLPETTE, SALSA VERDE

STRANGOLAPRETI DI SPINACI

FOCACCIA

HE'S OPEN WITH INFORMATION, CURIOUS ABOUT EVERYTHING, AND ALWAYS ON A MISSION TO KEEP PERFECTING HIS TECHNIQUE—HE NEVER FEELS LIKE HIS WORK IS DONE.

— Jessica Koslow

EVAN FUNKE

WILLIAM GLEAVE & GIUSEPPE BELVEDERE

YOTAM OTTOLENGHI

MENU

PIZZA FRITTA

RAW MACKEREL AND GOOSEBERRY KOSHO

PHEASANT SOPA DE LIMA

TAGLIATELLE AND CHICKEN OFFAL RAGÙ

POACHED TURBOT, VIN JAUNE, AND WINTER TRUFFLE

BAKED LEMON LEAF CREAM, CITRUS, AND JASMINE

Two chefs cooking in tandem can be a tricky proposition, but when it works, disparate visions can coalesce into something truly original. Working in harmony, Giuseppe "Peppe" Belvedere and William Gleave and have burned Bright—the aptly named restaurant they co-helm—into the minds of London diners, synthesizing their talents to create a dining experience that is at once timeless and of the moment.

The pair made their names in the growing realm of "cave bistronomy," which matches natural wines with thoughtful small plates that complement the honest, unvarnished flavors found in these bottles. Gleave came to prominence at the late Garagistes, in the Tasmanian capital of Hobart; Belvedere logged years under chef Ed Wilson at Brawn, the acclaimed London restaurant known for its smart wine list and Pan-European cuisine. But it was individual guest chef runs at P. Franco, the Clapton neighborhood wineshop founded by the team behind Bright, that first hipped East London to the exciting potential of both young chefs. Gleave's tenure, in 2015, saw him juggling techniques with umami-rich Asian flavors; Belvedere's 2017 stint showcased his Sardinian heritage, with seafood and handmade pastas.

At P. Franco, the chefs had just two electric induction burners, but now at Bright they have the space and equipment to express their ideas in an entirely new scope and context. The large charcoal grill gets plenty of work as the chefs turn out deceptively simple cuts of fish or meat, the unassuming appearance of which belies a deep understanding of live fire cooking. Gleave's skill with sauces, from classical French offerings to complex Cantonese XO, is a highlight, as are Belvedere's flawless pastas. Such strengths, taken together, make Bright one of London's most versatile dining rooms—the kind of place one can visit every day of the week without repeating a meal.

PHEASANT SOPA DE LIMA
Serves 4

For the broth and pheasant:
1 kg chicken wings* • 2 small shallots • 2 cloves garlic • 2 small green tomatoes • 2 jalapeño chilies, seeded • 2 dried morita chilies, seeded and lightly toasted • 1 pasilla chili, seeded and lightly toasted • 1 cascabel chili, seeded • 10 sprigs thyme • ½ bunch cilantro (fresh coriander) • 4 sprigs epazote 10 black peppercorns • Salt • 1 large female pheasant

For finishing and plating:
1 small white onion, finely diced and preserved in Meyer lemon juice • 1 jalapeño chili, finely sliced • 10 sprigs cilantro (fresh coriander), leaves picked and stems finely diced • Meyer lemon wedges

We use wings that we reserve from the chickens we use to make Chicken Offal Ragù (recipe follows)

Make the broth:
In a large pot, cover the chicken wings with 1.5 kg filtered water. Bring to a boil and skim off any impurities with a ladle. Add half of the shallots, garlic, green tomatoes, chilies, herbs, and peppercorns along with a pinch of salt. Cover and gently simmer for 2 hours. Remove from the heat and allow to cool. Strain the broth into a bowl and set aside.

Prepare the pheasant:
Remove the head, innards, and feet from pheasant. Debone the pheasant, keeping the breast, legs, fat, offal, and all the bones. Separate the legs into thighs and drumsticks and reserve the thighs for grilling.

In a large stockpot, combine all the pheasant bones, trimmings, and drumsticks. Cover with the strained broth and the remaining shallots, garlic, green tomatoes, chilies, and peppercorns. Cover and gently simmer for 2 hours. Remove from the heat and add the remaining herbs and pheasant breasts to poach in the residual heat of the broth. Allow to completely cool.
Carefully remove and reserve the pheasant breasts and dried chilies and set aside. Taste the broth and adjust the seasoning with salt. You should obtain a beautiful, concentrated broth that encapsulates the flavors of gamey pheasant and smoked chilies.

Finish and plate:
In a small pan, gently render the reserved pheasant fat and infuse with the reserved chilies. Transfer to a blender, puree, strain and keep warm.

PHEASANT SOPA DE LIMA

123

Grill the pheasant thighs over charcoal, using some of the chili-infused fat to glaze. Let rest before carving.

Meanwhile, shred the breast meat and divide into 4 warmed bowls. Add the warmed broth and garnish with a generous spoon of diced onion, cilantro (coriander), jalapeño, and finally the chili-infused fat.

Serve the thigh on the side with a little Meyer lemon wedge and a cold beer.

TAGLIATELLE AND CHICKEN OFFAL RAGÙ
Serves 4

For the pasta dough:
250 g fine semolina flour • 100 g tipo "00" flour • 3 large eggs • 4 egg yolks

For the chicken offal ragù:
150 g chicken hearts • 150 g chicken gizzards • 80 g chicken livers • 3 tablespoons chicken fat • Salt • 1 small white onion, finely chopped • 1 clove garlic, lightly crushed • 100 g white wine • 60 g Marsala • 50 g heavy (whipping) cream • 300 g brown chicken stock • 10 g dried porcini • 5 sage leaves • 1 sprig rosemary • Freshly ground black pepper • Freshly grated nutmeg • Grated Parmesan cheese, for serving

Make the pasta dough:
In an large bowl, combine the semolina and 00 flour. In a separate bowl, beat together the whole eggs and yolks. Add the eggs to the flours and working by hand, knead the dough until smooth. Wrap in plastic wrap (cling film) and allow to rest for 1 hour at room temperature.

Roll the dough with a pasta machine to a thickness of generous 1/16 inch (2 mm) and cut into tagliatelle. Dust with semolina and store on an uncovered tray until needed.

Make the chicken offal ragù:
Roughly hand-chop the hearts, gizzards, and livers separately as they will require different cooking times.

In a large Dutch oven (casserole), color off the hearts in a spoon of the chicken fat. Season with salt and set aside.

Repeat with the gizzards and when golden, deglaze by adding the chopped onion, the garlic, and the remaining spoon of chicken fat. Once the onion is translucent, deglaze first with wine, followed by the Marsala. Add the cream, 200 g of stock, the porcini, sage, and rosemary and simmer very gently until the gizzards are tender, about 15 minutes. At this stage add the colored hearts and the remaining 100 g stock and simmer for 5 minutes. Remove from the heat and add the chopped livers, stirring constantly to allow the livers to cook from the residual heat. Adjust the season with salt, pepper, and nutmeg to taste. Cover and let rest for 1 hour. Discard the sage, rosemary, and garlic.

When ready to serve, bring a large pot of salted water to a boil. Drop in the tagliatelle and cook for 1 minute.

Gently warm the ragù. Drain the pasta and add it to the Dutch oven and dress in the ragù. Sprinkle with Parmesan and serve.

BAKED LEMON LEAF CREAM, CITRUS, AND JASMINE
Serves 4

For the baked lemon leaf cream:
250 g heavy (whipping) cream • 35 g superfine (caster) sugar • Peel of 1 lemon • 6 fresh lemon leaves • 45 g egg white

For the sugar syrup:
200 g superfine (caster) sugar • 200 g filtered water

For the compressed kumquats:
8 kumquats, halved and seeded • 100 g Sugar Syrup *(above)*

For the dehydrated/rehydrated citrus:
1 navel orange • 1 unwaxed lemon • 100 g Sugar Syrup *(above)* • 50 g orange juice • 50 g lemon juice

For the fresh citrus fruit segments:
1 pink navel orange • 1 pink grapefruit • 1 blood orange • 1 mandarin

For assembly:
80 g Citrus and Jasmine Jelly (per portion; *recipe follows*) • Fruity olive oil

Make the baked lemon leaf cream:
In a saucepan, combine the cream, sugar, lemon peel, and lemon leaves and heat to about 194°F (90°C). Remove from the heat and allow to infuse for 30 minutes.

In a large bowl, gently whisk the egg whites to lightly break down the structure of the whites (the aim is NOT to incorporate air). Reheat the cream/sugar/lemon mixture to 194°F (90°C) and pour it over the whites, whisking as you go. Pass through a fine-mesh sieve, remove any foam, and divide among 4 bowls. Place the bowls into a combination oven set at 194°F (90°C) with 50% humidity; the cream should set in about 20 minutes. Once set, remove the bowls from the oven and allow to cool at room temperature. It is best served without visiting the fridge.

Make the sugar syrup:
In a saucepan, heat the sugar and water together over gentle until the sugar is dissolved. Let cool and refrigerate until needed.

Compress the kumquats:
Place the kumquats and sugar syrup in a vacuum bag and vacuum-seal under high pressure. Store under pressure for 30 minutes and then remove the kumquats and store in the fridge.

Dehydrate and rehydrate the citrus:
Using an electric meat slicer, cut both the blood orange and lemon into slices 1/8 inch (4 mm) thick. Then cut each slice into 4 pieces, removing any seeds as you go. Transfer to a bowl, add the sugar syrup, and macerate for 10 minutes.

Remove the fruit (keeping the syrup) and place in a dehydrator set at 140°F (60°C) to dry for about 8 hours.

When ready to use, rehydrate the orange pieces in the orange juice plus 50 g of the reserved sugar syrup. Rehydrate the lemon pieces in the lemon juice plus the remaining sugar syrup.

Prepare the fresh fruit:
Peel the citrus fruit with a knife, exposing the fruit and removing the outer membrane. Then cut the segments out from between the membranes using a sharp knife (saving excess juice as you go).

To plate:
Top each bowl of baked cream with layers of jelly and the different citrus fruits, adding a little of the reserved fresh citrus juice and a few drops of fruity olive oil.

CITRUS AND JASMINE JELLY
400 g filtered water • 150 g superfine (caster sugar) • 6 g jasmine pearl tea • 280 g lemon juice • 40 g orange juice • 40 g mandarin juice • 20 g lime juice • 5 sheets bronze gelatin

In a saucepan, combine the water and sugar and heat to 176°F (80°C). Add the jasmine tea and allow to steep for 5 minutes. Strain the tea through a sieve into a metal bowl set in an ice bath. Stir in the lemon, orange, mandarin, and lime juices and taste.

Soak the gelatin sheets in ice cold water. Add the soaked gelatin to the juices and let sit overnight.

AT BRIGHT, A CUT OF MEAT OR A PIECE OF FISH THAT MIGHT AT FIRST SEEM SIMPLY COOKED IN FACT TELLS OF A DEEP UNDERSTANDING OF FIRE AND THE GRILL ON WHICH IT'S BEEN COOKED, OF CLASSIC AND MODERN TECHNIQUES AND THE TRICKIEST SAUCES.
— Yotam Ottolenghi

TAGLIATELLE AND CHICKEN OFFAL RAGÙ

WILLIAM GLEAVE & GIUSEPPE BELVEDERE

MATT HARPER

HUGH ACHESON

"Modern classic" might sound like an oxymoron, but it is the best way to characterize Matt Harper's formidable food. At Kensington Quarters in Philadelphia, he cooks in a measured, technical manner grounded in fundamentals. But he always knows when to zag, engaging the ingredients of both local and global larders to create dishes that are at once familiar and unexpected.

Harper grew up in Arkansas, and was pursuing a college degree in communications when he realized hands-on work would suit him better. He enrolled in culinary school in Atlanta, home of Hugh Acheson's Empire State South, a formative early stop for Harper and where he began building his identity as a chef. Practicing whole-animal butchery and forging connections with independent growers and producers became priorities, and his heartfelt dedication to sustainability only grew as he advanced. As the chef de cuisine at Zahav, Michael Solomonov's acclaimed Israeli restaurant in Philadelphia, Harper took his next leap, achieving fluency in Middle Eastern cuisines and honing his managerial style, one built upon mutual respect.

At restaurant and butcher shop Kensington Quarters, Chef Harper stocks its meat locker, butcher case, refrigerators, and pantry with the best the region has to offer. Since every ingredient is selected for its unique merits, he is assertively restrained in manipulating them, emphasizing techniques that encourage clarity of flavor: a perfectly grilled Denver steak, house-made soppressata, flawless tortellini pinched by hand. Comforting food is a guiding principle, but that doesn't mean Harper plays it safe. For example, he takes Brussels sprouts up a notch with miso aioli and furikake-spiced puffed rice, and flashes his Southern experience with a "dirty rice" made of farro and sunchoke. And by minimizing the environmental impact of his kitchen, Harper does his part to encourage the health of local agriculture and to secure the future of farming. Harper and Kensington Quarters are a spiritual match.

MENU

CHARCUTERIE: ASSORTED MEATS AND ACCOUTERMENTS

PUMPKIN AND APPLE SALAD WITH PEPITAS AND BUTTERMILK DRESSING

LACE CORN BREAD WITH CREAMED CORN, OKRA, AND BACON

CHICKEN AND DUMPLINGS WITH ENGLISH PEAS

COAL-ROASTED BEETS WITH MOLE, TARDIVE, AND WINTER CITRUS

DRY-AGED PORK CHOP WITH SORGHUM, MISO, AND BITTER GREENS

LACE CORN BREAD WITH CREAMED CORN, OKRA, AND BACON
Serves 4–6

For the pickled okra:
1 pound (455 g) okra • 2 cups (475 ml) apple cider vinegar • 1 cup (240 ml) water • 4 tablespoons sugar • 1 tablespoon salt • 1 bay leaf • 1 tablespoon black peppercorns • 1 allspice berry

For the creamed corn:
3 ears corn, husked • 1 tablesoon oil • Salt • ½ cup (115 g) crème fraîche • 1 lemon • ½ teaspoon cayenne pepper

For the bacon:
¼ slab bacon (homemade or Benton's)

For the lace corn bread:
2 cups (475 ml) water • 1 cup (130 g) stone-ground cornmeal • 1 teaspoon kosher (flaked) salt

To finish:
Rosemary with blossoms, for garnish

Make the pickled okra:
Rinse the okra and place in 4-quart/liter heatproof container. In a saucepan, combine the vinegar, water, sugar, salt, bay leaf, peppercorns, and allspice and bring to a boil. Once the pickling liquid comes to a boil, pour over the okra. Weight down the okra if necessary to insure they are all submerged in liquid. Let cool and refrigerate overnight. Once pickled, thinly slice.

Make the creamed corn:
Prepare a wood or charcoal fire. Rub the corn kernels with the oil and sprinkle with 1 tablespoon salt. Grill. Once cooled, cut the kernels from the cobs. Transfer to a bowl and stir in the crème fraîche. Using a Microplane, grate the zest of the whole lemon in, then add the juice of ½ lemon. Season with the cayenne and salt to taste.

Prepare the bacon:
Cut the slab into large lardons and render in a cast-iron skillet. Remove the bacon from the pan and drain on paper towels. Reserve the bacon fat in the pan for cooking the corn bread.

Make the lace corn bread:
In a saucepan, bring 1 cup (240 ml) of the water to a boil. In a bowl, mix the cornmeal and salt. Whisk in the boiling water until smooth.
Set the cast-iron skillet over high heat and heat the bacon fat until it begins to smoke. Spoon in 1 cup (240 ml) cornbread batter being careful of splatter. Reduce the heat to medium and cook until golden brown, about 2 minutes.

To finish:
Place ½ cup (120 ml) creamed corn in the center of corn bread. Arrange pickled okra and bacon lardons around the edge of the corn. Garnished with tender young rosemary and blossoms.

PUMPKIN AND APPLE SALAD

MATT HAS QUIETLY BEEN SPONGING UP KNOWLEDGE TO BUILD HIS OWN VISION OF FOOD THAT, AT THE SAME TIME, COMFORTS OUR SOULS AND PIQUES OUR PALATE INTEREST.
— Hugh Acheson

CHICKEN AND DUMPLINGS

LACE CORNBREAD

128

PUMPKIN AND APPLE SALAD WITH PEPITAS AND BUTTER-MILK DRESSING
Serves 4

1 bunch chives, roughly chopped • Olive oil • 1 cup (130 g) hulled pumpkin seeds (pepitas) • Salt • 1 neck pumpkin • 2 Honeycrisp apples • 1 cup (240 ml) buttermilk • 1 lemon, quartered • Nasturtium flowers and thyme leaves, for garnish

Place the chives in a blender jar. In a small pan, heat 1 cup (240 ml) olive oil to 350°F (177°C), then pour over the chives in the blender jar. Blend on medium speed for 1–2 minutes until smooth. Strain through a fine chinois. Set aside.
Toss the pumpkin seeds with ½ teaspoon olive oil and ⅛ teaspoon salt. Spread out on a pan and toast in a 300°F (150°C) oven for 20 minutes.
Cut the neck off of the pumpkin and peel to remove any skin. Cut the neck into 3 or 4 pieces depending on size. Using a mandoline, shave the pumpkin into slices about ¼-inch (6 mm) thick. Using a chef's knife, cut the pumpkin slices into julienne. Toss in a bowl with some olive oil and salt.
In a small bowl, season the buttermilk with the juice of ¼ lemon· and salt to taste· Whisk in the reserved chive oil and reserve.
Core the apple, then shave on a mandoline into slices about ¼ inch (6 mm) thick. Using a chef's knife, cut the apple slices into julienne, making sure they are similar in size to the pumpkin. Toss in a bowl with some olive oil and salt.

To plate:
Arrange the pumpkin and apples, separately, in clusters on the plate. Squeeze ¼ lemon over the dish and garnish with the toasted pepitas, nasturtium flowers, and thyme leaves. Drizzle the plated salad with ¼ cup of the reserved dressing.

CHICKEN AND DUMPLINGS WITH ENGLISH PEAS
Serves 4–6

For the dumpling dough:
12 ounces (340 g) all-purpose (plain) flour • 1 tablespoon baking powder • 1 tablespoon salt • 1 tablespoon freshly ground black pepper • 8 ounces (225 g) very cold unsalted butter • 2 cups (475 ml) cold buttermilk

For the herb oil:
1 bunch parsley • 1 bunch chives • 1 cup (240 ml) olive oil

For the peas:
1 quart/liter fresh English peas • ¼ cup (60 ml) Herb Oil *(above)* or olive oil • Salt

For the chicken:
1 white onion • 1 carrot • 1 bunch celery • 1 whole chicken • 2 quarts/liters chicken stock • 2 bay leaves • 3 tablespoons salt • ¼ cup (60 ml) hot sauce (homemade or your favorite) • ¼ cup (50 g) sour cream • 2 cups (125 g) crispy chicken skin, for garnish • Dill and celery leaves, for garnish

Make the dumpling dough:
In a bowl, mix together the flour, baking powder, salt, and pepper. Using a box grater, shred the cold butter directly into the bowl with the flour. Mix the butter into the flour until pea-size pieces form. Mix in the buttermilk until a firm ball forms. Refrigerate for at least 2 hours.

Make the herb oil:
Roughly chop the parsley and chives and transfer to a blender jar. In a small pan, heat the olive oil to 300°F (149°C), then gently add to the blender. Start the blender on low, gradually increasing speed until the oil in smooth. Strain through a chinois and chill.

Prepare the peas:
Shell the peas and blanch for 1 minute 30 seconds in a pot of boiling water. Shock the peas in ice water, then drain and transfer to a bowl. Peel the outer membrane of the peas. Toss the peeled peas with ¼-cup herb oil and season with salt to taste.

Cook the chicken and dumplings:
Brunoise the onion, carrot, and celery. Save any vegetable scraps to add to the soup base. In a stockpot, combine the chicken stock, reserved vegetable scraps, bay leaves, and salt. Bring to a boil, then add the whole chicken and return to a simmer. Simmer the chicken until very tender, about 2 hours. Once the chicken is cooked, remove from the stock and allow to cool at room temperature. Strain the stock (discard the vegetable scraps) and set aside.
Preheat the oven to 300°F (150°C).
Once the chicken has cooled, carefully pull off the chicken skin and lay it out on a sheet pan. Transfer to the oven and bake until crispy, about 1 hour. Reserve the crispy skin. Meanwhile, shred all the chicken meat, discarding any bones. In a large pot, sauté the mirepoix for 1 minute over low heat or until soft. Add the reserved chicken stock and the shredded chicken. Bring to a simmer.
On a floured surface, roll out the dumpling dough to about ¼ inch (6 mm) thick. Cut the dough into 2-inch (5 cm) squares. Making sure the chicken stock with chicken and vegetables is simmering, add the dumplings in batches. Gently stir to ensure they do not stick together. Bring to a simmer and cook until the dumplings are cooked through and the stock thickened, 15 to 20 minutes. Season with salt and pepper to taste.
To serve, spoon 1–2 cups of the chicken and dumplings into a bowl. Drizzle herb oil around the edge of the bowl and top the dumplings with 1 cup of peas. Quenelle 1 spoonful of sour cream next to the peas. Drizzle hot sauce over then garnish with crispy chicken skin, dill and celery leaves.

MATT HARPER

JAMES HENRY

SKYE GYNGELL

LE DOYENNÉ
Saint-Vrain, France

James Henry's trajectory could perhaps have been predicted: he spent his childhood living in many different places around the world, including Canberra, Paris, Riyadh, and San Francisco. He credits his parents, whose globally inspired good cooking and itinerant cookbook collection did much to mold him into the chef he is today. Henry has helmed restaurants from Paris to Hong Kong, as his unceasing curiosity guided him to new projects and new locales—always bringing his trademark sensitivity and a style that is simultaneously classic and entirely modern.

Henry first cooked in restaurants in Australia (Cumulus Inc. in Melbourne, the Stackings in Tasmania) before relocating to Paris. There, his creative energy attracted fans and propelled him into the limelight. He first worked at Spring, under Chef Daniel Rose, then at Au Passage, where his vegetable-centered small plates helped drive the Parisian neobistro movement. His first solo restaurant, Bones, further realized the city's shift toward accessible dining. His cooking there was simple—without pretension, artifice, and distraction, says Henry—and made possible by high-quality produce. He served dishes such as veal rump with dandelions, onions, and anchovies, and smoked eel alongside beets, egg, and leeks. And in a city where making one's own bread and butter is nearly unheard of, Henry's sourdough became a signature.

Restlessness and a desire for novelty landed him in Hong Kong after a pair of restaurateurs asked him to come on as executive chef for a French-style bistro there called Belon. But his latest project drew him back to France and to an eighteenth-century estate in the village of Saint-Vrain, thirty miles south of Paris. There, with partner, Shaun Kelly, Henry is planning a farm-to-table restaurant in the estate's renovated stables. In advance, he has established the property's orchards and farm, cultivated with his preferred heirloom varietals. He and Kelly have been growing and selling produce to Paris restaurants in the meantime—a delicious foreshadowing of the menus to come at Le Doyenné.

MENU

FRESH AND PICKLED VEGETABLES AND SORREL CREAM

RAW CLAM, SALTED PLUM, AND COLD ALMOND SOUP

CRAYFISH AND HEIRLOOM TOMATO SALAD

GRILLED PORK NECK, BORLOTTI BEANS, AND CHILI SEAWEED CONDIMENT

GARDEN SALAD

HUNG YOGURT AND WILD BLACKBERRY GRANITA

LEMON VERBENA MILLEFEUILLE WITH WOOD-ROASTED PEACHES

RAW CLAM, SALTED PLUM, AND COLD ALMOND SOUP
Serves 4

500 g Palourde clams • 200 g blanched organic almonds • ¼ clove garlic, grated 200 ml extra-virgin olive oil, plus more for serving • 60 ml vin jaune vinegar • 2 umeboshi (salted Japanese plums) • Fresh fennel flowers

Shuck the clams and reserve all the juices. Strain the juice through cheesecloth (muslin), taking care to not let any sand or grit pass through. Reserve the raw clams in the fridge.
In a blender, combine the almonds, garlic, clam juice, and enough water to blend to a smooth velouté consistency. With the machine running, drizzle 200 ml of the olive oil to emulsify. Finish with the vin jaune vinegar and adjust seasoning as necessary. Place the cold soup in the fridge to chill.
Pass the umeboshi through a tamis to achieve a thick and jammy puree.
To plate, divide the clams evenly among 4 bowls. Place ¼ teaspoon of the umeboshi puree over the raw clams and cover completely with the cold almond soup. Add another drop of oil and the fennel flowers to finish the soup. Serve very cold!

CRAYFISH AND HEIRLOOM TOMATO SALAD
Serves 4

For the court-bouillon:
500 ml dry white wine (of drinking quality) • 1 large heirloom tomato • 1 leek • 2 stalks celery • 2 carrots • 1 bulb fennel • 8 sprigs thyme • 3 bay leaves • A few sprigs lovage • 1 tablespoon organic black peppercorns • Salt

For the crayfish:
8 large freshwater crayfish • 50 ml extra-virgin olive oil • 45 ml white Banyuls vinegar • Cracked black pepper and salt

For plating:
Bunch of lovage • 2 large heirloom tomatoes • Fleur de sel • 16 Piedmont hazelnuts, toasted and cracked in half • Assorted torn basil leaves, buds, and flowers • 150 ml olive oil

Make the court-bouillon:
In a heavy-bottomed pot, combine 2 quarts (liters) water, the wine, the tomato, leek, celery, carrots, fennel, thyme, bay leaves,

lovage, peppercorns, and 1 tablespoon salt.
Bring to a boil, then reduce to a simmer and
cook for 1 hour.

Prepare the crayfish:
Strain the court-bouillon, return to the pot,
and bring to a boil. Once at a rolling boil,
add the crayfish and then turn off the heat.
Leave for 4 minutes and then remove the
crays and leave to cool at room temperature. Once cool enough to handle, shell the
crayfish, keep the meat aside and return the
shells to the court-bouillon and cook for an
additional 30 minutes.
Take 100 ml of the court-bouillon and mix
it with the olive oil and the vinegar. Season
the vinaigrette with some cracked black
pepper and salt.

To plate:
Slice each crayfish tail lengthwise into three
pieces, arrange 6 slices on each of 4 plates.
Dress the crayfish with the vinaigrette.
Chiffonade the lovage leaves and sprinkle
over the dressed crayfish. Slice the tomatoes
into ¼-inch (4 mm) slices and completely
cover the crayfish. Season the tomatoes
with fleur de sel, add 8 hazelnut halves and
the torn basil leaves to each plate and finish
with olive oil.

HUNG YOGURT AND WILD BLACKBERRY GRANITA
Serves 4

400 g sheep or goat milk yogurt • 10 g salt
• 500 g wild blackberries • 3 tablespoons
dark, strong-flavored honey, such as a
wildflower or buckwheat • 200 ml sparkling
mineral water (or tap) • 100 ml hazelnut oil
• Oregano buds and flowers

Take a large sieve, line it with a wet tea
towel, and place it over a bowl. Mix the
yogurt with 5 g of the salt and place in the
lined sieve. Cover and place in the fridge to
drain overnight.
Place the berries in a large bowl, add the
honey, remaining 5 g salt, and the mineral
water and crush with your hands. Cover and
leave at room temperature overnight.
The next day, pass the berry mixture
through the fine plate of a food mill. Pour
into a shallow dish and place in the freezer.
Gently scrape the mixture with a fork every
30 minutes to create fine and even shards of
berry ice.
Remove the yogurt from the fridge and mix
until smooth. Divide the yogurt among 4
bowls and evenly distribute the berry granita
over the yogurt. Dress each bowl with
hazelnut oil and oregano buds and flowers.

A BEAUTIFUL, SENSITIVE
COOK WITH A CLASSIC
SENSIBILITY THAT
SOMEHOW MANAGES TO
FEEL ENTIRELY MODERN.
— Skye Gyngell

JAMES HENRY

JORDAN KAHN

VIRGILIO MARTINEZ

MENU

MACROCYSTIS PYRIFERA,
EMULSION OF ROASTED TURKEY
DRIPPINGS, HALOPHYTE PLANTS,
OCEAN HONEY

SAVORY COOKIE, ROASTED YEAST,
BLACK CURRANT, HYACINTH

LIVE SCALLOP, BALSAM FIR,
SMOKED BONE MARROW

HIRAME FIN, WILD YUCCA
BLOSSOM, ETROG

CARAMELIZED LAMB FAT,
OVERRIPE PLANTAIN, WOODRUFF

PEAR, OAK BARK FUDGE,
WINTERGREEN LEAF, PARSNIP

The praise, reviews, and musings describing American chef Jordan Kahn's Culver City gastronomic temple, Vespertine, often focus on a transporting sense of otherness: otherworldly, postmodern, supernatural. At Vespertine, a collaboration with architect Eric Owen Moss, guests are welcomed into an utterly immersive sensory experience, beyond anything familiar in the annals of dining out. The restaurant occupies parts of an entire multistory building, and the evening takes diners from floor to floor and from outdoor to indoor spaces and back. The late *Los Angeles Times* restaurant critic, Jonathan Gold, described Vespertine as Gesamtkunstwerk, or a "universal work of art" that synthesizes many art forms. Indeed, Vespertine fuses gastronomy with architecture, surrealistic elements, and sensorial experience, from the use of space to manipulation of light and sound.

Kahn's attraction to food as a medium started early: his first kitchen job was at age fifteen in his hometown of Savannah, Georgia. Kahn graduated from cooking school at Johnson & Wales in just eight months, an early harbinger of his exceptional ambition. At age seventeen, he got a job at Thomas Keller's fine-dining bastion the French Laundry, the youngest cook ever to work in Keller's kitchen there. He then went on to help open Keller's Per Se in New York City. Next, at Chef Grant Achatz's Alinea in Chicago, Kahn met and worked with his mentor, head pastry chef Alex Stupak, who encouraged Kahn to develop not just his craft but also his personal style. In 2012, Kahn opened his first restaurant, the French-Vietnamese Red Medicine in Los Angeles, where he parlayed the exacting principles of pastry to create savory dishes emphasizing artistic plating and foraged ingredients.

Now, with Vespertine—and its nearby more informal sibling, Destroyer, which is open for breakfast and lunch—Kahn's fluid skills are evident on every plate. His courageous desire to give guests one of the most avant-garde dining experiences in the world is undeniable. With dishes like halibut pounded thin over pickled Japanese plum and minced shallots and covered with a dusting of charred onion powder, things are rarely, if ever, what they seem, while the atmosphere creates a dizzying sensation of seeing everything from a new perspective. In a city known for its informal and laid-back lifestyle, Kahn's sensory maneuvers are particularly transporting and electrifying. Vespertine has two Michelin stars and received an Atmosphere of the Year Award at the World Restaurant Awards.

SAVORY COOKIE, ROASTED YEAST, BLACK CURRANT, HYACINTH

For the savory cookie dough:
150 g malted wheat flour • 150 g Red Fife whole wheat flour • 30 g onion ash • 170 g almond flour • 10 g dark-roasted malt, ground • 10 g freeze-dried onions, ground • 170 g unsalted butter, at room temperature • 25 g ground myrica gale • 70 g powdered sugar • 1½ tablespoons salt • 1 egg • 20 g raw onion juice • 6 g caramelized sake lees

For the black currant paste:
200 g shallots, minced • 200 g fennel, minced • 50 g canola (rapeseed) oil • 1 kg wild black currants, sorted and stemmed • 2 bay leaves • 4 g dried dulse, ground • 25 g dried smoked tomatoes, ground • Salt

For assembly:
Wild hyacinth blossoms • Wild everlasting pea blossoms

Make the savory cookie dough:
Sift the malted wheat flour, whole wheat flour, onion ash, almond flour, ground malt, and freeze-dried onions into a bowl.
In a stand mixer fitted with the paddle, beat the softened butter until soft and creamy.
Add the myrica gale, powdered (icing) sugar, and salt and continue to beat for 1 minute on medium speed.
Add the egg, onion juice, and sake lees and continue to beat for 3 minutes until all of the sake lees are integrated.
Add the flour mixture to the mixer and beat until the dough comes together. Wrap the dough in plastic wrap (cling film) and refrigerate overnight.

Roll the dough out into a sheet ³⁄₁₆ inch (5 mm) thick and cut into an isosceles trapezoid (trapezium) shape and place inside of a ring mold 3 inches (7.5 cm) in diameter and 1½ inches (4 cm) deep. Press the dough against the bottom and sides of the mold, then freeze for 30 minutes.
Preheat a combi oven to 300°F (150°C), medium fan, 0% steam.
Bake the cookie in the mold for 20 minutes. Allow the cookie to cool and remove from the mold. Store in an airtight container.

Make the black currant paste:
In a wide pot, sweat the shallots and fennel in the canola (rapeseed) oil for 20 minutes. Add the black currants, bay leaves, dulse, and smoked tomatoes to the shallot mixture and bring to a boil. Reduce to a simmer and cook over low heat until the currants are

YUCCA BLOSSOM

cooked down to a dark, rich paste, about 6 hours. Season with salt to taste

To assemble:
Brush the savory cookie with a generous layer of the black currant paste. Place 4 hyacinth blossoms and 4 everlasting pea blossoms on top adhering them to the paste.

MACROCYSTIS PYRIFERA, EMULSION OF ROASTED TURKEY DRIPPINGS, HALOPHYTE PLANTS, OCEAN HONEY

For the giant kelp chip:
2 blades Macrocystis pyrifera (giant kelp) • Canola (rapeseed) oil

For the roasted turkey drippings:
2 shallots • ½ bunch thyme • 4 bay leaves • 20 juniper berries • 4 pine buds • 1 teaspoon carrot seeds • 10 turkey wings, each split into 4 pieces • 50 g rendered duck fat

For the emulsion:
250 g roasted turkey jelly (from Turkey Drippings, *above*) • 50 g fresh lemon juice • 1 teaspoon salt • 1 g xanthan gum • 250 g rendered turkey fat (from Turkey Drippings, *above*), liquid but not warm

For plating:
Maritime/coastal honey crystals • 10 stems salicornia • 10 stems salsola soda • 4 Spanish dagger flowers • 4 stems sea aster • 12 sea rocket blossoms

Make the giant kelp chip:
Clean and trim the giant kelp blades and remove any sand, shells, or baby shellfish that may be clinging to the surface. Make sure to remove the bladder from the end of the kelp. Split the blade lengthwise into 2 pieces. Dehydrate the kelp at 120°F (49°C) overnight.
Heat a pot of canola (rapeseed) oil to 450°F (230°C).
Using 2 pairs of tweezers, pinch the kelp strips at both ends and dip into the hot oil while curving the shape of the kelp. Only hold in the oil for about 3 seconds, then transfer to a rack to cool. Hold in a dehydrator to stay crisp.

Make the roasted turkey drippings:
Preheat the oven to 350°F (175°C).
In a large roasting pan, place the shallots, herbs, and seeds in the bottom. Lay the turkey wings over the herbs and spices, then brush the wings with the rendered duck fat. Roast until the wings are golden brown and have rendered much of their fat and juices, about 1 hour.

Pour off the fat and roasting juices into a container, then strain them and place in the blast freezer for 1 hour. At this point, the liquid should be jellied and the fat congealed. Separate the turkey jelly and the fat and reserve separately.

Make the emulsion:
In a high-powered blender, blend the turkey jelly, lemon juice, salt, and xanthan gum for 30 seconds. With the machine running, slowly stream in the rendered turkey fat as if you are making a mayonnaise. Allow the machine's friction to warm the mixture to slightly above body temperature, ensuring all of the fat crystals are melted.
Transfer the emulsion to an ice bath and whisk constantly until cold. Store the emulsion in the refrigerator.

To plate:
In a small vessel, place a generous dollop of the roasted turkey emulsion. Lightly sift some coastal honey crystals over the top. Arrange the halophyte plants around the inside edge of the emulsion. Serve the giant kelp chip in a service piece on the side to use as a dip for the emulsion.

ALMOND

BURNT ONION

JORDAN PRESENTS A
FUTURISTIC VIEW OF
GASTRONOMY: DARING,
COURAGEOUS, RESOURCEFUL.
— Virgilio Martínez

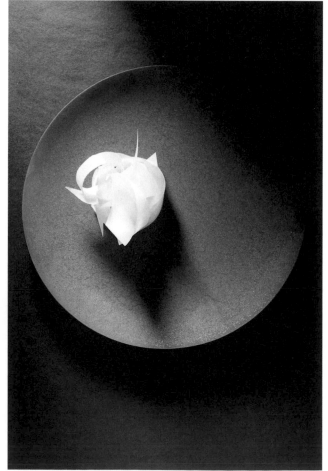

WHITE ASPARAGUS

JORDAN KAHN

MATTHEW KAMMERER

THE HARBOR
HOUSE INN
Mendocino, California,
United States

DAVID KINCH

Clinging to a wind-whipped seaside cliff in Elk, a town of about two hundred people, Harbor House Inn showcases Matthew Kammerer's culinary distillation of the Northern California coast. Kammerer forages all over the surrounding lands gleaning anything edible, which he then uses to create multicourse menus that capture the seaside terroir. In the final composition, his dishes also nod to the various other locales he has explored and been inspired by during his career, most notably Japan.

Kammerer relocated to Elk following three years at Saison, in San Francisco, where he directed the kitchen as the executive sous chef. It was not until his arrival in Elk that he started to develop the intimate knowledge of the California environment now so vividly reflected in his dishes. After a childhood in New Jersey, he attended culinary school at Johnson & Wales University, worked in restaurants in Boston, and then started jet-setting. He honed his craft with stints from Attica, in Melbourne (one of Australia's most acclaimed fine-dining destinations), and Nihonryori RyuGin in Tokyo, where he steeped in the techniques of *kaiseki*, a traditional multicourse haute cuisine, to In De Wulf in Belgium, where he manned the Spanish-style charcoal grill.

Fatigued by working at faraway restaurants and tired of the urban-chef life, Kammerer seized an opportunity to spearhead the cuisine at Harbor House Inn, a historic inn three hours north of San Francisco. It reopened in 2018 under new ownership; his partner, Amanda Nemec, runs the hotel. Kammerer no longer awaits trucks delivering produce; instead, he and his team grow and cull many of the ingredients they need. They harvest vegetables—mustard greens, artichokes, daikon, to name a few—from the garden beds they built and sow at the inn; chanterelles are plucked from neighboring redwood forests; seaweed is heaved and sea urchins fished from the cove at the base of cliffs. The team even uses seawater, which they evaporate to yield sea salt.

On a menu at Harbor Inn, one might find a "Mendocino stew" of red abalone, local wild rice, fermented turnip, and freshly harvested seaweeds. For dessert, perhaps a Calhikari rice pudding with matcha and black ginger, or seaweed ice cream with miso crust, cocoa, and bay nuts.

Michelin recognized Harbor House Inn with a star in 2019, and Kammerer has been recognized nationally as one of the best new chefs.

MENU

RED ABALONE, KELP CALHIKARI RICE, ABALONE OFFAL, NORI

MURDOC CABBAGE, SEA PALM, MAITAKE MUSHROOM

COPPER ROCKFISH-GRILLED LEEK, HEDGEHOG MUSHROOM, WATERCRESS

CELERIAC, HATCHO MISO, PURPLE SEA URCHIN, CELLARED HAM

PORK LEG SMOKED OVER CYPRESS, SHIITAKE JUS, ELK SPICE

SEAWEED ICE CREAM, BAY NUT, BATTERA KOMBU

RED ABALONE, KELP CALHIKARI RICE, ABALONE OFFAL, NORI

For the rice:
1 cup (195 g) Calhikari rice • 355 g kombu dashi • 30 g tamari • 30 g shiro shoyu • 70 g fresh shiitake mushrooms plus 1 shiitake for cooking • Salt • 1 bay leaf

For the poached abalone mushrooms:
150 g kombu dashi • 50 g shiro shoyu • 5 g salt • 50 g clarified butter • 4 abalone mushrooms

For the abalone offal sauce:
250 g kombu dashi • 50 g shiro shoyu • 2 g salt • 10 g katsuobushi • 5 g nori • 25 g sunflower oil • 4 abalone guts • 1 g xanthan gum • 1 g Ultra-Tex

For plating:
Sanshō powder *(recipe follows)* • Fermented Lettuce *(recipe follows)* • Aonori • Red giant mustard greens • Wasabi arugula

Make the rice:
Rinse the rice in a colander with cold water until the water runs clear.
In a pot, combine dashi, tamari, and shoyu and heat to just below a simmer. Cook for 15 minutes to bring the flavors together.
Cut the shiitakes into ⅜-inch (1 cm) slices. Add the shiitakes to the pot and remove from the heat. Let steep for 15 minutes.
Taste and adjust seasoning if necessary, then strain out the mushrooms.
In a rice cooker, combine 1 cup (240 ml) of the broth from the pot and the washed rice.

Close the cooker and cook. Open and fluff the rice and add 1 fresh shiitake and the bay leaf. Keep warm.

Prepare the abalone:
It is very important to make sure the abalone is relaxed before taking this step. If it is stressed it will not become tender and will only break the more you pound it.
Shuck the abalone by inserting a thin spatula behind the "foot" and releasing the adductor muscle from the shell. Be careful to not damage the guts (reserve for the offal sauce).
Pound the abalone for roughly 30 seconds each side focusing on the outside until it feels limp and is soft in texture. You should almost be able to bend it in half.
Cut off the adductor muscle to make a flat surface. Wipe the black mucus from around the edges and reserve.
Cut the mouth tentacles and anus off and cut the abalone horizontally into 4 slices. Soak the kelp in cold water until pliable.

> HE TOOK THE
> PLUNGE TO MOVE
> OFF THE GRID INTO
> RURAL CALIFORNIA
> AND IS STARTING
> TO CREATE THE
> FOUNDATION OF
> A REAL SENSE OF
> TIME AND PLACE.
> — David Kinch

WHOLE CRAB COOKED IN SEA WATER

Brush the middle of the kelp with clarified butter.

Add the sliced abalone and wrap the abalone twice starting with two vertical folds and then two horizontal folds. Keep the package closed with a skewer.

Poach the abalone mushrooms:
In a pan, combine the dashi, shoyu, salt, and clarified butter and cook over low heat for 10 minutes until the flavors become one. Rinse the abalone mushrooms quickly under cold water. Dry immediately, then vacuum-seal with the prepared liquid on 100%. On the top tier of a 3-tier steamer, steam the mushrooms until tender, about 10 minutes. Remove and cool at room temperature. Cut into ⅜ × 1½–inch (1 × 4 cm) strips. Reserve in the liquid until ready to use.

Make the abalone offal sauce:
In a pan, combine the dashi, shoyu, and salt and heat over low-medium heat for 10 minutes to combine the flavor.
Using a kezuriki, shave the katsuobushi à la minute. Add to the dashi and steep for 10–15 seconds. Strain the broth through a fine paper towel. Add the nori to the warm broth and steep 5 minutes.
In a heavy-bottomed pan, heat the sunflower oil over high heat. Add the abalone guts and cook, turning occasionally—the goal is to create a fond without overcooking. Remove from the heat and deglaze with the nori broth.
Transfer to a blender and blend on high until completely smooth. Taste for correct seasoning one last time. Add the xanthan gum and blend on high for 1 minute. Turn the blender to low and add the Ultra-Tex and blend for 1 minute. Strain through a fine-mesh sieve.

To finish, preheat the oven to 500°F (260°C).
Spray the top of the kelp package with water and lay flat on a wire rack over a sheet pan. Roast the kelp package for 10–13 minutes depending on the size of the abalone.
Warm the abalone mushrooms in the cooking liquid. Lightly warm the offal sauce.
To plate, add a small mound of warm rice to a preheated bowl. Dust with sanshō. Place 3 strips of abalone mushroom on top of the rice, then garnish the rice with the fermented lettuce, aonori, mustard leaf, and wasabi arugula. Add a side dish of warm offal sauce. Open the kelp packet and let the guests serve themselves.

SANSHŌ POWDER
Grind sanshō berries with a mortar and pestle until a fine powder is achieved. Pass through a fine-mesh strainer and store airtight.

FERMENTED LETTUCE
Lettuce • Salt

Add 2% salt by weight to lettuce, let ferment for 2 weeks or until desired sourness is achieved.

GRILLED SEAWEED ICE CREAM, BAY NUT, BATTERA KOMBU

For the wakame ice cream:
250 g heavy (whipping) cream • 85 g sugar • 2 g Cremodan 30 (ice cream stabilizer) • 4 egg yolks • 13 g dried wakame

For assembly:
Bay nut • Battera kombu

Make the ice cream:
Prepare an ice bath and set a bowl inside. Add the cream to the bowl.
In a small bowl, combine the sugar and Cremodan, being sure to mix well.
In a saucepan, heat the milk until small bubbles form on the edge. Remove from the heat and whisk in the sugar/Cremodan mixture. Temper the egg yolks into the milk. Place the mixture in a double boiler and heat to 181°F (83°C), whisking constantly. Once the temperature is achieved, pass through fine-mesh sieve and add to the cream.
Grill the wakame over medium heat until the seaweed begins to puff and bubble and a change in color is achieved, being careful not to burn it. It should become very brittle. Place the toasted wakame in a blender and blend to fine powder. Add the chilled ice cream base to blender and gently blend to incorporate the wakame. Transfer to Pacojet beakers and freeze overnight.

Preheat the oven to 500°F (260°C).
Place the bay nuts on a sheet pan and roast for 15 minutes. When cool enough to handle, crack the shell, and remove the nuts.
Grill the battera kombu over medium heat until it starts to puff and bubble and a change in color takes places, being careful not to burn. It will become very brittle. Store in an airtight container or dehydrator.

To plate:
Spin the ice cream up in the Pacojet. Scoop into prefrozen bowls. Microplane the roasted bay nut over the ice cream. Top with a piece of battera kombu.

CELERIAC, HATCHO MISO, PURPLE SEA URCHIN, CELLARED HAM

For the celeriac puree:
115 g unsalted butter • 400 g celery root, peeled and diced • 30 g hatcho miso • 5 g salt

For the celeriac noodles:
25 g peeled celery root per serving

For the poaching liquid:
325 g celery root • 20 g garlic • 50 g clarified butter • 350 g kombu dashi • 45 g tamari • 15 g shiro shoyu • 50 g chicken jus

For the shiitake powder:
Fresh shiitakes

For assembly:
50 g Celery Poaching Liquid *(above)* • 10 g butter • 1 purple sea urchin per serving • 2 slices Cypress Ham *(recipe follows)* per serving • 3 sprigs lovage per serving

Make the celeriac puree:
In a pot, melt the butter over low heat. Add the celery root, cover, and cook over medium heat—stirring often, making sure not to brown—until completely tender. Transfer to a blender, and the miso and salt, blend until completely smooth. Pass through fine-mesh sieve.

Make the celeriac noodles:
Using a turning slicer, sheet the celery root into ribbons. Cut the ribbons into 2¼ × 8–inch (6 × 20 cm) strips. Reserve in an airtight container

Make the poaching liquid:
Cut the celery root into 1 × 2–inch (2.5 × 5 cm) rectangles, reserving the trim for later use. Peel the garlic, split in half, and remove the germ.
In a pot, melt the clarified butter over high heat. Add the blocks of celery root and pan roast until a deep golden brown. Flip and continue to cook, add the garlic and pan roast until golden brown. Remove from the heat and let cool slightly, then add the dashi. Slice the reserved celery root trim into ⅜-inch (1 cm) batons and add to the pot. Add the tamari, shoyu, and chicken jus and bring up to a light simmer. Cook for 2 minutes and remove from the heat. Cover and steep for 10 minutes, until the sliced celery root has poached through and infused the broth.
Strain the poaching liquid and make an final adjustments to seasoning—it should be slightly overseasoned to adjust for the water content of the celeriac noodles when you poach them later on.

Make the shiitake powder:
Dehydrate fresh shiitakes in a dehydrator overnight. Pulverize in a mortar and pestle and reserve in an airtight container.

To assemble:
Heat the celeriac puree and reserve in a lidded pot in a warm place.
In a heavy-bottomed pot, combine the poaching liquid and butter. Add the celeriac noodles and poach until al dente and most of the cooking liquid is absorbed, stirring often. Transfer each bundle of noodles to a prewarmed tray. Dust with shiitake powder. Top with a sea urchin.
To plate, add some of the puree to a plate. Place the bundle of noodles next to the puree and top with the ham and lovage.

CYPRESS HAM
Cypress cones • Salt • Ham

At a ratio of 1:10, grind fresh cypress cones with salt until fragrant.

Pack the ham in a cooler with the salt for 3 months, checking regularly for air pockets.

Hang the ham in a cool dark place for at least 1 year.

GRILLED SEAWEED ICE CREAM

CELERIAC

RED ABALONE

MATTHEW KAMMERER

CHIHO KANZAKI & MARCELO DI GIACOMO

DAVID KINCH

VIRTUS
Paris, France

On a street in Paris's lively 12th arrondissement, Chiho Kanzaki and her partner, Argentinian Marcelo di Giacomo, have served bright, vegetable-focused menus anchored by rigorous technique since 2016. There, at Virtus, the dishes are grounded in simplicity, distilling the character of each ingredient with subtlety and precision. Having spent time as a child by her father's side watching him do his butchering work in Fujisawa, Japan, Kanzaki has long nurtured a passion for cuisine. In a culture that has historically encouraged women to pursue patisserie as a path rather than cuisine, Kanzaki, nonetheless, pursued her culinary ambitions and trained at the renowned Tsuji Culinary Institute in Osaka, Japan. After graduating, she moved to France to further develop her skills in French cuisine, eventually landing on the Mediterranean coast at Mauro Colagreco's now three-Michelin-starred restaurant Mirazur. She steadily rose to helm the team as chef de cuisine, embodying the restaurant's philosophy of respect for ingredients, and a lack of artifice or manipulation—think beetroots yanked straight from the garden, then steamed in a salt crust and drenched with caviar-specked cream; or Alpine lemons harvested from the restaurant's grounds and served as lemon confit or tarte au citron.

Even after almost a decade in the kitchen, Kanzaki felt that, as a woman, a single mistake could be ruinous. This pressure drove her to concentrate exclusively on her career, and ultimately, she shaped her own style, characterized by discipline, restraint, and intense precision. Kanzaki's seven years at Mirazur molded her as a chef and also gave her the leadership experience necessary to run her own restaurant. At Virtus, Kanzaki plies a longtime obsession with citrus: crab with kohlrabi and finger limes, veal in orange sauce, pollack and grapefruit. Before opening, she and di Giacomo, also her life partner, scoured France to locate the best producers and farmers. Consequently, Virtus stands out for its simple, candid but creative treatment of ingredients on menus that evolve with the seasons and by the day. The couples' constant collaboration results in a French cuisine laced with hints of each partner's respective homelands. In 2019, their labor of love received its first Michelin star.

MENU

SCALLOPS, CAULIFLOWER, GREEN APPLE SOUP

PIGLET, SALSIFY

COFFEE, COCONUT, PISTACHIO

SCALLOPS, CAULIFLOWER, GREEN APPLE SOUP
Serves 4

20 g unsalted butter • 300 g white cauliflower, cut into small florets • 200 ml milk • 50 g green cauliflower, cut into small florets • 50 gr yellow cauliflower, cut into small florets • 300 g green apple, unpeeled and cut up • 1 tablespoon apple cider vinegar • 2 tablespoons extra-virgin olive oil • Pinch of salt

For finishing:
50 g purple cauliflower • 1 green apple, scooped into small balls • 8 scallops, diced • 1 makrut lime • Crystalline ice plant shoots

In a saucepan, heat the butter, then add the white cauliflower and cook it for 20 minutes without browning. Add the milk and mix until it becomes a smooth puree. Let cool. In a large pot of boiling salted water, blanch the green and yellow cauliflower for 30 seconds, then shock in a bowl of ice cold water. Place the apple in a blender and puree, then press through a fine chinois.
In a small bowl, whisk together the vinegar, olive oil, and salt.

To finish:
To plate, put some white cauliflower cream in the bottom of the plate, add the cooked

cauliflower and raw purple cauliflower, and the diced scallops. Dot with some green apple balls and add some makrut lime zest. Add young ice plant shoots. Pour the dressing delicately on top and spoon the green apple soup around.

COFFEE, COCONUT, PISTACHIO
Serves 4

For the coffee ice cream:
600 g whole milk • 300 g heavy (whipping) cream • 120 g sugar • 12 g ice cream stabilizer • 65 g glucose • 33 g coffee beans, coarsely crushed

For the coconut espuma:
150 g full-fat coconut milk • 50 g heavy (whipping) cream • 50 g egg whites • 20 g sugar

For the coconut ganache:
50 g full-fat coconut milk • 25 g heavy (whipping) cream • 12.5 g egg yolk • ¼ sheet gelatin • 37.5 g white chocolate, chopped up • 125 g coconut puree

For the pistachio ganache:
62 g whole milk • 62 g heavy (whipping) cream • 12 g glucose • 45 g pistachio paste • 185 g ivory chocolate, cut up

For the coffee opaline:
50 g fondant • 50 g glucose • 50 g white chocolate, cut up

For finishing:
Roasted pistachios • Ground coffee

Make the coffee ice cream:
In a saucepan, combine the milk, cream, sugar, stabilizer, and glucose. Heat to 183°F

(84°C), then remove from the heat. Stir in the crushes coffee and refrigerate for 24 hours to infuse. Strain out the coffee ground and freeze in Pacojet beakers.

Make the coconut espuma:
Mix together all the ingredients and refrigerate in the canister of a cream whipper.

Make the coconut ganache:
In a saucepan, combine coconut milk, cream, and egg yolk. Heat to 185°F (85°C). Stir in the white chocolate to melt. Refrigerate to chill, then beat the mixture with a whisk or an electric mixer and incorporate the coconut puree.

Make the pistachio ganache:
In a saucepan, combine the milk, cream, and glucose. Bring to a boil, then remove from the heat and add the pistachio puree then the white chocolate and stir well until everything is well incorporated. Mix to have a ganache and place in the fridge.

Make the coffee opaline:
In a saucepan, heat the fondant and glucose to 365°F (185°C). Stir in the white chocolate and pour the preparation onto a silicone baking mat to cool and harden.
Meanwhile, preheat the oven to 320°F (160°C). Line a sheet pan with a silicone baking mat.

Break the opaline into pieces and grind to a super fine powder. Place the powder in a small sieve and gently hit it on the baking mat to make small disks of powder. Transfer to the oven and bake for 3 minutes.

To finish:
On each plate, place some whipped coconut ganache, pistachio ganache, some roasted pistachios, and a scoop of coffee ice cream. Place 2 opaline disks on either side. Top with some coconut espuma. Place a last opaline and finish with some ground coffee.

COFFEE, COCONUT, PISTACHIO

VIGOROUS TECHNIQUE, BRIGHT, FLAVORFUL, WITH A COMPLEX SIMPLICITY THAT MAKES THEM STAND OUT.
— David Kinch

CHIHO KANZAKI & MARCELO DI GIACOMO

KUNIHIKO KATO

UBUKA
Tokyo, Japan

YOSHIHIRO NARISAWA

Kunihiko Kato loves crab so much, it occurred to him as a young man that if he worked at Kani Doraku, the Japanese chain restaurant known for its crab, he would be able to eat as much of it as he wanted. And so, he landed himself a job there forthwith. Years later, at the helm of his own restaurant, Ubuka, Kato's food still evokes the influence of Kani Doraku. Opened in Tokyo in 2012, Ubuka specializes in crustaceans, which Kato handles with unparalleled techniques and thoughtfulness, earning him acclaim for serving some of Tokyo's best seafood.

After his start at Kani Doraku in his hometown of Sendai, Kato moved to Kyoto, where, for several years, he apprenticed at a *ryotei* (the Japanese term for a certain kind of high-end and often exclusive restaurant) studying traditional Japanese cuisine. He subsequently spent time at a Japanese restaurant in New Zealand, then at the Chinese restaurant Renge, in Tokyo.

Returning to his crustacean roots, Kato's daily immersion has deepened his knowledge of both procurement and preparation of those prized live ingredients. He sources shrimp and crab from all over Japan (via both local fisherman and the famed Tsukiji Market), and as they vary by season, he uses upwards of thirty different species in a year. Colleagues say that they have yet to meet a chef who knows as much about crustaceans as Kato does.

At Ubuka, the eight-course omakase (chef's choice) menu changes seasonally. In autumn, Kato serves the freshwater Shanghai crab; in winter, snow crab. In spring, his menu offers sweet shima-ebi shrimp, and in summer, uni and pike eel. A mainstay throughout the year is breaded, deep-fried king prawns—particularly juicy thanks to the prawn viscera they are coated in before frying—accompanied by a sansho pepper–flecked tartar sauce. And the meal, as is traditional in Japan, concludes with rice. When the rice is almost done, Kato stirs in vegetables and crab for a fragrant and steaming conclusion to his tour of crustaceans.

MENU

JAPANESE MIXED RICE WITH CABBAGE AND CRAB

SOFT-BOILED EGG WITH CURSTACEAN DASHI

JAPANESE-STYLE FRIED PRAWN

For the fried prawns:
1 large (about 50 g) head-on tiger prawn • Salt • 1 spring roll wrapper • Freshly ground black pepper • 10 g Ebi-Miso (*above*) • Egg, beaten • Rice oil • Flour • Panko bread crumbs • 15 g *miazansho* (Japanese peppercorns) tartar • 3 g Prawn Salt (*above*) • Lemon wedge

JAPANESE MIXED RICE WITH CABBAGE AND CRAB (TAKIKOMI GOHAN)
Serves 5

For the crab broth:
250 g hairy crabs • Salt • 20 ml sake • 5 cm square dried kombu

For the rice:
1 kg rice • 900 g Crab Broth (*above*) • 150 g shredded cabbage • 100 g kani-miso (crab innards) • Sake (moderate amounts, to adjust the taste)

To make the crab broth:
In a pot of salted boiling water, cook the crabs. Remove the carapace with the kani-miso (crab innards) and set aside. Remove the crabmeat from the shells and set the meat aside.
Spread the shells on a sheet pan and broil (grill) until nice and fragrant. Place the shells in a pot and add 1.5 liters water, the sake, and kombu and bring to a boil. Skim the foam that forms on the surface of the broth. Reduce the heat to low and cook for another 20 minutes. Strain the broth.

To make the rice:
Place the rice in a sieve and rinse well. Add to a rice pot along with the crab broth and cook until tender.
In a pot of salted boiling water, cook the cabbage. Drain and cut into fine strips. Serve the cooked rice topped with the shredded cabbage and crabmeat. Finally, add the kani-miso as topping.

JAPANESE-STYLE FRIED PRAWN
Serves 1

For the prawn salt:
Prawn shells • Salt

For the ebi-miso:
Tiger prawn heads • Rice oil • Tiger prawn innards

To make the prawn salt:
Roast prawn shells with some salt. Then grind them in a mixer to make the prawn salt.

To make the ebi-miso:
Slowly fry tiger prawn heads in some oil. Put them in a masher together with the prawn innards. Strain.

To prepare the fried prawn:
Remove the head, peel, and devein the prawn. Reserve the shells and head. Sprinkle the prawn with some salt and rinse under running water. Pat the prawn dry and make a shallow cut in the ventral side of the prawn to stretch and lengthen out the prawn.
Place the prawn on the spring roll wrapper and lightly sprinkle with salt and pepper. Cut the ebi-miso into appropriate sizes and place on the edge of the shrimp's head. Fold and roll up the roll and apply some beaten egg to the edges of the spring roll skin to hold together.

In a deep pot, heat rice oil to 350°F (180°C). Set up a dredging station: one bowl with beaten egg, another bowl with flour, and a third bowl with panko. Dredge the roll first in the flour, then in the beaten egg, and finally in the panko. Drop the prawn into the hot oil and cook until crispy and nicely browned.

Place the fried prawn in a plate. Season with *miazansho* tartar and a sprinkle of prawn salt and garnish with the lemon.

147

SOFT-BOILED EGG WITH CRUSTACEAN DASHI

JAPANESE-STYLE FRIED PRAWN

148

HIS KNOWLEDGE
ABOUT CRUSTACEANS
IS WONDERFUL
—I HAVE NEVER
MET ANY CHEF WHO
KNOWS MORE
THAN CHEF KATO.
— Yoshihiro Narisawa

KUNIHIKO KATO

GAVIN KAYSEN

SPOON AND STABLE
Minneapolis, Minnesota,
United States

A series of chance encounters sparked Gavin Kaysen's interest in becoming a chef. One day, while working at a sandwich shop in Bloomington, Minnesota, a man named George Serra began coming in and ordering tuna sandwiches from him, only to throw them away. He kept coming back each Saturday, and when Kaysen asked him why he'd been tossing the sandwiches, Serra replied that he simply wanted to see Kaysen's skills in action—the new pasta place next door was Serra's, and he ultimately recruited Kaysen to come work for him. It was there that Kaysen's relationship with food transformed, learning from Serra the art of cooking with feeling and emotion.

Kaysen's story is a heartwarming one, though judging by his drive, it is likely he would have found his way to the top on his own. Armed with his degree from the New England Culinary Institute, he went on to cook for Robert Curry at Domaine Chandon in Yountville, California, then in Europe at L'Auberge de Lavaux in Lausanne and L'Escargot in London under Marco Pierre White. Kaysen returned to the United States to work as executive chef at El Bizcocho in San Diego, earning a Best New Chef honor from *Food & Wine* in 2007; that same year, he represented the United States in the international competition the Bocuse d'Or and moved to New York to work for Chef Daniel Boulud.

At Café Boulud, Kaysen gained an entirely new perspective on what it meant to be a chef—this period of his career was pivotal in how he now defines hospitality. Under Boulud's tutelage, Kaysen continued to garner praise, earning the James Beard Award for Rising Star Chef of the Year in 2008 and rising up the ranks in the restaurant until his departure in 2014.

Today, Kaysen brings his spin on French cuisine to Minnesota with Spoon and Stable, Bellecour Bakery, and Demi in Minneapolis; he earned the James Beard Foundation's Best Chef: Midwest honor in 2018. He is also the president of the Ment'or BKB Foundation.

MENU

BISON TARTARE

SPAGHETTI NERO

TAMARIND-GLAZED
PORK CHOP

DOROTHY'S POT ROAST

HONEY AND CREAM CAKE

DOROTHY'S POT ROAST
Serves 4–6

For the mushroom confit:
1 pound (455 g) button mushrooms, stems trimmed and reserved • 2 cups (475 ml) hot water • 1 pound (455 g) unsalted butter, melted • 1 sachet of thyme, bay, rosemary

For the pommes aligot:
2 pounds (910 g) Yukon Gold potatoes • Salt • 8 ounces (225 g) unsalted butter • 1 quart/liter heavy (whipping) cream • 1 cup (110 g) shredded Gruyère cheese • Rosemary, garlic, thyme

For the braised top blade:
2 beef top blade or flat iron steaks • Salt and freshly ground black pepper • Canola oil • 1 onion, chopped • 1 carrot, chopped • 2 stalks celery, chopped • 2 tomatoes • 1 cup mushrooms • 4 tablespoons tomato paste (puree) • 2 cloves garlic • 1 (750 ml) bottle red wine • Veal stock or chicken stock • 1 sachet of thyme, bay leaf, black peppercorns • 1 cup large-diced bone marrow

Make the mushroom confit:
Rinse the mushrooms and stems. Keep separate. Drain and pat dry. In a small saucepot, cover the mushroom scraps with the hot water. Bring to a boil, reduce the heat to medium, and cook for 20 minutes. Strain out the mushroom scraps and reserve the broth.
Using the same pot, add the melted butter over medium heat and bring the temperature of the butter up slowly. Add the rinsed mushroom caps and cook over medium heat until the mushrooms are cooked through, about 10 minutes. In a sieve set over a bowl, drain the mushrooms and reserve the liquid. Return the liquid to the same pot. Combine with the mushroom broth and cook over high heat, reducing until 1 cup (240 ml) of liquid remains. Add the mushrooms back into the glaze and stir until coated.

Make the pommes aligot:
In a 4-quart/4-liter pot, combine the potatoes and warm water to cover. Add 2 tablespoons salt and bring to a boil. Reduce the heat to medium and cook until the potatoes are tender when easily pierced with a knife.

There should be little to no resistance. Allow the potato to cool slightly, then peel and pass through a food mill or ricer back into the dry cooking pot. Season the potato with a small amount of salt.
In a saucepan, melt the butter and cream together. Stir just enough butter/cream mixture into the potato to loosen the potato. Add the Gruyère and remaining butter/cream mixture. Stir vigorously until the cheese has melted and the potato takes on a stringy texture. Adjust seasoning if needed.

Make the braised top blade:
Preheat the oven to 325°F (160°C).
Season the meat thoroughly. Place a large sauté pan over high heat. When hot, add the canola oil and the steaks and sear until caramelized on one side, about 4 minutes. Repeat on the other side.
In a large Dutch oven (casserole) over high heat, roast the onion, carrot, celery, tomatoes, and mushrooms for 5 minutes. Add the tomato paste (purée) and cook just so the bottom of the pot gets sticky but doesn't burn. Add the wine and reduce until almost dry. Return the beef to the pot and cover with stock. Bring to a boil, add the sachet, and cover with a lid.
Transfer the pot to the oven and cook until the beef is tender and can easily be pierced by a knife with little to no resistance, about 3 hours.

Remove the meat and vegetables. Strain the broth, return to the Dutch oven, and cook until reduced to half the original volume. Just before pulling off the heat, add the diced bone marrow and cook, stirring to emulsify the fat.

Pour the reduced broth over the beef. Season with salt and pepper.

Serve the beef and vegetables with mushroom confit and pommes aligot.

HONEY AND CREAM CAKE
Serves 4–6

For the sponge cake (makes 2 half-sheets):
1 cup (290 g) egg yolks • 1¾ cups (350 g) sugar • 1 pound (455 g) egg whites • ⅓ cup (45 g) all-purpose (plain) flour, sifted

For the honey mousse:
2 cups (475 ml) heavy (whipping) cream • ½ cup (145 g) egg yolks • Pinch of salt • ½ cup (100 g) sugar • ½ cup (120 ml) honey • ½ cup (120 ml) water • 4 sheets gelatin, bloomed in ice water

For the sweetened condensed milk ice cream:
2 cups (475 ml) whole milk • 2 cups (475 ml) heavy (whipping) cream • ½ cup (145 g) egg yolks • 1 pound (455 g) sweetened condensed milk

For the milk crumble:
8 tablespoons (115 g) cold unsalted butter, cubed • 1 cup (130 g) all-purpose (plain) flour • 4 tablespoons sugar • 4 tablespoons malted milk powder • Kosher (flaked) salt

For the milk soak:
1 cup (240 ml) heavy (whipping) cream • 1 cup (240 ml) sweetened condensed milk • 1 cup (240 ml) evaporated milk

For the crispy honey meringues:
½ cup (120 ml) egg whites • ½ cup (120 ml) honey

Make the sponge cakes:
Preheat the oven to 350°F (180°C). Line two half-sheet pans with parchment paper. In a stand mixer fitted with the whisk, whip the yolks and 1 cup (200 g) of the sugar for 5 minutes. Scrape out of the bowl and set aside. Clean and dry the mixer bowl. With the whisk attachment, whip the egg whites until frothy. Slowly add the remaining ¾ cup (150 g) sugar. Whip until medium stiff peaks. Fold half of the whipped yolks into the whites to lighten it up, then fold in the rest of the yolks and the flour, just until everything is combined. Do not overmix. Divide the batter between the half-sheet pans and level the batter with an offset (icing) spatula.

Transfer to the oven and bake until lightly golden and the cake is set not jiggly. Let cool. This is best to make a day ahead.

Make the honey mousse:
In a stand mixer fitted with the whisk, whip the cream to medium peaks, scrape out and set aside. Clean and dry the bowl.

In the mixer with the whisk, whip the yolks and salt on high until thickened. Meanwhile, in a small saucepan, combine the sugar, honey and ¼ cup (60 ml) of the water and heat to an amber color. Immediately add the remaining ¼ cup (60 ml) of water, whisk rapidly to incorporate. Remove from the heat (be careful, it will splash out). With the mixer on medium-slow speed, pour the hot honey caramel down the side of the bowl (do not let it hit the whisk). Add the bloomed gelatin sheets and increase the mixer speed to high until thick and cooled. When cooled, fold in the whipped cream and set aside.

Make the sweetened condensed milk ice cream:
In a saucepan, combine the milk and cream, bring up to a simmer, then remove from the heat.

In a bowl, whisk the egg yolks and sweetened condensed milk together until combined. Whisking constantly, whisk some of the hot milk/cream mixture into the yolks to temper them, then add to the saucepan of milk/cream. Cook, stirring constantly with a heatproof spatula until slightly thickened. Remove from the heat and strain through a chinois. Then chill in an ice bath. Let sit for 24 hours. Freeze according to the directions for your ice cream maker.

Make the milk crumble:
Preheat the oven to 350°F (180°C).
In a food processor, combine the butter, flour, sugar, malted milk powder, and some salt. Pulse until crumbly. Spread on a sheet pan and bake until just very lightly golden,

5–10 minutes, stirring constantly so it stays crumbly. Let cool and store in airtight.

Make the milk soak:
In a bowl, whisk everything together and refrigerate.

Make the crisp honey meringues:
Preheat the oven to 180°–200°F (80°–90°C). Line a baking sheet with a silicone baking mat. In a stand mixer with the whisk, whip the egg whites and honey on high until thick/ stiff peaks form. Transfer to a piping bag fitted with a plain tip (nozzle) and pipe rounds ¾–1 inch (2–2.5 cm) in diameter onto the baking mat. Dry in the oven for 2 hours. Remove from the oven and let it sit for 1 minute and then peel off. Store airtight.

TAMARIND-GLAZED PORK CHOP

SPAGHETTI NERO

HONEY AND CREAM CAKE

GAVIN IS REACHING A
WHOLE NEW GENERATION
OF COOKS IN THE MIDWEST,
ENCOURAGING THEM TO
BECOME GREAT CHEFS.
— Daniel Boulud

153

GAVIN KAYSEN

JAMES KENT

CROWN SHY
New York, New York,
United States

DANIEL BOULUD

James Kent is a chef who truly embodies the spirit of New York City. Raised in the Greenwich Village neighborhood, Kent found his calling early on, working in kitchens from a young age—and as luck would have it, Chef David Bouley happened to live in his building.

It was a birthday dinner (his fourteenth) at Bouley that solidified Kent's future in the field, and at fifteen he sought and landed a coveted *stage* at the restaurant in 1993. Post–high school graduation, Kent went on to study food service management, culinary arts, and marketing at Johnson & Wales University in Providence, Rhode Island. In 2001, he studied at Le Cordon Bleu in London and Paris. It was just a matter of time before he returned to his roots to work in some of Manhattan's most sought-after kitchens.

Jean-Georges, Babbo, and Gordon Ramsay at The London were some of Kent's first gigs in this phase of his career. In 2007, he began working at Eleven Madison Park, one of the most prestigious restaurants in the world, where he would stay until 2013. Chef Daniel Humm became his mentor, teaching him the value of focus, diligence, and working toward goals— applying this, he competed in 2010 at the Bocuse d'Or USA and won, going on to represent the United States in Lyon the following year, placing tenth in the world.

From 2014 to 2017, Kent served as executive chef at The NoMad, sister restaurant to Eleven Madison Park and acclaimed in its own right. The following year was a defining one for him—Kent, along with Jeff Katz of Del Posto, opened Crown Shy in Manhattan's Financial District. Crown Shy is a stunning, sprawling space with an open kitchen, a profoundly personal stage for Kent to showcase his soulful, globally inspired cuisine. The menu is a product of his team's travels, memories, and experiences, executed with European techniques, hardly confined to any traditional boxes.

MENU

GRUYÈRE FRITTERS, CHILI, LIME

FLUKE CRUDO, CITRUS, SESAME TUILE

CHARRED CARROTS, RAZOR CLAMS, LEMON THYME

ROASTED CHICKEN WITH CHILIES, BABY GEM LETTUCE, AND CILANTRO

ROASTED SHORT RIB, BRAISED ENDS, SUNCHOKES, CHIMICHURRI

STICKY TOFFEE PUDDING FOR TWO, PECAN, APPLE SORBET

CHARRED CARROTS, RAZOR CLAMS, LEMON THYME
Serves 6

For the roasted carrots:
10 orange carrots • 100 g grapeseed oil • Kosher salt

For the lemon-thyme oil:
100 g lemon thyme • 25 g parsley • 350 g grapeseed oil

For the razor clams:
3 pounds (1.36 kg) razor clams • 20 g grapeseed oil • 35 g shallots • 15 g tarragon • 10 g chervil • 15 g chives • 9 g garlic • 150 g white wine • 30 g unsalted butter

For the clam foam:
500 g liquid from cooking the clams • 3 sprigs thyme • 200 g canned clam pieces • 50 g unsalted butter • 100 g onion, sliced • 30 g shallots, sliced • 30 g leeks, sliced • 100 g celery, sliced • 2 g garlic, sliced • 3 g Fresno chili, sliced • 50 g Yukon Gold potato, sliced • 350 g heavy (whipping) cream • 25 g lemon juice • 0.5 g cayenne pepper • Salt • Old Bay seasoning • 5 g soy lecithin

For the onion soubise:
30 g unsalted butter • 250 g yellow onion, thinly sliced • 1 g thyme sprigs • 250 g heavy (whipping) cream • 50 g whole milk • Salt • 0.75 g xanthan gum

To finish:
5 Roasted Carrots *(above)* • 3 lemon thyme

Roast the carrots:
Preheat a combi oven to 180°F (82°C) at 100% steam.
Scrub the carrots clean. Pat dry, drizzle with the oil and season with salt. Place the carrots on a wire rack in a sheet pan and cook in the combi oven until tender, about 20 minutes. Once the carrots are fully tender, torch the outside until crisp. Cut in half and portion.

Make the lemon-thyme oil:
In a medium saucepan, combine the thyme and oil, bring up to 180°F (82°C). Turn off the heat and allow to steep for 10 minutes. Transfer the oil to a blender, add the parsley, and blend for about 5 minutes or until all the water in the parsley is cooked out. The oil should be vibrant green. Strain and reserve.

Prepare the razor clams:
Purge the clams in water for at least 1 hour before cooking.
In a very hot rondeau, add the oil and clams. Cover for 1 minute. Add the shallots and herbs and cook 1 more minute. Deglaze with the white wine and add the butter. Cover and let the clams cook for 2–3 minutes. Once the clams start to open, strain through a perforated pan set over another pan to catch the cooking liquid. Wrap in plastic wrap (cling film) and let steam and then cool. Clean the razor clams from their shells and hold them in their cooking liquid.

Make the clam foam:
In a saucepan, cook the clam liquid until reduced to 200 g. Make a sachet with thyme and canned clam pieces and set it aside. In a medium rondeau, melt the butter and add the sliced onion, shallots, leeks, celery, and garlic. Cook until translucent. Do not get any color on the vegetables. Add the Fresno, potato, and the thyme/clam sachet. Add the reduced clam stock and cream. Keep at a simmer until all the vegetables are soft, to extract the flavor but not reduce. Strain the cream. Season with the lemon juice, cayenne, salt and Old Bay to taste. Finish with soy lecithin before service.

Make the onion soubise:
In a medium rondeau, heat the butter until melted but not browned. Add the onions and cook until translucent. Add the thyme and continue to cook. Add the cream and milk and cook until the onions are completely soft. Discard the thyme springs. Strain the liquid and reserve. Blend the onions in a blender and add salt to taste. Blend until smooth. Add cream if consistency needs to be adjusted.

GRUYÈRE FRITTERS

To finish:
For each serving, place 30 g of the onion soubise in the center of a plate, and shingle 5 razor clams over the top. In a row lay 5 bias-cut roasted carrots. Using a hand blender, froth the foam. Spoon the foam and 40 g of the razor clam cooking liquid over the carrots. Finish with several drops of thyme oil and leaves of fresh lemon thyme.

ROASTED CHICKEN WITH CHILES, BABY GEM LETTUCE, AND CILANTRO
Serves 6

For the fermented red habaneros:
3% salt brine • 1 kg red habanero pepper, halved and seeded

For the fermented red peppers:
3% salt brine • 1 kg red bell peppers, halved and seeded

For the fermented orange peppers:
3% salt brine • 1 kg orange bell peppers, halved and seeded

For the chicken marinade:
120 g fresh jalapeño pepper • 60 g fresh habanero pepper • 400 g grapefruit juice • 600 g orange juice • 200 g lemon juice • 80 g lime juice • 40 g ginger juice • 124 g salt • 84 g shallots • 20 coriander seeds • 20 black peppercorns • 4 whole star anise • 3 whole chickens

For the hot sauce:
50 g grapeseed oil • 150 g onions, sliced • 10 g garlic, sliced • 150 g fresh fennel, sliced • 750 g red bell peppers, sliced • 150 g peeled and segmented orange • 450 g orange juice • 50 g extra-virgin olive oil • 30 g Fermented Red Habaneros *(above)* • 300 g Fermented Red Peppers *(above)* • 50 g Fermented Orange Peppers *(above)*

For the gastrique:
175 g sugar • 3 whole star anise • 135 g lemon juice and zest • 150 g lime juice and zest • 215 g orange juice and zest

For assembly:
900 g chicken jus • Gastrique *(above)* • Fresh orange juice • Fresh lemon juice • Sliced jalapeños • Sliced watermelon radishes • Picked cilantro (fresh coriander) • Little Gem lettuce tops • Lemon vinaigrette

Ferment the habaneros:
Make a brine with 3% kosher salt. Place the chilies in clean glass jars and pour the brine over to cover, leaving at least 3 inches (7.5 cm) of headspace. Place the lids on and store for at least 7 days. Open the jars to release gas every other day.

Ferment the red bell peppers:
Make a brine with 3% kosher salt. Place the peppers in clean glass jars and pour the brine over to cover, leaving at least 3 inches (7.5 cm) of headspace. Place the lids on and store for at least 7 days. Open the jars to release gas every other day.

Ferment the orange peppers:
Make a brine with 3% kosher salt. Place the peppers in clean glass jars and pour the brine over to cover, leaving at least 3 inches (7.5 cm) of headspace. Place the lid on and store for at least 7 days. Open the jars to release gas every other day.

Marinate the chicken:
In a blender, lightly pulse the chilies and spices with a portion of the juice. Halve the chickens (you will have 6 pieces) and bone out the drumsticks and thighs. Combine with the marinade and marinate for 24 hours. Remove from the marinade and dry on a rack for 12 hours.

Make the hot sauce:
In a rondeau, heat the grapeseed oil over medium heat and sweat the onions, garlic, fennel and bell pepper, making sure not to let the vegetables brown. Add the orange flesh and orange juice and reduce until all the liquid is evaporated and the peppers are very soft. Transfer to a blender and add all the fermented peppers and the olive oil. Blend, then pass through a chinois.

Make the gastrique:
In a dry medium pan, caramelize the sugar. Add the star anise and toast. Add the citrus juices to dissolve the caramel. Reduce by half. Mix in the citrus zest. Cool.

To assemble:
In a saucepan, reduce the chicken jus by one-fifth. Add the gastrique to taste and finish with fresh orange juice and lemon juice if needed. Roast the chicken on the grill and finish cooking in the oven. Pull from the oven and rest for 10 minutes. To plate, dress jalapeños, radishes, watercress, and cilantro (fresh coriander) with lemon vinaigrette and place on top of chicken.

JAMES'S CUISINE IS IDENTIFIED WITH CREATIVE PRESENTATION, GREAT SKILL, FLAVORFUL COMBINATIONS, AND SOULFUL TASTE; HIS RESTAURANT IS A PLACE WHERE CASUALNESS MEETS FINESSE, WHERE CREATIVE CUISINE HAS NO BORDERS.

— Daniel Boulud

ROASTED CHICKEN

STICKY TOFFEE PUDDING

JAMES KENT

IZUMI KIMURA

SUSHIJIN
Toyama, Japan

YOSHIHIRO NARISAWA

When Izumi Kimura discovered that the bay off the coast of his home prefecture was the provenance of much of the best seafood he enjoyed in Tokyo, he quit his job and moved back north to the coastal city of Toyama, famed for waters hosting around five hundred species of fish. He had recently been transformed by a meal at Tokyo's Ginza Kyubey, a renowned sushi restaurant—so much so that he reconsidered his career as a salaryman in the construction industry and began his self-taught journey to becoming a sushi chef.

From in 2005—and including two failed attempts to create his own restaurant—Kimura trained himself in the craft of sushi, and, as an autodidact, he doesn't hesitate to do things his own way. For him, a big part of that means paying close attention to his natural environment and the rhythms of the sea. Kimura now runs an eighteen-seat restaurant in Toyama called Sushijin, acclaimed as the home of some of the best sushi in Japan.

Kimura's knowledge of the sea shines in his omakase menu. He serves blackthroat seaperch as two dishes: the male, lean and firm in texture, is served on skewers with green onions, sansho peppers, and boiled snow crab; the more delicate female is served shabu-shabu style, briefly boiled in soup. Another ode to the sea is his bite-size firefly squid, a local specialty, served with uni and a mixture of crab, sushi rice, and nori and covered in a cod milt sauce. Kimura also champions the local in his selection of other ingredients: rice, grown by his in-laws, hails from the base of the nearby Tateyama mountains; the red rice vinegar he uses is the local vintage; salt comes from the coast of nearby Noto Peninsula. And in place of traditional miso soup, he serves a seafood broth he calls "Toyama bouillabaisse."

Kimura's renown has brought invitations to culinary events around the world. When traveling, he prepares only fish local to each country—an ongoing challenge he maintains for both himself and his craft.

MENU

CHAWANMUSHI WITH UME SAUCE

AMAEBI AND SHIRO EBI NIGIRI

BAIGAI SASHIMI WITH FRESH WASABI AND SUDACHI CITRUS

NODOGURO

CHAWANMUSHI WITH UME SAUCE

For the dashi:
45 g kombu • 150 g katsuobushi • 2 liters cold water

For the chawanmushi:
8 eggs • 50 g light soy sauce • 60 g mirin • 600 g Dashi *(above)*

For the ume sauce:
3 umeboshi • 300 ml water • 5 g kudzu or arrowroot powder

Make the dashi:
In a pot, combine the kombu, 100 g of the katsuobushi, and the water and refrigerate overnight.
Set over heat and bring to 203°F (95°C). Add a of splash of cold water to lower the temperature to 185°F (85°C) and add another 50 g katsuobushi and keep at that temperature for 10 minutes. Strain the dashi (discard the solids).

Make the chawanmushi:
In a bowl, whisk together the eggs, soy sauce, mirin, and dashi. Strain through a fine-mesh sieve. Divide the custard among 50 g cups. Set up a steamer and steam the custards until just set, 5–6 minutes.

Make the ume sauce:
Pit (stone) the umeboshi and blend into a sauce/paste texture.
In a small saucepan, slowly heat the water with the kudzu powder. When the mixture turns clear, stir in the blended ume paste. Remove from the heat and let cool to room temperature before refrigerating until use.

To serve, spoon 5 grams of chilled ume sauce on top of the egg custard.

SHARI (SUSHI RICE)

1 kg Koshihikari rice • 110 g red rice vinegar • 50 g white rice vinegar • 35 g sea salt • 25 g natural radish sugar

The rice is the most important part, so be careful. Wash the rice four times gently. The first time make sure you use a lot of water and be quick so the rice doesn't soak up all the starch that comes out. Wash three more times and after the last time, let the rice sit in a bowl under running water for 13 minutes 30 seconds.
Drain the rice in a sieve and let it sit in the sieve to air-dry for 12 minutes. Refrigerate overnight.
In a large pot, bring 800 ml water to a boil. Add the washed rice and cook over high heat for 3 minutes. Reduce the temperature and continue to cook for 7 minutes. Remove from the heat and let it rest for 1 minute. In a bowl, combine both vinegars, the salt, and sugar. Mix the rice with the vinegar blend.

BURI (YELLOWTAIL)

AMAEBI AND SHIRO EBI NIGIRI (SPOT PRAWN AND GLASS SHRIMP NIGIRI)

Glass shrimp, peeled • Seaweed • Spot prawns, peeled • Shari *(see above)*

The glass shrimp is cured in seaweed for 2 hours for more umamai taste.

BAIGAI SASHIMI WITH FRESH WASABI AND SUDACHI CITRUS

Baigai (whelk/sea snail) • Salt • Sudachi juice • Sea salt • Fresh wasabi

Remove the whelks from their shells. Wash three times with salt to get more umami. Dry and thinly slice.
To serve, add sudachi juice and finish off with sea salt and wasabi.

NODOGURO (BLACKTHROAT SEAPERCH)

1 whole blackthroat seaperch • Salt • Scallions (spring onions) • Sake (in a spray bottle) • Soy sauce

Fillet the fish and remove the scales. Salt the fillets for 5 minutes to remove water and add more umami. Wash off the salt and cut into smaller pieces. Thread on a skewer

with the scallions (spring onions).
Set up a charcoal fire (preferably using *binchōtan* charcoal). Spray the fish with sake and grill skin-side down over the coals. Brush with soy sauce toward the end of cooking.

FEMALE NODOGURO, SHABU-SHABU STYLE

HORSE MACKEREL

CHEF KIMURA STRUGGLED TO CREATE HIS STYLE WITHOUT THE GUIDANCE OF A MAESTRO, BUT HE HAS CREATED WHAT A SUSHI RESTAURANT SHOULD BE. HE HAS SUCH DEEP KNOWLEDGE OF THE SEA.

— Yoshihiro Narisawa

IZUMI KIMURA

KEITA KITAMURA

ERH
Paris, France

YOSHIHIRO NARISAWA

MENU

SCALLOP, BERGAMOT,
PURPLE TURNIP

FOIE GRAS, MANGO,
AND BEET

SEA BASS TEMPURA,
MUSSEL BROTH, COCKLES,
PUNTARELLE, CIME DI RAPA

ROE DEER, PEAR,
CHERVIL ROOT

PIÑA COLADA

Keita Kitamura can trace his passion for good food back to the age of three. During his childhood in Japan, his mother's cooking hooked him first; later a popular television series featuring international cuisines further stirred his interest. Especially excited by French food, he set off in pursuit of mastering it. Now, as chef of the restaurant ERH in Paris, he is realizing his passion in tasting menus that showcase his mastery of precise French technique.

After studying French cuisine at the Tsuji Culinary Institute, from which he graduated at the age of nineteen, Kitamura spent eight years working in Japan under acclaimed chef Yoshihiro Narisawa. Kitamura's consistent interest in French cuisine inevitably spurred his move to Paris, where he gleaned experience at the three-Michelin-starred Pierre Gagnaire and the modern bistro Au Bon Accueil. When he was approached by the owner of La Maison du Saké, an elegant sake shop in the center of Paris, to open a restaurant within the shop, Kitamura jumped at the opportunity. Not only would he have command of the kitchen, but he could collaborate in food and sake pairings. ERH stands for the words "Eau, Riz, Hommes"—water, rice, and men, once the fundamental elements of sake.

While Kitamura's cuisine showcases his admiration and mastery of French techniques, there are frequent nods to Japan and elsewhere. Tempura-fried monkfish, for example, is served with clams, blue-foot mushrooms, and chard in broth. His signature foie-gras dish, balanced atop a hunk of brioche secured in a swirl of mango puree and veal juice, is flavored with sakura cherry tree smoke. A dessert of poached figs is served with an unctuous ice cream made with Fourme d'Ambert cheese; his "piña colada" arrives as a mélange of pineapple, passion fruit, and coconut granitas.

Having received a Michelin star only one year after opening ERH—earlier than any chef would imagine for a new venture—Kitamura's passion continues as he works toward his second.

SCALLOP, BERGAMOT, PURPLE TURNIP
Serves 4

For the scallop fumet:
80 g scallop mantle • 15 g carrot • 15 g leek • 15 g white celery • 2 sprigs thyme • 2 sprigs parsley • 15 g white pepper • 30 g white wine • Water

For the scallop sauce:
30 g shallots • 200 g white wine • 600 g Scallop Fumet (above) • 200 g heavy (whipping) cream • Lemon juice • Salt

For the bergamot coulis:
130 g bergamot, zest grated, peeled, and cut into rings • 43 g sugar • 200 g water • 40 g olive oil

To finish:
4 scallops • 1 purple turnip • Zest and juice of 1 bergamot • 2 tablespoons olive oil • Fleur de sel • Chickweed and watercress, for garnish

Make the scallop fumet:
In a large pot, combine all the ingredients and bring to a boil. Reduce the heat and simmer for 15 minutes. Strain through a fine-mesh sieve.

Make the scallop sauce:
In a saucepan, reduce the shallots and wine. Add the fumet and reduce again. Add the heavy (whipping) cream and bring to a boil. Strain in a fine-mesh sieve. Adjust taste with lemon juice and salt.

Make the bergamot coulis:
In a saucepan, combine the bergamot zest, flesh, sugar, and water and cook on low heat for about 2 hours.
Transfer the mixture to a blender and mix. With the machine running, emulsify in the oil. Pass through a fine-mesh sieve.

To finish:
Cut the scallops horizontally into 3 thin slices. Very thinly slice the purple turnip. Cut into rounds with a ring cutter.
Season the scallops and turnips with bergamot juice, olive oil, and fleur de sel.

Spread the scallop sauce on a plate, and place the scallop and turnip on top. Garnish with watercress and chickweed, and dress with the bergamot coulis and bergamot zest

FOIE GRAS, MANGO, AND BEET
Serves 4

For the red beet puree:
3 red beets • Salt • Sugar • Olive oil • Water • Chinese five-spice powder • Salt

For the ravioli dough:
300 g cake (soft) flour • 300 g all-purpose (plain) flour • Margarine • 100 g Red Beet Puree (above) • 150 g egg whites

For the Modena sauce:
200 g sugar • 800 g red wine vinegar • 600 g veal stock • 80 g balsamic vinegar • Salt • Freshly ground white pepper

For the mango coulis:
80 g mango • 5 g Sichuan pepper • 20 g olive oil • Fleur de sel

DUCK, BLACK TRUMPET MUSHROOM, CABBAGE, AND HAM

FOIE GRAS, MANGO, AND BEET

ROE DEER, PEAR, CHERVIL ROOT

163

PIÑA COLADA

> # HE FOCUSES ON DEVELOPING ORIGINALITY BASED ON FRENCH TECHNIQUE, BUT INEVITABLY INCORPORATING HIS JAPANESE HERITAGE.
>
> — Yoshihiro Narisawa

For the smoked foie gras:
Foie gras • 15 g cherry wood

For finishing:
Fresh mango, sliced, for filling • Red oxalis, for garnish

Make the red beet puree:
Preheat the oven to 400°F (200°C).
Set the beets on a square of foil. Dress with salt, sugar, and olive oil. Close the package and roast for about 2 hours. Remove from the oven and set aside to cool.
When the beets are cool enough to handle, peel and dice small. Transfer the beets to a Thermomix and add the water. Heat it for 30 minutes at 221°F (105°C). Blend well and add five-spice powder and salt to taste.

Make the ravioli dough:
In a Thermomix, blend together the flours and margarine. Add the beet puree and mix. Add the egg whites and mix. Work the dough and then vacuum-seal it. Let it rest overnight.

Make the Modena sauce:
In a saucepan, combine the sugar and red wine vinegar and reduce.
Add the veal stock and reduce again to 550 g. Stir in the balsamic vinegar and salt and white pepper to taste.

Make the mango coulis:
In a Thermomix, combine the mango and Sichuan pepper and blend. With the machine running, slowing emulsify in the oil. Adjust with fleur de sel to taste. Pass through a fine-mesh sieve.

Smoke the foie gras:
Separate the big and small lobes of the foie and clean up the veins.
Smoke it with cherry wood for about 4 minutes. Wrap it up and cool it down.

To finish:
Roll out the dough and fill the ravioli by layering mango (15 g), 2 slices (15 g) of foie gras, and some Modena sauce for each raviolo. Seal and cut the dough.
In a large pot of boiling water, cook the ravioli for 5 minutes.
Set the mango coulis and beet puree on a plate and place the ravioli on top. Garnish with red oxalis.

ROE DEER, PEAR, CHERVIL ROOT
Serves 4

For the deer marinade and stock:
300 g carrots • 120 g white celery • 150 g shallots • 150 g onion • 60 g garlic • 5 liters red wine • 1 bouquet garni • 900 ml red wine vinegar • 5 kg venison bones • Veal stock • Chicken stock

For the sauce poivrade:
20 g blueberry jelly • 60 g red wine vinegar • 120 g Deer Marinade *(above)* • 80 g Deer Stock *(above)* • Butter • Cream • Salt and freshly ground black pepper • Blueberries • Marc de Bourgogne

For the chervil confit:
2 tonka beans, crushed • Butter • Sugar • Fine salt • 2 chervil roots, halved lengthwise

For the caramelized pear:
Sugar • 1 conference pear • Calvados

For the salsify confit:
Ascorbic acid • 2 salsify • Grapeseed oil

For the fried parsnips:
Grapeseed oil • 2 parsnips, sliced lengthwise

For finishing:
Venison backstrap • Butter for sautéing • Oil for sautéing • Red currants, for garnish

Make the deer stock:
Cut all the vegetables into ¾ to 2-inch (1–5 cm) pieces. In a sauté pan, fry the vegetables.
In a large pot, heat the wine until the alcohol cooks off. Add the fried vegetables, bouquet garni, and vinegar. Heat the marinade for 5 minutes, then cool down. Add the venison bones and soak overnight.
Remove the venison bones from the marinade and fry it in a pan.
Measure out half of the marinade, pass through a fine-mesh sieve, cool down, and set aside.
Mix the remaining half of the marinade with the venison bones and cook to reduce the liquid by half. Add veal stock and chicken stock and let it cook for 6 hours.

Strain the deer stock and pass through a fine-mesh sieve. Return to a pot and cook until reduced by 90 percent.

Make the sauce poivrade:
In a small saucepan, combine the jelly and vinegar and bring to a boil. Add the marinade and bring to a boil. Add the stock and cook until reduced by half.
Stir in the butter and cream and adjust the taste with salt and black pepper. Add the blueberries and Marc de Bourgogne.

Roast the chervil confit:
Preheat the oven to 350°F (180°C).
In a small bowl, blend the tonka beans, butter, sugar, and salt. Arrange the chervil roots on a baking sheet and spread the tonka/butter mixture on them. Wrap the whole pan with foil and bake it for 50 minutes.
Uncover, turn the roots over, return to the oven for 20 minutes.

Make the caramelized pear:
In a saucepan, cook the sugar until caramel in color.
Add the pear and caramelize. Add the Calvados to stop the cooking.

Make the salsify confit:
Set up a bowl of water acidulated with ascorbic acid. Peel the salsify and dip in the acidulated water.
In a sauté pan, heat several inches of oil to 230°F (110°C). Add the salsify and cook for 30 minutes. Fry it with the oil at 350°F (180°C).

Fry the parsnip:
In a sauté pan, heat a few inches of oil to 350°F (180°C). Add the parsnips and fry.

To finish:
In a frying pan, sauté the venison backstraps in the butter and oil. Let it rest wrapped in foil until ready to slice.

To serve, plate the chervil confit, and fried parsnip. Add the sliced venison and pour on the sauce poivrade. Garnish with the caramelized pear and some red currants.

KEITA KITAMURA

ANTONIA KLUGMANN

DOMINIQUE CRENN

MENU

WHITE TURNIP AND QUINCE

BROKEN SPAGHETTI, CAULIFLOWER, AND CHAMOMILE

FIG, TOMATO SAUCE, AND LAUREL

SMOKED SQUID HAM BROTH, SAUSAGES, AND SESAME OIL

ESCARGOT OMELET WITH HERBS AND MAYONNAISE

CLEMENTINE

Few chefs are pushing the boundaries of culinary arts quite like Antonia Klugmann of L'Argine a Vencò in Italy. Born in 1979 to a family of doctors in Trieste, Klugmann's career began in a drastically different direction—while studying law, she became interested in food. In 2001, after taking a few patisserie classes, Klugmann was officially hooked and moved back home to pursue a career as a chef. She started out strong, learning the ropes under the tutelage of Raffaele Mazzolini, with whom she spent five years before tragedy struck. A car accident confined Klugmann to her home to recover for nearly a year. Klugmann spent this time planting and tending to her own garden, and through this, she fell in love with a new facet of the culinary world and developed a plan to one day open her own restaurant.

Once she was back on her feet, Klugmann got back to work, and in 2006 opened the Antico Foledor in Conte Lovaria, in Pavia di Udine, northwest of Trieste. It was then that she began to capture the attention of the country's critics with her knack for expertly manipulating aroma while channeling her own personal experiences and emotions through food. She went on to become the chef at Il Ridotto in Venice in 2012, and then was executive chef at the Michelin-starred Venissa in Burano. In 2014, Klugmann and her sister, Vittoria, opened the doors to L'Argine a Vencò in Dolegna del Collio. Within months of its debut, L'Argine a Vencò earned its first Michelin star, and things have only picked up from there.

In recent years, Klugmann has become both a decorated chef (she won Best Female Chef recognitions from both Identità Golose and Guida Espresso in 2016 and 2017, respectively) and a regular on culinary television programs. Klugmann, who is perhaps best known for her signature dish of bluefish and anchovies, often uses ingredients not commonly found in the luxury dining sphere, seeking to redefine what flavor and ingenuity mean.

WHITE TURNIP AND QUINCE
Serves 4

5 quince

For the daikon:
1 medium daikon radish (for 6 people), sliced • Salt • Extra-virgin olive oil • 4 tablespoons brown sugar • 2 tablespoons unsalted butter

For the chicory:
1 puntarelle chicory per person • Pinch of chili pepper • Salt • Oil

In a juice extractor, juice the quince. Transfer the juice to a saucepan and reduce the liquid by half.

Prepare the daikon:
Preheat the oven to 410°F (210°C).
In a pot of boiling salted water, cook the daikon for 5 minutes. Spread out on a sheet pan and sprinkle with salt and a little bit of olive oil. Bake for 5 minutes on one side

and 4 minutes on the other. Remove from the oven and reduce the oven temperature to 390°F (200°C).
Sprinkle half of the brown sugar on one side of the daikon and spread with half of the butter. Return to the oven for 4 minutes. Turn the daikon, top with the remaining brown sugar and butter. Bake for 4 minutes longer.
Transfer the daikon in a copper or aluminum pan. Gradually add the juice and cook until the daikon is nicely glazed. When the turnips are evenly cooked through, remove and finely chop them.

Cook the puntarelle:
Finely chop the puntarelle. In a pot of boiling salted water, cook the daikon for 3 minutes.
Serve the daikon with the puntarelle and reduced quince juice.

BROKEN SPAGHETTI, CAULI-FLOWER, AND CHAMOMILE
Serves 2

100 g unsalted butter • 3 tablespoons dried chamomile flowers • 1 cauliflower, broken into florets, plus ¼ cauliflower, whole • 500 ml milk • Extra-virgin olive oil • 100 g broken spaghetti • Bigroot geranium leaves

Vacuum-seal the butter and 2 tablespoons of the chamomile flowers. Cook at 131°F (55°C) for 3 hours.
In a pan, cook the cauliflower in the milk until tender. Reserving the milk, drain the cauliflower. Transfer the cauliflower to a food processor and puree to a smooth cream with some olive oil.
In a cast-iron pan, roast the ¼ cauliflower for just a couple of minutes with a pinch of salt and some extra-virgin olive oil.
In a separate pan, quickly toast the spaghetti with a pinch of salt and some extra-virgin olive oil. Cook the pasta for 8 minutes in the reserved cauliflower milk. Halfway through, add half of the roasted cauliflower. Remove from the heat and let them rest for 1 minute. Season with the chamomile butter.

ESCARGOT OMELETE WITH HERBS AND MAYONNAISE

To serve, put 1 tablespoon cauliflower puree onto a plate and add the spaghetti. Sprinkle some dried chamomile flowers on top of the spaghetti and top with a couple of leaves of bigroot geranium.

SMOKED SQUID HAM BROTH, SAUSAGES, AND SESAME OIL
Serves 1

1 squid per person (200 g)

For the ham broth:
1 onion, halved, unpeeled • 250 g ham, trimmed of fat • 800 g water

For the sauce:
1 musky octopus or 1 little octopus per person • 1 onion • 1 carrot • 1 stalk celery • 1 tomato • 1 bay leaf • 2 juniper berries • Squid trimmings • 20 g vinegar • 20 g olive oil

For the sausage cream:
1 onion, halved, unpeeled • 1 semidry smoked pork sausage, chopped • Olive oil • 1 fresh chili pepper • 1 red bell pepper • 1 teaspoon sweet paprika • 1 dried chili pepper • 2 cloves garlic • 100 g apple juice • 1 teaspoon honey • 20 g lard

For serving:
Toasted sesame oil • Salt • 1 teaspoon wine vinegar

Prepare the squid:
Clean the squid and save the trimmings for the sauce. If necessary, dry them in the fridge. Smoke them finely chopped until the desired taste and aroma are obtained.

Make the ham broth:
In a dry cast-iron skillet, roast the onion cut-sides down until browned. Vacuum-seal the ham, roasted onion, and water and cook at 131°F (55°C) for 5 hours. Strain (discard the solids).

Make the sauce:
Lay out all the ingredients in a pot large enough to avoid overlapping. Add the vinegar and a little bit of olive oil. Set the pot over heat. To favor the coming out of the water add a couple of spoons of fresh water. Cover airtight and cook over low heat for 45 minutes. Strain and return to the pot. Cook until reduced to a glaze.

Make the sausage cream:
In a dry cast-iron skillet, roast the onion cut-side down until browned.
Combine the chopped sausage and a little olive oil in a cold pan and bring up to heat. Brown the sausage and add the fresh chili, bell pepper, paprika, dried chili pepper, the powders, apple juice, honey, and roasted onion. Cook until the sausage is very soft. Blend with the lard. Strain.

To serve:
Season the smoked squid with a little bit of sesame oil, some sauce, and salt. Serve it on some sausage cream. Finish the dish with the ham broth.

ESCARGOT OMELET WITH HERBS AND MAYONNAISE
Serves 6

For the tomato sauce:
1 tablespoon extra-virgin olive oil • 1 clove garlic • 1 green chili pepper, chopped • 200 g tomatoes, halved • Salt • 1 onion, julienned

For the escargots:
1 onion, halved, unpeeled • 3 liters cold water • 1 carrot • 1 stalk celery • 1 bay leaf • Sprig of rosemary • Black peppercorns • Juniper berries • 1 kg escargot • Salt • Flour • Olive oil • Salted butter • 2 tablespoons balsamic vinegar • 3 tablespoons soy sauce, plus more if needed • 2 tablespoons stravecchio balsamic vinegar from Modena

For the mayonnaise:
3 egg yolks • Pinch of salt • 1 tablespoon red wine vinegar • 200 g seed oil • 50 g cold water

For the green omelet:
50 g unsalted butter, at room temperature • 60 g parsley • 10 g Silene vulgaris • 3 egg whites • Pinch of salt

To finish:
Butter • Salt and freshly ground black pepper • Extra-virgin olive oil • 3 small plantain leaves, blanched • 2 stellaria tops • 3 nigella leaves

Make the tomato sauce:
In a saucepan, heat some olive oil, the garlic, and chili over high heat. When the garlic clove starts turning brown, add the tomatoes and continue cooking. When they start releasing their liquid, add some salt and the onion. Cook for a couple of minutes. Keep warm while you prepare the escargots.

Prepare the escargots:
In a dry cast-iron skillet, roast the onion cut-side down until browned.
In a pot, combine the cold water, carrot, roasted onion, celery, bay leaf, rosemary, and peppercorns, and juniper berries to taste. Cook over low heat without letting it boil.
Bring the broth to a boil and cook the escargots in it just a few at a time, for 4–5 minutes. Drain the escargots and strain the broth.
In a cast-iron skillet, sauté the shelled escargots with a pinch of salt and a little bit of flour and olive oil. Halfway through, add a knob of butter.

Once braised, add the escargots to the tomato sauce. Cover with the strained broth. Stir them and continue cooking, covered, for about 30 minutes.
Stir in the balsamic vinegar, soy sauce, and stravecchio balsamic vinegar and continue cooking for 10 minutes. Adjust with soy sauce if needed.
Scoop the escargots out of the liquid with a slotted spoon. Strain the broth through a chinois and reserve.

Make the mayonnaise:
Season the egg yolks with salt and vinegar. Beat with a hand blender and add three-quarters of the oil very gradually, just a little bit at the time. Add the cold water and the remaining oil to taste, and continue mixing with the blender. Let the mayonnaise rest for at least 2 hours before serving.

Make the green omelet:
Beat together the butter, parsley, and Silene to make a green butter.
To make one omelet at a time, in a bowl, with an electric mixer, beat the egg whites, parsley leaves, and salt at high speed for a couple of minutes.
Heat a small frying pan with a knob of butter. Remove from the heat, pour the egg white mixture into the hot pan, and cover with a lid so the omelet cooks delicately and the moistness and color of the omelet is preserved. If necessary, return the pan to heat for just a couple of seconds. The omelet is ready when firm, but still soft. Repeat to make more omelets.
Position an omelet on plastic wrap (cling film) with the unbrowned side facing up. Spread a small layer of green butter onto the omelet. Roll the omelet, using the plastic wrap to help, trying not to close the ends. Once cool, cut into slices. Repeat.

To finish:
Reduce the reserved strained broth and add the escargots. Season with butter, pepper, a pinch of salt, and olive oil if necessary. Create a stripe of mayonnaise on the plate, position the escargots at the extremities of the plate with 3 omelet rolls on each side. Complete the plate by topping the escargots with 3 small plantain leaves, 3 stellaria tops, and 3 small nigella leaves.

SMOKED SQUID HAM BROTH, SAUSAGES, AND SESAME OIL

BROKEN SPAGHETTI, CAULIFLOWER, AND CHAMOMILE

SHE IS SO INTELLIGENT AND CREATIVE THAT SHE USED HER PAST AS A SPRINGBOARD INTO THE FUTURE.
— Dominique Crenn

ANTONIA KLUGMANN

ZACH KOLOMEIR

DREYFUS
Toronto, Ontario, Canada

DAVID MCMILLAN

MENU

CROQUE CUBANO

POMMES DAUPHINE

BAKED OYSTERS KAMOURASKA

SALADE D'HOMARD, LOBSTER VINAIGRETTE

CHICKEN WING FRICASSEE, CUCUMBER, AND KOSHER SALAMI

WHOLE GRILLED LAMB SHOULDER AND ACCOUTREMENTS

FRESH MADELEINES AND VALDEÓN

The Dreyfus Affair might not ring any immediate bells for the nonhistory buff, but Montreal native Zach Kolomeir calls back to the nineteenth-century political scandal with each daily unlocking of his Toronto restaurant's doors. The series of injustices took place during the beginning of the rise of antisemitism in Europe—something Kolomeir seeks to defy in his everyday work by flipping the narrative of history's missteps to create modern joy.

Kolomeir's cooking style at his restaurant Dreyfus, in the heart of Toronto's Harbord Village, is a nod to his Jewish upbringing in Montreal mixed with French and broadly European influences. Montreal is a cohesive smorgasbord of culture, and he aims to bring that sentiment to his place in Toronto—it was also in Montreal that he cut his teeth in the culinary scene. A Liverpool House and Joe Beef veteran, where he began as a busboy and left a chef de cuisine in 2018, Kolomeir is widely regarded for his ability to cook on a deep, soulful level. His specialties today ranging from challah to pommes dauphine. He is also certainly not shy when it comes to cooking with butter. As one of the few French-Jewish restaurants in North America, Dreyfus hits all the right notes on both facets of its dual identity.

Named "Toronto's best new bistro" by *Toronto Life* magazine in 2019, Dreyfus's handwritten daily menu is perpetually evolving, a reflection of the dynamic offerings sourced from local purveyors and at the mercy of the seasons. Kolomeir, a graduate of the Culinary Institute of America, works alongside his partner, Carmelina Imola, the wine buyer and manager. Together, they are subtly bringing a social statement to the city through European-accented and refined Jewish deli fare, proving that food and politics can coexist.

CROQUE CUBANO
Makes 30 sandwiches

3 kg pork shoulder, deboned • 450 g salt • 300 g ground white pepper • 1 tablespoon pink curing salt • Neutral oil • 1 loaf Harbord Bakery rye bread • 1 cup béchamel • 2 cups mustard • 500 g Swiss cheese • 10 dill pickles • Vegetable oil

Season the pork with salt, white pepper, and curing salt. Let sit for 2 days covered.
Preheat the oven to 285°F (140°C).
Place the pork in a nonreactive dish and cover with neutral oil. Bake until tender. Pull from the oil and place in a square vessel lined with plastic wrap and press overnight. Once the pork is pressed and cooled, remove from the container and cut bricks the size of fish sticks (or your desired shape).
Cut the rye bread very thin and trim to the same size as the pork sticks. Brush half of the slices with béchamel and half of the slices with mustard and place one of each on each side of the pork.
Cut the Swiss cheese and pickles very thin to the same length as the sandwiches.
Set a sauté pan over medium heat and add some vegetable oil. Add the sandwiches meat-side down and sear on all sides. Once crispy, top with mustard and a slice of Swiss. Melt the Swiss and top with a slice of pickle.

BAKED OYSTERS KAMOURASKA
Makes 24 oysters

2 onions, diced • 1 head celery, diced • 4 cloves garlic, diced • 2 teaspoons unsalted butter • 3 lb (1.4 kg) spinach • 1 cup (240 ml) white wine • 1 cup (250 ml) cream • ½ cup (28 g) fresh bread crumbs • ½ cup (120 ml) mayonnaise • 1 cup (90 g) grated Parmesan cheese • 1 cup smoked shrimp • 1 cup diced smoked eel • 1 cup diced smoked sturgeon • Salt and freshly ground black pepper • Cayenne pepper • Fresh lemon juice • 24 East Coast oysters (deep cup for more stuffing) • Rock salt and lemon wedges, for serving

In a sauté pan, sweat the onion, celery, and garlic in the butter and cook slowly until translucent.
In large pot of boiling water, blanch the spinach. Cool and chop.
Add the chopped spinach to the sweated vegetables, bring back up to heat, and add the white wine. Reduce by half. Add the cream and reduce by half again. Set aside and cool. Once chilled, add the bread crumbs, mayonnaise, and ½ cup (45 g) of the Parmesan to the mix. Add all the smoked fishes to the filling. Season with salt, pepper, cayenne, and lemon juice. Set aside.
Preheat the oven to 425°F (220°C).

FRESH MADELEINES

Line a sheet pan with foil that's been crumpled so it has little spots for the oysters to sit on while they bake.

Shuck the oysters and top with the filling. Bake until bubbling, 5–6 minutes.

Garnish with the rest of the grated Parmesan and serve on top of rock salt with a lemon wedge.

CHICKEN WING FRICASSEE, CUCUMBER, AND KOSHER SALAMI
Serves 4

12 chicken wings • Neutral oil • Salt and ground white pepper • 1 onion, diced • 1 clove garlic, minced • 1 tablespoon brandy • ½ cup (120 ml) white wine • 1 cup (240 ml) white chicken stock • 1 tablespoon coriander seeds • 1 tablespoon black peppercorns • 1 teaspoon paprika • ⅓ cup (75 ml) sherry vinegar • 1 cup (240 ml) sunflower oil • ½ cup (65 g) diced Lebanese cucumber • ½ cup (60 g) sliced Lebanese cucumber • 1 cup diced kosher salami • 1 dill pickle, diced • ½ cup (60 g) sliced lemon cucumber • 15 sprigs of picked dill • 3 tablespoons brown butter

Bone the chicken wings. (Probably the hardest part, but so rewarding to eat a boned-out chicken wing.) It's fine if the skin tears a bit as we are not stuffing them. Preheat the oven to 350°F (180°C). Heat a sauté pan over medium-high heat and add some neutral oil. Season the chicken wings with salt and white pepper. Add to the pan and sear until golden. Once the wings are golden, pour the fat out of the pan, leaving the wings. Add the onion, garlic, and a small amount more of the neutral oil to the pan and cook over low heat until translucent. Add the brandy and flambé. Add the white wine and reduce by half. Add the white stock and as it is reducing, add the pan with wings and liquid to the oven and bake for 12–15 minutes. Meanwhile, dry-toast the coriander seeds and peppercorns in a pan. Coarsely grind the spices. In a bowl, mix the ground spices with the paprika, sherry vinegar, and sunflower oil for the coriander vinaigrette. Pull the chicken out of the oven after the allotted time and glaze with the liquid. Add the diced and sliced Lebanese cucumbers, salami, and dill pickle to the pan and toss to glaze everything and warm it through. Serve 3 wings on each plate with a lot of the sauce and garnish. Garnish with fresh lemon cucumber, fresh dill, a spoon of the coriander vinaigrette, and a touch of brown butter. (I sometimes like to also add a spoonful of yogurt or sour cream and a spoonful of spicy horseradish mustard from Kozlik's.)

SALADE D'HOMARD, LOBSTER VINAIGRETTE

CHICKEN WING FRICASSEE

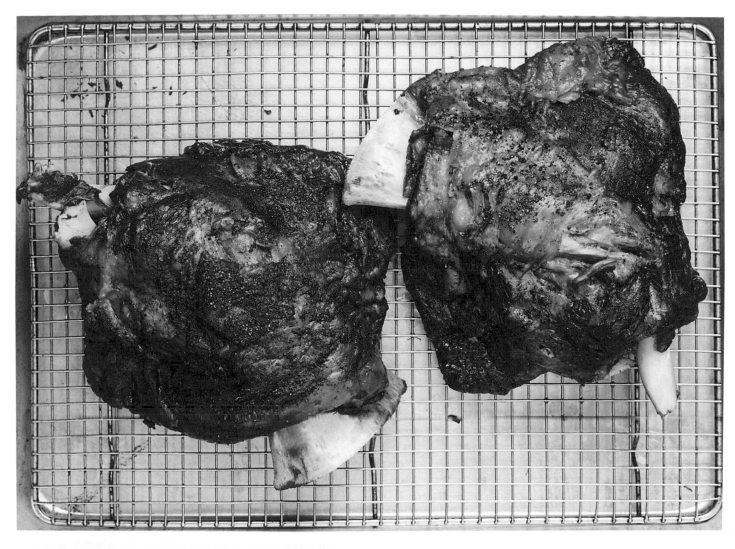

Guitar Lessons
416-975-9035

THE COMBINATION
OF THESE TWO
BACKGROUNDS—
FRENCH AND JEWISH—
IS EXTREMELY
UNIQUE. HE'S COOKING
FROM HIS SOUL; IT'S
BRILLIANT.
— David McMillan

ZACH KOLOMEIR

BERNARD KORAK

ANA ROŠ

Bernard Korak is the chef of the Korak Family Estate—the family vineyards in the Samobor Highlands of Plešivica, Croatia. His grandfather founded the winemaking enterprise, and in 2019, Bernard launched a restaurant there. Plešivica is known for its progressive wines, and the Korak vineyards produce what are considered some of the finest Croatian wines on the market. But the food program at the vineyard was focused on catering before Korak decided to up the ante by creating the first fine-dining establishment in the region.

Korak came to cooking relatively late. Growing up on his family's vineyard, he helped with the viticulture and vegetable farming. While he sometimes lent a hand as a waiter or cook at his family's small restaurant near their vineyard, he was more focused on training as a structural engineer. Still, the world of the kitchen called to him, and so he hired on for a two-month cooking gig in a seasonal restaurant in Zabar to see how it felt. Despite the long hours and hard work, the job agreed with him, and Korak got an internship at Dubravkin Put, in Zagreb, under Chef Priska Thuring. She eventually offered Korak a job, at which he remained for a year. Similarly, an internship at Ana Roš's acclaimed Hiša Franko in Slovenia led to a job offer and he accepted, under the condition that Roš would help arrange an internship for him when Hiša Franko was closed for the season. He wanted to train at Osteria Francescana, Massimo Bottura's restaurant in Modena, Italy, at the time ranked first on the World's 50 Best Restaurants list. Roš made good on this promise, and Korak was also able to cook under and learn from Bottura.

Korak has never seen his lack of formal culinary education as a hindrance. His innate curiosity and tenacity set him apart and made him a coveted addition to the kitchens of some of the finest chefs in the world. Now Korak is his own master, creating tasting-menu meals that he strives to make unfold like a suspenseful thriller, each course giving way to new sensations and possibilities.

MENU

MIRAS MILK-FRESH CHEESE WITH SWEET PAPRIKA FAT

SKUTA—TOASTED POLENTA IN SOUR WHEY

RAVIOLI—FERMENTED HOMEMADE RICOTTA

TEPKA PEAR—PEAR, PARSLEY ROOT, FOIE GRAS

TROUT—BLACK CHESTNUTS, CLEMENTINE

WILD DUCK—ROSE HIP, SUNCHOKE, AND SHALLOTS

BITTER ALMOND ICE CREAM

TEPKA PEAR—PEAR, PARSLEY ROOT, FOIE GRAS
Serves 4

For the tepka pear:
2 tepka pears (120 g each) • Salt and freshly ground black pepper • 100 g rendered duck fat • 4 large sage leaves

For the parsley root puree:
200 g parsley roots, peeled and cut into pieces • 100 ml heavy (whipping) cream

For the sage oil:
100 g sage leaves • 300 g grapeseed oil

For the foie gras sauce:
100 g long duck jus • 100 g chilled foie gras (marinated in salt, pepper, and wild pear–infused grappa)

To finish:
Duck fat • Sage leaves • 50 g wild pear–infused grappa • 10 g butter • 10 g verjus • Fleur de sel • Cracked black pepper

Prepare the pears:
Preheat a combi oven to 185°F (85°C) at 100% steam. Prepare an ice bath.
Halve and core the pears, season with salt and a generous amount of black pepper. Vacuum-seal with the duck fat and sage leaves. Cook in the oven until tender, about 30 minutes. Shock the pears in the ice bath.

Make the parsley root puree:
In a heavy-bottomed pot, combine the parsley roots and cream (it should barely cover the pieces) and cover with a cartouche. Cook over low heat until most of the cream evaporates and the parsley roots soften. Blend with a blender and strain through a chinois. Season with salt.

Make the sage oil:
Prepare an ice bath. In a blender, combine the sage leaves and oil and puree on high speed for about 2 minutes. Transfer to a saucepan and slowly bring to a simmer. Simmer for 30 seconds. Immediately chill the oil over the ice bath. Strain through a coffee filter.

Make the foie gras sauce:
In a saucepan, bring the duck jus to a boil. Remove from the heat and add the cold foie gras, then blend with a hand blender until the foie gras melts and the sauce foams.

To finish:
Cut the cooked tepka pear into quarters. Preheat a heavy cast-iron skillet, drizzle with duck fat, and sear the tepka pear quarters on both cut sides. Add the sage leaves and deglaze the skillet with the grappa. Remove from the heat and add the butter. Swirl the pear with the butter and sage until the butter melts down. Season with fleur de sel and black pepper.
To plate, add a spoonful of parsley root puree to the middle of a plate and set 2 pear quarters on top of it. Cover the pear with the foamy foie gras sauce and 2 drops of sage oil.

WILD DUCK — ROSE HIP, SUNCHOKE, AND SHALLOTS

Serves 2

For the wild duck:
1 wild duck (about 600 g)

For the rose hip sauce:
3 liters wild duck stock • 300 g rose hips •
100 ml apple juice

For the rose hip glaze:
Rose hips (reserved from Rose Hip Sauce,
above) • 1 liter apple juice • 100 g forest honey

For the sunchoke foam:
4 large Jerusalem artichokes (about 400 g) •
300 ml wild duck stock • 100 ml whole milk
• Salt

For the shallots:
2 shallots • 30 g Rose Hip Glaze *(above)*
• Salt

To finish:
Salt and freshly ground black pepper •
Duck fat • Rose Hip Sauce *(above)*

Prepare the wild duck:
Using hooks, hang the duck by its neck in the
refrigerator with good air circulation until
the skin of the duck is dried, 7 to 10 days.

Make the rose hip sauce:
In a wide-bottomed stockpot, combine the
duck stock, rose hips, and apple juice and
bring to a simmer over high heat. Reduce
the heat to low and simmer until the stock is
reduced by half. Strain the stock and reserve
the rose hips for the glaze.

Transfer the stock to a pot and simmer until
it reduces to 500 ml. Strain **through** a sieve
lined cheesecloth (muslin) and chill over an
ice bath.

Make the rose hip glaze:
In a saucepan, combine the rose hips and
apple juice and bring to a simmer. Process
the rose hips and liquid through a food mill,
then strain through cheesecloth. Place the
strained mixture in a pot and cook until
reduced by half. Mix in the honey and chill
over an ice bath.

Make the sunchoke foam:
Preheat the oven to 320°F (160°C).
Wrap the Jerusalem artichokes in foil and
bake for 45 minutes.
When cool enough to handle, halve the
roots. Use a spoon the scrape out the meat.
(Reserve the skins to use in a different
recipe.)
In a pot, combine the Jerusalem artichoke
meat, duck stock, and milk and simmer over
low heat for 30 minutes.
Transfer to a blender and blend on high
speed. Pass through a fine-mesh sieve.
Season with salt.
Transfer to a whipper siphon and charge
twice.

Prepare the shallots:
Preheat a combi oven to 185°F (85°C) at
100% steam. Prepare an ice bath.
Peel the shallots, leaving the root ends so
they keep their shape while cooking. Vacuum-seal the shallots, and rose hip glaze,
and salt to taste. Cook in the oven for 35
minutes. Shock in the ice bath.

To finish:
Preheat a convection oven to 400°F
(200°C), high fan.
Cut the head, the neck, the wing tips and
midwing section from the duck, reserving
the neck and wing pieces for stock. Remove
and discard the wishbone. Truss the duck
with butcher's twine. Rub the duck with
the rose hip glaze evenly, and coat it evenly
with salt and black pepper. Roast the duck,
hanging by the legs, for 9 minutes. While
roasting, brush the duck with a single layer
of the rose hip glaze. Remove from the oven
and let it rest at room temperature for 15
minutes before carving.
With a sharp knife, remove the breast and
brush the meat side with the rose hip glaze.
Reserve the carcass for stock.
Halve the shallots lengthwise, making
sure to cut through the middle of the root.
Heat up a skillet over medium heat and
sear the shallots in duck fat on the flat side.
Remove from heat when the shallots are
heated through.
To plate, dispense a spoonful of sunchoke
foam onto the middle of the plate. Season
with a pinch of black pepper. Place the
shallots on one side of the plate seared-side
up, and the duck breast on the other side of
the plate. Drizzle the rose hip sauce around
the plate.

A YOUNG CHEF WHOSE CAREER WAS SUPPOSED TO BE SOMETHING COMPLETELY DIFFERENT— BUT THROUGH HIS DEDICATION HE IS GOING TO BECOME ONE OF THE BEST BALKAN CHEFS.

— Ana Roš

TEPKA PEAR

MIRAS MILK

177

BERNARD KORAK

LUKA KOŠIR

ANA ROŠ

MENU

TROUT ROE, KOJI BRIOCHE, SMOKED EGG YOLK, ROSA DE GORIZIA

ADRIATIC SEA BREAM COOKED IN BEESWAX AND PRESERVED FLOWERS

CABBAGE REBLOCHON

DUCK AND PITURALKA PEARS

GOAT COLOSTRUM WITH PRESERVED FRUITS AND BEECH LEAVES

Since 2009, Luka Košir of restaurant Grič has helped define Slovenian cooking through his love of exceptional local produce. Tucked away in a small village near Slovenian capital Ljubljana, Grič has become one of the country's finest restaurants since Košir took the helm. He is prized for his unfussy ingredient-focused style, making his restaurant a destination for Ljubljana food lovers.

Košir's career began at JB Restaurant in Ljubljana, where he was mentored by chef-owner Janez Bratovž. Košir decided to return to Grič, the then-humble restaurant that his father had started in 1993. Under Košir's direction, Grič evolved from a local lunch spot, which people visited on bike rides, to a full-blown, reservation-only tasting-menu establishment. Simply decorated with exposed beams, wood surfaces, and white accents; Grič is traditional yet contemporary, a perfect reflection of Košir's food ethos. Košir sources 80 percent of the menu from the Košir family farm, local gardens, and the wild. As such, the menu is ever-changing with the seasons and relies heavily on house-made preserves to supply variety. Traditional preserving techniques, such as pickling, fermentation, salting, drying, smoking, curing, and conserving, help maintain a larder of proprietary ingredients that he draws from year-round.

Košir's contribution to Slovenian cuisine extends past his kitchen to the land: he also created Slovenia's first certified organic duck farm on the slopes of Lavrovca, where he cultivates free-range ducks that breed naturally. In doing so, he is paving the way for other Slovenian producers and farmers to embrace ecological husbandry practices by showing them that it is not only possible, it is preferable.

Košir refers to Grič as a family-run restaurant, and indeed, with four young children—who will perhaps someday join him in the kitchen—he is a family man. Thanks in large part to his contributions, Slovenia was awarded the official title European Region of Gastronomy 2021.

TROUT ROE, KOJI BRIOCHE, SMOKED EGG YOLK, ROSA DE GORIZIA
Serves 8

For the koji brioche:
250 g all-purpose (plain) flour • 150 g eggs • 30 g granulated sugar • 7 g salt • 14 g active dry yeast • 100 g blackened barley koji • 200 g unsalted butter • 1 egg yolk

For the smoked egg cream:
8 Muscovy duck eggs • 500 g applewood-smoked salt • 500 g brown sugar • 100 g poppyseed miso

For plating:
Brioche cut 1½ inch (4 cm) wide and ⅜ inch (1 cm) thick • 50 g softened butter • 4 heads Rosa de Gorizia radicchio, broken into petals • 80 g brown trout roe • 20 ml fig vinegar in a spray bottle

Make the brioche:
In a stand mixer fitted with the dough hook, knead together the flour, eggs, sugar, salt, and yeast. Add the koji and butter in three separate additions. Continue kneading until the dough stops sticking to the sides of the bowl and becomes smooth, elastic, and firm. Finish by folding in the egg yolks. Let sit for 1½ hours.
Punch the dough down. Divide up and mold. Let rise at room temperature, until the dough reaches almost twice its size. Meanwhile, preheat the oven to 375°F (190°C).
Bake the brioche until the tops are lightly browned, about 7 minutes.

Make the smoked egg cream:
Crack the eggs and separate the yolks from the whites.
Mix together the smoked salt and brown sugar. Spread half of the mixture on a sheet pan, put the yolks directly on the salt/sugar mixture, then sprinkle them with the remaining salt/sugar mixture. Store in a dry refrigerator for 24 hours.
Wash the egg yolks under lukewarm water to remove all the excess salt mixture. Arrange them on a parchment-lined tray and put into well-ventilated refrigerator to dry for 5 hours.

Take two 8-inch (20 cm) squares of cheesecloth (muslin) and rub the miso paste into them. When the cloth is saturated with miso, put one cloth on the tray and spread the yolks over it, then cover the yolks with the second cloth. Leave the yolks in the miso for a minimum of 24 hours.
Press the yolks through a fine-mesh sieve and store in refrigerator for up to 1 week.

To plate:
Brush each brioche with butter and warm up over embers until it becomes crusty. Spread egg cream on the brioche, top the egg cream with petals of Rosa de Gorizia and a spoon of trout roe. For the finish, gently spray each brioche with fig vinegar.

CABBAGE REBLOCHON
Serves 8

1 kg water • 20 g salt • 10 g trout garum • 50 g fresh goat milk whey • 1 head cabbage (about 1.5 kg) • 3 kg aged beef tallow, for coating • 200 g raw sheep butter • 185 g sheep milk reblochon cheese, cut into 8 slices (a generous ⅛ inch/4 mm thick)

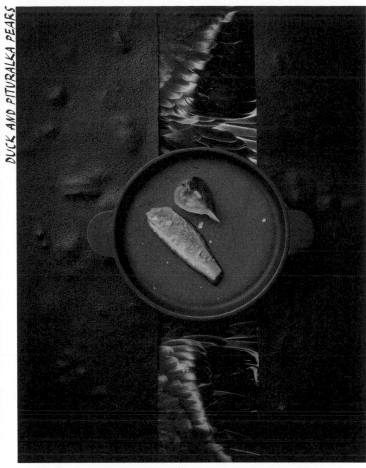

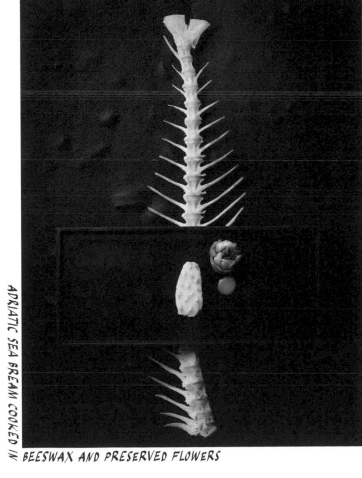

ADRIATIC SEA BREAM COOKED IN

BEESWAX AND PRESERVED FLOWERS

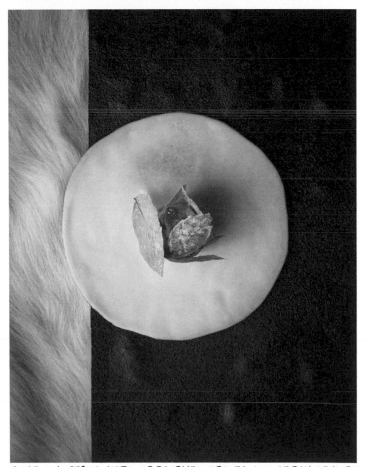

GOAT COLOSTRUM WITH PRESERVED FRUITS AND BEECH LEAVES

179

In a bowl, mix together the water, salt, garum, and goat whey, stirring until the salt dissolves. Vacuum-seal the cabbage and the brine on 100%. After 5 hours unpack the cabbage and dry it for 2 hours.

In a deep pot, warm the beef tallow over low heat.

Tie a string around the cabbage (this will make it easier to handle) and holding it by the strings, immerse the whole cabbage in the warm beef tallow until it is completely covered. Repeat this a few times, so there are no cracks left on the surface. Leave one part of the string outside for the repressure. Let the cabbage age for at least 2 weeks. The temperature should not exceed 59°F (15°C). Turn it regularly and remove all excess fluid. After the aging, peel the tallow and save it. The smell of the cabbage should be pleasant, lightly acidic, and fruity.

Cut the cabbage in half, cook it sous vide at 90°C for 30 to 40 minutes,. Cool it down in an ice bath.

Open the bag and remove the cabbage, reserving all the cabbage liquid. Core the halves and cut each half into four wedges 2 inches (5 cm) thick. Put the cores and all the trimmings into a juicer and mix it with the reserved cabbage cooking liquid. Transfer the mixture to a pan and cook until reduced by half. Emulsify the liquid with the raw butter and save the cabbage butter sauce for later.

Tie the cabbage wedges with butcher's twine. In a sauté pan, heat one spoon of reserved tallow from the cabbage over medium heat. Add the cabbage pieces and pan roast until golden brown on both sides. Put the cabbage in deep plates. Bake the reblochon cheese in a nonstick pan on both sides so the outside is crispy and the middle still melting. Put two spoonfuls of cabbage butter sauce in each plate and top with the reblochon.

DUCK AND PITURALKA PEARS
Serves 8

For the rub:
50 g pumpkin seed shoyu • 50 g acacia honey • 15 g salt • 10 g garlic • 15 g fermented blue plum paste

For poaching:
2 liters water • 200 g pumpkin seed shoyu • 50 g acacia honey • 20 g juniper berries • 12 g bay leaf • 10 g fennel seeds • 10 g whole cloves • 10g black peppercorns • 20 g garlic

For the duck:
1 Rouen Clair drake (about 3+ kg), aged with innards 7–8 days • 100 ml birch syrup • 50 ml oatmeal stout • 2 kg mountain hay • 4 Pituralka pears • Vegetable oil, for frying
For serving:
20 g fermented birch water syrup • 25 g heather–olive oil infusion • Flaky salt (optional)

Make the rub:
Combine the shoyu, honey, salt, garlic, and fermented plum paste and blend to a paste.

Make the poaching liquid:
In a stockpot, combine the water, shoyu, honey, and spices. Bring a boil and boil for 10 minutes before using.

Prepare the duck:
Clean the duck, tie the neck with a string, being careful not to damage the neck. Reserve the heart, liver. and gizzard to make duck pâté. (Reserve the head to prepare the following way: Cut the head on half and bake it over a wood fire until the brains slightly pop out. Serve it on crusty brioche with mountain ash jam.) When the duck is clean, separate the skin from the flesh using an air compressor. Rub the duck's cavity with the rub and truss it. Hang the duck over the pot of boiling poaching liquid and carefully ladle the hot liquid over the duck so the skin firms up. Let the duck air-fry.

In a bowl, stir together the birch syrup and stout. Brush the duck with half of the mixture. Allow the duck to hang in cool and well-ventilated chamber for 4–5 days so the skin dries up well.

Preheat the oven to 345°F (175°C). Before baking the duck, open the cavity and let it dry, brush it with the remaining birch and beer liquid. Fill a deep roasting pan with hay and pears, put the duck inside and cover it with more hay. Cover the pan tightly but leave one-quarter of it open. Transfer to the oven and bake the duck for about 30 minutes. Remove from the oven and hang it for a few minutes over the pan so the juices from the cavity drip out. (Leave the oven on.) Remove the pears from the hay and store them in duck juice in a pan. Return the duck to the oven with hay and bake it until the internal temperature of the breast core is 131°F (55°C). Hang the duck somewhere warm to rest.

In a deep pot, heat the vegetable oil. Suspend the duck over the pot and ladle the oil over the skin so it gets crispy.

To serve:
With the duck on its back, carve off the wings and legs, then the wishbone and the breasts. Reserve the wings and legs. (We save the wings and legs for another preparation, hanging them with the neck over Jerusalem artichokes on light embers, and serving them with the duck carcass–pressed juice.)

Put the pan with the pears and duck-fat juices over medium heat and stir it so the sauce thickens and caramelizes.

Brush the duck breasts with fermented birch syrup, cut it into portions, and serve it with the pears. Finish the dish with few drops of heather oil infusion and sprinkle with salt flakes.

GOAT COLOSTRUM WITH PRESERVED FRUITS AND BEECH LEAVES
Serves 8

For the beech leaves:
Spring beech leaves • Apple cider vinegar • Simple syrup

For the goat colostrum:
120 g brown or muscovado sugar • 300 g heavy (whipping) cream, divided • 500 g goat colostrum • 3 egg yolks • 15 g salt

For serving:
80 g preserved quince • 40 g honey vinegar-preserved rowan berries

Prepare the beech leaves:
Pick young, soft spring beech leaves, put them in a jar, and cover them with apple cider vinegar. Seal the jar with a lid. After 10 months, take out as much as you need, dry them with a paper towel, and put them in simple syrup. To use, drain the excess syrup from the leaves. Place them on a baking mat and let dehydrate at 113°F (45°C) for 24 hours.

Prepare the goat colostrum:
In a saucepan, melt the brown sugar. Add 100 g cream and whisk constantly over medium heat until all the sugar is dissolved. Bring to a boil and allow to boil for about 3 minutes, but no more. Set the caramel aside to cool.

In a separate bowl, mix together the goat colostrum, remaining 200 g cream, egg yolks, and salt. Add the cooled caramel and stir until all the ingredients are blended. Pour the mixture into four 4 ounces (120 ml) ramekins. Cover each one of them with a lid or foil and place them in a baking dish. Steam in a steamer or combi oven at 194°F (90°C) until the centers are barely set, 25–30 minutes. Cool completely. Refrigerate for several hours and up to a couple of days.

To serve:
Top the custards with preserved quince, preserved rowan berries, and beech leaves.

HE CAN TALK ABOUT EVERY WALL
OF THE RESTAURANT AND WHERE
THE WALL COMES FROM, BUT THIS
IS THE SAME WAY THAT HE TALKS
ABOUT HIS DISHES.

— Ana Roš

LUKA KOŠIR

PATRICK KRISS

ALO, ALOETTE
Toronto, Ontario, Canada

DANIEL BOULUD

Channeling the character and sophistication of a simpler time, Chef Patrick Kriss has become a veritable culinary icon of Canada. His masterpiece, Alo Restaurant, is a contemporary French spot with a classic feel and a whisper of Japanese influence.

Kriss, a native of Toronto, did not grow up with culinary roots. Giving in to the pull of a life in the kitchen, he worked various cooking jobs, including an internship at Rosedale Golf Club. He then landed a position at Auberge du Pommier after studying culinary arts and hospitality at George Brown College. Kriss was then hired at Restaurant Daniel in New York City. From there he made his way to France, where he perfected his rich yet minimalist technique at Régis Marcon and La Maison Troisgros (now known simply as Régis & Jacques Marcon), south of Lyon. Kriss briefly reprised his role at Daniel upon his return to North America in 2009 before then returning to Toronto as chef de cuisine at Splendido.

Known by colleagues as a chef of humility and integrity, Kriss is now back home in Toronto, where his 2015 solo venture Alo Restaurant continues to thrive after being recognized as a best restaurant in Toronto and Canada during its early days. Today, he oversees a trifecta of widely beloved French-accented spots: cozy bistro Aloette and Alobar, a cocktail bar and kitchen focusing on raw cuisine and grilled fare, joined Alo in 2017 and 2019, respectively.

At Kriss's restaurants, guests are met with dishes that are both bold and refreshingly uncomplicated, finessed with his signature minimalist touch. His passions lie not just in creating good food, but in ensuring comfort, warmth, and unmatched hospitality for his guests.

MENU

HOKKAIDO SEA SCALLOP, HIDDEN ROSE APPLE, LEMON THYME, FENNEL POLLEN

KANPACHI, NORI BUTTER, PONZU, YUZU

CAROLINA GOLD RICE, BLACK TRUMPET MUSHROOM, SHIO KOJI, CURED HEN EGG YOLK

EAST COAST LOBSTER, SHIITAKE MUSHROOM, TOM YUM, CELTUCE

SNAKE RIVER FARMS BEEF RIBCAP, MYOGA, PURPLE MUSTARD, BEEF FAT JUS

ONTARIO WILDFLOWER HONEY, MEYER LEMON

HOKKAIDO SEA SCALLOP, HIDDEN ROSE APPLE, LEMON THYME, FENNEL POLLEN
Serves 4

For the apple vinegar:
2 Granny Smith apples, unpeeled, cored and roughly chopped • 2 Gala apples, unpeeled, cored, and roughly chopped • 500 ml white wine vinegar • 100 ml apple cider (cloudy apple juice) • 2 tablespoons Cognac • Salt • Sugar

For the lemon thyme crème fraîche:
500 ml heavy (whipping) cream (35%) • 150 ml buttermilk • Juice of 1 lemon • 1 bunch lemon thyme, roughly chopped and bruised • Salt

For the lemon thyme oil:
1 bunch lemon thyme • Vegetable oil

For the dried apple:
1 Granny Smith apple • 50 ml simple syrup • Lemon juice

For assembly:
250 g Hokkaido scallops • 1 Hidden Rose apple • 1 Gala apple • 1 teaspoon crushed chili flakes • 1 teaspoon fennel pollen • Fleur de sel • Lemon juice • Fennel fronds, for garnish

Make the apple vinegar:
In a bowl, combine the apples, vinegar, cider (cloudy apple juice), Cognac, a pinch of salt, and a few pinches of sugar. Blend with a hand blender. Cover and let sit out at room temperature covered for up to 1 week to slightly ferment. Strain through fine cheesecloth (muslin) or towel. Discard the solids.

Make the lemon thyme crème fraîche:
In a bowl, combine the heavy cream, buttermilk, lemon juice, and lemon thyme. Let sit overnight in the fridge. Strain the thyme. Leave the mixture out at room temperature in a warm place (few degrees higher than room temperature) for up to 3 days to thicken. Season with salt.

Make the lemon thyme oil:
In a pot, combine the lemon thyme and oil to cover. Bring the oil to 140°F (60°C) and maintain for 1 hour to infuse gently. Strain.

IT IMPRESSES ME THAT PATRICK'S FOCUS IS TO EXPAND HIS CULINARY ART THROUGH SMALL RESTAURANTS, SHOWCASING HIS STYLE THAT COMBINES THE CLASSIC ELEGANCE OF FRENCH CUISINE WITH A JAPANESE ELEMENT. — Daniel Boulud

HOKKAIDO SEA SCALLOP

Make the dried apple:
Cut the Granny Smith apple into medium dice. Dress in the simple syrup and a squeeze of lemon juice. Dehydrate in a low oven until chewy in texture and half their original size.

To assemble:
Halve the scallops horizontally. Cut the Hidden Rose apple into thin slices and punch out with a ring cutter to get rounds. Add a dollop of the lemon thyme crème fraîche to a plate. Season the scallops with the chili flakes, fennel pollen, fleur de sel, and a few drops of lemon juice. Add the scallops to the plate. Dress the scallops with a bit of the lemon thyme oil. Garnish the scallops with the dried apple, fresh apple, and the fennel fronds, 3-4 pieces each. Froth the vinegar using a hand blender and blanket the scallops with it.

KANPACHI, NORI BUTTER, PONZU, YUZU
Serves 4

3 yuzus

For the ponzu:
3 sheets kombu • 2 limes • 1 orange, sliced into rounds • 1 lemon, sliced into rounds • 100 ml bonito flakes

For the yuzu rind condiment:
2 yuzus • Salt • Sugar

For the nori butter:
4 sheets nori • 100 ml heavy (whipping) cream (35%) • 200 g unsalted butter, cubed • Salt

For the fish:
500 g kanpachi, skin on • 100 ml barley miso • Oil • 500 ml high-quality soy sauce • Juice of 1 sudachi • 1 pink lemon, segmented and cut into small triangles • Fleur de sel • 100 g red radish, julienned

Remove the peel from the 3 yuzus and reserve for the condiment along with one of the fruits for juicing. Set aside one of the yuzus to be juiced for the ponzu and the remaining fruit to be juiced for the fish.

Make the ponzu:
Toast the kombu in an oven for a few minutes. Slice 1 of the limes (reserve the other for juice). In a bowl, combine the sliced citrus, bonito, kombu, and soy sauce. Refrigerate for 1 day or more to infuse. Juice the reserved yuzu and reserved lime and stir into the ponzu. Strain.

Make the yuzu rind condiment:
Juice one of the reserved yuzus. Dress the yuzu rind with the juice, a pinch of salt, and a pinch of sugar. Macerate for 1 hour. Chop the rind into a fine paste with the juice and reserve.

Make the nori butter:
Toast the nori sheets. In a small saucepan, reduce the cream by three-quarters. Mount in cubes of butter to emulsify. Transfer this mixture to a blender and blend in the toasted nori sheets. Season with salt.

Prepare the fish:
Cut the fish into 100 g portions, leaving the skin on. Mix the barley miso with the juice of the remaining yuzu. Brush the flesh of the fish with this mixture and let sit at room temperature for 30 minutes. Do not brush the skin.
In a hot pan with oil (or on a grill if preferred), cook the fish skin-side down until the skin is crispy. Remove and torch the flesh until the miso marinade caramelizes and slightly cooks the fish. Cut the portions in half after cooking.

To plate:
Add a spoon of the ponzu in the center of the plate. Add a few swirls of nori butter to the ponzu so it sits on top. Lay the halved fish portions flat to expose the cut side. Dress with the sudachi juice, some segments of the pink lemon, fleur de sel, yuzu rind condiment, and the radish. Place the fish on top of the 2 sauces.

EAST COAST LOBSTER, SHIITAKE MUSHROOM, TOM YUM, CELTUCE
Serves 4

For the lobster:
3 East Coast lobsters (about 1½ lb/680 g each)

For the garnish:
1 pound (455 g) shiitake mushrooms • Vegetable oil • Salt • 2 tablespoons basil seeds • 1 pound (455 g) celtuce, brunoise • 2 tablespoons rice wine vinegar • Sugar • ½ bunch cilantro (fresh coriander) • 1 bunch parsley

For the sauce:
150 g unsalted butter • 250 ml dry white vermouth • 3 cloves garlic, smashed • 1 shallot, sliced • 1 piece galangal, roughly chopped • 1 Thai chili, halved • 2 stalks lemongrass, roughly chopped • 1 liter chicken stock • ½ bunch Thai green basil • ½ bunch cilantro (fresh coriander) • 5 makrut lime leaves • Jasmine rice • Lime juice

For plating:
1 bunch Thai purple basil or cress, leaves picked • 1 bunch lemon balm or cress, leaves picked

Prepare the lobster:
Bring a large pot of water to a boil to cook the lobster. Separate the heads from the bodies and set aside for the sauce. Separate the claws and tails. Cook the tails for 3½ minutes, small claw for 4½ minutes, large claw for 6 minutes. Crack the meat from the various parts and cut into ¼-inch (6 mm) chunks. Reserve.

Make the garnish:
Discard the shiitake stems and put the caps in a saucepan with vegetable oil to cover. Lightly season with salt and poach as gently as possible until tender. Cut each cap into sixths to make triangles. Set aside.
Bloom the basil seeds by adding tepid water. Drain. Season the celtuce with the rice vinegar, some salt, some sugar, and the hydrated basil seeds to taste. It should taste like a light pickle. Set aside.
In a blender, combine the cilantro (coriander) and parsley, cover with vegetable oil, and blend on high for 5 minutes. Strain the cilantro oil through fine cheesecloth (muslin) or a coffee filter (discard the solids).

Make the sauce:
Take the reserved lobster heads and break apart as much as you can. In a stand mixer fitted with the paddle, combine the lobster heads and the butter and blend together. In a pot or large saucepan, heat a splash of vegetable oil. Sauté and sweat the lobster in the hot oil for 5 minutes. Add the vermouth and deglaze until dry and fully evaporated. In a pressure cooker, heat some vegetable oil. Add the garlic, shallots, galangal, chili, and lemongrass and sweat for 5 minutes. Once translucent add the lobster mix. Sweat 1 minute. Add the chicken stock, Thai basil, cilantro, and lime leaves. Pressure cook everything for 30 minutes.
Strain the broth and weigh in grams. Take 5% of that weight and weigh out the jasmine rice. Cook the rice in the broth until tender. Blend the rice into the broth on high to thicken. Strain again. Add another few sprigs of cilantro and Thai basil while hot to infuse some fresh aromatics into the broth. Season the broth to taste with salt and lime juice. Reserve.

To plate:
Use a bowl-type vessel. Place the shiitake triangles in first, followed by the reserved lobster meat, gently heated. Heat the broth and add 4–5 tablespoons of the cilantro oil to it. Mix the oil throughout the broth and liberally dress and cover the lobster and mushrooms in it. Scatter the celtuce over the lobster meat. Garnish with the purple basil and lemon balm.

PATRICK KRISS

MERLIN LABRON-JOHNSON

SKYE GYNGELL

OSIP
London, England

MENU

TREACLE AND ALE BREAD, POTTED PHEASANT

SMOKED BEET TARTARE, CULTURED CREAM AND AMARANTH

LEEKS WITH A CHOPPED EGG VINAIGRETTE AND FRIED CROUTONS

ROAST CELERY ROOT, MACADAMIA NUT AND CAVALO NERO SAUCE

JERUSALEM ARTICHOKES, ROAST CHICKEN JUICES AND DIVER SCALLOP

WILD DUCK, HAY BAKED APPLE, CABBAGE AND SOURDOUGH BREAD SAUCE

HAZELNUT PRALINE ÉCLAIR

Chef Merlin Labron-Johnson is on a mission: he is determined to use food as his means for leaving the world a better place than he found it. Uninterested in academics as a youth, Labron-Johnson got his start cooking while helping out in his school's cafeteria kitchen. Exploring further, Labron-Johnson got a job as a chef's assistant at the Ashburton Cookery School. Next, his first real restaurant work was at the Elephant in Torquay under Simon Hulstone, followed by a stint at ABode in Exeter, under chef Michael Caines. Labron-Johnson spent the next four years cooking abroad, first in Switzerland and then in France. But after all that training and experience, it was the two years that Labron-Johnson spent at In De Wulf, Chef Kobe Desramaults's renowned contemporary restaurant in the Belgian countryside, that was most formative for him; that's also where Labron-Johnson developed his love of fermentation.

The opportunity to open the London restaurant Portland came while he was at In De Wulf, and led to a seminal first experience as executive chef. In 2015, at age 24, Labron-Johnson became the youngest British chef to receive a Michelin star. With his Portland partners, Labron-Johnson opened the more informal Clipstone, also in the Fitzrovia neighborhood. In 2018, Labron-Johnson was included in the Forbes 2019 Europe 30 Under 30: Arts & Culture list. Now, as executive chef-owner of Osip, a tiny restaurant in Bruton, Somerset, he sources hyper locally from farmers, hunters, and foragers nearby for his seasonal dinner and à la carte lunch tasting menus. Additionally, he and his staff cultivate a biodynamic garden at the restaurant.

When Labron-Johnson is not in the garden or the kitchen, he is in the field with grassroots movements working to change our food system. In 2018 and 2019 he spent time in Greece, cooking 1,000 meals a day at a refugee camp, and working to inspire displaced male youths with an interest in cooking to foster their employability. He's also a regular cook at Refettorio Felix at St. Cuthbert's Centre, the community kitchen started by Massimo Bottura. Labron-Johnson is the rare chef whose talent is matched by an indefatigable commitment to his community.

LEEKS WITH A CHOPPED EGG VINAIGRETTE AND FRIED CROUTONS
Serves 4 as a starter

2 medium leeks, thoroughly cleaned and dark green tops removed (reserve for stock) • Salt • 2 duck eggs or 3 hen eggs, boiled for 6 to 7 minutes depending on size • 2 gherkins, diced • ½ shallot, diced • Handful of tarragon, chopped • Handful of parsley, chopped • Freshly ground black pepper • Lemon juice • Olive oil • 2 slices stale bread, cut into cubes • Mustard leaves, for garnish

Find a pot big enough to accommodate the leeks and fill it with water. Bring to a boil and add a healthy handful of salt. The water should taste as salty as the sea! Boil the leeks until they show no resistance when pierced with a knife, about 7 minutes. Refresh in cold water and pat dry.
Peel the eggs and finely chop until you have a sloppy, eggy mixture. Mix with the gherkins, shallot, tarragon, and parsley. Season with salt, pepper, and a squeeze of lemon juice.
In a frying pan, heat a little olive oil and fry the bread cubes until crispy and golden, then drain on paper towels.
Cut the leeks into rounds or long pieces depending on your mood. Or split them lengthwise. Divide among 4 plates and

dress them with the chopped egg vinaigrette so that they are completely covered. Top each plate with a handful of croutons and a scattering of mustard leaves.

SMOKED BEET TARTARE, CULTURED CREAM, AND AMARANTH
Serves 4

2 large beets • Salt • Olive oil • Organic hay, for smoking • 1 liter beet juice • 100 ml red wine vinegar • 3 tablespoons beet ketchup • 1 tablespoon chopped red onion • Freshly ground black pepper • 120 g cultured cream • 1 bunch amaranth leaves • Vinegar • Toast or flatbreads, for serving

Preheat the oven to 425°F (220°C).
Season the beets with salt, dress with
olive oil, and wrap them in foil. Roast in
the oven until tender when pierced with a
knife, 1 to 1½ hours. Leave to cool in the
foil for 20 minutes before using a cloth to
rub off the skin.

Gently smoke the beets over organic hay in a
covered grill (barbecue) or using the smoke-
box in a combi oven.

Meanwhile, in a saucepan, combine the beet
juice and vinegar and boil until reduced to
a loose syrup. Pass through a sieve and leave
to cool. The mixture should thicken a little
more as it cools.

Finely chop the beet and toss together with
the beet ketchup, red onion, and salt and
pepper to taste.

Plate the mixture in a ring mold and place
a spoonful of cultured cream in the middle.
Finish with a small spoonful of the beet juice
in the middle of the cream. Lightly dress the
amaranth leaves with oil and vinegar and set
over the beet. Serve with toast or flatbreads.

HAZELNUT PRALINE ÉCLAIR
Serves 6

For the choux pastry:
250 ml whole milk • 270 ml water • 200 g
unsalted butter • Pinch of salt • 150 g bread
(strong) flour • 150 g all-purpose (plain)
flour • 4 eggs

For the hazelnut cream:
500 ml whole milk • 120 g sugar • 90 g
organic hazelnut praline paste (or house-
made) • 150 g egg yolks • 50 g all-purpose
(plain) flour • 50 g cornstarch (corn flour) •
1 sheet gelatin, soaked in cold water • 100 g
unsalted butter, diced, at room temperature
• Sea salt

For the milk jam:
1 liter raw milk • 100 g cane sugar • 1 tablespoon baking soda (bicarbonate of soda) •
Sea salt

To finish:
**Handful of organic hazelnuts or cobnuts,
toasted and roughly chopped • Sea salt •
Powdered (icing) sugar**

Make the choux pastry:
Preheat a convection oven to 375°F (190°C)
with medium fan.

In a saucepan, bring the milk, water, butter,
and salt to a boil. Stir in both flours, mix
well with a spatula, and continue to cook
until the paste comes away from the sides
of the pan, about 4 minutes. Transfer the
mixture to the bowl of a stand mixer and
leave to cool. When cool, attach the paddle
and slowly incorporate the eggs, one by one
while mixing continuously.

Line a baking sheet with parchment paper
or a silicone baking mat. Transfer the choux
paste to a piping bag and pipe onto the
lined pan into éclair shapes. The éclairs will
double in size during cooking so be careful
to pipe them smaller than the desired end
product. Bake for 9 minutes, then reduce
the temperature to 340°F (170°C) without
opening the oven door and bake for another
10 minutes with lower fan. Remove from the
pan to cool on a rack.

Make the hazelnut cream:
In a saucepan, combine the milk, sugar, and
hazelnut paste and bring to a boil. In a bowl,
whisk the egg yolk, all-purpose flour, and
cornstarch (corn flour) together. Whisking
constantly, incorporate the hot milk into the
mixture. Return the mixture to a saucepan
and cook over medium heat until the mixture
becomes very thick. Make sure you whisk the
mixture while it is thickening to prevent it
from becoming lumpy. Pass through a fine-
mesh sieve and stir in the bloomed gelatin
and the diced butter. Mix well and refrigerate for at least 6 hours to chill.

In a stand mixer fitted with the whisk, whip
the chilled mixture until it is very creamy
and unctuous. Season with a pinch of sea salt
and place in a piping bag.

Make the milk jam:
In a saucepan, bring the milk to a boil and
add the sugar and baking soda (bicarb).
Whisk well and reduce the heat to low.
Cook slowly for a few hours while whisking
occasionally until the mixture is reduced
and taking on a caramel color. It should
start to thicken. When you are happy with
the consistency (like dulce de leche), remove
from the heat and blend with a hand blender
so that it is extra smooth. Season with a good
pinch of sea salt.

To finish:
Slice the éclairs horizontally in half and drizzle the top half with some of the milk jam.
Sprinkle some toasted hazelnuts over the top
and add a pinch of sea salt and a dusting of
powdered (icing) sugar. Pipe the hazelnut
cream onto the bottom half of the éclair and
cover with the top half like a sandwich.

HAZELNUT PRALINE ÉCLAIR

WILD DUCK TOURTE

SMOKED BEET TARTARE

MERLIN IS REALLY
COMMITTED TO THE
BIGGER PICTURE—
SUSTAINABILITY, FOOD
SECURITY, AND FOOD-
WASTE ISSUES. HE FEELS
VERY MUCH LIKE
A CHEF OF NOW.
— *Skye Gyngell*

MERLIN LABRON-JOHNSON

THI LE

ANCHOVY
Richmond, Australia

JESSICA KOSLOW

Thi Le opened the 30-seat Anchovy in the Melbourne, Australia, suburb of Richmond in 2015 with her partner, Jia-Yen Lee. They had only a couple of pots, one pan, and two pizza trays. Le had never led a kitchen, and didn't think she was ready. Lee managed to convince her otherwise, and indeed, Anchovy quickly attracted attention and accolades. The menu, self-described as "modern Asian," "modern Australian," and "a little bit in between," is full of flavor-packed, category-flaunting dishes, and displays a compelling pastiche of influences, from Le's Vietnamese heritage to the contemporary Australian dining scene.

Le honed an interest in food at a young age. She points to her mother's beef tartare, served in an effort to not waste meat after making pho, as making an early impression. In high school, she experimented with Australian grocery-store staples, like Old El Paso taco shells and KanTong chicken sauces, which for Le, raised in the kitchen of her refugee mother, were novel. Later, travelling in Europe as a design student, she found that she took more interest in uncovering food stories than in looking at architecture. When she returned to Sydney, she enrolled in culinary studies at TAFE, Australia's largest vocational institution. Le went on to work for Christine Manfield, known as "The Spice Queen," at Universal, where she developed a familiarity with using bold flavors, and honed her palate. Later, Le was spellbound by the pared-down, simple dishes of Andrew McConnell, who she worked for at Cumulus and the now-closed Luxembourg. McConnell also fostered Le's relationship with fresh produce, and taught her to lead a kitchen.

Now, the menu at Anchovy showcases a culinary proficiency that still melds Le's personal and professional histories. She's known for her dish of Vietnamese blood pudding, served crispy and brightened with herbs and pickled ginger; a salad of pickled sardines, green mango, pomelo, and *rau dang* (knotweed); a wallaby-tail-stuffed savory pastry served with tomato relish; and Le's own version of raw beef, inspired by her childhood, served carpaccio-style, with pencil leeks and *mam*.

MENU

DUCK, RHUBARB, AND PENCIL LEEK KIMCHI

EGGPLANT, COCONUT, PEANUT, AND THAI BASIL

HOUSE-MADE NOODLES, SPANNER CRAB, WARRIGAL GREENS, CURRY SPICE

LOBSTER, KAMPOT PEPPER, AND CURRY LEAF

LAMB, MANCHURIAN SPICE, SERVED WITH HERB GARDEN, PICKLES, CONDIMENTS, BÁNH HOI

BANANA ICE CREAM, GINGER GRANITA, AND GRAPEFRUIT

sliced duck over the rhubarb, then tuck some pencil leek kimchi between each layer of duck. Spoon 1 tablespoon fermented kimchi juice over the duck, then top with 4 or 5 pieces of very thinly sliced raw rhubarb.

EGGPLANT, COCONUT, PEANUT, AND THAI BASIL
Serves 2–3

For the green chili dressing:
35 g garlic • 7–10 g bird's eye chilies • 35 g cilantro (coriander) root • 55 g superfine (caster) sugar • 75 g lime juice • 55 g fish sauce

For the smoked coconut cream:
100 g coconut cream • 2 tablespoons Tea Smoke Mix *(above)*

For assembly:
1 Fairy Tale eggplant • 50 g Green Chili Dressing *(above)* • 2½ tablespoons Smoked Coconut Cream *(above)* • 1 tablespoon fig leaf oil • 2½ tablespoons crushed roasted peanuts • 1 tablespoon pickled shallots • 1 makrut lime leaf, finely slivered • Thai basil

Make the green chili dressing:
Pound the garlic and chilies in a mortar and pestle until smooth. Add the cilantro

DUCK, RHUBARB, AND PENCIL LEEK KIMCHI
Serves 2–3

For the pencil leek kimchi:
35 g garlic • 35 g ginger • 3 bird's eye chilies • 50 g fish sauce • 50 g sugar • 8 g salt • 25 g sriracha sauce, house made • 500 g pencil leeks, cleaned and trimmed to batons • 60 g shrimp paste

For the rhubarb chutney:
60 g shallot, brunoised • 200 ml rice vinegar • 100 g palm sugar • 450 g rhubarb, cleaned and diced • 50 g ginger, brunoised • Mirin

For the tea smoke mix:
60 g tea leaves • 10 g mandarin peel • 50 g jasmine rice • 140 g brown sugar • 40 g star anise • 15 g Sichuan pepper • 20 g cassia bark

For the smoked duck:
1 duck breast • Sea salt • Tea Smoke Mix *(above)*

Make the pencil leek kimchi:
In a blender, combine the garlic, ginger, chilies, fish sauce, sugar, salt, and sriracha to make a rough paste—you do not want it super smooth. Stir in the leeks and shrimp paste. Vacuum-seal and let sit for 1 to 2 months.

Make the rhubarb chutney:
In a pot, combine the shallots, vinegar, and palm sugar. Cook until reduced by half. Add the rhubarb and ginger and cook until the rhubarb is just cooked. Remove from the heat and add mirin to taste.
Season the duck breast with sea salt. Smoke over the tea smoke mix in a wok for 12–15 minutes over medium to low heat. Set aside to rest, then cut lengthwise into 6 slices. To serve, spoon 2 tablespoons of the rhubarb chutney in the center of a plate. Drape the

(coriander) root and pound until smooth. Add the sugar and incorporate until dissolved. Add the lime juice and fish sauce. Check the seasoning—this dressing should be hot.

Make the smoked coconut cream:
Smoke the coconut cream with tea smoke mix for 2 minutes. Set aside.

To assemble and plate:
Steam the eggplant for 5–8 minutes, depending on size. When cool enough to handle, peel and cut into chunks. Place in a bowl and marinate with the green chilli dressing and smoked coconut cream for 1 minute. The eggplant should absorb the

dressing. Add the fig leaf oil. Check the seasoning and adjust if required.
Place the eggplant on plate, cover with the peanuts, shallots, and lime leaf. Garnish with a Thai basil sprig.

LOBSTER, KAMPOT PEPPER, AND CURRY LEAF
Serves 1–2

½ lobster, about 600 g • Cornstarch (corn flour) • Rice flour • Oil • 2 tablespoons minced garlic • 2 tablespoons minced ginger • 2 tablespoons minced shallot • Butter • 2 tablespoons coarsely ground Kampot pepper • 10 g curry leaf • Fish sauce • ½ lime

Lightly dust the lobster in cornstarch (corn flour) and rice flour.
In a wok, fry the lobster in oil over medium heat until just opaque, 4–5 minutes.
Remove from the wok and drain out the oil. Add 3 tablespoons fresh oil to the wok, add the garlic, ginger, and shallot and fry until fragrant. Add 100 g butter, the pepper, and curry leaf and cook to burnt butter stage, taking care to not burn the curry leaf. (The curry leaf should be crispy but not burned.) Season with fish sauce to taste.
To serve, plate the lobster and pour over the pepper sauce. Garnish with lime.

LE USES HONEST INGREDIENTS AND THEIR TEXTURES TO CREATE PUNCHY FLAVOR, AND HER DISHES REALLY DENOTE PLACE. I WANT TO EAT THEM EVERY DAY.
— Jessica Koslow

BANANA ICE CREAM, GINGER GRANITA, AND GRAPEFRUIT

EGGPLANT, COCONUT, PEANUT, AND THAI BASIL

HOUSE-MADE NOODLES, SPANNER CRAB, WARRIGAL GREENS

LAMB, MANCHURIAN SPICE, SERVED WITH HERB GARDEN

LOBSTER, KAMPOT PEPPER, CURRY LEAF

THI LE

PÍA LEÓN

VIRGILIO MARTÍNEZ

In 2018, when Peruvian chef Pía León opened Kjolle in Lima, Peru, she was finally stepping into the spotlight. Before launching Kjolle, León worked for ten years at Central, the internationally acclaimed restaurant that her husband, chef Virgilio Martínez, created and which was awarded Best Restaurant in South America on the World's 50 Best Restaurants list three times.

León always knew she wanted to be a chef. She attended Le Cordon Bleu Peru in Lima, then understook an internship at the Michelin-starred El Celler de Can Roca in Girona, Spain, followed by a stint in at the Ritz-Carlton in New York. A desire to return to her homeland brought León back to Lima. At the time, everyone in their restaurant community was talking about Martínez, who was in the process of starting Central. In 2008, at age 21, León approached Martínez and asked him for a job, a decision that would prove seminal in both her professional life and their personal trajectories.

Now, with Kjolle, León has her own stage on which to direct her culinary vision. She maintains a focus on the products and biodiversity of Peru, from produce to handcrafted plateware, in a relaxed environment that Lima locals can afford to frequent often. León's love of color is expressed throughout the menu with bright ingredients such as flowers, golden squash, purple tubers, and a variety of pink accents, served on colorful custom ceramics.

Kjolle has already landed at number 21 on Latin America's 50 Best Restaurants list and won the Highest Climber Award. León is the recipient of the Elit Vodka Latin America's Best Female Chef Award and has played a critical role in making Lima the culinary destination that it is today.

MENU

SEABASS AND RAZOR CLAMS—
BLACK MASHUA,
AMAZONIAN NUT, ZAPALLO
MACRE SQUASH

SQUASH AND CRUSTACEANS—
LOCHE, RIVER PRAWN,
BITTER ORANGE

MANY TUBERS—
YUCA, OLLUCO, POTATO

BEEF AND CORN—
BURNT CORN, SHICA SHICA, PAICO

CACAO FROM MIL—
CHERIMOYA, AMAZONIAN HONEY

SEABASS AND RAZOR CLAMS
Serves 50

100 razor clams • 200 slices seabass fillet • 15 Amazonian nuts

For the purple tiger's milk:
250 g classic tiger's milk • 250 g black mashua pickling juice • 250 g razor clam stock • Olive oil • Salt

For the pickled mashua:
150 g distilled white vinegar • 150 g water • 150 g panela • 75 g purple corn reduction • 200 g black mashua, thinly sliced

For the pickled squash:
150 g distilled white vinegar • 150 g water • 150 g panela • 200 g Zapallo Macre squash

For the chalaquita sauce:
70 g brunoise tomato • 70 g brunoise cocona • 70 g brunoise red onion • Salt • 30 ml lime juice • 5 g cilantro (fresh coriander), cut into a chiffonade

Clean and cut the razor clams into ⅜-inch (1 cm) pieces. Store them with dry paper. Clean and fillet the fish. Slice the fish sashimi-style and refrigerate.
Toast the Amazonian nuts and then slice as thin as possible on a mandoline.

Make the purple tiger's milk:
In a blender, blend together the tiger's milk, mashua pickling juice, stock, and olive oil. Check the seasoning. Transfer to a squeeze bottle and refrigerate.

Make the pickled mashua:
In a pot, combine the vinegar, water, panela, and corn reduction and bring to boil.
Place the mashua in a heatproof container. Pour the hot pickling juice over the mashua and cool it down. Store in the refrigerator.

Make the pickled squash:
In a pot, combine the vinegar, water, and panela and bring to a boil. Let cool.
Cut the squash into 3½ × 1-inch (9 × 2.5 cm) rectangles and thinly slice on a mandoline. Pour the cold pickling juice over the sliced squash and let it sit for up to 3 days.

Make the chalaquita sauce:
In a bowl, mix together the tomato, cocona, and onion. Season them with salt and add the cilantro (fresh coriander) and lime juice.

To plate, place 5 pieces of fish in the center of the dish leaving a small separation between them. Spread the tiger's milk in the bottom of the dish. Garnish with 3 slices of squash and 3 slices of mashua. Finish by topping with the chalaquita sauce and 3 slices of Amazonian nuts.

MANY TUBERS
Serves 50

For the kañihua dough:
720 g kañihua flour • 1.18 kg all-purpose (plain) flour • 1.32 kg cold butter • 24 g brown sugar • 42 g salt • 572 g cold water

For the goat cheese filling:
1.5 kg goat cream cheese • 1.2 kg mashed potato • 3 eggs • 6 egg yolks • 300 g heavy (whipping) cream • Salt

For the sautéed ollucos:
1 kg yellow ollucos • 1 kg red ollucos • 300 g butter • 100 g honey

To finish:
Raw ollucos

Make the kañihua dough:
In a stand mixer fitted with a dough hook, combine the kañiwa flour, all-purpose (plain) flour, butter, brown sugar, salt, and water and knead until the dough becomes homogeneous. Wrap it in plastic wrap (cling film) and refrigerate.
Preheat the oven to 320°F (160°C).
Roll out the dough and fit into tart molds. Prick the dough all over with a fork. Line the dough with parchment paper and put in pie weights. Bake for 17 minutes. Remove the paper and weights and bake for another 4 minutes.

Let the tart shells cool in the molds before filling. (If continuing to bake the tarts, leave the oven on.)

Make the goat cheese filling:
In a Thermomix, combine the goat cheese, mashed potato, whole eggs, egg yolks, cream, and salt to taste. Blend together and heat to 149°F (65°C). Let cool down, then fill half of the tarts. Bake for 16 minutes in a 608°F (320°C) oven. Let the tarts cool in the molds.

Sauté the ollucos:
Slice the ollucos lengthwise on a mandoline. In a large pan, sauté the yellow ollucos with half the butter and honey. In a separate pan, sauté the red ollucos in the remaining butter and honey. Let them cool down.
Slice the raw ollucos with a mandoline and store them in wet paper.

To serve, reheat the tarts in the oven. Garnish the top of the tarts with the sautéed ollucos.

PÍA HAS SHOWN GREAT CRAFTMANSHIP, COOKING IN A UNIQUE MANNER WITH THE ADDITION OF COLORS, TECHNIQUES, AND TEXTURES ONLY SHE COULD THINK OF.
— Virgilio Martínez

CACAO FROM MIL

SEABASS AND RAZOR CLAMS

MANY TUBERS

PÍA LEÓN

YUVAL LESHEM

EYAL SHANI

MENU

FAVA BEAN MASABAHA SURROUNDED WITH A VEGETABLE CROWN

MAITAKE ENTRECOTE STEAK

BURNED BEET TORTELLINI WITH SAGE BUTTER, POPPY SEEDS, AND PARMESAN

PRECISE DIVINE ROOTS OF EARTH, STEAMED GENTLY

OCEAN TREASURES: LIVE COQUILLE ST. JACQUES, JAPANESE UNI, OSCIETRE CAVIAR, JAPANESE YELLOWTAIL, GIANT OCTOPUS, STORMY WATER SEAWEEDS, RAW TROUT, KING CRAB LEG, HORSERADISH

At HaSalon in New York City's Hell's Kitchen neighborhood, just west of the theater district, dinner is the show. There, with theatrical flourishes, they serve up a taste of Tel Aviv's internationally influenced culinary and nightlife scenes all in one—though the party itself is no distraction from what is quite possibly some of the city's best Israeli food, as realized by executive chef Yuval Leshem.

Leshem opened this outpost of Chef Eyal Shani's Tel Aviv hot spot of the same name in 2019. Prior to that, during his time in the food arena in Israel, Leshem built his career under Shani's gastronomic umbrella, having worked closely with him since the early days of Shani's restaurant group and for more than a decade since as the prolific group grew, leading up to the New York debut of HaSalon. Leshem, who is primarily self-taught, served as culinary director for the group's Tel Aviv restaurants, making him a natural pick for Shani when the opportunity in New York arose.

At HaSalon in NYC, Leshem seems to imbue each meal with his personal stories of New York experiences, using ingredients largely sourced from local greenmarkets and prepared using Israeli and Mediterranean styles and techniques. Japanese and French accents are also layered in.

While the menu changes nightly, HaSalon is beloved for many of its star mainstays: "naked tomato sashimi," a hydroponic tomato peeled, sliced, drizzled in olive oil, and sprinkled with sea salt; avocado bruschetta served on challah bread; and a single twelve-foot-long pici noodle spun into a neat mound and topped with sage. Meats and whole fish are roasted in a *tabun*, a centuries-old style of cone-shaped clay oven, and Middle Eastern wines on tap complement the food.

Leshem's cooking is familiar yet inventive, comforting in a way that, especially in this festive spot, is likely to make you want to dance.

FAVA BEAN MASABAHA SURROUNDED WITH A VEGETABLE CROWN

For the lamb bone broth:
2 kg lamb or goat bones • Olive oil • 2 carrots, roughly chopped • 1 onion, roughly chopped • 1 parsley root, roughly chopped • 1 bulb fennel • 1 tomato, halved • Mineral water

For the favas:
1 kg shelled young fava beans • 3 liters Lamb Bone Broth *(above)* or mineral water

For plating:
Favas *(above)* • 3 spoons tahini • Raw vegetables (such as cucumber, tomato, onions, roots, green chile), cut into elongated shapes • Olive oil

Make the lamb bone broth:
Coat the bones with a little olive oil and roast them in an oven or a tabun preheated to medium-high heat.
Meanwhile, in a large heavy-bottomed pot, caramelize the vegetables in olive oil. Add the roasted bones and add enough mineral water to cover everything in the pot. Bring to a boil, skimming off the foam. Reduce the heat to medium-low and cook for 3–4 hours. Strain.

Prepare the favas:
Pour the fava beans into a heavy pot. Add the bone broth or mineral water and bring to a boil. Cover the surface with a round of parchment paper and foil. Reduce the heat to a minimal flame and cook for 3 hours, until the beans are soft.

To plate:
In a frying pan, heat the beans and reduce the liquids.
With a circular motion, smear tahini in the middle of a plate and pile the fava beans on top of it. Arrange the raw vegetables in concentric circles. Pour on a little bit of olive oil.

BURNED BEET TORTELLINI WITH SAGE BUTTER, POPPY SEEDS, AND PARMESAN

For the tortellini dough:
1¾ cups (220 g) Pivetti pasta flour • ¼ cup (45 g) semolina flour • 1 cup (240 ml) water • 2 g Atlantic sea salt, finely crushed • 1 spoon olive oil • 1 egg

For the beet tortellini:
10 small beets, preferably with some stems still attached • Freshly crushed black pepper (in a mortar and pestle) • Butter • Semolina, for dusting

For assembly:
Salt • 5 Beet Tortellini *(above)* • ¼ cup mineral water • 25 g butter • A fragment of shatta pepper • Pinch of Atlantic sea salt • 2 sage leaves • Parmesan cheese, for grating • Poppy seeds, toasted

Make the tortellini dough:
In a stainless steel bowl, whisk together ¾ cup (95 g) of the pasta flour, the semolina, water, salt, and olive oil until you get a smooth mixture. Place the bowl in

a bain-marie and stir, scraping the sides of the bowl with a spatula, until you have a firm and elastic dough.

Take the dough out of the bowl and cool it by kneading and folding on a work surface of marble or stainless steel.

When the dough has cooled, return it to the bowl and add the egg. Knead the egg into the dough with your palms and fingers, until it comes apart into large independent lumps. Add the remaining 1 cup (125 g) flour and knead until the dough is elastic and somewhat shiny.

Wrap it with plastic wrap (cling film) and chill for at least 2 hours or preferably overnight.

Make the tortellini:
Roast the beets for 3 hours in the oven or tabun on maximum heat, until the skins become charcoal-like and the beets lose half of their weight. Take them out to cool. Peel off the charred exteriors and slice the beets into paper-thin slices with a sharp knife. Make piles of 4 or 5 slices of beet each (depending on their size). Each pile will fill one tortellini. After you've arrange an entire tray, scatter crushed black pepper on the piles. Roll the pasta dough out on a floured surface (marble is best), so thin that you can almost see the marble's veins through it. With a floured champagne glass, cut out rounds. Immediately cover with a tea towel to keep the dough from drying out. Take a round of dough in your hands and stretch it a little. Place a dot of butter in the center along with a pile of beet slices. If you're right-handed, move the round of pasta to your left hand (if you're left-handed, then to your right) and fold it in half with your right-hand fingers, trapping the beets inside the dough. Seal the edges by pressing together with floured fingers and close the far sides of the half-moons by pinching them. Arrange the tortellini on a tray heavily dusted with semolina. Keep covered with a towel and in a dark spot.

It's important to keep your hands dry throughout all this! Work while constantly drying your hands on a towel and flouring them.

To assemble:
Bring a large pot of lightly salted water to a boil. Slide the tortellini into the boiling water and cook until the tortellini turn bright purple and float, about 2½ minutes. Meanwhile, in a frying pan, combine the water, butter, shatta pepper, and sea salt and bring to a boil. Add the sage. Scoop the tortellini out of the water and transfer to the frying pan. Cook until the sauce is reduced and an emulsion has formed. The extra semolina stuck to the ravioli should help with thickening. Slide to a plate with a spoon. Grate Parmesan over everything and scatter evenly with the toasted poppy seeds.

MAITAKE ENTRECOTE STEAK

1 large maitake mushroom (an average large mushroom will give you 2–3 steaks) • Olive oil • Atlantic sea salt • Freshly ground black pepper

For the sauce:
½ cup chicken stock (see Note) • 1 clove garlic • 30 g butter

Preheat the oven to 350°F (180°C). Choose a large and beautiful maitake mushroom. Figure out how you can cut steaks from it: The object is to get as much surface area as possible while still maintaining the look of the whole mushroom. The steak thickness should be about 1¼ inches (3 cm). If any scraps of mushroom fall away, save them for the sauce. Once we cut our "steak," we treat it like an entrecote. Put olive oil, black pepper, and sea salt on both sides. Set a plancha or a grill pan over high heat. (I like to use a Le

Creuset ridged plancha.) Add the steak to the hot pan and roast until you get a golden brown color on both sides. Transfer the pan to the oven and continue roasting for 5–7 minutes.

Meanwhile, make the sauce:
Because the oven-roasted mushroom will lose some liquids, we want to give it some juiciness at this point by making a sauce, a kind of a glaze that will bring back the shine and juiciness. This sauce will give a feeling of the great fat you usually have on rib-eye steaks.
In a saucepan, combine the chicken stock, garlic, and butter and reduce to a glaze. (If you have any mushroom scraps from cutting the steak, add them to the sauce as well.) The reduced sauce goes surprisingly well with mushrooms, as it has some fat to replace the fat lost in the mushroom roasting.

To plate:
When the maitake steak is ready, take it out from the oven and place it on a cutting board that you use for eating steaks. Brush it with a lot of sauce.

Note: Usually we don't really prepare a stock, instead we use the pan juices from the chickens that we roast slowly throughout the day in our slow-cook oven.

200

BURNED BEET TORTELLINI

YUVAL CREATED HIS
COOKING FROM A
SENSUAL TOUCH THAT
REVEALS TO HIM
MOTHER NATURE'S
SECRETS. HE IS
OF ONE THE MOST
UNIQUE CHEFS I HAVE
EVER EXPERIENCED.
— Eyal Shani

201

YUVAL LESHEM

MEI LIN

HUGH ACHESON

MENU

OYSTERS, PASSION FRUIT LECHE DE TIGRE

SCALLOPS

SEA BREAM AGUACHILE

SHRIMP TOAST, CANTONESE CURRY

CONGEE

BRANZINO

What does American cuisine taste like? That's an enormous and intimidating question—but one Mei Lin answers, simply by being herself. With Nightshade, her restaurant in downtown Los Angeles, the chef at last has the platform to cook precisely what she wants, how she wants. Drawing from a vast library of taste memories she has been cultivating since childhood, Lin looks to food to unspool the thread of her own American story.

Lin was just three months old when her family emigrated from China to Dearborn, Michigan. She discovered her love for cooking working alongside her father at their family restaurant, Kong Kow, which is still going strong today. Although her parents urged her to consider other careers, Lin didn't waver. She earned a culinary degree and left Dearborn, quickly landing at restaurants to work for Michael Symon, Marcus Samuelsson, and Wolfgang Puck. Eventually settling in Los Angeles, Lin was the sous-chef at Michael Voltaggio's Ink when she was cast on Bravo's *Top Chef: Boston*, which she won in 2015. Instead of immediately investing her prize money in a restaurant, Lin spent several years living as a culinary nomad of sorts—eating, cooking, and learning across Europe, Asia, and the United States.

This chronology is key to understanding the essence of Nightshade, which opened in 2019: authoritative and accessible, cosmopolitan but homey, and modern but never in a fussy or extreme way, her style is shaped by her journey. Lin's flavors are both technically flawless in their balance and unapologetically bold. Expressions of umami, heat, acid, and earth are omnipresent on her border-blurring menu. Under her watch, Italian spaccatelli skews Japanese, while chicharróns flavored with Thai tom yum serve as a vessel for American caviar. She seasons a Spago-inspired pork schnitzel in the style of Taiwanese fried chicken, and looks to both Sichuan and Nashville for the lingering spice of her fiery "hot" quail. This is soul-stirring food that sticks with you—the work of a chef with a truly global point of view.

OYSTERS, PASSION FRUIT LECHE DE TIGRE
Serves 6

For the passion fruit leche de tigre:
75 g passion fruit juice, seeds strained out • 80 g tangerine juice • 55 g fresh lime juice • 10 g ají amarillo • 30 g fresh ginger, smashed • 10 g garlic, smashed • 10 g serrano chili, smashed • 10 g simple syrup (equal parts water and sugar)

For the charred garlic oil:
95 g garlic • 200 g grapeseed oil • 15 g kosher (flaked) salt

For the cucumber basil seeds:
4 tablespoons basil seeds • 1 cup (240 ml) cucumber juice

To serve:
Oysters • Coriander blooms • Onion blossoms

Make the passion fruit leche de tigre:
In a bowl, combine the passion fruit juice, tangerine juice, lime juice, and ají amarillo. Add the smashed ginger, garlic, and serrano and let steep for 1 hour. Strain, reserve and keep very cold.

Make the charred garlic oil:
In a small saucepot, combine the garlic, grapeseed oil, and salt and cook until the garlic turns black (charred). Remove from the heat and let cool.
Once cooled, transfer the contents to a high-powered blender and blend on high until the garlic has ground up. Put in an eye dropper bottle.

Make the cucumber basil seeds:
In a small bowl, soak the basil seeds in the cucumber juice. Add a bit more juice if it seems too dry.

To open an oyster:
Wrap a tea towel over one hand and use it to hold the oyster firmly. Using an oyster shucking knife in the other hand, place the tip of the shucking knife at the base of the hinge, twist the knife using pressure, then without the pressure, lever the knife upward, or carefully twist it to prise the hinge open.

SEA BREAM AGUACHILE
Serves 2

For the sea bream:
1 sea bream, filleted and skinned
Kosher (flaked) salt

For the celery aguachile:
820 g celery juice • 150 g fresh lime juice • 130 g ayu fish sauce • 65 g fresh ginger, smashed • 30 g garlic, smashed • 140 g serrano chili • 130 onion • 35 g cilantro (fresh coriander) stems

LIN'S FOOD IS TECHNICALLY SPOT-ON, FULL OF ENERGY AND SPICE. SHE IS A CHEF WHO SHOWS HAPPINESS IN ALL SHE DOES, AND THAT IS A RARITY.
— Hugh Acheson

BRANZINO

203

For the celery oil:
600 g celery leaves, blanched • 400 g grape-seed oil • 20 g salt

For the pickled green papaya:
500 g rice vinegar • 100 g sugar • 15 g salt • 1 green papaya

For garnish:
Julienne of sweet onion • Pink celery batons

Cure the fish:
Lightly sprinkle the fillets with salt. Cure the sea bream for 7 minutes. Rinse and pat dry on paper towels.

Make the celery aguachile:
In a bowl, combine the celery juice, lime juice, and fish sauce. Add the ginger, garlic, serrano, onion, and cilantro (coriander) stems to the liquid and let steep for 30 minutes. Strain and keep very cold.

Make the celery oil:
Blend all the ingredients in a high-powered blender until it warms up. Pass through a chinois lined with a coffee filter.

Pickle the green papaya:
In a saucepan, heat up the vinegar and sugar until the sugar dissolves.
Peel the green papaya, quarter, and seed.
On a mandoline, slice the papaya thinly lengthwise.
Once the pickling liquid is cooled, vacuum-seal with the green papaya.

To plate:
Slice the cured fish and, in a bowl, lay 2 ounces (55 g) of fish, covering the bottom of the bowl. Evenly space some celery batons and sliced onions on top of the fish. On a cutting board, shingle the pickled papaya and use a ring cutter to stamp out a circle. Transfer to the top of the fish. Dress with the celery aguachile and celery oil.

SHRIMP TOAST, CANTONESE CURRY
Serves 2–4

For the shrimp mousse:
1.14 kg 21/25 shrimp (prawns), peeled and deveined • 55 g pork fat, cold • 85 g schmaltz, cold • 8 g toasted sesame oil • 50 g fresh ginger, brunoise • 50 g garlic, minced • 50 g cilantro (fresh coriander) stems • 20 g fish sauce • 20 g Shaoxing wine • 65 g egg whites • 15 g cornstarch (corn flour) • 15 g salt • 55 g sugar • 20 g white pepper

For the Cantonese curry:
50 g garlic • 130 g shallots • 50 g fresh ginger • 215 g onion • 45 g lemongrass • 20 g Fresno chilies • 15 g serrano chilies • 14 g Madras curry powder • 2 tablespoons oil • 50 g palm sugar or rock sugar • 390 g chicken stock • 5 g salt • 1 liter Kara coconut milk • 35 g fish sauce

For the shrimp toast:
8 slices pain de mie or other white sandwich bread • Shrimp Mousse *(above)* • neutral oil, for frying

For garnish:
Fried curry leaves

Make the shrimp mousse:
In a meat grinder or food processor, grind or pulse the shrimp (prawns) to a paste. Add all the ingredients to make the mousse.

Make the Cantonese curry:
In a food processor, blitz the garlic, shallots, ginger, onion, lemongrass, and chilies until it forms a paste. Transfer to a bowl and add the curry powder.
In a soup pot, heat the oil and toast the curry paste until fragrant. Add the palm sugar, chicken stock, and coconut milk and reduce until it's thick enough to coat the back of a spoon.
Strain through a chinois. Add fish sauce at the end.

Make the shrimp toast:
Cut the bread into slices ¼ inch (6 mm) thick. Trim off the crusts. Let it dehydrate until semi-dry. If it dries out too much it will become brittle and will break.
In a fryer or deep cast-iron pan over medium-high heat, pour the oil and heat to 350°F (175°C).
Scoop 3 ounces of shrimp mousse onto a slice of dried bread and evenly spread it to the edges.
Place a rack into a sheet pan and set aside. Place the toast mousse side-down in the hot oil. Fry until the edges start to turn golden brown, then flip. Using a spider, remove the shrimp toast and place it on the rack to drain.

To plate:
In a coupe bowl, ladle 3 ounces of Cantonese Curry. Cut the fried shrimp toast in thirds and place on top of the curry. Garnish with a healthy number of curry leaves.

BRANZINO
Serves 4–6

1 branzino, butterflied *(see Note)*

For the Sichuan chili paste:
160 g chili crisp (pulp from our housemade chili oil) • 2 g green peppercorns, toasted • 2 g red peppercorns, toasted • 5 g brown sugar • 30 g black garlic cloves • 50 g black vinegar

For the chive ginger sauce:
310 gm fresh ginger • 290 g chives • 170 g oil • 10 g salt

For the bone broth:
500 g sake • 1 kg mirin • 2 kg reserved fish bones • 200 g ginger, smashed • 75 g garlic, smashed • 100 g scallions (spring onions)

• 200 g light colored soy sauce (such as Kikkoman) • 50 g bonito

For garnish:
Chervil • Cilantro (fresh coriander) • Scallion grass • Radishes • Bibb (round) lettuce cups

Make the Sichuan chili paste:
In a blender, blend everything until smooth.

Make the chive ginger sauce:
Puree all ingredients in a high-powered blender. Transfer to a saucepan and cook until green.

Make the bone broth:
To a large stock pot add the sake and mirin and bring to a boil. Flambée to burn off all the alcohol. Once the flame has subsided, add the fish bones, ginger, garlic, scallions, and soy sauce and simmer for 30 minutes until the liquid has reduced. Stir in the bonito then strain and cool the broth.

Cook the fish:
Pat the skin dry on each fillet with paper towels (this will help keep the fish from sticking). season the flesh side with kosher salt. Place a 12-inch (30 cm) nonstick pan on medium heat; add a bit of grapeseed oil to the pan once its heated. Add in the branzino.
Once the fish is halfway cooked, Spread the left fillet with ¼ cup of Szechuan chili paste each, making sure to coat the entire surface. Repeat process with the right fillet using chive ginger sauce this time.
Carefully with a wide spatula; take the fish out of the pan and place flesh side up on a platter. Garnish with herbs and radishes. Serve with bibb lettuce and bone broth on side.

Note:
To butterfly a fish, start by freeing the ends of the backbone from the fish's body. Use kitchen shears to snip the backbone right behind the head and right in front of the tail. Use the knife to free the backbone from the meat. Be careful not to slice all the way up to the top of the fish and through the skin.

SCALLOPS

SHRIMP TOAST, CANTONESE CURRY

OYSTERS, PASSIONFRUIT LECHE DE TIGRE

205

MEI LIN

ROSETTA LIN

VOISIN ORGANIQUE
Shenzhen, China

MAY CHOW

MENU

GREEN WOOD
TIME AND NATURE
CREATES DAINTINESS

PINE TREE
MATSUTAKE "FO TOAO QIANG"
SOUP, WONTON

RED RAY
TOMATO, FERMENTED
TOMATO SOUP, BASIL

SEA WAVE
PRAWN-STUFFED SEA
CUCUMBER WITH STEAMED EGG

FIRE
SMOKED STEAK TARTARE,
BEEF CHIPS AND
DRY-AGED DAN DONG RIB EYE,
"MAPO" TOFU, SMOKED BRAISED
OX TONGUE

LAND
MARA CAKE AND
MATSUTAKE ICE CREAM

Rosetta Lin, executive chef of Voisin Organique in Shenzhen, China, is no stranger to doing things her own way and to nonconformism. She found her path to making food for people not through traditional training or education, but serendipitously and organically, coming from a world of music, vocals, language, and dance. After working as a jazz singer in London, Lin began to gravitate to the city's farmers' markets and their bounty, and upon returning to China, she found herself tasting tomatoes at an organic farm run by entrepreneur Tina Chen. From there on, her life and career were forever changed.

In 2017, Lin and Chen opened the first iteration of Voisin Organique in Shenzhen, joining forces to bring organic ingredients and the concept of sustainable farming to a city that was far better known for its technology manufacturing than for its food scene. Over the next two years, in a lovely, peaceful setting, the restaurant built a loyal base of supporters and regulars, most of whom followed them when the restaurant moved into a bigger space in late 2019, in the towering development known as Upperhills. Today, Voisin Organique remains quite unlike anything Shenzhen has ever seen, tasted, or felt—a testament to Lin's goal of making her space and food an all-around sensory experience.

Stepping inside Voisin Organique's striking, serene space is like entering another world. The design, music, art, and energy work together to set a calm yet engaging stage for the food, unwaveringly the star of Lin's show. As with music, a hybrid of formula and feeling is what makes Lin's cuisine so visceral. She uses the scientific makeup of each ingredient to draw out its unique qualities, and combines them with the emotional connections inherent within these ingredients. The results are a modern farm-to-table expression of Cantonese cuisine and Chinese culture. While Lin is unattached to tradition, she is filled with respect for it. Her tasting menu called "Fragments of Memory 2.0—Autumn," arguably her most notable, brought to the forefront Lin's own childhood memories of travel and terroir, highlighting the farm's organic ingredients, such as chestnuts, sweet osmanthus, mountain-foraged matsutake, and more. The menu is, of course, dictated by the season—though change doesn't tend to deter this chef in any element of her life.

RED RAY
Serves 1

For the fermented tomato soup:
500 g tomato, chopped • 10 g salt

For the tomato jelly:
125 ml tomato consommé • 8 g konjac flour

For the basil granita:
35 g basil leaves • ⅓ cup (80 ml) filtered water • 8 g sugar • Pinch of salt

For the seasoned tomato:
5 drops of dill oil • 3 tomatoes, peeled • Chopped preserved tangerine peel

For plating
Grated green lemon zest • Sun-dried cherry tomatoes • Mini basil sprigs • Dill oil

Make the fermented tomato soup:
In a bowl, combine the tomato and salt and let sit at room temperature for 7 days. Strain the juice.

Make the tomato jelly:
In a small pan, mix the tomato consommé with the konjac flour. Bring to a boil and then reduce heat. Simmer until flour is fully dissolved. Transfer the jelly to a plastic container set on ice, and let stand until solid.

Make the basil granita:
In a pot of boiling water, blanch the basil. Drain, add to a blender with the water, sugar, and salt and blend until smooth. Strain the juice and freeze for 24 hours and shave it with a fork.

Make the seasoned tomato:
Cut the tomatoes into thick moon-shaped slices. Mix them with the chopped preserved tangerine peel and tomato.

To plate:
For each serving, pour 10 g fermented tomato soup into a deep plate. Add seasoned tomato and 10 g tomato jelly with ¼ teaspoon green lemon zest. Add 3 sun-dried cherry tomatoes and mini basil on top. Drizzle with 5 drops dill oil. Add 1 tablespoon of basil granita to the plate.

SEA WAVE
Serves 1

For the shrimp mousse:
1 kg whiteleg shrimp (prawn) • 200 g egg white • Diced ham • Diced scallions (spring onions) • Diced celery • Hua diao wine • Sesame oil • Diced lard • Pinch of salt • Pinch of freshly ground white pepper

For the sea cucumber:
Sea cucumber • 500 g chicken stock • 30 g lean ham, diced

For the seafood foam:
Vegetable oil • 1 tablespoon tomato paste (puree) • 15 g garlic and scallion (spring onions) • 800 ml seafood broth • Clam broth • Light (single) cream • Xanthan gum

For the steamed egg:
2 eggs • Seafood stock

To finish:
Fermented glutinous rice • Chicken oil • Hua diao wine

Make the shrimp mousse:
Peel and devein the shrimp (reserve the shells for seafood broth). Hand mix some salt and dry.
Chop the shrimp. In a blender, combine the shrimp, egg whites, ham, scallions (spring onions), celery, wine, sesame oil, lard, salt, and white pepper. Blend the mixture until smooth. Refrigerate for 2 hours to chill.

Boil the sea cucumber:
Soak the sea cucumber. In a pot, combine the sea cucumber, chicken stock, and diced ham and bring to a boil, then poach for 30 minutes and fire juices until the sea cucumber become soft and the juice coated on it evenly.
Brush the corn starch inside the sea cucumber and stuff with the shrimp mousse.

Make the seafood foam:
In a sauté pan, heat the oil and sauté the garlic and scallion (spring onion). Stir in the tomato paste (puree) and seafood broth and cook to reduce the broth by half. Strain the sauce and transfer to a pot. Add the clam broth and blend it with xanthan gum, then blend the seafood sauce until foamed.

Make the steamed egg:
Weigh the shelled eggs and use double or triple that weight of seafood stock. Whisk the eggs with the seafood stock, then strain. Wrap the mixture in plastic wrap (cling film) and steam for 4 minutes. (30 g per portion.)

To finish:
Steam the sea cucumber for 3 minutes, then turn off the heat and let rest for 1 minute. Put the shrimp-stuffed sea cucumber on the steamed egg, pour some chicken oil, fermented glutinous rice, and hua diao wine on top. Top with the seafood foam and spray the hua diao wine on the top of the sea cucumber.

HER LEVEL OF
CREATIVITY AND
FORWARDNESS IS
DEFINITELY AN
AMAZING INJECTION
INTO THE MODERN
CULINARY CUISINE
IN CHINA.
— May Chow

SEA WAVE

ROSETTA LIN

MAT LINDSAY

PALISA ANDERSON

ESTER, POLY
Sydney, Australia

At the tender age of fifteen, Mat Lindsay participated in a two-week internship at a restaurant kitchen, and was told that he wasn't cut out for the hospitality industry. Nevertheless, Lindsay has gone on to become one of the celebrated young chefs whose food most embodies modern Australian cuisine: inventive but uncomplicated, unfailingly delicious, and a special marriage of European, Southeast Asian, and indigenous influences that guide both the choice of ingredients and the methodology.

A few years after that initial kitchen stint, Lindsay moved to Sydney, intending to work as a graphic designer. But he still felt the pull of the joy of cooking; when he landed a job waiting tables at Wockpool, an acclaimed Asian noodle bar, he convinced its chef, Kylie Kwong, to transfer him to the kitchen. Subsequently, Lindsay became Kwong's head chef at her famed Chinese restaurant, Billy Kwong, and worked at the Italian 121BC Cantina & Enoteca, both of which imprinted a breadth of techniques and talent for balancing flavors on his cooking. Next, Lindsay opened Ester, the first restaurant of his own and where he quickly became known for the ubiquitous wood-fire treatment that metamorphosizes almost everything on the menu. One moment he's tucking smoked oysters between cucumber and crispy pig's tail; a moment later, he sets roasted cabbage leaves bulging with chopped brassicas in a broth of clarified Parmesan and sansho pepper. He went on to open Poly, a food-driven wine bar. Like Ester, its freestyling menu is intelligent and well executed: dishes such as tea-smoked quail, king prawns bathed in a sauce of salted egg yolk, and a heap of grilled peppers and pickled green tomatoes in a puddle of stracciatella and kombu oil.

Lindsay's establishments have appeared on nearly every "best restaurant" list in Sydney and Australia. In 2019, he opened a small takeaway place called Shwarmama, offering Middle Eastern classics like shawarma and falafel. Lindsay's constellation of projects, and the cross-pollination between them, demonstrate the energy and innovation with which he has contributed to the transformation of Sydney's cuisine, all the while catching the attention of food lovers around the world.

MENU

FERMENTED POTATO BREAD WITH DASH JELLY, KEFIR CREAM, AND TROUT ROE

ROASTED OYSTERS WITH PEPPERBERRY AND SAKE BUTTER

BLOOD SAUSAGE SANGA

ROASTED, FRIED, AND POPPED CORN WITH PARMESAN CUSTARD

CALAMARI AND LARDO SKEWERS

EGGPLANT, WATTLESEED, AND ENOKI

ROASTED KING PRAWNS WITH FERMENTED SHRIMP PASTE BUTTER

BURNT PAV

ROASTED OYSTERS WITH PEPPERBERRY AND SAKE BUTTER
Serves 4–6

For the pepperberry/sake butter:
1 liter sake • 1 liter brown rice vinegar • ½ cup (95 g) superfine (caster) sugar • 2 tablespoons Australian pepperberries • 500 g unsalted butter, at room temperature

For the oysters:
Rock salt • 1 dozen Sydney rock oysters, scrubbed clean • 4 tablespoons Pepperberry/Sake Butter (above)

Make the pepperberry/sake butter:
In a heavy-bottomed saucepan, combine the sake, vinegar, sugar, and pepperberries. Reduce over medium heat until thick and syrupy and tastes sweet and sour and spicy from the berries. Let cool slightly.

In a blender, emulsify the butter into the reduction (this will make more than you need for this amount of oysters).

Prepare the oysters:
Prepare a very hot wood-fired oven. Fill a heavy-bottomed pan or roasting tray with ½ inch (1.25 cm) rock salt. Warm the salt in the oven. Arrange the unopened oysters on top of the warm salt, pushing them in slightly but not covering the tops. Roast in the oven for until the first oyster starts to open, about 1½ minutes. Remove from the oven and shuck the lids from the oysters. Top each oyster with 1 teaspoon of the pepperberry/sake butter and return to the oven until the butter starts to bubble and the oyster flesh starts to trim up.

CALAMARI AND LARDO SKEWERS
Serves 4–6

For the skewers:
2 whole calamari • 100 g lardo di Colonnata, cut into ¾-inch (2 cm) squares

For the dressing:
Reserved calamari trim • Olive oil, as needed • Chinese red rice vinegar • 1 tablespoon squid ink

Prepare the skewer:
Clean the calamari. Set the wings, tentacles, skin, innards, and ink aside to make the dressing. Lay the calamari hoods (bodies) on a tray and freeze slightly just to firm up. Slice the calamari on a very fine angle into pieces just slightly larger than the lardo slices. Using metal skewers, thread the pieces of calamari and lardo, alternating 4 pieces of calamari to 1 piece of lardo.

EGGPLANT, WATTLESEED, AND ENOKI

AUSTRALIAN CUISINE IS TOUCHED BY EUROPEAN COLONIAL, SOUTH EAST ASIAN, AND INDIGENOUS INFLUENCES IN BOTH OUR PRODUCE AND METHODOLOGIES. IT IS INCREDIBLY UNIQUE, AND MAT'S COOKING UNFAILINGLY EMBODIES THE MARRIAGE OF ALL THESE ELEMENTS AND MORE. — *Palisa Anderson*

BLOOD SAUSAGE SANGA

FERMENTED POTATO BREAD

ROASTED, FRIED, AND POPPED CORN

ROASTED KING PRAWNS

Make the dressing:
Roughly chop the reserved pieces of calamari trimmings. Get a pan smoking hot in the wood oven, add a little oil, and fry the trimmings in batches, making sure not to overcrowd the pan, until the pieces smell roasted and start to release a little liquid. Transfer to a heatproof bowl and cover with plastic wrap (cling film). Let sit at 140°F (60°C) for 1 hour until the meat releases all its juice. Strain, keeping the liquid.
Season the squid liquid with red rice vinegar. Add more squid ink to improve the color.
To serve, prepare a hot wood or charcoal grill (barbecue). Grill the skewers until the calamari just turns opaque and starts to caramelize slightly. The lardo will render and season the meat at the same time.
On the plate, dress liberally with the dressing and olive oil.

EGGPLANT, WATTLESEED, AND ENOKI
Serves 4–6

For the marinated eggplant:
4 large eggplants • 1 clove garlic, peeled but whole • 50 g wattleseeds, roasted and ground • 125 g white miso paste • 5 g superfine (caster) sugar • 60 ml tamari • 30 ml lemon juice • 400 ml dashi • 10 ml toasted sesame oil

To finish:
1 bunch fresh enoki mushroom • 1 cup (240 ml) dashi, warmed • Extra-virgin olive oil • Sea salt

Prepare the eggplant:
Over fire or coals, completely blacken the eggplant skins, taking care to not cook the eggplants too much at this stage. Transfer to a heatproof container, cover tightly with foil, and let steam until the flesh is just softened.
Meanwhile, to make the marinade, in a blender, combine the garlic, ground wattleseeds, miso, sugar, and tamari and blend until combined. Add the lemon juice, dashi, and sesame oil and blend until well combined.

Peel away the blackened eggplant skins, keeping the eggplants whole. While still warm, completely cover the eggplants with the wattleseed-miso marinade and marinate for at least 2 hours.

To finish:
Preheat the oven to 480°F (250°C).
Scrape excess marinade from the eggplant. Cover the eggplant with a blanket of the raw enoki. Heat in the oven until the eggplant is just warm through and the enoki are slightly wilted.
Transfer to a bowl with warmed seasoned dashi, a generous bit of olive oil and finish with some sea salt.

MAT LINDSAY

NORMA LISTMAN & SAQIB KEVAL

JESSICA KOSLOW

MENU

SAMOSAS DE SUADERO,
CHUTNEY VERDE,
VERDOLAGAS

PRAWNS, BERBERE, PICKLED
JICAMA, GREEN MANGO

CHINAMPA SALAD,
TAMARIND VINAIGRETTE,
SMOKED DUCK

LAMB BARBACOA
MASALA Y MAÍZ

"OLD FASHIONED" DONUT

Masala y Maíz is more than just a place to eat. The Mexico City restaurant is also a pancultural waypoint, a practicum of ethical labor, and an engine for meaningful outreach. Building equity at the intersection of art, cuisine, and activism, Norma Listman and Saqib Keval are united in their desires to tackle issues overlooked by the industry. The pair met and fell in love in Northern California, and found they were kindred spirits in their approach to heritage cuisines and activism through cooking. Originally conceived as an event series, Masala y Maíz evolved into a brick-and-mortar based in the Colonia Juárez neighborhood of the Mexican capital.

Each day at Masala y Maíz, there are potent, commingling traditions at work, a synergy captured with great economy by the restaurant's name. "Masala" refers to Keval, the American-born son of East African immigrants who trace their ancestry to Kutch, India. "Maíz," meanwhile, refers to Listman, a native of Texcoco, Mexico, who champions Mexican culinary history through hands-on evangelization and academic engagement. Their rebellious mixing of flavors is a *mestizaje,* an intermingling of disparate cultures with a mind toward revolution. This dynamic conversation materializes in dishes like esquites, the corn-based Mexican street snack, reimagined with fresh coconut milk, ginger, and turmeric in a nod to Kenyan makai pakka; and uttapam, a dosa, or fermented Indian flatbread, made there with a base of nixtamalized blue corn and cooked with squash blossoms and nutty salsa macha.

Listman and Keval harness the unifying power of food as a tool in the struggle for justice, liberation, and creating community. The chefs source locally and ethically, and take care of staff with the same care, offering employees equitable wages, comprehensive health care, overtime pay, fixed schedules, and ownership in a worker-owned cooperative grocery store. It is an ambitious and difficult undertaking, but Listman and Keval have found a way to make it work—for their city, their team, and themselves.

LAMB BARBACOA MASALA Y MAÍZ
Serves 8

For the lamb:
Salt • 5.2 kg lamb (leg, loin and neck, bones included)

For the masala:
2 tablespoons cumin • 1½ tablespoons coriander seeds • 1½ tablespoons fenugreek seeds • 1 tablespoon fennel seeds • 1 tablespoon green cardamom seeds • 2 teaspoons yellow mustard seeds • 5 cm cinnamon stick • 2 black cardamom pods • 2 whole star anise • 2 dried banana leaves

For the adobo:
2 black chilhuacle chilies • 4 guajillo chilies • 3 chiles de árbol • 5 Roma tomatoes • 5 cloves garlic • 2 bay leaves • 1 cup (240 ml) virgin olive oil • 3 white onions, cut into medium cubes • 3 tablespoons finely chopped peeled fresh turmeric • 3 tablespoons finely chopped peeled fresh ginger ½ cup (180 g) tamarind paste •

3 tablespoons quince • ½ cup (120 ml) pineapple or apple cider vinegar • 4 tablespoons sea salt

For finishing the barbacoa:
8 avocado leaves • 1 large maguey leaf (or 4 large banana leaves) • About 7 liters water • 3 fresh banana leaves

For the consommé:
3 liters water • 4 tomatoes, halved • 2 onions • 2 chiles de árbol • Salt

For serving:
500 g limes • 250 g radishes • 1 white onion • 1 bunch cilantro (fresh coriander) • 24–32 tortillas

Prepare the lamb:
Two nights before cooking, salt the lamb all over, cover with film paper, and let sit in the refrigerator.

Make the masala:
Toast each spice separately, being careful not to burn them, then grind them with a mortar and pestle or in a spice grinder until a homogenous powder is formed.

Make the adobo:
In a saucepot, boil the chilies, tomatoes, garlic, and bay leaves until the chilies are softened. Set a sieve over a bowl and drain the chiles, reserving the broth. Remove the chile stems.
In a frying pan, heat the oil over low heat. Add the onion, turmeric, and ginger and sauté until the onion is translucent. Add the tamarind paste, quince, vinegar, and salt. Cook for 10 more minutes, then let cool. Once everything is at room temperature, blend the masala and chilies and sauté using a little of the broth the chilies were cooked in. The consistency should be thick and velvety.

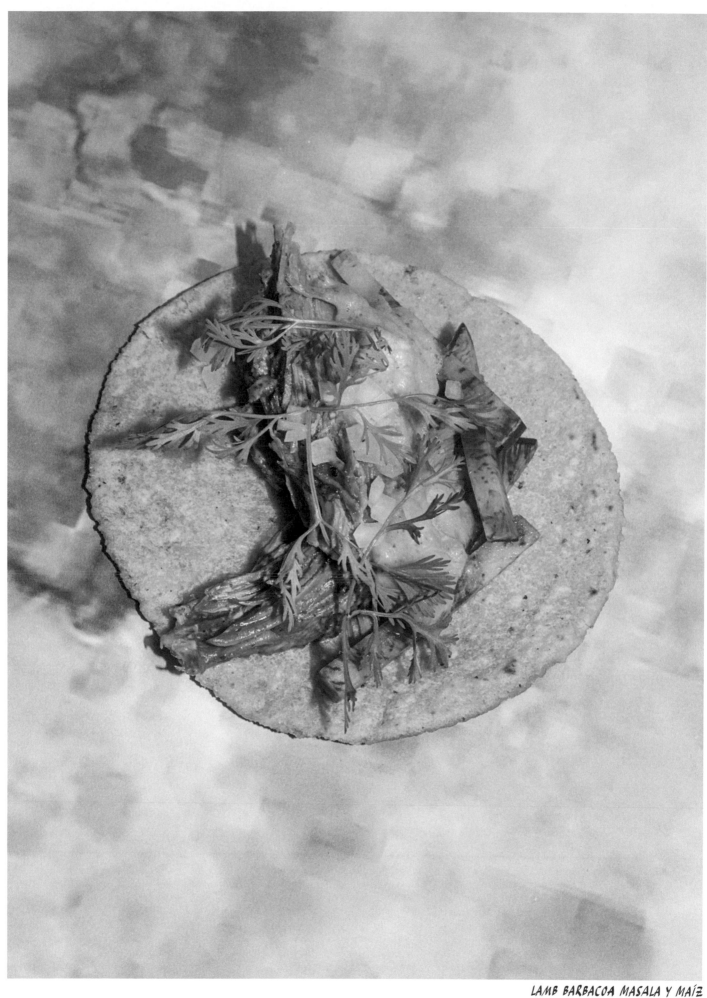

LAMB BARBACOA MASALA Y MAÍZ

Cook the barbacoa:

Measure out and set aside 1 cup (240 ml) adobo. Generously cover the meat with the remaining adobo and the avocado leaves. Let sit for 24–48 hours.

With a sturdy sharp knife and a pair of thick gloves, cut off the thorns along the edges maguey leaf: Start at the base and work toward the tip. Then, remove the thick rib that runs from the base to a little beyond halfway up the leaf. In a large pot, bring about 7 liters water to a boil. Poach the maguey until it's flexible and its color has changed to a dark, dull green.

Preheat the oven to 300°F (150°C).

In a wide, deep, and ovenproof pot (like a Dutch oven), place the leaf lengthwise. The ends of the leaf can stick up above the sides of the pan—that's okay, they will be folded in over the meat later. Arrange one banana leaf at a time to fully cover the bottom and spill over the sides. The goal here is to create a completely sealed pouch of leaves that you will cook the barbacoa in.

Place the meat in the center of the banana leaves, layering the meat with avocado leaves. Add the reserved cup of adobo. Cover the meat with the banana leaves. If there are uncovered corners, grab an extra piece of banana leaf and cover any holes, making sure no meat is left uncovered. Finally, use the excess parts of the maguey to wrap around the banana leaf packet. Pour as much water as your pot will fit around the barbacoa packet. Cover tightly with 3 layers of foil to make it airtight and keep the steam from leaving. Set a sheet pan on top and then place a brick on top. Transfer to the oven to bake for 2 hours. Increase the temperature to 450°F (230°C) and bake for 2 more hours. Then reduce to

250°F (120°C) for the 4 final hours. It is important to check the water level and make sure it does not evaporate. You can add water as needed. (This will later turn into the consommé!)

Make the consommé:

Once the barbacoa is ready, separate the bones from the meat and place them in a deep stockpot. Pour the cooking liquids from the barbacoa into the pot. If there is anything stuck to the bottom of the pot, deglaze it and add it to the stockpot. Add the water, tomatoes, chilies, and salt. Bring to a hard boil and keep it going for about 2 minutes. Check the salt. Strain and serve warm along with the barbacoa. Reserve about 500 ml of consommé in case you need to reheat your barbacoa. Serve the barbacoa warm and moist (if it starts to dry out, bathe it in a couple spoonfuls of consommé), with a stack of warm corn tortillas, salsa borracha, tomatillo salsa, finely chopped onions and cilantro, cut limes, and pickled onions. Make tacos with the barbacoa and all your fixings. Serve a hot cup of consommé for each person.

SALSA BORRACHA
Serves 8

½ cup (120 ml) vegetable oil • 5 mulato chilies, stemmed • 5 pasilla chilies, stemmed • 1 large white onion, cut into rounds • 2 cloves garlic, peeled • 2 teaspoons sea salt • ½ cup (120 ml) water • 2 tablespoons rice vinegar • ¾ cup (175 ml) pulque or beer • ¼ cup (60 ml) espadín mezcal

In a heavy-bottomed pan, heat the oil over medium heat. Add the mulato chilies and fry them on both sides until they have a toasted color, being careful not to burn them. Remove them and add the pasilla chilies, following the same procedure. In the same oil, fry the onion and garlic until browned. Reserve the cooking oil.

In a blender, combine the chilies, sautéed onion/garlic mixture, the frying oil, salt, water, mezcal, and vinegar. Blend until homogenous, with a velvety texture. Transfer to a bowl to rest for 30 minutes. If you're throwing a party, this can be done the day prior. After the sauce has rested, stir in the pulque little by little. Check for salt.

"OLD-FASHIONED" DONUTS
Serves 8

For the dough:
18 g unsalted butter • 120 g sugar • 45 g egg yolks • 190 g whole-milk yogurt • 300 g all-purpose (plain) flour, plus more for the work surface • 8 g baking powder • 6 g salt • Oil for the bowl • 1.5 liters vegetable oil, for deep-frying

For the topping:
Ground cinnamon • Freshly grated nutmeg • Raw sugar

Make the dough:

In a stand mixer, beat together the butter, sugar, and egg yolks. Once everything is mixed well, add the yogurt.

In a bowl, mix together the flour, baking powder, and salt. With the mixer on low speed, add the flour mixture to the yogurt mixture one spoon at a time. Once you have added all the dry ingredients, increase the speed to high for a couple seconds and stop. You are going to end up with a moist and sticky dough—this is what you want.

Place a spoonful of vegetable oil in a bowl and cover the whole surface by spreading it with your fingers. The idea is that you will be putting the dough into the bowl and you do not want it to stick to the metal sides. Place the dough in the greased bowl and cover tightly with plastic wrap. Rest for 25 minutes in the fridge.

As the dough is resting, get the following steps ready. Heat the oil to 340°F (171°C). Start the oil at a very low heat in a deep cast-iron pan so that the oil comes up to temperature slowly and is more stable. Set up a sheet pan and dust it with flour. Dust the work surface with a very healthy amount of flour. Unwrap the dough onto the floured work surface and dust additional flour on the top of the dough. Press the dough ball slightly with your hands. With the help of a spatula, fold the dough once. Repeat this one more time. Roll out the dough to about 1½-inch (4 cm) thickness and cut out donuts. Transfer the donuts to the floured sheet pan as you cut them. Reroll the scraps and cut out more donuts. Keep refolding and cutting the donuts until you are out of dough.

Chill the donuts for 15 minutes in the refrigerator or 5 minutes in the freezer. When the oil is hot, start frying. The raw donuts will sink to the bottom and then slowly rise to the surface. Once you see a little color on the edges, turn it over. The donuts will increase in size and start to form beautiful "creases." Turn the donuts one more time. They should be a beautiful golden brown color and cooked through (check with a cake tester). Transfer the donuts to a wire rack to cool slightly.

In a bowl, stir together cinnamon, nutmeg, and raw sugar to taste. Toss the warm donuts in the cinnamon-sugar. Enjoy warm.

Glazed Coconut Donuts
100 g whole milk • 400 g extra-fine powdered (icing) sugar (sifted) • Toasted shaved coconut

Make the donuts as directed and let cool to room temperature.

In a bowl, slowly whisk the milk into the powdered (icing) sugar. Keep whisking until the glaze sticks to the whisk and is uniformly thick.

Once the donuts are fully cooled, dip one side into the glaze. Sprinkle the glaze with toasted coconut.

GLAZED COCONUT DONUTS

TO ME, THE FUTURE IS
ACCEPTING OUR HERITAGES
AND REFLECTING IT IN OUR
WORK. THIS IS EXACTLY
WHAT NORMA AND SAQIB
ARE DOING.
— Jessica Koslow

217

NORMA LISTMAN & SAQIB KEVAL

LISA LOV

ANA ROŠ

TIGERMOM
Copenhagen, Denmark

In 2018, when Chef Lisa Lov opened Tigermom in the Nørrebro neighborhood of Copenhagen, her goal was to serve her compatriots the food she had been missing while living and working in Denmark. Raised in New Zealand by Chinese-Cambodian refugee parents, who had fled the Khmer Rouge regime, Lov associates Asian dishes such as *laab* and Hainan chicken with home and comfort. When she prepared these classic dishes for her friends and for family meals at the restaurant, her Denmark chef community immediately encouraged her to open a restaurant of her own so she could put such meals on center stage.

Before landing in Northern Europe, Lov worked around the world: at Maenam in Vancouver; at Nahm and at Bo.Lan in Bangkok; in Australia, she staged at Ben Shewry's Attica in Melbourne and the Royal Mail Hotel in Dunkeld under Dan Hunter. And in Copenhagen, Lov worked at AOC under Ronny Emborg and then for eight years at Christian Puglisi's acclaimed Restaurant Relæ, where she was sous chef for six years before eventually opening Tigermom.

Tigermom is a manifestation of Lov's personal history as a Chinese-Cambodian and curious chef with wanderlust on a quest for excellence, as well as of her warm, generous nature. The food marries her favorite Asian flavors with a sustainable approach to sourcing, in a light-hearted environment: a set menu of dishes meant to be eaten family-style with "bottomless rice." While she works with local farms to procure the best Danish beef and pork, Lov also sources the Asian ingredients meticulously from places she herself has visited and approved—products such as Red Boat Fish Sauce from Phu Quoc in Vietnam and organic rice from a collective in northeastern Thailand. This spirit makes plates like coconut cream curry of grass-fed Danish beef, local Hokkaido pumpkin, and home-grown hydroponic Thai basil, a perfect expression of Lov's vision and identity.

Tigermom—Lov's nickname at Relæ, where she was at first shy but quickly became a force to be reckoned with—is fulfilling her mission to show Copenhageners that Asian food can be much more nuanced and simply excellent than they may have ever understood it to be while also offering a taste of her home and heritage.

MENU

PIKE PERCH CEVICHE, LEMONGRASS, LIME LEAF, CORIANDER, AND AROMATIC TIGER'S MILK

NORWEGIAN HAND-DIVED SCALLOPS, XO SAUCE, AND BUTTER

WILD AND CULTIVATED LOCAL MUSHROOMS, AROMATIC COCONUT CREAM DRESSING, AND PUFFED RICE

STEAMED BRILL, GINGER, SEASONAL HERBS, AND SOY AND SESAME OIL "SIZZLE SAUCE"

BLACK SESAME AND COCONUT WAFFLES AND TOASTED WHITE SESAME ICE CREAM

WILD AND CULTIVATED LOCAL MUSHROOMS, AROMATIC COCONUT CREAM DRESSING, AND PUFFED RICE
Serves 6

400 g coconut cream • 150 g fresh galangal, lightly smashed • 35 g shallots, peeled and lightly smashed • 500 g mixed local mushrooms (we use oyster, enoki, king, shiitake, and seasonal wild mushrooms) • 100–150 g coconut milk • A pinch of white pepper • A pinch of crushed chili flakes, dry toasted • Fish sauce • Fresh lime juice • 100–150 g mixed fresh herbs (we use mint, cilantro, Vietnamese mint, amaranth, shingiku, nasturtium, watercress, marigold, and other seasonal herbs) • 2 small shallots, thinly sliced • 60 g puffed rice • 60 g fried shallots Marigold or nasturtium flowers, for garnish

In a saucepan, warm the coconut cream, smashed galangal, and smashed shallots over medium-low heat and simmer for 25–30 minutes to infuse. Remove the galangal and shallots. Increase the heat to medium-high, add the mushrooms and simmer until just cooked, 2–5 minutes. Add the larger mushrooms (such as king mushrooms) first as they take longer to cook, and add the smallest mushrooms last. Add coconut milk while simmering the mushrooms to adjust the consistency of the sauce and prevent the coconut cream from splitting. Season with the white pepper, chili flakes, fish sauce to taste, and lime juice to taste. It should taste sour, spicy, and salty. In a large bowl, combine the mixed herbs and sliced shallots. Add the warm mushroom coconut cream mixture and toss. Add more fish sauce and lime juice if necessary. Gently mix in half of the puffed rice and

fried shallots and plate the salad. Top the salad with the rest of the puffed rice and fried shallots and garnish with flowers. Serve warm.

STEAMED BRILL, GINGER, SEASONAL HERBS, AND SOY AND SESAME OIL "SIZZLE SAUCE"
Serves 6

Salt • 600 g brill fillet, skin on • 50 g fish stock reduction • 40 g soy sauce • 50 g mixed fresh herbs, finely chopped (we use ramson leaves, garlic chives, chives, cilantro, scallion, Vietnamese mint, lovage, and other seasonal herbs) • 30 g fresh ginger, peeled and julienned • 30 g fresh mild chili, seeded and julienned • 80 g toasted sesame oil • Fresh lime juice • Ramson or chive flowers, for garnish

218

Lightly salt the fish. In a bamboo steamer, set over a pot of simmering water, steam the brill skin-side up, until just cooked, 6–8 minutes. Transfer to a serving dish. Dress with the fish stock reduction and soy sauce. Cover the fish completely with the chopped herbs and top with ginger and fresh chili slivers.

In a saucepan, heat the sesame oil over high heat until it just starts to smoke. Remove from the heat and carefully pour over the brill to sizzle and wilt the toppings. The foaming oil should also emulsify slightly with the fish stock and soy sauce. Season with lime juice to taste. Garnish with ramson or chive flowers.

BLACK SESAME AND COCONUT WAFFLES

LISA IS SO FULL OF KNOWLEDGE, AND AT THE SAME TIME SO FULL OF THAT CHILDISH CREATIVITY.
— Ana Roš

PIKE PERCH CEVICHE

LISA LOV

JAMIE MALONE

GRAND CAFÉ
Minneapolis, Minnesota,
United States

JESSICA KOSLOW

MENU

CHILLED POACHED SHELLFISH WITH LEMON MAYONNAISE

3 YEAR-AGED WEDGE OAKS FARM MANGALISTA HAM

PORCINI AND FOIE GRAS CUSTARD WITH MUGOLIO SYRUP AND PARMESAN

WHOLE ROAST BASS STUFFED WITH PORK CHEEK RAGU AND CAPERBERRIES

FRENCH PRUNES PRESERVED IN ARMAGNAC WITH VANILLA ICE CREAM

Jamie Malone is an evangelist for the urbane and understated dining scene in Minneapolis–St. Paul, Minnesota. The native Minnesotan has built an inspiring model for female chefs all over, proving that you do not need to decamp to a coast or compromise your vision to make a nationwide splash.

Malone expanded her range before completing culinary school, traveling solo throughout Asia and Europe to immerse herself in as many cultures and cuisines as possible. These worldly experiences gave her many advantages once she began her local career in earnest, starting with interning under Chef Tim McKee at La Belle Vie, an influential fine-dining restaurant in Minneapolis. Malone broke through in her own right in 2011 as the chef de cuisine of Sea Change, another collaboration with McKee. Here, her clever and whimsical cooking, as well as her vocal advocacy for sustainable seafood practices, earned her a *Food & Wine* Best New Chef 2013 nod, among other honors.

In 2017, Malone put her idiosyncratic stamp on Grand Café, a Minneapolis fixture that had been operating under various owners for seventy years. Her reimagining remains true to the space's Gallic roots—bountiful raw bar, French-heavy bottle list, Gauguinesque antique wallpaper—but Malone has also asserted her own unique sense of style. She has managed to blend the romance of the Belle Epoque with her own brand of upper Midwestern pluck, setting a fun, feminine tone that is undeniably her.

The vintage-modern mix found throughout the room's decor informs the menu at Grand Café. Malone's king crab omelet comes with a side of Japanese *shokupan* toast. Typically a dessert, Paris-Brest becomes a savory starter here, with luscious chicken liver mousse standing in for sweet cream. Order a perfect classic cheeseburger, or spring for a posh tasting of three-year-old Mangalitsa ham.

Malone's limber skills and attention to detail in both food and aesthetics coalesce in an invigorating experience—they are imbued with qualities you could never replicate in any another city with any another chef, and that is what makes her restaurant so special.

PORCINI AND FOIE GRAS CUSTARD WITH MUGOLIO SYRUP AND PARMESAN
Serves 8

For the porcini cream:
50 g butter • 500 g fresh or frozen porcini • 4 cloves garlic, unpeeled • 4 sprigs thyme • 100 g chicken stock • 700 g heavy (whipping) cream

For the porcini and foie gras custard:
600 g Porcini Cream *(above)* • 400 g button mushroom stock • 300 g dark chicken stock • 15 g cornstarch (corn flour) • 5 eggs • 200 g foie gras, cut into 1-inch (2.5 cm) chunks • 10 g Madeira • Salt • Sugar

For the Parmesan cream:
225 g whole milk • 225 g heavy (whipping) cream • 3 sprigs rosemary • 3 g shallot • 100 g Parmesan cheese, broken into small pieces • 3 g fresh lemon juice

For assembly:
Mugolio (pine bud syrup) • Fleur de sel

Make the porcini cream:
In a saucepan, heat the butter. Add the porcini, garlic, and thyme and cook until the porcini and garlic are caramelized. Deglaze with the chicken stock. Add the cream, bring to a boil, remove from the heat, and let infuse for 1 hour. Strain.

Make the porcini and foie gras custard:
In a medium pot, combine the porcini cream, mushroom stock, and cornstarch (corn flour). Bring to a boil, then let cool slightly. Blend the eggs in a blender on low speed. Slowly blend half of the hot cream and stock mixture into the eggs. Add the foie gras to the blender and blend on high to fully puree and emulsify.
Transfer the foie gras puree to a large bowl and whisk in the remaining cream and stock mixture. Season with the Madeira and salt and sugar to taste. Pass through a chinois and cool over an ice bath.

Make the Parmesan cream:
In a saucepan, simmer together the milk, cream, and rosemary. Let steep for 10 minutes. In a blender, combine the shallot, Parmesan, and lemon juice. Strain the milk/cream mixture into the blender and blend well. Pass through a chinois and transfer to a 1-pint whipper siphon canister. Charge twice.

To assemble and plate:
Preheat the oven to 400°F (200°C). Fill small ramekins (or topped eggshells) with 100 g of custard. Set on a sheet pan. Bake until fully set, about 25 minutes, rotating the pan front to back halfway through. Cool slightly at room temperature. Top each custard with a thin layer of Mugolio syrup and a sprinkling of fleur de sel. Finish with a thick layer of charged Parmesan cream and serve.

WHOLE ROAST BASS STUFFED WITH PORK CHEEK RAGU AND CAPERBERRIES
Serves 8

For the pork cheek ragu:
1 lb (455 g) pork cheeks, cleaned and braised until tender, left whole • 100 g barrel-aged apple cider vinegar, plus more to taste • 50 g hacher shallots • 20 g Calabrian chilies, seeded and finely chopped • 250 g darkly browned butter, warmed, plus more if needed • Sugar (optional) • Salt • 4 tablespoons finely chopped mixture of flat-leaf parsley and chives

For assembly:
1 whole bass (about 1.5 kg) • Neutral oil • Kosher (flaked) salt • Apple cider vinegar • Juice of 1 lemon • Coarsely ground black pepper • 12 oil-preserved caperberries, halved • Handful of flat-leaf parsley leaves

Make the pork cheek ragu:
In a small rondeau, combine the pork cheeks, vinegar, shallots, and Calabrian chilies. Reduce to au sec. Gently pull the pork into about 1-inch (2.5 cm) chunks. Stir the pulled pork together with the brown butter. Adjust the seasoning with

additional brown butter, sugar (if necessary), salt, and vinegar.
Just before serving, finish with the parsley/chives mixture.

To assemble and plate:
Remove the rib bones and backbone from the fish, leaving the skin and the flesh intact. Once the bones are removed, the fish should still look whole.
Brush the fish with neutral oil and sprinkle generously with kosher salt.
Place the fish on its side directly into a large cast-iron skillet, or plancha, over medium-high heat. Cook until the skin begins to brown and releases from the surface of the pan or plancha. Flip and cook on other side until the skin is browned. The flesh in the belly should be just about cooked through at this point. If not, turn the heat down and cook until the flesh just starts to turn opaque.
Remove from the heat and brush with a little apple cider vinegar and a spritz of fresh lemon juice.
Place the fish on a large oval-shaped platter. Carefully fill the belly with pork cheek ragu, allowing a little to spill out onto the platter. Garnish with black pepper, caperberries, and parsley leaves and serve.

FRENCH PRUNES PRESERVED IN ARMAGNAC WITH VANILLA ICE CREAM
Serves 8

For the preserved prunes:
200 g sugar • 250 g water • Zest strips from 1 lemon • 3 vanilla beans, split lengthwise • 500 g demisec prunes • 750 g Armagnac

For plating:
Homemade or high-quality store-bought vanilla ice cream

Make the preserved prunes:
In a saucepan, combine the sugar and water and cook until the sugar is dissolved. Add the lemon zest and vanilla beans. Boil for 45 seconds.
Place the prunes in a heatproof container and pour the boiling liquid over them. Let cool completely.
Pour in the Armagnac and stir to combine. Transfer the prunes and liquid to a glass jar. Seal and allow to sit for at least 1 week.

To plate:
Place one scoop of vanilla ice cream in a petite glass bowl or ice cream dish. Top with 2 or 3 prunes and drizzle generously with the Armagnac syrup.

GRAND CAFE IS THIS WHIMSICAL YET HIGH-END RESTAURANT THAT'S REALLY PLAYING WITH MULTIPLE FACTORS—SETTING, VIBE, CUISINE. JAMIE PAYS SUCH CAREFUL ATTENTION TO DETAIL AND HAS SUCH A BEAUTIFUL CARE FOR WHAT SHE'S DOING. — Jessica Koslow

WHOLE ROAST BASS

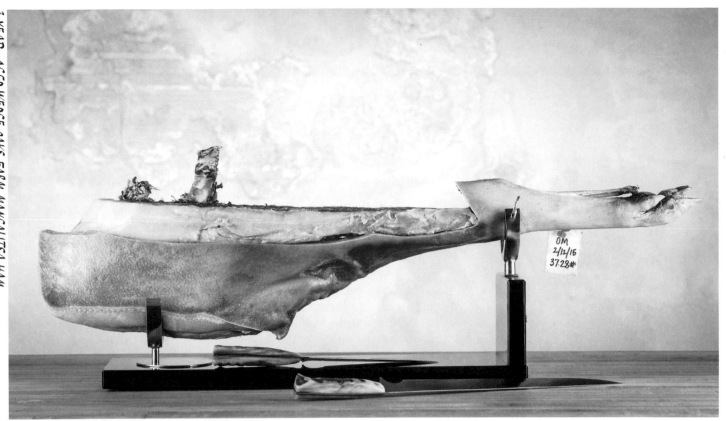

3 YEAR–AGED WEDGE OAKS FARM MANGALITSA HAM

OM
2/12/15
37.28#

CHILLED POACHED SHELLFISH

JAMIE MALONE

DIEUVEIL MALONGA

SELASSIE ATADIKA

MENU

HOMELAND
NILE PERCH FILLET, UGANDAN AVOCADOS, MORINGA FROM IVORY COAST, GHANAIAN SHITO, MANGO ROUGAIL FROM REUNION ISLAND

GHANAIAN PEPPER SOUP
VICTORIA NILE PERCH, IMAMBA FISH FROM LAKE RWERU, PEPPER SOUP, GHANAIAN SHITO & CASSAVA

IBISHYIMBO N'AMAVUTA Y'INKA
BEANS PUREED WITH TRADITIONAL COW BUTTER FROM EASTERN RWANDA PEAS & ODIKA SAUCE FROM GABON

MWAMBA NGUMBA
FREE RANGE POULTRY, CONGOLESE PEANUT SAUCE, BANANA RAVIOLI AND BITEKUTEKU FROM BUKAVU

MANANASI
4-SPICE PINEAPPLE, CONGO VANILLA, PEANUT CRUMBLE, CARAMELIZED PINEAPPLE WITH AMARULA FROM SOUTH AFRICA, COCONUT MERINGUE

For Dieuveil Malonga, food is full of dichotomy. It is an interpretation that is perhaps a reflection of his upbringing, one that began in the early 1990s in the Republic of the Congo. Born in Linzolo, Malonga was raised largely by his grandmother until the age of thirteen, when he went to Warstein, Germany, where he quickly gravitated toward cooking and music, graduating from the Adolph-Kolping-Berufskolleg, a vocational school in Münster, with a concentration on Afro-Fusion cuisine. Africa clearly defined his roots and was an integral part of his adulthood and career, with the intersection of Africa and Europe eventually shaping Malonga's approach to his craft.

Malonga worked in some of Germany's most revered kitchens, launching his career at Schote, Life, and Aqua, all Michelin-starred. He has won a variety of culinary competitions and been honored throughout the world, including as a finalist of the Basque Culinary World Prize—honored for his contribution to the world of gastronomy after having launched his Chefs in Africa initiative, dedicated to supporting African culinary talent through training.

Malonga firmly believes that education is the key to bringing the cuisines and cultural nuances of Africa to the international culinary stage. To him, it is a political matter and the catalyst for much of his recent work—in 2017, he teamed up with professor Sissi Johnson to design and implement an African gastronomy course within the International Fashion Academy Paris' MBA Luxury Brand Management program, where students learn about what defines African cuisine.

Malonga's most recent venture, Meza Malonga, has brought him back to Africa, where he is currently focusing on a physical manifestation of his passion for Afro-fusion in the form of his own restaurant in Kigali, Rwanda. In showcasing the richness of Rwanda's earthly bounty, Malonga's mission is clear, rewriting the story of how Africa fits into the global culinary scene.

HOMELAND
Serves 4

For the Nile perch:
600 g Nile perch fillets • Juice of 1 lime • Pinch of salt (from Lake Rose, Senegal) • 1 tablespoon Algerian olive oil

For the avocado:
1 avocado (preferably from Uganda), halved and pitted • 1 tablespoon wild honey • 1 clove garlic • 5 g fresh ginger • 5 g basil • 1 teaspoon moringa • Pinch of ground Penja pepper • Pinch of salt

For the shito (Ghanian black chili sauce):
500 ml vegetable oil • 3 red onions • 70 g dried black chili (with seeds) • 8 cloves garlic, finely chopped • 50 g dried shrimp • 50 g smoked fish powder • 100 ml chicken stock • Salt • 8 Guinea peppers • ginger • thyme

For the lemongrass-marinated cucumber:
2 cucumbers • 2 tablespoons honey • Juice of 3 limes • 2 tablespoons olive oil • 2 stalks lemongrass, crushed • Pinch of salt

For the mango rougail:
2 mangoes, finely diced • 10 g red onions, finely diced • 1 fresh chili, finely diced • 4 g cilantro (fresh coriander) chiffonade • 4 g fresh basil chiffonade • 1 tablespoon oil • Pinch of salt • Lime juice

For plating:
1 mango, cut into large cubes • Decorative assortment of wild edible flowers and cresses

Prepare the perch:
Clean and remove the skin of the fish. Cut the fish into 2-inch (5–6 cm) pieces. In a bowl, toss the fish with the lime juice and a pinch of salt.
Grill fish with olive oil for about 1 minute per side.

MANANASI
Serves 4

For the 4-spice pineapple:
2 pineapples • 1 vanilla bean, split length-wise • 6 g cinnamon • 6 cardamom seeds • 6 Penja peppercorns • 10 g butter • 30 g brown sugar

For the coconut meringue:
20 g coconut flour • 3 large egg whites • 40 g powdered (icing) sugar

For the ginger caramel:
3 tablespoons brown sugar • 3 tablespoons cold water • Salt • 2 tablespoons heavy (whipping) cream • 10 g butter • 1 table-spoon fresh ginger juice

Prepare the 4-spice pineapple:
Trim and peel both pineapples. Cut one pineapple into pieces. Transfer to a high-powdered blender, puree, and strain to get the juice.
Pour the juice in a saucepan and add the vanilla seeds and pod, cinnamon, carda-mom, and peppercorns. Boil the mixture until reduction.
Slice the second pineapple into rounds. In a sauté pan, heat the butter and brown sugar. Add the pineapple and cook until caramelized. Transfer the caramelized pine-apple to the pineapple reduction. Refriger-ate for 6 hours.

Make the coconut meringue:
Preheat the oven to 300°F (150°C).
Spread the coconut flour on a baking sheet and bake until golden, about 5 minutes. Remove from the oven. Leave the oven on but reduce the temperature to 200°F (90°C).
In a stand mixer, beat the egg whites until they form soft peaks. Slowly sprinkle in the powdered (icing) sugar while beating until the whites are stiff and glossy.
Transfer the meringue to a piping bag with a large plain tip (nozzle). Pipe the meringue into shapes onto an ungreased or parch-ment-lined baking sheet.
Sprinkle with toasted coconut flour and bake for 1 hour. Turn the oven off and let meringues dry inside the oven until crisp.

Prepare the avocado:
Scoop the avocado into a blender. Add the honey, garlic, ginger, basil, moringa, Penja pepper, and salt and blend all together to your desired taste.

Make the shito:
In a saucepan, heat the oil, add the onions, dried chili, garlic, dried shrimp, and smoked fish powder and fry for 3–4 min-utes. Add the chicken stock, Guinea peppers and salt. Simmer over low heat for about 30 minutes. Transfer to a blender and puree.

Marinate the cucumbers:
Peel and seed the cucumbers. Make cucum-ber balls using a melon baller.
In a bowl, combine the honey, lime juice, olive oil, and lemongrass. Add the cucum-ber balls and toss to mix. Refrigerate for 6 hours.
When ready to use, drain off the marinade.

Make the mango rougail:
In a bowl, stir together the mangoes, onions, chile, cilantro (coriander), and basil. Dress with the oil and salt, and lime juice to taste.

Make the ginger caramel:
In a small saucepan, combine the brown sugar, water, and salt. Bring to a simmer over medium heat, stirring every so often until the sugar is dissolved, about 5 minutes. Increase the heat to medium-high and cook until deeply golden, without stirring, 4–5 minutes more.
Once the caramel is a deep copper color, remove from the heat and immediately stir in the cream, butter, and ginger juice. The mixture will bubble up so be careful! Let cool slightly in pan, then transfer to a container to cool off completely.

WITH CHEF MALONGA'S ROOTS NOW SET IN AFRICA, I LOOK FORWARD TO SEEING HOW HIS CUISINE WILL DEVELOP AND GROW.
— Selassie Atadika

MANANASI

DIEUVEIL MALONGA

JUAN JOSÉ MARQUÉS GARRIDO

RAQUEL CARENA

MARAN RESTAURANT –
MARQUÉS & ANSESA
Girona, Spain

MENU

PARTRIDGE PATÉ COATED IN
PEDRO XIMÉNEZ

FOIE AND MISO CREAM WITH
SMOKED EEL AND
ARTICHOKE ROYALE

LIVER, MUSHROOM, AND
TRUFFLE-STUFFED
CABBAGE ROLLS

CONFIT BASS WITH CARDAMOM
SAUCE AND RED ENDIVE
GLAZED WITH BUTTER

HARE À LA ROYALE WITH
SICHUAN PEPPER FOAM

MASCARPONE MILLE-FEUILLE
AND GLAZED CHERRIES WITH
VANILLA AND KIRSCH

Watching Juan José (Juanjo) Marqués Garrido prepare a light and fresh sofrito, you understand the patient and laborious determination behind his cooking. To the classic Latin-cooking base of onions, garlic, and red bell pepper, lightly embellished with grated tomato and a drizzle of water, he adds finely chopped cuttlefish with its ink. A few hours later, the mixture is rendered into a powerful concentrate that goes as well with lobster as with pigeon, and also with the Catalan rice dishes Garrido executes perfectly.

This conviction, and Garrido's renowned kitchen proficiency, is not the result of chance. He grew up in Aragon and Andalusia, disparate regions in the north and south of Spain, and at the age of seventeen, started to train in big kitchens: Casa Irene in Arties in the Pyrenees, the Guggenheim Museum Bilbao, and, in particular, El Celler de Can Roca, the prestigious neighbor of his restaurant Maran in Girona, where he spent five years.

A master of Catalan cuisine, Garrido is also recognized as a skillful artisan in Andalusian tradition, producing gems crafted in his own way such as his ajo blanco, a popular cold soup made from lightly roasted almonds—more beige than white—which he combines with watermelon and basil. A culinary player as focused as he is tenacious, locally sourced products help him excel—for example, the fish that flourish in this region. A pristine fresh tuna inspires Garrido in myriad ways, especially the parts that are often overlooked. From gill to fin, he creates a miracle of textures according to the cooking methods he applies. He also creates new dishes with whole fishes like cod, whose innards he trims like a suckling pig and cooks at low temperature in a terrine.

Juanjo opened Maran in 2016 with his friend Ferran Ansesa Batallé, the top-notch sommelier responsible for the natural Catalan and European wine list that caters to fans of the best wines from Xérès. Juanjo has a keen understanding of how to orchestrate the cuisine he loves and that inspires him, picking the best ingredients from each season. When the hunting season begins and the partridges return, for example, this chef pays homage to his maternal Andalusian grandmother, reviving a pâté that she served to him as a child.

PARTRIDGE PÂTÉ COATED IN PEDRO XIMÉNEZ
Serves 50

3 large onions • 500 g Iberian pork fat • 500 g white mushrooms • 3 partridges, boned • 3 cloves garlic • 2 bay leaves • 1 heaping tablespoon peppercorns • 1 heaping tablespoon dried thyme • 250 g heavy (whipping) cream • 1 kg partridge livers • 1 glass (300 ml) Cognac • 1 liter chicken stock • 1 glass (300 ml) port • 10 g kappa-carrageenan • 1 liter Pedro Ximénez

In a pan, sweat the onions until soft. Add the pork fat, mushrooms, partridges, garlic, bay leaves, peppercorns, thyme, and cream. In a sauté pan, sauté the livers. Deglaze the pan with the Cognac. Add to the pan containing the other ingredients and cover with chicken stock. Cook for 1 hour 30 minutes. Blend everything and leave to stand for 24 hours.
Fill molds with the pâté and freeze.
In a saucepan, stir the carrageenan into the Pedro Ximénez and bring to a boil for 2 minutes.
Dip the frozen pâtés into the Pedro Ximénez mixture to coat.

LIVER, MUSHROOM, AND TRUFFLE-STUFFED CABBAGE ROLLS
Serves 15

1 head Savoy cabbage • 1 kg pork liver, finely chopped • 1 kg bacon (streaky), finely chopped • 3 large onions, finely chopped 1 garlic bulb, finely chopped • 500 g chard leaves, cooked and finely chopped • Salt and freshly ground black pepper • 1 glass (300 ml) Manzanilla sherry • 300 g white mushrooms, sliced • Truffle (as needed)

Remove the leaves from the cabbage and blanch in boiling water for 1 minute. Refresh in iced water.
Preheat the oven to 350°F (180°C).
In a large bowl, combine the liver, bacon, onions, garlic, and chard. Season with salt and pepper and add the sherry. Mix everything together and shape the mixture into balls each weighing about 200 g. Wrap in the cabbage leaves to form rolls.
Set on a baking sheet and bake for 30 minutes.

PARTRIDGE PATÉ COATED IN PEDRO XIMÉNEZ

Scatter the mushrooms over the stuffed cabbage rolls. Grate truffle over the sliced mushrooms.

HARE À LA ROYALE WITH SICHUAN PEPPER FOAM
Serves 40

For the forcemeat:
750 g bacon (streaky) • 350 g duxelles • 400 g pork liver, finely chopped • 250 g duck foie gras, finely chopped • 200 g bread, finely chopped • 150 g black truffle, finely chopped • 300 g blood • 200 g pasteurized egg whites • 100 g heavy (whipping) cream • 60 g Cognac • 60 g salt

For the hare:
1.5 kg hare

For the Sichuan pepper foam:
1 liter milk • 200 g Sichuan peppercorns

Make the forcemeat:
Cook the bacon and set aside.
In a bowl, mix together all the ingredients.

Prepare the hare:
Bone out the hare. Cut it open completely and put in a little of the forcemeat. Wrap tightly in several layers of plastic wrap (cling film) and chill in a blast freezer.
When very cold, vacuum-seal the hare and cook in a circulating water bath set at 63ºC for 30 hours.

Make the Sichuan pepper foam:
In a saucepan, infuse the milk with the Sichuan pepper for 15 minutes and strain. Froth the surface of the milk with a hand blender.

LIVER, MUSHROOM, AND TRUFFLE-STUFFED CABBAGE ROLLS

232

JUANJO'S CUISINE IS A UNIQUE BLEND OF GASTRONOMIC KNOW-HOW AND BISTRO STYLE. HE IS THE KING OF SOFRITO (THE BASIS FOR THOSE RICE RECIPES HE MASTERS SO WELL) AND ANDALUSIAN SOUPS!

— Raquel Carena

MASCARPONE MILLE-FEUILLE

JUAN JOSÉ MARQUÉS GARRIDO

AMAIUR MARTÍNEZ ORTUZAR

RAQUEL CARENA

GANBARA
San Sebastián, Spain

MENU

NATURAL, SEASONAL VEGETABLE SOUP

SEASONAL FUNGI WITH EGG YOLK AND FOIE

SEASONAL TRUFFLE SALAD

BAKED SPIDER CRAB TARTLETS

GRILLED SEASONAL WILD FISH

GRILLED TXULETA STEAK

STRAWBERRIES WITH BLACK PEPPER AND YOGURT ICE CREAM

Ganbara, diminutive and yet unmissable, is a place in San Sebastián that is impossible to classify. Nestled in the Old Town district, the location attracts people for drinks as well as those who come in for the pintxos (small snacks) that have made the restaurant's reputation. Born into the institution where he now cooks, Amaiur Martínez is the third generation of a family of chefs to take over the kitchen. It was for this legacy that he gave up his career in the audio/visual industry in Barcelona, where he lived for ten years. Back at home in San Sebastián, he proved himself in the most demanding of classrooms—the kitchen of his mother Amaia Ortuzar, the soul of the Ganbara. Here Amaia and her husband, José Ignacio Martínez, began cooking together over a quarter century ago. For fifteen years before that, José worked in his family's restaurant, Bar Martínez, while Amaia was working in a well-known restaurant right across the street.

For Ganbara, Amaiur and his team rely on local fishermen for line-caught seafood, forage for wild ingredients like mushrooms, and know where to find the most beautiful specimens of vegetables. Diners eat standing at the bar upstairs or sitting at the few tables downstairs—either way, always within a merry whirlwind, noisy and fast, buzzing with life. Martínez executes the pintxos in front of the guests: classics like *ensalada rusa*, such as is rarely seen anymore, the potatoes stacked like a cake, coated with white mustard-free mayonnaise; an array of seasonal mushrooms; warm, crispy cod croquettes that rival the beloved version made with ham; and the tradition green olives, anchovies, and gildas—small sweet peppers in vinegar. Another Basque essential at Ganbara is seen in the range of *kokotxas* (cod or hake cheeks), cooked in three ways: grilled, stuffed, or *al pil pil*, all deliciously gelatinous.

The attention to detail is also reflected in the drinks, and Amaiur's touch is there, too. Loosening the limiting Basque traditions of *txakolís* (white wines) and glasses of beer, he added a selection of natural wines—bottles from upstart vineyards anchored on the other side of the Pyrenees or bold novelties from Galicia, as well as sherry, Italian wines, and even champagne. Ganbara is first and foremost a story of family—and values in and out of the kitchen that have been handed down through the generations.

SEASONAL TRUFFLE SALAD

Wild lettuce (Lactuca quercina) • Lamb's lettuce • Arugula • Potatoes • Truffle (20 g per person) • Truffle juice • Peanut oil • Wine vinegar or sherry vinegar • Salt • Green asparagus • Pomegranate seeds

Clean the greens well.
Roast the potatoes and slice them into rounds.
Shave the truffles and set aside.
Make a vinaigrette with truffle juice, peanut oil, vinegar, and salt. Dress the greens with the vinaigrette.

Place the potato rounds on a plate. Top with the dressed greens, asparagus, and pomegranate seeds. To finish, place the shaved truffle on top.

BAKED SPIDER CRAB TARTLETS

Olive oil • Onion, finely chopped • Carrot, finely chopped • Spider crab, cooked and shredded • Salt and freshly ground black pepper • Fish fumet • Brandy • Puff pastry tartlet shells • Parsley, finely chopped • Butter

In a skillet, heat some olive oil over low heat and cook the onion and carrot until soft. Add the crabmeat, season with salt and pepper, and stir. Add a bit of fish fumet and allow to boil for 5 minutes. Finish with the brandy (previously flambéed).
For presentation, place the crab mixture in a tartlet shell or in a porcelain gratin dish. Sprinkle with the parsley and top with a small cube of butter and bake.

NATURAL, SEASONAL VEGETABLE SOUP

FROM THE CHAOS AND CROWDS AT THE GANBARA BAR, A KITCHEN OF UNEXPECTED GENEROSITY AND PRECISION EMERGES.
— Raquel Carena

STRAWBERRIES WITH BLACK PEPPER AND YOGURT ICE CREAM

AMAIUR MARTÍNEZ ORTUZAR

DULCE MARTÍNEZ

EL MOLÍN DE MINGO
Peruyes, Spain

JOSÉ ANDRÉS

MENU

HAM CROQUETTES

CHICKEN GIBLETS PATÉ AND SPICED FOIE

ASSORTED CORN "TORTOS"

GREEN FAVA BEANS WITH COD

WILD CHICKEN WITH RICE

PEAR TART

FRENCH TOAST

Dulce Martínez is the Asturian chef of El Molín de Mingo, a once humble *casa de comidas* that Martínez has elevated into a shrine to traditional Spanish, and particularly Asturian, gastronomy. From quintessentially Spanish dishes, such as her croquetas, to the uniquely Asturian arroz con pitu featuring a local breed of free-range chicken, Martínez pays tribute to indigenous classics in meals that many a great chef would choose as their last on Earth. Hidden in the hills of the town of Peruyes, El Molín de Mingo has an "end of the world" atmosphere, a magical energy; at the same time, Martínez makes you feel as if you're right at home.

Housed beside a creek in an old mill, El Molín de Mingo's food tastes as if it's from family recipes, cooked with love. Wild boar, sausages specific to the region, jamón Iberico, giblets from locally raised chickens, tortos, and creamy Gamonéu cheese are all trademarks of this distinctive region. Martínez has a singular way of using traditional elements to create dishes rooted in the history of Asturias that are at once familiar and intriguing.

HAM CROQUETTES

250 ml mild olive oil • 250 g Serrano ham, diced • 250 g all-purpose (plain) flour • 3 liters whole milk, heated to scalding • 5 g salt • Eggs, beaten • Fine white bread crumbs • oil, for deep-frying

In a saucepan 12 inches (30 cm) in diameter (for proper evaporation), heat the olive oil. Add the ham and fry it until it turns golden. Add the flour and stir well while cooking for another 10 minutes. Add the very hot milk and cook for another 50 minutes, stirring often to prevent sticking.
Transfer the béchamel/ham mixture to a sheet pan, filling it to a depth of 1½ inches (4 cm). Stir every 10 minutes until it cools completely. Cover with plastic wrap (cling film), in direct contact with the sauce so that no skin forms, and refrigerate.
Form the ham mixture into oval croquettes of the desired size. Dredge in beaten egg and bread crumbs, shaking them briskly in the bowl to remove any excess.
Rest in the refrigerator for 3 hours.
In a deep fryer, heat oil to 355°F (180°C). Fry the croquettes by immersing them in the oil, a few at a time so as to prevent them from breaking.

WILD CHICKEN WITH RICE

For the pitu de caleya chicken stock:
4 pitu de caleya chicken carcasses • 4 pitu de caleya chicken necks • 6 g salt • 50 ml (olive oil • 5 liters water • 1 medium carrot • 1 medium leek • 2 cloves garlic • 1 sprig fresh parsley • 200 g solids

For the chicken and rice:
18 g pitu de caleya chicken fat • 40 ml pitu de caleya sauce • 1 piquillo pepper • 0.5 g saffron • 150 g bomba rice • 500 ml Pitu de Caleya Chicken Stock *(above)* • 1 pitu de caleya chicken drumstick • 2 pitu de caleya chicken rib cages

Make the stock:
Preheat the oven to 340°F (170°C).
Put the chicken carcasses and necks on a sheet pan and add the salt and oil. Roast for 30 minutes.
Transfer to a stockpot and add the water, carrot, leek, garlic, parsley, and solids. Simmer for 1 hour 30 minutes. Adjust the seasoning with salt.

Cook the rice and chicken:
In a 10-inch (25 cm) diameter paella pan, combine the chicken fat and the sauce,

piquillo pepper, and saffron. Cook for 2–3 minutes to enhance the color and concentrate the flavors of the mixture. Remove the piquillo and add the rice. Sauté well, then add the hot stock and chicken pieces. Cook for 5 minutes over high heat, then reduce the heat and simmer for another 14 minutes. Remove from the heat, cover the pan with a sheet of foil in direct contact with the contents, and let sit for 3 minutes. Serve hot.

WILD CHICKEN WITH RICE

HAM CROQUETTES

GREEEN FAVA BEANS WITH COD

THE CARE DULCE
PUTS INTO EACH DISH
AND INTO OPENING
HER DOORS TO ALL
WHO VENTURE
PAST, MAKES THE
JOURNEY WORTH IT.
— José Andrés

RICE PUDDING

DULCE MARTÍNEZ

JUAN LUIS MARTÍNEZ & JOSÉ LUIS SAUME

VIRGILIO MARTÍNEZ

In 2018, Venezuelan chefs Juan Luis Martínez and José Luis Saume, who both hail from Caracas, opened Mérito, in the Barranco neighborhood of Lima. The restaurant, a compact two-floor space with an industrial feel and original adobe walls, offers an astute fusion of two Latin American cuisines, Venezuelan and Peruvian, with smooth, coherent, and playful results. Seemingly without effort, the chefs update Venezuelan dishes such as arepas and quesadillas by incorporating local Peruvian ingredients; similar twists characterize such presentations as the seared cherimoya, often cooked on a Josper grill (the legendary charcoal grill from Spain) and served on handmade ceramic plates by local artisan Taller Dos Ríos. Dishes such as razor clams with celeriac and yacón and yucca quesadillas with mashuas (an Andean tuber) springing forth from the chefs' imaginations of Venezuelan cuisine in Peru are nuanced and may be hard to pinpoint, but they are definitely easy to love.

An emphasis on sharing and a sense of camaraderie and informality pervade the Mérito dining experience, making it a favorite of both Barranco neighbors, farther-flung locals, and even chefs from elsewhere in Lima, all of whom appreciate the unpretentious, rustic energy. Ever-changing playlists of grunge and reggae music are expected at Mérito, where everyone, including the cooks, seem to be having fun experimenting. Indeed, accessibility is also at the heart of the restaurant, where lunch can cost as little as $10. Lima locals don't often queue up for meals, but the combination of flavors and affordability—and the no reservations policy—mean there's often a line outside Mérito.

Juan Luis originally moved to Lima to join Vergilio Martínez's team at Central, and before that he worked at two three-Michelin-star restaurants in Spain. At Mérito, together with Saume, the collaboration yields food that exudes a confidence and quality that's hard to master: original, approachable, and technically astute.

MENU

SEA URCHIN, PURPLE CORN AREPA

BONITO TARTARE AND TREE TOMATO

NATIVE POTATO GYOZAS, AND CARAPULCRA FILLING

SCALLOPS AND CORN

CATCH OF THE DAY WITH AREPAS AND CHICHA DE JORA BUTTER

CHOCOLATE ROCK

BONITO TARTARE AND TREE TOMATO
Serves 8

For the tree tomato water:
1 kg tree tomatoes (tamarillos) • 1 liter water

For the tree tomato barbecue sauce:
500 g seedless tree tomato (tamarillo) pulp • 100 g distilled white vinegar • 100 g sugar • 5 g salt • 5 g ground Sichuan pepper • 1 g ground clove

For the tree tomato powder:
500 g seedless tree tomato (tamarillo) pulp

For the tree tomato "leche de tigre:"
500 ml Tree Tomato Water (above) • 2 cloves garlic • 100 g red onion • 5 g fresh ginger • 50 g celery shown on bottom • 2 g ají limo, red • 15 g salt

For the tartare:
400 g fresh bonito cut in 2 cm dice • 50 g red onion, cut in brunoise • 20 g yellow chili, cut in brunoise • 25 g scallions (spring onions), minced • 15 g cilantro (fresh coriander) leaves, minced • 60 g Tree Tomato Barbecue Sauce (above) • 50 g Tree Tomato "Leche de Tigre" (above) • 10 ml good-quality olive oil • Salt to taste

Make the tree tomato water:
Peel the tamarillos and quarter. Dehydrate at 158°F (70°C) for 6 hours.

Place the dried tamarillo segments in the water and steep for 48 hours. In a sieve set over a bowl, drain the tamarillos. Reserve the liquid and pulp separately. Use the pulp for the barbecue sauce and the tree tomato powder below.

Make the tree tomato barbecue sauce:
In a bowl, stir together the tamarillo pulp, vinegar, sugar, salt, Sichuan pepper, and cloves. Spread on a pan and smoke for 2 hours. Blend in a Thermomix and set aside.

Make the tree tomato powder:
Spread the tamarillo pulp on a silicone baking mat and dehydrate.
Blend in a Thermomix and reserve.

SEA URCHIN, PURPLE CORN AREPA

CATCH OF THE DAY WITH AREPAS

NATIVE POTATO GYOZAS

SCALLOPS AND CORN

Make the tree tomato "leche de tigre:"
Roughly cut all the vegetables.
In a bowl, combine all of the ingredients
and refrigerate for at least 2 hours. Strain
the liquid and set aside (discard the solids).

Make the tartare:
In a bowl, mix together all the ingredients.

To assemble, spread the tartare mixture on
a plate of choice preferably one that has a
shallow surface. With a fine-mesh sieve sift
the tree tomato powder over the tartare.
Garnish with seasonal flowers of choice.

AREPAS AND CHICHA DE JORA BUTTER
Serves 10

For the white corn arepas:
1.18 kg water • 390 g masarepa (precooked
cornmeal) • 11 g salt

For the chicha de jora butter:
200 g butter, at room temperature • 22 g
chicha de jora reduction • 6 g salt

Make the arepas:
Heat water to about 122°F (50°C).
Mix the masarepa and salt into the water
and mix in a stand mixer for at least 10 minutes or until the dough becomes a bit elastic.
Roll the dough to a ½-inch (1.5 cm) thickness. Cut out 4-inch (10 cm) rounds with
a ring cutter.
Preheat the oven to 425°F (220°C).
Cook the arepas in a skillet making sure
that each side is lightly colored.
Place the seared arepas on a baking pan and
transfer to the oven.
Bake the arepas until they puff up and get
a nicely toasted.

Make the chicha de jora butter:
In a stand mixer fitted with the whisk,
combine the butter, chicha de jora reduction, and salt. Whisk at high speed in order
to incorporate air into the mixture resulting
in a very light butter.

Serve the arepas with the butter on the side.

POTATO GYOZAS
Serves 24

For the filling:
250 g dried Peruvian potato • 1 liter water
• 50 ml olive oil • 250 g pork shoulder,
cut into ¾-inch (2 cm) cubes • Salt and
freshly ground black pepper • 200 g onions,
brunoise • 30 g garlic, minced • 10 g
dried oregano • 5 g ground cumin • 100 g
homemade ají panca paste • 10 g homemade
ají amarillo paste • 10 g roasted peanuts,
ground almost to a powder • 1 liter chicken
and pork stock

Make the filling:
Rehydrate the dried potatoes in the water
for 24 hours in the fridge.
Preheat a nonstick frying pan over high heat.
Add the pork and cook until golden brown.
Season with salt and pepper. Remove the
meat from the skillet and set aside.
In the same nonstick pan, cook the onions
and garlic with olive oil over medium heat
until fragrant. Add the oregano and cumin.
Add the two chili pastes and cook over
medium-low heat until all the liquid has
evaporated and the mixture becomes dry
and toasted. Add the roasted peanuts and
return the meat to the pan. Add the chicken
and pork stock and adjust the salt taste.
Drain the rehydrated potatoes and add them
to the pan with all the other ingredients.
Cook over medium heat until the stew-like
mixture gets to the right consistency, not
too thin nor too thick and the meat its tender, at least 1 hour. Let cool and set aside.

Assemble the gyoza:
Preheat the oven to 280°F (140°C).
Thinly slice the potatoes on a mandoline.
Line a baking sheet with a silicone baking
mat. Arrange the slices on the mat to form a
round 4 inches (10 cm) in diameter, placing
the slices overlapping in a spiral shape (this
is a gyoza skin). Repeat to make multiple
rounds. Cover the potato rounds with a
second baking mat.
Transfer to the oven and bake for 4 minutes.
Take out of the oven and uncover them as
quickly as possible to avoid overcooking.
Let the cooked potatoes air out and cool for
at least 5 minutes.
Brush the edges of the potatoes with some
egg yolk as if you were making ravioli. Place
a spoonful of the filling in the center of
each potato round. Fold the edges to form
the gyoza-like half-moon and make sure
it's well sealed on all sides. Refrigerate the
gyozas in a container until time for service.
When ready to serve, preheat the oven to
350°F (180°C).
Arrange the gyozas on a baking sheet and
bake until golden and crispy, about 8 minutes.

CHOCOLATE ROCK
Serves 12

For the chocolate pastry cream:
400 ml milk • 100 ml heavy (whipping)
cream • 4 egg yolks • 100 g sugar • 20 g
cornstarch (corn flour) • 170 g chocolate
(75% cacao)

For the sacher:
125 g egg whites • 65 g granulated sugar
• 50 g chocolate (75% cacao) • 50 g butter
• 105 g egg yolks • 2 eggs • 108 g powdered
(icing) sugar, sifted • 108 g Brazil-nut
flour • 50 g all-purpose (plain) flour • 25 g
unsweetened cocoa powder

For the mousse de chocolate:
169 g chocolate (75% cacao) • 65 g unsweetened cocoa powder • 391 g heavy (whipping) cream • 104 g whole milk • 78 g egg
yolks • 130 g granulated sugar • 78 g egg
whites

For the nibs de cacao:
100 g cacao nibs

Make the chocolate pastry cream:
Place the milk and the heavy cream in a
sauce pot. Bring to a boil and then set aside.
Place the egg yolks, sugar, and cornstarch in
a bowl and whisk until fully incorporated.
Melt the chocolate over a bain-marie.
Add the milk and cream mixture to the egg
mixture and then return to the sauce pan.
Heat over medium heat whisking vigorously, until the mixture thickens. Add in
the melted chocolate and using a whisk or
electric beater, mix until completely smooth.

Make the sacher:
Wisk the egg whites with the white sugar
until firm peak stage and set aside.
In a bowl, melt the chocolate and butter
together and set aside.
In the bowl of a stand mixer, beat the egg
yolks with the 2 eggs at high speed until
tripled in volume. Add the powdered sugar
and Brazil nut flour and mix at medium
speed fully incorporated.Remove the bowl
from the mixer.
Sift together the flour and cocoa and gradually add to the egg mixture bit by bit until it
becomes smooth and evenly mixed. Gradually whisk in the egg white/sugar mixture.
Place mixture into a baking pan and bake
at 320°F (160°C) for 15 minutes.

Make the mousse de chocolate:
Place the chocolate and cocoa in a bowl.
Heat the cream and milk until boiling, then
add to the chocolate and cocoa mixture.
Using an electric beater, mix until the
chocolate is fully melted, then mix in the
egg yols and the sugar. Mix in the egg
whites, then let the mixture cool to room
temperature.Place the mixture in a 1-liter
ISI whipper with two charges of gas.

Process the nibs de caco:
This should be done by hand so the nibs do
not turn into a paste. Using a very sharp
knife, finely chop the nibs to the consistency
of fine sugar. Sift and set aside.

To assemble, start with a river rock as your
base. Alternate layers of the sacher, the
pastry cream, and the mousse on top of the
base to create a round form. Use a small
spatula to shape the outside of the finished
form to look like a rock. Dust with the
chopped nibs de cacao.

THEY HAVE EXHIBITED THE TECHNICAL CAPACITY TO FUSE TWO LATIN AMERICAN CUISINES, PERUVIAN AND VENEZUELAN, WITH SMOOTH, COHERENT, AND INTERESTING RESULTS. — *Virgilio Martínez*

CHOCOLATE ROCK

JUAN LUIS MARTÍNEZ & JOSÉ LUIS SAUME

FLYNN MCGARRY

GEM
New York, New York,
United States

HUGH ACHESON

MENU

PEAS WITH FRESH CHEESE AND VERBENA

DIVER SCALLOPS WITH PICKLED WHITE ASPARAGUS AND PINE

EGGPLANT WITH EGG YOLK, BLACK GARLIC, AND CHERRY BLOSSOMS

BEETS WITH MAITAKE AND BORDELAISE

BEE POLLEN SEMIFREDDO WITH BEESWAX AND HONEY

So much of the conversation swirling around Flynn McGarry—glowing blog write-ups, newspaper and glossy magazine profiles, photo shoots, and even a documentary film—has focused overwhelmingly on his age. That's understandable, considering he set his sights on becoming one of the best chefs in America when most of his peers were still playing with toys. Everyone loves a prodigy—but McGarry, who turns twenty-two in 2020, has single-handedly reshaped his narrative through relentless dedication to the one thing that matters most to him: the food.

By the time he was in seventh grade, McGarry had already mastered the *French Laundry* and *Le Bernardin* cookbooks cover to cover, his natural talent shepherded along by his supportive parents and older sister. He began hosting elaborate private dinners in his family's California home, and it didn't take long for the food media to pounce on his irresistible trajectory. These meals were replete with artful, intricate, modernist dishes that looked and tasted like they came from a Michelin-starred galley, not the practice kitchen his parents built for him in his tween bedroom. This led to impressive staging jobs, formative part-time gigs, and sold-out pop-ups, all en route to the 2018 opening of the then nineteen-year-old's fully realized restaurant on New York's Lower East Side.

Inside the inviting, living room-like Gem—his mother Meg's name spelled backwards—McGarry keeps his head down and focuses on moving forward, his well-received, rapidly maturing cooking serving as an edible retort to detractors who dismissed him. Featuring twelve to fifteen courses, McGarry's tastings showcase a nuanced understanding of how ingredients work together, juggling flavors and techniques. His "aged beet," a longtime signature, has an entire culinary degree's worth of techniques behind it, all means to the end of elevating its earthbound essence to unforeseen heights. Strawberries with geranium or mussels with verbena may not sound like natural matches, but they click when he gets ahold of them. McGarry is an attentive and intensely thoughtful chef who is only just beginning to share his gifts.

EGGPLANT WITH EGG YOLK, BLACK GARLIC, AND CHERRY BLOSSOMS
Serves 4

For the eggplant:
1 large eggplant • 2 (12-inch/30 cm) sheets kombu • Salt

For the egg yolk gel:
4 eggs • 2 g *yuzu koshō* • Salt

For the black garlic leather:
200 g peeled black garlic • 20 g water • Salt

For the vinegar salted cherry blossoms:
8 salted cherry blossoms • Champagne vinegar

To finish:
Brown butter, for brushing • 16 pieces fresh kombu, cut into ½-inch (1.25 cm) squares • 16 leaves opal basil • *Yuzu koshō*

Prepare the eggplant:
Grill the eggplant with its skin on until it is fully charred. Place in a covered container for 20 minutes to steam. Peel the skin off and cut the eggplant into 1-inch (2.5 cm) cubes. Place in between the sheets of kombu, salt to taste, and let sit for 4 hours.

Make the egg yolk gel:
Cook the eggs in a water bath at 148°F (64.5°C) for 1 hour 10 minutes. Clean off the whites and pass the yolks through a tamis. Season with *yuzu koshō* and salt to taste. Reserve in a piping bag.

Make the black garlic leather:
Tamis the black garlic and whisk with water and salt to taste. Spread it paper thin on a silicone baking mat and dehydrate at 140°F (60°C) until dry but still pliable. Cut into ¾-inch (2 cm) squares.

Make the vinegar-salted cherry blossoms:
Rinse the cherry blossoms to remove the salt and let them sit in champagne vinegar for 24 hours.

To finish:
Brush the eggplant with brown butter and warm on a grill. Brush with a small amount of *yuzu koshō* and plate with 4 dots of egg yolk, 2 cherry blossoms, 4 squares of fresh kombu, 4 squares black garlic leather, and 4 leaves opal basil.

PEAS WITH FRESH CHEESE AND LEMON VERBENA OIL
Serves 4

For the peas:
Sugar snap peas

For the mussel stock:
500 g mussels • 250 g white wine

For the fresh cheese:
250 g whole milk • Salt • 12.5 g heavy cream • 7 g buttermilk • 2 g rennet

For the pea broth:
Pea pods (reserved from shucking sugar snaps) • 40 g Mussel Stock *(above)* • 3 g lemon verbena

For the lemon verbena oil:
100 g neutral oil • 30 g lemon verbena

To finish:
Lemon juice • Olive oil • Salt • Maldon sea salt • 20 lemon thyme blossoms

Make the peas:
Shuck enough sugar snap peas for 40 g per person and sort into large and small peas. Save the pods for the broth. You will need 80 g each of small and larger peas.
In a pot of boiling water, blanch the large peas for 30 seconds. Shock in ice water. Reserve the small peas raw.

Make the mussel stock:
Cover the mussels with wine and bring to a boil, simmer for 10 minutes, and strain.

Make the fresh cheese:
In a saucepan, combine the milk and salt to 85°F (29°C). Stir in the cream and buttermilk. Add the rennet and pour into a container sitting in a 98°F (36°C) water bath. Let cook for 1 hour 20 minutes, then let cool.

Make the pea broth:
Juice the pea pods in a juicer and strain. Weigh out 100 g of pea juice. Mix with the mussel stock. Blend the pea and mussel liquid with the lemon verbena and strain.

Make the lemon verbena oil:
Blend the oil and verbena together until lightly smoking. Strain through a tea towel.

To finish:
Separately season the raw and cooked peas with lemon juice, olive oil, and salt. Scoop 20 g of raw peas and 20 g of cooked peas into each bowl, making sure they stay separate. Spoon over a large spoonful of pea broth and drizzle with some of the verbena oil. Scoop one small spoonful of cheese into the bowl and season with Maldon salt. Arrange the thyme flowers on top.

BEETS WITH MAITAKE AND BORDELAISE

EGGPLANT WITH EGG YOLK

PEAS WITH FRESH CHEESE

248

FLYNN WAS CROWNED AS A PRODIGY OF THE CULINARY WORLD AT THE AGE OF TWELVE. INSTEAD OF FALLING UNDER THE WEIGHT OF THAT EXPECTATION, HE PUT DOWN HIS HEAD, TOSSED AWAY THE CROWN HE DIDN'T ASK FOR, AND LEARNED AN INCREDIBLE AMOUNT ABOUT FOOD, BEVERAGE, AND HOSPITALITY.

— Hugh Acheson

249

FLYNN MCGARRY

VICTOR MORENO

MORENO
Caracas, Venezuela

JOSÉ ANDRÉS

Before returning to his native Venezuela to champion and educate about the food traditions of his home country, Victor Moreno traveled the world to perfect his culinary craft. His eponymous restaurant, Moreno, in Caracas, is a love letter to his national cuisine, but also reflects his extensive international travel and experiences cooking with some of the world's greatest chefs. Traditional Venezuelan elements—plentiful meats and seafood, plus Latin American spices and produce—form the backbone of Moreno's thoughtful menu, where pork ribs are served with ripe banana and arepas and grilled beef tenderloin is paired with traditional cassava cake and *chistorra*.

Moreno graduated from the revered Center for Gastronomic Studies (CEGA) in Caracas, and the experience instilled in him not only a passion to learn but also to teach. Following his studies there, Moreno cooked under gastronomy legends Andrés Madrigal and the late Santi Santamaría in Spain. After his tutelage with these greats, Moreno returned to Latin America to cook in Peru, Mexico, and Colombia, gaining insights into neighboring countries' culinary traditions that inform his cooking in Venezuela. Hence, Moreno has a knack for expressing the essence of his country—its history, culture, traditions, and flavors—employing astute cooking techniques collected and comprised from further afield.

Perhaps being the son of an academic and culinary historian helped Moreno identify that his craft was not enough, and that his goal should be to educate others about why he does what he does. With this in mind, Moreno has hosted and participated in myriad television and radio shows, where he articulately and passionately shares what he has learned in the kitchen.

MENU

BOLLOS PELONES

RED CEVICHE

PASTEL DE CHUCHO BY MORENO

FUSIÓN ARROZ CHAUFA

BIENMESABE

PUYAO CHOCOLATE

stew, seal, and set aside. Repeat this process with the remaining dough balls.
The bollos can be fried, baked, or boiled in broth. Serve hot with tomato sauce. Garnish the bollos with raisins and olives.

PASTEL DE CHUCHO BY MORENO
Serves 6 to 8

For the dogfish stew:
Oil • 10 g garlic, minced • 40 g white onion, finely chopped • 40 g bell pepper, finely chopped • 20 g sweet ají peppers, minced • 15 g tomato paste (purée) • 1 tablespoon Worcestershire sauce • 350 g dogfish, cooked and shredded • Salt and freshly ground black pepper • 20 g cilantro (coriander), minced

For the béchamel sauce:
50 g unsalted butter • 50 g all-purpose (plain) flour • 500 ml milk, warmed

For the sweet plantain slices:
4 very ripe plantains • Oil

For the cheese mix:
125 g shredded mozzarella cheese • 125 g shredded Gouda cheese

Make the dogfish stew:
In a large pot, heat enough oil to cover the bottom. Add the garlic and cook until browned. Add the onion and cook until translucent. Add the bell pepper and sweet ají peppers and cook over low heat for about 10 minutes.

BOLLOS PELONES
Serves 6

For the bollo dough:
300 ml warm water • 1 teaspoon salt • 2 tablespoons adobo seasoning • 200 g yellow corn flour • Oil

For the pork stew:
Oil • 100 g bacon, finely diced • 100 g white onion, finely chopped • 4 cloves garlic, minced • 100 g chives, minced • 50 ml sweet red wine • 1.5 kg pork • 250 ml tomato sauce • Freshly ground black pepper • 2 tablespoons Worcestershire sauce • 250 ml vegetable stock • 40 g pimiento-stuffed olives, finely chopped • 40 g raisins, finely chopped • 1 tablespoon capers, finely chopped • Salt

For assembly:
Tomato sauce • Finely chopped raisins • Finely chopped olives

Make the bollo dough:
In a bowl, mix together the water, salt, and adobo. Add the corn flour and knead

until the dough is smooth. Cover the bowl with plastic wrap (cling film) and let rest for about 20 minutes.
With dampened hands, separate the dough into small balls of 40 g (about 12 balls).
Place the dough balls on a tray with a bit of oil, cover with plastic wrap, and refrigerate until needed.

Make the pork stew:
In a large frying pan, heat the oil and lightly fry the bacon. Add the onion, garlic, and chives and continue cooking for about 10 minutes.
Stir in the red wine. Add the pork and cook for another 10 minutes, stirring constantly. Add the tomato sauce, pepper to taste, and the Worcestershire sauce. Cook for another 20 minutes.
Remove from the heat and stir in the olives, raisins, and capers. Set aside until ready to use.

To assemble:
Take one of the dough balls and make a hole in the middle. Fill the hole with the

250

PASTEL DE CHUCHO BY MORENO

BIENMESABE

251

HE IS SPREADING THE WORD ABOUT THE FOODS OF HIS HOME COUNTRY TO A WIDER AUDIENCE. IT IS SOMETIMES DIFFICULT FOR A CHEF TO BE WELL-REGARDED AND SUCCESSFUL IN THE KITCHEN WHILE ALSO BEING A POPULAR PERSONALITY IN THE MEDIA, BUT VICTOR HAS DONE AN AMAZING JOB TO BE BOTH.

— José Andrés

252

Add the tomato paste (purée) and the Worcestershire sauce. Add the dogfish a little at a time and stir until fully incorporated. Season with salt and pepper to taste. Add the cilantro (coriander), allow the mixture to cool, and refrigerate until ready to use.

Make the béchamel sauce:
In a pot, melt the butter. Add the flour all at once and mix vigorously until browned (make a roux). Add the milk a little at a time, mixing constantly. Cook until thickened. Allow to cool and set aside.

Make the sweet plantain slices:
Peel the plantains, cut them in half lengthwise, then slice, cutting diagonally and not too thickly.
In a large pot, heat some oil over high heat. Once very hot, fry the plantain slices until golden brown.
Transfer the plantains to paper towels to drain. Set aside.

Make the cheese mix:
In a bowl, mix together the mozzarella and Gouda. Set aside.

Assemble the dish:
Cover the bottom of a deep, ovenproof dish with some of the béchamel sauce. Add a fair amount of the stew, then place plantain slices over the stew. Cover with more béchamel sauce, and repeat the process until the dish is filled to within a finger's width of the top. Cover the casserole with the cheese mix.
Bake and serve hot.

BIENMESABE
Serves 6 to 8

For the coconut dacquoise:
72 g almond flour • 54 g all-purpose (plain) flour • 110 g powdered (icing) sugar • 54 g shredded (desiccated) coconut • 200 g egg whites • 30 g granulated sugar

For the coconut pastry cream:
200 g coconut milk • 120 g heavy cream • 60 g milk • 1 egg • 75 g granulated sugar • 30 g all-purpose (plain) flour • Pinch of salt • 10 g butter, cold • 45 g shredded coconut, toasted

For the rum syrup:
100 g water • 50 g granulated sugar • 50 g rum

For the tuiles:
80 g butter • 80 g granulated sugar • 80 g egg whites • 80 g all-purpose (plain) flour

For the coconut kisses:
60 g shredded (desiccated) coconut • 35 g powdered (icing) sugar • 40 g water • 10 g vegetable shortening • 10 g Coconut Pastry Cream *(above)* • 100 g water • 50 g granulated sugar

Make the coconut dacquoise:
Preheat the oven to 360°F (180°C). Grease an 8 × 10-inch (20 × 25 cm) baking pan.
In a bowl, stir together the almond flour, all-purpose (plain) flour, powdered (icing) sugar, and shredded (desiccated) coconut.
In a separate bowl, with an electric mixer, beat the egg whites and granulated sugar until the mixture achieves a foamy texture. With a spatula, fold in the dry ingredients a little bit at a time.
Spread the mixture evenly in the greased baking pan. Bake for 15 minutes. Remove from the oven and allow to cool.

Make the coconut pastry cream:
In a pot, mix the coconut milk, cream, and milk and warm over low heat. Set aside.
In a bowl, with an electric mixer, beat the egg and granulated sugar until the mixture turns white. Mix in the flour and salt.
Add the warm milk mixture a little at a time, mixing constantly to cool the mixture. Pour the mixture into a pot and cook over low heat, stirring constantly, until it acquires a creamy texture. Remove from the heat, add the butter and toasted coconut, stirring gently until incorporated. Cool and set aside.

Make the rum syrup:
In a pot, combine the water and granulated sugar. Cook over low heat, without stirring, until the sugar dissolves. Once cool, add the rum.

Make the tuiles:
In a bowl, with an electric mixer, whip the butter, adding the granulated sugar a little at a time. While still beating the mixture, pour in the egg whites in a thin, steady stream. Once incorporated, add the flour and mix until fully incorporated.
Let the mixture rest for 30 minutes in the refrigerator.
Preheat the oven to 360°F (180°C). Line a sheet pan with wax paper.
With the help of a spatula, spread the batter into thin rounds on the lined sheet pan. Bake until the tuiles are golden brown, then remove from the oven. Once cooled, carefully remove the wafers with a thin spatula or palette knife.
The wafers should be stored in an airtight container to keep them dry.

Make the coconut kisses:
In a pot, combine the coconut, powdered sugar, water, and vegetable shortening. Cook over low heat, stirring constantly, until the mixture becomes paste-like. Remove from the heat, cool, add the pastry cream, and mix.
Form into small balls. Set them in the freezer for 2 hours.
In a small pot, prepare a caramel with the water and sugar, cooking until golden. Skewer the coconut balls, immerse them in the caramel, and allow to set.

To plate:
In a short glass (like a whiskey glass), pour a small amount of the rum syrup. Add a bit of the coconut pastry cream.
Chop the dacquoise and add some to the glass. Cover the glass with the tuile, placing a coconut kiss in the center of the wafer. Sprinkle with a few drops of rum syrup.

VICTOR MORENO

TAKAYUKI NAKATSUKA

NAKATSUKA
Kyoto, Japan

YOSHIHIRO NARISAWA

MENU

CRÊPE CARBONARA

AMBERJACK AND SCALLOP, ORIENTAL

MUSHROOM PASCADE

PIGEON TART, RECONSTRUCTION

FRESH FISH AND WHISKERED VELVET SHRIMP BOUILLABAISSE

PARIS-BREST

At the counter of his restaurant's open kitchen, Takayuki Nakatsuka bends over to perfect the last flourishes on the plates in front of him before sending them to his guests; his service is carefully orchestrated so he can deliver dishes at the temperature that best accentuates each ingredient's aroma. Nakatsuka has performed his culinary magic in his eponymous restaurant in Kyoto, Japan, since 2017. The restaurant's dark wood exterior, emblematic of the traditional Kyoto townhouse, belies the modern blond-wood-paneled walls and contemporary French tasting menus found within. Nakatsuka's many years steeped in French cooking and careful selection of ingredients are evident in dishes that stimulate all five senses of his guests.

Deeply intrigued by French cuisine early on, Nakatsuka elected to study French cooking at Osaka's Tsuji Culinary Institute. After school, he trained under revered chef Yoshihiro Narisawa at La Napoule, in the Kanagawa Prefecture, and then at Narisawa, in Tokyo. Next he set off for Paris, where he cooked at places ranging from classic fine dining (Le Pré Catelan, Le Grand Véfour) to more contemporary and creative outposts (Chez L'Ami Jean, Ze Kitchen Galerie). He worked his way around Europe—Spain (Arzak), Italy (Hotel Ferraro), and Belgium (Pastorale)—before returning to Japan to refamiliarize himself with Japanese kitchens and ultimately to open his own place.

Every one of Nakatsuka's dishes reflects his philosophy—the centrality of smell—playing with elements such as herbs, citrus, and spices to coax forth the subtle uniqueness of different ingredients. For example, he may accent a chilled corn soup with a dusting of coffee powder, or enliven peony shrimp with a sauce based on calamansi, a Southeast Asian citrus. His version of bouillabaisse—a wedge of fish bathed in a coppery orange broth, crowned with a cluster of vibrant green herbs—constantly evolves as Nakatsuka riffs on the shifts in flavor and ingredients that accompany the changing seasons.

CRÊPE CARBONARA

Pork belly • Salt • Sugar • Pimenton • Fresh paprika peppers • Onions • Chorizo, cubed • Bouillon • Sherry vinegar • Eggs • Sugar • Buckwheat flour • All-purpose flour • Browned butter • Milk • Salt • Poached eggs, for serving • Green salad dressed with vinaigrette, for serving • Parmesan, for garnish • Freshly ground black pepper, for garnish

Cut the pork belly into blocks and coat with salt and sugar. Vacuum pack the pork blocks and cook sous vide for 2 days.
Remove the pork from the bath, remove packaging, and wipe all the moisture off the meat. Season with imenton powder and vacuum cook once again.
Remove the pork and cook in a steam oven at 60°C for 70 minutes. Then, use a smoke machine to smoke the pork fragrant. Cut the bacon into 3mm slices and sear its surface with a burner.
In the oven, Bake the peppers. Then, remove the skin and seeds and transfer to a blender. Puree the peppers.
Saute the onions with butter, then add the chorizo. Add the bouillon, then cook for 30 minutes. Transfer the onion-chorizo mixture to a blender and puree, then strain. Combine with the pepper puree and season to taste with sherry vinegar and salt.
In a bowl, beat together the eggs and sugar. Sift both flours into the mixture and stir. Add the browned butter and the milk and mix thoroughly. Adjust the flavor with salt. Bake thin crepes with the batter.
To serve, place a folded crepe on a plate and top with bacon, pochaed eggs, chorizo puree, and salad. Garnish with grated Parmesan cheese, more pimenton, and freshly ground black pepper.

FRESH FISH AND WHISKERED VELVET SHRIMP BOUILLABAISSE

Olive oil • Garlic, thinly sliced • Vegetables, thinly sliced • Fish scraps, finely chopped • Tomato paste • Tomatoes, sliced • Lobster • Powdered saffron • Whiskered velvet shrimp, heads removed and reserved • Rice bran oil • Fresh fish

In a pan, heat the olive oil and saute the garlic. Add the vegetables and stir fry. Add the fish scraps and cook until the mixture starts to soften into a puree. Add some tomato paste and the tomatoes.
In a separate pan, stir-fry the lobster until fragrant. Add water to cover, bring up to a simmer, and cook for 15 minutes. Strain the broth and add saffron.
Fry the reserved shrimp heads until fragrant and then transfer them to a mixer with the rice bran oil. Blend well, then strain.
Fry the fish and shrimp until fragrant.
To serve, pour the broth over the fish and shrimp. Garnish with shrimp-head oil, and olive oil.

PIGEON TART, RECONSTRUCTION

CHEF NAKATSUKA SERVES
CAREFULLY COOKED DISHES
IN A CASUAL ATMOSPHERE.
HE HAS QUITE A TALENT—
IT WILL BE VERY EXCITING
TO SEE WHERE HE GOES
FROM HERE.
— Yoshihiro Narisawa

TAKAYUKI NAKATSUKA

TOYOMITSU NAKAYAMA

RAQUEL CARENA

TOYO
Paris, France, and
Tokyo, Japan

In 2009, Toyomitsu Nakayama, who goes by Toyo, opened his eponymous restaurant on a Paris street not far from Montparnasse. The refined, elegant venue reflects the singular cuisine of this Japanese chef. Born in the south of Japan, after culinary school Toyo trained in Kobe at Jean Moulin, a restaurant inspired by classic French cuisine. Ironically, it was in Paris, at Isse, that Nakayama finally returned to Japanese food culture. Discovered by the couturier Kenzo Takada, Toyo was Kenzo's personal chef for seven years before opening his own place in Paris, and then another in Tokyo.

Since then, Nakayama has never ceased to build bridges between French and Japanese cultures. Both cuisines emphasize not imposing the strength of one ingredient upon another, while playing up their special qualities and maintaining the clarity of a recipe. At the counter, face to face with his customers, Nakayama uses the same large Japanese knife to prepare even the simplest of ingredients, such as a daikon or turnip. He cuts or slices them differently depending on whether they will be served lightly roasted, grilled, candied, cooked al dente, or raw and barely touched. Mushrooms are gently brushed to perfect their texture. Toyo's approach is almost ceremonial, performed in silence. Minimalism is the guiding principle, eschewing overuse of sauces and seasonings.

Toyo embodies balance: exquisite French cuisine with Japanese aesthetics and spirituality. The multicourse meals, which follow the tradition of kaiseki, are as much a journey as an experience. Nakayama allies himself with faithful suppliers to find the best the seasons and terroirs have to offer, including Hugo Desnoyer's meats; fish and shellfish from the Poissonnerie du Dôme; and vegetables from the Marché Président Wilson. Every element is important—the contrast of textures and flavors, the composition, even the succession of plates all display an intricate balance, definitive of his cooking. The menu finishes with an incredible Japanese paella that combines rice and seaweed with shellfish or chicken. Fruit sorbets and sake granita are offered for dessert, and are completed by the "signature infusion" that bursts with the flavors of ginger and candied kumquat.

MENU

RAW TUNA WITH
SALMON EGGS

SAINT-JACQUES SALAD

KANPACHI WITH TOMATO
SAUCE AND PARMESAN

KINMEDAÏ WITH
CHICKEN BROTH

PAELLA TOYO STYLE

PEACH SOUP WITH
YOGURT GRANITA

PAELLA TOYO STYLE
Serves 4

For the clams:
20 clams • 1 clove garlic, smashed • 1 fresh or dried chili pepper • Oil • 10 g shallots, chopped • 25 g fennel, coarsely chopped • 50 ml white wine • 100 ml chicken stock

For the onsen tamago:
4 eggs

For the paella:
150 g mixed mushrooms (such as shiitake, oyster mushrooms, or chanterelles) • Salt • Sake • 200 g Japanese rice • 10 g yellow carrot, very finely grated (on a Japanese grater) • 5 g unsalted butter • 200 g skin-on chicken thighs • Grapeseed oil • 50 g shimeji mushrooms • 2 or 3 drops soy sauce

For finishing:
5 g seaweed butter • A few scallion (spring onion) tops • 10 g sanshô (Japanese pepper) • 1 lime

Prepare the clams:
Check that the clams are fresh and discard any dead ones. Wash them in running water, rubbing them together. Let them soak for at least 1 hour in a salt solution made with 3.5% salt by weight (35 g of salt per 1 liter of water, like seawater) to remove sand and dirt. In a saucepan, sauté the garlic and chili in a little oil. Add the clams, shallots, fennel, and white wine. Put over high heat and cover. When the clams open, remove from the heat. Cover the pan and let sit to continue cooking.
Shuck the clams and strain the cooking juices through a chinois. Pour 100 ml of this juice into a saucepan and add the chicken stock. This broth will be used to cook the paella.

Make the onsen tamago:

Place the eggs in a small saucepan and add just enough water to cover them. Heat over medium-low heat and maintain the water temperature at 147°F (64°C) for 40 minutes. Set aside.

Make the paella:
Preheat the oven to 284°F (140°C). Clean and slice the mushrooms. Arrange on a baking sheet. Salt them and pour a little sake over them, then put into the oven for 10 minutes to remove any liquid. Meanwhile, rinse the rice thoroughly and let it soak in water for 15 minutes. Drain. In a saucepan, combine the mushrooms, drained rice, grated carrot, butter, and broth (reserved from cooking the clams). Cover and bring to a boil over medium heat for 10 minutes. Increase the heat to high for 30 seconds, the reduce the heat to low and cook for 10 minutes. Remove from the heat and let sit covered for 10 minutes. Lightly salt the chicken thighs on all sides

PAELLA TOYO STYLE

259

EVERYTHING IS CALM WITH HIM, PRECISE, BALANCED. EVERYTHING TAKES PLACE QUIETLY, UNDER CONTROL. AND YET THERE IS SOMETHING VERY ENERGETIC IN HIS CUISINE, A COMING AND GOING OF FLA-VORS, UNEXPECTED MARRIAGES THAT ALWAYS WORK.
— Raquel Careua

CARPACCIO TOYO STYLE

to remove any odor. Wrap them in paper towels and let drain for about 10 minutes. Heat a sauté pan and pour in a little oil. Add the chicken skin-side down (do not crowd the pan) and sear—it should be half cooked through. Dice.

In another sauté pan, quickly sauté the shimejis. Season them with soy sauce.

To finish:

Add the seaweed butter, clams, chicken, and shimejis to the pan with the rice. Cover and cook over high heat for 30 seconds. The chicken will continue to cook off the heat in the covered pan.

Just before serving, sprinkle with finely chopped chives and stir well to mix. Accompany with onsen tamago, fresh sanshō, and lime, if you like.

SAINT-JACQUES SALAD
Serves 4

4 sea scallops • Guérande salt • Seasonal mushrooms • Citron • A few chive flowers • Aromatic herbs of your choice • Olive oil

Cut the scallops in half.
Season a serving dish lightly with salt. Arrange the scallops, mushrooms, a small piece of citron, chive flowers, and herbs on the salt. Add a little olive oil.

PEACH SOUP WITH YOGURT GRANITA
Serves 8

For the yogurt granita:
125 g yogurt (with a full-flavored taste) • Pinch of salt

For the peach soup:
1 lemon, thinly sliced • 6 white peaches • 300 g powdered sugar • 100 ml white wine • 2 sheets gelatin (2 g each) • Juice of 1 lemon • 100 g powdered (icing) sugar • 100 ml whole milk • 1 sprig mint

For plating:
8 bunches sea grapes • Mint leaves • 1 yellow peach, sliced

Make the yogurt granita:
Drain the yogurt in a colander for about 30 minutes in the refrigerator.
Pour the drained yogurt into a container and stir it well with the salt. Place in the freezer for 30 minutes, then stir with a fork to break up the ice crystals. Repeat this procedure three times.

Make the peach soup:
In a small pot, bring about 250 ml of water to a boil. Add four of the peaches to the water with the sugar, and place the lemon slices over the surface. Cover with

a cartouche and return to a boil. Add the wine and remove from the heat, then let cool to room temperature.
Soak the gelatin sheets in a bowl of ice water for 5 minutes to soften them.
In a small saucepan, heat 600 ml of the cooking liquid from the poached peaches over low heat. When the juice reaches about 140°F (60°C), squeeze out the gelatin sheets and add them to the juice. Stir until the gelatin dissolves, then remove from the heat and strain it through a very fine sieve.
Rinse the remaining peaches briefly. Without peeling them, make 6 vertical cuts at regular intervals into each one and remove the pits. Transfer the peaches to a blender. Working quickly to preserve their color, add half the lemon juice and sugar, then the gelatin mixture. Stir in half the milk and blend again.
Taste and add the rest of the lemon juice, milk, and sugar, depending on the sugar content of the peaches and your preferences. Strain the soup through a fine-mesh sieve. Lightly mash the stem of the mint sprig and add it to the soup.

To finish:
Place 2 tablespoons of yogurt granita on each serving plate. Pour 3 tablespoons of peach soup over it and garnish with sea grapes, a few mint leaves, and a few slices of yellow peach.

TOYOMITSU NAKAYAMA

JOSH NILAND

SAINT PETER, FISH BUTCHERY
Paddington, Australia

SKYE GYNGELL

MENU

GOLDBAND SNAPPER SCOTCH EGGS

HAND-FILLETED SARDINES IN VIVIDUS EXTRA-VIRGIN OLIVE OIL AND BBQ O COUTO PEPPERS

ROCK OYSTER, SCARLET PRAWN AND SEA URCHIN

BBQ RED MULLET, BURNT TOMATO, MARJORAM, AND ANCHOVY

A SELECTION OF FISH BUTCHERY CHARCUTERIE

16-DAY AGED ALBACORE, BBQ FENNEL, BULL KELP, AND ALMONDS

CHOCOLATE AND COBIA FAT CARAMEL SLICE

Australian chef Josh Niland of Saint Peter restaurant in Sydney has made a significant contribution to changing the way we think about fish consumption. In 2016, Niland opened Saint Peter to critical acclaim; then, he and his business partner and wife, Julie, also a chef, followed up by launching the Fish Butchery, a contemporary fishmonger selling only local, line-caught species. Taking a cue from the nose-to-tail movement in butchery, Niland and his like-minded colleagues apply a gill-to-fin philosophy in cutting fresh fish. The technique reduces the ratio of waste from the traditional fillet-focused approach, which yields only 40 to 50 percent of the edible parts of the fish. Additionally, both Saint Peter and Fish Butchery introduce lesser-known varieties to customers to help take the pressure off overfished species.

Given Niland's fish focus, it's ironic that he grew up in a landlocked region of Australia. In fact, it was the challenge of being an eight-year-old with cancer that led to Niland's initial interest in food: watching cooking shows on television was a respite from his illness. Then, at age fifteen, Niland attended a children's cancer charity lunch, where he was given a certificate for dinner for two at Fish Face, Steve Hodges's lauded Sydney seafood restaurant. By seventeen, Niland had secured work in various busy Sydney eateries, including Est. from Peter Doyle, who eventually introduced him to Hodges. Niland's story came full circle when Hodges hired and mentored him. Later, a stint at Heston Blumenthal's Fat Duck development kitchen helped cement Niland's vision of what he hoped to do with fish.

Saint Peter has been shortlisted for the World Restaurant Award for Ethical Thinking and made the long list for both Ethical and Original Thinking. Niland and his team have received numerous other accolades as well as much critical acclaim, winning him an international coterie of kindred-spirit devotees.

GOLDBAND SNAPPER SCOTCH EGGS
Makes 8 eggs

30 g ghee • 1 onion, finely diced • 125 g ocean trout or sea trout belly • 125 g skinless white fish fillet (such as ling, cod, grouper or snapper), cut into ¼-inch (5 mm) dice • 4 g fine salt • 2 g freshly ground black pepper • 2 g ground fennel • 1 tablespoon finely chopped parsley • 1 tablespoon finely chopped chives • 12 eggs • 150 g rice flour • 150 g white panko bread crumbs • Flaky salt • Cottonseed oil, for deep-frying

In a small saucepan, heat the ghee over medium heat and sweat the onion for 6–7 minutes, then cool completely. Cut the trout belly into large chunks and chill for at least 2 hours until completely cold. Working in small batches, blend the trout belly in a food processor until smooth. If the mix seems too oily, add a splash of chilled water to help emulsify. Transfer to a bowl and add the diced white fish, sautéed onion, salt, pepper, fennel, parsley, and chives. In a large deep saucepan, bring 2 liters of water to a boil. Once at a boil, carefully add 8 of the eggs to the water and cover with a fitted lid. Cook for 5 minutes 30 seconds. Transfer the eggs to an ice bath to stop the cooking. Once the eggs are completely cold, peel them. This is very challenging when the eggs are this soft, so be patient and ultimately if it proves to be too difficult, then cook the egg for 1 minute longer. Set the peeled eggs aside in the fridge. (These eggs can be done the day before if necessary.) Using a square of plastic wrap (cling film), place 70 g of the fish mixture into the center of the square. Pat down gently with clean hands to create an even platform for the egg to sit on about ⅛ inch (3–4 mm) thick. Set the peeled egg in the center of the fish mix. Carefully pull up the 4 edges of the plastic and form an egg shape by twisting the plastic together to bring the fish around the soft egg. Be careful not to twist too tight as the egg may break. Once the eggs are assembled, refrigerate for about 1 hour to allow to set. Set up a dredging station: Flour in one container, the remaining 4 eggs whisked together in a second, and the panko in a third. Dredge the eggs first in flour, then egg wash, then panko, each egg once only. Allow to set again for another hour in the refrigerator. Pour oil into a deep-fryer or deep heavy pot, Heat to 356°F (180°C) over medium heat. Lower the egg into the hot oil and fry for 2 minutes, then remove from the oil to a wire rack to drain well. Season with salt flakes. Let rest for 2 minutes longer, then using a sharp serrated knife cut the Scotch egg in

GOLDBAND SNAPPER SCOTCH EGGS

16-DAY AGED ALBACORE

half and serve with cocktail sauce, tartar sauce, or mustard with bitter greens like dandelion, endive, and nasturtium.

BBQ RED MULLET, BURNT TOMATO, MARJORAM, AND ANCHOVY
Serves 4

For the tomato dressing:
300 g cherry tomatoes, halved • 75 g capers • 125 g shallot, thinly sliced into rings • 2 teaspoons superfine (caster) sugar • 100 ml Chardonnay vinegar (or white wine vinegar with a pinch of sugar) • 80 g salted anchovy fillets • 200 ml extra-virgin olive oil

For the mullet:
4 boneless butterflied red mullet (about 200 g each), skin on, head and tail on • 60 ml extra-virgin olive oil • Flaky sea salt and cracked black pepper

Make the dressing:
Heat a cast-iron skillet over high heat. Working in batches if necessary, add the tomato halves, cut-side down, and let sit until darkly colored, about 6 minutes. Once all tomatoes are burnt, add the capers, shallot, sugar, vinegar, anchovies, and olive oil and set aside for 30 minutes before serving. Keep warm.

Grill the mullet:
Prepare a hot charcoal grill, with the charcoal burnt down to hot embers. Level out the embers so the heat is even.
Brush the fish with olive oil and season the skin liberally with salt. Place the fish, skin-side down, on the grill rack, add a fish weight *(see Note)* on top of the flesh closest to the head and grill for 2 minutes. Reposition the fish weight to the center of the fish and cook for a minute longer.
When the fish is 70 percent cooked, serve with warm tomato dressing. The remainder of the cooking will happen when the fish is garnished. Trust that this heat will finish the cooking. If mullet is overcooked, it will result in a neutral flavor profile and texture comparable to overcooked chicken

> *Note: A fish weight is a stainless-steel weight that I specifically designed for fish cookery. It brings efficiency to the method of cooking fish by the transfer of heat from the skin to the flesh. Along with evenness of cooking and coloration of the skin when pan-frying or grilling.*

16-DAY AGED ALBACORE, BBQ FENNEL, BULL KELP, AND ALMONDS
Serves 4

For the fennel dressing:
1 large bulb fennel, stalks intact • 170 ml extra-virgin olive oil • 80 g dried kelp powder • Pinch of salt • 1 teaspoon superfine (caster) sugar • 60 g French shallot, thinly sliced into rings • 50 ml Chardonnay vinegar (or white wine vinegar with a pinch of sugar) • 100 g bull kelp (or best alternative, such as samphire), finely sliced • 80 g almonds, halved and toasted

For the albacore:
400 g albacore top loin • 50 ml extra-virgin olive oil • Flaky sea salt

Shave the fennel on a mandoline, starting at the head and cutting down to the base. In a bowl, toss the fennel with 30 ml of the olive oil until it is lightly dressed.
Heat a grill pan (griddle pan) or a cast-iron skillet over high heat. Add a little of the fennel in a single layer and cook for 1–2 minutes, turning the fennel over halfway. Transfer to a large bowl and season with the kelp powder. Set aside. Repeat with the remaining fennel.
In a separate bowl, combine the salt, sugar, and shallot. Set aside for 10 minutes, then stir in the remaining 140 ml oil and the vinegar. Add this dressing to the fennel along with the sliced kelp and almonds and leave in a warm place.

Prepare the albacore:
Brush the loin with the olive oil lightly coat.
Season lightly with salt flakes.
Heat a grill pan (griddle pan) or a cast-iron skillet over high heat. Place the albacore loin on the hot pan and being sure to count 5 seconds for each side of the albacore, sear briefly until every raw surface of the fish has been seared for an even amount of time. Remove from the pan and allow to stand at room temperature.

When ready to serve, carve the albacore loin: Take 16 slices from the loin giving 4 thin slices and about 100 g total per portion. Place a spoonful of the fennel dressing in the center of a plate. Drape the albacore slices delicately atop the warm fennel dressing. Season well with salt flakes. Serve warm.

CHOCOLATE AND COBIA FAT CARAMEL SLICE
Serves 16

For the chocolate base:
190 g unsalted butter, at room temperature • 215 g superfine (caster) caster sugar • 15 g unsweetened cocoa powder • 105 g egg yolks • 75 g eggs • 225 g dark chocolate (at least 70% cacao), melted • 340 g egg whites

For the chocolate custard:
235 g unsalted butter • 345 g dark chocolate (at least 70% cacao), broken into pieces • 6 eggs • 210 g superfine (caster) sugar

For the chocolate glaze:
8 sheets titanium gelatin • 500 ml ice-cold water • 140 ml water • 180 g superfine (caster) sugar • 120 g single (light) cream • 60 g good-quality high percentage cocoa powder • 100 g Valrhona neutral glaze (buy online)

For the cobia fat salted caramel:
125 g fish fat (cobia or cod) • 500 g superfine (caster) sugar • 250 g double cream • 2 vanilla beans, split open lengthwise • 75 g liquid glucose • 200 g unsalted butter • 3 g flaky sea salt

For assembly:
4 glazed chocolate cakes *(above)* • 4 strips Cobia Fat Salted Caramel *(above)* • Flaky sea salt • 120 g sour cream

Make the chocolate base:
Preheat the oven to 340°F (170°C). Line two 12 × 8-inch (30 × 20 cm) baking pans with parchment paper.
In a stand mixer fitted with the paddle, beat the butter, 90 g of the sugar, and the cocoa until pale and the sugar has dissolved. Gradually add the egg yolks and whole eggs on medium speed in 3 batches, making sure they are incorporated after each addition. Stop the mixer and add the melted chocolate. Turn the mixer back

on gradually to a medium speed until the chocolate is incorporated.
In a separate bowl, whisk the egg whites with the remaining 125 g sugar for 4 minutes, or until stiff peaks form, then gently fold through the chocolate base until incorporated.
Divide the batter between the prepared baking pans and bake until the cake is just set and a skewer inserted into the center comes out clean, about 20 minutes. Refrigerate for 1 hour.

Make the chocolate custard:
Preheat the oven to 340°F (170°C). Line a 12 × 8-inch (30 × 20 cm) baking pan with parchment paper.
Melt the butter and chocolate together in a heatproof bowl set over a saucepan of simmering water. When melted, mix well to combine.
In a stand mixer, whisk the eggs and sugar together in a stand mixer until the sugar has dissolved. Fold the chocolate into the egg mix, then pour into the prepared baking pan. Place the baking pan in a larger baking pan or roasting pan, then pour in enough hot water to come halfway up the sides of the smaller pan. Cover the larger pan with foil, making sure it is sealed and bake until the custard is just set, about 40 minutes. Remove from the oven, uncover and, if the custard isn't set, leave it in the warm water. Refrigerate overnight to set.

To assemble the cake, lay a cake layer on a cutting board. Invert the pan of set custard upside down on top and tip the custard out onto the cake. Firmly push down to stick them together. Peel the parchment paper off the custard and, using a very hot sharp knife, cut the cake into bars about 4 inches (10 cm) long and 1½–2 inches (4–5 cm) wide. Arrange the bars on a wire rack set over a sheet pan and refrigerate for 1 hour.

Meanwhile, make the glaze:
Soften the gelatin in the ice-cold water for 15 minutes.
In a saucepan, combine the 140 ml water, sugar, and cream and bring to a boil. Add the cocoa and mix well.
In a separate small pan, melt the neutral glaze over low heat. Add the neutral glaze to the cream mixture, return to a boil, and boil for 5 minutes. Remove from the heat

and add the softened gelatin. Combine and set aside in a warm place, if not using immediately. The glaze needs to be warmed to 95°F (35°C) to be pourable.
Pour the warm glaze over the bars, then refrigerate for 1 hour on a wire rack until set. Once set, trim off any glaze that has stuck to the base and chill in an airtight container until required.

Make cobia fat salted caramel:
Line two 12 × 8-inch (30 × 20 cm) baking trays with parchment paper.
In a saucepan, melt the fat over low heat until liquid, 10–12 minutes. Keep warm.
In a separate saucepan, combine 250 g of the sugar and the cream. Scrape in the vanilla seeds and add the pods. Warm over low heat until the sugar has dissolved, about 5 minutes. Cool. Remove the vanilla pods.
In a large heavy-bottomed pot, mix the remaining 250 g sugar and the liquid glucose together and cook over medium-high heat for 10 minutes, without stirring until the sugar has dissolved. Cook until the caramel has reached the desired color, then add the vanilla cream in three batches, being careful as it will spit and boil rapidly. Cook until it reaches a temperature of 262°F (128°C), then remove from the heat and, using a whisk, whisk in the butter, melted cobia fat, and salt. Pour the caramel across the prepared baking pans in a thin layer, about ¼ in (5 mm) thick and cool completely at room temperature for 2 hours. Refrigerate overnight to set.
The next day, tip the caramel onto a cutting board and, using a very hot sharp knife, cut the caramel into 4 × ¾-inch (10 × 2 cm) strips. Refrigerate in an airtight container until required.

To assemble:
Place the 4 glazed chocolate bars down in front of you. Arrange the caramel strips in the center of each chocolate bar and a few salt flakes. Place the sour cream in a piping bag fitted with a fluted tip (nozzle) and pipe the sour cream down both sides of the caramel. There should be a gap of ¾ inch (2 cm) between the edge of the caramel and the edge of the chocolate. Serve at room temperature.

> VERY RARELY SOMEONE COMES ALONG AND MAKES YOU THINK ABOUT THINGS IN A VERY NEW AND DIFFERENT WAY. JOSH IS ONE OF THOSE CHEFS. — Skye Gyngell

A SELECTION OF FISH BUTCHERY CHARCUTERIE

HAND-FILLETED SARDINES

JOSH NILAND

JESSICA NOËL

DAVID MCMILLAN

MON LAPIN
Montreal, Quebec, Canada

MENU

CARROTS, 'NDUJA, POLLEN

DUCK HEARTS, SUNCHOKE
CHARCUTIÈRE

ONION GALETTE, GREEN ONION
BAGNA CAUDA

"POMME AU FOUR"
PROFITEROLE

MACKEREL, HABANADA, WHEY

When it comes to vegetables, Mon Lapin's Jessica Noël is an expert by way of obsession. Mon Lapin's fine fare is an extension of Noël's undying love of seasonal produce, which she complements with oft-neglected seafood and cuts of meat. She helms the restaurant's open kitchen alongside chef-partner Marc-Olivier Frappier, and pairs the ever-changing seasonal menu with an extensive natural wine list full of idiosyncrasy. The experience, a manifestation of Noël's robust talent and larger-than-life passion, is belied only by the tiny, cozy dimensions of the restaurant itself.

Noël found her way into a white coat after spending several years working in the fashion industry. In 2012, she took her career in a different direction, drawing inspiration from childhood memories of watching her mother and grandmother cook, and enrolled in a cooking course at the Institut de tourisme et d'hôtellerie du Québec, from which she graduated. Throughout her studies, she worked in the restaurant business, including restaurant Toqué! in Montreal and Blue Hill at Stone Barns in New York state. In 2014, after receiving a Relais & Châteaux scholarship, Noël ventured to Europe to *stage* at Steirereck im Stadtpark in Vienna, Frantzén in Stockholm, and Maison Pic in Valence, France. She then returned to New York to work again at Blue Hill at Stone Barns.

Mon Lapin opened its doors in 2018, and Noël has been there from the very beginning. Her belief that vegetables, grains, and legumes should serve as the stars of a dish has helped to define the restaurant's identity—it is by no means limited to vegetarian cuisine, but meat and seafood certainly take a backseat here, and ingredient sourcing by season always shines. Tucked away in Montreal's Little Italy neighborhood, Mon Lapin lives up to its accolades, and with Noël at the helm, it can only go up from there.

CARROTS, 'NDUJA, POLLEN
Serves 4

For the chewy carrots:
6 large carrots • 1 tablespoon grapeseed oil • Salt and freshly ground black pepper • 2 sprigs thyme

For the 'nduja/carrot sauce:
1 onion, diced • 100 g 'nduja (to taste, depending on how spicy your 'nduja is) • 500 ml carrot juice (including the roasting juices from Chewy Carrots, *above*) • 100 g olive oil • Smoked apple cider vinegar • Salt

For the pollen mix:
1 tablespoon black peppercorns • 2 tablespoons bee pollen • 2 tablespoons fennel pollen • Sea salt

To assemble:
Oil • Garlic-infused honey

Make the chewy carrots:
Preheat the oven to 375°F (190°C). Season the carrots and seal in a foil papillote. Roast until soft but not too far. Take the carrots out of the papillote and reserve the cooking juices for the sauce. Place the carrots on a tray and dehydrate at 158°F (70°C) for 12 hours.

Make the 'nduja/carrot sauce:
In a sauté pan, sweat the onion until translucent. Add the 'nduja and cook through. Deglaze with the 500 ml carrot juice (which includes the reserved roasting juices) and let reduce by one-third.
Blend the mixture, mounting it with the olive oil. Pass through a fine chinois. Finish the seasoning with the vinegar and salt. The end result should be sweet and slightly spicy. Reserve at room temperature until ready to serve.

Make the pollen mix:
In a blender, pulse the peppercorns to uniform size. Shake first in a chinois and then in a fine chinois to get rid of the fine dust and keep only what is left between both sifting procedures.
Pulse the bee pollen to break up the larger pieces.
In a bowl, mix together the bee pollen, peppercorns, and fennel pollen. Finish with sea salt to taste.

To assemble:
Heat the oil in a fryer to 375°F (190°C). Cut the chewy carrots into manageable pieces. Add to the fryer and cook until golden and warmed through. They should have a meaty texture.
Place the garlic-honey in a bowl and cover the fried carrots. Spread the pollen mixture on a tray and dip one side of the carrots to completely cover them.
Pour the 'nduja/carrot sauce into a plate and place each piece of carrot.

MACKEREL, HABANADA, WHEY
Serves 4

For the grilled habanada pepper pickle:
200 g habanada peppers • 250 ml apple cider vinegar • 140 g water • 80 g sugar • 25 g salt

For the whey and fermented habanada vinaigrette:
Habanada peppers • Salt • 1 tablespoon plus 150 ml yogurt whey

CARROTS, 'NDUJA, POLLEN

DUCK HEARTS, SUNCHOKE CHARCUTIÈRE

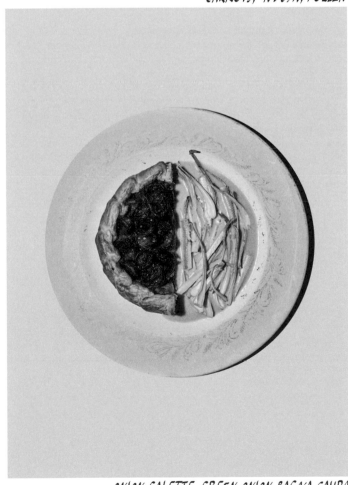

ONION GALETTE, GREEN ONION BAGNA CAUDA

"POMME AU FOUR" PROFITEROLE

MACKEREL, HABANADA, WHEY

For the smoked yogurt:
250 g drained plain yogurt (housemade) • Handful of hay • Salt

For the cured mackerel:
50 g smoked salt • 50 g sugar • 750 g mackerel, filleted and skinned

For assembly:
Lemon juice • Salt • Camelina oil

Make the grilled habanada pepper pickle:
Grill the peppers over charcoal for a few seconds to get slightly charred. Cool down and place in a heatproof container.
In a saucepan, combine the vinegar, water, sugar, and salt and bring to a boil. Pour the brine over the peppers and refrigerate until ready to use.

Make the whey and fermented habanada vinaigrette:
In a saucepan, cook down the habanada peppers slowly. Blend until smooth. Place in a vacuum bag and add 1.5% salt and the 1 tablespoon whey. Seal and let ferment for 5–7 days.
Mix 150 ml of the fermented pepper puree with the remaining 150 ml whey to make a vinaigrette. It should already be sour and salty. If needed you can add some of the habanada pickling liquid to adjust the seasoning.

Make the smoked yogurt:
Set the strained yogurt in a perforated pan on parchment paper. Cover with foil.
Place the hay in a hotel pan (gastro) and torch to get smoky. Place the perforated pan on top and smoke for about 30 seconds or until smoky enough.
Transfer to a bowl and season with salt.

Make the cured mackerel:
In a small bowl, combine the smoked salt and sugar. Place the mackerel fillets on a tray and cover with the sugar/salt mix. Let sit for 20 minutes.
Rinse off the cure. Dice the mackerel into 50 g portions.

To assemble:
Season the mackerel dice with lemon juice, salt, and camelina oil.
At the bottom of the plate, place a dollop of smoked yogurt. Cover with the mackerel. Place the halved of habanada pickles on top. Pour over the whey vinaigrette.
Drizzle everything with cold-pressed camelina oil (this oil brings a mustardy kick).

"POMME AU FOUR" PROFITEROLE
Serves 12

For the pâte à choux:
240 g water • 120 g unsalted butter • 66 g sugar • 3 g salt • 175 g all-purpose (plain) flour • 5 eggs

For the craquelin:
85 g unsalted butter • 100 g brown sugar • 100 g all-purpose (plain) flour • Salt

For the baked apple:
125 g unsalted butter • 200 g brown sugar • 2 tablespoons ground cinnamon • ¼ teaspoon freshly grated nutmeg • Freshly ground black pepper to taste • Fleur de sel to taste • 6 Cortland apples, halved and cored

For the yogurt cream:
2 sheets gelatin • 250 g heavy cream (35%) • Malt syrup • 250 g drained plain yogurt

For the pink apple puree:
3 very red Cortland apples, halved and cored

For the apple-whey caramel:
250 g apple juice (clarified) • 250 g yogurt whey • 100 g sugar • 125 g heavy cream (35%) • 50 g unsalted butter • Fleur de sel

Make the pâte à choux:
In a pot, bring the water, butter, sugar, and salt to a boil. Add the flour in one shot. Mix to combine and cook out the flour.
Transfer the mixture to a stand mixer with the paddle and beat to release the steam. Add one egg at a time on medium speed. Place in a piping bag with a large plain tip (nozzle). Pipe 2-inch (5 cm) spheres onto a silicone baking mat on a pan.

Make the craquelin:
Preheat the oven to 375°F (190°C) low fan.
In a bowl, cream the butter and brown sugar until well combined and soft. Beat in the flour and salt to taste until homogenous. Place the mixture in a sous vide bag and roll out to fill the bag. Place in the freezer. Once frozen, let stand at room temperature to temper, then cut 2-inch (5 cm) rounds. Place a round of craquelin on top of each choux. Bake the choux for 28 minutes.

Make the baked apple:
Preheat the oven to 375°F (190°C).
In a stand mixer with the paddle, beat the butter, brown sugar, and spices until well combined and soft.
Cover the half apples with the butter mixture. Bake until soft but still holding their shape, about 15 minutes.
Flip the apple to really soak in the syrup and let rest in a warm place.

Make the yogurt cream:
Soften the gelatin in 50 g of the cream.
In a stand mixer with the whisk, combine the remaining 200 g cream, the gelatin mixture, and malt syrup to sweeten and whip to firm peaks.
In another bowl, whisk the yogurt to loosen it up. Gently fold in the whipped cream. Keep in the fridge.

Make the pink apple puree:
Vacuum-seal the half apples and cook in an 80°C water bath for 30 minutes.
Transfer the apples and their juices to a blender and blend until smooth. Adjust the seasoning if needed. Chill until use.

Make the apple-whey caramel:
In a pot, combine the apple juice and yogurt whey and cook to reduce by half. Add the sugar and boil until caramelized. Once amber in color, add the cream and let simmer a few minutes to incorporate. Mount with the butter and finish seasoning with the fleur de sel. Keep warm.
To assemble, cut the top off a choux. Fill with a baked apple half. Cover with the whipped yogurt cream and close with the top.
Place a spoonful of the cold apple puree on a plate. Set a filled choux on top. Cover with the apple-whey caramel.

EACH SEASON
SHE ANALYZES
NEW PRODUCE,
SOURCES THE
BEST GROWERS,
RESEARCHES
EVERYTHING THAT
HAS EVER BEEN
DONE WITH IT,
AND COMES UP
WITH A NEW WAY
TO DO IT.
— David McMillan

JESSICA NOËL

OSWALDO OLIVA

LOREA
Mexico City, Mexico

VIRGILIO MARTÍNEZ

Lorea, opened in 2017 by Mexican chef Oswaldo Oliva, is one of the most eminent fine-dining establishments in Mexico City, one of the world's most enthralling culinary hubs. Accessed through a discreet townhouse doorway in the Roma Norte district, Lorea's contemporary dining room is a sleek backdrop for Oliva's inspired modern Mexican cuisine. His credo is to challenge preconceived notions about Mexican food, which drives his inventiveness and often means taking risks and surprising diners.

Oliva hails from Andoni Luis Aduriz's illustrious modernist restaurant Mugaritz in Spain, where he did research and development along with cooking. A 2014 trip with Aduriz to Mexico City surprised and inspired Oliva. While he had been cooking abroad, Mexico City's dining scene had changed, and Oliva wanted to be a part of his hometown's culinary movement. He decided to return to Mexico City and create his own restaurant. The goal from the start was to challenge preconceived notions of fine dining and contribute to the Mexico City food scene. Oliva created Lorea as an extension of himself: a place where he could continue to grow as a chef by changing the menu daily. He committed to giving his teams a good quality of life, insisting that everyone take two days off each week.

At Lorea, guests can guide their own experience, choosing from nine- to fifteen-course tasting menus, or coming just for a drink and some snacks from the à la carte menu. Everything is sourced from Mexican ingredients in peak season, and designed to challenge the palate with innovative flavors and techniques. However, the thread running through all of Lorea's offerings is corn, be it in a broth or sauce, or in the form of a tortilla freshly cooked on the comal that stands in the middle of the dining room. With Lorea, Oliva has created a space meant to inspire trust so diners can take risks. Each meal tells a story: of Oliva's passion, of his history and his place, and of the future of Mexican gastronomy.

MENU

ROASTED TENDONS AND FISH-BONE HOLLANDAISE

HUITLACOCHE, BARLEY BROTH AND CORN SILK

OUR WAGYU BARBACOA

HONEY AND ARBEQUINA

HIBISCUS IN A MOUTHFUL

HONEY AND ARBEQUINA
Serves 10

For the frozen yogurt:
192 g whole milk • 42 g heavy (whipping) cream • 151 g dextrose • 33 g fat-free powdered milk • 78 g sugar • 4 g ice cream stabilizer • 500 g whole-milk yogurt

For the watermelon rind:
400 g watermelon

For the honey:
10 g honey

For plating:
Extra-virgin arbequina olive oil (or a fragrant mild olive oil) • Fleur de sel

Make the frozen yogurt:
In a large pot, whisk together the milk, cream, dextrose, and milk powder. When everything is well dispersed, start cooking and take constant reads of the temperature using a thermometer. In a small bowl, mix together the sugar and ice cream stabilizer.

When the temperature of the milk mixture gets to 104°F (40°C), add the ice cream stabilizer/sugar mixture and disperse well. Keep cooking up to 185°F (85°C), then remove from the heat. Chill down over an ice bath and when the temperature gets below 104°F (40°C), add the yogurt and mix well. Refrigerate well covered for at least 6 hours and then churn in an ice cream machine. Keep well covered in a 12°F (−11°C) freezer.

Prepare the watermelon rind:
Cut the fruit off the rind and save the red pulp for other uses but make sure to keep the white rind. Peel off the dark-green skin. Make small dice (petit brunoise) of the rind and store in a clean container.

Prepare the honey:
If available, use whole honeycombs that must be portioned before serving, if not, try to use organic honey. Put the honey inside in a pastry bag and reserve at room temperature.

To plate:
Use frozen shallow plates to make it more beautiful. Smear a portion (around 80 g) of ice cream on the center of a plate and make space in the center to hold a spoonful of olive oil. Sprinkle the diced watermelon rinds over the ice cream and some grains of fleur de sel. Finish with a portion of honey comb or the equivalent of 2 spoonfuls of honey.

OUR WAGYU BARBACOA
Serves 30

For the barbacoa:
3 kg Mexican wagyu suadero *(see Notes)* • 4 kg rendered pork fat • 200 g demi-glace

For the chili demi-glace:
250 g demi-glace • 50 g dried whole unstemmed chilies *(see Notes)*

For the garlic confit:
500 ml olive oil • 1 bulb garlic, separated but unpeeled

OUR WAGYU BARBACOA

CHEDDAR CAULIFLOWER AND FISH-HEAD EMULSION

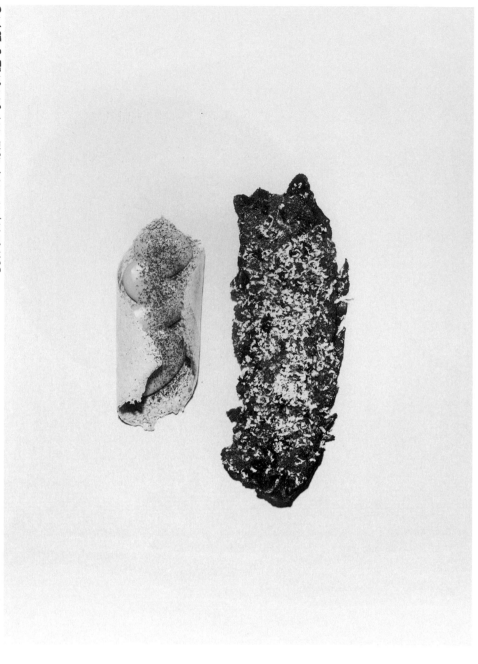

the oil is warm, place the unpeeled garlic cloves in the oil and poach them gently for about 2 hours. They should be tender, easy to peel, and lightly browned. When ready, drain off the oil, peel the garlic gloves, crush them, then pass them through a fine-mesh sieve and leave at room temperature.

Make the aioli:
Put the garlic confit and egg yolk in a tall beaker and use a hand blender to form a paste. Slowly drizzle the oil in, being careful that the emulsion does not lose stability. Once ready, add salt to taste and set aside in a covered bowl.

To plate:
Dress the Suaeda and cilantro (coriander) with the aioli and toss together.
Heat a sauté pan until it is very hot. Add just enough canola oil to coat the bottom and pour out any excess. Place a portion of chopped meat (about 80 g) in the hot pan trying to keep it concentrated in a bunch or bundle (do not spread it), this will ensure only a portion of it will be seared and get crispy. After the layer in contact with the pan is crispy, transfer the meat to a service tray and place under the salamander to keep warm.
To plate, in a shallow bowl, place the portion of seared suadero (crispy-side facing up) and add a spoonful of chili demi-glace. Place the aioli-dressed suaeda/cilantro mix on top and finish with a spoonful of chili demi-glace.

Notes:
• Suadero is a cut of beef between the belly and leg that is composed of very long fibers. It can be very tough when raw, but very tender when cooked for a long time. It is super tasty.
• The best chilies for this recipe will be the ones with smoky notes and not so much heat. It is crucial that the dried chilies be whole and unbroken. The whole chilies are soaked in the hot demi-glace in order to infuse the outside of the chili into the sauce. Mind that if the chilies are broken or pierced, the spiciness will invade the demi-glace and the result might be too hot.

For the aioli:
40 g Garlic Confit *(above)* • 1 egg yolk • 60 ml extra-virgin olive oil • Salt

For plating:
250 g clean Suaeda maritima or samphire • 250 g picked cilantro (fresh coriander) leaves • 50 g Aioli *(above)* • Canola oil • Fleur de sel

Make the barbacoa:
Cut the meat into big chunks of about 5 inches (12 cm) long. Place them in a large pot with the melted pork fat and water about 3 fingers deep to maintain. Cook over low heat until fork-tender, 4–6 hours. Take the meat out of the liquid just before service and drain on top of a griddle. Chop the meat using a big knife and combine the fattier sections with the leaner ones.

Put the chopped meat in a medium pot with some of the confit liquid and the demi-glace and keep warm during service.

Make the chili demi-glace:
This technique will give the demi-glace a beautiful smoky and chili aroma without making it spicy. Wash the chiles being careful not to break them in any way. After washing, check each chile to make sure it is not pierced or broken. Bring the demi-glace sauce to a boil and then take off the heat. Add the chiles and steep them in the demi-glace for 30 minutes. Pick or strain out the chiles, again being careful not to break them.

Make the garlic confit:
Pour the oil into a small, deep saucepan and place over very low and steady heat. When

OSWALDO'S COOKING IS TECHNICALLY AND CONCEPTUALLY A MODERN WAY TO SEE REFINED MEXICAN COOKING. IT IS THE GENERAL CONSENSUS THAT HE IS A PROMISE IN THE CURRENT MEXICAN FINE DINING SCENE.
— Virgilio Martínez

OSWALDO OLIVA

TOMOS PARRY

YOTAM OTTOLENGHI

MENU

FLATBREAD, BROWN GARLIC BUTTER, AND ANCHOVIES

SMOKED COD ROE, FENNEL BUTTER, AND TOAST

WHOLE TURBOT

CHEESECAKE AND WOOD-ROASTED PEACHES

More than a thousand miles separate Tomos Parry's home island of Anglesey, Wales, from Basque Country. A visit to Brat, his celebrated London restaurant, makes this distance seem to disappear, but that is just part of the magic. Paying profound respect to the traditions that inspire him, the Welshman has conjured a destination all his own, enlivened by the epicurean zeal of modern London.

Named for an old Northumbrian term for turbot, the flatfish that is a signature of the menu, Brat is not a traditional Basque restaurant, but can't quite be categorized as British either. Instead, Parry pulls together a multitude of ideas with an understated grace reflective of well-rounded experiences. Working in kitchens since his teens, Parry chose to pursue full-time cooking after several years in Cardiff at Le Gallois, under mentor Grady Atkins. He found his way to London, spending time at the River Cafe, the Ledbury, Climpson's Arch, and Kitty Fisher's, in addition to training in Spain and at Noma in Copenhagen.

All these experiences led Parry to create Brat, his Michelin-starred ode to the family-run Basque restaurants he loves. In Basque Country, leaning on local products is the fundamental and logical way things have been done for centuries, and this approach has plenty in common with the simple cooking that defined Parry's coastal upbringing. Parry has transmitted this energy to East London, working with a small circle of Welsh and Cornish farmers, fishermen, and producers to source his ingredients, many of which find glory over an open flame.

Inspired by Basque hearth masters like Aitor Arregui of Elkano and Victor Arguinzoniz of Asador Etxebarri, Parry has made his grill the physical and spiritual centerpiece of Brat. Locked between custom metal grills, the turbot cooks to transcendence in the live fire; the same goes for throats of hake, immaculate Jersey oysters, muttonchops, wood pigeon, and myriad other specialties of the house. Parry has perfected the wood-fired grill, realizing that showcasing the unparalleled beauty of ingredients is best achieved by minimizing his intervention.

FLATBREAD, BROWN GARLIC BUTTER, AND ANCHOVIES
Serves 6

For the flatbread:
10 g instant yeast • About 300 ml water • 500 g bread (strong white) flour • 10 g salt • 30 g unsalted butter

For the brown garlic butter:
Garlic • Butter

For finishing:
Anchovies • Chives

Make the flatbread:
Combine the yeast with 100 ml of the warm water and stir. Cover and leave at room temperature for 2–3 hours. This will start to ferment, adding a depth of flavor to the bread.
Put the flour in a large, warm bowl and add the salt and the yeast mixture. Add the butter and most of the remaining water, then mix with your hands to bring the mixture together. Gradually add the remaining water until all the flour is mixed in.

Put the dough on a lightly floured board and knead for 5–10 minutes. When the dough feels smooth and silky, return it to the bowl, cover it with a tea towel, and leave it in a warm place to rise until the dough has doubled in size, at least 1 hour.
Tip the dough onto a floured surface, fold repeatedly until all the air is knocked out of it, then tear it into 12 equal pieces. Roll each piece into a ball.

Make the brown butter:
In a saucepan, melt the over medium heat and whisk until it turns brown, then remove from the heat. Add the thyme and crushed garlic. Transfer to a metal bowl and allow to cool, stirring occasionally.

To finish:
Preheat the oven (wood oven if you're using one) to 480°F (250°C). Place a baking sheet lightly dusted with flour in the oven to preheat.
Dust a work surface with flour and roll out a piece of dough to a 6-inch (15 cm) round.

Place on the preheated baking sheet. Place in the oven and cook for 4–5 minutes. It should start to blister and rise.
When ready, take out and brush with the brown garlic butter, drape the anchovies over, and season with sea salt and chives.

SMOKED COD ROE, FENNEL BUTTER, AND TOAST
Makes about 12 sticks

For the whipped smoked cod roe:
250 g best-quality smoked cod roe • 1 egg yolk • Juice of 2 lemons • 10 g salt • 500 ml neutral oil, such as canola (rapeseed) • 50 ml cold water

For the fennel butter:
½ bulb fennel, roughly chopped • 10 ml canola (rapeseed) oil • Pinch of fennel seeds • Very small pinch of crushed chili flakes • 20 ml Pernod • 50 ml water • 150 g cold unsalted butter, diced • 15 g sea salt

1 whole wild turbot • Fine salt

Make the light vinaigrette:
Make the vinaigrette with about 50% fish stock, 20% light wine vinegar, 10% lemon juice, and 20% oil (many of these elements are to taste). Transfer to a spray bottle.

For the turbot:
Set up a charcoal fire and burn down the charcoal to embers, making sure they are giving a gentle glowing and even heat. Remove the gills from the turbot and season with salt, only inside the head.
Place the turbot in a turbot basket, generously spritz with the vinaigrette, and place over the grill.
Keep turning every 8–10 minutes for 30–40 minutes, constantly basting with the spray and making sure the fire and heat are gentle. In order to melt the natural collagen in the fish into a delicious gelatinous sauce, the ideal internal temperature to maintain the fish at is 131°F (55°C).
Once the fish is cooked, cut out the spine of the fish, season with more salt and place on a large white plate, adding more vinaigrette. Gently move the plate to release the gelatin from the fish. The gelatin will combine with the vinaigrette to make a pil-pil-style sauce to serve with the fish.

CHEESECAKE AND WOOD-ROASTED PEACHES
Serves 6

360 g cream cheese • 160 g superfine (caster) sugar • Grated zest of ¼ orange • 4 organic eggs • 225 ml double cream • 20 g all-purpose (plain) flour • Grilled fruit (such as rhubarb or peaches), for serving • Crème fraîche, for serving

Preheat the convection oven to 350°F (180°C) or a regular oven to 390°F (200°C).
In a bowl, whisk the cream cheese, sugar, and orange zest until light and glossy. Whisk in the eggs one at a time. Gently whisk in the cream, then slowly sift in the flour and mix thoroughly.
Line a 10-inch (25 cm) cast-iron skillet with parchment paper. Pour in the mixture and bake for 30 minutes, then rotate front to back and cook for 15 minutes longer. The aim is for the cheesecake to rise like a soufflé and caramelize, almost burning on the top.
Once the cheesecake is out of the oven, leave it to cool for 1 hour (it will sink a bit). Slice and serve it with grilled fruit and a dollop of crème fraîche on the side.

For assembly:
Day-old sourdough bread, cut into 4½ × ½-inch (12 × 1.5 cm) sticks • Lemon juice • 50 ml good-quality olive oil • 50 g English sandwich cress

Make the whipped smoked cod roe:
The cod roe will come in its lobe skin. It is important to scrape all the smoked roe from within the lobe, not wasting any. Use a kitchen spoon to do this; it may take some time, but it's worth it.
In a bowl, combine the roe, egg yolk, lemon juice, and 5 g salt (keep 5 g back to add later if needed) and begin to slowly whisk.
Once the ingredients are mixed, start to add the oil gradually while continuing to whisk to emulsify (as you would with mayonnaise). Stop with 100 ml oil to go. Now add the water—this will lighten the mix and alter the color.
Add the remaining 100 ml oil and 5 g salt. The mixture should be nice and moussey by now. Transfer to a piping bag and make a ½-inch (1.5 cm) cut at the end.

Make the fennel butter:
Sweat the chopped fennel in the canola (rapeseed) oil until soft. Add the fennel seeds and chili flakes and cook for 1 minute. Add the Pernod and cook over high heat for another minute.
Add the water, and when the fennel mixture comes to a boil, gradually add the cold butter. Stir in the salt. Allow to cool, then strain.

To assemble:
Toast the bread sticks (ideally on a charcoal grill, but a domestic grill will work or on top of a toaster). Once toasted, brush liberally with the fennel butter. Pipe or spoon on the whipped cod roe. Season with lemon juice and olive oil and place the cut English cress on top.

WHOLE TURBOT
Serves 6

For the light vinaigrette:
Fish stock • Light wine vinegar • Lemon juice • Canola (rapeseed) oil

FLATBREAD, BROWN GARLIC BUTTER, AND ANCHOVIES

STAYING TRUE TO
THE QUALITY OF THE
INGREDIENTS, NOT TOO MUCH
FUSS GOES INTO THE FOOD
HERE. BUT THAT'S NOT
TO SAY THAT THERE ISN'T
TALENT AND INTUITION BY
THE BUCKETLOAD.

— Yotam Ottolenghi

TOMOS PARRY

NATALIE PAULL

BEATRIX
Melbourne, Australia

PALISA ANDERSON

Nat Paull, Melbourne's queen of cakes, recalls the first cake she baked: a heavy, flat butter cake enrobed in bright blue icing, speckled with gelatinous banana "lolly" candies. She was seven years old. The moment was a landmark.

After years of practice, Paull is still making cakes with flair. She is the mastermind behind Beatrix, the tiny café and bakery in North Melbourne, Australia, known since its opening in 2011 for old-school, traditional baked goods that reach beyond their sweet-dominant flavor profile to nuance and balance. The shop is quaint and cozy, and upon entering, one may get the feeling of having passed into a sacred space—a magical cake realm that overwhelms the senses. Paull thought the name "Beatrix" was an appropriate reference to herself, a woman who beats things—like cake batter.

Paull's career officially began with a letter she wrote to Australian culinary icon Maggie Beer, at a time when she should have been studying for a history exam. She failed the exam but landed a culinary apprenticeship. Paull credits her strong foundation to Beer's generous outpouring of time and know-how. She went on to work for Australian notables Stephanie Alexander, Greg Malouf, and Alex Herbert, learning her way around professional kitchens. She opened and ran Little Bertha, a wholesale bakery, for several years before closing it with visions of Beatrix in mind.

Paull's creations of cakes and desserts pull from her experience as a pastry chef, which instilled in her both a full gamut of techniques and the ability to improvise. Her version of double-tiered carrot cake is flecked with hazelnuts and split by a layer of cheesecake; her sweet rolls boast roasted pineapple, salted kaya (coconut jam) curd, and lime glaze. A fragrant lemon curd and pistachio cake is elevated by perfectly roasted cracked pistachios. Her favorite ingredients—Meyer lemons, passion fruit, muscovado sugar—make seasonal appearances. And she's a fiend for creamy textures in her baking: sabayon, brown-butter-soaked genoise, and buttercreams.

MENU

PRUNE, MASCARPONE, AND COCOA SPONGE TART-A-MISU IN A WALNUT BUTTER CRUST

ALMONDJAWS: TOASTED ALMOND SANDIES FILLED WITH SALTY DULCE DE LECHES

APPLE PIE LAYER CAKE WITH CINNAMON BUTTERCREAM AND CANDY APPLE CRISPS

PUREST PASSION FRUIT TART

DOUGHNUTS WITH BURST BLUEBERRRIES AND SWEET WHIPPED CREAM CHEESE

PISTACHIO AND LEMON CURD LAYER CAKE

VANILLA SOUR CREAM CHEESECAKE WITH HAZELNUT CRUMB AND ROASTED QUINCE

PUREST PASSION FRUIT TART
Makes one (9½-inch/ 24 cm) tart (Serves 8)

For the crust:
240 g pastry (soft) flour • 60 g superfine (caster) sugar • 2 g fine sea salt • 140 g unsalted cold butter, diced • 20 g egg yolk • 50 g heavy (whipping) cream • Beaten egg white, for the crust

For the filling:
250 g egg (about 5 large) • 150 g superfine (caster) sugar • 10 passionfruit, whizzed and strained to yield 180 g juice • 300 g heavy cream (35–45% butterfat) • 2 g fine sea salt

To finish:
1 passionfruit

Make the crust:
In a bowl, combine the flour, sugar, and salt. Add the butter cubes and squeeze until they are small flakes and the flour is taking on a yellow hue. In a small bowl, stir the yolk into the cream, then mix into the flour with your fingers until the dough is soft and pliable, like a ball of Play-Doh. Squeeze into a flat disk. Rest in the fridge if it's sticky, but if it's cool enough, roll out and line a 9½ inch (24 cm) tart pan 1¼ inches (3 cm) deep. (Save any dough scraps for patching the tart shell.)
Freeze the tart shell for 1 hour.
Preheat the oven to 350°F (180°C).
Blind bake the tart shell until it is deep biscuity brown. Pale pastry is pointless. (Leave the oven on but reduce the temperature to 250°F/120°C.) Let the pastry cool for 5 minutes and gently patch any large cracks or fissures with some softened leftover raw dough. Brush the inside with a lightly beaten egg white and place the tart shell, in its pan, on a heavy baking sheet.

Make the filling:
In a bowl, whisk the eggs and sugar together by hand until just combined but not airy. Whisk in the passion fruit juice, then the cream and salt. Strain the mixture into a measuring cup with a spout (a jug) and set aside.
Place the tart crust in the oven to dry the inside of the crust. Then pull the shelf out a little and carefully pour the filling in, only filling to the top of the lowest side of the crust. Don't let the custard slosh down the side between the crust and the pan.
Bake until there is a viscous, quivering, eggy wobble to the center, 20–40 minutes.

DONUTS WITH BURST BLUEBERRIES AND SWEET WHIPPED CREAM CHEESE

NAT'S PALATE AS A PASTRY CHEF IS MUCH MORE FAR-REACHING THAN JUST SWEET DOMINANT; THERE ARE NUANCES TO EVERYTHING YOU EAT AT BEATRIX THAT MAKE YOU SIT UP AND REALIZE YOU HAVE BEEN GRACED BY A TRUE FLAVOR MASTER.

— Palisa Anderson

Turn the oven off and leave the door ajar for the tart to cool for 15 minutes, then continue to cool for around 4 hours at room temperature. It is perfect to eat, unchilled with a slick of freshly pulped passionfruit on top. Best eaten on the day of baking. Chill any leftovers.

DOUGHNUTS WITH BURST BLUE-BERRIES AND SWEET WHIPPED CREAM CHEESE
Makes 12 doughnuts

For the dough:
600 g all-purpose (plain) flour • 10 g fine sea salt • 90 g powdered whole milk • 60 g superfine (caster) sugar • 200 g room temperature water • 40 g fresh yeast • 2 large eggs • 90 g unsalted butter, at room temperature • 1 liter rice bran oil, for deep-frying

For the dusting sugar:
250 g superfine (caster) sugar • Grated zest of 2 lemons • 75 g fine polenta

For the filling:
400 g full-fat cream cheese, at room temperature • 100 g superfine (caster) sugar • 50 g heavy (whipping) cream • ½ vanilla bean, split lengthwise

For the burst blueberries:
50 g superfine (caster) sugar • 450 g blueberries

Make the dough:
Weigh the dry ingredients together. Place the water in the bottom of a stand mixer bowl and add the yeast, whisking well to dissolve. Add the eggs and soft butter and then pour the dry ingredients on top. Attach the dough hook and knead the dough on just over low speed for around 10 minutes. You are looking for a slack, yet shiny dough that you may feel is too wet. Resist the urge to add more flour. Remove from the mixer and coat the top of the dough with cooking spray. Cover with plastic wrap (cling film) and set aside at warm ambient temperature until doubled in size, about 1 hour.
Scrape the dough out onto a lightly floured surface and gently portion into twelve 90 g pieces and roll into tight balls. Place on a sheet pan coated cooking spray. Lightly coat the tops, too, then cover with plastic wrap and allow to prove again in a warm place for around 30 minutes.
Meanwhile, heat the oil so you can be ready to fry as soon as the doughnuts are ready. If you own a countertop fryer, heat it to 338°–356°F (170°–180°C). Or heat a heavy (10-inch/25 cm diameter) pot of oil on the stove over very low heat.

Mix the dusting sugar:
Stir all the ingredients together in a baking pan large enough to roll 4 doughnuts at a time. Check the prove: The dough should look puffy and like it is stretching below the surface. Push a finger in and if the dough doesn't bounce back, it is ready.

Time to fry:
Place a few balls at a time in the oil. Avoid the temptation to fearfully pitch them in. You want to lay them down into the oil. Don't overcrowd. Fry for around 2½ minutes. Carefully flip the doughnuts over with tongs. The color should be a pale golden. Fry longer/increase heat/decrease heat as needed. Fry for another 2½ minutes. Pull the doughnuts out with tongs and drain for a minute on a cooling rack set over a tray. Then roll in the dusting sugar. Allow to completely cool before filling.

Prepare the filling:
In a food processor, combine the cream cheese, sugar, and cream. Scrape in the vanilla seeds. Whiz until smooth and creamy. Load into a piping bag.

Prepare the blueberries:
In a small saucepan, scorch the sugar until deep brown. Pour in a quarter of the blueberries and cook until they burst. Let cool and stir in the remaining blueberries.

To assemble, make a deep incision in each doughnut and pipe in a little cream cheese. Load a spoonful of blueberries on top and serve. Best eaten within 3 hours of frying.

NATALIE PAULL

CARLA PEREZ-GALLARDO & HANNAH BLACK

DAVID MCMILLAN

The US state of Alabama and South America come together in the unexpectedly harmonic partnership that is Hannah Black and Carla Perez-Gallardo. Their cooking is a joint expression of their personalities, and the two would not have it any other way.

Perez-Gallardo and Black met in 2014 while working at a Vietnamese food truck in the Catskills region of New York state; both came from arts backgrounds and had found a creative outlet through cooking. A native of Queens in New York City, Perez-Gallardo grew up learning her way around cuisine with her family and their Ecuadorian and Argentine roots. Black was born and raised in Alabama, and the ideals of Southern hospitality were instilled in her from a young age. Perez-Gallardo's studies were focused on studio arts, particularly installation and performance, which she has translated to her approach to food. Upstate New York drew Black with its bucolic charm and community-oriented nature, a sort of calm after working in some of North America's busiest kitchens (she is a veteran of New York City's Mission Chinese, and Hartwood, in Tulum, Mexico). The two began hosting pop-up dinners at an old-school diner up state, which quickly garnered buzz among community members and beyond. When owner Debbie Fiero retired, she offered the space to Perez-Gallardo and Black. They accepted without hesitation, and the blank canvas of Lil' Deb's Oasis soon became a work of art brimming with transportive kitsch as a backdrop to smart, playful cuisine.

The product of these two personalities is "tropical comfort food," as they describe it. But at Lil' Deb's Oasis, the food and space are a combined catalyst for a bigger conversation about inclusion. The restaurant is wholly inclusive, especially for the queer community, underscoring the need for addressing social inequalities in the food world. Their efforts have been widely recognized. At the intersection of great food, thought-provoking art, and a welcoming embrace for guests from all walks of life, Perez-Gallardo and Black bring so much more than just an enjoyable meal to the table.

MENU

CEVICHE DEL DIA IN A HABANERO-LIME AGUA

SWEET PLANTAINS WITH CILANTRO YOGURT

COCONUT SHRIMP, HERBS, AND CITRUSY NUOC CHAM

CITRUS SALAD WITH UMEBOSHI-CHILE VINAIGRETTE

SEAFOOD MOQUECA, SILKY COCONUT AND TOMATO BROTH

WHOLE FRIED FISH WITH GINGER-CITRUS VINAIGRETTE

For the nuoc cham dipping sauce:
2 cups (475 ml) fresh lime juice, plus all the zest • 2 cups (475 ml) yuzu juice* or 1 whole grapefruit, its juice and segments • 1 cup (240 ml) fish sauce • ½ cup (100 g) grated palm sugar or granulated white sugar • 4 tablespoons diced shallot or red onion • 4 tablespoons thinly sliced garlic (lengthwise, on the mandoline) • 4 tablespoons carrot pulsed in a food processor until fine but not a paste • 1 Fresno chili, seeded and thinly sliced into rounds • 1 serrano chili, seeded and thinly sliced into rounds

For the batter:
2 cups (315 g) rice flour • 4 tablespoons tapioca flour • 1 cup coconut flakes, toasted • 1 teaspoon ground allspice • Salt • Sugar • Seltzer (sparkling water)

For the shrimp:
Coconut, grapeseed, or canola oil, for frying • ½ pound (225 g) shrimp (prawns), deveined, tails on • Salt and freshly ground black pepper • 8–12 lettuce leaves (butter lettuce or chicories, really anything with color and firm flexibility!) • 3–4 sprigs mint, parsley, cilantro, dill, leaves picked • Toasted coconut

CEVICHE DEL DIA IN A HABANERO-LIME AGUA
Serves 2–3

6 ounces (170 g) sushi-grade salmon • Salt • 4 tablespoons extra-virgin olive oil • 3 passion fruit • 2 cups (475 ml) lime juice • 1 cup (240 ml) orange juice • 1 habanero chili • 2 satsuma oranges, peeled and cut into round slices • 1 purple daikon radish, peeled and sliced into thin rounds on the mandoline, and then cut into quarter triangles • A few sprigs cilantro (fresh coriander), for garnish • 2 teaspoons Maldon salt

Cut the salmon into ½-inch (1.25 cm) cubes, season with salt and 1 tablespoon of the olive oil. Set aside.
Scoop out the passion fruit flesh stir together with the remaining 3 tablespoons olive oil. Set aside.

In a blender, combine the lime and orange juices. Blend in the habanero ½ at a time, since spice levels vary from pepper to pepper. Season the habanero-lime agua with salt. In a bowl, mix together the salmon, satsuma segments, and daikon. Season lightly with a little salt and plate. Pour the habanero-lime agua on the edges of the plate until it pools around the salmon. You want to do this right before serving or the salmon will turn gray. Spoon the passion fruit pulp across the plate. Garnish with a few sprigs of cilantro (coriander) and sprinkle some Maldon salt to finish.

COCONUT SHRIMP, HERBS, AND CITRUSY NUOC CHAM
Serves 3–4

COCONUT SHRIMP

SEAFOOD MOQUECA

CEVICHE DEL DIA

If you have access to fresh yuzu, even better!!!

Make the nuoc cham:
Combine all the ingredients in a bowl, mix together and taste for seasoning. You want to achieve a tangy sauce with lots of umami, the flavor of fresh citrus and a blooming heat from the chilies. This sauce can be easily altered as you wish—add more chilies for extra heat, or more lime juice if you like it extra acidic! (Leftover sauce will store well up to 1 week in your refrigerator, and use in combination with pretty much anything—rice, noodles, salads!)

Make the batter:
In a medium bowl, mix together the rice flour, tapioca flour, coconut flakes, allspice, and salt and sugar to taste.
Use seltzer to mix the batter before frying. Add in slowly, you want to achieve the thickness of lumpy pancake batter.

Make the shrimp:
In a deep cast-iron skillet, heat 3–4 inches (7–10 cm) of oil and heat over medium-high heat to 350°F (177°C).
While the oil is warming up, season the shrimp generously with salt and pepper. Once your oil is close to reaching the correct temp, drop 4–6 shrimp in the batter, coating them thoroughly, and begin lowering them into the oil. The shrimp should immediately begin to sizzle. Cook each shrimp 1–2 minutes on each side, or until golden brown, and bubbling subsides. Lift the shrimp out of the oil, draining on paper towels (or we like to recycle paper grocery store bags!) and season with a bit more salt.
Set up a plate with your gorgeous lettuce leaves on the upper left-hand quadrant. When you've finished frying all your shrimp, make a pile of them on the bottom right quadrant, and place a small bowl of dipping sauce on the bottom left. Garnish with herb sprigs and a pinch or two of toasted coconut, making little wraps for each shrimp with the lettuces and herbs. Dip in!

SEAFOOD MOQUECA, SILKY COCONUT AND TOMATO BROTH
Serves 4–6

2 pounds (910 g) mixed mussels and clams • 1 pound (455 g) firm white fish, bones removed and cut into 2–3-inch (5–7.5 cm) chunks • Lime juice • Salt • 1 tablespoon coconut oil • 1 medium yellow onion, small diced • 3 cloves garlic, minced • 2 cups (475 ml) confit of summer tomatoes (or canned crushed) • 1 red bell pepper, chopped or sliced • 4 tablespoons chopped scallions (spring onions) • 1 large bunch of cilantro (fresh coriander), chopped with some set aside for garnish • 1 tablespoons sweet paprika • 2 cups (475 ml) fish or shrimp stock • 1 can (14 fl oz/414 ml) full-fat coconut milk • 4 tablespoons fish sauce, or to taste • 2 stalks hearts of palm, cut into rounds ½ inch (1.25 cm) thick • 2 tablespoons butter • Cooked rice, for serving • Chili oil, for serving

Rinse the mussels and clams in cold water and scrub clean. Separate into two bowls. Season the fish with lime juice and salt. Place all the seafood in the refrigerator. Start to make the sofrito base: In a heavy-bottomed pot, heat the oil. Add the onions and sweat until translucent. Add the garlic, tomatoes, bell pepper, scallions, half the cilantro, and the paprika and cook until the vegetables are soft.
Stir in the stock and coconut milk and add fish sauce a splash at a time to season. Cover and bring to a boil.
Take the seafood out of the fridge. Add the clams first, cover and steam until they begin to open, about 5 minutes. Add the mussels next, cover, and steam until open. Finally, add the fish and hearts of palm, cover and steam until just cooked through, another 1–2 minutes. Stir in the butter.
Season to taste with lime juice and serve over rice. Garnish with cilantro and chili oil.

YOU HAVE TO HAVE A LOT OF CONFIDENCE TO MAKE FOOD THAT SPEAKS DIRECTLY TO WHO YOU ARE AS A PERSON, AND RARELY DOES IT HAPPEN, BUT THAT'S EXACTLY WHAT HANNAH AND CARLA HAVE ACHIEVED.
— David McMillan

CARLA PEREZ-GALLARDO & HANNAH BLACK

CAROLE PEYRICHOU

LA NAUTIQUE
Narbonne, France

RAQUEL CARENA

Every spring, Carole Peyrichou reopens her seasonal bistro, La Nautique. Moored on the edge of L'Étang de Bages, a lake just under 4 miles south of Narbonne, France, the restaurant's terrace overlooks a small marina, with masts and sails on the horizon. The dishes that Carole and her team serve with great enthusiasm tell the story of this in-between place that combines coastline and hinterland.

La Nautique is the culmination of a series of serendipitous encounters for Peyrichou, who trained in Paris—first as a server while she was working to finance her film studies, then in the kitchen, piqued by Raquel Carena's cooking at Le Baratin. After Paris, she cooked for three years alongside Fabien Lefebvre at L'Octopus in Béziers. When Peyrichou was promoted to chef de partie, Lefebvre encouraged her to study for her *certificat d'aptitude professionnelle* to formalize her promising instincts as a chef and perfect her technique. Given wings by this success, Peyrichou then looked for a place of her own where she could work with seasonal produce to create an inexpensive cuisine. The result was La Nautique, made in her image: enticing, sincere, and lively.

Peyrichou has made a reputation for her sharing dishes, whether the incredible "seafood chips" made from fried anchovy bones, or her fried joels, smelts caught right next to the restaurant and drizzled with lemon. Other dishes reflect her penchant for southern French cuisine, such as octopus fried with chile pepper, crispy on the outside and melting on the inside, and roasted vegetable escalivada. An exceptional cod liver dish, a nod to the North, shows admirable restraint, served practically "as is." Every day, fish and shellfish come to the feast: cuttlefish stew and soup of cranquette (green crabs from the Gulf of Lion), razor clams cooked on the embers of the outdoor oven, pasta with shellfish, often with Valencian-style rice. And from the farm comes offal meats, the legacy of her mentors—the menu of the day may include brains, kidneys, or grilled rolled calf's head. Carole's portside cuisine is well worth a trip.

MENU

OUR FAMOUS
DEEP-FRIED FISH BONES

GRILLED OYSTERS

CALÇOT-STYLE LEEKS

CUTTLEFISH IN INK

CHOCOLATE MOUSSE

CALÇOT-STYLE LEEKS
Serves 4

4 medium leeks • Olive oil • Salt • Pepper

For the "Salvitxada" vinaigrette:
2 tablespoon sherry vinegar • 1 spoon of sweet mustard • 3 tablespoon olive oil • Salt • Pepper • 10 g toasted almonds, crushed • 10 g toasted hazelnuts, crushed • 10 g toasted pine nuts, crushed • 1 small red chili, finely chopped • ½ green garlic bulb, finely minced

Preheat oven to 350°F (180°C) in grill or broil mode. Rinse leeks to remove any dirt or grit. Remove half of the leek's green leaves. Place leeks on a baking sheet lined with aluminum foil. Using a brush, brush leeks with olive oil and season with salt and pepper. Put them in the oven for about half an hour, turning them over as soon as tops are well-blackened. Check the doneness of the leeks by pricking them with the tip of a knife. They should be well-charred and melting inside. Take them out of the oven and cover them with aluminum foil or newspaper for about 10 minutes.

Make the vinaigrette:
In a salad bowl, mix the sherry vinegar, mustard, salt and pepper. Then add the olive oil little by little to make the vinaigrette. Taste, adjust seasoning with salt and pepper if necessary. Then add the chopped chili, and the green garlic (if the season permits); then finish with the roasted and crushed nuts.

To serve, arrange the leeks on a plate and split them lengthwise. Garnish with the vinaigrette.

CHOCOLATE MOUSSE
Serves 10

600 g chocolate • 240g butter • 12 eggs • 120g sugar

Cut the chocolate into pieces and combine with the butter in a saucepan inside a hot water bath. Let melt until smooth, remove from the heat and let cool.
Separate the whites from the yolks.
Add the egg yolks to the butter and chocolate mixture. Make sure it has cooled so as not to cook the eggs. Mix.
Beat the egg whites to soft peaks. Then add the sugar and continue to beat until smooth and stiff peaks have formed.
Add a third of the egg whites to the chocolate and egg yolk mixture and mix vigorously with a spatula to loosen the chocolate. Then fold in the remaining whites to a smooth mousse.
Transfer to a serving container and refrigerate for at least 3 hours.

CHOCOLATE MOUSSE

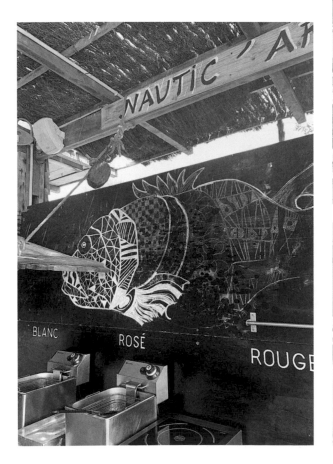

OF COURSE, IT'S CAROLE'S COOKING THAT BRINGS PEOPLE TO LA NAUTIQUE. BUT THE CUSTOMERS ALSO COME FOR HER, HER SURE HAND, THE ATMOSPHERE THAT EMANATES FROM THIS SINGULAR PLACE THAT HAS NOT YIELDED TO THE SIREN CALL OF TOURISM, A PLACE THAT DOES NOT EXIST ANYWHERE ELSE.
— Raquel Carena

CAROLE PEYRICHOU

JAKOB PINTAR

ANA ROŠ

TABAR
Ljubljana, Slovenia

MENU

DEER

PUMPKIN

CARP

BEAR AND SHEEP

Slovenian chef Jakob Pintar, a rising star of his country's food scene, is reinventing tapas for Slovenian palates at TaBar in Ljubljana. In conceptualizing TaBar, Pintar recognized the similarities between Slovenia and Spain, the birthplace of tapas: both countries have deep historical roots with and proximity to influences from Italy, Austria, Croatia, and the Mediterranean. At TaBar, Pintar expresses his love for the paradigm of national foodstuffs by serving the finest local ingredients, including cured meats from lauded Slovenian producer BioSing and cheeses made by Valter Kramar of Hiša Franko. Traditional tapas presentations of hot and cold composed small plates are available either à la carte or as three- or five-course tasting menus. Impeccable sourcing from well-regarded and traceable local producers extends to the wine list, where biodynamic and ecological selections are prevalent, with a particular emphasis on Slovenian wines, a category that is gaining international attention.

Pintar honed his craft at gastronomic institutions such as Gordon Ramsey's Maze in London and L'Atelier de Joël Robuchon in London, as well as under Heinz Reitbauer at Steirereck in Vienna. In 2019, Pintar was the only Slovenian finalist in the San Pellegrino Young Chef competition, for which he submitted a dish called Alpine Ostrich that was emblematic of his craft. By incorporating ostrich—an animal that seems incongruous with Slovenia's terroir, but is actually sourced from a local producer—with foraged wild ingredients such as coastal greens and fermented carrots, Pintar communicated a pointed message: Slovenia must embrace the notions of new and foreign, as much as what is traditional and familiar.

At TaBar, Pintar manages to maintain the relaxed, approachable atmosphere associated with tapas, while simultaneously challenging his diners. He has a fondness for unusual ingredients and offal, which fits with his commitment to sustainability, sometimes offering offcuts such as heart and brain. Still, Pintar's signature style is streamlined and ingredient-driven. He doesn't try to overexert his prowess in a single dish, instead leaving diners wanting more with a deft sense of restraint—a hallmark of great cooking and the reason he is considered one of the best chefs in Slovenia.

DEER HEART WITH TROUT ROE MAYONNAISE, SMOKED OYSTER MUSHROOMS, AND PINE VINEGAR
Serves 10

For the pine vinegar:
1 liter water • 140 g sugar • 200 g pine tips • 5 g dried ale yeast

For the trout roe mayonnaise:
100 g trout roe • 100 g canola (rapeseed) oil • 20 g white wine vinegar • Salt • Grated lime zest

For the fried yeast:
80 g fresh yeast • 50 ml water • Frying oil

For the smoked mushrooms:
500 g oyster mushrooms • 300 g pine sawdust • 2 liters frying oil • Salt

For the heart:
300 g deer heart

Make the pine vinegar:
In a saucepan, heat the water and sugar to dissolve the sugar. Let it cool.
In a blender, combine the pine tips and sugary water and coarsely blend. Pour in the yeast and mix well.
Let it rest for 1 month at room temperature (68°F/20°C) so it turns into vinegar.
Strain and dilute with water, if necessary.

Make the trout roe mayonnaise:
In a Thermomix, grind the roe into a smooth thick liquid. Heat for 20 minutes at 158°F (70°C) to become creamy then let cool.
Emulsify the oil into the cooled roe cream. Season with the vinegar and salt and lime zest to taste.

Fry the yeast:
Dissolve the yeast in the water.
In a large, deep saucepan, heat the oil over low heat until medium-hot.
Pour the dissolved yeast into the hot oil and fry it while stirring constantly.

Smoke the mushrooms:
Tear the mushrooms into thin strips and smoke over the pine sawdust for 2 hours.
Before serving, fry them in oil and season with salt and fried yeast.

To serve:
Before serving, clean the deer heart and cut it into cubes. Mix with the trout roe mayonnaise.
Cover with smoked oyster mushrooms. Pour a spoonful of pine vinegar over it. Finish the plate with olive herb oil and add some fresh olive herb sprigs.

CRUNCHY HOKKAIDO PUMPKIN WITH APRICOT, CANDIED KUMQUAT, AND PUMPKIN OIL EMULSION
Serves 10

For the fermented apricots:
200 g fresh apricots • 4 g salt • 50 ml maple syrup • 150 ml sunflower seed oil

For the candied kumquats:
10 kumquats • 500 ml simple syrup

For the pumpkin oil emulsion:
100 ml soy milk • 200 ml pumpkin seed oil • 20 ml white wine vinegar • Salt

For the pumpkin seeds:
30 g pumpkin seeds • 20 ml soy milk • Salt

For the pumpkin:
2 kg Hokkaido pumpkin (red kuri squash/onion squash) • 3 liters brown butter • 4 whole star anise • Salt • Frying oil

To serve:
Ground red pepper

Ferment the apricots:
Pit the apricots and salt them. Let them ferment for 7 days at 140°F (60°C).
Add the maple syrup to the fermented apricots and puree it with the oil to make an emulsion.

Candy the kumquats:
Halve the kumquats and remove the pulp. Candy the kumquat rinds in syrup for 3–4 hours.

Make the pumpkin oil emulsion:
Pour the soy milk into a Thermomix and slowly add the pumpkin oil, but with full speed to emulsify. Add the vinegar for acidity and season with salt.

Make the pumpkin seeds:
Soak the pumpkin seeds in the soy milk for 30 minutes.
Preheat the oven to 340°F (170°C).
Drain and rinse the pumpkin seeds. Season with salt, spread on a pan, and bake until they puff, stirring constantly every 2 minutes.

Prepare the pumpkin:
Peel the pumpkin, scoop out the seeds and strings, and cut the flesh into scant ¹⁄₁₆-inch (1 mm) slices.

Stick the slices one at a time, packing them closely together, onto a wooden skewer until you reach 4 inches (10 cm) in length. Repeat.
Combine the brown butter and star anise. Add the skewered pumpkin and confit until soft. Let it cool.
When ready to serve, fry the pumpkin in 320°F (160°C) oil until it's crispy outside and soft, buttery inside. Season with salt.

To serve:
Set a pumpkin skewer on a plate. Coat with the fermented apricot emulsion. Cover with candied kumquat, puffed pumpkin seeds, and ground red pepper. Smear the pumpkin oil emulsion on the side of the plate.

CARP BAKED ON GOAT CHEESE, FERMENTED ROMAINE LETTUCE WITH WILD MUSHROOMS AND SOURDOUGH SAUCE
Serves 10

For the fermented romaine:
40 g salt • 1 liter water • 10 romaine lettuce leaves • 50 g horseradish

For the fried scales:
100 g fish scales • Frying oil • 20 g ground dried capers

For the wild mushrooms:
150 ml water • 80 ml white wine vinegar • 50 ml fresh apple juice • 20 g brown sugar • 1 clove garlic • 2 curry leaves • 5 g salt • 2 g

black pepper • 2 g mustard seeds • 1 juniper berry • 200 g mixed wild mushrooms

For the sourdough sauce:
300 ml sunflower seed oil • 3 dark-green lettuce leaves • 100 g spinach • 300 ml buttermilk • 50 g sourdough bread • 2 egg yolks • 1 lime • Salt

For the carp:
100 g soft goat cheese • 1 kg carp fillet • 10 g unsalted butter

For serving:
1 black radish, grated • Lettuce leaves • Salt

Ferment the romaine lettuce:
Dissolve the salt in the water. Submerge the romaine lettuce and horseradish in the water. Let it ferment at room temperature for 7 days.

Fry the scales:
In a pot of boiling water, blanch the scales. Drain, spread out, and dehydrate.
When dry, fry them in 428°F (220°C) oil. Dust with dried caper powder.

Pickle the wild mushrooms:
In a saucepan, combine the water, vinegar, apple juice, brown sugar, garlic, curry leaves, and all the spices. Bring to a boil and let it infuse for 30 minutes.
Strain the pickling liquid. Clean the mushrooms and pickle with the strained liquid.

BEAR AND SHEEP

Make the sourdough sauce:
Puree the oil, lettuce, and spinach. Strain to get green oil. Save part of the oil for serving. In a saucepan, cook the buttermilk to reduce by half. Add the sourdough, mix, and let it cool. Mix in the egg yolks.
Transfer to a bain-marie and heat at 165°F (74°C). Slowly mix in green oil. Season with salt.

Prepare the carp:
Put a thin slice of goat cheese into a hot pan. When the cheese is partly melted, put the carp on top of it and pan roast until nicely browned. Add the butter and baste to roast the carp from all sides.

To serve:
Plate the carp and cover with grated black radish and fried scales. Chop the pickled mushrooms, wrap in lettuce and place on the plate. Gently mix the sourdough sauce with the reserved green oil and pour onto the plate in a ring made of fermented romaine lettuce.

BRAISED BROWN BEAR PAW, MEDLAR, SPRUCE TIPS, ROSE HIP AND SHEEP TRIPE SAUCE WITH RAW BEESWAX, RAMARIA FLAVA
Serves 10

For the braised bear paws:
4 bear paws • Salt • Oil • 2 kg mirepoix • 500 ml port

For the candied rose hips:
50 g rose hips • 20 ml simple syrup

For the tripe:
500 g sheep tripe • 500 ml chicken stock • 50 g leek, diced • 50 g celery, diced • 50 g shallot, diced • 50 g garlic, minced • 20 g fresh ginger, diced • 20 red peppercorns • 20 black peppercorns • 10 juniper berries • Salt • 1 kg pure raw beeswax

For the medlar emulsion:
500 g medlars • 7 g salt • 20 g sugar • 100 ml camelina oil • 20 g brown butter

For the ramaria flava mushrooms:
Ramaria flava mushrooms (called bear paws in Slovenian) • 20 g unsalted butter • 50 ml verjuice

For plating:
Hairy bittercress • Bee pollen • Thyme leaves

Braise the bear paws:
Season the bear paws with salt. In a roasting pan, heat the oil. Add the bear paws and roast them in the oil. Add the mirepoix and cook until dark. Deglaze with the port. Cover and braise the paws until the meat separates from the bone, about 2 hours. Debone and trim the meat. Reserve the drippings and juices.

Candy the rose hips:
Halve the rose hips and seed them. Candy the rose hips in the simple syrup.

Make the tripe:
Slowly cook the tripe in the chicken stock until very tender. Blend the tripe.
Add all of the vegetables and seasonings to the thick sauce and let it infuse for 30 minutes. Season with salt.
Strain the sauce. Vacuum-seal the sauce with the beeswax and cook at 140°F (60°C) for 2 hours.
Let it cool and separate it from the beeswax.

Make the medlar emulsion:
In a bowl, toss the medlars with the salt, sugar, and oil. Spread on a tray and bake over embers at a very low temperature for 2 hours. Let it cool.
Emulsify the spread so the oil blends in.

Prepare the bear paw mushrooms:
Cut the mushrooms in half. In a sauté pan, cook the mushrooms in the butter. Deglaze with verjuice and season with salt.

To plate:
Heat the bear meat in the reserved juices. Plate the bear, glaze with the medlar emulsion, and cover with candied rose hips. Garnish with hairy bittercress and dust with bee pollen. Serve the tripe sauce on the side. Serve the mushrooms with thyme leaves.

A YOUNG, TALENTED CHEF WHO BELIEVES IN COLLABORATION AND FRIENDSHIP BETWEEN CHEFS.
— Ana Roš

JAKOB PINTAR

SEBASTIÁN PINZÓN GIRALDO & JAIME RODRÍGUEZ CAMACHO

VIRGILIO MARTÍNEZ

MENU

BOCANA MUSSELS IN COASTAL PICKLE, PORK RINDS, AND SEAWEEDS

CURED AND MATURED LOBSTER IN COCONUT OIL WITH PICKLED CASHEW FRUIT AND CREAMY CASHEW NUT

CARIBBEAN BEANS WITH CREOLE HERBS DRESSING, SMOKED EGGPLANT, AND MORINGA (FLOWERS AND LEAVES)

GOAT STEWED IN COCONUT MILK AND SUN-DRIED SHRIMP RICE IN TWO WAYS

FLOWERS AND HERBS "SALPICON" WITH JAMAICA LEAVES SHERBET

PUMPKIN AND PLANTAIN MINGUI WITH COASTAL GRANOLA AND COCONUT LEMONADE SORBET

In 2018, Sebastián Pinzón and Jaime Rodríguez opened Celele with a visionary goal: to showcase the little-known cuisine of Caribbean Colombia. Located in the hip Getsemaní neighborhood of Cartagena, a city that the pair sees as the gateway to the Caribbean coastal region, Celele is colorful and vibrant, both on the plate and within its cozy interior, reflecting the co-chefs' boundless creativity. Caribbean Colombian is often misunderstood and minimized as fried food and plantains, but Celele's contemporary tasting menus (either five or ten courses) showcase the diverse influences—Lebanese, Syrian, African, European, and native Indian—that coexist in the region. The chefs' elegant, intriguing plating and flavor combinations defy preconceived notions about food from that area.

Pinzón and Rodríguez, both natives of Andean Colombia, were cooking at two different restaurants when they met in Cartagena. They realized immediately that they shared a common curiosity about the region's culinary roots and began to explore the notion that Cartagena was a portal to Caribbean Colombia and its unique culinary lexicon. First, the pair had to decipher the influences. Using funds raised by their first pop-up, they set out for the islands to research. Together they launched Proyecto Caribe Lab, a roving workshop and pop-up designed to explore and educate people about the culture and biodiversity of Caribbean influences. They learned traditional cooking methods from indigenous families, experimented with foraged ingredients and contemporary techniques, and invited others to enjoy their journey through their pop-up series in Cartagena.

Cartagena's singular locale as a port city, through which myriad cultures have immigrated and settled, makes it the perfect spiritual home for Celele. The biodiverse region, tropical climate, and proximity to both sea and rich farmland offer the ultimate panoply from which to source. In 2019, Celele was honored with the Miele One to Watch Award by Latin America's 50 Best Restaurants.

BOCANA MUSSELS IN COASTAL PICKLE, PORK RINDS, AND SEAWEEDS
Serves 15 (tasting menu)

For the mussels in coastal pickle:
15 large mussels (about 1.2 kg) • 200 ml olive oil • 5 g garlic • 10 g annatto seeds • 0.5 g Jamaican peppercorns • 150 ml sugar cane rum • 300 ml plantain vinegar • 30 g ground Caribbean sweet pepper • 0.5 g ground cumin • Salt • 5 g cilantro (fresh coriander) leaves

For the pork rinds:
1 pound pork skin • Salt, as needed • Oil, for deep-frying

Pickle the mussels:
Place the mussels in a sheet pan and steam in a 190°F (90°C) oven for 8 minutes. Take out of the oven and let them cool. Clean one by one and reserve the mussel juices.

In a small pot, combine the olive oil, garlic, annatto seeds, peppercorns, and cilantro (coriander) leaves. Cook over low heat at about 167°F (75°C) for 30 minutes. Strain the oil.
In a saucepan, heat the rum and let it evaporate for a little bit, then add the plantain vinegar, ground sweet pepper, and 150 ml mussel juices and let it boil. Season with the cumin and salt to taste before taking off the heat.
Place the mussels in a bowl and cover them with the rum/vinegar brine and then add the flavored oil. Refrigerate for 3 days so they can absorb the flavors.

Make the pork rinds:
Clean the pork skin without damaging it, removing all the fat (reserve it for another preparation).
Season the skin with enough salt and pack it lengthwise into vacuum bags. Cook in the sous vide at 93°C for 8 hours. Lay the

BOCANA MUSSELS

CURED AND MATURED LOBSTER

THEY CREATE UNIQUE MESSAGES BASED ON THE TERRITORY, SO THEY ARE GENERATING A NEW TREND OF HOW PEOPLE CAN SEE THEIR REGION.
— *Virgilio Martínez*

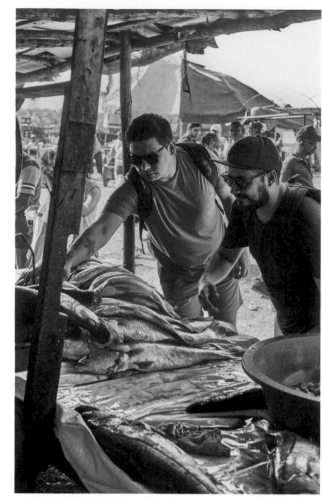

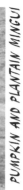

cooked skin on silicone sheets and dehydrate it at 145°F (63°C) for 12 hours. Store it in a sealed container until ready to fry.
In a deep-fryer or deep heavy pot, heat oil to 392°F (200°C). Submerge the skin in the oil, handling with tongs so it stays as flat as possible. Drain on paper towels and place in a dehydrator until plating.
To serve, remove the mussels from the pickled mixture. Emulsify the remaining cooking water and oil with a blender and pour over the mussels upon plating. Cut up the pork rinds and use them to garnish.

CURED AND MATURED LOBSTER IN COCONUT OIL WITH PICKLED CASHEW FRUIT AND CREAMY CASHEW NUT

Serves 4 (tasting menu)

For the lobster:
400 g sugar • 200 g sea salt • 1 g mandarin lemon zest • 400 g cleaned lobster tail meat • 500 ml cold-pressed coconut oil

For the pickled cashew fruit:
100 g cashew fruits • 300 ml filtered water • 200 ml cashew vinegar • 100 g block cane sugar • 1 g Jamaican pepper

For the creamy cashews:
100 g cashews • 100 ml filtered water • 50 ml olive oil • Salt

Cure the lobster:
In a bowl, mix together the sugar, salt, and zest. Cover the lobster with the mixture. and refrigerate for 4 hours. Rinse the lobster to remove the rub.
Dry the lobster thoroughly and submerge it in the coconut oil at room temperature. Lower the temperature until the coconut oil solidifies. Without removing any oil, cover and refrigerate for 3 days.

Make the pickled cashew fruit:
Cut the cashew fruit in half and place in a glass jar,
In a pot, combine the water, vinegar, cane sugar, and pepper and bring to a boil. Pour the liquid over the cashew fruit. Let it cool down and refrigerate until use.

Make the creamy cashew nut:
Vacuum-seal the nuts with the water and refrigerate for 12 hours.
Place the soaked nuts and any remaining liquid in a processor. Pour in the olive oil slowly until a creamy smooth texture develops. Season with salt to taste.
When ready to serve, break the coconut oil block and remove the lobster tail. Serve slices of the lobster layered with slices of pickled cashew fruit, with creamy cashew on the side.

PUMPKIN AND PLANTAIN MINGUI WITH COASTAL GRANOLA AND COCONUT LEMONADE SORBET

Serves 10 (tasting menu)

For the mingui:
300 g yellow plantain, grilled • 150 g steamed pumpkin • 300 ml coconut milk • 80 ml condensed milk • 1 g Caribbean five-spice

For the coconut lemonade sorbet:
100 g sugar • 50 g Totalbase stabilizer • 450 ml coconut milk • 0.5 g grated lemon zest • 95 ml lemon juice • 10 ml coconut oil

For the coastal granola:
5 g sorghum, popped • 50 g hulled pumpkin seeds, toasted • 50 g dried pineapple, chopped • 20 g grated coconut, toasted • 20 g crushed toasted corn • 1 g sweet five-spice • 20 g cane sugar

Make the mingui:
In a food processor, blend all the ingredients until smooth and homogenous.

Make the sorbet:
In a bowl, mix the sugar with the stabilizer. Add the coconut milk, lemon zest, lemon juice, and coconut oil. Divide in two parts and turbine each one for 45 minutes. Store in metal containers in the freezer.

Make the granola:
Preheat the oven to 210°F (100°C).
In a bowl, combine all the ingredients. Spread out on a sheet pan and bake for 10 minutes, mixing around 4 times. Take out of the oven and let it cool down.
Serve the mingui topped with granola and a quenlle of sorbet.

SEBASTIÁN PINZÓN GIRALDO & JAIME RODRÍGUEZ CAMACHO

ANNA POSEY & DAVID POSEY

JESSICA KOSLOW

ELSKE
Chicago, Illinois, United States

Anna and David Posey are gifted chefs and tremendous storytellers. To take part in a tasting at Elske, their Chicago restaurant, is to immerse yourself in a narrative, one rich in beauty, brains, risks, and surprises. From start to finish, each successive dish seems to complete a sentence started by the plate that preceded it—a through line driven by Anna and David's individual quirks and unified talents. From the big picture to the small details, Elske offers a level of thoughtfulness that is rare, the type of care that separates good meals from great ones.

Plenty of chefs work with their significant others, but the Poseys, both veterans of Paul Kahan's empire, have figured out how to weave together their distinct and respective strengths in a way that feels natural and beneficial. Elske, fittingly, is Danish for "love." Alhough Elske is not a Danish restaurant, David, a Los Angeles native, finds subtle ways to honor his Scandinavian heritage: his mother Gunde's pickles and cucumber salad recipes have made appearances, enhancing dishes like an elegant beef tartare that playfully evokes rød pølse, the hot dogs served by Copenhagen street vendors. With her fine-art background and Midwestern upbringing, Wisconsinite Anna offers an entirely different aesthetic, influencing both the mood of the room and the timbre of the bread and pastry programs.

The way in which sweet and savory flavors interact across Elske's menu is refreshing and unexpected, the by-product of two creative souls open to constant collaboration. It is a special energy, and you don't need special training to recognize and appreciate it. Anna and David's efforts have managed to charm everyone from *Michelin Guide* inspectors (they received one star in 2017) to West Loop locals who have become regulars, thanks to the accessible price point Elske strives to maintain. All told, the most vibrant feature of Elske might be how personal it is at every juncture. The Poseys are doing exactly what they want to do, and it turns out that what makes them happy makes their guests ever happier.

MENU

DUCK LIVER TART WITH SALTED RAMPS AND BUCKWHEAT

KOMBU-CURED FLUKE WITH TURNIP, ASIAN PEAR, AND SESAME

SUNFLOWER SEED PARFAIT WITH SOUR HONEY, BEE POLLEN, AND LICORICE

DUCK LIVER TART WITH SALTED RAMPS AND BUCKWHEAT
Serves 20 as an hors d'oeuvre

For the buckwheat tart dough:
300 g all-purpose (plain) flour • 150 g buckwheat flour • 140 g powdered (icing) sugar • 8 g salt • 240 g unsalted butter • 2 eggs • 10 g water

For the duck liver tart filling:
8 ounces (225 g) unsalted butter • 1 pint shallots, sliced • 2 cloves garlic, sliced • 1 cup (240 ml) heavy (whipping) cream • 2 pounds (910 g) duck livers, cured with 1% pink curing salt • 8 ounces (225 g) foie gras • Salt • Cayenne pepper

For the salted ramp gel:
2 cups (475 ml) chicken consommé (*see Notes*) • ½ cup pickled ramp liquid (*see Notes*) • 3 sheets gelatin, bloomed in ice water

For the parsley powder:
2 bunches of parsley, leaves removed from stems

Make the tart dough:
In a food processor, combine the all-purpose (plain) flour, buckwheat flour, sugar, and salt and pulse to mix. Add the butter and blend until the texture of cornmeal. Mix in the eggs and water until just combined. Portion the dough into five 200 g disks. Refrigerate for 1–2 hours.

Preheat the oven to 375°F (190°C). Roll out a portion of dough to ¼ inch (6 mm) thick. Line a 4 × 13 inch rectangular tart mold. Repeat.
Place a sheet of parchment on a the tart dough and fill with baking weights (rice or dried beans work well) and blind bake for 15–20 minutes. (Leave the oven on but reduce the temperature to 200°F/90°C.)

Meanwhile, make the filling:
In a large pan, heat 1 ounce of the butter and sweat the shallots and garlic until tender. Add the cream and cook until the cream is reduced by about one-quarter and let cool to room temperature.
In a high powered blender, blend the cream and livers until smooth. Mount in the foie and then the remaining 225 g of butter. Season with salt and cayenne.
Portion about 12 ounce of filling into each tart shell. Transfer to the oven and bake until the center registers 165°F (74°C), about 20 minutes. Cool in the refrigerator.

DUCK LIVER TART

Make the salted ramp gel:
Season the consommé with the pickled ramp liquid. Set the consommé with the gelatin.

Make the parsley powder:
Heat a dehydrator to 125°F (52°C). Place the parsley leaves in an even layer on a dehydrator tray, and place in dehydrator. Dehydrate until parsley is dried and bright green, about 3 hours.
Cool to room temperature and grind into a fine powder in a spice grinder or blender.

To assemble:
Warm the ramp gel over low heat until it turns liquid but is not hot. (It should be slightly above body temperature.) Gently spoon 2 ounces of the warmed gel over a chilled tart, and let the gel set overtop the duck liver. Repeat the gelling process once more, until you have a nice even layer of gel covering the whole tart. Let the gel fully set for 1 hour. Using a fine-mesh strainer, dust the top of the gelled tart with the parsley powder.
Remove the tart from the pan, and slice into wedges using a warm knife.

Notes: Make a chicken consommé using a traditional meat raft of 10% meat to liquid. We use the liquid left over from our ramp pickles, which we use elsewhere on the restaurant's menu.

SUNFLOWER SEED PARFAIT WITH SOUR HONEY, BEE POLLEN, AND LICORICE
Serves 36

For the sunflower seed praline:
800 g sucrose • 160 g water • 800 g sunflower seeds, toasted until very golden • 80 g neutral oil, as needed

For the caramelized sunflower seed parfait:
1.325 g heavy (whipping) cream • 475 g whole milk • 20 g vanilla paste • 320 g sugar • 7 g salt • 80 g glucose syrup • 330 g egg yolks • 720 g Sunflower Seed Praline *(above)* • 20 g gelatin, bloomed

For assembly:
Honey vinegar • Licorice crumble • Powdered bee pollen

Make the praline:
Line a sheet pan with a silicone baking mat. Make a wet caramel with the sugar and water, using a lid or bowl to build condensation in the beginning stages as the organic sucrose crystallizes easily. Once the caramel is a dark amber, pour out onto the pan to cool. When completely at room temperature, break into 1–2 inch (2.5–5 cm) pieces. In a food processor, blend the toasted sunflower seeds and caramel pieces until it forms a smooth paste. This blending process will take a long time. The heat generated by the food processor will help the mixture blend smoothly. Add oil as needed.

Make the parfait:
Lightly coat three quarter-sheet pans (12 × 8 inches/30 × 20 cm), line with acetate, and set aside.
In a mixer, whip the cream to medium peaks (not firm!) and chill while preparing the base.
In a saucepan, bring the milk, vanilla, sucrose, glucose, and salt to a simmer. Stir some of the hot milk into the yolks to temper them, then stir the yolks into the milk and cook until thickened, about 180°F (82°C). Quickly take off the heat, add the praline, and whisk very well. Strain the mixture into the bowl of a stand mixer fitted with the whisk, then whip until cool.
Fold the whipped cream into the cooled praline base in stages. Once the base is mixed together, ladle about 1 kg of the base onto each prepared quarter-sheet pan. Make sure the parfait is completely smooth and even. Freeze overnight, then cut into ¾-inch (7 cm) squares and reserve until needed.

To assemble:
Place a square of the frozen parfait onto a cold plate. Top the parfait with a few drops of honey vinegar. On the side sprinkle a large spoonful of licorice crumble dusted with powdered bee pollen.

> IT'S REALLY RARE TO HAVE A MEAL THAT'S AS THOUGHTFUL FROM THE BEGINNING TO THE END. IT'S ALMOST LIKE EACH DISH IS PICKING UP A SENTENCE WHERE IT LEFT OFF. — *Jessica Koslow*

KOMBU-CURED FLUKE

ANNA POSEY & DAVID POSEY

PHILIP RACHINGER

RESTAURANT
MÜHLTALHOF
Unternberg, Austria

ANA ROŠ

MENU

RAW CARP BELLY WITH KOHLRABI AND PINE SPROUTS

CURED SALMON TROUT WITH CHERVIL ROOTS, TANGERINES, AND PUMPKIN SEED OIL

CARP LEBERKÄSE AND SOURDOUGH BREAD

"SCHWEIZER KRACHER" POTATO DUMPLING WITH KALE AND JERSEY BLUE

HARE SHOULDER, HAUNCH, AND RACK WITH BLOOD SAUCE AND BLOOD ORANGE

GRANITA

Cooking runs in Philip Rachinger's blood. A native of Upper Austria, Rachinger grew up at Mühltalhof, the acclaimed hotel and restaurant in Unternberg that has been in his family for generations. He became the head chef there in 2018. Considering his hereditary connection to the land and region, it makes perfect sense that Rachinger's cuisine is a love letter to his environs. He grows herbs for the restaurant in the hotel garden, and has also cultivated relationships with the best farmers and producers nearby. But his food also has a modernity influenced by his travels and training abroad in foreign chefs' kitchens.

Rachinger's first professional experience was under Heinz Reitbauer, at the Pogusch Country Inn and Steirereck in Vienna. Then Rachinger moved to London, where he worked under Pierre Gagniere before becoming sous chef for Isaac McHale at Upstairs at the Ten Bells. From there, he went to Paris, where he cooked with Sven Chartier at Saturne.

In 2013, Rachinger returned to Mühltalhof. He joined his father, Helmut, a legendary chef in his own right, in the Mühltalhof kitchen. The pair cooked together there for five years, after which Helmut left to open another small restaurant nearby, officially passing the torch to his son.

Now, as the sixth generation of chefs at Mühltalhof, Rachinger's elegantly streamlined, modern cooking style has a chance to shine. Particularly beloved dishes that have garnered international attention include Fillet of Fish on a Hot Wood Shingle and Beetroot with Saddle of Hare and Smoked Cream. At Mühltalhof, guests have the option to let Rachinger choose for them or to select their own menu, but by all accounts, the best way to enjoy the experience is to put oneself in the chef's capable hands and submit to his vision. Rachinger has three toques from Gault Millau and is considered one to watch in the global culinary world.

RAW CARP BELLY WITH KOHLRABI AND PINE SPROUTS

3 limes • 10 g fresh ginger, peeled and minced (scant ¹⁄₁₆ inch/1 mm) • 15 g pine sprout honey • 30 g preserved pine sprouts, chopped • Salt • 1 kohlrabi • 2 carp bellies • 45 ml celery green oil

Peel the limes and remove the fillets. Thinly slice them so they start to fall apart. And keep the leftover for the juice. Combine the ginger, lime segments, lime juice, pine honey, and pine sprouts. Add a pinch of salt. Set the vinaigrette aside.
Use a vegetable sheeter to make a continuous kohlrabi sheet. Roll it up again and slice it crosswise into ¹⁄₁₆-inch (1.5 mm) noodles. Refresh them in ice water for 2 hours. Thinly slice the carp belly at a slight angle like Jiro Ono.
To finish, rinse the kohlrabi noodles. When they are dry, marinate them with the vinaigrette.

To plate, place 8 or 9 long slices of carp belly on the kohlrabi. Roll it up to form a fluffy ball.

CURED SALMON TROUT WITH CHERVIL ROOTS, TANGERINES, AND PUMPKIN SEED OIL

For the cured fish:
Coriander seeds • Mustard seeds • 120 g sugar • 200 g salt • 1 salmon trout fillet

For the confited chervil roots:
250 g unsalted butter • 4 chervil roots, peeled

For the sauce:
Olive oil • 2 shallots, julienned • Garlic • Juice of 10 tangerines • 2 lime leaves • 1 stalk lemongrass • Salt • Cayenne pepper • Ponzu sauce • 20 ml Styrian pumpkin seed oil

For plating:
200 g trout caviar • 1 pomelo, segmented • Pumpkin seeds, toasted

Cure the fish:
Toast the coriander seeds and mustard seeds in a dry pan. Let them cool down and grind them. Mix the sugar and salt with the ground seeds. Spread on a tray.
Skin the fillet and dip each side in the cure. Anything that doesn't stick on the fish is too much—keep it for the next batch. Let the fish cure overnight.
Wash off the cure and cut the fish into slices a generous ⅛ inch (4 mm) thick.

Make the confited chervil roots:
Heat up the butter and make a beurre noisette. Add the chervil roots and confit them at 266°F (130°C) for about 25 minutes.

Make the sauce:
In a sauteuse, heat up some olive oil.
Add the shallots and garlic and slightly

RAW CARP BELLY

PHILIP IS DIGGING INTO THOSE REAL TRADITIONS OF AUSTRIAN CUISINE, WHICH IS A MOTHER OF ALL CENTRAL EUROPEAN CUISINE ITSELF.
— Ana Roš

CURED SALMON TROUT

CARP LEBERKÄSE

roast them. Deglaze with the tangerine juice. Add the lime leaves and lemongrass. Cook to reduce by half and season with salt, cayenne, and a little bit of ponzu sauce. Let it cool down. At serving time, let it split with a bit of Styrian pumpkin seed oil.

To plate:
Arrange the trout and confited chervil root in the middle of the plate. Don't be shy with the caviar and add some pomelo segments. Finish it with toasted pumpkin seeds and sauce.

"SCHWEIZER KRACHER" POTATO DUMPLING WITH KALE AND JERSEY BLUE

For the dumpling dough:
500 g Agria potatoes • 220 g T700 flour • 80 g unsalted butter, melted • 4 egg yolks • Muscat • Salt

For the kale filling:
Salt • 1 bunch kale, stemmed • Baking powder • 3 leeks • Butter • 2 white onions, finely diced • 4 cloves garlic, minced • Freshly ground black pepper • 10 g nori powder • 5 g ramson powder • 140 g Jersey Blue cheese, cut into ⅜-inch (1 cm) cubes

For the pear puree:
3 pears • 200 ml white wine • 1 stick cinnamon • 2 whole star anise • 1 fresh horseradish root

Make the dumpling dough:
In a large pot of boiling water, cook the potatoes. Peel them and press them through a ricer. Refrigerate overnight. The next day, make a nice dough with your hands. Start with the pressed potatoes and add the flour, melted butter, and egg yolks. Season with Muscat and salt.

Make the kale filling:
In a large pot of boiling salted water, cook the kale with some baking powder until it starts to fall apart. Scoop out the kale (reserve the cooking water) and squeeze the kale to get all the liquid out.
Cook the leek greens in the same water until soft and make a cream out of it.
In a sauté pan, heat a knob of butter.
Add the onions and garlic and cook until browned. Add the kale and the leek cream. Season with salt, pepper, nori powder, and ramson powder.
Add the Jersey Blue cheese to the kale filling and mix it gently. Form 1¼-inch (3 cm) balls. Freeze them so it's easier to form dumplings.

Make the pear puree:
Peel the pears and roughly chop. In a saucepan, combine the pears, wine, cinnamon, and star anise. When the pear is soft,

"SCHWEIZER KRACHER" POTATO DUMPLING

blend it to a smooth puree. Before serving, peel the horseradish and grate in as much as you can handle in the puree.

GRANITA

For the poppy seed ice cream:
500 ml whole milk • 75 ml heavy cream • 75 g superfine (caster) sugar • 3 egg yolks • 33 g ground poppy seeds • 10 ml poppy-seed oil

For the beechwood charcoal crumbles:
325 g all-purpose (plain) flour • 250 g unsalted butter, at room temperature • 200 g powdered (icing) sugar • 7 g salt • 30 g ground black sesame seeds • 15 g charcoal powder (from beechwood)

For the vinegar meringue:
100 g egg whites • 100 g superfine (caster) sugar • 100 g powdered (icing) sugar • 30 g vinegar powder

For the grilled Williams pear:
2 ripe Williams pears • 10 cl Gölles balsamic vinegar

Make the poppy seed ice cream:
In a saucepan, combine the milk and cream and bring to a boil.
Meanwhile, in a stand mixer, whisk together the sugar and egg yolks until pale and very fluffy.
When the milk and cream have come to a boil, remove from the heat. Add the yolk/sugar mixture to the milk/cream. Return to

the heat and cook, stirring constantly, until it reaches 180°F (82°C). Strain into a bowl set on an ice-cooled tray.
Transfer to Pacojet beakers and freeze overnight.

Make the beechwood charcoal crumbles:
In a bowl, mix together the flour, butter, powdered sugar, and salt to form a smooth dough. Let it rest for 4 hours.
Preheat the oven to 300°F (150°C).
Roll the dough out between two sheets of parchment paper a scant ¼ inch (5 mm) thick. Transfer to a pan and bake for 14 minutes.

Make the vinegar meringue:
In a stand mixer, whisk the egg whites to half stiff peaks. Then add the superfine (caster) sugar and whisk to stiff peaks. Beat in the powdered (icing) sugar and vinegar powder. Dehydrate it at 230°F (110°C) for 2 hours.

Grill the pears:
Grill the pears and dress with the vinegar.

PHILIP RACHINGER

ELENA REYGADAS

DANIELA SOTO-INNES

ROSETTA, PANADERÍA ROSETTA
Mexico City, Mexico

Since 2010, at her restaurant Rosetta, behind the plant-flanked wooden doors of an elegant Beaux Arts mansion, Elena Reygadas's dishes blend Mexico's seasonal produce and culinary traditions with Italian sensibilities and technique, yielding transcendent food that is fresh and contemporary.

Reygadas learned to love food during her upbringing in Mexico City. Her grandmother taught her to cook, and her parents imparted to her their pleasure in hosting meals and discovering new foods. After college, where Reygadas studied English literature, she catered for her filmmaker brother's production crew. The experience got her hooked, and she set off for New York City, where she enrolled at the International Culinary Center. Next, she moved to London, where she landed at Locanda Locatelli under the tutelage of Giorgio Locatelli. She became versed not only in Italian cuisine, but in the significance of superb and seasonal ingredients. When she gave birth to her first daughter, she returned to Mexico, where she organized pop-up events and private dinners. Increasing demand prompted her to open something stable: Rosetta.

Rosetta has always been strongly defined by Italian technique, but while Reygadas's pastas are renowned, her name was arguably made through her innovation with Mexican ingredients. She spotlights those often not considered hallmarks of Mexican food, such as fennel, *hoja santa*, beets, and chicatana ants. Others she serves using European techniques—gnocchi with *huitlachoche* and Ocosingo cheese, or risotto with wild Mexican mushrooms. And Reygadas is a fiend for disregarding rules: she serves mole for dessert, rather than with meat, and *chicozapote*, a typical ice cream flavor, in salad.

The restaurant's breads became so sought-after that Reygadas opened a bakery, La Panadería Rosetta; later came her casual café, Lardo, and her French-themed sandwich-and-salad joint, Café Nin. As she transforms the Mexican gastronomic scene, Reygadas has garnered acclaim from around the world.

MENU

MORNING SWEET TOOTH:
CONCHA

ENDIVES, VANILLA, LEMON
AND PIXTLE

POTATO AND EPAZOTE
TORTELLONI WITH CORN BROTH

HOJA SANTA MOLE AND
QUELITES TAMAL

WHITE HEIRLOOM CACAO
CHOCOLATE AND HOJA SANTA

CONCHA
Makes 4 conchas

For the vanilla crust:
10 g all-purpose (plain) flour • 10 g vegetable shortening • 5 g sugar glass • 5 g sugar • 0.5 g baking powder • Pinch of salt • Seeds from ½ vanilla bean

For the conchas:
4 g fresh yeast • 15 g whole milk • 180 g wheat flour • 25 g sugar • 1 g fine sea salt • 45 g eggs • 40 g butter • Egg wash

Make the vanilla crust:
In a bowl, combine all of the ingredients and beat with an electric mixer at a low speed until well blended. Don't overmix. Once the mixture is uniform, let stand at room temperature while you make the conchas.

Make the conchas:
Dissolve the yeast in the milk. In a large bowl, combine the flour, dissolved yeast, sugar, salt, eggs, and butter and mix with your hands, making small circles. Once everything has blended together, knead the dough, lightly striking it against the surface until it becomes smooth and elastic.
Place the dough in a covered container and let it sit at room temperature for 10 minutes. Divide the dough into 4 pieces and shape each into a ball.
Divide the vanilla crust into 4 portions; they should be about 20 g. Form each portion into a ball and then use your palm to flatten it into a disk large enough to cover one of the dough balls.
Glaze each ball of dough with egg and cover with a disk of vanilla crust. Press a shell-pattern mold into the crust or make the traditional pattern with a knife. Dip each concha in sugar and place on a baking sheet. Cover the conchas with a lightly

floured cloth and let sit at room temperature for 1½–2 hours, preferably in a humid environment between 70–75°F (20–25°C). Preheat the oven to 350°F (175°C). Bake the conchas for 18 minutes.

POTATO AND EPAZOTE TORTELLONI WITH CORN BROTH
Serves 4

For the corn broth:
1 ear white corn, unhusked • 20 g leek • 25 g onion • 600 ml water

For the potato and epazote puree:
160 g potato • 65 g butter, melted • ½ egg yolk • 20 g epazote, chopped • 20 g Parmesan cheese • Pinch of salt

For the potato and epazote tortelloni:
100 g tipo "00" flour • 1 g salt • 5 ml extra-virgin olive oil • 40 g egg yolks • 5 g egg white • Egg wash • 230 g Potato and Epazote Puree *(above)*

For finishing:
10 g brown butter

Make the corn broth:
Grill the corn directly over a flame. Roast the leek and onion in the oven until golden.

Scrape the kernels from the corn cob and place in a saucepan. Add a few of the charred husks as well as the cob. Add roasted leek and onion and the water and bring to a boil over high heat. Reduce the heat and let simmer until it reduces to half its volume. Remove from the heat and strain.

Make the potato and epazote puree:
In a pot of boiling water, cook the potatoes until tender, about 20 minutes. Drain and peel while still warm.
In a food processor, combine the potatoes, butter, egg yolk, epazote, Parmesan, and salt and process until smooth.

Make the potato and epazote tortelloni:
Pour the flour into a large bowl and add the salt. Make a well in the center and add the oil, egg yolks, and egg whites.
Using your fingers, incorporate the wet ingredients into the flour until everything is well mixed. If the pasta mixture is very dry, add a little more egg white. Cover the pasta mixture with plastic wrap (cling film) and refrigerate for 2 hours.
With a rolling pin, roll the pasta dough out until ⅜ inch (1 cm) thick. On your pasta rolling machine, starting with the widest possible opening, run the pasta through to get a long strip. Fold the pasta strip over into thirds and run the pasta through again. The next time, fold the pasta strip again, but this time feed it into the machine in the opposite direction, so that the fold is perpendicular to the roller. Keep running it through, alternating direction of the folded pasta, until you reach the narrowest opening.
Repeat this process once more until the pasta is smooth and glossy ¹⁄₁₆ inch (1.5 mm) thick.
Cut the pasta into 1½-inch (4 cm) squares and brush with a beaten egg. Add about 8 g of potato and epazote puree to the center of each square. Fold in half diagonally and trim the edges of the triangle in order to form a half-moon shape.
Take both ends and fold them into the center in order to form the shape of a tortelloni.

To finish:
In a large pot of salted boiling water, cook the tortellini. When the tortellini float, scoop them out of the water.
Heat the corn broth. Place 7 tortelloni on each of four plates. Add a few drops of brown butter and pour 60 ml corn broth into each plate and serve.

HOJA SANTA MOLE AND QUELITES TAMAL
Serves 4

For the quelites tamal:
Oil • 40 g quelites • 2 g garlic • Pinch of salt • 90 g fresh masa • 40 g olive oil • 4 banana leaves

For assembly:
12 g purple quelites • 15 ml olive oil • 5 ml lemon juice • 240 g Hoja Santa Mole *(recipe follows)*, warmed • 32 g purslane

Make the quelites tamal:
In a sauté pan, stir-fry the quelites, garlic, and salt. Remove from the heat and add to a bowl with ice to stop the cooking process. Remove the excess of water with your hand. Pull the masa apart into crumbs with your fingers and place it in a mixer bowl. With the mixer running at low speed, gradually add the oil and beat the masa until fluffy. Add the quelites to the masa and mix well. Cut the banana leaves into squares and place them directly over a flame until they are flexible.

Using a pastry ring set in the center of each banana leaf, add 30 g of masa and form into a round tamal. Fold in the edges.
Cook in a steamer for about 20 minutes.

To assemble:
Season the purple quelites with olive oil and lemon. Place the warm tamal at the center of the plate. Top the tamal with 60 g hoja santa mole. Garnish with the purslane and the purple quelites.

HOJA SANTA MOLE
Makes 500 grams

30 g safflower oil • 50 g onion, cut into large cubes • 10 g garlic, halved • 65 g blanched almonds • 10 g pine nuts • 20 g pumpkin seeds

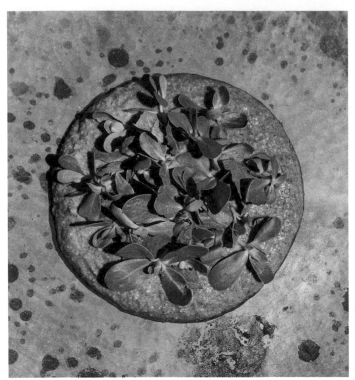

HOJA SANTA MOLE AND QUELITES TAMAL

• 65 g plantain • 1 g cumin • 1 g coriander seeds • 1 g black pepper • 3 bay leaves • 1 g avocado leaf • 5 g sesame seeds • 200 g tomatillo, quartered • 1 serrano chili • 60 g poblano pepper • 15 g chaya • 30 g hoja santa • 12 g parsley • 8 g cilantro (coriander) • 6 g epazote • 10 g salt

In a sauté pan, heat the oil over medium heat. Add the onion and cook until tender, then remove from the pan. Sauté the garlic in the same pan and remove once cooked. Add the almonds and cook until golden and remove. Do the same with the pine nuts and the pumpkin seeds. Add the plantain and cook until tender, then remove from the pan. Pour all the ingredients together in a bowl.

In another pan, without oil, toast the cumin, coriander seed, and black pepper over low heat. Let them cool and then grind with them with the bay leaves and avocado leaf. Separately, toast the sesame seeds and then grind into a paste, adding a bit of water if necessary.

In a pot of boiling water, blanch the tomatillos and serrano. Halve the serrano, seed, and derib. Don't discard the cooking water.

In a blender, combine the sautéed vegetable/nut/seed mixture with the tomatillo and serrano. Once you get the texture of a puree, add the sesame paste and the spice powder. Mix well, adding a bit of the reserved cooking water if necessary. Pour this mixture into a large bowl and set aside.

Place the poblano pepper directly over a flame to char the skin all over. Place in a bag and allow to steam for at least 15 minutes. Remove from the bag, peel, and derib the poblano.

In separate pots of boiling water, blanch the chaya and hoja santa. Place in a bowl with ice water to stop the cooking process. Scoop out the greens and squeeze with your hands to make them as dry as possible.

In a blender, blend the poblanos, chaya, hoja santa, parsley, cilantro (coriander), and epazote until you get the consistency of a puree and add the salt.

Pour this poblano/herb mixture into the bowl with the vegetable/nut/sesame mixture and mix well with a whisk.

WHITE HEIRLOOM CACAO CHOCOLATE AND HOJA SANTA
Serves 4

For the crystallized hoja santa:
20 g water • 20 g sugar • 4 hoja santa leaves

For the hoja santa ice cream:
100 g milk • 65 g heavy (whipping) cream • 20 g glucose • 2 g ice cream stabilizer • 60 g yogurt • 20 g hoja santa

For the chocolate sauce:
180 g heavy (whipping) cream • 1 vanilla bean, split • 20 g hoja santa • 65 g heirloom white cacao chocolate

For the heirloom white cacao nibs:
20 g heavy (whipping) cream • 1 g pectin • 20 g sugar • 10 g glucose • 30 g heirloom white cacao nibs • 20 g butter

Make the crystallized hoja santa:
In a saucepan, heat the water and sugar to make a syrup.
Line a dehydrator tray with parchment paper. Select the biggest and prettiest hoja

santas and clean them. Varnish them on both sides with the syrup and place them on the tray. Dehydrate for 24 hours.

Make the hoja santa ice cream:
In a saucepan, combine the milk, cream, glucose, and stabilizer and heat to 185°F (85°C). Place over an ice bath and stir to bring the temperature down to 39°F (4°C). Add the hoja santa and blend with a hand blender. Strain into a bowl and stir in the yogurt. Churn it in an ice cream machine.

Make the chocolate sauce:
In a saucepan, bring the cream, vanilla seeds and pod, and hoja santa just to a boil, then remove from the heat and let sit for 15 minutes. Discard the vanilla pods. Blend, then strain in a chinois. Melt the chocolate into the mixture with the help of a hand blender and let it sit.

Prepare the heirloom white cacao nibs:
Preheat the oven to 350°F (180°C). Line a sheet pan with parchment paper.
In a saucepan, heat the cream, pectin, sugar, and glucose until it reaches 217°F (103°C). Remove from the heat and stir in the cacao nibs and butter. Spread the mixture in the lined pan and bake for 9 minutes. Let cool until set, then break into small pieces.

To plate:
Place 30 g of cacao nibs in the center of each plate. Spoon 60 g of chocolate sauce on top and add a quenelle of hoja santa ice cream. Garnish with a crystallized hoja santa leaf.

*ELENA'S PASTRIES
ARE MY FAVORITE—
WHEN I HAVE A BITE
OF HER GUAVA PASTRY,
EVERYTHING JUST
STOPS. HER PASSION
FOR ITALIAN-MEXICAN
CULTURE SHOWS.*
— Daniela Soto-Innes

ELENA REYGADAS

JONATHAN "JONNY" RHODES

MARCUS SAMUELSSON

INDIGO
Houston, Texas,
United States

There were times during the challenging lead-up to the opening of his Houston restaurant, Indigo, that Jonny Rhodes considered leaving cooking behind to teach history. Lucky for us, he has developed a way to do both, relying on his gifts in the kitchen to educate and uplift. To him, food is the ideal medium for forging an incisive dialogue about inequality in the United States.

Rhodes came to the restaurant life relatively late. He enlisted in the United States Marine Corps out of high school, but his priorities shifted once he met his wife, Chana, a fellow Marine. He completed culinary school, then cut his teeth at a series of Houston restaurants, including Oxheart with Chef Justin Yu. After working for Chef Michael Anthony at New York's Gramercy Tavern, Rhodes came home and partnered with Chana to launch the Jensen Chronicles, a pop-up series with dishes that illuminated Houston's Northside—the blueprint for a permanent location, which in 2019 *TIME* would dub one of the World's Greatest Places.

Indigo, Rhodes's thirteen-seat tasting-menu restaurant, is a subversive force in dining today. Its Lindale Park location is a statement in itself. Rhodes's restaurant is an incubator for efforts like community gardening, with the long-term goal of increasing availability of fresh, local food in this under-resourced area. His activism has grown organically, as has his cuisine, and through it he shares insights gleaned from his studies of the African diaspora and American slavery.

Indigo serves "neo–soul food" with purpose. On one plate, he captures the story of the simple yam, from its agricultural origins in Nigeria to preservation techniques detailed in the antebellum writings of Frederick Douglass. On another, he presents smoked turnips with his rendition of "slabber sauce," an oil, flour, water, and pepper mixture invented as a means of survival by slaves traversing the Middle Passage. A conscientious keeper of unsung stories, Rhodes is exhaustive in his research and generous with his time. He is dedicated to amplifying the social, political, and historical tragedies and triumphs of the African American experience.

MENU

LOCAL DRY-AGED SHEEPSHEAD FISH COOKED OVER EMBERS, CITRUS PEEL GEL, ALLIUM EXTRACT

ASH-AGED POTATO ASHCAKES WITH CARAMELIZED POTATO CRÈME, OKRA CONDIMENT, CRISPY SHALLOTS, HERBS

CURED, HUNG, SMOKED PICKLED CARROTS WITH YELLOW BARBECUE SAUCE, HERBS

SOFKI STEW WITH PECAN EMULSION, RABBIT CONFIT CROQUETTE, COLLARD GREENS, PRESERVED MUSHROOMS

CHARCOAL-ROASTED CANDIED YAM SEMIFREDDO

ASH-AGED POTATO ASHCAKES

For the cured smoked potatoes:
25 lb (11.3 kg) new potatoes •
1 lb (455 g) salt

For the ash-aged potatoes:
20 lb (9 kg) Cured Smoked Potatoes *(above)*

For the smoked potato syrup:
5 lb (2.26 kg) Cured Smoked Potatoes *(above)*

For the ashcake mix:
1.11 kg milled Ash-Aged Potatoes *(above)* • 3 eggs • 45 g spice mix of choice • 950 g fine sweet cornmeal • 150 g garlic confit paste • 28 g salt, plus more for sprinkling • Oil, for drizzling

For the caramelized clabber milk:
Raw heavy (whipping) cream • Buttermilk • Vinegar of choice

For the caramelized clabber milk sauce:
850 g Caramelized Clabber Milk *(above)* • 500 g Smoked Potato Syrup *(above)* • 85 g garlic confit • 135 g caramelized onions • 1 cured, smoked boiled potato (about 150 g) • 1–2 teaspoons xanthan gum (optional)

For plating:
Fried shallots • Fresh oregano

Make the cured smoked potatoes:
Rinse the potatoes thoroughly in cold water. Pat dry and cure in the salt for 72 hours. In a vertical smoker over a wood fire (with the smoker at least 6 feet above the embers), smoke the potatoes at 200°F (93°C) for 12–16 hours.

Make the ash-aged potatoes:
Once the potatoes have cooled and all the wood and charcoal have turned into ashes, take 20 pounds (9 kg) of the potatoes and layer them, alternating with ashes, in a clear, airtight container: Place a layer of

potato, bury with ashes completely, repeat. Be sure to end with 2–4 inches (5–10 cm) of ashes at the top and to leave no airspace in the container. Ash-age the potatoes in a cool area for 10 months.

Make the smoked potato syrup:
Take the remaining 5 pounds (2.26 kg) of cured smoked potatoes and create a stock. Strain the stock and reduce to a syrup.

Make the ashcake mix:
In a bowl, combine the potatoes, eggs, spice mix, cornmeal, garlic confit paste,

ASH-AGED POTATO ASHCAKES WITH CARAMELIZED POTATO CRÈME

CURED, HUNG, SMOKED PICKLED CARROTS

and salt and mix thoroughly. Scoop 1 ounce (28 g)—more or less to your desired size—and roll into a ball. Using a tortilla press, or any other flat surface, flatten the ashcake to your desired thickness. Drizzle with oil and sprinkle with salt.

Using a live fire pit, set up a cast-iron griddle over the flames to heat up. Once the griddle is heated and oiled, lay an ashcake salted-side down in the pan. Once the edges start to crisp up and become brown, flip to the other side to brown. Your ashcake should be a nice golden brown. Repeat to make multiple ashcakes.

Make the caramelized clabber milk:
Mix the raw cream and buttermilk together. Measure out vinegar to equal one-third of total product and mix together with a whisk. Cover and leave at room temperature for 36 hours.

Once cultured, place the clabber milk in mason jars filled three-quarters of the way. Screw on the lids extremely tightly and place in a water bath in a metal pan. Place in 350°F (180°C) oven for 10–12 hours for the dairy to caramelize. Once the milk solids and whey separate, allow to cool overnight. Drain off the whey.

Make the caramelized clabber milk sauce:
In medium saucepot, combine the caramelized clabber milk, potato syrup, garlic confit, onions, and potato. Bring to a simmer and simmer for 5–8 minutes. Transfer to a blender and puree until completely smooth. If still loose, add the xanthan gum. Do not pass or strain.

To plate:
Stack ashcakes to desired height and pour the caramelized clabber milk sauce over them. (Or alternatively you can pour sauce between the layers.) Garnish with fried shallots and fresh oregano.

CHARCOAL-ROASTED CANDIED YAM SEMIFREDDO

For the candied yam puree:
10 lb (4.5 kg) yams (orange sweet potatoes) • 250 g grapeseed oil • 150 g salt • 2 kg brown sugar • 50 g ground cinnamon • 35 g ground cloves • 25 g grated nutmeg

For the semifreddo:
618 g heavy (whipping) cream • 110 g brown butter • 30 g vanilla paste • 422 g Candied Yam Puree *(above)* • 157 g sugar • 90 g water • 3 egg whites

For garnish:
Spiced nuts

Make the candied yam puree:
Set up a wood or charcoal fire and wait until the coals turn white. On large sheet pan, arrange the yams (sweet potatoes) in a single layer. Drizzle with the oil and sprinkle on the salt. Grill until tender and caramelized. Transfer to an airtight container, seal, and steam the yams for 7 minutes. Peel the yams and cut into rounds 3 inches (7.5 cm) thick. In a large pot, combine the brown sugar, spices, and 1 liter water. Stir over medium heat until the sugar dissolves. Add the yam

rounds and simmer until they are candied, 30 minutes to 1 hour.

With a slotted spoon, transfer the candied yams to a blender. Puree, adding syrup from the pot as needed.

Make the semifreddo:
In a saucepan, heat the cream over medium-low heat, whisking frequently. As soon as the cream comes to a boil, remove from the heat and whisk in the brown butter. Add the vanilla paste and yam puree. With a hand blender, blend until emulsified. Transfer to a large bowl, cool, cover, and set aside in the refrigerator.

In a small saucepan, combine the granulated sugar and water and heat over medium heat. At the same time, in a stand mixer fitted with the whisk, whip the egg whites to medium peaks. When the syrup has reached 210°F (99°C), stream it into the egg whites, with the mixer running. Whip until the meringue is shiny with stiff peaks.

Fold the meringue into the chilled yam mixture. Using a hand blender, blend until smooth. Pour the mixture into desired molds and freeze 4–8 hours.

To serve:
Temper the semifreddo for 5 minutes. In a chilled serving bowl, place 1 portion semifreddo. Garnish with spiced nuts.

AS HOUSTON BEGINS TO TRULY MAKE A NAME FOR ITSELF AS A PRIME CULINARY AND RESTAURANT DESTINATION, JONNY IS LEADING THE PACK. THERE IS NO OTHER CHEF IN THE CITY DOING WORK AS IMPORTANT AND TASTY AS HIS.
— Marcus Samuelsson

JONATHAN "JONNY" RHODES

MELISSA RODRIGUEZ

DEL POSTO
New York, New York,
United States

DANIEL BOULUD

MENU

CHILLED VEAL AND TUNA
WITH LEMON BASIL AND
VINAIGRETTE (VITELLO
TONNATO CON COLATURA)

GRILLED LETTUCES WITH
FENNEL, CUCUMBER, AND
CUTTLEFISH (LATTUGA
GRIGLIATA CON FINOCCHIO
E SEPPIE)

LITTLE EARS WITH BROCCOLI
RABE AND PUGLIAN SHEEP'S
MILK CHEESE (ORECCHIETTE
CON RAPINI E PECORINO
CANESTRATO)

HANDKERCHIEF WITH HERBS,
MUSSELS, AND SAFFRON
(FAZZOLETTO DI SETA CON
COZZE E ZAFFERANO)

THIN RIBBON PASTA WITH
GEODUCK AND LEMON
(LINGUINE ALLE VONGOLE
GIGANTI)

Melissa Rodriguez is the kind of chef who makes an impact everywhere she goes. Her reputation as a true team player precedes her, as does her affinity for a healthy, positive kitchen culture, which she has brought with her to some of the best restaurants in New York City.

Rodriguez grew up in northern New Jersey, often cooking for herself from a young age. Her family taught her the value in table manners and dining etiquette, and when she was in elementary school, her mother took her Girl Scout troop to the Culinary Institute of America (CIA) for lunch—it was an intimidating experience for a second grader, but it stuck with Rodriguez, and in 1997 she returned to the CIA as a student, then graduated in Culinary Arts and Chef Training.

Her first professional kitchen experiences were in New York and California. In 2006, she went to work for Daniel Boulud at Restaurant Daniel, where she was quickly promoted to sous chef. In 2011, Rodriguez moved on to Del Posto, working under Executive Chef Mark Ladner. In 2015, she was promoted to chef de cuisine, and when Ladner left, Rodriguez was named his successor, becoming the first female chef at a kitchen with four stars from the *New York Times*.

Since taking over at Del Posto, Rodriguez has worked to make things her own. From tightening up the restaurant's presentation and updating hallmark dishes, to working with new suppliers and updating ingredient sourcing methods, she has struck a delicate balance between preserving the soul of Del Posto and embracing the idea of fine Italian dining. Her cuisine style is soulful, inventive, and refined, with strong Italian roots accented by the occasional nod to French cooking, thanks to her time with Boulud. And her work doesn't end when she leaves the kitchen—Rodriguez is passionate about working with community organizations including the Edible Schoolyard, City Harvest, Ment'or BKB, Cookies for Kids' Cancer, Citymeals on Wheels, and God's Love We Deliver, where her entire team at Del Posto volunteers together.

GRILLED LETTUCES WITH FEN-NEL, CUCUMBER, AND CUTTLE-FISH (LATTUGA GRIGLIATA CON FINOCCHIO E SEPPIE)
Serves 4–6

For the grilled and marinated Gem lettuces:
5 tablespoons white balsamic vinegar •
1 cup (240 ml) extra-virgin olive oil, plus more for grilling • Salt • 8–10 Gem lettuces

For the roasted fennel puree:
3 bulbs fennel, cut into medium dice •
2 onions, cut into medium dice • Olive oil •
Salt • Water • Sherry vinegar

For the vinaigrette:
1 cup (240 ml) olive juice • 1 cup (240 ml) white balsamic vinegar • 1 cup (240 ml) extra-virgin olive oil • 1 teaspoon ground pepperoncini • 2 teaspoons salt

For the cuttlefish:
6–8 cuttlefish, cleaned, cuttlebone removed
Olive oil • Salt • 1 cup (150 g) finely diced fennel • 1 cup (130 g) finely diced cucumber

For assembly:
Vinaigrette *(above)* • Small bunch mint, minced, plus torn mint for garnish • Small bunch basil, minced, plus torn basil for garnish • 1 teaspoon small marjoram leaves • Juice of 1 lemon • Black pepper • Agretti

Grill and marinate the lettuces:
In a bowl, whisk together the vinegar, olive oil, and salt to taste. Set the marinade aside.

Halve each lettuce lengthwise and wash by soaking and rinsing under cold water. Allow to air-dry on paper towels.
Season the lettuces liberally with olive oil and salt on both sides.
On a grill (barbecue), lightly char the lettuce on each side. (Alternatively, pan-sear on a grill pan or griddle.) Place in a single layer in a shallow container and spoon the marinade over them until well dressed. If the lettuce is hardy, this will last 2–3 days in the refrigerator.

Make the roasted fennel puree:
Preheat the oven to 375°F (190°C).
In a large bowl, combine the fennel and onions. Coat with just enough olive oil to evenly cover and season with salt to taste. Spread out evenly on a sheet pan and roast until caramelized. During the cooking, add water as needed and stir to loosen any golden bits stuck to the pan. The vegetables should be deeply roasted and very tender. While the vegetables are still hot, puree them in blender while emulsifying in olive oil (use a small amount of water if needed

314

HANDKERCHIEF WITH HERBS

to get the blades of the blender to spin). Finish with sherry vinegar and salt to taste. Keep refrigerated until serving.

Make the vinaigrette:
In a bowl, whisk together all the ingredients until well combined.

Make the cuttlefish:
Dress the cuttlefish with olive oil and salt. Quickly cook on a grill. Cut it into pieces to match the size of the diced raw fennel and cucumber.
In a bowl, combine the fennel, cucumber, and grilled cuttlefish. Dress with the vinaigrette and add the minced mint, minced basil, marjoram, and lemon juice. Season with salt to taste.

To assemble:
Swoop a generous spoonful of roasted fennel puree on a plate/platter. Spoon the dressed salad over the puree and set the grilled Gem lettuces on the top. Drizzle with remaining vinaigrette and garnish with *agretti* and more fresh torn mint and basil.

HANDKERCHIEF WITH HERBS, MUSSELS, AND SAFFRON (FAZZOLETTO DI SETA CON COZZE E ZAFFERANO)
Serves 4–6

For the herb pesto filling:
Salt • 2 small bunches basil • 1 small bunch parsley • Ice cubes, as needed • 2 ½ cups (590 ml) Primo olive oil • ¾ cup (175 ml) Agrumato lemon olive oil

For the mussels:
4 tablespoons olive oil • 1 garlic bulb, halved horizontally • 4 sprigs thyme • 2 quarts/liters white wine • 10 lb (4.5 kg) mussels • 2 tablespoons saffron

For the fresh egg pasta dough:
1½ cups (190 g) Caputo tipo "00" flour, plus more for dusting • ¾ cup (95 g) durum wheat flour, plus more for dusting • 15 egg yolks

For assembly:
Salt • Cold butter, cut into pieces • Chives, cut into ½-inch (1.25 cm) lengths • Celery leaf • Parsley leaves • Opal basil leaves

Make the herb pesto filling:
In a large pot of boiling salted water, quickly blanch all of the herbs and shock in an ice bath.
Set a glass or metal bowl into a larger bowl filled with ice. Set aside.
In a blender, add the blanched herbs in batches, 3 ice cubes, a splash of olive oil, and just enough water to get the blades to spin. Blend the puree as smooth as you can without heating the pesto and immediately pour out into the chilled bowl to preserve the deep green color.

Prepare the mussels:
In a large, deep pot, heat the olive oil over medium-low heat. Add the garlic bulb and toast until golden brown. Add the thyme. Add the white wine and cook over high heat until the raw alcohol flavor is completely cooked off.
Add the mussels and stir. As the mussels open, remove them immediately with tongs. After all of the mussels are removed, taste the liquid to ensure that it has not over-reduced in the cook time. If so, add a splash of water. Remove from the heat and, while hot, add the saffron to steep and draw out the flavor. Strain through a fine chinois or cheesecloth (muslin). Cool and reserve the saffron broth and mussels separately.

Make the fresh egg pasta dough:
In a large bowl, use your hands to mix together the "00" and durum flours, then form a well in the center. Add the egg yolks to the well. Using a fork, gently break up the yolks and slowly incorporate the flour mixture from the inside rim of the well. Continue until the liquid is absorbed (about half of the flour will be incorporated). With both hands, using your palms primarily, begin kneading the dough until it forms a mostly cohesive mass.
Transfer the dough and any flour or bits remaining in the bowl to a clean work surface and continue kneading and occasionally pulling apart the dough to expose moisture, then pressing it back together, until the dough is smooth and firm, 7–10 minutes. (You want a firm dough. If you are having trouble kneading, wrap the dough tightly in plastic wrap/cling film and let it rest for 10–15 minutes, then knead again. An additional yolk can be added if the dough is too dry.)
Wrap the dough tightly in plastic wrap and let rest at room temperature for at least 15 minutes or up to 1 hour before using. (The dough can be made ahead and kept tightly wrapped and refrigerated for up to 1 day, or frozen for up to 1 month. Thaw frozen dough in the refrigerator before using.)
To roll out the dough, unwrap and cut the pasta dough into 4 pieces. Flatten one piece so that it will fit through the rollers of a pasta machine (rewrap the remaining pieces). Set the rollers of the pasta machine to the widest setting, then feed the pasta through the rollers three or four times, folding and turning the pasta until it is smooth and the width of the machine. Roll the pasta through the machine, decreasing the setting one notch at a time (do not fold or turn the pasta) to the thickness desired. Cut the sheet in half crosswise, then lightly dust with "00" flour. Layer the sheets between dry, clean, "00" flour-dusted towels to keep them from drying out.
Using a 6-inch (15 cm) round cutter or plate, cut out 12 rounds from the sheeted dough. You will have leftover pasta, which you can cut into desired shapes and keep refrigerated or frozen for soup!

Dollop 1 tablespoon of pesto filling in the center of half of the pasta rounds. Using an offset spatula or the back of a large spoon, spread the filling over the round, leaving ½-inch (1.25 cm) border. Using a finger dipped in water or a water-filled spray bottle, lightly dab or mist the pasta rounds to dampen, then top with the remaining dough rounds. Gently press the rounds together to eliminate any air bubbles. Dust with semolina flour. Layer the finished fazzoletti between sheets of semolina-dusted parchment paper.

To assemble:
Bring a large pot of generously salted water to a gentle boil.
Working in batches of 2 fazzoletti at a time (or whatever is an appropriate batch size for the pan you have, but no more than 3 at one time), add the pasta to the gently boiling water and cook for 1 minute.
Meanwhile, in a 12-inch (30 cm) sauté pan, bring the reserved saffron and mussel broth to a boil. Whisk in cold pieces of butter until silky, then taste for seasoning. Add the reserved cooked mussels and gently warm through in the hot sauce.
Using a large slotted spoon, transfer the pasta to the butter sauce and gently swirl the pan for 30 seconds to coat evenly with sauce. Use the slotted spoon to transfer the fazzoletti to serving plates, laying them flat, then drizzle with some sauce from the pan and add 3 or 4 mussels. Garnish with the finishing herbs. Serve immediately.

316

CHILLED VEAL AND TUNA

LITTLE EARS WITH BROCCOLI RABE

MELISSA RODRIGUEZ

DIEGO ROSSI

MAY CHOW

TRIPPA
Milan, Italy

Diego Rossi's fun-loving spirit is reflected in his dynamic food and his energetic restaurant, a deliberately ungrand Milan trattoria where Rossi—unrestricted by his training at highly awarded gastronomic restaurants—chooses to cook free-form, using impeccable seasonal ingredients with no tweezers and no fuss. These are the kinds of things that excite him: taking an ingredient such as lamb intestines and cooking it just to a crispy sear with bite and juice intact; or taking an underappreciated vegetable such as *broccoletti di Custoza*—a rare brassica grown near Diego's native Verona—and serving it roasted with a grilled pig's ear.

Born and raised in Verona, Rossi worked his way from a high-class fish restaurant to a five-star hotel in Venice, then joined the now three-starred Restaurant St. Hubertus in Alta Badia. He continued to cook in gastronomic kitchens around Italy, but following his arrival in Milan in 2013, he realized he wanted to do something very different. He planned to create his own restaurant where the experience would be as important as the food. It would also be defined by his strong leaning towards a zero-waste "gill to fin" ethos, wherein every part of a fish is eaten except the bones (although he does not waste bone marrow).

Trippa, the name of Rossi's trattoria in the Porta Romana neighborhood, has double significance: meaning tripe or offal, parts of the animal Rossi champions not to be wasted, *trippa* also connotes substance and solidity, apt for his opposition to culinary flights of fancy. Instead, Rossi demonstrates a mastery of ingredients cooked to perfection in ways that are fluid and subject to constant change. There may be off-menu surprises for those who care to find out, and regulars know not to rely on encountering the same dish repeatedly. Rossi's approach is to respect his produce rather than to embellish it. He cites Italy's vast natural biodiversity as inspiring ceaseless research, and he promotes humble and overlooked vegetables, as well as butcher's offal. Rossi's vitality brings his project vividly to life: he elevates the spirit of the trattoria and classic Italian dishes to create a seemingly traditional restaurant that is entirely refreshing and forward thinking.

MENU

FRIED TRIPE

CHICKEN LIVER TERRINE

VITELLO TONNATO

SARDINIAN FREGOLA WITH MUTTON RAGU, 'NDUJA, SMOKED PECORINO, AND BERGAMOT

BLOOD CIPOLLATA AND POLENTA

ZABAIONE CRÈME BRÛLÉE

FRIED TRIPE
Serves 4

600 g veal honeycomb tripe, boiled and sliced • 2 liters peanut (ground nut) oil • Black pepper • Rosemary

In a large pot, deep-fry the tripe in the oil for about 4 minutes. Season with salt, pepper, and rosemary before serving.

CHICKEN LIVER TERRINE
Serves 8

10 g shallot, julienned • 1 clove garlic, minced • 1 sprig thyme • 250 g butter • 100 g Marsala wine • 50 g port wine • 250 g cleaned chicken livers • 3 eggs • 8 g salt • Saba (grape must reduction) • Rustic bread, for crostini

In a sauté pan, cook the shallot, garlic, and thyme in the butter. Add the Marsala and port and reduce by 80 percent.

In a Thermomix, combine the mixture from the pan, the chicken livers, eggs, and salt and blend. Strain the mixture and pour into a terrine.
Steam at 167°F (75°C) for 1 hour. Serve with crostini.

VITELLO TONNATO
Serves 4

For the veal:
Neutral oil • Salt • 500 g veal leg (round or tri-tip roast) • 1 sprig thyme • 1 clove garlic, peeled • Extra-virgin olive oil

For the tonnato sauce:
1 egg • 3 egg yolks • 2 teaspoons fresh lemon juice • 1 teaspoon vinegar • 1 teaspoon Dijon mustard • 500 ml sunflower oil • Salt • 250 g oil-packed jarred tuna • 5 oil-packed anchovy fillets • 1 teaspoon capers

For plating:
Extra-virgin olive oil • Maldon salt • Black pepper • capers

Prepare the veal:
Heat a nonstick frying pan and grease with a drizzle of oil. Salt the veal and sear it on both sides. Cool the meat.
Vacuum-seal the veal with the thyme, garlic, and a drizzle of olive oil. Set a circulating water bath to 52°C, immerse the bag, and cook for 15 hours.

Prepare the tonnato sauce:
Make a mayonnaise with the whole egg, egg yolks, lemon juice, vinegar, mustard, sunflower oil, and salt to taste.
In a Thermomix, combine the mayonnaise with the tuna, anchovies, and capers and blend everything. Transfer the sauce to the canister of a whipper siphon and charge it with nitrogen. Set it in the refrigerator to chill.

To plate:
Remove the veal from the vacuum bag and reserve the jus.
Cut the meat into thin slices and arrange them in the center of the plate in a concentric way and alternate them with the tonnato sauce. Finish the dish with the veal jus, the capers, a drizzle of extra-virgin olive oil, Maldon salt, and black pepper.

VITELLO TONNATO

BLOOD CIPOLLATA AND POLENTA

CHICKEN LIVER TERRINE

HIS CULINARY MASTERY IS SHOWN
THROUGH HIS PASSION TO SHOWCASE
THE BEST ITALIAN INGREDIENTS
COOKED TO PERFECTION IN A FUN,
FLUID AND EVER-CHANGING MANNER.
— May Chow

FRIED TRIPE

DIEGO ROSSI

PRATEEK SADHU

MASQUE MUMBAI
Mumbai, India

MENU

CORN PANI PURI

MACKEREL ON BUCKWHEAT TOAST

YAKHNI BROTH WITH RAISIN-GLAZED QUAIL AND SPRUCE OIL

LAMB NECK, RAGI ROTI

SEA BUCKTHORN, BLACK PEPPER MOUSSE

BLACKENED SUNCHOKE AND HONEY ICE CREAM

A pioneer of progressive cooking who is changing the face of his national cuisine, Prateek Sadhu was inspired by his time at Noma in Copenhagen to develop new ways of thinking about Indian produce and its preparation. A trailblazer in India, he is among the most innovative of chefs, fostering international connections and looking ever more closely at sustainable practices.

Growing up around family farms in Kashmir, Sadhu studied at the Culinary Institute of America and worked stints at the French Laundry in California, Alinea in Chicago, and Le Bernardin in New York City. During his subsequent European odyssey, during which he staged at Noma, Sadhu's own interest in sourcing and showcasing local ingredients was given a fillip by René Redzepi's sublimely fastidious approach. In 2012, he returned to India to become sous-chef at Le Cirque Signature in Bengaluru, knowing he was ready for something big. As soon as he connected with his business partner, Aditi Dugar, they came up with the idea for Masque, which opened in Mumbai in 2016 following a two-year research and development trip around India. The pair sought out the most superb ingredients around the subcontinent, and set about building strong relationships with farmers and growers.

Some of the methods Sadhu uses are down-home—he keeps a mango-wood spit at Masque for finishing meat, game, and seafood and for smoking pork to serve with Goan sausage and pickled mango. Other methods, such as sous vide, are about attaining world-class perfection on the plate. This duality reflects Sadhu's identity as a chef who has won international acclaim, yet someone who is not cut off from his Northern Indian roots.

There is no menu as such at Masque; instead, diners learn what they have eaten at the end of service. At one dinner, this included a dish of pickled peaches with almond-milk ice cream, and for a pumpkin course, the dried guts of the pumpkin became a sour powder that was dusted on top of the dish, with the rind used as a base. This take on responsible cooking with an eye to zero waste is the kind of innovation the world has come to expect from the chef behind India's first tasting menu.

CORN PANI PURI
Serves 10

For the semolina puri:
215 g semolina • 50 g neutral oil • Pinch of salt • ½ cup (120 ml) lukewarm water • Oil, for frying

For the corn salsa:
1 ear corn • 30 g onion, chopped • 30 g tomatoes, chopped

For the kale/green apple gel:
40 g kale • 1 green apple, cut up • 20 g celery, cut up • 25 g onion, cut up • 1 fresh green chili, cut up • 130 g fresh lime juice • 8 g salt • 14 g sugar • 4 ice cubes • 2 g xanthan gum

For the corn foam:
200 g corn kernels • 50 g salted butter • 100 g cream

For the onion ash:
4 red onions • 5 white onions • 1 teaspoon ground red chilies • Salt

For assembly:
Small sprigs of cilantro (coriander)

Make the semolina puri:
Measure out 15 g semolina and set aside. In the bowl of a stand mixer, combine the remaining 200 g semolina with the neutral oil and salt. Add the lukewarm water and let rest for 30–45 minutes.
Set the bowl on the mixer and snap on the paddle attachment. Mix well, adding the remaining 15 g semolina as you do. Transfer to a work surface and knead by hand for 5 minutes, then roll dough out to a ¹⁄₁₆-inch (1–2 mm) thickness. Cut with a round cutter.
In a sauté pan, heat the oil over medium-low heat. Add the puri and cook until puffed up and golden.

Make the corn salsa:
Cook 1 ear of corn directly over a flame until charred. Slice the kernels off the cob. Stir together the corn, onion, and tomatoes.

Make the kale/green apple gel:
In a blender, combine all the ingredients and blend until smooth. Strain and keep over an ice bath.

Make the corn foam:
In a pan, cook the corn in the butter. Transfer to a blender and puree, then push through a sieve. Stir in the cream. Transfer to the canister of a whipper siphon and charge twice.

Make the onion ash:
Burn the red onion until blackened. Dehydrate the white onions. In a blender,

CORN PANI PURI

combine the charred onions, dehydrated onions, ground red chilies, and salt to taste and grind to a powder.

To assemble:
Make a small hole in the puri, put the salsa as the base, then add the corn foam and kale/apple gel and top it with onion ash and a sprig of cilantro (coriander).

MACKEREL ON BUCKWHEAT TOAST
Serves 12

For the buckwheat bread:
350 ml lukewarm water • 98 g eggs • 30 ml oil • 5 g vinegar • 10 g yeast • 10 g sugar • 5 g salt • 250 g buckwheat flour • 250 g all-purpose (plain) flour

For the mackerel:
12 mackerel fillets • 1 liter water • 40 g salt • 20 g sugar

For the mackerel chutney:
1 mackerel fillet, skinned • 4 chilies (soaked) • 4 cloves garlic, peeled • 20 ml fresh lemon juice • Salt • Sugar

For the lemon emulsion:
2 egg yolks • 5 ml vinegar gastrique • 125 g clarified butter • 2 lemon zests • 1 teaspoon fresh lemon juice • Salt

For assembly:
Banana leaf sheets • Ghee • Baby arugula (rocket) leaves • Flowers

Make the buckwheat bread:
In a large bowl, whisk together the water, eggs, oil, vinegar, yeast, sugar, and salt. Mix in both flours. Grease an 8-inch (20 cm) square pan. Add the bread mixture to it. Leave to proof for 1 hour.
Preheat the oven to 350°F (180°C) with 30% steam.
Bake until golden brown, 20–25 minutes.

Prepare the mackerel:
Pull the pin bones out of the mackerel fillets. In a container that will fit the mackerel, mix the together the water, salt and sugar. Brine the fish in the solution for 5 minutes. Pat the fish dry and store for service.

Make the mackerel chutney:
In a blender, combine the mackerel, chilies, garlic, and lemon juice and blend into a smooth chutney. Season with salt and sugar to taste.

Make the lemon emulsion:
In a double boiler, stir together the egg yolks and the gastrique. Emulsify in the clarified butter in small batches. Stir in the lemon zest, lemon juice, and salt to taste.

To assemble:
Spread a sheet of banana leaf with ghee. Put a mackerel fillet, skin-side down, on the leaf. Brush a generous amount of mackerel chutney over it. Cook in a smoker. (Alternatively, place the wrapped fish in a sauté pan, cover, and cook about 5 minutes on each side.)
Toast a slice of bread with some ghee. Spread the lemon emulsion on the toast. Place the mackerel over the slice of toast with seasoned garnishes. Serve warm.

YAKHNI BROTH WITH RAISIN-GLAZED QUAIL AND SPRUCE OIL
Serves 2

For the yakhni broth:
300 g yogurt • 30 g ground fennel • 15 g ground ginger • Ghee • 6 green cardamom pods • 3 black cardamom pods • 3 bay leaves • 5 g fennel seeds • 2 cinnamon sticks • 2 bay leaves • 600 ml quail stock

For the brined quail:
1 liter water • 40 g salt • 40 g sugar • 30 g veri masala spice blend • 1 quail

For the black raisin glaze:
250 g black raisins, soaked • 30 g veri masala spice blend • 100 ml orange juice

For the spruce oil (optional):
1 part fresh spruce • 2 parts neutral oil

For assembly:
Ghee • Black pepper • Arugula (rocket) flowers

Make the yakhni broth:
In a bowl, whisk together the yogurt, fennel, and ginger.
In a sauté pan, heat a little ghee over medium heat. Add the whole spices. As they cook, add the yogurt mixture and let it simmer over low heat until the oil separates, 30 to 45 minutes. Add the quail stock and remove from the heat. Blend to a smooth puree, then strain.

Brine the quail:
In a container that will fit the quail, mix the water, salt, sugar, and veri masala. Brine the quail in the solution for 12 hours, then portion into legs and breasts.

Make the black raisin glaze:
In a saucepan, combine the raisins, veri masala, and orange juice. Simmer together, then blend to a smooth glaze. Strain if necessary.

Make the spruce oil:
In a blender, puree the spruce and oil together, then strain through cheesecloth (muslin).

To assemble:
Portion the yakhni broth into mugs or bowls and drizzle with spruce oil (if using). In a sauté pan, fry the quail in a little ghee and brush with the black raisin glaze. Finish with black pepper and garnish with arugula (rocket) flowers. Serve alongside the broth.

BLACKENED SUNCHOKE AND HONEY ICE CREAM
Serves 12

For the blackened sunchoke mousse:
500 g sunchokes (Jerusalem artichokes) • 100 g water • 50 g sugar • 5g xanthan gum

For the honey ice cream:
250 g milk • 250 g cream • 120 g egg yolks • 1 teaspoon vanilla extract • 80 g honey

For the brown butter crumbs:
200 g unsalted butter • 75 g superfine (caster) sugar • 95 g brown sugar • 192 g flour • 64 g wheat flour • 1¼ teaspoons salt

For plating:
Damask rose petals

Prepare the sunchoke mousse:
Wash the sunchokes. Vacuum-seal them in a bag and leave at 140°F (60°C) for 1 month. Remove when they have blackened. Transfer to a blender and blend with the water, sugar, and xanthan gum and pass the mousse through a fine-mesh sieve.

Make the honey ice cream:
In a saucepan, heat the milk and cream together.
Meanwhile, in a bowl, whisk together the yolks and vanilla.
Whisking constantly, add the hot milk mixture to the yolks. Return the mixture to the saucepan, set back over heat, and stir with a spatula until the custard thickens. Strain and cool it down. Stir in the honey. Freeze and churn as needed.

Make the brown butter crumbs:
Preheat the oven to 320°F (160°C).
In a sauté pan, heat the butter until deeply browned.
In a bowl, stir together both sugars, both flours, the salt, and browned butter. Spread on a sheet pan.
Bake until golden brown, about 15 minutes.

To plate:
Place a spoon of sunchoke mousse on one side of a bowl. Garnish with rose petals to cover. Add some brown butter crumbs next to the mousse and quenelle the honey ice cream over it.

MACKEREL ON BUCKWHEAT TOAST

YAKHNI BROTH WITH RAISIN-GLAZED QUAIL

HIS PASSION IS CLEAR THAT HE WANTS TO CHANGE THE PERCEPTION OF DINING CULTURE IN INDIA.

— May Chow

PRATEEK SADHU

LENA SAREINI

MARCUS SAMUELSSON

SELDEN STANDARD
Detroit, Michigan, United States

MENU

KALAMATA OLIVE TART WITH HONEY CUSTARD

OLIVE OIL CAKE WITH ZA'ATAR AND SESAME

CAMPFIRE SUNDAE

PINE NUT CHEESECAKE WITH SPICED PEARS

Lena Sareini was just twenty-two years old when she was hired at Selden Standard in Detroit, wowing management with a lemon tart so good, restaurant partner Evan Hansen licked his plate to finish. It was an auspicious start for a marvel wise beyond her years, a gifted pastry chef whose natural instincts, paired with a hunger for perpetual improvement, set a high standard for America's next generation of cooking talent.

A native of Dearborn, Michigan, Sareini is the daughter of a Lebanese father and an Irish mother, and kitchen influences from both sides of her family steered her toward a professional cooking path early in life. After high school she enrolled at Schoolcraft College, and it didn't take long for Joseph Decker, the decorated instructor who conceived the institution's Culinary Baking and Pastry Arts curriculum, to recognize her potential. He brought on Sareini as his sous-chef while she was still a student, fast-tracking her growth in preparation for her entering the professional world of restaurants.

Since landing at Selden Standard in 2015, Sareini has earned well-deserved national attention for her dessert menu, on which she never repeats a dish—a self-imposed stricture that motivates her to continue challenging herself, in addition to keeping diners intrigued. Adhering closely to the local and seasonal ethos of the restaurant, Sareini possesses an uncanny knack for marrying Middle Eastern flavors, classical French pastry techniques, and her own original ideas, simultaneously celebrating her culture and showcasing her skills on the plate.

Her spin on *kanafeh* comes topped with a quenelle of *ashta*, rich and fragrant clotted cream, though traditional feta is swapped for tangy goat cheese. Simple Lebanese-style rice pudding gets a fine-dining makeover with *dukkah* spice, pine-nut brittle, and green strawberries. Savory ingredients not typically associated with dessert, including cumin, bay leaf, olive, and squid ink, make their way into her meringues, ice creams, crumbles, and many other surprising dishes. While her upbeat personality might create the impression that her desserts are effortless, there is a massive amount of preparation, creativity, and perspective apparent in all of Sareini's work.

KALAMATA OLIVE TART WITH HONEY CUSTARD
Makes 60 tarts

For the tart dough:
1.3 kg cold unsalted butter • 822 g powdered (icing) sugar • 72 g vanilla extract • 1.434 kg all-purpose (plain) flour • 20 g salt • 336 g Kalamata olives, finely chopped

For the filling:
6 eggs • 600 g egg yolks • 1.8 kg heavy (whipping) cream • 400 g honey

For the candied olives:
1.8 kg granulated sugar • 350 g water • 900 g Kalamata olives, pitted

For the lavender honey caramel:
350 g honey • 225 g unsalted butter • 150 g brown sugar • 1 can (14 oz/386 g) sweetened condensed milk • 2 g lavender • Pinch of sea salt

For the whipped crème fraîche:
960 g heavy (whipping) cream • 4 lemon zest • 60 g powdered (icing) sugar • 48 g vanilla bean paste • 4 g salt • 400 g crème fraîche

For plating:
Almonds • Lavender • Powdered (icing) sugar, for sprinkling

Make the tart dough:
In a stand mixer, cream the butter and powdered (icing) sugar until smooth, mixing down with a spatula when necessary. Add the vanilla and mix just to combine. Add the flour, salt, and olives. Mix just to combine. Divide the dough into 4 equal portions, wrap in plastic wrap (cling film), and chill until firm. Roll to desired thickness, cut into rounds, and fit into tart molds. Chill until firm.
Preheat the oven to 300°F (150°C), fan speed at 50%.
Line the tarts shells with rounds of parchment. Bake until slightly golden, 20–22 minutes. Remove the parchment and continue to bake until golden brown, 5–6 minutes. Cool. (Leave the oven on, increase the temperature to 325°F/160°C, no fan.)

Make the filling:
In a large mixer fitted with the whisk, combine the whole eggs, egg yolks, cream, and honey and beat on high to full volume. Pour into the tart shells, filling to the top.

(If not using all the custard mixture, save the remainder and use as needed, just make sure to rewhip before using each time.) Transfer to the oven and bake for until golden, about 15 minutes. Cool.

Make the candied olives:
Set a wire rack into a half-sheet pan. In a saucepan, bring the granulated sugar and water to 240°F (115°C). Wet the sides of the pot with a pastry brush to prevent crystallization. Add the olives to the boiling sugar, stirring every few minutes until the temperature has returned to 240°F (115°C). Fish olives out of the pot with a slotted spoon and place on the rack in the sheet pan to drain away any excess sugar. Transfer to a dehydrator and dehydrate at 200°F (93°C) overnight.
The next day, chop the olives to desired size and dehydrate for an additional day. Cool completely and store in an airtight container.

Make the lavender honey caramel:
In a saucepan, bring the honey, butter, and brown sugar to a boil. Cook for 2 minutes. Whisk in the sweetened condensed milk and lavender and cook, constantly whisking, until golden. Remove from the heat and strain. Cool completely and stir in the salt.

Make the whipped crème fraîche:
In a stand mixer fitted with the whisk, combine the cream, lemon zest, powdered sugar, vanilla paste, and salt and beat on high until tracks begin to form. Add the crème fraîche and whisk to soft peaks.

To plate:
Add a spoonful of lavender honey caramel to the top of the plate off center. Using a small offset spatula, scrape the caramel down in a line. Place the tart in the center of the plate. Sprinkle almonds and lavender over the caramel. Sprinkle powdered sugar and candied olives over the tart. Spoon soft whipped crème fraîche over the tart and allow it to fall over the left side of the tart.

OLIVE OIL CAKE WITH ZA'TAR AND SESAME
Makes eight 8-inch (20 cm) cakes

For the olive oil cake batter:
1.136 kg tipo "00" flour • 16 g baking soda (bicarbonate of soda), sifted • 8 g baking powder, sifted • 8 g salt • 12 orange zest • 1.952 kg sugar • 12 eggs • 1.412 kg buttermilk • 1.244 kg olive oil • Za'atar *(recipe follows)*

For the honey sesame brittle:
250 g sugar • 250 g honey • 2 g salt • 275 g sesame seeds, toasted

For plating:
Labneh • Orange segments • Za'atar *(recipe follows)* • Candied oranges • Fresh flowers

Make the cake batter:
Preheat the oven to 325°F (160°C), convection (fan-assist) on. Coat eight 8-inch (20 cm) cake pans with cooking spray, then coat with flour and line with a round of parchment paper.
In a bowl, blend together the flour, baking soda (bicarbonate of soda), baking powder, and salt. In a separate bowl, whisk together the orange zest, sugar, eggs, buttermilk, and olive oil. Add the flour mixture to the wet ingredients in three additions. Whisk together until just incorporated. Pour 800 g of batter into each prepared cake pan. Tap out any lingering air bubbles. Sprinkle enough za'atar on each cake to cover the top layer.
Bake for 15 minutes. Rotate the pans front to back and bake until cooked through, 20–30 minutes. Cool, cut each cake into 8 slices, and store individually in airtight containers.

Make the sesame brittle:
In a saucepan, combine the sugar, honey, and salt and caramelize to medium-light amber. Add the sesame seeds. Pull off the heat and immediately pour out onto

a silicone baking mat. Cover with a second and mat and roll thin. Let cool. Break into shards.

To plate:
Level two layers of olive oil cake. Spread labneh on top of one layer, place segments of oranges on top of the labneh, and sprinkle with za'atar. Sandwich another layer of cake on top. Spread more labneh on top and garnish to your liking. Add another sprinkle of za'atar, orange segments, candied oranges, honey sesame brittle, fresh flowers (and if you're feeling fancy: gold leaf!).

ZA'ATAR
140 g ground sumac • 60 g ground thyme • 75 g sesame seeds, toasted • 30 g ground marjoram • 30 g ground oregano • 30 g sea salt

Place all the ingredients in a bowl and dry blend together.

CAMPFIRE SUNDAE
Makes 4 quarts each ice cream and sorbet

For the marshmallows:
Powdered (icing) sugar and cornstarch (corn flour) • 22 sheets silver strength gelatin • 910 g sugar • 120 g glucose syrup • 200 g water • 5 g salt • 220 g egg whites • 10 g vanilla extract

LENA HAS AN UNCANNY SKILL OF EFFORTLESSLY INFUSING LEBANESE FLAVORS INTO CLASSIC FRENCH PASTRY TECHNIQUES, CREATING BAKED GOODS THAT ARE QUINTESSENTIALLY AMERICAN.
— *Marcus Samuelsson*

For the toasted marshmallow ice cream:
500 g Marshmallows *(above)* • 1.8 kg heavy (whipping) cream • 400 g granulated sugar • 10 g salt • 1 kg whole milk • 10 g vanilla • bean paste • 360 g egg yolks

For the marshmallow creme:
250 g granulated sugar • 350 g glucose syrup • 200 g water • 5 g salt • 150 g egg whites • Pinch of cream of tartar • 16 g vanilla extract

For the chocolate sorbet:
800 g sugar • 2.22 kg water • 320 g Dutch-process cocoa powder • 10 g salt • 680 g dark chocolate • 32 g vanilla extract • 60 g vodka

For the graham crackers:
300 g all-purpose (plain) flour • 140 g whole-grain pastry (soft) flour • 210 g granulated sugar • 6 g baking soda (bicarbonate of soda) • 3 g salt • 100 g unsalted butter • 115 g honey • 70 g whole milk • 20 g vanilla extract • Cinnamon sugar

Make the marshmallows:
Make a mixture of equal parts powdered (icing) sugar and cornstarch (corn flour). Line a sheet pan with parchment and dust with the mixture.
Bloom the gelatin in ice water.
In a saucepan, cook the sugar, glucose syrup, and water to 245°F (118°C).

In a stand mixer fitted with the whisk, whip the egg whites three-quarters of the way. With the machine running, pour the hot sugar solution into the whipping whites. Whip until the heat is dissipated. Spread the mixture onto the lined and dusted sheet pan. Dust the top of the marshmallows with more of the mixture. Allow to cool. Cut into squares and coat in more of the powder, then shake in a sieve to remove any excess coating.

Make the ice cream:
Place the marshmallows in the bottom of an 8-quart/liter pot and toast thoroughly with a torch until all the marshmallows are completely toasty. Add the cream, granulated sugar, and salt to the pot.
In a separate pot, combine the milk and vanilla paste with a chinois on top. Warm the milk mixture to a scald.
When the marshmallows float to the top, torch them again until they are a deep golden caramel color. Whisk together. Continue to do this every so often to really incorporate a good roasted marshmallow flavor. Stir some hot cream mixture into the egg yolks to temper, then return to the pot and cook to the texture of an anglaise. Strain the custard through the chinois into the scalded milk. Chill over an ice bath. Let set overnight.
Whisk/immersion blend, then spin in an ice cream machine. Freeze.

Make the marshmallow creme:
In a saucepan, combine the granulated sugar, glucose, water, and salt and bring to 240°F (116°C).
In a stand mixer fitted with the whisk, whip the egg whites three-quarters of the way. With the machine running, slowly pour in the hot sugar mixture while whipping on high. Add the vanilla.

Make the chocolate sorbet:
In a saucepan, combine the sugar, water, cocoa, and salt and bring to a boil. Add the chocolate, vanilla, and vodka and stir to melt. Pull off the heat and blend with immersion blender until completely smooth. Chill. Blend again. Spin in an ice cream machine. Freeze.

Make the graham crackers:
Preheat the oven to 300°F (150°C).
In a bowl, combine the flours, granulated sugar, baking soda (bicarb), and salt. Cut in the butter. In a separate bowl, whisk together the honey, milk, and vanilla. Add the honey mixture to the flour mixture and stir until just combined. Roll dough about ⅛ inch (3 mm) thick and dock. Cut into 1½-inch (4 cm) squares and dust with cinnamon sugar.
Bake a until completely crisp all the way through, 20–30 minutes. Let cool, then buzz into a powder.

To plate, spread marshmallow fluff on the bottom of a bowl. Torch until golden brown. Place 2 scoops of toasted marshmallow ice cream and 2 scoops of chocolate sorbet on top of the toasted fluff. Sprinkle with crushed up graham crackers.

PINE NUT CHEESECAKE WITH SPICED PEARS
Makes 60 mini cheesecakes

For the baklava filling:
4 cups (475 g) cashews, toasted and cooled • 2 cups (265 g) pine nuts, toasted and cooled • ¾ cup (150 g) granulated sugar • Salt

For the baklava:
4 sheets phyllo (filo) dough • Clarified butter, as needed • Baklava Filling *(above)* • Orange blossom simple syrup • Pistachios, for sprinkling

For the pine nut cheesecake:
2.835 kg full-fat cream cheese, at room temperature • 780 g granulated sugar • 4 g salt • 780 g sour cream, at room temperature • 500 g pine nuts, toasted and cooled • 10 eggs, at room temperature

For the pine nut cream:
1.8 kg heavy (whipping) cream • 150 g powdered (icing) sugar • Pinch of salt • 100 g pine nuts, toasted and cooled

For the spiced pears:
12 pears • Lemon juice • 80 g brown sugar • 4 g ground cardamom • 4 g ground cinnamon • 4 g salt

For plating:
Ground pistachios • Pomegranate molasses

Make the baklava filling:
In a food processor, combine the nuts, sugar, and a pinch of salt and pulse until the nuts are ground enough to clump up in your fist.

Make the baklava:
Preheat the oven to 300°F (150°C).
Brush a sheet of phyllo (filo) dough with clarified butter and lay another sheet of dough on top. Repeat this two more times. In total there should be 4 layers of phyllo with clarified butter brushed in between. Spread the baklava filling in a ½ to ¾-inch (1½–2 cm) line going across the sheet of phyllo. Press the nut mixture so that it holds its shape in a line. Carefully roll one-third of the dough over the filling into a log and slice off. Repeat the process two more times. You should get three logs of baklava out of the stacked phyllo. Brush the logs with clarified butter. Cut the baklava logs into 1-inch pieces.
Bake for 24 minutes. Immediately brush with the orange blossom simple syrup and sprinkle with pistachios. Cool completely before serving.

Make the pine nut cheesecake:
Preheat the oven to 350°F (180°C). Coat silicone molds with oil spray.
In a large mixer fitted with the paddle, combine the cream cheese, granulated sugar, and salt and cream on the lowest speed until fully incorporated, stopping to scrape down the paddle and sides of the bowl often.
In a blender, process the sour cream and pine nuts until smooth. Strain the mixture

into the cream cheese mixture and beat until incorporated, again stopping to scrape down often. Add the eggs 1 or 2 at a time. Scrape down for a final time and mix until fully incorporated. Try to mix as little as possible to avoid any aeration.
Scrape the batter into the molds and place the molds in a water bath. Bake until the cheesecake's internal temperature reads 180°F (82°C), about 14 minutes. Let cool, then freeze before removing from the molds.

Make the pine nut cream:
In a saucepan, heat the cream, sugar, and salt. Whisk the pine nuts into the warming cream mixture and heat until it begins to steam, just before a simmer. Transfer to a blender and blend until completely smooth. Strain through a chinois. Cool over an ice bath. Once cool, whip to desired whipped cream consistency.

Make the spiced pears:
Peel, halve, and core the pears and rinse them in lemon juice to avoid oxidation. Cut the pears into small dice and transfer to a medium pot. Add the brown sugar, cardamom, cinnamon, and salt. Cook until the sugar is dissolved and bubbling and the pears no longer taste raw but still have some texture to them.

To plate:
Place a piece of cheesecake on the plate. Sprinkle ground pistachios in a line on the right side of the cheesecake. Place three mini pieces of baklava on top of the line of pistachios. Pipe dots of pine nut cream randomly going up the plate. Spoon spiced pears over the cheesecake, falling over the left side of it. Drizzle the pears with pomegranate molasses.

LENA SAREINI

JASON SAXBY

RAES ON WATEGOS
Byron Bay, Australia

MENU

ZUPPA DI GAMBERI

TAGLIOLINI AL GRANCHIO

ARAGOSTA CON POLENTA

MAIALE AL LATTE

PIZZA BIANCA AI FORMAGGI

IL MANGO

PALISA ANDERSON

For being part of such a studied and steady professional trajectory, Jason Saxby's relocation to Byron Bay in New South Wales, Australia, unfolded rather precipitously. On a first visit to the area, he was charmed enough to buy a property, thinking of future ambitions down the road. But the move ended up happening within months, after he received an offer to head the kitchen at Raes on Wategos.

Saxby explains that his roots as a country boy ultimately propelled him to Byron Bay and its slower pace. He grew up in the small New South Wales town of Bathurst, where he studied hospitality and won a regional cooking competition. Moving to Sydney, Saxby received a crash course in regional Italian cooking, working at Park Hyatt Sydney under Lombardian chef Alessandro Pavoni, and at Pilu at Freshwater, learning Sardinian cuisine from Giovanni Pilu. Ensuing travels sent him to New York (Per Se) and London (The Ledbury, Pollen Street Social). Returning to Sydney, he honed his kitchen leadership as sous chef at the Bridge Room and head chef at both Osteria di Russo & Russo and Pilu at Freshwater.

Saxby fashions precise yet comforting dishes. His menus tilt toward Italy—think tagliolini pasta with bottarga and prawns, or chestnut cake with pears and rosemary. But he strives for his food to reflect its time and place, so his menus naturally merge coastal Australia with the Italian techniques. The quiet synergy of his dishes can sometimes bely their inventiveness: camel's milk fromage blanc oozing between coral prawns in chilled tomato broth; kangaroo tartare tucked beneath a mantle of radishes. He is known for his use of indigenous ingredients, including native limes, tropical lobsters, lemon myrtle, and Davidson's plums.

After many hardworking and peripatetic years, Saxby reevaluated his balance between work and family, and decided to leave the city. Now he cooks inside a white stucco Spanish-mission-style boutique hotel, with the sea and sandy beaches in view, and Raes has already been pegged as one of the region's best kitchens.

ZUPPA DI GAMBERI: CURED RED CORAL PRAWNS WITH CHILLED TOMATO CONSOMMÉ, HEIRLOOM TOMATO, CAMEL FROMAGE BLANC, AND WILD FENNEL
Serves 4

For the cured prawns:
32 small coral/red/scarlet prawns • 250 g sugar • 250 g fine salt

For the tomato consommé:
1 kg very ripe tomatoes, cut into pieces • 500 g red bell peppers, cut into pieces • 3 fresh long red chilies, cut into pieces • 20 g basil leaves • 2 cloves garlic, peeled • 1 teaspoon sugar • 1 teaspoon salt • 50 ml verjuice • 25 ml chardonnay vinegar

For the prawn oil:
Shells and heads reserved from Cured Prawns *(above)* • 50 g tomato paste (puree) • 50 g canola (rapeseed) oil • 50 g olive oil

For the fennel oil:
100 g fennel fronds • 1 bunch dill • ½ teaspoon fennel seeds • 100 ml extra-virgin olive oil

For assembly:
20 tiny heirloom (heritage) cherry tomatoes (various colors), halved • 6 cucamelons, sliced into rounds • 6 caperberries, sliced into rounds • 100 g camel milk fromage blanc • 32 sprigs bronze fennel • 32 wild fennel flowers

Cure the prawns:
Peel the prawns and remove the heads. Reserve the shells and heads for the prawn oil.
In a large bowl, mix together the sugar and salt. Toss the prawns in the cure mix and cure in the fridge for 45 minutes. Rinse off and lay on absorbent cloth or paper to dry. Place in an airtight container until ready to serve.

Make the tomato consommé:
In a large bowl, combine the tomatoes, bell peppers, chilies, basil, garlic, sugar, salt, verjuice, and vinegar. Working in batches, blend until it is small pieces. Do not overblend.
Strain through a coffee/oil filter or cheesecloth (muslin) into a bowl.
Adjust the seasoning and balance as needed. Store in the fridge until needed.

Make the prawn oil:
In a small pot, combine the prawn shells and heads, tomato paste (puree), and oil and gently cook for 1 hour. Strain and set aside to cool.

Make the fennel oil:
Pick the fennel and dill free of any thick stems.
In a pot of boiling water, blanch the herbs for 30 seconds. Refresh in ice water. Squeeze completely dry of all water with a tea towel or cloth.
Place the herbs, fennel seeds, and oil in a blender and blend until you see steam coming out of the jar. Strain through a coffee/oil filter. Set aside in the fridge until serving time.

To assemble:
Place the cured prawns flat on a plate. Arrange 8 cherry tomato halves around the plate. Add the cucamelon and caperberry slices artfully. Pipe 8 dots of fromage blanc. Place bronze fennel sprigs and fennel flowers around the plate.
Drizzle the prawn oil over the cured prawns to dress them. Drizzle little pools of the fennel oil around the bowl.
Pour 40 ml per serving of the consommé into a pouring jug, and pour the consommé at the table. This dish must be served chilled.

TAGLIOLINI AL GRANCHIO: TAGLIOLINI WITH SPANNER CRAB, MACADAMIA, SALTED FINGER LIME, SCAMPI CAVIAR, AND SOFT HERBS

Serves 4

For the pasta dough:
175 g tipo "00" flour • 75 g macadamia flour • 75 g buckwheat flour • 100 g semolina • 170 g egg yolks • 50 g eggs

For the crab and crab stock:
2 spanner crabs, steamed • 1 onion, finely diced • 2 tomatoes, finely diced • 1 carrot, finely diced • 2 stalks celery, finely diced • 1 garlic bulb, minced • 1 bulb fennel, finely diced • Oil • 2 bay leaves • 1 teaspoon fennel seeds • 1 teaspoon freshly ground black pepper • 3 liters water • 100 ml white wine

For the macadamia cream:
250 g macadamia nuts • 100 g water • 30 ml fresh lemon juice • Salt

For the salted finger lime skins:
100 g finger lime skins (left from your finger lime pearls for the oysters) • 50 g good-quality aged white wine vinegar • 50 g sugar • 50 g water • 50 g butter • 50 g fresh lime juice • Salt

For the soffritto:
100 g butter • 1 bulb fennel, finely diced • 1 onion, finely diced • 2 cloves garlic, minced • 1 fresh long red chili, finely chopped

To finish:
50 g salt • 50 ml extra-virgin olive oil

For plating:
50 g toasted macadamia nuts • 30 g scampi caviar • 20 g chervil leaves • 20 g dill leaves • 20 g mint leaves • 20 g sorrel leaves • 40 ml lemon oil

Make the pasta dough:
In a stand mixer with the paddle, combine all four flours. In a separate bowl, mix the yolks and whole egg together. With the mixer running, slowly pour in the egg mixture and mix until a dough forms. Turn the dough out onto a work surface and knead until smooth. Wrap and rest in the fridge until ready. When ready, roll the pasta through a pasta roller until you have sheets ¹⁄₁₆ inch (1 mm) thick. Cut into scant ⅛-inch (2 mm) strands to create tagliolini. Weigh into 50 g portions and set aside until ready to cook.

Make the crab and crab stock:
Pick the crabmeat and remove any small bits of shell. Set the white crabmeat aside for later. Reserve the brown meat and shells for the stock.
Preheat the oven to 350°F (180°C).
Spread the crab shells and vegetables together in a roasting pan and toss with a little oil. Transfer to the oven and roast for 20 minutes.

ZUPPA DI GAMBERI

Transfer the roasted vegetables and shells, aromatics and tomatoes to a stockpot. Add the water and set over high heat.
Meanwhile, place the roasting pan over a burner and heat up, then deglaze with the white wine. Cook until reduced by half.
Add the deglazed pan juices to the stockpot and bring to a boil. Reduce the heat and simmer for 2 hours. Strain and set the crab stock aside for later use.

Make the macadamia cream:
Preheat the oven to 320°F (160°C).
Spread the macadamias in a sheet pan and roast for 12 minutes.
Transfer to a blender, add the water, and blend until completely smooth. Season with the lemon juice and salt to taste. Place in an airtight container until needed.

Make the salted finger lime skins:
Place the finger lime skins in a saucepan of cold water and bring to a boil. Drain and repeat this step five times.
In a blender, combine the blanched skins, vinegar, sugar, water, and butter. Blend on high until smooth. Finish with fresh lime juice and season with salt. Place in a small squeeze bottle or piping bag.

Make the soffritto:
In a sauté pan, heat the butter and gently sweat the vegetables down until translucent, soft, and sweet. No color. Set aside.

To finish:
In a large pot, bring 5 liters water with the salt to a boil.
In a separate pan, bring the crab stock to a boil. In a large pasta pan, heat the olive oil and add the soffritto. Deglaze with 250 ml of crab stock.

Add the pasta to the pot of boiling salted water and cook for 2 minutes. Scoop the pasta out of the boiling water and place in the pan with the stock. Add half of the reserved crabmeat. Simmer for 2 minutes while gently tossing the pasta. Adjust the seasoning and set aside to rest for 30 seconds.

To plate:
Smear 2 spoonfuls of macadamia cream on the base of each bowl.
Twirl the pasta into long, tight, and neat piles and place on top of the macadamia cream. Divide the remaining reserved crab among the plates. Pipe 8 small dots of salted finger lime artfully around the dish.
Divide the toasted macadamias among the plates. Divide the caviar onto each plate in little piles. Top with 8 leaves of each of the herbs. Finish with a drizzle of lemon oil.

PIZZA BIANCA AI FORMAGGI: PANE CARASAU, PYENGANA CHEDDAR, PICKLED BABY FIG, AND NATIVE PEPPERBERRY

Serves 4

For the carasau base:
60 ml extra-virgin olive oil • 1 teaspoon finely chopped rosemary • 4 wedges pane carasau • 1 teaspoon salt • Freshly ground black pepper

For the Pyengana cheddar crema:
1 sheet gelatin • 500 ml heavy (whipping) cream • 250 g Pyengana cheddar cheese, finely grated • Salt • 2 g native pepperberries, ground

For the fig and native pepper jam:
500 g very ripe figs, cut into chunks • 150 g sugar • 150 ml good-quality aged red wine vinegar • 3 g native pepperberries, ground • 3 g freshly ground black pepper

For the pickled baby figs:
100 ml aged red wine vinegar • 100 g sugar • 100 g dried baby figs

For plating:
100 g Pyengana cheddar cheese • 2 g native pepperberries, ground • 40 ml extra-virgin olive oil

Prepare the carasau base:
In a small bowl, mix the oil and rosemary. Brush this mixture onto the pane carasau. Cook on a charbroiler (chargrill) until lightly charred. Season with salt and pepper while still hot. Set aside to cool and store in an airtight container until ready to serve.

Make the Pyengana cheddar crema:
Soak the gelatin in cold water until soft. In a small pot, heat the cream to 158°F (70°C). Squeeze the gelatin of any excess water and add to the pot with the cream. Using a stick blender, blend in the cheddar until completely melted. Season with salt to taste and the native pepper. Let cool and then transfer to a piping bag.

Make the fig and native pepper jam:
In a pot, combine the figs, sugar, vinegar, native pepper, and black pepper. Cook until the figs have broken down.
Blend with a stick blender and adjust the acidity and sweetness as needed.

Make the pickled baby figs:
In a small pot, bring the vinegar and sugar to a boil. Add the baby figs and cook in this syrup until they are coated. Transfer to a container and store at room temperature until needed.

To plate:
Slice the pickled figs into 24 perfect rounds. Pipe a ⅛ inch (3 mm) thick layer of Pyengana crema on top of the pane carasau wedges. Spread it with an offset spatula to ensure it reaches to the edges. It should look like you have a slice of pizza.
Pipe 8 dots of fig jam randomly on top of each piece. Using a Microplane, shave a thick shower of Pyengana cheddar over each piece. Place 6 rounds of pickled baby figs on top. (They should resemble slices of tomato.) Sprinkle some native pepper on top and drizzle with a little olive oil. Serve quickly to ensure it retains its crunch.

IL MANGO: TOASTED MACADAMIA SEMI-FREDDO, MANGO SORBET, HONEYCOMB, AND SALTED MACADAMIAS
Serves 4

4 Kensington Pride mangoes • 100 g dried mango

For the macadamia semifreddo:
200 g macadamia nuts • 1 teaspoon salt • 600 ml thickened cream • 2 eggs • 4 egg yolks • 215 g superfine (caster) sugar

For the honeycomb:
365 g superfine (caster) sugar • 140 g glucose • 80 g honey • 30 g water • 16 g baking soda (bicarbonate of soda)

For the macadamia and honeycomb crumble mix:
3 g sea salt • 50 g dried mango • 50 g Honeycomb *(above)*

For the mango sorbet:
105 g superfine (caster) sugar • 45 g glucose powder • 2 g sorbet stabilizer • 95 g water • Juice of 1 lime

Prepare the mango skins:
Halve the mangoes, remove the pits, and scoop the flesh completely away from the skins. Pick the 4 most perfect skins and reserve them for the semifreddo. Store the skins in a straight and natural way until ready to fill them, as you want their shape to look real.
Cut the mango flesh off the pits. Measure out 400 g of the mango flesh and reserve for the sorbet.

Make the macadamia semifreddo:
Preheat the oven to 320°F (160°C).
Spread the macadamia nuts on a sheet pan and toast in the oven until golden brown, about 10 minutes. Immediately sprinkle the salt over the nuts while still hot.
Transfer the toasted nuts to a pot and add the cream. Gently heat until it is just warm. Pulse the mixture with a stick blender. Be careful not to overblend. (This is just to release some oils out of the macadamias. If you overblend, they will absorb too much of the liquid.) Refrigerate the cream overnight to chill and infuse.
Strain the cream into the bowl of a stand mixer, reserving the macadamias. With a whisk, whip the cream on high speed until peaks form. Transfer to a bowl and refrigerate to chill.
Set aside half of the reserved macadamias for the crumble mix. Blend the remaining half into a smooth paste and reserve for mixing into the semifreddo.
In the bowl of a stand mixer, combine the whole eggs, egg yolks, and sugar. Set the bowl over a small pot of simmering water and whisk until it is warm. Transfer the bowl to the mixer and whisk until it is light and airy but thick and has cooled down, 6–8 minutes.
Quickly and gently fold in the chilled whipped cream and the reserved macadamia paste.

Scoop the semifreddo into the emptied mango skins until halfway up the sides and spread flat. Place in the freezer to freeze until firm.

Make the honeycomb:
In a medium pot, mix together the sugar, glucose, honey, and water. Gently heat, stirring to dissolve evenly.
Meanwhile, line a large hotel pan (gastronorm) with paper and spray with oil. Place over another pan of iced water. When the sugar mixture turns golden, quickly whisk in the baking soda (bicarb) and whisk for 5 seconds to make sure it's mixed in well. Pour immediately into the pan over ice.
When completely cooled, break into pieces and store in an airtight container.

Make the macadamia and honeycomb crumble mix:
Preheat the oven to 284°F (140°C).
Spread the reserved macadamias (from the semifreddo mix) on a sheet pan and transfer to the oven to dry and retoast, 20–30 minutes.
Sprinkle the sea salt onto the nuts while they're still hot and toss around to ensure an even seasoning. Set aside to cool down. Cut the dried mango into generous ¼-inch (7–8 mm) dice. Break the honeycomb into pieces the same size as the mango and macadamia halves.
Measure out 50 g of the macadamias and mix with the dried mango and honeycomb pieces. Store in an airtight container.

Make the mango sorbet:
In a small bowl, mix together the sugar, glucose powder, and stabilizer.
In a small saucepan, heat the water over medium heat until it reaches 113°F (45°C), then rain in the sugar mixture while whisking. Bring to 185°F (85°C) while whisking. Do not let boil.
Remove from the heat and place in containers in the fridge to cool and properly activate overnight.
In a blender, combine the reserved 400 g mango, the lime juice, and chilled syrup and blend until smooth. Churn or process the sorbet according to the manufacturer's directions. Store in a container in the freezer.

To finish:
Remove the mango skins filled with macadamia semifreddo from the freezer. Sprinkle in a nice even layer of the crumble mix. Fill the mango skins with the mango sorbet and spread the top completely flat with a spatula.
Score the top in a diamond pattern. Make sure the semifreddo and sorbet are both at the correct soft consistency and serve.

JASON SOURCES IMPECCABLY, THE VERY BEST OF AUSTRALIAN INGREDIENTS SEASONALLY THAT HE TRANSFORMS INTO DISHES THAT ARE SO SOIGNÉ, THEY ARE IMMEDIATELY RECOGNIZABLE AS TRULY EXCEPTIONAL.

— Palisa Anderson

KANGAROO TONNATO

PIZZA BIANCA

JASON SAXBY

RAMAEL SCULLY

YOTAM OTTOLENGHI

Few chefs embody the staggering cosmopolitanism of today's UK quite like Ramael Scully. Born in Malaysia and raised between there and in Australia by a Balinese-Irish father and Chinese-Indian mother, he has constructed a culinary identity by building exhilarating bridges between traditions. His cooking is so much more than "fusion," as anyone who has dined at Scully St. James's, his London restaurant, can attest.

Scully's friends affectionately label him a "food nerd," a cerebral, ever-tinkering creative who will rewrite a menu after an impromptu Chinatown shopping trip, or slow-cook a carrot for weeks just to see what happens. It might be more accurate, though, to describe him as a sponge. While the intricate and personal cuisine of Malaysia serves as Scully's cornerstone, he has spent his career absorbing lessons from the global canon and commingling them to create something entirely new.

He was already well-versed in French, Italian, and Southeast Asian ingredients and techniques in 2005, the year he first entered Yotam Ottolenghi's orbit. With the Israeli-English chef/restaurateur and his business partner, Palestinian chef Sami Tamimi, Scully found kindred kitchen spirits. Deftly folding their beloved African and Middle Eastern flavors into his repertoire, Scully excelled and was tapped to open Ottolenghi's internationally inclined NOPI in London, in 2011.

Now on his own, the full scope of Scully's culinary vision is on display. The food at Scully is thoughtful but never self-serious, authoritative but never heavy-handed. Eggplant *sambal* served atop bergamot-infused *labneh* links Malaysia and the Middle East; an accompanying *arepa* made from corn fermented with *koji* speaks for Venezuela and Japan. Crispy sea bream comes with dollops of a complex sauce that is equal parts Mexican mole (chiles, dark chocolate) and South Asian curry (Makrut limes, lemongrass). Dishes like these exemplify Scully's singular style, penchant for taking risks, and breadth of expertise—he is a chef that is not merely interested in the possibilities, but exhilarated by them.

MENU

PUFF BEEF TENDONS/TOMATO PANCETTA KILPATRICK/ OYSTER MAYO

CHAR-GRILLED BROCCOLI/ONION BARLEY VINEGAR/SALTED EGG YOLK

TOMATOES/COCONUT SAMBAL/ TOMATO SHRUB/GREEN CHILI OIL

OCTOPUS/SALT-BAKED AVOCADO/ BLACK GARLIC

BEEF SHORT-RIB PASTRAMI/ BUTTERSCOTCH HORSERADISH/ PISTACHIO PESTO

CARAMELIZED WHITE CHOCOLATE/ PINK PEPPERCORN/GRAPEFRUIT

OCTOPUS/SALT-BAKED AVOCADO/BLACK GARLIC
Serves 4

1.8 kg octopus • 1 tablespoon salt • 250 ml olive oil • 150 ml white wine • A few sprigs thyme • A few bay leaves • 1 teaspoon black peppercorns

For the salt-baked avocado:
4 firm-ripe avocados • 300 g rock salt • 1 teaspoon Yuzu Koshō (recipe follows) • 1 tablespoon crème fraîche • 30 ml avocado oil • Grated zest and juice of 1 lime

For the black garlic dressing:
200 g Black Garlic (recipe follows) • 100 ml grapeseed oil • 1 tablespoon lemon juice • 1 tablespoon rose water • 2 teaspoons unsweetened cocoa powder • 1 teaspoon harissa paste • 1 teaspoon pomegranate molasses • ¼ teaspoon urfa chile • Salt

For the cherry tomato jerky:
250 g cherry tomatoes on the vine • 200 ml white balsamic vinegar • 50 g superfine (caster) sugar • Salt

For garnish:
200 g red quinoa • 50 g dashi • 1 tablespoons shallot confit (see Note) • 1 teaspoon finely chopped chives

Prepare the octopus:
Clean and scrub the octopus with the salt. Rinsed under water, portion the tentacles and heads separately. Vacuum-seal the octopus, olive oil, wine, herbs, and peppercorns and cook sous vide at 77°C for 5–6 hours.

Make the salt-baked avocado:
Preheat the oven to 185°F (85°C). Layer rock salt on a sheet pan.
Nestle the avocados firmly on the rock salt. Bake for 1 hour and let avocado cool completely on rock salt.

Scoop the avocado flesh out into a blender, add the yuzu koshō, crème fraîche, avocado oil, lime zest, and lime juice and blend to a smooth puree.

Make the black garlic dressing:
In a blender, combine the black garlic, oil, lemon juice, rose water, cocoa, harissa, and salt to taste and blend to a smooth paste

Make the cherry tomato jerky:
Vacuum-seal the tomatoes and balsamic and let sit for 24 hours. Drain the tomatoes gently, capturing the juices. Transfer the juices to a pan, add the sugar and salt to taste, and cook to reduce to a light thick glaze.
Lay the cherry tomatoes on dehydrator sheets, lightly glaze the tomatoes with the reduction, and dehydrate to a jerky like texture.

OCTOPUS/SALT-BAKED AVOCADO/BLACK GARLIC

CARAMELIZED WHITE CHOCOLATE/PINK PEPPERCORN/GRAPEFRUIT

Prepare the garnish:
In a pot of boiling water, cook the red quinoa for 8 minutes. Drain and cool. When ready to plate, lightly reheat the quinoa with the dashi, shallot confit, and chives.

To serve:
Place a griddle on a high heat. Lightly toss the octopus with some olive oil and a pinch of salt and grill for 1-2 minutes, turning once, so that the octopus is warmed through and charred.
Spread the avocado puree in the middle of a plate. Add the warm quinoa and a couple of dots of black garlic dressing and plate the octopus on top of the quinoa. Garnish with 2 or 3 pieces of cherry tomato jerky.

Note: For shallot confit, finely dice shallots and slow-cooked with olive oil, garlic, and bouquet garni.

FERMENTED BLACK GARLIC
Whole garlic bulbs

Peel the outer skin of the garlic bulbs so that you can see the separation of garlic cloves. Put the whole bulbs in one layer in a rice cooker. Close the lid on the rice cooker and press the button "keep warm." Leave it as is for 10 days. Then dehydrate at 100°F (38°C) for 2 days.
Separate and peel the black garlic cloves and store in the refrigerator in an airtight container.

YUZU KOSHŌ
300 g of a mixture of lime, lemon, grapefruit, and orange zest • 150 g yuzu Juice • 200 g green chilies, seeded and minced • 100 g salt

In a bowl, toss together all the ingredients. Vacuum-seal and ferment at room temperature for 1 month. Blitz the paste and store in the refrigerator.

CARAMELIZED WHITE CHOCOLATE/PINK PEPPERCORN/GRAPEFRUIT
Serves 4

For the macaroon:
150 g granulated sugar • 150 g water • 100 g egg whites • 150 g powdered (icing) sugar • 150 g almond flour • 1 teaspoon raspberry powder • 1 teaspoon pink peppercorns

For the white chocolate ganache:
480 g white chocolate • 150 g whole milk • 120 g double cream

For the grapefruit sorbet:
500 ml grapefruit juice • 65 ml water • 315 g glucose

For the Aperol "sherbet":
750 ml Aperol • 50 g powdered (icing) sugar • 15 g cream of tartar • 15 g citric acid

For the grapefruit gel:
250 g grapefruit juice • 3 g agar agar • Touch of salt

For the burnt grapefruit:
Grapefruit segments • Demerara sugar

Make the macaroon:
In a saucepan, combine 150 g sugar with 150 g water bring it to 244°F (118°C). In a mixer fitted with the whisk, beat 50 g of the egg whites at full speed, add the hot syrup slowly and beat until it drops to

95°–97°F (35°–36°C), body temperature. In a separate bowl, mix together the remaining 50g egg whites, the powdered (icing) sugar, almonds flour, and raspberry powder. Fold the dry mixture into the meringue.
Spread the mixture on silicone baking mat in thin layers and sprinkle the pink peppercorns on top. Let rest for 10 hours at room temperature.
Preheat the oven to 240°F (115°C). Bake the macaroon for 15 minutes.

Make the white chocolate ganache:
Preheat the oven to 250°F (130°C). Place the chocolate on a baking sheet lined with a silicone mat. Bake for 1 hour, stirring every 10 minutes, until the chocolate is caramelized. In a saucepan, heat up the milk and cream. Add the caramelized white chocolate and use a hand blender to mix all the ingredients. Pass the ganache through a sieve and then reserve in the refrigerator until set.

Make the grapefruit sorbet:
In a saucepan, combine the juice, water, and glucose and bring to a light boil, making sure the glucose is fully melted. Let the mixture cool, then blend with an immersion blender and transfer to Pacojet cannisters to freeze.

Make the Aperol "sherbet":
Pour the Aperol into a shallow metal tray and dry on top of your coffee machine for 1 week. Using a fork, scrape the dehydrated aperol into fine crystals.
In a small bowl, blend together the powdered (icing) sugar, cream of tartar, and citric acid. Measure out 30 g of this mixture and stir together with 70 g of the dehydrated Aperol. Store in a cool, dry place.

Make the grapefruit gel:
In a saucepan, heat up the juice. Add the agar and salt and cook for 2 minutes to thicken the liquid. Cool down, blitz, and pass through a fine-mesh sieve.

Make the burnt grapefruit:
Sprinkle the segments with demerara sugar, and torch to caramelize.

One hour before serving, take the ganache out of the refrigerator to temper.
On either side of a shallow serving bowl, scatter some of the Aperol sherbet. Place a quenelle of ganache on one side of the bowl, a few dots of grapefruit gel next to it, and scatter caramelised grapefruit segments. Break the macaroon into various size pieces and place a few around the plate ending with a large one on top. Finish with a quenelle of grapefruit sorbet on top of the largest macaroon piece.

HE'S CRAZY ENOUGH TO THINK NOTHING OF SPENDING WEEKS SLOW-COOKING A CARROT TO LEATHERY, UMAMI-RICH PERFECTION, BUT SANE ENOUGH TO BE ABLE TO REIGN THINGS IN WHERE NEEDED.
— Yotam Ottolenghi

CHAR-GRILLED BROCCOLI/ONION BARLEY VINEGAR/SALTED EGG YOLK

RAMAEL SCULLY

ELDAD SHMUELI

EYAL SHANI

An alum of two Tel Aviv favorites—hot spot Claro, and Eyal Shani's North Abraxas—Eldad Shmueli followed his calling away from the city and up the coast to open his own boutique bakery near Pardes Hanna-Karkur in 2016. Situated at the entrance to a kibbutz, Elchanan Bread Culture is Shmueli's ode to the traditions and ingredients of yore. Geography, time, and politics are mere constructs in Shmueli's eyes—his science-backed techniques, though French-inspired, are preindustrial at heart and involve yeast as a key flavor element. Israeli and Palestinian cultures converge harmoniously at his bakery, a nod to the locale, and recipes that were previously lost are not only preserved, but extremely popular.

Shmueli, who previously trained under Alain Ducasse, is a modern messiah of natural sourdough, an old-school recipe made up of just water, flour, and wild yeast—his croissants and pretzels are made in this style. And of course, no Israeli bakery would be complete without some version of challah; Shmueli's calls for no added yeast and is baked in a stone oven. Reducing food waste is also a priority at Elchanan. Baked goods that are less than fresh take on new forms like granola and bread pudding, and breads that aren't repurposed are either donated to the local kibbutz as food for the animals or used for an experimental ale, the product of nearly a year of research by Shmueli.

In Israeli cuisine, breakfast is king, especially in kibbutz culture. Alongside his free-spirited baking endeavors, Shmueli puts his chef training to use to bring comforting morning dishes to locals and tourists alike. Roasted vegetables, charred cauliflower, thoughtful cheese boards, classic Israeli salads, locally sourced eggs, and more showcase the land and his passion for tradition—and the roots thereof—as the foundation of his vision. In other words, all things that are not-so-coincidentally perfect accompaniments to a freshly baked hunk of crusty bread.

MENU

BUTCHER BLOCK BREAKFAST

POACHED EGGS

KUNAFE CROISSANT

"HOT" SANDWICH WITH MATBUCHA AND TAHINI

POTATO PIZZA BIANCA

BREAD SALAD

FISH BALLS AND BREAD "STEAKS"

POACHED EGGS

For the hollandaise sauce:
6 egg yolks • 4 tablespoons water • 2 tablespoons white wine vinegar • 1 teaspoon sea salt • 1 teaspoon Dijon mustard • 400 g butter, clarified and strained

For the poached eggs:
1 tablespoon vinegar • 8 eggs

For the green chili in oil:
2 green chilies, finely mined • ½ clove garlic, finely minced • Pinch of sea salt • ½ cup (120 ml) olive oil

For assembly:
Cherry Tomato Perfume Sauce *(recipe follows)*, reduced to a thick consistency • Sea salt and cracked black pepper • 4 sprigs za'atar, leaves only • Thick slices sourdough bread, lightly grilled, for serving

Make the hollandaise:
In a bowl, whisk together the egg yolks, water, vinegar, salt, and mustard until

foamy. Put over a bain-marie and continue to whisk until about 149°F (65°C) and the mixture is fluffy and a little thick. Remove from the heat and start pouring in the clarified butter, whisking constantly. When well emulsified, check and adjust the seasoning. Keep warm.

Poach the eggs:
Bring a wide pot of water to a boil and add the vinegar. Crack the eggs into small cups. Make a whirlpool in the water and gently pour the eggs one by one into the water. Cook for about 5 minutes. Drain and stop the cooking of the eggs in cold water.

Make the green chili in oil:
In a small bowl, mix everything together.

To assemble:
Warm the tomato perfume sauce. Warm the eggs for 1 minute in hot water. Put about ½ cup (120 ml) hollandaise sauce into each plate and 2 tablespoons of the tomato perfume. Arrange the heated poached eggs on top. Spoon some of the

green chilies in oil around. Season with salt and pepper and some of the za'atar leaves. Serve with a thick slice of lightly grilled sourdough bread.

CHERRY TOMATO PERFUME SAUCE
2 tablespoons olive oil • 1 green chili, cut into ⅜-inch (1 cm) slices • 10 cloves garlic, roughly chopped • 1 kg mixed cherry tomatoes, halved • Sea salt

In a large pot, combine the olive oil, green chili, and garlic. Sweat over high heat for 1 minute, then add the tomatoes and salt and cook just until the tomatoes collapse, but don't overcook. Strain through a chinois.

BREAD SALAD

For the roasted vegetables:
8 tomatoes, halved • 4 onions, quartered • 2 long green chilies, torn in half • 8 cloves garlic, peeled • 1 sprig sage • ¼ cup (60 ml) olive oil • Cracked black pepper and sea salt

• 1 tablespoon sea salt • Cherry Tomato Perfume Sauce *(above)* • 1 teaspoon salt

For the spinach:
1 tablespoon olive oil • 4 sage leaves • 2 cloves garlic, sliced • 500 g spinach leaves, washed but not dried • 100 g butter

For the toasted bread "steaks:"
1 large loaf sourdough bread, halved and crusts cut off • 4 tablespoons olive oil • Sea salt and cracked black pepper

For serving:
100 g butter • 200 g whole-milk Greek yogurt

Make the fish balls:
In a sauté pan, heat the olive oil over low heat. Add the leek, onion, garlic, chili, sage, and black pepper and cook until soft and sweet but not browned.
Transfer to a food processor and mix for about 2 minutes. Form small balls of the mixture using oiled hands and put on a sheet pan.
Transfer to a preheated oven and roast for 3 minutes. (Leave the oven on for the toasted bread.)
In a pan, heat the cherry tomato sauce and gently put the fish balls inside. Cook on low for 8 minutes.

Make the spinach:
In a large pan, heat the olive oil over medium heat. Add the sage and garlic and cook for 1 minute. Add the spinach and cook until wilted and soft, about 10 minutes. Stir in the butter and cook for 2 more minutes.

Toast the bread "steaks:"
Place the bread on a sheet pan. Drizzle with the olive oil and sprinkle with salt and pepper. Toast in the oven for 1–2 minutes. (Leave the oven on for serving.)

To serve:
Into oven-to-table pans, divide the fish balls with the sauce (if too runny, reduce a little). Put the bread "steaks" in the middle and the cooked spinach in 1 or 2 corners in each pan. Put butter in some areas on the fish balls and on the bread. Transfer to the oven until nicely charred and heated, 3–6 minutes.
Serve with some of the yogurt spooned on the side of the bread "steaks."

For the tahini sauce:
1 cup (240 ml) tahini • 1 cup (240 ml) water • ½ teaspoon sea salt • ½ teaspoon fresh lemon juice

For the toasted bread:
500 g sourdough bread, torn into irregular chunks (about the size of ping-pong balls) • 2 tablespoons olive oil • Sea salt and cracked black pepper

For assembly:
Juice of 2 medium tomatoes • 2 tablespoons olive oil • 4 sprigs za'atar, leaves only • Sea salt and cracked black pepper

Roast the vegetables:
Preheat the oven to 425°F (220°C). Line a sheet pan with parchment paper.
In a large bowl, toss together the tomatoes, onions, chilies, garlic, sage, olive oil, and salt and pepper to taste. Arrange on the lined pan. Transfer to the oven and roast until browned and even blackened in places, about 30 minutes. (Leave the oven on for the toasted bread.)

Make the tahini sauce:
Mix all the ingredients well and adjust the water to achieve a creamy consistency.

Toast the bread:
In a bowl, toss together the bread, oil, and salt and pepper to taste. Arrange in a sheet pan and roast until slightly charred, 2–3 minutes.

To assemble:
In a large bowl, mix the roasted vegetables, charred bread, tomato juice, olive oil, za'atar leaves, and salt and pepper to taste. Serve on top of the tahini sauce.

FISH BALLS AND BREAD "STEAKS"

For the fish balls:
½ cup (120 ml) olive oil • 1 large leek (white part only), finely sliced • 1 medium onion, finely sliced • 3 cloves garlic, sliced • 3 slices (⅜ inch/1 cm) green chili • 2 sage leaves • ¼ teaspoon cracked black pepper • 1 kg fresh sardines, cleaned • 3 salted black olives, pitted, • 1 thick slice bread, soaked in water 10 minutes, then squeezed and dried • 1 egg

HE DOES NOT
HURRY THE BREAD,
HE WHISPERS TO IT.
HIS BREADS AND
PASTRIES ARE
FLAWLESS IN THEIR
BAKING, TASTE,
AND SOUND.

— Eyal Shani

BUTCHER BLOCK BREAKFAST

FISH BALLS AND BREAD "STEAKS"

"HOT" SANDWICH

POTATO PIZZA BIANCA

ELDAD SHMUELI

RYAN SMITH

STAPLEHOUSE
Atlanta, Georgia, United States

HUGH ACHESON

Orchestrating a delicate harmony of flavor and texture across a multicourse tasting menu is a demanding task; safeguarding the physical and mental health of all the people whose energies make it possible is another challenge altogether. It is rarely a simple undertaking, but Ryan Smith, chef and partner at Staplehouse in Atlanta, Georgia, has found a way to do both. A native of Pennsylvania, Smith started cooking while studying at Penn State University in his hometown of State College. After graduating from the Culinary Institute of America in 2000, Smith relocated to Atlanta and began building his repertoire in some of the city's most respected restaurants, including Bacchanalia, Canoe, Empire State South, and Holeman and Finch Public House.

It was at Staplehouse, which opened in 2015, that Smith came into his own, both as a culinary original and as a leader. There, he celebrates locally sourced, heirloom, and often foraged Southern ingredients in season—and sometimes out of it, given his penchant for clever preservation. Despite his Northern origins, he displays an innate kinship with these ingredients and traditions, and incorporates them into his dishes in ways that are grounded in history and thoughtful innovation. A simple chicken liver tart, deftly glazed with honey gelée, is a thing of beauty and precision. In his tribute to his grandmother Lillian's potato bread, Smith ferments the tubers before combining them with red wheat flour from DaySpring, an organic farm just outside Atlanta. He also pays close attention to the progression of a meal; he will follow an airy plate of corn, crab, and finger lime, for example, with an earthy aged beef, keeping diners intrigued and their palates engaged.

Smith understands that balance on a menu must be bolstered by balance in the lives of the people behind it. He has a reputation for going above and beyond as a mentor, cultivating an environment centered around learning, encouragement, and work-life equilibrium. Moreover, Staplehouse is the for-profit subsidiary of the Giving Kitchen, a nonprofit organization that provides emergency assistance to food workers in crisis. Expanding the tenets of American Southern cuisine while giving back to the community he has helped build, and prioritizing time for himself and his family, Smith sets an inspiring example in the industry.

MENU

CRAB, SUNFLOWER, HOT PEPPER VINEGAR

CARROT, CASHEW, SORREL

COBIA, SCALLOP GARUM, FENNEL

CHICKEN LIVER TART

SQUASH, COUNTRY HAM, GREEN CORIANDER

BEEF, ONION, FISH-SAUCE CARAMEL

the xanthan and incorporate the salt and vinegar. With the blender running slowly, emulsify in the sunflower oil until smooth and creamy. Adjust the seasoning with salt as needed.

Set a circulating water bath to 85°C. Vacuum-seal the carrots and the carrot juice emulsion in a flat even layer. Cook the carrots for 45 minutes to 1 hour, depending on size. Once cooked, chill the bag in an ice bath. Once the carrots are cold, take them out of the bags and drain off the emulsion, reserving both.

Prepare the cashews:
Preheat the oven to 325°F (163°C). Spread the cashews out on a sheet pan in an even layer. Dress the cashews with 10 g of the cashew oil and sprinkle with sea salt. Transfer to the oven and slowly roast until evenly golden brown, 20–25 minutes. Cut one cashew in half to ensure that it's toasted all the way through. Allow the cashews to cool to room temperature.
Measure out a quarter of the roasted cashews, chop them very finely and evenly, and reserve. Place the remaining cashews in a blender with a small amount of water and blend. Once the cashews begin to get smooth, start emulsifying in the remaining 110 g cashew oil. Once smooth, pass the puree through a fine-mesh sieve or chinois. Chill over an ice bath. Fill a small piping bag with the puree and reserve.

CARROT, CASHEW, SORREL
Serves 6

For the carrots:
12 young carrots (Nantes variety), well scrubbed • Sea salt • 300 g carrot juice • 100 g distilled white vinegar • 1.25 g xanthan gum • 100 g sunflower oil

For the cashews:
450 g cashews • 120 g cashew oil • Sea salt

For the sorrel sauce:
225 g sorrel, preferably French • 400 g buttermilk • Sea salt • 2 g xanthan gum • 60 g powdered egg whites

For the garnish:
Cosmic Purple carrots • Small sorrel leaves (wood sorrel, French sorrel, or other varieties of oxalis)

For plating:
Cashew oil • Sea salt

Prepare the carrots:
It's important to find young carrots that are equal in size and shape to ensure they cook uniformly and evenly. Weigh the carrots and season them with 2 g sea salt per 100 g carrots. Set aside.
In a blender, combine the carrot juice, vinegar, salt, and xanthan gum. Blend the juice on high speed to hydrate

Make the sorrel sauce:
In a blender, combine the sorrel and buttermilk and blend on high until smooth. Strain the puree through a fine-mesh sieve or chinois and return to the blender. Blend in some sea salt and the xanthan gum. Once incorporated, slowly add the egg white powder until completely smooth and incorporated. Chill over an ice bath. Transfer the mixture to a whipper siphon canister and charge two times. Shake to ensure that it's incorporated and refrigerate until needed.

Prepare the garnish:
Shave the purple carrot into thin rounds on a mandoline straight into an ice bath. While the carrot slices are in the ice bath, place the container into a Cryovac machine and run on high pressure two or three times. Immediately drain the carrots and dry in a salad spinner. Store between paper towels to absorb any residual moisture.
Trim the sorrel leaves to the desired size/shape and place in an ice bath. Place the container into the Cryovac machine and run on high pressure two or three times. Immediately drain and gently spin in a salad spinner. Store between paper towels to absorb any residual moisture.

To plate:
Gently warm the carrots in the reserved carrot emulsion, using just enough emulsion to coat them. Place on a tray and coat them in the reserved chopped roasted cashews.
Arrange on a plate and pipe the cashew puree along the tops (this is to season the carrot, but it also acts as glue for the shaved purple carrot). Lightly dress the shaved purple carrots with cashew oil and sea salt and shingle along the top of the carrots. Off to the side, dispense a small amount of the sorrel sauce from the siphon. Garnish the sauce with raw sorrel leaves.

COBIA, SCALLOP GARUM, FENNEL
Serves 6

For the garum:
900 g scallops • 600 g rice koji • 152 g sea salt • 400 g distilled water

For the fennel oil:
450 g fennel fronds • 150 g grapeseed oil

For the grilled fish broth:
1 lb (455 g) cobia bones *(see Note)*, cut into small even pieces • 1 onion, thinly sliced • 1 bulb fennel, thinly sliced

For the garum sauce:
200 g Garum *(above)* • 20 g fresh lime juice • 300 g Grilled Fish Broth *(above)* • 3 g sucrose • Sea salt • 100 g Fennel Oil *(above)*
For the cobia:

CARROT, CASHEW, SORREL

6 cobia fillets, 3–4 oz (85–155 g) each *(see Note)* • 2 cups (475 ml) shio koji • Sunflower oil

For the fennel:
6 bulbs young fennel • Sea salt • 20 g sunflower oil • 3 g fennel pollen

For the herb powder:
60 g fennel fronds • 30 g parsley • 30 g dill • 30 g chives • 30 g chervil • Sea salt

For the greens:
60 g tetragonia • 30 g young arugula (rocket) • 30 g fennel fronds

For assembly:
Sea salt • Lime juice

Note: If purchasing fillets, ask your fishmonger for bones for the broth. Or start with a whole cobia and break it down: Remove the loins from the bones and reserve the bones for the

broth. Butcher the fillets to achieve loins that have been cleaned of surface connective tissue, blood line, and skin. Portion the loins into pieces that are 3–4 oz (85–115 g) each.

Make the garum:
Grind the scallops and the rice koji through a meat grinder. Season with the sea salt and add the water. Transfer the mixture to a sterilized airtight container and store at room temperature for 2–3 months, or until the desired flavor is produced.
Strain the garum through a chinois lined with cheesecloth (muslin). Pasteurize the garum by slowly bringing it to a boil. Boil for 3 minutes, then strain again through a chinois lined with cheesecloth. Chill and reserve.

Make the fennel oil:
In a blender, combine the fennel fronds and grapeseed oil and blend on high speed. It needs to be blended for 2–4 minutes. The friction will cook the fennel and set

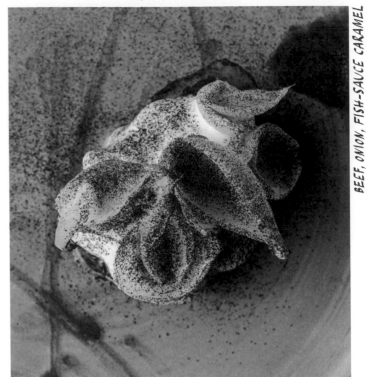

BEEF, ONION, FISH-SAUCE CARAMEL

CRAB, SUNFLOWER, HOT-PEPPER VINEGAR

RYAN SMITH IS A MODERN, METICULOUS, ASSERTIVE, AND TECHNICAL CHEF. HE COOKS IN A CONTEMPORARY AND STUDIED WAY, GLEANING IDEAS FROM HISTORY AND TECHNIQUES, RATHER THAN POACHING ITEMS FROM AU COURANT MENUS.

— Hugh Acheson

the chlorophyll. The color will deepen and it will appear to be separated or broken. At this point, stop the blender and strain through a chinois lined with a coffee filter. Chill and reserve.

Make the grilled fish broth:
Set up a wood-fire grill (barbecue) with hardwood charcoal or *binchōtan* for indirect grilling. When it's at medium heat, grill the cobia bones over indirect heat to gently cook the flesh and render its residual fat. Be sure not to achieve much, if any, color as the goal is not to get deep flavor from the broth but rather a delicate flavor.
Transfer the grilled bones to a stockpot and add cold water to just barely cover them. Slowly bring the broth to 180°F (82°C). Once at temp, add the sliced onion and fennel. Maintaining a temperature of 180–185°F (82–85°C), continue to cook for 20–25 minutes.
Remove from the heat and allow to rest for 30 minutes at room temperature.
Using a large ladle, pull the broth from the top of the pot so as not to disturb the bones and sediment that have settled while resting. Strain the broth through a chinois lined with cheesecloth. Chill and reserve.

Make the garum sauce:
In a blender, combine the garum, lime juice, fish broth, sucrose, and sea salt to taste. Blend until all the ingredients are fully incorporated. With the blender running slowly, emulsify in the fennel oil. Reserve.

Prepare the cobia:
Marinate the fish portions in the shio koji for 3–4 hours.
Gently rinse the cobia fillets with cold water and pat dry with paper towels. Vacuum-seal each portion in an individual bag with a small amount of sunflower oil and reserve.

Prepare the fennel:
Halve the fennel lengthwise and season with sea salt. Vacuum-seal the fennel with the sunflower oil and fennel pollen. Set a circulating water bath to 85°C. Cook the fennel for 45 minutes to 1 hour, or until desired doneness. Chill the bags of fennel in an ice bath. Once fully chilled, remove the fennel from the bags and cut across the grain of the fennel into strips ¼ inch (6 mm) wide and reserve.

Make the herb powder:
Pick all of the herbs to remove any stems. Evenly lay out all the herbs on a dehydrator tray and dehydrate at 120°F (49°C) until completely dry. Place the dried herbs and sea salt in a blender and blend to a fine powder. Reserve.

Prepare the greens:
Gently wash all of the different greens in cold water. Submerge the cleaned greens in an ice bath and place the container in the

Cryovac machine and run the machine on high pressure two or three times. Immediately remove the greens from the water and gently spin in a salad spinner. Place the greens between two paper towels and reserve.

To assemble and plate:
Gently warm the garum sauce in a deep saucepot. Keep warm while the fish cooks. Set a circulating water bath to 70°C and cook the fish for 4–5 minutes. Take the bags out of the bath and allow the fish to rest for 1 minute. Take the fish out of the bag and slice each portion into 4 equal pieces. Place the sliced fish in the base of the bowl and add the fennel strips. Dress the greens with a small amount of sea salt and lime juice and place them on top of the fish to cover and keep any residual warmth in. Using a stick blender, blend the garum sauce at a slight angle to allow air to be incorporated into the sauce and create froth/bubbles. Spoon some of the froth over the greens. Using a small sifter or sieve, dust the top of the dish with the dried herb powder.

BEEF, ONION, FISH SAUCE CARAMEL
Serves 6

For the fish sauce caramel:
300 g sugar • 50 g sherry vinegar • 200 g fish sauce • 20 g fresh lime juice • Ultra-Tex 3

For the onions:
6 small sweet onions • Sea salt • 200 g butter • 2 bay leaves

For the beef fat sauce:
200 g beef stock • 200 g whole milk • 5 cloves garlic, peeled • 3 bay leaves • Sea salt • White pepper • 1.6 g xanthan gum • 2 g citric acid • 100 g aged beef fat, rendered and strained • 36 g powdered egg whites

For the onion powder:
2 onions, cut into ½-inch (1.25 cm) slices • Sea salt • Grapeseed oil • Citric acid

For assembly:
One 24–30 oz (680–850 g) beef ribeye • Sea salt and cracked black pepper • Grapeseed oil

Make the fish sauce caramel:
In a medium saucepot, combine the sugar and water. Bring to a boil over high heat and cook until the sugar caramelizes evenly to desired color. Reduce the heat to low and deglaze the caramel with the vinegar, then add the fish sauce. Slowly incorporate the fish sauce until homogenous. Bring the sauce back up to a boil and cook until reduced by half.
Transfer to a blender and add the lime juice. Blend on high and slightly thicken with Ultra-Tex 3 until the desired texture is achieved. Refrigerate until needed.
Prepare the onions:

Set a circulating water bath to 85°C. Halve the onions from root to stem. Peel the skin, keeping the halves intact. Season the onions with sea salt. Vacuum-seal them with the butter and bay leaves. Cook in the water bath for 45 minutes to 1 hour, or until the desired texture is achieved.
Chill in an ice bath. Once chilled, remove the onions from the bag and reserve the liquid. Pull the onions into individual petals, making sure each petal remains intact, and reserve.

Make the beef fat sauce:
In a medium stockpot, combine the beef stock, milk, garlic, bay leaves, and some sea salt. Slowly bring the mixture to a boil. Once it comes up to a boil, reduce the heat to low and very gently poach the garlic until sweet and tender.
Discard the bay leaves and transfer the mixture to a blender. With the machine on high, season with sea salt and white pepper. Add the xanthan gum and citric acid and blend until fully hydrated. Slowly emulsify in the melted aged beef fat. With the blender still on high, slowly add the egg white powder until fully incorporated. Adjust the seasoning with sea salt. Transfer the sauce to the canister of a whipper siphon and charge. Reserve warm until ready to use.

Make the onion powder:
Preheat a grill to medium heat. Season the onion slices with sea salt and dress with grapeseed oil. Place the onions on the grill and cook to achieve a dark caramelized color. Transfer the grilled onions to a dehydrator tray and dehydrate until completely dry of any moisture.
In a blender, blend the dried onions, sea salt, and citric acid. Blend on high until a fine powder is achieved. Place the powder in a small fine-mesh sieve and reserve.

To assemble:
Preheat a sauté pan or cast-iron skillet over medium-high heat. Once hot, add a small amount of grapeseed oil and add the beef. Sear each side of the beef for 1–2 minutes depending on size and level of heat. Each side should be evenly caramelized. Cook until the desired doneness is achieved and remove from the pan. Allow the beef to rest until warm to the touch.
Slice the rested beef for one slice per portion. Place the slice of beef on a plate and spoon the fish sauce caramel directly over the beef. Dispense the beef fat sauce to cover the top. Place the gently warmed onions on top of that and dust the top with the onion powder.

RYAN SMITH

JOHNNY SPERO

REVERIE
Washington, DC,
United States

JOSÉ ANDRÉS

Johnny Spero is the chef-owner of Reverie, a modern American restaurant in Washington, DC's Georgetown district. Reverie is notable for its impeccable sourcing with global accents in dishes such as Japanese-inspired *maitake* mushrooms with egg-yolk fudge or Nordic-leaning *rugbrød* with miso, leek ash, and the famed Spanish jamón Ibérico. All are testaments to Spero's wanderlust and the culinary curiosity that guides him even when he's not in the kitchen. Another Reverie trademark is its very open kitchen, where chefs serve diners directly—hence promoting interaction and approachability, and demonstrating how Spero eschews any intimidation between chefs and patrons.

A Maryland native, Spero moved to DC in 2008, where he first worked at Johnny Monis's fine-dining flagship Komi for two years—one cooking savory and one in pastry. In 2010, his desire to explore other cultures and their cuisines took him abroad and eventually to Copenhagen for a two-month tenure at Noma, where he was forever changed by the restaurant's sourcing doctrine and original methods. Back in the United States, Spero worked with John Shields at Town House in Chilhowie, Virginia, before opening his own restaurant, Suna, in DC That first venture was short-lived but impressive: Spero's skills at Suna caught the eye of José Andrés' company, ThinkFoodGroup, and led to a position as executive sous-chef at Andres's DC fine-dining bastion Minibar, for which he received a perfect four-star review from the *Washington Post*.

Next, Spero decided once again to travel. He spent a season staging at Andoni Luis Aduriz's legendary temple to fine dining, Mugaritz, in Spain, before returning to DC to plan his new restaurant. Reverie has been much lauded and Spero has been featured on *The Final Table*.

MENU

UNI TORTILLA

BARBECUE KANPACHI LOIN
WITH SUNCHOKE AND MOSS
DASHI

KANPACHI COLLAR WITH
POTATO PITA

ROASTED PEAR ICE CREAM

UNI TORTILLA
Serves 4–6

For the sake kasu crème fraîche:
2 kg heavy (whipping) cream • 200 g house-made buttermilk (reserved from our butter production) • 75 g sake kasu

For the confit onion and potato:
2 quarts/liters grapeseed oil • 1 whole Spanish onion, cut into medium dice • 2 Yukon Gold potatoes, peeled and cut into medium dice

For the uni egg mixture:
6 eggs • 50 g fresh uni, pureed smooth • 20 g dashi • 5 g sunchoke tamari (or whatever you have available) • 100 g potato egg mixture

For plating:
Reserved tongues from 2 whole uni • Sunchoke tamari • Maldon sea salt • Plum sorrel • Wood sorrel

Make the sake kasu crème fraîche:
Sterilize a plastic container large enough to fit the cream mixture.

In a bowl, mix all the ingredients until combined and pour into the sterilized container. Cover the container with a few layers of cheesecloth (muslin) and let stand at room temperature (65°–75°F/18°–24°C) for 24–48 hours, until the desired consistency is achieved.

Pass the cream through a tamis to make sure there are no bits of *sake kasu* remaining. Line a sieve with cheesecloth, spoon in the cream, and drain the mixture overnight to remove any excess liquid.

Make the confit onion and potato:
In a medium soup pot, gently heat the oil over medium-low heat.

Add the onion and potatoes and cook slowly. You are not trying to deep-fry, so keep the temperature regulated, stirring constantly and not allowing any color. Cook until both the onion and potato are soft but not mushy, 25–30 minutes.

Drain, reserving the oil, and lay the potatoes and onion on a tray to cool.

Make the uni egg mixture:
In a bowl, beat the eggs with a fork, gently so you do not incorporate a lot of air. Gently

whisk in the uni puree until combined completely with the egg (this is important so the uni cooks evenly with the egg and does not create unevenness in the tortilla).

Stir in the dashi, tamari, and potato egg mixture.

In a nonstick medium sauté pan, heat 1 tablespoon of the oil reserved from the confit and heat over high heat. While constantly agitating the pan, slowly pour in the egg mixture, keep the pan moving so the egg does not stick to the bottom.

With a spatula, constantly scrape the bottom of the pan and move the egg so it does not brown, also folding down the sides to keep the shape of the tortilla. After 2–3 minutes, when the egg is mostly cooked on the bottom and has begun to solidify, stop stirring so the tortilla can take its shape. When the egg is almost cooked through but the center is still runny, use a plate to cover the pan, flip the pan over to release the tortilla. Return the pan to heat and slide in the tortilla cooked-side up. It is important that during this stage you use the spatula to keep the shape of the tortilla tight and only allow it to cook for less than a minute so the interior does not overcook.

Remove the tortilla from the pan and place on a plate for service.

To plate:
Cover the top of the tortilla with the fresh uni tongue, seasoning them with a small amount of tamari. Place a small dollop of the crème fraîche directly next to the uni, seasoning with Maldon salt. Garnish the uni and crème fraîche with a mixture of both sorrels.

BARBECUE KANPACHI LOIN WITH SUNCHOKE AND MOSS DASHI

Serves 4–6

For the tomato "Marmite:"
25 lb (11.33 kg) heirloom (heritage) tomatoes (we prefer seconds or any ugly ones) • Salt • 1 lb (455 g) fresh yeast

For the kanpachi loin:
1 whole kanpachi • 500 g salt • 500 g sugar • 100 g Sichuan peppercorns, cracked • Grated zest of 1 lime

For the moss dashi:
4 quarts/liters filtered water • 2 sheets kombu • 100 g dried and cleaned moss • 10 g lacto-fermented and dried plums • 10 g bonito flakes

For the sake kasu oil:
1 kg sunflower oil • 250 g sake kasu

For assembly:
Sunchoke tamari • Salt • 1 oz (28 g) caviar or paddlefish roe • Raw sunchokes (Jerusalem artichokes), shaved paper thin, reserved in water • Salad burnet, leaves picked

Make the tomato "Marmite:"
Gently rinse the tomatoes to clean off any dirt or residue. With the tip of a small knife, gently remove the cores from the tomatoes. Fill several large vacuum bags with the tomatoes. Set each bag on a scale and add 2% salt by weight. Seal on high and let sit at room temperature for 2 weeks, occasionally piercing the bag to "burp," then resealing. Pour the tomatoes into a sieve lined with cheesecloth (muslin) set over a bowl to catch the juices and let drain (reserve the tomato pulp for another use).

Preheat an oven to 400°F (205°C). Line a sheet pan with a Silpat.
Spread the fresh yeast on the lined pan and roast until golden brown.
In a saucepan, combine the reserved tomato water and the yeast and reduce down until sticky and tacky. It will be very salty, but only a few drops are needed for the dish.

Cure the kanpachi loin:
Break down the kanpachi, reserving the bones, head, and collars for additional dishes (such as Kanpachi Collar with Potato Pita, *below*).
In a bowl, combine the salt, sugar, peppercorns, and lime zest. Cure the loins in the salt mixture for 1 hour. Gently rinse and place on a wire rack set in a sheet pan to dry.

Make the moss dashi:
In a large stockpot, combine the water and kombu and bring to a slow simmer. Add the moss and plums, reduce the heat to very low (just enough to keep the water warm), and gently cook uncovered for 1 hour.
Add the bonito flakes and remove from the heat. Cover and let cool at room temperature for 1 hour. Strain through a coffee filter to ensure the broth is clear and no sediment from the moss has transferred through. Refrigerate until needed.

Make the sake kasu oil:
Vacuum-seal the oil and *sake kasu*. Set a circulating water bath to 85°C and cook for 3 hours.
Let the oil cool overnight. The next day strain through a coffee filter.

To assemble:
Set up a charcoal fire using a few pieces of *binchōtan*, just enough to fill one side of a small konro grill.

Cut the kanpachi into 100 g portions and pierce with 3 metal skewers, this will ensure the fish does not lose its shape during the quick high-heat cooking.
Rub the fish with a small amount of the tomato "Marmite," just enough to coat.
Cook over the coals, gently turning and fanning so the fish does not burn but just gets an even layer of caramelization. Remove from the heat and immediately take out the skewers.
In a saucepan, gently warm up the moss dashi (without boiling), season to taste with some sunchoke tamari and a little salt if needed. Add a few generous drops of the sake kasu oil, but do not whisk in.
Place the fish in a bowl, adding a small amount more of the tomato "Marmite." Spread the caviar to cover the fish and top with the 6 pieces of raw shaved sunchoke. Pour the warm dashi over the top to finish cooking the fish, and garnished with the salad burnet leaves.

KANPACHI COLLAR WITH POTATO PITA

Serves 2–4

For the kombu/miso paste:
4 sheets kombu • 1 quart/liter sunflower oil • 150 g sunchoke miso

For the charcoal emulsion:
2 quarts/liters sunflower oil • 1 brick *binchōtan* charcoal, heated to red hot • 1 egg • 1 egg yolk • 10 g sherry vinegar • Salt

For serving:
1 kanpachi collar • Grated zest of yuzu or lemon (depending on availability) • Potato Pita *(recipe follows)* • Borage cress • Fresh yuzu

Make the kombu/miso paste:
Set a convection oven to low heat. Lay out the kombu on a sheet pan and slowly bake until crispy.
Once dried, break up the seaweed and pulverize to a powder in a blender. With the blender running, slowly pour in the oil to create a paste.
Transfer to a bowl and whisk in the miso until incorporated.

Make the charcoal emulsion:
In a small soup pot with a lid, heat the sunflower oil over low heat so it is slightly above room temperature.
Ensuring that the piece of coal is red hot, use tongs to place it directly into the oil, then immediately cover the pot so the oil does not ignite. Remove from the heat and allow it to smoke and smolder for about 1 hour until the oil has cooled down.
Strain through a coffee filter to make sure no bits of charcoal seep through. Refrigerate for a few hours to chill.
In a blender, combine the whole egg, egg yolk, vinegar, and a pinch of salt and blend until smooth. With the blender running, emulsify in the charcoal oil until thick.
Transfer to a piping bag and refrigerate until needed.

To serve:
With a brush, cover the flesh side of the collar with the kombu/miso paste until completely covered—it should look almost entirely black. Let sit at room temperature to dry slightly.
Make a fire with *binchōtan* charcoal on one side of a grill. Place the collar skin-side down over the hottest part of the coals.
After 2–3 minutes, flip the collar over onto the flesh side, flipping back and forth until cooked, which should take only about 10 minutes. The flesh will look almost burnt because of the kombu/miso paste. Remove from the heat and immediately season with the citrus zest.
Place the collar flesh-side up on a plate. Place a small amount of the charcoal emulsion on the potato pita and cover it with borage cress. Serve with two forks, instructing the guests to scrape the meat from the bone of the collar, place on the pita, and eat like a gyro.

POTATO PITAS
1.2 kg Yukon Gold potatoes, peeled • Salt • 16 g active dry yeast • 10 g warm water • 600 g whole-milk Greek yogurt • 1.25 kg all-purpose (plain) flour • Oil

In a medium soup pot, combine the potatoes and cold salted water to cover. Bring to a boil, then reduce to a simmer and cook until tender.
Meanwhile, in a small bowl, hydrate the yeast in the warm water.
Drain the cooked potatoes and process through a ricer while still warm.

In a stand mixer with the paddle, combine the riced potato, yogurt, and yeast mixture and beat until combined. Slowly add the flour until just combined. Do not overwork. Transfer the dough to a lightly oiled bowl, cover with plastic wrap (cling film), and let sit in the fridge overnight.
Portion into 100 g balls and set in small plastic containers with a small amount of oil. Cover and let sit again for 1 hour.
Set up a charcoal grill (or if no grill is available, preheat the oven to 450°F/230°C).
On a floured surface, quickly roll each ball of dough into an 8-inch (20 cm) round, flipping over only once so as to not overwork.
Heat up a plancha or large pan with a small amount of oil over medium-high heat. Gently place a pita, shaking off any excess flour, in the pan and sear on each side for about 1 minute.
Set the bread over the coals on the grill (or bake in the oven) to finish the cooking.

ROASTED PEAR ICE CREAM
Serves 6–8

For the roasted pears:
12 Seckel pears • 500 g elderflower syrup

For the ice cream base:
750 g heavy (whipping) cream • 500 g whole milk • 200 g sugar • 2 g salt

For the ice cream:
600 g Ice Cream Base *(above)* **• 128 g egg yolks • 6 Roasted Pears** *(above)*, **stems removed**

For the cilantro oil:
1 lb (455 g) cilantro (coriander), leaves picked, stems reserved for garnish • 500 g sunflower oil

For the pear juice:
1 kg water • 4 g ascorbic acid • 6 Bosc pears • 0.5 g xanthan gum

For plating:
4 apple slices, punched with a small ring mold • Cilantro (coriander) stems and leaves • Pear brandy (in a spray bottle) • ½ Roasted Pear *(above)*, **stemmed and cored**

Roast the pears:
Preheat a convection oven to 400°F (200°C).
Cut a small amount of the bottom from each pear so it can sit flat on a sheet pan. Place the pear on a sheet of foil, glaze with a generous amount of elderflower syrup, and wrap tightly.
Roast the pears until the inside is soft and the skin begins to wrinkle, about 2 hours, checking every 30 minutes.
Let them sit covered in the fridge for several hours to the absorb the caramelized syrup. Set aside 6 of the pears for garnish and the other 6 for the ice cream. Reserve all the juices and elderflower syrup as well.

Make the ice cream base:
Measure out 90 g of the elderflower syrup and juices from the roasted pears. In a saucepan, combine the elderflower syrup, cream, milk, sugar, and salt. Bring to a boil, stirring to be sure the sugar and salt are dissolved. Strain and refrigerate.

Make the ice cream:
In a saucepan, heat the ice cream base to 181°F (83°C). Immediately pour into a blender and on high speed slowly pour in the egg yolks. Let run until thick.
Place 2 roasted pears in each Pacojet beaker. Divide the ice cream mixture evenly among the beakers. Freeze overnight.
Spin and freeze again to make sure the pear is combined.

Make the cilantro oil:
Bring a small pot of water to a boil. Add the cilantro (coriander) leaves and blanch for 30 seconds. Scoop out and immediately place in an ice bath to cool for 10–15 minutes. Remove the leaves from the water, wrap in a tea towel, and squeeze until all the excess water is removed.
In a blender, combine the oil and leaves and run on high speed for 2 minutes. Pour the mixture into a stainless steel bowl and cool over an ice bath, stirring with a spatula. Allow the oil to sit in the sediment overnight. The next day, strain through a coffee filter.

Make the pear juice:
Set up a bowl with the water and 2 g of the ascorbic acid. Quarter and core the pears, dropping them into the acidulated water as you work.
Juice the pears in a centrifugal juicer into a container and add the remaining 2 g ascorbic acid.
Transfer the juice to a blender and on high speed slowly sheer in the xanthan gum to thicken. Strain and reserve.

To plate:
Spin the ice cream in the Pacojet, then place a small scoop on the bottom of a frozen bowl. Garnish the ice cream with the apples and cilantro leaves and stems and spray with pear brandy.
Cover the ice cream with the pear half, leaving some of the cilantro stems and apple exposed.
Add a small amount of the cilantro oil to the pear juice, not fully combining but just barely mixing together so it is not emulsified. Pour the juice on the side of the bowl, not directly on top of the pear.

JOHNNY CAN EDIT HIMSELF TO MAKE SURE HIS PLATES ONLY HAVE ON THEM WHAT IS NECESSARY. HE IS AN INTELLECTUAL, MAYBE EVEN A CHEF'S CHEF, SOMEONE WHO CHALLENGES YOU TO THINK WHILE YOU ARE EATING. — José Andrés

UNI TORTILLA

ROASTED PEAR ICE CREAM

JOHNNY SPERO

JEREMIAH STONE &
FABIÁN VON HAUSKE VALTIERRA

DANIELA SOTO-INNES

MENU

BEEF TARTARE, SMOKED CHEDDAR, HORSERADISH

POTATO DARPHIN, UNI, JALAPEÑO

OYSTER, LAPSANG SOUCHONG

RYE PORRIDGE, UNI, LOVAGE

PORK, GOOSEBERRIES, SUCCULENTS

APRICOT, BITTER ALMOND, ANISE HYSSOP

CHOCOLATE TART

It is safe to say that New York City's Lower East Side would not be the culinary heavy hitter it is today without chefs like Jeremiah Stone and Fabián von Hauske Valtierra. The duo, who were jointly named *GQ*'s Chefs of the Year in 2018, are best friends, business partners, and pioneers of the unpretentious fine-dining movement. Stone and von Hauske Valtierra opened Contra, a forty-four-seat space in 2013 to much acclaim and media attention—at twenty-eight and twenty-three, respectively, it was clear that the pair was one to watch from the very beginning.

It was New York's French Culinary Institute (now the International Culinary Center) that brought the chefs together by way of Dave Arnold in 2008, under whom von Hauske Valtierra was interning at the time. Stone, who is from Maryland, graduated from the Culinary Arts program in 2007 and was working as a sous chef for the school's events; von Hauske Valtierra, a Mexico City native, had enrolled in the school's Culinary Arts and Pastry Arts programs. The two first discussed future collaboration back in 2010.

After each chef briefly explored the culinary world independently— Stone at Le Chateaubriand and Rino in Paris, and at Isa in Brooklyn; and von Hauske Valtierra at Noma, Faviken, and Attica—they reunited, and the seeds they planted began to sprout. Contra's opening was the product of plenty of brainstorming, about a year's worth of searching for the perfect space, and some travel through Europe in search of more inspiration for the project. The restaurant's unpretentious tasting menu gained traction in the New York culinary scene, and in 2015, the duo opened the doors to their second project, Wildair, focusing on natural wines and simple yet sophisticated American fare. Both restaurants and the chefs have received numerous accolades.

In 2019, Stone and von Hauske opened Peoples Wine Shop and Bar inside the Lower East Side market space called The Market Line. As the duo's restaurant group continues to earn recognition, the future of casual fine-dining in New York City is a bright one.

BEEF TARTARE, SMOKED CHEDDAR, HORSERADISH
Serves 4

50 g unsalted butter • 100 g raw buckwheat groats • 250 g top sirloin • 150 g fattier cut, such as coulotte, strip loin, or ribeye • 12 g pickled shallots, finely chopped • 40 g pimentón oil • Kosher salt and freshly ground pepper • 10 chervil sprigs • 100 g fresh horseradish • 150 g smoked cheddar cheese • 40 g raw chestnuts, peeled

Melt the butter in a medium frying pan over medium-high heat and add the buckwheat. Toss until the butter has started to brown and the buckwheat is smelling toasty, like popcorn, about 4 minutes. Remove from the heat, drain off the butter, and set the buckwheat aside.
Using the sharpest knife possible, slice the sirloin into slices about ¼ inch (6 mm) thick. Slice again into strips ¼ inch (6 mm)

wide, then crosswise into ¼-inch (6 mm) dice. Don't break out a ruler or anything. We do it by hand to get a mix of sizes and textures, so don't stress. Do the same with the coulotte. Set the raw meat in a bowl set over another bowl filled with ice, then refrigerate it. You want to keep this meat as cold as possible.
Combine the shallots, beef, and pimentón oil and toss to coat. Season with salt and pepper. To plate, spoon the beef mixture onto each plate and use the back of a large spoon to kind of flatten it into a disklike shape. You don't want to smush it, but it should be wider than taller, to give the toppings a place to sit without falling off. Sprinkle with the buckwheat and scatter some chervil on top. Using a Microplane, grate some horseradish over, followed by the smoked cheddar, then chestnuts (in that order).

OYSTER, LAPSANG SOUCHONG
Serves 4

For the gelée:
10 sheets bronze gelatin • 5 g lapsang souchong tea leaves • 330 g water • 20 g sugar • 10 g shoyu • 15 g mirin

For the spruce vinegar:
150 g young spruce tips or rosemary • 300 g unseasoned rice vinegar

For the oysters and assembly:
4 large East Coast oysters • 20 g chives, finely chopped • 25 g chervil • 100 g house-made almond milk • 15 g American osetra (white sturgeon) caviar

For the gelée:
Place the gelatin in a large bowl of ice water to soften. Set aside.
Bring a medium pot of water to a simmer and remove from the heat. Add the tea

APRICOT, BITTER ALMOND, ANISE HYSSOP

PERSIMMON, TANGERINE, BOURBON

POTATO DARPHIN, UNI, JALAPEÑO

BEEF TARTARE, SMOKED CHEDDAR, HORSERADISH

351

THE REFRESHING APPROACH THAT THEY HAVE TOWARD INGREDIENTS AND AMBIANCE IS SO FUN TO WATCH. THE DUO IS A PERFECT EXAMPLE OF TEAM BUILDING AND TEAM EFFORT.
— Daniela Soto-Innes

leaves and blanch for 20 seconds. Drain off and discard the water (this step removes some bitterness from the tea) and set the leaves aside. Heat the 330 grams of water to 190°F (88°C). Add the tea leaves and steep for only 5 minutes (if you oversteep, it'll be bitter). Strain the brewed tea into a bowl (discard the leaves). Squeeze the water out of the gelatin sheets and add to the hot tea along with the sugar and stir to dissolve. Stir in the shoyu and mirin. Pour into a shallow bowl or baking dish to set up. Once properly chilled, it should be similar to Jell-O (original recipe, not jigglers); scoopable but not too firm or crunchy.

For the spruce vinegar:
Blend the spruce with the vinegar in a blender until well combined. Strain and set aside.

For the oysters:
Bring a large pot of water to a simmer and remove from the heat. Gently lower the oysters into the water and leave them in there for about 5 seconds. This step doesn't open the shell and it doesn't cook them, all it does is slightly firm the oysters up for the perfect texture. Shuck the oyster (don't bother saving the liquor for anything, it won't stay fresh) and place in a small bowl with the spruce vinegar for about 2 minutes. Using a slotted spoon, remove the oyster. Cut it in half (or thirds if it's especially large). To plate, place the oyster in a bowl with a few small spoonfuls of the lapsang souchong gelée, chives, and chervil. Spoon almond milk around and top with caviar.

CHOCOLATE TART
Serves 4

For the pâte sucrée:
83 g all-purpose (plain) flour, plus more for dusting • 15 g buckwheat flour • 23 g cornstarch (corn flour) • 1 g kosher salt • 62 g unsalted butter • 41 g sugar • 1 g vanilla extract • 50 g eggs

For the praline feuilletine:
100 g hazelnuts • 100 g sugar • 20 g glucose • Canola (rapeseed) oil • 50 g feuilletine • 6 g kosher salt

For assembly:
Chocolate-Hazelnut Crémeux *(recipe follows)* • Flaky sea salt

For the pâte sucrée:
Whisk together the all-purpose (plain) flour, buckwheat flour, cornstarch (corn flour), and salt in a medium bowl. In a bowl, with an electric mixer on medium-high speed, cream the butter, sugar, and vanilla. Add the eggs, scrape down the sides of the bowl, and continue to beat until well combined. With the mixer on low, add the flour mixture and beat until well combined. Wrap the dough in plastic wrap (cling film) and pat to a square 1 inch (2.5 cm) thick. Refrigerate for at least 20 minutes. Preheat the oven to 320°F (160°C). Line a baking sheet with a silicone baking mat. Roll the dough on a lightly floured surface to a thickness of about ¹⁄₁₆ inch (1.5 mm). Using a 5-inch (12.5 cm) ring cutter, punch out rounds (you can chill it if it's feeling

too soft to cut). Shimmy four rounds of dough into four 4-inch (10 cm) ring molds, pressing to get into the edges of the ring mold. Place on the lined baking sheet. Bake until the dough is evenly golden brown, 12–15 minutes. Feel free to do this with the remaining dough and eat them as snacks.

For the praline feuilletine:
Preheat the oven to 320°F (160°C). Spread the hazelnuts on a sheet pan and bake until golden brown and fragrant, 10–15 minutes. Line a second sheet pan with a silicone baking mat. Combine the sugar, glucose, and just enough water to make the texture of wet sand in a large frying pan over medium heat. Once the caramel is a light amber-honey color, add the hazelnuts and stir to coat. Remove from the heat and quickly transfer the hazelnuts to the lined sheet pan and let cool completely. Break up the praline and transfer to a food processor. Pulverize until the texture is slightly grainy and chunky but won't break down further. Add a bit of canola oil and continue to process until the praline is smooth and the consistency of loose peanut butter (the longer you pulverize, the runnier it will become; be careful not to overprocess or add too much oil too fast). Transfer to a large bowl with the feuilletine and salt and mix to coat the feuilletine evenly (it'll look a bit wet, like a weird Rice Krispies treat). Set aside.

For the assembly:
Spoon a bit of the praline feuilletine into the bottom of the tart shell, using the bottom of a spoon to make an even layer. Pipe a generous amount of chocolate-hazelnut crémeux into the shell however you like. Finish with flaky sea salt.

CHOCOLATE-HAZELNUT CRÉMEUX
Makes about 600 g

1 sheet silver gelatin • 166 g milk • 166 g heavy (whipping) cream • 230 g gianduja chocolate, chopped • 60 g unsalted butter • Flaky sea salt

Soak the gelatin in a medium bowl of ice water until completely softened. Bring the milk and cream to a simmer in a medium pot. Squeeze the water from the gelatin, add to the pot, and stir to dissolve. Pour the hot milk/cream mixture over the chocolate in a heatproof bowl and use a hand mixer to blend until completely smooth. Add the butter and blend until smooth. Season with flaky sea salt and transfer to a large bowl (or pastry bag if piping) and place in the refrigerator to chill completely, at least 3 hours.

JEREMIAH STONE & FABIÁN VON HAUSKE VALTIERRA

JONATHAN TAM

DANIELA SOTO-INNES

RESTAURANT RELÆ
Copenhagen, Denmark

Noma has served as an incubator for some of the world's most extraordinary talent, and Jonathan Tam is no exception. The humble chef, a native of Edmonton in Alberta, Canada, arrived at Noma in 2007—little did he know that his first interaction there would end up shaping his career.

When Tam set foot inside Noma, the first person to greet him was the then sous-chef, Christian Puglisi. Tam was a recent graduate of Northern Alberta Institute of Technology's culinary arts and chef training program. He and Puglisi became close during their time together. In 2009, Tam (who by then was chef de partie at Noma) had internships in New York City at Corton, wd~50, and Momofuku Ko. In 2010, Puglisi opened the doors to another establishment in Copenhagen, Relæ. Tam returned to Denmark for the restaurant's opening, working alongside Puglisi once again.

The open kitchen at Relæ is a nod to its functionality, foreshadowing the transparency of its cuisine style. This speaks to what Tam and Puglisi set out to do in the beginning: to be free and spontaneous in their quest to bring accessible and progressive gastronomy to the city, and that is exactly what they have done over the past decade. Tam transitioned to head chef in 2016 when Puglisi shifted his focus to oversee all of the Relæ community including the team's newly acquired "Farm of Ideas." This farm supplies the restaurants with produce, meat, and raw milk, bringing hyper-seasonality and an element of sustainability to the business.

Under Tam's reign, the fare is clever yet unfussy and takes on a more freestyle approach than that of his predecessor. Generally speaking, Tam lets a core ingredient shine, with a maximum of three flavor elements in any dish. There is a minimalist feel to his cooking, though there is always more than meets the eye. And if Relæ's current accolades are any indication, the next decade (and those after it) will be good to this bright, young chef.

MENU

PIKE PERCH, SAVOY CABBAGE, AND BERGAMOT

SQUID DUMPLING

CROWN PRINCE PUMPKIN AND HABANADA PEPPER

POACHED DUCK, MUSHROOM, AND BRASSICAS

PUMPKIN AND SEA BUCKTHORN

BARLEY AND SOURDOUGH

PIKE PERCH, SAVOY CABBAGE, AND BERGAMOT
Serves 4

For the pike perch:
1 large pike perch • Salt • Juice of
1 bergamot

For the Savoy cabbage rolls:
1 head Savoy cabbage • 100 g lacinato kale (cavolo nero) leaves, blanched • 50 g black radish, julienned • 10 g preserved bergamot skin, julienned • Salt • Bergamot juice

Prepare the pike perch:
Clean, fillet, and skin the fish. Save the bones for the stock. Keep the loin and tail for this dish and reserve the rest of the fish for another dish.
Lightly season the fish with salt and allow to cure for 12 hours. This is just to firm up the fish, so it's better to use less salt, since we will season it more later on.
Meanwhile, place the fish bones in a large pot and cover with water. Bring to a simmer and cook for 30 minutes. Remove from the

heat and let the stock steep for 30 minutes, then discard the bones. Season with salt and bergamot juice, then strain through a fine-mesh sieve. Chill until ready to serve.

Make the Savoy cabbage rolls:
Separate the head of Savoy cabbage into individual leaves and wash well. Blanch the leaves in salted water until tender but still has its vibrant green color, shock in ice water. Pick out 8 large leaves. (Set aside 100 g of the remaining leaves to be used in the stuffing.)
Place these leaves on a cutting board and cover with a tea towel. Take a rolling pin and roll on top of the towel to flatten the leaves and soften the stem. Leave resting in the towel to absorb the excess water.
Slice the fish into thin slices.
Take 2 of the flattened cabbage leaves and overlap to form one large sheet. Lay out 6 slices of pike perch in the center of the leaf. Cut the Savoy and lacinato kale leaves into the same size as the fish. Then layer both on top of the fish. Make a thin line of julienned black radish down the center. Top the line

of radish with a few strips of the preserved bergamot. Season with salt and fresh bergamot juice.
Now we roll it, as if we are making a maki roll. Repeat to make 4 rolls in total.
To serve, trim off the ends of each roll, then cut into 5 equal pieces. Form a circle with the rolls, leaving space in the center of the plate for the broth. Spoon a bit of pike broth onto each piece, then add 3 tablespoons to the center of the plate. Season with a bit of salt and fresh bergamot juice on each piece. Serve at room temperature.

CROWN PRINCE PUMPKIN AND HABANADA PEPPER
Serves 4

For the confited pumpkin:
1 large Crown Prince pumpkin • Grapeseed oil, to cover

For the pumpkin and habanada puree:
3 habanada peppers • Grapeseed oil • Salt • 50 ml pear vinegar

To plate:
100 ml brown butter • Salt • Pear vinegar

Confit the pumpkin:
Preheat the oven to 300°F (150°C).
Halve the pumpkin horizontally to get a top and bottom piece. Scoop out the seeds.
Using a 2½-inch (6 cm) ring cutter, punch a hole in the center of each half to remove the core at the stem and blossom ends.
Cut into 4–6 triangle wedges depending on the size of pumpkin. Use a turning knife to remove the stringy wet parts from the surface of the flesh. Then take a peeler and remove the skin.
With the turning knife again, "turn" the pumpkin into a smooth and natural rounded oval shape: Think of the shape of a small mango. Reserve all of the skinless pumpkin trim for the pumpkin puree.
Each piece of turned pumpkin should weigh about 100 g (you will have more than 4 pieces).
Place 4 pieces of the pumpkin into a deep roasting pan. Cover the pumpkin with grapeseed oil until completely submerged in the oil.
Bake until tender, about 35 minutes. Test with a skewer, when you have reached the soft texture, remove from the oven and reserve in the warm oil until it's time to plate.

Make the pumpkin and habanada puree:
In a large pot, combine the reserved pumpkin trim, 1 whole habanada pepper, and the grapeseed oil. Bring to a light simmer over medium heat, then reduce to low and cook until the pumpkin is completely soft, about 30 minutes.
Drain off the oil (reserve it for the next time you cook pumpkin so it can be cooked in a flavorful pumpkin oil). Transfer the cooked pumpkin and pepper to a blender and add the remaining 2 (raw) habanada peppers and blend until smooth, adding water if necessary. Pass through a fine-mesh sieve. Season the pumpkin puree with salt and the pear vinegar. Keep warm.

To plate:
Place 2 spoonfuls of the warm pumpkin and habanada pepper puree in the center of the plate, gently spread the puree to make a round.
Carefully take the cooked pumpkin pieces out of the oil with a slotted spoon. Season the pumpkin with a good amount of salt and brush with pear vinegar and melted brown butter.
Gently place the pumpkin on the puree. Match the outside edge of the pumpkin wedges to the round line of the pumpkin puree so the pumpkin sits within the circle. Serve warm.

SQUID DUMPLING
Serves: 4

For the lompe dough:
600 g peeled russet potatoes, cut into large cubes • 18 g salt • 600 g tipo "00" flour

For the fried quinoa furikake:
100 g quinoa • Oil, for frying • 1 g chili powder • 1 g seaweed powder • 1 g dried shiso powder

For the "bulldog sauce:"
150 g onion, diced • 100 g celeriac, diced • 150 g crab apples, stemmed • 15 g garlic, minced • 40 g sugar • 40 ml black currant vinegar • 150 g tomato, diced • Water, as needed • Salt • 1 g freshly ground black pepper • 1 whole star anise • 2 g ground cumin • 4 g yellow mustard seed • 1 g cloves

For the squid:
500 g squid, cleaned with tentacles removed • "Bulldog Sauce" *(above)*

Make the lompe dough:
Steam the potato at 212°F (100°C) until completely cooked, about 15 minutes.
In a bowl, toss the potato with the salt. Vacuum-seal and let the potato ferment at room temperature for 10 days. (After this stage of fermentation, you can seal the potato in a new vacuum bag and keep in the fridge for another week.)
Pass the fermented potato through a tamis. Weigh out the potato then add an equal weight of flour. Knead by hand until thoroughly mixed and slightly sticky. Leave in a covered container to rest for 1 hour.

Make fried quinoa furikake:
Soak the quinoa in water overnight.
Drain off the water and let the quinoa dry on a paper towel.
Pour oil into a heavy pot and bring to 392°F (200°C). Working in small batches, fry the quinoa until golden brown. Drain on paper towels.
Toss the fried quinoa with the chili powder, seaweed powder, and shiso powder.

Make the "bulldog sauce:"
In a large pot, pan-roast the onion and celeriac until dark brown. Add the crab apples and continue roasting for 10 more minutes. Add the garlic and sugar and let the sugar caramelize lightly. Deglaze with the vinegar and tomatoes and cook until the tomatoes break down and reduce a bit. Transfer to a blender and blend until smooth by adding just enough water to allow for the vegetables to blend. Season with salt. Pass through a fine-mesh sieve and allow to cool down.

Prepare the squid:
Cut the squid bodies into 3 × 2-inch (8 × 6 cm) pieces. Score the squid diagonally on both sides. Marinate the squid pieces in just enough "bulldog sauce" to coat the squid.

To form the dumplings, on a floured surface, roll out the lompe dough to ¹⁄₁₆ inch (1.5 mm) thick. Cut into 4 × 3-inch (10 × 7 cm) rectangles.
Roll a piece of squid from a long side to form a cylinder. Place a cylinder of squid on one long edge of a rectangle of lompe and wrap the squid up in the dough so it's completely covered. Pinch both ends to resemble a wrapped piece of candy. Repeat to make all the dumplings and store in the fridge.
Steam the squid dumpling in a bamboo steamer on full steam for 2 minutes. Carefully remove the dumpling from the basket and let it rest for 2 minutes.
Sear the dumpling in a hot pan, on the bottom side until golden brown.
Place the dumpling roasted-side down on a cutting board and cut each dumpling down the middle crosswise into two pieces. Season each piece with a bit of salt and sprinkle some fried quinoa furikake on top.

To plate, place the two dumpling halves on a plate, one half showing the golden roasted side and the other showing the quinoa furikake side. Keep the two pieces together so it looks like one large dumpling. Serve right away.

POACHED DUCK, MUSHROOM, AND BRASSICAS
Serves 4

For the elderflower and padrón koshō:
100 g pickled elderflowers, stemmed and finely chopped • 50 g padrón pepper, seeded and finely diced • 40 g salt • 30 g water

For the master stock:
1 kg duck bones • 8 liters water • 200 g fennel • 45 g apple • 25 g onion • 10 g garlic • 10 g fresh ginger • 25 g fresh anise hyssop • 10 g dried shiitake mushrooms • 3 g juniper berries

For the brassicas:
100 g lacinato kale (cavolo nero) • 100 g green cabbage • 100 g Savoy cabbage • 100 g napa cabbage • 4 liters water • 15 g dried kelp • 15 g apple cider vinegar

For the duck:
1 duck crown (whole duck breast on the bone), aged for 3 weeks

For the mushrooms:
100 g fresh shiitake mushrooms • 100 g Judas ear mushroom • Salt • Apple cider vinegar • 20 g juniper oil • Duck fat • 100 g yellowfoot chanterelles • 100 g oyster mushrooms

> # JONATHAN'S COOKING IS THE TYPE OF FOOD I WANT TO EAT ALL THE TIME: LOTS OF VEGETABLES, FISH, AND HERBS.
> — Daniela Soto-Innes

SQUID DUMPLING

Make the elderflower and padrón koshō:
In a blender, combine the elderflowers, padrón pepper, and salt and blend together. It will be fine but not completely smooth. Store in airtight container and allow to ferment at room temperature for 3 days. After 3 days, mix in the water. Store in airtight container until ready to use. This *koshō* will hold for many weeks.

Make the master stock:
Place all the ingredients in a large stockpot and simmer for 10 hours. Strain through a fine-mesh sieve. Chill until use.

Prepare the brassicas:
Prep the kale and cabbages into bite-size strips around 1½ × ¾ inch (4 × 2 cm). Only use the tender soft leafy parts and remove any thick midribs and stems. Wash and keep each type separate.
In a pot, combine the water and keep and cook on a light simmer for 30 minutes. After 30 minutes, strain out the kelp. Remove half of the seaweed broth and refrigerate. Keep the other half warm. Bring the seaweed broth to a simmer, and adding each vegetable separately, blanch for about 1 minute (depending on the vegetable) just enough to soften but still have a bite. Each type of cabbage will require a different cooking time.

Add the cooked vegetables to the cold seaweed broth and leave to marinate in the refrigerator for at least 1 hour.
One hour before serving time, add the vinegar to the vegetable and seaweed brine. Take 1 teaspoon of the elderflower koshō and spread a thin layer on the bottom of a serving bowl. Layer the different cabbages on top of the koshō. Repeat to make 4 bowls and keep chilled until ready to plate.

Poach the duck:
In a pan, heat the master stock to 167°F (75°C) and keep at this temperature. Place the duck in the stock and let it poach until the duck reaches an internal temperature of 113°F (45°C), about 25 minutes, but check routinely during this cooking time. Remove the duck from the poaching liquid and let rest for 10 minutes in a warm spot.
Heat up a sauté pan and add the duck crown to crisp up the skin until golden. This will also cook the duck, so be careful not to leave it on the heat for too long. Aim to have the duck reach 118°–120°F (48°–49°C), then let rest for about 15 minutes. With carryover the duck should reach 124°F (51°C). Keep warm.

Prepare the mushrooms:
Bring a small pot of the master stock to a low simmer. Place shiitake and Judas ear

mushrooms in the warm broth and let simmer until tender, about 3 minutes. Remove the mushrooms from the poaching liquid and season with salt, cider vinegar, and the juniper oil.
In a sauté pan, heat some duck fat. Add the chanterelle and oysters mushrooms and sauté. Season with salt and cider vinegar.

To serve, remove the duck from the bone and cut into thin slices. Each portion should weigh 100 g.
Place one portion of duck in the center of a warm serving plate. Make 4 small (20 g) bundles of each type of mushroom. Place the mushrooms around the sliced duck. Strain the duck-poaching liquid and sauce on top of the duck and mushrooms. Serve with cabbage on the side.

Note: Each day after cooking we refresh the master stock with new aromatics if needed, bring up to boil, and chill before storing in fridge. After each use it will be more flavorful and aromatic. If the stock is treated properly it can be used for a very long time. There are chefs that specialize in Chinese cooking that have kept a "master stock" for years.

JONATHAN TAM

OMAR TATE

SELASSIE ATADIKA

HONEYSUCKLE PROJECTS
Phildelphia, Pennsylvania,
United States

MENU

AMERICAN SALAMI

PAISLEY PARK

NEW YORK OYSTER
CIRCA 1826

A LINE CATCH

Omar Tate spent the first phase of his career pushing forward on the same journey as many chefs before him: head down, long hours, learning constantly, and trying to get ahead. His work landed him in some of the most notable kitchens in New York City and Philadelphia, from A Voce and Meadowsweet to Russet and Runner & Stone. But a moment of clarity in 2017 led Tate to take a step back and pursue a journey of his own—both figurative and literal—away from the usual grind of chef life. This began with diving into his roots through literature, and ultimately brought him back to his childhood home in Philadelphia, then to South Carolina to visit the site of the plantation on which his ancestors were enslaved.

This profound exploratory period of Tate's life has had a lasting impact on his subsequent work. For him, it was a matter of honoring his Black heritage in the same way chefs have historically told stories behind the food they make through their own culturally rooted nostalgia. In 2018, Tate launched Honeysuckle, a series of immersive pop-up dinners that seeks to communicate the narrative—past, present, and future—of Black culture in America. The name itself is inspired by Tate's memories of the smell of honeysuckle swirling around him when he opened the front door to his house as a young boy. Memories of his mother's fried fish, his neighborhood's deli sandwiches, and just-stirred drinks at home are also woven into the fabric of Honeysuckle, with Black history as its pattern. For Tate, a poet at heart, combating stigma through it all is a main motivator.

Guests of Honeysuckle have experienced Tate's tangible interpretations of history and society through dishes such as 1980s-inspired smoked turkey necks; "Cart of Yams" (charred sweet potatoes slow-cooked with yam molasses); honeysuckle ice cream; and "Clorindy," a powerful all-black take on tartare made of cubed meat, bell pepper, candied lemon peel, grilled scallions, and squid ink.

From day one, Honeysuckle has sought to redefine how soul food and traditional Southern cooking has historically been regarded.

AMERICAN SALAMI

For the live culture:
Salami • ½ cup (120 ml) water, at room temperature

For the salami:
5 lbs (2.2 kg) of lean pork • ½ lb (226 g) pork fat • 1 oz (20 g) of garlic clove • 2 oz (40 g) of dried sage • ½ oz (10 g) dried Carolina chile pepper • ½ oz (10 g) cracked black pepper • 3 oz (85 g) sea salt • Live culture *(above)* • About 12 corn husks

Make the live culture:
To create wild fermentation, use pieces of old salami that have live culture in them to inoculate the sausage. To do this, place the end of an old piece of salami into the water and give it a slight stir. Allow the meat to sit in the water for about 1 hour. Reserving the water, discard the meat.

Make the salami:
You will need a meat grinder, a ⅜-inch (1 cm) diameter grinding die, and a 3/16-inch (5 mm) diameter grinding die. You must begin this process by making sure that all of your meat and equipment are very cold. Grind half of the lean pork through the ⅜-inch (1 cm) diameter grinding die. Set aside when finished.
Dismantle the grinder and attach the 3/16-inch (5 mm) grinding die to the unit and grind the remaining lean pork, pork fat, and garlic all together.
In a bowl, mix together the coarsely ground lean pork, the finer pork/fat/garlic mixture, the sage, chile, black pepper, and salt. Sprinkle the mixture with the live culture water.
Stuff the sausage mixture into the corn husks. Use about 8 ounces (226 g) sausage per husk. (Over the course of curing, the sausage will decrease in diameter by 30 percent.)

To ferment your links, you will need to keep them warm and moist. Do this by putting a humidifier under the hanging sausages and then tenting everything with big garbage bags (bin liners) that are sliced open on one end. Use a water sprayer to spritz the sausages a couple times a day. Doing this prevents the casings from hardening. Keep the sausages hanging at room temperature (65–80°F/18–26°C) for 2 to 3 days, until you begin to see mold development on the husks.
Now you need to dry the sausages and turn them into salami. Hang them in a place that is about 50–60°F (10–15°C) with about 80–90% humidity (in most cases you will need to put a humidifier under your links). Spritz them with water once a day for the first 2 weeks.
If at any time you see black mold developing throw the sausages away. Black or green mold is dangerous. White mold is safe and a signifier of a healthy product.

After the first week of hanging, drop the humidity to 70–80%. On the third week, drop it again to 65–70% and hold it there until a total of 5 to 10 weeks has elapsed from the time the salami went into the chamber. After this amount of time you should have a servable salami.

PAISLEY PARK

4 small red beets • 2 blood oranges • 8 sprigs thyme, preferably lemon thyme • 2 cloves garlic • Extra-virgin olive oil • Sea salt • 1 head Romanesco cauliflower • 1 bunch parsley • Juice of 2–3 lemons • 1 head purple cauliflower • 1 purple carrot, purple radish, or both, tops reserved • Ground white pepper • ½ small shallot, brunoised • Raspberry vincotto (like a raspberry beret) • 1 bunch fennel fronds • 1 oz (28 g) Bull's Blood micro lettuce

Start a fire from oak wood and reduce to embers and ash (this is for roasting the beets). Meanwhile, cut the blood oranges into supremes, reserving the spent centers and peels. Squeeze the juice from the spent orange centers. Set aside half of the juice for roasting the beets and the other half for the vinaigrette.

Use foil to create individual packages for each beet to include: 1 beet, 2 thyme sprigs, blood orange zest, ½ clove garlic, blood orange juice, olive oil, and a sprinkling of sea salt.

Wrap each beet tightly in a foil package and set them to roast in the fire. You will need to rotate them periodically to ensure even cooking. This will take 1½–2 hours. Meanwhile, blanch the Romanesco and parsley separately and shock them in ice water. Blend them thoroughly together with the parsley stems included. You may need to add a little water to get a smooth consistency, but use as little water as possible to ensure the most flavorful product. Blend until smooth and the consistency of cream. Add sea salt to this blend and some lemon juice. Strain through a sieve and chill in a metal bowl or container over ice. Stir the mixture until thoroughly cooled. It is very important to get the puree cold as soon as possible. Using a mandoline, thinly slice the purple cauliflower and carrot and/or radish and set aside.

Make a light citrus vinaigrette with the reserved blood orange juice, an equal amount of lemon juice and olive oil, and a dash of salt and white pepper.

Remove the beets from the fire and peel them immediately while they are hot. Pour any liquid remaining in the foil packages into a bowl. Finely dice the beets and add them to the bowl with the liquid. Add the shallot and toss. Mix the salad and add salt as needed.

Lightly dress the shaved vegetables with the citrus vinaigrette.

Plate as desired using the Romanesco puree

AMERICAN SALAMI

as your flavor base on the plate. Build the beets and drizzle raspberry vin cotto into the salad (you will not need to use all of the beets in one salad). Arrange the shaved vegetables and picked herbs and micro lettuce. Serve cool to room temperature.

NEW YORK OYSTER CIRCA 1826

For the oyster fat:
1 jar preshucked oysters • 1 quart (1 liter) organic non-GMO canola (rapeseed) oil

For the soup:
3 oz (85 g) Oyster Fat *(above)* • 1 small Spanish or Vidalia onion, thinly julienned • 2 stalks celery, thinly julienned • 2 cloves garlic, smashed • Sachet (½ oz/14 g toasted black pepper and 1 fresh bay leaf, crushed to release its oils) • ¼ bunch thyme • 1 quart (1 liter) oyster liquor or clam juice • 2 quarts (2 liters) heavy (whipping) cream • Salt • Lemon juice

For the celeriac confit:
4 oz (225 g) European butter • Grated zest of ½ lemon • Salt • 1 sprig thyme • 1 celeriac, brunoised

For the oyster crackers:
1 cup (128 g) all-purpose (plain) flour • Pinch of salt • ¼ cup (32 g) very cold European butter, shaved • About 2 tablespoons (16 g) cold water • Egg wash • Sea salt, for garnish

For plating:
Freshly shucked oysters (preferably from Long Island Sound, New York) • Thyme leaves • Cracked black pepper • 1 Honeycrisp apple, brunoised • Pickling liquid from sweet chow-chow pickles • 1 sprig rosemary, picked

Make the oyster fat:
The best equipment for this is a heavy-bottomed stainless steel pot over an induction burner.

Reserving the liquor from the jar, drain the oysters and lay them out onto food-safe sport towels. Pat them until as dry as possible. Place them in the heavy-bottomed pot and pour the oil directly over. Set your induction to 140°F (60°C) and cook for 4 hours. The oysters will shrivel and the oil should turn a hue of green and give off an amorous odor of sweet oyster.

OMAR TATE IS AN ARTISAN WHO IS ABLE TO MASTERFULLY CRAFT JOYS, PAIN, LAUGHTER, AND THE SOUNDTRACK OF THE BLACK EXPERIENCE INTO HONEST, THOUGHTFUL, AND DELICIOUS DINING EXPERIENCES.
— Selassie Atadika

After 4 hours, blend the oysters and oil in a blender. Strain through a fine chinois. The final product will look like a tannish to grayish color fat and have a consistency similar to a heavy aioli or mayonnaise. Allow to cool and refrigerate immediately. Or if you do not intend to use it immediately, it freezes very well.

Make the soup:
In a medium pot, combine the oyster fat, onion, celery, garlic, sachet, and thyme and sweat down the vegetables until they are soft and translucent. Be careful not to let the vegetables take on any color.
Pour in half the oyster liquor and reduce until it is almost evaporated. Add the other half and repeat. (It's useful to have more oyster liquor than necessary to add later for thinning or added flavor.)
Pour in half the heavy cream, increase the heat, and cook to reduce. Be careful not to allow the cream to rise and boil over. Reduce it until it becomes thick. You will notice that the cream will begin to caramelize as you reduce it. Use a wooden spoon to scrape the bottom of the pot and sides to reincorporate the caramelization back into the mixture. You want the sugars to add to the depth of the stew. It will require constant attention and stirring to ensure that the cream does not scorch and that the soup is evenly flavored.
Continue adding cream by the pint and reducing until all of the cream is incorporated. Remove the sachet and thyme and blend your soup thoroughly. Add salt and lemon juice to taste. Strain the stew through a chinois. Your final product will be amberish brown and have the consistency of a cream of mushroom soup. Reheat the soup to piping hot for serving.

Confit the celeriac:
In a sauté pan, melt the butter and add the lemon zest. Add a pinch of salt and the thyme. Add the celeriac and slowly cook over low heat until just cooked, 10–12 minutes.

Make the oyster crackers:
In a medium bowl, mix together the flour and salt until evenly distributed. Add the butter and cut in. Pour in the water and work the dough until it comes together. The dough should be slightly dry but will hold together and be workable.
Use a rolling pin to roll the dough out to about ⅛ inch (3 mm) thick. Use a ¾ inch (2 cm) diameter ring cutter to cut the crackers. Place the cut crackers into the freezer to chill for 15–20 minutes. Save the remaining dough for future use.
Preheat the oven to 425°F (218°C).
Arrange the crackers on a baking sheet. Use a pastry brush to coat the surface of the crackers with the egg wash and sprinkle gently with sea salt. Bake the crackers for about 8 minutes, rotating the pan halfway through.

To plate:
Place one raw oyster into a shallow 2½-inch (6 cm) diameter bowl. Add about a dime-size (¾ inch/2 cm) amount of celeriac confit directly atop the oyster and pour in boiling hot oyster soup to cover entirely and come just under the rim of the bowl. Garnish with two oyster crackers, tender leaves of thyme, and cracked black pepper.
Serve the soup alongside a raw oyster in the shell with a dime-size amount of Honeycrisp apple, a small amount of chow chow pickling liquid, and a small pinch of rosemary.

A LINE CATCH

1 medium whole perch, scaled and gutted, fins trimmed • Salt • 1 lb (450 g) young new potatoes • Fat of your choice (I like leaf lard) • Freshly cracked black pepper

For the beer butter:
1 can (12 oz/355 ml) American pilsner • ½ onion, sliced • 1 clove garlic • 1 sprig rosemary, lightly charred • 1 tablespoon (15 g) Creole mustard • 1 tablespoon (15 g) raw Ethiopian honey • ½ lb (225 g) cold European butter • Salt • Raw apple cider vinegar

For the greens:
3 cloves garlic, smashed • 1 small Spanish or Vidalia onion, thinly julienned • Fat of choice (I use leaf lard) • 1 bunch turnip greens • 1 bunch tatsoi • 1 bunch wild lamb's quarters • 1 bunch chard • 1 bunch wild mustard greens • Salt and freshly ground black pepper

For plating:
Black walnuts • Celery leaves • Lemon, for squeezing

Season the fish lightly with salt 2 days prior to cooking.
The day of cooking, start a fire of oak wood and reduce to hot coals.
When the coals are ready, add the potatoes directly to the coals at the perimeter of the heat. You will need to monitor this carefully and rotate the potatoes during the process to ensure that they are cooked evenly and avoid any burning. This will take 45 minutes to 1 hour.
Once the potatoes are close to being finished, oil the fish with the fat and season with salt and freshly cracked black pepper. Gently grill over the coals and potatoes until cooked through.

Meanwhile, make the beer butter:
In a saucepan, combine the beer, onion, garlic, and rosemary and cook until reduced by three-quarters.
Add the mustard and honey to the beer reduction and set over low heat. Begin to add the cold butter little by little until it is all incorporated and emulsified. Season with salt and apple cider vinegar to taste.

Prepare the greens:
In a large pot, combine the garlic, onion, and fat. Stir and cook to sweat. Once sweated, add the greens and lightly season with salt. Cook the greens down until just done. They should still have a deep green hue and fresh texture.
By this point your potatoes should be finished. Brush any excess ash off of them with a clean towel. Smash them and add them to the pot of greens off the heat. Toss them to coat in flavor and greens and add more salt and pepper to taste.

To plate:
Spoon out a bit of potatoes and greens. Place the grilled fish over the vegetables and shave the black walnut directly over the fish. Spoon the mounted beer butter over the fish and garnish with celery leaves and a squirt of lemon juice.

AMERICAN SALAMI

A LINE CATCH

OMAR TATE

PIM TECHAMUANVIVIT

KIN KHAO, NARI, NAHM
San Francisco, California,
United States, and
Bangkok, Thailand

DAVID KINCH

While working in Silicon Valley after graduate school, Pim Techamuanvivit longed for the home cooking of her native Thailand. The Thai restaurants she went to in the United States did not evoke any of the tastes she was searching for, but she knew nothing about reproducing those flavors herself. She decided then that she must learn to cook, and each time she visited Thailand, she added at least one of her grandmother's recipes to her repertoire, learning from her aunts and other family cooks.

Meanwhile, work had her jet-setting around Europe and dining solo. It was the early 2000s, and she began collecting her thoughts and photographs in a widely read food blog called Chez Pim. In 2014, she opened her first restaurant, Kin Khao, in San Francisco. There, Techamuanvivit serves Thai food as she remembers it from home, with the use of local California ingredients; in a green curry, for instance, in place of chicken she substitutes rabbit, closer in texture to Thailand's chewy poultry. On the menu, the nam prik long rua—spicy shrimp paste relish with caramelized pork jowl and catfish—apprises diners that it is not for Thai food novices.

A couple of years and many accolades later, Techamuanvivit was invited to lead Nahm, a Michelin-starred restaurant in Bangkok known for melding traditional Thai cooking and fine dining. She doubled down on the kitchen's commitment to small artisans and farmers across Thailand. The restaurant now makes all its curries in-house, sources ingredients such as heirloom rice and small-batch fish sauces, and serves versions of dishes she remembers as a child, such as kanom jeen nam prik (fermented rice noodles in a spicy sweet sauce of coconut, makrut lime, and shrimp).

Techamuanvivit opened Nari in San Francisco in 2019. Here she designs menus to more fully showcase the depth and breadth of Thai cooking, including dishes like kapi plah, a mash of prawns and shrimp paste with green Meyer lemon and samphire. The name Nari means "woman" in both Sanskrit and Thai, and for Techamuanvivit, this articulates who is at the heart of Thai cuisine.

MENU

MIANG

CHRYSANTHEMUM AND GREEN MANGO SALAD

SQUID AND PORK JOWL

NAM PRIK ONG

SQUID AND PORK JOWL
Serves 4

For the jowl:
10 oz (283 g) palm sugar • 2 cups (475 ml) fish sauce • 3 lb (1.4 kg) pork jowl • 5 shallots, roughly chopped

For the squid sauce:
10 cloves garlic, roughly chopped • 6 green bird's-eye chilies, seeded and roughly chopped • ½ cup (100 g) palm sugar • 5 tablespoons fish sauce • 4 tablespoons fresh lime juice

For assembly:
2 lb (905 g) squids, cleaned • Chopped peanuts • Roughly chopped cilantro (coriander)

Prepare the jowl:
In a pot, melt the palm sugar into the fish sauce over low heat until the sugar fully dissolves. Because the sweetness of the palm sugar and the salinity of the fish sauce vary from brand to brand, please taste the sauce first. The balance here should be the balance you're aiming for in the finished dish. It should be equally sweet and salty.
Add the jowl, shallots, and enough water to just cover. Bring to a boil and reduce to a bare simmer. Cook the jowl until tender, 4–5 hours.
Remove the jowl from the cooking liquid and reserve the liquid. Set the jowl aside to chill in the fridge. When the jowl is cold, cut it into 2- to 3-inch (5 to 7.5 cm) chunks. Reduce the cooking liquid until caramelized and thick. Set the fish sauce caramel aside.

Make the squid sauce:
Pound the garlic and chilies in a mortar and pestle to form a rough paste. (Chopping is fine if you don't have a mortar and pestle.) Push the paste to one side of the mortar. Add the sugar to the middle of the mortar and grind until the sugar has dissolved. Add the fish sauce and lime juice and stir everything to combine. Set the sauce aside.

To assemble the dish:
Warm 4 pieces of the jowl in the fish sauce caramel.
Grill 6–10 squid until just cooked.
Place the squid and the jowl on the plate. Drizzle the fish sauce caramel over the pieces of the jowl. Spoon the squid sauce over the squid and a little more on the plate. Garnish with peanuts and cilantro (coriander).

NAM PRIK ONG
Serves 4

For the paste:
20 g puya chili, seeded and chopped • 50 g shallots, chopped • 50 g garlic, chopped •

SQUID AND PORK JOWL

15 g galangal, chopped • 15 g lemongrass, chopped • 25 g red miso or Thai fermented bean paste

For the pork:
½ cup (120 ml) rice bran oil or neutral oil • 500 g ground pork • 500 g tomatoes, peeled and roughly chopped • Fish sauce

For serving:
Fresh vegetables • Fried pork rinds

Make the paste:
Process all the paste ingredients in a mortar and pestle or in a food processor until fine.

Prepare the pork:
In a saucepan, heat the oil and the paste and cook until fragrant. Add the pork, stir to mix well with the paste, and cook for a couple of minutes. Add the tomatoes and cook over low heat until the pork is tender and the tomatoes soft. Season with fish sauce to taste.

To serve:
Serve with fresh vegetables and pork rinds.

MASSAMAN CURRY OF LAMB SHANK

NAM PRIK ONG

CHRYSANTHEMUM AND GREEN MANGO SALAD

A DYNAMO OF A WRITER, AND POSSESSOR OF A WEALTH OF INFORMATION AND CULTURAL KNOWLEDGE ABOUT THAILAND, SHE IS CREATING NEW BENCHMARKS FOR WHAT THAI RESTAURANT CUISINE CAN BE.
— David Kinch

MIANG

PIM TECHAMUANVIVIT

KWANG UH

MAY CHOW

MENU

KIMCHI FRIED RICE

NOOROOK (KOJI)

GIM (SEAWEED)

CELERIAC PASTA

PICKLE SAMPLER

HOUSE-FERMENTED
KOMBUCHA AND TEPACHE

BAROO
*Los Angeles, California,
United States*

He is unlikely to say it himself, but Kwang Uh epitomizes Los Angeles. An immigrant from South Korea celebrated for cooking astonishingly detailed comfort food in a bare space in a strip mall in a nondescript part of the city, he melds modern Korean and Los Angeles farmers' market with Buddhist leanings and much fermentation. His first venture, Baroo, opened in 2015 and captivated LA diners. After a sojourn at a Korean monastery with monk Jeong Kwan, he followed up his by-then-closed restaurant with the pop-up Baroo Canteen, a tiny experimental and developmental eatery inside the Union Swapmeet in East Hollywood, which ran through the end of 2019. This was a venture with his new wife, Korean-American Mina Park, whom he'd met at the monastery. They are currently working on a fast-casual concept, Shiku, and a new Baroo.

When Uh first opened Baroo with Matthew Kim, whom he met at hospitality school, their budget only included one staffer, a dishwasher; the menu was written on a blackboard. Baroo was a restaurant with no sign, but before long, a queue. In this humble setting, Uh prepared kimchi fried rice with a dozen components, starting with basmati rice instead of the traditional short-grain white rice; fermented pineapple to replace the pungent cabbage; and bacon, Peruvian potato chips, and gremolata in the mix, all topped with a slow-cooked egg. Diners came craving the house-made kombucha tea, vivid pickles, nourishing grains, and heady smacks of *gochujang* aioli, kombu dashi, aged Parmesan, and shiso-fermented *mu* radishes.

Weaving methods and flavors from his experiences cooking in New York, Denmark, Spain, and Italy together with lessons learned from Jeong Kwan, Uh creates a cuisine that is all-embracing, thrilling, and finely balanced. Uh always intended Baroo to be an experimental kitchen and cites "connnectedness and energy" in the Buddhist sense as more important to his restaurants than service or ambiance.

KIMCHI FRIED RICE
Serves 4–6

For the pineapple salsa:
¼ pineapple, peeled and brunoised • ½ Granny Smith apple, peeled and brunoised • 2 stalks celery, peeled and brunoised • ½ jalapeño chili, chopped • 1 teaspoon Tabasco sauce • 1 teaspoon Himalayan pink salt • 90 ml citrus champagne vinegar • 1 tablespoon yuzu juice • 2 tablespoons extra-virgin olive oil

For the gremolata:
4 tablespoons pine nuts • 3–5 cloves garlic, sliced • 3 cups (70 g) fresh basil leaves, rinsed and spun dry • 1 cup (20 g) fresh flat-leaf parsley leaves, rinsed and spun dry • ½ teaspoon kosher (flaked) salt • 1 cup (90 g) finely grated Parmigiano-Reggiano cheese • 120 ml extra-virgin olive oil

For the sous vide eggs:
1 egg per serving

For the fried purple potato chips:
3 medium purple potatoes • 2 liters canola (rapeseed) oil • Kosher (flaked) salt

For the steamed basmati rice:
Basmati rice • Kosher (flaked) salt

For the pineapple kimchi:
1 medium napa cabbage • 2.5% kosher salt (ratio to cabbage) • Strained juice of 1 pineapple • 1½ cup pineapple kimchi liquid (from previous batch) (optional)

For the sautéed pineapple kimchi:
Fermented pineapple kimchi • Extra-virgin olive oil • Wild sesame oil • Salt • Fermented green plum syrup

For plating:
1 tablespoon olive oil • 30 g sautéed Pineapple Kimchi *(above)* • ½ teaspoon yondu (Korean umami essence) • 150 g steamed Basmati Rice *(above)* • Smoked paprika • Koji powder • 1 Sous Vide Egg *(above)* • A pinch each of mixed buckwheat (roasted) and quinoa (popped) • A pinch of

Maldon salt • ½ tablespoon Pineapple Salsa *(above)* • ½ tablespoon Gremolata *(above)* • 7–10 Fried Purple Potato Chips *(above)* • A pinch of shredded roasted seaweed • 4 pinches of microgreens

Make the pineapple salsa:
In a large bowl, combine the diced pineapple, apple, celery, and jalapeno. Stir in the Tabasco, salt, vinegar, yuzu juice, and oil.

Make the gremolata:
Toast the pine nuts and sliced garlic in a toaster oven for about 5 minutes. In a food processor, roughly mince the toasted pine nuts and garlic. Add the basil, parsley, and salt and pulse several times more until well mixed. If needed, use a rubber spatula to scrape the sides of the bowl. Transfer the mixture to a bowl, add the Parmigiano-Reggiano and olive oil, and mix all together.

CELERIAC PASTA

Make the sous vide egg(s):
Set a circulating water bath to 62.5°C. Gently add the egg to the water bath and cook for 1 hour 7 minutes.

Make the fried purple potato chips:
Peel the potatoes and cut into slices a scant ¹⁄₁₆ inch (1 mm) thick on a mandoline. As you work, transfer the potatoes to a bowl with enough cold water to cover them, and stir to release starch. (Let them sit about 2 hours.) Drain the potatoes and pat dry.
Pour 4 inches (10 cm) oil into a deep-fryer and heat the oil to 338°F (170°C).
Fry the potatoes, turning occasionally to cook evenly, until crisp, about 2 minutes. Using a slotted spoon or sieve, transfer to paper towels to drain. Season with salt.

Make the basmati rice:
Rinse the rice under running water for at least 10 minutes to remove starch and impurities, then soak in cold water for at least 30 minutes.
In a saucepan, combine the rice, cold water, and salt. Bring to a boil, then remove from the heat and let it sit until just before al dente, 3–6 minutes. (This takes into account the carryover cooking and the time of stir-frying when serving. It's basically the boiling method of cooking rice but it's an easier way to control the doneness.)
Drain in a large sieve and spread the rice out to cool down, stirring from time to time to flip the rice over for an even cooling process.

Make the pineapple kimchi:
Chop the napa cabbage into 1-inch (2.5 cm) pieces, rinse thoroughly and drain. In a large sterilized bowl, toss cabbage with salt and let sit for 2–4 hours, until the cabbage is wilted and has released its liquid. Transfer the cabbage and the liquid to a sterilized jar and pour in the pineapple juice and kimchi liquid to cover. Place a lid on the jar and store in a cool, dry place for 1–2 weeks.

Sauté the pineapple kimchi:
Drain the kimchi to remove excess juice at least before 30 minutes before cooking. Heat a wok on a turbo stove for stir-frying until it's almost smoking hot. When the wok is ready, drizzle in the oil and add the drained kimchi. Stir-fry quickly by making instant fire using traditional wok technique. Season lightly with wild sesame oil, salt, and fermented green plum syrup.

To plate:
In a wok, heat the olive oil, add the sautéed kimchi, and cook about 20 seconds. Season with the Yondu. Add the rice and stir-fry all together in the wok for 1 minute.
Put the fried rice in a bowl and sprinkle evenly with smoked paprika and koji powder. Place a sous vide egg in the center of the fried rice, scatter with the buckwheat and quinoa, and sprinkle Maldon salt on the egg.
Put the pineapple salsa on the right side of the egg, a quenelle of gremolata on the left side, fried purple potato chips on the top side, and shredded roasted seaweed on the bottom side. Put a pinch of microgreens on four points between the garnishes.

CELERIAC PASTA
Serves 4–6

For the vegetable kombu mushroom dashi:
Vegetable trim, leftover from other dishes (e.g., carrot, leek, celery, fennel, onion; avoid strong aromatic ingredients) • Filtered water, preferably low mineral content • 20–40 g high-quality dried kelp • 8–10 medium-large dried shiitake mushrooms

For the celeriac puree:
1 medium to large celeriac, peeled and cleaned • Milk • 1 teaspoon celery salt • 1 teaspoon pink sea salt, plus more to taste • 80 g butter • 40 g heavy (whipping) cream, warmed • 160 g Vegetable Kombu Mushroom Dashi *(above)* • Yondu, Bragg liquid aminos, or other soy or fermented vegetable essence (optional)

For the pasta:
520 g flour, preferably tipo "00" • 170 g semolina flour • 4 eggs, preferably organic • 8 egg yolks • 1 tablespoon sea salt • 1 tablespoon extra-virgin olive oil • Rice flour, for dusting

For the lemon crème fraîche:
Grated zest and juice of 2 lemons (juice strained) • 225 g crème fraîche

For the celery crudité:
5 stalks celery • ½ Granny Smith apple • 1 teaspoon yuzu juice • ½ teaspoon good-quality olive oil • Pink sea salt

For the celery ash:
7 stalks celery

For serving:
1 quart **Vegetable Kombu Mushroom Dashi** *(above)* • Celery leaves (picked from stems but light yellow leaves only)

Make the vegetable kombu mushroom dashi:
In a stockpot, combine the vegetable trim with four times the amount of water by volume. Add the kelp and mushrooms. Set over heat to come to a boil, but when it's just about to boil, remove from the heat and cover with a lid. Let sit for 10 minutes, then take out the kombu and let it sit for another 30 minutes. Strain the dashi and save the mushrooms for another use.

Make the celeriac puree:
Cut the celeriac into rough 2-inch-ish (5 cm) chunks. Put them in a bowl, add milk to cover, and add the celery salt and pink sea salt. Cover with plastic wrap (cling film) and steam until fork-tender, 45 minutes to 1 hour. Drain the celeriac and reserve both the celeriac and the cooking liquid. Meanwhile, in a saucepan, make a beurre noisette, whisking constantly.
In a food processor, combine the cooked celeriac chunks, beurre noisette, and dashi. Season with salt and Yondu (if using), then blend all together. Adjust the consistency of liquid by adding some celeriac cooking liquid or kombu broth. Adjust with more salt if needed. Strain through a chinois and let it cool in an ice bath, then portion into a container.

Make the pasta:
In the bowl of a stand mixer, mix the "00" flour and semolina together and make a well in the center. Put the whole eggs and yolks in the well and add the salt and oil. Mix the egg mixture in the well with chopsticks.

Attach the dough hook and mix the dough on speed level 2 until the dough forms a ball shape and leaves no trace in the bowl as it is kneaded.
Hand-knead the dough for about 10 minutes, until it's not sticky and forms a shiny surface. Then let it rest wrapped in plastic wrap (cling film) for at least 3 hours at room temperature.
When it's ready, use the roll and fold method a few times to shape the dough into a square. In a pasta roller, start to roll the dough out gradually increasing the thickness settings from 1 to 6 (roll the pasta dough 3 times each on settings 1 and 2; then once each on settings 3 through 6). Place the sheet of dough on a work surface dusted with rice flour and cover with a damp towel.
Set up the pasta shape attachment (tagliatelle), then cut the pasta into noodles. Portion it, then semi-dry the pasta on wooden boards at room temperature.

Make the lemon crème fraîche:
In a bowl, whisk together the lemon zest, lemon juice, and crème fraîche. Reserve in a container.

Make the celery crudité:
Peel off the fibrous layer of celery, then cut into 2½-inch-ish (6 cm) lengths. Cut the lengths into 1/16-inch (1.5 mm) julienne. Peel the apple and cut into 1/16-inch (1.5 mm) julienne. Toss with the yuzu juice to prevent oxidization.
Combine the celery and apple and season with sea salt to taste.

Make the celery ash:
Preheat the oven 450°F (230°C).
Slice the celery as thinly as possible. Spread evenly on a sheet pan. Roast until an even charcoal-like color, 40–50 minutes.
Let cool, then grind to a fine powder in a spice grinder.

To serve:
In a pot, simmer the vegetable dashi (do not boil) until reduced almost by half.
Bring a large pot of water to a boil. Meanwhile, in a large sauté pan, heat the celeriac puree and a splash of the concentrated dashi. Lower the pasta in a pasta basket into the boiling water and cook to just shy of al dente. Pull the pasta out of the water and add to the celeriac puree. Season to taste. Plate the pasta in a shallow pasta bowl or plate. Place the celery crudité in the center, sprinkle the celery ash evenly over the pasta, drizzle with the lemon crème fraîche. Garnish with several celery leaves around the dish.

KWANG'S OBSESSION THAT GREAT NOURISHING FOOD FOR THE SOUL SHOULD BE SERVED TO THE EVERYDAY PEOPLE IS HEARTWARMING.

— May Chow

KWANG UH

COŞKUN UYSAL

TULUM
Melbourne, Australia

YOTAM OTTOLENGHI

Coşkun Uysal's cooking is so exceptionally modern, it's easy to forget that his culture is one of civilization's most ancient. A native of Istanbul, the chef and owner of Tulum in Melbourne makes eye-opening Turkish food, an often misunderstood cuisine he exalts with equal parts care and flair. With each plate, Uysal reveals truths about his homeland, his upbringing, and his own journey.

Outside its birthplace, Turkish food is frequently abbreviated, over-simplified to its greatest hits: kebab, *pide*, dips. At his ambitious Tulum, in the suburb of Balaclava, Uysal fearlessly expands these limits, exploring the culinary scope of his country in a truly intimate and original manner. The diners of Melbourne, one of the most discerning and diverse food cities in the world, have taken notice, entranced by Uysal's inimitable point of view. In 2019, the *Herald Sun* selected the restaurant as the best in all of Australia, just one of many accolades it has earned since opening in 2016.

Tulum, which Uysal owns with Turkish-Australian chef-restaurateur Kemal Barut, is named after the cave-aged cheese produced in myriad styles across Anatolia, a practical metaphor for the breathtaking regionality of Turkish gastronomy. But it is also a personal statement—*tulum* with fresh-baked bread and olive oil was one of many family meals prepared by Uysal's mother, Emine, who is his greatest inspiration in the kitchen. The chef's interpretation of her simple snack is a sliver of cheese topped with a jet black crisp of olive lavash, aside pinches of *dukkah* seasoning and a textbook-perfect quenelle of tomato jam.

This very dynamic cuisine—with timeless flavors enhanced by modernist technique and cutting-edge presentation—defines Tulum. Examples of Uysal's dishes are the ethereal beef dumplings called *manti* and the lauded *çilbir*, a humble dish of poached eggs in yogurt, all raised to stratospheric heights via fine-dining acumen gleaned through training in Turkey, the UK, and Australia. Uysal's enthusiasm for integrating stellar Antipodean meat, fish, and produce into his approach speaks to a chef who understands both where he has been and where he is.

MENU

COLD YOGURT SOUP (AYRAN AŞI)

OLIVE OIL AND ORANGE BRAISED LEEKS (ZEYTINYAGLI PIRASA)

BRAISED AND GRILLED OCTOPUS, BLACK OLIVE BISCUIT (AHTAPOT)

THE SULTAN'S FAVORITE LAMB, SMOKED EGGPLANT (KUZU)

CANDIED BABY EGGPLANT (PATLICAN REÇELI)

SEMOLINA YOGURT CAKE (REVANI)

For the braised leeks:
10 large leeks • 200 g olive oil • 2 onions, chopped • 3 g coriander seeds • 5 bay leaves • 3 g salt • 200 g orange juice • 250 g vegetable stock • 5 g sugar • Juice of 2 lemons

For the puffed wild rice:
250 g vegetable oil • 50 g wild rice • 2 g vinegar powder • 2 g sea salt

For the baby carrots:
2 baby red carrots • 2 baby yellow carrots • 2 baby purple carrots • 10 g olive oil • 5 g pomegranate molasses • 1 g sea salt

For the Turkish tea prunes:
250 g dried prunes • 300 ml water • 5 g black tea leaves • 1 cinnamon stick

Braise the leeks:
Trim the leeks and remove a few of the outer layers, then slice, discarding the tough green parts, and wash under running water. In a saucepan, heat 100 g of the olive oil, then stir in the onions, coriander seeds, bay leaves, and salt. Cook for 5 minutes. Add the leeks and cook for another 5 minutes.

COLD YOGURT SOUP (AYRAN AŞI)
Serves 6

For the cold yogurt soup:
500 g yogurt • 2 liters water • 50 g cooked chickpeas • 50 g cooked barley • 1 cucumber thinly sliced • 1 radish thinly sliced • 10 fresh mint leaves finely chopped • 10 fresh sprigs dill finely chopped • 2 g salt • 10 g olive oil • Juice of 1 lemon

For the dill granita:
1 liter water • 150 g fresh dill • 50 g apple cider vinegar • 2 g xanthan gum

Make the cold yogurt soup:
In a bowl, stir all the ingredients together until it reaches a thick, soupy consistency. Refrigerate so that it's cold, ideally ready for use the next day.

Make the dill granita:
Set up an ice bath. In a small pot of boiling water, blanch the dill, then shock. Squeeze any excess water from the dill, then put into a blender with the 1 liter water, the vinegar, and xanthan gum. Blitz for 3 minutes until the water becomes bright green. Strain into a container and transfer to the freezer. Run a fork through it every 20 minutes to obtain a granita.
To serve, pour the cold soup straight from fridge into a very cold soup bowl, and add the granita on top.

OLIVE OIL AND ORANGE BRAISED LEEKS (ZEYTINYAĞLI PIRASA)
Serves 12

For the spiced milk:
500 ml whole milk • 100 g honey • 50 g glucose • 5 cinnamon sticks • 10 whole cloves • 3 whole star anise • 1 cardamom pod • 2 g grated nutmeg

For the spiced milk granita:
500 ml whole milk • 100 g honey • 50 g glucose • 5 cinnamon sticks • 10 whole cloves • 3 whole star anise • 1 cardamom pod • 2 g grated nutmeg • 2 g sorbet stabilizer • 2 g xanthan gum

Prepare the baby eggplant:
In a deep bowl, mix 4 liters of the water and the lime and refrigerate for 24 hours. The lime will sink and the clear water on the surface will be used.
Cut the baby eggplants in half.
Carefully scoop the clear water from above the lime sediment over the eggplants and soak in the fridge for another 24 hours.
The next day, remove the eggplants from the fridge and drain, then wash under cold running water for 10 minutes.
In a large pot, combine the eggplant, sugar, cloves, cinnamon, and remaining 3 liters water and cook over medium heat for 2 hours.
Add the lemon juice and cook for 5 more minutes. Remove from the heat and leave to cool.

Make the mulberry molasses ice cream:
In a saucepan, heat the milk and cream to 185°F (85°C).
Add the milk powder, molasses, and glucose, then simmer over medium heat for 5 minutes until the glucose dissolves. Add xanthan gum and stabilizer and whisk for 5 minutes over medium heat.
Pour the mixture into a blender and blitz. Strain into a Pacojet beaker and freeze. Remove from the freezer and spin the ice cream up in the Pacojet. Return to the freezer for 1½ hours before use (this extra 1½ hours ensures the perfect consistency).

Make the spiced milk:
In a deep saucepan, combine the milk, honey, glucose, and spices and simmer over medium heat for 30 minutes to infuse the milk.
Remove from heat and leave the spices in the milk until the mixture reaches room temperature. Strain and keep at room temperature to serve.

Make the spiced milk granita:
In a saucepan, combine the milk, honey, glucose, and spices and to 185°F (85°C) over medium heat for 30 minutes. Add the stabilizer and xanthan gum and whisk until the powders are dissolved.
Strain into a Pacojet beaker and freeze. Remove from the freezer and spin the granita up in the Pacojet. Return to the freezer for 1½ hours before use (this extra 1½ hours ensures the perfect consistency).

Add the orange juice and vegetable stock, then cover and simmer over medium heat for 30 minutes.
Remove the leeks from heat and add the sugar, lemon juice, and the remaining 100 g olive oil.
Let stand at room temperature.

Make the puffed wild rice:
In a pot, heat the oil to 374°F (190°C). Add the wild rice, which will first sink to the bottom and then, after about 2 minutes, it will puff and rise to the surface. Once all the rice has done so, remove from the heat and drain the rice. Transfer to paper towels to remove any excess oil. Add the sea salt and vinegar powder to the rice. Set aside.

Prepare the baby carrots:
Peel the carrots and use a Japanese mandoline to cut the carrots thinly. Dress them with the olive oil, pomegranate molasses, and salt. Set aside.

Make the Turkish tea prunes:
Place all ingredients in a saucepan and boil until the prunes are soft, about 10 minutes. Remove from the heat, cover, and let steep for 30 minutes.

Remove the cinnamon stick and blitz the rest with a blender to a fine purée. Strain and keep in a container for future use.

To serve, arrange the leeks in a circle on each of twelve warm plates, then cover with the baby carrots. Divide the puffed rice between the plates, next to and on top of the carrots. Pour the leek sauce next to the vegetables and add a coin-sized dollop of prune purée to each plate.

CANDIED BABY EGGPLANT (PATLICAN REÇELI)
Serves 12

For the baby eggplant:
7 liters water • 300 g hydrated lime (calcium hydroxide) • 3 kg baby eggplant • 3 kg sugar • 10 whole cloves • 2 cinnamon sticks • Juice of 2 lemons

For the mulberry molasses ice cream:
800 ml whole milk • 200 g heavy (whipping) cream • 60 g whole milk powder • 120 g mulberry molasses • 20 g glucose • 2 g ice cream stabilizer • 2 g xanthan gum

To serve, place one eggplant on each of twelve very cold plates. Add a scoop of ice cream next to each eggplant and divide the granita between the plates. Pour the spiced milk in the middle of each plate and serve.

SEMOLINA YOGURT CAKE (REVANI)
Serves 12

For the sugar syrup:
500 ml water • 400 g sugar • Juice of 1 lemon

For the revani:
4 eggs • 250 g sugar • 250 g semolina • 500 g all-purpose (plain) flour • 10 g baking powder • 10 g shredded coconut • 250 g yogurt • 250 g vegetable oil • Grated zest of 1 lemon

For the coconut water wafer:
350 g coconut water • 90 g egg whites • 60 g powdered (icing) sugar • Grated zest of 1 lemon • 2 g xanthan gum

For the coconut milk sugar syrup:
500 ml water • 400 g sugar • 500 g coconut milk • Juice of 1 lemon • 10 g rose water

For the coconut milk granita
125 ml water • 90 g sugar • Juice of 1 lemon • 200 g coconut milk • 200 g yogurt

Make the sugar syrup:
In a deep saucepan, bring the water and sugar to a boil over medium-high heat. Reduce the heat to low and stir constantly for 3–5 minutes until the sugar dissolves completely and the mixture is clear. Stir in the lemon juice and remove from the heat. Refrigerate for at least 1 hour to chill.

Make the revani:
Preheat the oven to 320°F (160°C). Grease a 10-inch (25 cm) square cake pan with butter.
In a mixer, blend the eggs and sugar for 5 minutes until the sugar dissolves and the eggs become pale and fluffy.
In a bowl, mix together the semolina, flour, baking powder, and shredded coconut. In a separate bowl, mix the together the yogurt, oil, and lemon zest. Add the yogurt mixture to the flour mixture, and then add this to the egg mixture. Whip slowly so that it becomes an airy cake batter.
Pour the batter into the baking pan and bake for 40 minutes.
Pour the cold sugar syrup over the hot cake and let it soak in. Cool to room temperature.

Make the coconut water wafer:
With a blender, combine the coconut water and egg whites and blitz. Add the powdered (icing) sugar and lemon zest and blitz until the sugar dissolves. Add the xanthan gum and blend thoroughly.
Strain the mixture into the bowl of a stand mixer, attach the whisk, and whisk for 10 minutes, or until stiff peaks form.
Line a dehydrator tray with a silicone mat or parchment paper. Smooth the wafer batter to a scant ⅛-inch (2 mm) thickness. Dehydrate at 66°C for 4 hours or until crisp.

Make the coconut milk sugar syrup:
In a deep saucepan, bring the cold water and sugar to a boil, then immediately reduce the heat to low. Stir constantly until the sugar dissolves and the mixture is clear, 3–5 minutes.
Add the coconut milk, lemon juice, and rose water. Remove from the heat and let the syrup cool in the fridge for 1 hour.

Make the coconut milk granita:
In a deep saucepan, bring the cold water and sugar to a boil over medium-high heat, then immediately reduce the heat to low. Stir constantly until the sugar dissolves and the mixture is clear, 3–5 minutes. Add the lemon juice and remove from the heat. Let the syrup cool in the fridge for 1 hour.
In a blender, combine the coconut milk and yogurt and blitz. Add the cold sugar syrup until combined. Strain into a container, freeze, and run a fork through it every 20 minutes to obtain a granita.

To serve, cut the cooled cake into 4 cm squares. In each of 12 very cold bowls, pour some of the syrup, then place a square of cake on top. Cover half of each cake square with granita. Cut or break off large pieces of wafer and balance on the lip of each bowl. Cut a large piece of wafer and arrange on the lip of the bowl and serve.

THIS IS WHAT IS SO
COMPELLING ABOUT
COŞKUN'S COOKING:
IT'S TURKISH, IT'S
AUSTRALIAN, AND
IT'S ACHINGLY
CONTEMPORARY.
— Yotam Ottolenghi

CANDIED BABY EGGPLANT

COŞKUN UYSAL

DAVE VERHEUL

EMBLA, LESA
Melbourne, Australia

YOTAM OTTOLENGHI

MENU

HEIRLOOM BEET, RED ONION,
OLIVE, SALTED ELDERBERRY

WHITE BEEFSTEAK TOMATO,
COMTÉ, WILD FENNEL,
OLIVE BLOSSOM

WOOD ROAST RAINBOW
TROUT, CAFÉ DE
MELBOURNE BUTTER

FROZEN RICOTTA,
RHUBARB, ROSE GERANIUM,
FERMENTED BLOOD PLUM

KOMBU, CHOCOLATE,
PORCINI, LEMON THYME,
AND SOUR APPLE

Dave Verheul's favorite meal to cook for himself is chicken broth crowded with green vegetables and overcooked rice, finished with a drizzle of olive oil and a pinch of lemon zest. For dinner parties, it is fresh pasta. If he were consigned to eat one cuisine for the rest of his days, it would be Italian. All that for someone who had never eaten pasta until he was a teenager—and who then went on to become one of Australia's most esteemed chefs.

Verheul is the head chef of Embla, a food-centric natural wine bar in Melbourne, and Lesa, its upstairs sister restaurant. The establishments, simultaneously highly professional and casual, go beyond their on-point modern Australian menus and offer something ineffable. This unique touch can be attributed to his upbringing in Mosgiel, New Zealand, the next-to-farthest-south city on the globe—far afield from any global culinary capital. He was never especially interested in food; in fact, he was an amateur skateboarder and snowboarder from age fourteen until twenty-two, when a skating accident ended those careers. Feeling lost, he enrolled in university, where he found he enjoyed more cooking for his roommates than studying. He began working as a dishwasher at a Lebanese restaurant, and he soon learned to cook.

Verheul's culinary curiosity spurred a trip to London, where he worked at Gordon Ramsay's Michelin-starred Savoy Grill for a couple of years. His next stop was Sydney, in the kitchen of Brent Savage at Bentley, whose take on fine dining in a laid-back environment influenced Verheul's own projects. Around then, restaurateur Christian McCabe proposed to Verheul that the two open a restaurant. They called it the Town Mouse, and its innovative menu earned it international acclaim. In 2015, Verheul opened Embla (again with McCabe) to much excitement.

The small plates emphasize the use of their wood oven and fermentation of all kinds: beef tartare is dressed with ginger, coastal arugula, and lemon shio koji; smoked trout rillettes come with fermented tomato and a dusting of rose petals; a wood-roasted whole rainbow trout sops up "café de Melbourne" butter. At Lesa, opened in 2018, the food is more cerebral: preserved chicken is adorned with red orach (mountain spinach, in the amaranth family), grapefruit blossom, and pine nuts; lamb aged in koji is served with handfuls of green peas, eucalyptus, and borage leaves. Verheul has earned himself worldwide recognition, and his tireless creativity makes one wonder what else he has in store.

HEIRLOOM BEET, RED ONION, OLIVE, SALTED ELDERBERRY
Serves 6

For the beet terrine:
1 kg purple beets • 1 kg Chioggia beets • 1 tablespoon picked thyme • Sea salt

For the red onion cream:
100 g red onion, diced • 3 tablespoons cherry vinegar • 1 teaspoon Dijon mustard • ½ teaspoon sea salt • 1 teaspoon sugar • 35 g grapeseed oil

For assembly:
3 tablespoons preserved salted elderberries • 3 tablespoons chopped dried black olives • 3 tablespoons picked bronze fennel leaves • 6 tablespoons mixed dried cornflowers

Make the beet terrine:
Preheat the oven to 360°F (180°C). Wash and peel the beets, keeping the two types separate. Using a meat slicer or mandoline, slice the Chioggia beets as finely as possible, followed by the purple. In an appropriately sized square baking dish, start layering the purple beet slices. Every few layers add a little thyme and season

with salt. When you get toward the middle, start alternating the purple beets with the Chioggias, eventually graduating into solely Chioggias. Cover the top of the beets with parchment paper, then wrap the dish in foil. Bake until tender when tested with a skewer, 1–1½ hours. Remove from the oven and remove the foil.
Find a place in fridge where it will be safe from being knocked, place something on top to weight it down and compress the layers together as it cools, and leave overnight. The following day, gently unmold and slice into slabs ⅓ inch (1 cm) thick.

WHITE BEEFSTEAK TOMATO

FROZEN RICOTTA

VERHEUL'S FOOD HAS LEFT ME BREATHLESSLY IMPRESSED BY DISHES THAT ARE EITHER FERMENTED, COOKED OVER FIRE, OR OFTEN BOTH. IT IS INIMITABLE, AND UNFORGETTABLE.
— Yotam Ottolenghi

SESAME CLOUD

Make the red onion cream:
In a small pot, combine the red onion with cold water to cover. Slowly bring to a boil over medium heat. Once it has come up, remove from the heat and drain off the water. Transfer the onion to a stand blender and add the vinegar, mustard, salt, and sugar. Blend until smooth. With the machine running, slowly stream in the oil. Pass through a fine sieve and cool.

To assemble:
On your plate of choice, place a spoon of the red onion cream, scatter a teaspoon of the elderberries and dried olives over the cream, place a few fennel leaves around, then sprinkle liberally with the dried flowers. Finally place a slab of the beet terrine slightly off to the side.

WHITE BEEFSTEAK TOMATO, COMTÉ, WILD FENNEL, OLIVE BLOSSOM
Serves 6

For the Comté sauce:
250 g 12-month Comté cheese • 250 g ricotta whey • 1 garlic clove, sliced

For assembly:
3 medium white beefsteak tomatoes • 30 g fermented yellow tomato juice • Salt and freshly ground black pepper • 10 g pickled young fennel stems, sliced • 10 g salted green plums, diced • 10 g fermented fennel flowers • 10 g pickled olive blossoms • 5 g lemon basil buds • 5 g thyme flowers

Make the Comté sauce:
Using a box grater, grate the Comté cheese into a small pot. Add the whey and garlic. Cook over low heat until the cheese melts and the curds solidify again. Remove from the heat and let rest 20 minutes. Pass through a fine sieve making sure you retain the split cheese fat. Keep warm.

To assemble:
Cut the top and bottom off each tomato, then slice in half horizontally. Dress with the fermented tomato juice and season to taste with salt and black pepper. Painstakingly arrange a selection of all the pickles around the edge of each tomato half. Place a couple of spoons of the hot Comté sauce into a hot bowl of your choosing and place the dressed tomato on top.

WOOD ROAST RAINBOW TROUT, CAFÉ DE MELBOURNE BUTTER
Serves 2

For the Café de Melbourne (CDM) butter:
100 g white wine • 75 g oxidative sherry • 7.5 g fenugreek • 500 g butter, at room temperature • 125 g fermented tomato paste • 100 g hazelnuts • 75 g shallots, diced • 35 g Dijon mustard • 30 g capers • 2 cloves garlic, chopped • 10 g Melbourne Bitter

vinegar • 10 g smoked paprika • 3 g dried oregano • 3 g rosemary chopped • 2 lemon zest • 3 g cumin, toasted • 5 g salt • 1 g black pepper

For assembly:
10 g vegetable oil • 1 rainbow trout (350 g), butterflied and boned • Salt • 25 g orange juice

Make the Café de Melbourne (CDM) butter:
In a small pot, combine the white wine, sherry, and fenugreek and reduce by one-third. Strain and chill.
In a blender, combine all of the remaining ingredients with the chilled reduction and pulse until combined. Season the CDM butter to taste.

To assemble:
You are going to need a wood oven for this one, sitting at around 500°C. Lightly oil a cast-iron skillet wide enough to hold the trout. Season the underside of the fish and place skin-side up in the pan. Slather with a layer of the CDM butter. Cook in the wood oven for around 1½ minutes, preferably in a spot where the flame will blast over the top of the fish. Remove from the oven and season with the orange juice. Transfer to a suitable plate.

FROZEN RICOTTA, RHUBARB, ROSE GERANIUM, FERMENTED BLOOD PLUM
Serves 6

For the ricotta puree:
350 g ricotta in whey

For the frozen ricotta:
275 g Ricotta Puree *(above)* • 200 g cream • 150 g egg whites • Pinch of salt • 135 g sugar

For the whey caramel:
500 g whey (reserved from Ricotta Puree, *above*) • 50 g sugar • 20 g butter

For the olive oil meringue:
75 g egg whites • 120 g sugar • Water • 75 g olive oil

For the rose geranium base:
180 g sweet Moscato wine • 180 g water • 75 g sugar • 10 g fresh rose geranium leaves • Xanthan gum

For the geranium-plum syrup:
100 g Rose Geranium Base *(above)* • 50 g sweet yeast-fermented blood plum juice

For the rhubarb:
6 very skinny forced rhubarb stalks • 150 g Geranium-Plum Syrup *(above)*

Make the ricotta puree:
Hang the ricotta in a sieve set over a bowl for 6 hours. Reserve the whey. In a blender, blend the drained ricotta with enough of the reserved whey to form a smooth puree. Reserve the rest of the whey.

Make the frozen ricotta:
Place the ricotta puree in a medium bowl. In another bowl, whip the cream to soft peaks. In a third bowl, whip the egg whites with the salt, slowly adding the sugar until you have a glossy medium peak meringue. Fold all three mixtures together and spread out in a tray that is the right size to give you a layer of ricotta mixture about ¾ inch (2 cm) deep. Freeze until hard.
Once fully frozen, cut into 2½-inch (6 cm) disks and hold frozen.

Make the whey caramel:
In a small pot, combine the whey and sugar and slowly reduce until it turns golden brown. Blend in the butter and set in the fridge.

Make the olive oil meringue:
Place the egg whites in the bowl of a stand mixer fitted with the whisk. In a small pot, combine the sugar and enough water to wet the sugar. Cook to 243°F (117°C). Start whisking the egg whites at high speed and slowly pour the hot sugar syrup down the side of the bowl as you whisk. Once all of the sugar is incorporated, reduce the speed and whisk until room temperature. Once cooled to room temp, slowly whisk in the olive oil. Remove the bowl from the mixer and use a spatula to beat the meringue down until it is glossy and dense. Transfer to a piping bag and hold in the fridge.

Make the rose geranium base:
In a medium pot, combine the wine, water, and sugar and heat to 176°F (80°C). Add the geranium leaves, cover, and steep until cool. Strain and use a stick blender to blend in enough xanthan gum to give it a little body.

Make the geranium-plum syrup:
Blend the rose geranium base and fermented plum juice together.

Prep the rhubarb:
Using a knife, thinly slice the rhubarb stalks as finely as possible and at such an angle that the slice will end up being 1½ inches (4 cm) long. Vacuum-seal the slices with the geranium-plum syrup. Set a circulating water bath to 80°C and cook for 2 minutes. Chill in an ice bath. Decant into a container and chill.

To plate:
In your favorite bowl, place a teaspoon-size lump of the whey caramel in the bottom, and a few rhubarb slices around this to help insulate the ricotta. Working quickly, take a disk of the frozen ricotta, pipe the olive oil meringue in a ⅓ inch (1 cm) wide ring around the edge, then place some rhubarb slices in a circular pattern on top. Place this in the bowl and dress with some of the geranium-plum syrup.

DAVE VERHEUL

AARON VERZOSA

MARCUS SAMUELSSON

MENU

ALASKEROS
IVORY KING KINILAW,
NORTHWEST VERJUS,
WATERMELON RADISH

ANAK NI BET
ALASKAN SPOT PRAWN,
WILD MUSHROOMS, PNW
BAGOONG, ASSORTED SQUASH

MIKI
SOURDOUGH RYE MIKI,
HABANERO CHILI, SMOKED
HALIBUT SARCIADO

MARIA OROSA
ARCTIC CHAR, BLACK GARLIC
TALONG, WILD BLACK RICE,
OROSA SAUCE

CEDAR PLANK SUMAN
WHEAT BERRY, HAZELNUT
BISKOTSO, PUMPKIN SEED
GINATAAN

In 2018, Washington State native Aaron Verzosa, along with his wife and partner, Amber Manuguid, opened Archipelago in Seattle's Hillman City neighborhood. With just eight seats, the restaurant is an intimate expression of the couple's shared identity: They are both Filipino Americans raised in the Pacific Northwest, and they both see food as a way of navigating and expressing their identity.

After completing culinary training, Verzosa cooked at Basque restaurants Harvest Vine and Txori in Seattle before taking a research and development position with innovative founder of the Cooking Lab, Nathan Myhrvold. He also staged with David Toutain in Paris to expand his knowledge of hyper-modern gastronomy. All the while, he and Manuguid, who met at the University of Washington, dreamt of reconnecting with their heritage in a manner that made sense to them.

There is nothing quite like the food of the Philippines. The Southeast Asian country's tumultuous colonial past means that Chinese, Spanish, American, and indigenous influences have coalesced across centuries to create a cuisine that is a hybrid, to say the least. Additionally, Filipinos are one of the largest Asian immigrant groups in the United States. At Archipelago, Verzosa shares his own version of this story, a new vision of Philippine cuisine using only ingredients sourced within the Pacific Northwest. Manuguid gracefully handles the front of house.

There are modernist techniques in play at Archipelago, but Verzosa's ten-course tastings are rooted most deeply in Filipino flavors. He bridges the distance between his ancestral and American homes by cooking lechon palapa with pristine pork from nearby Puyallup, or pinakbet with greens grown by Filipino farmers in Wapato, Washington. His sinigang, a soup usually made with tamarind, instead gets its sour backbone from Pacific Northwest cranberries or apples. Every meal is a deft, engrossing story that only a chef as self-assured as Verzosa could tell.

ALASKEROS
Serves 4–6

For the fish:
1 kg ivory king salmon fillet • 40 g raw honey • 30 g coarse salt

For the fried shallot oil:
250 g shallots, thinly sliced • 500 g neutral oil

For assembly:
100 g verjus • 20 g apple cider vinegar • 80 g Fried Shallot Oil *(above)* • Salt • Watermelon radish, for garnish • Micro dill, for garnish • Micro mustard greens, for garnish

Cure the fish:
Brush the fish with the honey. Coat evenly with the salt. With gloves, rub the salt into the honey layer. Wrap carefully in parchment paper, and refrigerate overnight to cure slightly.

Make the fried shallot oil:
Place the shallots and oil in a canning jar. Set the canning jar on a trivet in a pressure cooker. Fill the pressure cooker with water to just below the bottom of the jar. Close the lid and bring up to full pressure. Turn the heat down to low and infuse for 1 hour. Cool the jars and refrigerate overnight. Decant the infused oil layer.

To assemble:
Cut the salmon into small cubes and place in a nonreactive container. Add the verjus, vinegar, and shallot oil and for 15–20 minutes. Season with salt to taste.
Serve the kinilaw garnished with watermelon radish and the micro greens.

ANAK NI BET
Serves 4–6

For the squash soup:
100 g cultured butter • 35 g camelina oil • 20 g first squash juice • 4 g baking soda (bicarbonate of soda) • 20 g salt • 600 g butternut squash, cut into ½-inch (1.25 cm) cubes, seeds and peels reserved • 800 g second squash juice • Salt

For the mushrooms:
200 g black trumpets • 100 g matsutake, torn into small pieces • 20 g cultured butter • 10 g garlic, minced • 40 g dry cider • Sea salt

For assembly:
80 g blue hubbard squash, cut into small dice • 15 g bagoóng (salted shrimp paste) • Salt • 8 spot prawn • Chili oil • Micro arugula, for garnish • Castelfranco, for garnish • Treviso, for garnish

In a small pan, melt the butter in the oil. In a pressure cooker, combine the first squash juice, baking soda (bicarb), and salt. Stir in the squash and coat evenly with liquid. Close lid and bring to full pressure. Cook for 20 minutes.

Roast the reserved seeds and peels, then pressure-cook with the second juice for 5 minutes. Strain this squash stock through a fine-mesh sieve into a blender.

Add the caramelized squash to the stock and blend until smooth and desired consistency reached. Season to taste.

Prepare the mushrooms:
Place a large cast-iron skillet over high heat. Add the mushrooms and caramelize. Add the butter and mix in the garlic. Deglaze with the cider. Season to taste with sea salt.

To assemble:
Caramelize the squash gently, and add the salted shrimp paste just before the squash is cooked through. Season to taste with salt. In a sauté pan, fry the spot prawns in a light coating of chili oil.

Plate the squash and top with the mushrooms. Garnish with micro arugula and the radicchios. Pour soup and dress with extra chili oil as desired.

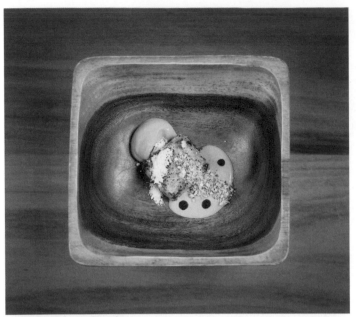

CEDAR PLANK SUMAN

ALASKEROS

ANAK NI BET

MARIA OROSA

MIKI

PAN DE SAL

ARCHIPELAGO IS
ONE OF THE MOST
UNIQUE AND
INTELLECTUALLY
INVIGORATING
RESTAURANTS
IN THE PACIFIC
NORTHWEST.
— Marcus Samuelsson

AARON VERZOSA

SILVANA VILLEGAS & MARIANA VILLEGAS

MASA
Bogotá, Colombia

DANIELA SOTO-INNES

Mariana and Silvana Villegas are a package deal. Both natives of Bogotá, Colombia, the sisters have forged their own paths in life, yet now have a growing culinary empire across their hometown. It is a joint venture that can be traced back to their mother's pastry business.

Martha Fernandez began her pastry production and supply operation, Morango, in 1990, catering to restaurants in the area before transitioning to management in the ice cream business. Morango continued to thrive as she balanced both efforts. Her husband (the girls' father), Juan Ramiro Villegas, left his job as a marine biologist to work alongside Fernandez on the production side of her baking business. Growing up with a front-row seat to this side of the industry inspired Silvana to pursue a culinary career and in 2003, at eighteen years old, she went to the Culinary Institute of America.

After two years at CIA, Silvana went to New York City for an externship at Jean-Georges, then returning to school for another year to complete her alma mater's pastry and baking program. After this, she returned to the city to work for Kurt Gutenbrunner and Gordon Ramsay and to hone her baking skills at Amy's Bread.

Meanwhile, her sister, Mariana, also moved to New York to begin her own culinary studies as a second career, ending up working at Cosme (opened by Mexican chefs Enrique Olvera and Daniela Soto-Innes) in various capacities. She settled into a front-of-house position and was opening general manager for its sister restaurant, Atla. After three years, she returned to Bogotá with Silvana to open their own bakery and restaurant, Masa. Silvana's vision of bringing European pastry to her hometown with Colombian ingredients became a reality, with Mariana serving as director of operations.

Masa quickly became a beloved mainstay in Bogotá, and three more locations have joined the portfolio. With their all-day bakery and restaurant concepts and open, minimalist design, the dynamic duo has gracefully captured the hearts of locals and visitors alike with no signs of slowing down.

MENU

BREAD BASKET: CINNAMON SUGAR TWIST, ROSEMARY AND SEA SALT TWIST, AREQUIPE CRUFFIN, FIVE-GRAIN WHOLE-WHEAT ROLL, COUNTRY SOURDOUGH, BUTTER CROISSANT

CHICHA DE PATILLA

PISTACHIO CROISSANTS

EGGS WITH SALSA MOLCAJETE, AVOCADO, AND FRESH CHEESE

TURKEY SANDWICH: SABANA CHEESE AND ROMESCO

CHOCOLATE CAKE WITH SINGLE-ORIGIN COLOMBIAN CHOCOLATE GANACHE

EGGS WITH SALSA MOLCAJETE, AVOCADO, AND FRESH CHEESE
Serves 4

For the salsa molcajete:
8 g ancho chilies • 600 g plum tomatoes • 96 g red onion • 3 cloves garlic • 10 g olive oil • 7 g salt

For assembly:
2 Hass avocados • 4 teaspoons butter • 8 eggs • 300 g Salsa Molcajete *(above)* • 120 g fresh cheese, grated • 4 slices sourdough bread, toasted • Cilantro (fresh coriander) • Salt

Make the salsa molcajete:
Preheat the oven to 572 °F (300 °C) Rehydrate the chilies in warm water.

Rub the vegetables with the olive oil and salt. Arrange on a sheet pan and roast until they are slightly burnt, about 20 minutes. Combine the roasted tomatoes, onion, garlic, and drained chilies in a molcajete or mortar, pound with a pestle until smooth.

To assemble:
Peel the avocado, halve, and pit. Place the halves flat and burn them with a torch. Cut each half lengthwise into ⅛-inch (4 mm) slices and fan out.
In a cast-iron skillet, heat the butter and add 2 eggs in each. Let the whites cook for few seconds, then spoon the molcajete sauce around. Add the cheese to half of the pan and let it melt while the eggs cook.
Serve with the avocado and the toasted bread. Sprinkle with cilantro (coriander) and salt.

TURKEY SANDWICH
Serves 8

For the romesco sauce:
2 g dried ñora chili • 400 g plum tomatoes, halved • 141 g red bell pepper, halved • 98 g onion, halved • 2 cloves garlic, peeled • 2.5 g salt, plus more to taste • 28 g olive oil • 35 g almonds, toasted and ground • 19 g bread crumbs • 10 g sherry vinegar • 2 g paprika • Pinch of freshly ground black pepper

To assemble:
360 g Romesco Sauce *(above)* • 16 (½-inch/ 1.5 cm) slices Whole Wheat Bread with Nuts and Raisins *(recipe follows)* • 140 g crisp green lettuce • 800 g Roast Turkey Breast *(recipe follows)* • 400 g Sabana cheese • 250 g avocado, sliced • 120 g cooked bacon slices

CHOCOLATE CAKE

TURKEY SANDWICH

I AM VERY CURIOUS TO SEE WHAT THE INCREDIBLY TALENTED SISTERS ARE GOING TO DO NEXT AS I'VE WATCHED THEM GROW TOGETHER WITH SO MUCH GRACE. — Daniela Soto-Innes

Make the romesco sauce:
Preheat the oven to 572°F (300°C).
Hydrate the ñora chili in warm water for 5 minutes.
Toss all the vegetables with salt and olive oil. Spread on a sheet pan and roast until they have some color, about 15 minutes.
Transfer the roasted vegetables to a blender, add the drained nora chili, and blend until smooth. Add the ground almonds, bread crumbs, vinegar, and paprika. Mix to combine. Season with salt and pepper.

Assemble the sandwiches:
Spread the romesco sauce on all the bread slices. Place some crunchy lettuce on 8 slices of bread.
Warm the turkey and the cheese together in the salamander or a broiler (grill). Place the turkey and cheese on top of the lettuce. Add some avocado slices, and crispy bacon.
Top with the remaining bread slices.

ROAST TURKEY BREAST
1.7 kg boneless turkey breast • 4 cloves garlic, smashed and peeled • 40 g Dijon mustard • 40 g soy sauce • 23 g salt • 8 g freshly ground black pepper • 1 tablespoon oregano • 1 tablespoon thyme • 2 bay leaves • 100 g red onion, sliced • 92 g celery, sliced • 72 g scallions (spring onions), chopped • 63 g carrots, sliced

Place the turkey breast in a medium high-sided roasting pan.
In a food processor, combine the garlic, mustard, soy sauce, salt, pepper, oregano, thyme, and bay leaves and blitz to combine. Place all the vegetables in a bowl, add the marinade and mix. Use your hands to spread all the mixture evenly under and over the turkey breast. Cover and refrigerate for at least 12 and up to 24 hours.
Preheat the oven to 365°F (185°C).
Roast for the turkey until the internal temperature is 165°F (75°C), 1 hour 30 minutes, basting every 20 minutes or so. Remove from the oven and set the turkey aside to rest before slicing. Strain the cooking liquid in the pan and reserve (discard all the vegetables).
When thinly slicing the turkey to make sandwiches, add some of the strained cooking juices to keep the turkey moist before serving.

WHOLE WHEAT BREAD WITH NUTS AND RAISINS
Makes 2 loaves

For the poolish:
105 g bread (strong white) flour • 1 g instant dry yeast • 105 g water (68°F/20°C)

For the bread:
335 g water (72°F/22°C) • 28 g panela, melted • 28 g honey • 213 g Poolish (above) • 262 g bread (strong) flour • 262 g whole wheat (wholemeal) flour • 4.62 g instant dry yeast • 19 g salt • 203 g raisins • 75 g walnuts, toasted • 58 g pecans, toasted • Butter for the pans • 26 g vegetable oil

Make the polish:
In a bowl, mix the flour, yeast. and water with your hands. Cover and allow to rest for 12 to 16 hours at room temperature (68°F/20°C).
When the poolish is ready to use, it will be double in size, and it will be covered with large bubbles.

Make the bread:
In a stand mixer fitted with the dough hook, combine the water, panela, honey, poolish, flours, and yeast. Mix on low speed until combined, 3 to 5 minutes Add the salt and mix on medium speed until it releases from the sides of the bowl, 5 to 6 minutes.
Add the raisins, walnuts, and pecans and mix until it releases from the sides of the bowl again. Transfer the dough to a bowl and set it in a cool place (68°F/20°C) for 2 hours for the bulk fermentation.
Just before shaping the dough, coat the pans with butter.
With a bench knife, divide the dough evenly in half. Work each portion of dough into a round shape. Let rest for 15 minutes. Lightly flour the top surface of the dough rounds, flip it over and fold the third of the dough closest to you up and over the middle. Stretch the dough horizontally and fold the right third over the center and fold the left side over the previous fold.
Cup your hands around the dough and pull it toward you rounding it while creating tension to close the seam.
Place the shaped dough seam-side down in the mold. Let rise in a warm place (81°F/27°C) for 1½ to 2 hours.
Preheat the oven to 445°F (230°C).
Bake until the loaves are golden brown, 25 to 30 minutes. Unmold and let cool on a wire rack before slicing.

CHOCOLATE CAKE WITH SINGLE-ORIGIN COLOMBIAN CHOCOLATE GANACHE
Makes one 8-inch (20 cm) cake

For the chocolate cake:
Butter for the pan • 350 g sugar • 337 g cake (soft) flour • 98 g unsweetened cocoa powder • 10 g baking powder • 11 g baking soda (bicarbonate of soda) • 5 g salt • 135 g eggs • 12 g vanilla extract • 122 g vegetable oil • 245 g whole milk • 184 g hot water

For the chocolate ganache:
300 g Santander single-origin chocolate (53% cacao), chopped • 300 g heavy (whipping) cream

For the chocolate glaze:
61 g sugar • 32 g water • 18 g unsweetened cocoa powder • 1 g gelatin sheet, hydrated in ice water • 19 g heavy (whipping) cream

Make the cake:
Preheat the oven to 330°F (165°C). Butter an 8-inch (20 cm) round cake pan.
In a bowl, combine the sugar, flour, cocoa powder, baking powder, baking soda (bicarb), and salt.
In a stand mixer, combine the eggs, vanilla and oil. Alternate adding the flour mixture and the milk and scraping down the sides of the bowl. Beat in the hot water.
Scrape the batter into the pan and bake about 45 minutes.

Make the ganache:
Place the chocolate in a heatproof bowl.
In a saucepan, bring the cream to just simmering. Pour the warm cream over the chocolate and let the two sit for a few minutes before stirring. Stir until smooth.

Make the glaze:
In a small saucepan, bring the sugar, water, and cocoa powder to a boil. Add the hydrated gelatin and the cream.

Assemble the cake:
Cut the cake horizontally into three equal layers.
Arrange 1 layer on a cake stand and spread ganache evenly over it. Top with another cake layer and ganache, spreading evenly, then the third cake layer. Refrigerate the cake until the ganache filling is firm, about 1 hour.
Spread a thin layer of ganache over the top and sides of the cake to make a crumb coat, then chill for 30 minutes.
Cover the cake with the chocolate glaze.
Decorate with chocolate fans.

PISTACHIO CROISSANTS
Makes 10 croissants

For the pistachio cream:
82 g cold unsalted butter • 98 g sugar • 82 g eggs • 53 g pistachio paste • 1 g rum • 100 g pistachio flour • 16 g cake (soft) flour

For the croissant dough:
170 g water (64°F/18°C) • 355 g plus 18 g bread (strong) flour • 43 g sugar • 9 g salt • 71 g unsalted butter, at room temperature • 7 g instant dry yeast • 177 g cold unsalted butter, cut into cubes • 18 g bread (strong) flour • Egg wash

Make the pistachio cream:
In a stand mixer, beat the butter and sugar until fluffy. Beat in the eggs and then the pistachio paste and the rum. Beat in the pistachio flour and the cake flour. Refrigerate until ready to be used.

Make the croissant dough:
In a stand mixer fitted with the dough hook, combine the water, 355 g of the flour, and the sugar and mix on low speed until combined, 3 to 5 minutes. Add the salt and room-temperature butter and mix on medium speed until it releases from the sides of the bowl, 5 to 6 minutes.
Transfer the dough to a bowl and set it in a cool place (72°F/22°C) for 45 minutes for the bulk fermentation.
Transfer the dough to a half-sheet pan, press to flatten it into a rectangle, and chill it in the refrigerator for 2 to 3 hours.
In a stand mixer fitted with the paddle, combine the cold butter and the remaining 18 g flour and beat until they come together. You don't want to mix it too long—it's a very quick process.
Mold the butter into a rectangle measuring roughly 8½ × 12 inches (22 × 30 cm). Place it on parchment paper and refrigerate briefly.
Place the dough (wrinkled part facing up) on a floured surface. Place the butter block on one side of the dough and fold the other half over. With your fingers, seal the "envelope," pressing down the edges.
Place the dough in the pasta sheeter, with the spine facing the rollers. Roll the dough until it's the size of a half-sheet pan. Rotate the dough 90 degrees and roll it again until it's ½ inch (1.5 cm) thick, keeping the edges straight and the corners square.
Make a business letter fold, cover the dough, and refrigerate for 20 minutes to rest.
Turn the dough 90 degrees from its position before it was refrigerated and repeat the same process two more times.
After completing the final fold, refrigerate or freeze.
When ready to make the croissants, roll the dough to ½ inch (1.3 cm) thick, cut triangles measuring 3½ inches (9 cm) on one side, with two long sides measuring 8¼ inches (21 cm). Roll the triangle up from the base, exerting gentle pressure with your fingertips.
Line a sheet pan with parchment paper. Place the croissants seam-side down in a warm place until they double their size.
Preheat the oven to 375°F (190°C).
Egg wash the pastries. Bake them for 12 to 15 minutes, with 5 seconds of steam. (Leave the oven on, but reduce the temperature to 350°F/175°C.)
Slice the croissants horizontally in half and spread some pistachio cream in the center. Replace the top and cover with sliced almonds. Refrigerate for 15 minutes.
Place the croissants on a parchment-lined sheet pan and bake until golden brown, about 12 minutes.
Sprinkle with powdered (icing) sugar and serve.

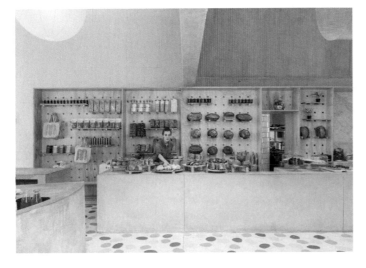

SILVANA VILLEGAS & MARIANA VILLEGAS

FRANCESCO VINCENZI

EYAL SHANI

MENU

"COME UN CARPIONE:" STURGEON, POMEGRANATE, SAGE

CAULIFLOWER, KALE, AND PECORINO CHEESE

PASSATELLI WITH BOURGUIGNON SNAILS AND ARTICHOKE BROTH

EMILIA BURGER BY MASSIMO BOTTURA

RISOTTO ALLA CACCIATORA

DUCK À L'ORANGE

SFOGLIATINA WITH LEMON, CAPERS, AND COFFEE

Franceschetta58 in Modena is a contemporary bistrot in the family of Massimo Bottura's three-Michelin-star Osteria Francescana. But like most younger siblings, it has inevitably come into its own, thanks to Francesco Vincenzi. Born in the northern Italian region of Emilia-Romagna, understanding and honoring the country's bounty of ingredients is at the top of his priority list. This is the foundation upon which his career as a chef has been built, his research processes and skills honed under the tutelage of Bottura himself.

Vincenzi, it can be said, is on the fast track to culinary stardom. His dreams of becoming a chef can be traced back to middle school, when a visit to Modena's esteemed Scuola Alberghiera e di Ristorazione di Serramazzoni sparked inspiration, compounded by the strong collective passion for cooking and family dining traditions in his hometown. He went on to study at the Scuola, and this would prove to be an integral career move, as the school became his connection to Bottura. Between his second and third years there, Vincenzi went to Osteria Francescana as a stagiaire (trainee). He was originally assigned to a front-of-house position, then talked his way into the kitchen for a second internship. In 2017, Vincenzi went to Franceschetta to trail then-chef Bernardo Paladini for six months, and when Paladini went to work on another project, Vincenzi settled into his new role.

Vincenzi often cites his family's cooking (particularly his mother's and great aunt's) as part of his story, their approach one of comfort and love, free of pretentiousness. Today, Vincenzi's own signature style combines his deep research of ingredients with personal travel experiences and memories, all while on a constant quest for growth and improvement. In 2019, Vincenzi was honored by international chef congress Identità Golose with a Best Italian Chef Under 30 award for his accomplishments thus far. In a way, Vincenzi is an ambassador for the cuisine of Emilia-Romagna, with pasta among his greatest strengths and passions alongside beans and rice. Like Vincenzi himself, his cooking has a strong, classic Italian identity, and its refreshing edge shines with youthful excitement.

PASTA E FAGIOLI
Serves 5

For the cooked beans:
100 g dried Trasimeno beans • 100 g dried Zolfino beans • 100 g dried red beans

For the cannellini cream sauce:
500 g dried white cannellini beans • 4 pieces Parmesan rind • 1 onion, julienned • 200 g Villa Manodori olive oil, plus more for the onion • 4 cloves garlic • 50 g fresh sage • 1 sprig rosemary

For the parsley powder:
1 bunch parsley

For assembly:
2 carrots, diced • 1 stalk celery, diced • Villa Manodori olive oil • Cooked Beans *(above)* • White Cannellini Cream Sauce *(above)* • 400 g mixed pasta

Prepare the beans:
Soak the three different types of beans separately in water (three times their weight) overnight.
Drain the beans and, keeping them separate, cook them in boiling water.

Make the cannellini cream sauce:
Soak the white cannellini beans in water (three times their weight) overnight.
Wash the Parmesan rind pieces and boil them in a pot of water for about 1 hour. Reserving the cooking liquid, drain the Parmesan rinds and let cool to room temperature. Cut them into ⅓-inch (1 cm) cubes and set aside.
Drain the cannellini beans. Brown the onion in a pan with a little oil. Add the beans to the onion and stir for a few minutes, then cover the ingredients with the reserved Parmesan rind cooking liquid and cook over low heat for about 2½ hours. While the cannellini beans cook, in a small pot, heat the 200 g olive oil to 154°F (68°C). Add 3 cloves of garlic, the sage, and rosemary and leave to infuse for 15 minutes. Strain the oil through a fine-mesh sieve and set aside until the beans are done.

ANGLER FISH, SUNCHOKE, RAPINI

TORTELLINI WITH PARMIGIANO REGGIANO SAUCE

Once cooked, blend the cannellini beans in a Thermomix with the flavored oil for about 5 minutes at medium speed. Strain the sauce.

Make the parsley powder:
Wash the parsley and remove the leaves. Chiffonade the leaves and set aside. Spread the parsley stems on a tray and dehydrate overnight at 113°F (45°C). Blend the dried stems to a powder.

To assemble:
Brown the carrots and celery in a little oil and set aside.
Drain the cooked beans and add them to the white cannellini cream sauce.
In a pot of boiling water, cook the pasta. Drain and return to the pot. Add the beans and cannellini cream sauce and toss the pasta over low heat. Add the celery and the diced onion, the Parmesan cubes, and the reserved parsley chiffonade.
Plate the pasta and finish with a dusting of parsley powder.

RISOTTO ALLA CACCIATORA
Serves 4

For the red pepper juice:
2 kg red bell peppers

For the red pepper powder:
Red pepper pulp (from Red Pepper Juice, *above*)

For the caper powder:
200 g capers from Pantelleria

For the capon stock:
1.5 kg capon, cleaned • 1 stalk celery • 1 carrot • 1 white onion • 3 bay leaves • 1 sprig thyme • 10 g freshly ground black pepper • 30 g sea salt • 200 g Parmigiano-Reggiano rinds

For the cacciatora rabbit sauce:
1 whole rabbit • 100 g black olives • 50 g capers from Pantelleria • 400 ml tomato sauce • 2 onions, thinly sliced • 3 cloves garlic, sliced • 2 red bell peppers, thinly sliced • Capon Stock *(above)* • Rosemary • Thyme

For the rabbit liver and heart:
200 g mixed rabbit heart and liver • Villa Manodori extra-virgin olive oil • 20 g Marsala

For assembly:
300 g Vialone Nano rice • Villa Manodori extra-virgin olive oil • Red Pepper Juice *(above)*, warmed • Aged (30 months) Parmigiano-Reggiano

Make the red pepper broth:
Clean the peppers and cook them in the combi oven at 320°F (160°C) and 40% steam for 3 hours.
When cool, juice them in a centrifugal juicer to separate the juice from the pulp.

The red pepper juice will be used to cook the risotto and the pulp to make the powder.

Make the red pepper powder:
Spread the pulp in a baking tray and dry in the oven at 167°F (75°C) overnight. Once dried, blend to a powder.

Make the caper powder:
Rinse the capers and spread on baking tray and dry in the oven at 167°F (75°C) overnight. Blend to a powder.

Make the capon stock:
In a stockpot, cover the capon with 10 kg cold water. Add the vegetables, herbs, pepper, and salt. Grate in the Parmigiano, bring to a boil, and simmer for about 5 hours. Strain through a chinois.

Make the cacciatora rabbit sauce:
Break the rabbit down into pieces. Place all the pieces in a bowl and add the olives, capers, tomato sauce, onions, and garlic and marinate overnight.
Remove the rabbit pieces (reserving the marinade) and blanch the individual pieces of meat. Transfer the rabbit to a large pan. Add the reserved marinade, capon stock to cover, and rosemary and thyme and cook until the rabbit is cooked through.

Meanwhile, prepare the rabbit liver and heart:
Purge the rabbit heart and liver in the milk for 3 hours in the fridge, then clean them with a knife by removing the veins. Cut them into small pieces, wash, and pat dry with paper towels.
In a hot pan with a drizzle of olive oil, pan-roast the heart and liver. Toss them with the Marsala.

To assemble:
After the rabbit has cooked, let it cool and then remove the meat from the bones. Finally blend the meat with the cooking juice of the livers.
In a pot, toast the rice with some olive oil. When the rice is toasted, add some hot water, then continue to cook risotto style, using the hot red pepper juice. Once the risotto is cooked, remove from the heat, stir in the creamy rabbit sauce, and add some extra-virgin olive oil and a little Parmigiano.
Put the heart and liver in a plate, cover them with the risotto, and garnish with the caper powder and red pepper powder.

FRANCESCO PERPETUATES ITALIAN TRADITIONS THAT
THE WORLD REMEMBERS BECAUSE OF THE FLAVORS
THAT PEOPLE LIKE HIM PRESERVE.
— Eyal Shani

EMILIA BURGER

FRANCESCO VINCENZI

TAKAYOSHI WATANABE

TERUZUSHI
Kitakyūshū, Japan

YOSHIHIRO NARISAWA

MENU

BLUEFIN TUNA TARTARE
WITH SEA URCHIN, CAVIAR,
AND SHISO FLOWERS

JAPANESE BLUE CRAB SHIP

JAPANESE LONGTOOTH
GROUPER SASHIMI

MUSHI AWABE
(STEAMED ABALONE)

KITA KYUSHU OYSTER WITH
WHISKEY JELLY

SABA BUTTERFLY
(MARINATED MACKEREL)

SAWARA ZUKE (SOY-DASHI
MARINATED MACKEREL)

KURUMA EBI (JAPANESE
TIGER PRAWN)

TENNEN HON-MAGURO
(WILD BLUEFIN TUNA)

GYOKU (JAPANESE SWEET
SOUFFLÉ-STYLE EGG)

Hidden away in Tobata, a coastal district of Kitakyūshū, on the southern island of Kyushu, Takayoshi Watanabe has made an international name for himself. Known for his theatrical performances and his embrace of local seafood, Watanabe has transformed his family's sushi business, Teruzushi, into a destination restaurant.

As a child, Watanabe never imagined becoming a celebrated chef. He grew up in his family's restaurant, and studied how to run chain restaurants at university. But he missed his hometown, and returned to Tobata to begin a rigid apprenticeship selected by his father. His next job, at a hotel, had him preparing sashimi for up to one thousand people a day. When he subsequently started to work at his family's business, it was also focused on catering and banquets. Soon, however, Watanabe realized he was seeking something more. He wanted to break out of the traditional, old-fashioned modes and delineate his own style. And so, he started breaking the rules of sushi restaurants.

When he began working at Teruzushi, Watanabe took on various non-cooking roles at first, then honed his vision and style as a sushi chef for many years after his predecessor asked him to take over. Now, Teruzushi is known for featuring unusual local ingredients. Every day Watanabe visits the market, selecting fish that almost exclusively come from either the Kyushu or the Yamaguchi coast. His signature dish is the "unagi burger"— hot rice enveloping a piece of charcoal-grilled eel, enclosed by a band of seaweed. In another trademark move, Watanabe carves raw mackerel into the form of a warbler to make a creation called "Butterfly."

Rather than the typical quiet and calm expected of sushi restaurants, the counter at Teru stages a rowdy show. Watanabe employs a dramatically long knife the curvature of which influences the sashimi's texture—and instead of setting the sushi on the counter in front of his guests, Watanabe balances sushi on his fingers for diners to pop into their mouths. He has become world-renowned, recasting the image and expectations of the traditional sushi experience with his own idiosyncratic flair.

GYOKU (JAPANESE SWEET SOUFFLÉ-STYLE EGG)

50 g cooked, peeled tiger prawn (or regular shrimp) • 50 g scallop • Salt • 30 g grated mountain yam (yamaimo) • 12 egg yolks • 100 g sugar • 7 egg whites

Preheat the oven to 300°F (150°C).
In a food processor, combine the shrimp, scallop, a pinch of salt, and mountain yam. Pulse to combine. Add the egg yolks and sugar and mix well.
In a bowl, whisk the egg whites into meringue, then add it to the food processor. Spread the egg mixture in a copper container lined with parchment paper.
Bake for 25 minutes. Rotate the pan and bake for 5 minutes more.

MUSHI AWABI (STEAMED ABALONE)

1 live abalone (Japanese recommended) • Kombu • Water • Sake • Salt • Japanese fish sauce

Plunge the whole abalone into 122°F (50°C) water for 10 seconds. Let the abalone cool for 5 minutes, then remove from the shell. Cut off the black parts encircling the abalone. Remove the liver and reserve it for the sauce. Pull out the mantle.
Put kombu in the bottom of the bowl, place abalone on top of it, and pour in water and sake in a ratio of 10:1 to cover abalone. Wrap the bowl with plastic wrap (cling film), then put it in a steamer at 210°F (99°C) for 6 hours. Reserve the cooking liquid to use in the liver sauce.
To make the liver sauce, boil the abalone liver in sake for 10 minutes. Push the liver through a sieve and add reserved abalone stock until desired thickness. Add salt and Japanese fish sauce to taste.

SABA BUTTERFLY (MARINATED MACKEREL)

1 fresh Japanese mackerel • Salt • Well-chilled rice vinegar • Battera • Seaweed

BLUEFIN TUNA TARTARE WITH SEA URCHIN, CAVIAR, AND SHISO FLOWERS

JAPANESE BLUE CRAB SHIP

KURAMA EBI

Fillet the mackerel, but leave the bones in. Cover the fillets completely with salt and let sit for 1 hour in the summer (2 hours in the winter) to remove the fishy smell and excess moisture from the fish. Wash the fish with cold water. Wipe with paper towel so completely dry, then rinse with vinegar. Cover fish with cold rice vinegar and marinate for 15–20 minutes.

Remove from the vinegar and rest it in the fridge for 1 day.

Remove the rib bones, pin bones, and skin before serving.

FUGU SHIRAKO (LOW-TEMPERATURE STEAMED BLOWFISH MILT)

Blowfish milt or cod milt •
Dashi • Usukuchi (light soy sauce)
• Mirin

Trim the veins off the milt, then cut into small pieces. Put it in ice water for 30 minutes.

Make a happo dashi by combing 8 parts dashi to 1 part usukuchi and 1 part mirin. Put the milt in the happo dashi and steam at 149°F (65°C) for 20 minutes. Serve immediately.

NODOGURO FISH TACOS

GOLD QUINTET

HE IS MAKING DAILY
EFFORTS IN DEVELOPING
NEW TECHNIQUES, AND
CREATING A STYLE OF
SUSHI ORIGINAL TO HIM
AND TO KITAKYUSHU.
HIS TALENT FAR
EXCEEDS THE THEATRICS
HE IS KNOWN FOR.
— Yoshihiro Narisawa

GYOKU

393

TAKAYOSHI WATANABE

DYLAN WATSON-BRAWN

ERNST
Berlin, Germany

EYAL SHANI

MENU

GOLDEN FRILLS

ENDIVE

ONION/WHEY

WALNUT/MILK/WALNUT OIL

DUCK

PEAR/SYRUP/PEAR
SCHNAPPS

Rich texture and deep, earthy tones serve as a visual welcoming committee at Ernst, Watson-Brawn's restaurant in Berlin. Beyond what meets the eye, the theme of the land continues into a deeper narrative. Close partnerships with local producers, many in the restaurant's immediate backyard of the German state of Brandenburg, drive the hyper-seasonal menu––an approach that makes Ernst a pioneer of the city's farm-to-table movement.

At seventeen, Watson-Brawn, a native of Vancouver, travelled to Japan with his father. At restaurant Ryugin, he was captivated by the meticulous, specialized, and simplistic approach to cuisine, and took the opportunity to stay and train under the guidance of Seiji Yamamoto. Another trip, this one to Paris, had a similar effect on him, and the combined cultural takeaways—both steeped in tradition and rooted in time and place—planted a seed in Watson-Brawn. After his experience in Japan, he spent some time in the great kitchens of New York and Copenhagen (including Eleven Madison Park and Noma), before moving to Berlin, where in 2014 he started Ernst as a pop-up with his partner and fellow Canadian Spencer Christenson, cooking for six guests in his apartment. During that time, they began sourcing from and building lasting relationships with producers from the region. The pop-up led to opening a permanent restaurant in 2017. At Ernst, the intimacy of the twelve-seat space (twice the size of the apartment setting it started in) is offset by the bevy of thoughtful courses—there are typically around thirty—though no two experiences are quite the same, because Watson-Brawn adheres strictly to the vicissitudes of microseasons.

There is a deeply personal element to dining at Ernst that comes with the nature of the team's sourcing, which translates to a close relationship with each producer. Guests are privy to frequent anecdotes and stories behind dishes and ingredients from the chefs, who can all speak to the details of their purveyors (and who sometimes forage wild ingredients themselves), bringing Watson-Brawn's passion and philosophy full circle.

ONION/WHEY

Kombu dashi • Small onions • Whey • Fennel fronds • Fleur de sel

Make the kombu dashi: Heat 500 ml filtered water and 6 g rishiri kombu to 140°F (60°C) and hold for 2 hours.
Find your favorite onions. Something not too sharp. Peel and halve. Grill over good charcoal until just blackened on the cut side. Cover the onions with whey and steam at 194°F (90°C) until just cooked through. The onions should retain bite but not be crunchy.
Blend fennel fronds with a bit of dashi immediately before plating. Pass through a fishnet sieve or Superbag.
Cut onion halves in half again. Plate and pour warm fennel dashi over them before finishing with a pinch of fleur de sel.

WALNUT/MILK/WALNUT OIL

Walnuts • Hazelnuts • Milk • Fleur de sel • Walnut oil

Find your favorite walnut tree. Ours is also on the dairy farm we work with. Buy all the walnuts.
Blend the best hazelnuts you can find with the best milk you can find. Raw milk if possible, high fat content preferable.
Crack the walnuts and blanch in boiling water seven times, being sure to change the water each time. This will leech out any bitterness. Peel the walnuts.
Warm the milk and season with fleur de sel. Toast the walnuts in a pan.
Pour the warm milk over the toasted walnuts and finish with walnut oil.

PEAR/SYRUP/PEAR SCHNAPPS

Pear • Hay • Simple syrup • Pear schnapps • Fleur de sel

Find your favorite variety of pear from your favorite farmer. In general, older trees will produce more complex fruit. Our favorite is from one tree from an orchard at the dairy farm we work with. Variety unknown. The best for this recipe would be a ripe, but firm pear with balanced acidity.
Juice pears and smoke the juice with hay. Make a simple syrup. (We use 150 g sugar to 250 g water.)
Peel the pears, remove the cores through the base, and completely cover with syrup. Cover and steam at 140°F (60°C) for 30 minutes. (After being held at this temperature, the pears will sustain eventual cooking at a higher temperature.)
Remove the pears from the syrup, leaving a bit of syrup in the container. Turn the oven to 320°F (160°C), no steam, and baste the pears every 5 minutes until they can be easily cut with a spoon and the syrup is reduced.
Remove the pears and brûlé until nicely caramelized on the outside.
Blend together the smoked pear juice, reduced syrup, and pear schnapps (we use Gräfin von Paris from Stählemühle) to taste.
Pour over the pears and serve with a pinch of fleur de sel.

PEAR/SYRUP/PEAR SCHNAPPS

395

DYLAN HAS A SECRET LANGUAGE WITH HIS PRODUCE, ESPECIALLY WITH THE VEGETABLES. IT IS AS IF HE WERE A GARDENER.

— Eyal Shani

397

DYLAN WATSON-BRAWN

BRADY WILLIAMS

CANLIS
Seattle, Washington, United States

DAVID KINCH

Since 1950, from atop Seattle's Queen Anne Hill, the iconic restaurant Canlis has held steady its glass-fronted gaze over Lake Union and the Cascade Mountains in the distance. The kitchen, now overseen by the founding family's third generation of owners, is helmed by Brady Williams. His way of delicately weaving tradition into his contemporary, place-based menus has breathed new life and energy into this institution of a restaurant.

When Williams started working at Canlis in 2015, he became the restaurant's youngest-ever chef, handpicked in a sweeping cross-country search. He was a last-minute contender, and when he was flown to Seattle to cook a test run, he didn't, like many others, come with suitcases filled with prepped ingredients. But he captivated the Canlis owners, and a few short months later, he started at his new post.

Williams was far from the presumed candidate. He had been working for two years as Carlo Mirarchi's sous-chef at hip Brooklyn pizzeria Roberta's and its sister two-Michelin-starred tasting-menu restaurant, Blanca. Prior to that, in Dallas, Texas, he helped Matt McCallister open FT33, considered one of the city's best restaurants and known for its artful, experimental cuisine.

At Canlis, Williams is creating head-turning menus that simultaneously channel the restaurant's storied past, invoke the bounty of the Pacific Northwest, and are infused with his own character and Japanese heritage. A barley porridge is topped with raw geoduck, shiso, green strawberries, and sorrel; a carrot is jacketed in cashew bits and celery and served alongside cashew pudding. One of the restaurant's historic mainstays, Wagyu beef, is served with kohlrabi, gooseberries, and horseradish jus.

Williams's unassuming audacity has earned him attention. He led Canlis to a rare four-star review from the *Seattle Times* and, in 2019, won a James Beard Award for Best Chef: Northwest.

MENU

CHAWANMUSHI
JAPANESE EGG CUSTARD WITH HEDGEHOG MUSHROOM AND GEODUCK

DUNGENESS CRAB RICE

SPOT PRAWNS
WILTED SPINACH IN A SAUCE OF SHELLFISH AND VERMOUTH

DUCK
ROASTED WINTER LUXURY SQUASH, QUINCE JAM, AND PUMPKIN SEED GOMASHIO

JAPANESE SWEET POTATO
BEE POLLEN GARAM, YUZU SHERBET, AND COCOA BUTTER CAKE

CHAWANMUSHI
Serves 4

For the dashi:
1 liter filtered water • 400 g kombu • 300 g shaved bonito

For the chawanmushi:
325 g eggs • 545 g Dashi *(above)* • 44 g mirin • 53 g white shoyu

For the geoduck:
1 live geoduck (from the Washington coast)

For the hedgehog mushrooms:
6 g grapeseed oil • 100 g hedgehog mushrooms • Salt • 10 g butter • 1 lemon, halved

Make the dashi:
Combine the filtered water and kombu bring up to 146°F (63°C). Once up to temp, remove and let steep for 30 minutes. Strain out the kombu, return the broth to 180°F (82°C) and add the shaved bonito. Once the bonito sinks, strain the dashi through a coffee filter.

Make the chawanmushi:
Use chopsticks to stir the eggs, being careful not to whisk too much air into them. Stir in the dashi, mirin, and shoyu.
Set a combi oven to steam at 195°F (90°C). Portion the custard into the cups of a yakumi pan (55 g per portion). Pour 202°F (94°C) water into the pan to come until halfway up the sides of the cups. Steam uncovered until the sides are set and the center is slightly jiggly when agitated, about 7 minutes 28 seconds. Allow chawanmushi to rest for 5 minutes.

Prepare the geoduck:
Set up an ice bath large enough for the geoduck to fit. Heat a large pot of water to simmering (around 180°F/82°C). Blanch the geoduck for 10 seconds in the hot water to release the outer membrane, then plunge in the ice bath until chilled. Using a paring knife, remove the geoduck siphon from the shell. Slide the membrane off the siphon. Using a sharp knife, thinly slice geoduck into slices a generous ⅛ inch (2 mm) thick.

Prepare the hedgehog mushrooms:
In a sauté pan, heat the grapeseed oil over medium-high heat until smoking. Add the mushrooms and a pinch of salt. Reduce the heat to medium and cook until the mushrooms are seared and starting to get tender. Add the butter and swirl the mushrooms in the pan until just cooked through. Finish with a small squeeze of lemon juice.
To serve, evenly place individual hedgehog mushrooms and geoduck slices on top of chawanmushi. Garnish with sliced chives.

SPOT PRAWNS
Serves 4

For the sea lettuce butter:
25 g kombu, cut into 1-inch (2.5 cm) strips • 25 g dried sea lettuce or wakame • 454 g clarified butter

DUNGENESS CRAB RICE

a single layer. Add a touch of very nice olive oil to the bags. Compress.

Make the shellfish nage:
In a saucepan, sweat the shallots and garlic until tender. Add the crab shells and toast until fragrant. Deglaze with the vermouth and vinegar and reduce until the liquid is evaporated. Add the chicken stock and miso and cook until reduced by half. Add the cream and reduce by half.
Pass through a fine-mesh sieve. Mount with butter and season to taste with salt and lemon.

Make the prawn butter:
In a large pan, toast the prawn heads. Add the butter and tarragon and cook until the butter starts to foam. Strain and cool.

Make the spot prawns:
In a small pot, heat the prawn butter to 140°F (60°C). Add the spot prawns and poach for 48 seconds. Transfer to a towel-lined tray and remove heads and shells.

Make the spinach:
To a shallow pan over medium heat add the oil and spinach. Add the shellfish nage and agitate spinach with chopsticks frequently to wilt. Finish with lemon juice.

To serve:
Place three spot prawns in a shallow bowl. Top with three slices of kohlrabi and some wilted spinach with its sauce. Add additional sauce to pool in the bowl and finish with a pinch of sea lettuce powder.

For the compressed kohlrabi:
1 medium-sized kohlrabi

For the shellfish nage:
140 g shallots • 60 g green garlic • 150 g crab shells • 250 ml vermouth • 100 ml white wine winegar • 600 ml chicken stock • 75 g green garlic miso • 500 ml heavy (whipping) cream • 115 g butter • Salt • Lemon juice

For the prawn butter:
1 kg prawn heads or shells • 4 pounds (1.8 kg) butter • 1 bunch tarragon

For the spot prawns:
500 ml of Prawn Butter *(above)* • 12 live spot prawns from the Salish Sea

For the spinach:
1 g grapeseed oil • 250 g Malabar spinach • 25 g shellfish nage • 1 g lemon juice

To serve:
Pulverized ulva (sea lettuce)

Make the sea lettuce butter:
Steep all seaweeds in the clarified butter at 145°F (63°C) for 1 hour. Strain out the seaweeds.

Compress the kohlrabi:
Trim the kohlrabi and shave into one long unbroken ribbon using a vegetable sheet cutter. Trim the ribbon into sections 5 inches (12.5 cm) long. Lightly salt the ribbons and arrange in vacuum bags in

KING CRAB WITH KANI MISO AND SAKE

MANGALITSA PORK WITH SPRING GARLIC AND TURNIP

HE HAS BREATHED
NEW LIFE AND ENERGY
INTO CANLIS, FORGING
HIS OWN STYLE WHILE
HONORING THE
TRADITIONS OF AN
AMERICAN INSTITUTION.
— David Kinch

BRADY WILLIAMS

JUSTIN WOODWARD

CASTAGNA
Portland, Oregon, United States

DAVID KINCH

Justin Woodward arrived at Castagna in 2009. The restaurant, a neighborhood fixture in Portland's Hawthorne District, had been host over the previous decade to a roster of celebrated chefs. Woodward initially worked as sous-chef to the wunderkind chef Matt Lightner. When Lightner left in 2011, Woodward stepped up as executive chef, quietly and efficiently forging his own style.

Woodward brought to Castagna a thick portfolio of experience. Since beginning his career in San Diego as a culinary student at the Art Institute of California, he acquired a breadth of technique and influences. He learned pastry at New York City's famed wd~50, soaked up contemporary sensibilities at Noma in Denmark and Mugaritz in Spain, and absorbed classic French technique at Eleven Madison Park and Corton in New York City.

A shining star among Portland restaurants, Castagna bills itself as progressive fine dining. Woodward's "snacks"—two-bite edible sculptures served at the beginning of the meal (one is described as "crab, fried sourdough, *wakame, shio koji,* lemon verbena")—bely his direct lineage to European Modernist cuisine. Nevertheless, Woodward's food is recognizably of the Pacific Northwest. Seasonal variations determine the menu, as does a survey of the weather and even current events. On one sweltering summer day, his "terrarium" consisted of summer beans, Sungold tomatoes, heirloom garlic, *kinome,* fennel fronds, and onion custard.

Sansho, agastache, and society garlic aren't the likeliest botanicals to find in the middle of a city. So when Woodward couldn't source them from the local markets, he lined the sidewalks outside Castagna with garden beds and sowed them with seeds to match his culinary intentions. This tenacious ambition and creativity is characteristic of Woodward, who instills the restaurant's menus with high technical caliber, artfulness, and a distinctive expression of Pacific Northwest bounty. Woodward's steadfast pushing of the envelope has earned him recognition. In addition to lavish local admiration, he has received several James Beard Award nominations.

MENU

OYSTER WITH SAVORY GELÉE OF CRAB AND WHITE SOY

CHANTERELLES, MALT, WILTED SORREL, CHANTERELLE CREAM

MADAI IN PAPILLOTE, BRAISED TREVISO, SAUCE BLANCHET

FOIE GRAS, PRESERVED MOUNTAIN HUCKLEBERRIES

AGED DUCK, SESAME LEAF

BEEF ZABUTON, TOASTED NIRA, PICKLED ONIONS, SEA BEANS, FENNEL

TOFFEE, PINE, MEYER LEMON, CINNAMON

OYSTER WITH SAVORY GELÉE OF CRAB AND WHITE SOY
Makes 30 oysters

For the poached oysters:
30 Shigoku oysters (1 per serving)

For the dashi:
1 kg water • 25 g kombu • 10 g fines herbes • 50 g brown butter • 12 g mirin • 25–50 g bonito flakes

For the crab consommé:
Dashi *(above)* • Shells, guts, and juices from 2 Dungeness crabs

For the shiitake tea:
3 dried shiitake mushroom caps • 300 g water

For the crab gelée:
3 sheets gelatin • 100 g heavy (whipping) cream • 35 g white soy sauce • 300 g Crab Consommé *(above)* • 5 lemon • 30 g Shiitake Tea *(above)*

Poach the oysters:
Prepare an ice bath. Bring a large pot of water to a boil and poach the oysters for 1 minute. Cool them in the ice bath.
Shuck the oysters into a small pan and reserve the shells and the oyster liquor. Cut off the adductor muscle from the shells. Strain the oyster liquor to remove shell fragments, then "wash" the poached oysters in the liquor. Strain the liquor again and repeat the "washing" process. Clean the oyster shells with an oyster knife. Place over kosher salt and reserve in a cooler.

Make the dashi:
Set a circulating water bath to 60°C. Bag the water, kombu, fines herbes, and brown butter and cook for 1 hour.
In a saucepan, bring the dashi and mirin to a boil. Add the bonito flakes and strain immediately through a chinois.

Make the crab consommé:
In a pot, simmer the dashi with the crab shells, guts (gills removed), and juices for 30 minutes.

Portion into delis and freeze, then ice-filter over cheesecloth (muslin) in the walk-in overnight to make a consommé.

Make the shiitake tea:
Place the shiitakes in a small bowl. Bring the water to a boil and pour over the mushrooms. Cool and strain.

Make the crab gelée:
Bloom the gelatin in ice water till softened. Squeeze out excess moisture. Warm the cream, crab consomme, and shiitake tea, add gelatin and stir to dissolve.

To assemble and serve:
Place a poached oyster into a cleaned oyster shell. Gently warm crab gelée over low heat until just melted. Pour into oyster shells and let set in cooler.
Serve set oyster over more oyster shells.

OYSTER WITH SAVORY GELÉE

BEEF ZABUTON

FOIE GRAS

CHANTERELLES, MALT, WILTED SORREL, CHANTERELLE CREAM
Serves 15

For the chanterelles:
800 g cleaned chanterelles (for the cream) • 30 g chanterelle mushrooms per serving

For the chanterelle cream:
250 g butter • 800 g chanterelles, cured (*above*) • 1 bay leaf • 6 g thyme sprigs, tied with twine • 400 g shallot • 8 g garlic • 75 g sherry vinegar • 15–20 g salt • 600 g white wine • 1 kg heavy (whipping) cream • 3 g xanthan gum

For finishing:
1 head Catalogna chicory • Olive oil • Maldon salt • Juice of 1 lime • 30 g chanterelles per serving (cured, *see above*) • Butter • 1 bunch sorrel leaves • Black malt powder

Cure the chanterelles:
Clean the chanterelles and cure for several days in a cool place.

Make the chanterelle cream:
Get a rondeau hot, then add the butter and mushrooms. Add the bay leaf and thyme. Cook the water out of the mushrooms and get some color on them. Add the shallot, garlic, vinegar, and salt and sweat until cooked. Deglaze with the wine, then reduce until almost dry. Add the cream and cook down to a semi-thick paste, 15–20 minutes. Puree in two batches, adding half of the xanthan gum to each batch. Pass through a chinois and cool in an ice bath. Taste and adjust salt and acid as necessary.

To finish:
Cut the chicory into 1-inch (2.5 cm) piece and soak in ice water. Drain and dress the chicory in olive oil, salt, and lime juice. Warm the chanterelle cream.
Sauté the mushrooms in butter. Remove from the pan and add the sorrel leaves to wilt slightly.
Spoon the warmed cream onto warmed plates and dust with black malt powder. Arrange the sautéed mushrooms next to the cream, place 3 pieces of chicory on the mushrooms and scatter with 2 pieces of sorrel.

JUSTIN STEPPED INTO
SOME BIG SHOES WHEN
HE TOOK OVER CASTAGNA,
AND HE HAS QUIETLY AND
EFFICIENTLY CREATED HIS
OWN STYLE.
— David Kinch

JUSTIN WOODWARD

AITOR ZABALA

SOMNI
Beverly Hills, California,
United States

JOSÉ ANDRÉS

Barcelona native Aitor Zabala is the chef at Somni in Los Angeles, California, a dinner-as-theater avant-garde restaurant in the Bazaar by José Andrés in Beverly Hills. Somni, which means "dream" in Catalan, is a ten-seat chef's-counter restaurant that offers guests an epicurean journey through a twenty-course prix fixe. As the name implies, Zabala's food is free from any constraints. Seasonality or sourcing locally are less important than creativity, playfulness, and commitment to excellence. Dishes that appear conceptual never disappoint in terms of deliciousness, and diners leave Somni satisfied.

In Spain, Zabala cooked at Ferran Adrià's molecular gastronomy temple, el Bulli, at three-Michelin-starred Arzak, with Chef Xavier Pellicer at ABaC, and with Pedro Subijana at Akelarre. Then in 2010, Zabala launched the forty-seat SAAM at the Bazaar with José Andrés, which he ran for eight years before turning the same space into its current iteration as Somni.

At Somni, guests enjoy concoctions that only Zabala could dream up. Powdered egg whites and clarified tomato are whipped into meringue and topped with mozzarella mousse and basil; the diner understands it as pizza, but the experience is more like eating an Italian cloud. Red fruit explodes into Aperol and strawberry in one's mouth. The menu imparts Zabala's identity, his Basque and Catalan roots, his training in Michelin-starred Spanish kitchens, and his love of his adopted home, Los Angeles, where he has been for a decade. The semicircular shape of the chef's counter is itself a nod to a distinctly Los Angeles spectacle, where simply by showing up, the diner becomes part of the show.

Somni is one of the most coveted reservations in Los Angeles and earned two Michelin stars. Zabala was named Chef of the Year in 2018 by Eater LA.

MENU

GUACAMOLE

TRUFFLECINI

PIZZA MARGHERITA

POTATO CROISSANT

FAVA BEANS

COW AND HER MILK

FRESAS CON NATA

PIZZA MARGHERITA
Serves 4

For the tomato water:
1 kg Roma (plum) tomatoes

For the Metil base:
1 kg filtered water • 30 g Metil powder

For the tomato meringue:
300 g Tomato Water *(above)* • 40 g Metil Base *(above)* • 18 g simple syrup • 10 g Trisol • 30 g powdered egg whites • Xantana • Crutomat (dehydrated tomato flakes)

For the tomate:
6 tomatoes • 2 cloves garlic • 1 bay leaf • Olive oil • Salt and pepper

For the burrata puree:
1 ball burrata cheese

For the browned burrata:
1 ball burrata cheese

For plating:
Powdered oregano • Chili flakes • Petite basil leaves • Olive oil • Maldon salt

Make the tomato water:
Cut up the tomatoes and buzz in a blender for a couple of minutes. Pass through a chinois to get rid of the pulp and seeds. Pass through a Superbag to get clear tomato water. Set aside.

Make the Metil base:
Heat the water up and place in a bowl. Set up another bowl with ice. When the water has cooled to 158°F (70°C), whisk in the Metil powder. Once the Metil is fully mixed, place the bowl into the ice bath. Cool the mixture down. Let it rest overnight to remove all the air bubbles.

Make the tomato meringue:
In the bowl of a stand mixer, stir together the tomato water, Metil base, and simple syrup. With a hand blender, add the Trisol and egg white powder and blend thoroughly. Add 0.45 Xantana and blend. Measure out 100 g of the meringue base and blend with 0.45 Xantana, then set this part aside.
Set the mixer bowl in the mixer and beat at speed 4, gradually increasing to 6, until the mixture is halfway up the sides of the bowl.

Add the reserved 100 g of meringue base and increase the speed to 8 until the bowl is filled with meringue.
Line baking sheets with silicone baking mats.
Wet a ring mold, pipe in the meringue, and cover top with the tomato flakes. Remove mold and repeat.
Dehydrate the meringues at 122°F (50°C) for 8 hours. Remove and keep in an airtight container.

Prepare the tomate:
Halve the tomatoes and grate them with a cheese grater. Set the grated tomato in a sieve set over a bowl. Drain the tomato of all excess water (reserve the tomato water for another use).
In a bowl, combine the drained tomatoes, garlic, thyme, bay leaf, olive oil, and salt and pepper to taste and marinate at room temperature for 2 hours before serving.

Make the burrata puree:
Open up the ball of burrata and place in a sieve. Stir it to open up and let sit for 30 minutes to let excess water drain off. Place the burrata in a container and blend with a hand blender until smooth. Reserve in a squeeze bottle.

Brown the burrata:
Open up the ball of burrata and divide between two sheet pans. Place under a salamander until browned but not burned. Remove and have at the ready.

To plate:
Torch the outside of meringue. Place some marinated tomato on top of the meringue. Place browned burrata cheese on top. Sprinkle with oregano powder and chili flakes. Squeeze 3 dots of burrata puree and garnish with 3 basil leaves. Finish with olive oil and Maldon salt. Serve immediately.

POTATO CROISSANT
Serves 10

For the picada:
30 g Marcona almonds • 40 g bread • 30 g pine nuts • 40 g parsley leaves

For the lobster:
Salt • 2 lb (910 g) lobster

For the potato croissant:
4 lb (1.8 kg) Chipperbec non-GMO California potatoes • 2 cups (475 ml) clarified butter • Salt and white pepper • Truffle • 1 egg, beaten

For the lobster sauce:
2 teaspoons olive oil • 300 g lobster shells and head • 190 g onion, chopped • 3 g garlic, smashed • 50 g white wine • 1 bay leaf • 60 g tomato, grated • 5 saffron threads • ¼ teaspoon sweet smoked paprika • 30 g brandy • 150 g russet potatoes, cut into ½-inch (1.25 cm) dice • 1 kg fish stock • 40 g Picada *(above)*

For assembly:
100 g Lobster Sauce *(above)* • 50 g butter • Salt and white pepper • Garlic flower or rosemary flowers, for garnish (depending on availability)

Make the picada:
Preheat the oven to 350°F (180°C). Spread the almonds and bread on a sheet pan and bake until golden brown and crispy, about 5 minutes.
Place the almonds, bread, pine nuts, and parsley in a molcajete and grind into a paste and reserve.

Prepare the lobster:
Fill a tall pot with water and enough salt to taste like the sea. Bring to a rapid boil.
Set up an ice bath with salted water.
Run a wooden skewer inside the lobster tail toward the head to prevent the tail from curling up. Pull off the claws and place the lobster and claws in the boiling water. Cook the tail for 3 minutes and the claws for 5 minutes. Shock the lobster in the ice bath. Remove the tail meat from the shell and reserve all the shells and claws for the sauce.

Make the potato croissant:
Peel the potatoes. In a vegetable sheeter, make long strips of potato. Coat the potato strips with clarified butter, salt, white pepper, and truffle. Cut into very long triangles and start rolling from widest to small. Make sure

to roll very tightly. Poke a skewer through to push out ends to form more like a croissant. Place the croissants in round molds to help them keep the crescent shape and cover with clarified butter to submerge. Steam at 176°F (80°C) until tender, about 1 hour 10 minutes. Pour the butter out of the molds and reserve the butter. Return the potato to the mold and brush with some of the beaten egg.
Bake (no steam) at 392°F (200°C) for 15 minutes. Remove from the oven. Brush with the egg wash again and return to the oven until golden brown, another 5 minutes.

Make the lobster sauce:
In a medium saucepan, heat the oil until smoking. Add the lobster shells and once a fond forms and caramelization begins, add the onion. Lightly caramelize the onion,

then add the garlic. Deglaze with the white wine and reduce to au sec. Add the bay leaf and grated tomatoes and cook until all the liquid is evaporated.
Add the saffron and smoked paprika and stir so as not to burn. Add the brandy and once hot, flame to burn off the alcohol. Add the potatoes, fish stock, and picada and simmer for 30 minutes.
Remove from the heat and let rest for 30 minutes. Strain and smash bodies. Return the sauce to heat and simmer until reduced by half. Skim any scum that forms. Pour into a Superbag to strain.

To assemble:
Heat up the lobster sauce and emulsify in the butter. Finish with some salt and white pepper and strain.

AITOR HAS DEVELOPED HIS OWN STYLE THAT NEARLY ESCAPES DESCRIPTION. HE IS ONE OF THE MOST MATURE VOICES IN THE INDUSTRY TODAY, CREATING ABSOLUTELY INCREDIBLE, MIND-BLOWING DISHES.
— José Andrés

TRUFFLECINI

FRESAS CON NATA

Place a potato croissant on a plate and pour some of the sauce in front of it. Garnish with petals from the garlic flowers.

COW AND HER MILK
Serves 10

For the blue cheese base:
500 g heavy (whipping) cream • 90 g blue cheese

For the whipped blue cheese:
250 g Blue Cheese Base *(above)*

For the vanilla syrup:
500 g filtered water • 500 g sugar • 1 vanilla bean, split lengthwise

For the apple puree:
5 Pink Lady apples, peeled and thinly sliced • 1 vanilla bean, split

For the apple dice:
2 Granny Smith apples, cut into ¼-inch (6 mm) dice • 150 g Vanilla Syrup *(above)*

For the cow cookies:
480 g butter, melted • 480 g all-purpose (plain) flour • 480 g sugar • 480 g egg whites • 4 g white food coloring • 2 g black food coloring

For the hazelnut split:
500 g hazelnuts

For plating:
Nutmeg

Make the blue cheese base:
In a saucepan, warm the cream to 120°–140°F (50°–60°C).
Transfer the warmed cream to a blender, add the blue cheese, and blend. Pass through a chinois and cool over an ice bath.

Whip the blue cheese:
In a bowl, with an electric mixer, whip the blue cheese base to medium peaks. Set aside in a container until ready to use.

Make the vanilla syrup:
Heat up water until hot enough to dissolve the sugar. Combine the water and sugar. Scrape the vanilla seeds into the sugar syrup and add the pod. Let infuse for 24 hours. Strain and discard the vanilla pod.

Make the apple puree:
Vacuum-seal the apples and vanilla bean and steam at 212°F (100°C) for 20–30 minutes.
Remove the vanilla pod. Puree the apples, strain, and reserve in a squeeze bottle.

Make the apple dice:
Vacuum-seal the diced apple and vanilla syrup. Let infuse for at least 3 hours.

Make the cow cookies:
In a blender, combine the melted butter, flour, sugar, egg whites, and white food coloring and blend until smooth (no lumps!). Measure out 960 g and transfer to a piping bag for the white cow base. Stir the black food coloring into the remaining mixture for the black cow base and transfer to a piping bag.
Preheat the oven to 338°F (170°C), low fan, 30% steam.
Line a baking sheet with a silicone baking mat. Set a cow stencil on the mat and pipe some of the black-and-white base in different places on the cow to make a pattern. Use an offset spatula to wipe off the excess (make sure to save the excess of black-and-white mixture to make more black base). Repeat to make more cows.
Bake until fully cooked, about 5 minutes. Let cool, then keep in a dehydrator until ready to serve.

Make the hazelnut split:
Preheat the oven to 350°F (180°C).
Toast the hazelnuts until golden brown, 10–20 minutes, checking periodically. Let the hazelnuts cool down and with a knife or a spatula split the hazelnuts in half.

To plate:
Place 5 pieces of apple dice in a circle. In between the apple dice, place 4 hazelnut halves. Pipe 1½–2 ounces (42–57 g) of whipped blue cheese, then squeeze apple puree on top of the blue cheese. Grate a very small amount of nutmeg onto the purees, then drizzle hazelnut praline in a zigzag pattern on the purees as well. Top it off with a cow cookie.

AITOR ZABALA

EMERGING CHEF BIOGRAPHIES

DANIELLE ALVAREZ

FRED'S
380 Oxford Street
Paddington, NSW 2021
Australia

Danielle Alvarez was born in Miami, Florida into a Cuban-American family. After a brief stint in the art world, Danielle enrolled in cooking school and then moved to California to learn about produce-driven cooking. Her next move was to Sydney, Australia to open Fred's Restaurant with the Merivale group. Danielle also contributes monthly recipes to *Good Food* magazine and is the author of the cookbook *Always Add Lemon*.

LUIS ARELLANO

CRIOLLO
Francisco I. Madero 129
Centro, 68000 Oaxaca de Juárez
Mexico

Luis Arellano's style of cooking reflects a deep knowledge and respect for Oaxacan produce. Born and raised in a small borough twenty minutes outside Oaxaca's downtown, where he now owns Criollo, Luis developed his baking and cooking techniques at his parents' bakery. Soon after, he became an intern at the acclaimed Casa Oaxaca with chef Alejandro Ruiz and eventually became the chef de cuisine. Afterward, he moved to Mexico City to work with chef Enrique Olvera, at Pujol.

SUZANNE BARR

TRUE TRUE DINER
169 King Street East
Toronto M5A 1J4 Ontario
Canada

Suzanne Barr has a flair for fresh comfort food and passion for local community, food security, and advocacy for people of color and LGBTQ communities. She was most recently the Chef/Owner at True True Diner, which closed in 2020. Previously, she was owner of the Saturday Dinette and chef-in-residence at the Gladstone Hotel. She also had a residency at Sand and Pearl Oyster Bar in Prince Edward County, Canada. In 2018, she was a MAD Symposium panelist, and she was featured in the documentary *The Heat: A Kitchen (R)evolution*.

DAVE BERAN

DIALOGUE
1315 3rd Street Promenade Suite K
Santa Monica, CA 90401
USA

PASJOLI
2732 Main St
Santa Monica, CA 90405
USA

Dave Beran is the chef/owner of the Michelin-starred restaurant Dialogue and the award-winning Pasjoli in Santa Monica, California. Prior to moving to California, Beran was the chef de cuisine at Alinea and executive chef at Next in Chicago where he received a James Beard Award for Best Chef Great Lakes and was named one of *Food & Wine* magazine's Best New Chefs in 2014. Additionally, Next won a James Beard Award for Best New Restaurant under Beran's leadership.

NEIL BORTHWICK

THE FRENCH HOUSE
49 Dean Street
Soho, London W1D 5BG
United Kingdom

Born in Edinburgh, Neil Borthwick has been working in the kitchen from the age of 14. Since then, he has honed his skills at the Connaught, Maison Pic, as well as Michel Bras and The Square, where he was sous chef. He went on to win the Nestlé Toque d'Or in 2000 and the Young Chef of the Year award in 2005. Neil was head chef at Merchants Tavern in Shoreditch for five years. He is now head chef at the Soho, London institution the French House.

BÉRANGÈRE BOUCHER

NOMIKAÏ
14 rue Crozatier
75012 Paris
France

Bérangère Boucher was a publisher, but tiring of her work she started to make bento for her office. One thing to another, and she applied to a cooking class. She earned a culinary degree, and worked anywhere that she could learn: private parties, bistros or gastronomic restaurants. She then became a private chef in order to work nomadically, but in summer 2017 decided to settle somewhere. She opened Nomikaï in 2018.

ANNIE BRACE-LAVOIE

BAR KISMET
2733 Agricola Street
Halifax B3K 4E2 Nova Scotia
Canada

Annie Brace-Lavoie has been cooking professionally for more than ten years and has groomed her skills in Montreal, Toronto, and London. She has worked in many of Canada's best restaurants, and is now a co-owner of Bar Kismet (fifteenth in Canada's Top 100 Restaurants in 2019) in Halifax, with her husband Jenner Cornier who runs the front of house and bar program. Annie has a passion for working with seafood and fresh pasta with is a strong focus on classic techniques as well as seasonal ingredients.

PAMELA BRUNTON

INVER RESTAURANT
Strathlachlan, Cairndow PA27 8BU
Scotland, UK

Pam Brunton's twenty-year career in food bounces from books to kitchens and back again; from remote Scottish islands to Scandinavia, via London, Belgium and France. After abandoning a philosophy degree, Pam started cooking. A decade later she returned to university to gain a masters in Food Policy, spent several years campaigning for reform in the farming and food industries, and learned to think anew about restaurants and their role in the world. She and partner Rob came home to Scotland to open Inver in spring 2015. Currently, Pam is the *Good Food Guide's* Chef of the Year and Inver holds the Menu of the Year "Catey" for 2020, the latest in a series of awards and accolades for the restaurant.

MANOELLA BUFFARA

MANU
Alameda Dom Pedro II, 317
Batel, Curitiba PR, 80420
Brazil

ELLA
436 West 15th Street
New York, NY 10011
USA

Manoella "Manu" Buffara is executive chef and owner of Manu located in Curitiba, Brazil, which has received critical acclaim for its tasting menu that has been recognized by World's 50 Best. Paving the way for gastronomy in Brazil, Manu celebrates the culture and produce unique to the region of Paraná. In 2021, Manu plans to launch Ella, her first restaurant in New York City. Manu plans to bring her interpretation of the cuisine and Brazilian soul to the city.

DANIEL CALVERT

BELON
41 Elgin St, Central
Hong Kong

Daniel Calvert brought his passion and precision to Belon after more than ten years working in Michelin-starred kitchens, building strong foundations with placements at the Ivy, Pied à Terre, Per Se and Epicure. With access to the best produce and the freedom to cook whatever he likes, Calvert's work at Belon is a continuation of this excellence. Calvert and Belon were awarded one star in the Michelin Guides for 2019 and 2020 and jumped from 40 to 4 on Asia's 50 Best Restaurants between their debut in 2018 to 2020.

PAUL CARMICHAEL

MOMOFUKU SEIŌBO
Pyrmont Street
Pyrmont NSW 2009
Australia

Paul Carmichael has worked in many exciting restaurants around the world including wd~50, Aquavit and the Tasting Room in New York, and Perla in Puerto Rico. His formal training began at the Culinary Institute of America but his true love and passion for food started at home in Barbados. He started working for the Momofuku group in New York City at Má Pêche in 2010 and landed in Sydney in 2015 to take up the position of executive chef at Momofuku Seiōbo. His cooking at Seiōbo honors his Caribbean heritage.

MARTINA CARUSO

HOTEL SIGNUM
Via Scalo 15, 98050
Malfa Salina, Messina
Italy

Martina Caruso is the chef and co-owner of Hotel Signum in Salina, which she runs with her parents and her brother. She is in charge of the restaurant, where she first started helping her father, then the chef, as a child. She has worked under acclaimed chefs in Italy and abroad, and her work at Signum has been widely recognized, including being awarded a Michelin star. In 2019 she became the youngest chef to earn the Michelin Female Chef Award from the Veuve Clicquot Atelier des Grandes Dames.

JEREMY CHAN

IKOYI
1 St James's Market
London, SW1Y 4AH
UK

Jeremy Chan was born in the UK to a Canadian mother and Chinese father and grew up in Hong Kong and the UK. He decided to open Ikoyi in 2017 with best friend and business partner, Ire Hassan Odukale. Jeremy explores hyper seasonal produce from local organic farms in combination with a focus on spice and umami. He aims to cook purely creatively with an artistic sensibility.

ALEX CHEN

BOULEVARD KITCHEN &
OYSTER BAR
845 Burrard street
Vancouver BC V6Z 2K6
Canada

A classically trained chef, Alex Chen led Team Canada to a top-ten in the world at the 2013 Bocuse d'Or in Lyon, France, prior to opening Boulevard Kitchen & Oyster Bar in 2014. In 2018, Alex was named Chef of the Year by the *Vancouver Magazine* restaurant awards and became the first challenger to beat an Iron Chef when he defeated Hugh Acheson on the inaugural season of *Iron Chef Canada*. In 2019, Alex led Boulevard to the number thirty-one on the prestigious annual list of Canada's 100 Best Restaurants.

MIA CHRISTIANSEN

BARR
Strandgade 93
1401 Copenhagen
Denmark

Mia has worked as a chef for twelves years, and has been head chef at Barr since it opened in the summer of 2017. After years of traveling and working as a chef abroad, she is thrilled to be back in Denmark leading the team at Barr and developing a menu inspired by grandmas and star chefs alike.

CARLOTA CLAVER

LA GORMANDA
Carrer d'Aribau 160
08036 Barcelona
Spain

For such a young chef, Carlota Claver has extensive experience in the kitchen. After graduating from the Hofmann Culinary School, she spent years working in the family business at Alba Granados and Alba Paris. Now running her own restaurant, at La Gormanda Claver reinterprets classic dishes with a wealth of inventive production techniques.

NATALIA CROZON

LA COURTILLE
208 Chemin des Cravailleux
30126 Tavel
France

Natalia Crozon is the chef and proprietor of La Courtille, in the village of Tavel, in the southern Rhône-wine region of France. Prior to opening her restaurant in 2018, she worked in Paris at the wine shop La Carte des Vins and at Le Baratin, where she met La Courtille cofounder Marie Lézouret, and was mentored by chef Raquel Carena. A selection of local, natural wines are on offer at Crozon's seasonal restaurant, housed in a historic farm building, with extensive terrace dining.

DIANA DÁVILA

MI TOCAYA ANTOJERÍA
2800 West Logan Boulevard
Chicago, IL 60647
USA

Diana Dávila is the chef and owner of Mi Tocaya Antojería in Chicago, IL. She was named one of *Food & Wine* magazine's Best New Chefs (2018), a James Beard semi-finalist for Best Chef: Great Lakes (2018), and finalist in the same category in 2019. At Mi Tocaya guests are invited to enjoy Dávila's takes on familiar Mexican favorites, lesser-known regional specialties, and completely new dishes that are inspired by her Mexican heritage.

CLARE DE BOER & JESS SHADBOLT

KING
18 King Street
New York, NY 10014
USA

Clare de Boer and Jess Shadbolt are co-chefs at King where they serve a daily changing menu inspired by regional Italian cooking and food from the south of France. Having met in London while working at The River Cafe, they opened King in Soho, New York in 2016 with their partner Annie Shi. In 2017 the *New York Times* restaurant critic Pete Wells awarded King a two-star review, and later included it in his annual list of "Best Restaurants of 2017." In 2018 Clare and Jess were named *Food & Wine*'s Best New Chefs for 2018.

MACA DE CASTRO

MACA DE CASTRO
Carrer Tritons, 4
07400 Alcúdia
Illes Balears
Spain

Maca de Castro was born in 1981 to a family already in the food industry. She began her career as a server at the family owned Jardín in Port d'Alcúdia, but soon gravitated toward the kitchen and worked her way up to the role of head chef, securing her first Michelin star in 2012. De Castro has always valued training highly, and has carried out stints with Hilario Arbelaitz, Andoni Luis Aduriz, and Julián Serrano. She has also attended various courses at elBulli and trained with Wylie Dufresne, Jean Coussau, and Juan Mari Arzak.

BEN DEVLIN

PIPIT RESTAURANT
Shop 4, 8 Coronation Ave
Pottsville, NSW 2489
Australia

Ben Devlin is the chef and owner of Pipit Restaurant. Pipit celebrates local produce in an open plan, wood-fired kitchen, and was named Australia's Best Regional Restaurant (*Good Food Guide 2020*) as well as being a finalist for Best New Restaurant in 2020's *Gourmet Traveler* Restaurant Awards. In 2014, Ben won QLD's Young Chef of the Year while working at Esquire in Brisbane; previous to that he spent two years as chef de partie at Noma in Copenhagen. He returned to the Northern Rivers region in 2015 to lead the award-winning restaurant Paper Daisy at Halcyon House, before realising his dream to open his own restaurant, Pipit, in 2019.

FANNY DUCHARME

RESTAURANT L'ÉPICURIEUX
2270 rue de L'église
Val-David J0T 2N0 Quebec
Canada

Born and raised in the Laurentians, just an hour north of Montreal, Fanny Ducharme obtained her diploma at the École Hôtelière des Laurentides. She spent time in the kitchens of Martin Picard at The Sugar Shack at Pied-de-Cochon, where she met Dominic Tougas, with whom she opened Restaurant l'Épicurieux in 2016. At her restaurant, she works with fresh products, local artisans, and buys from local farmers to create her signature dishes.

MICHAEL ELÉGBÈDÉ

ÌTÀN TEST KITCHEN
6 Moor Road
Ikoyi, Lagos
Nigeria

Born in Nigeria in 1989, Michael Elégbèdé emigrated to America with his family as a teenager. He studied at the Culinary Institute of America and worked with Daniel Humm at Eleven Madison Park and the NoMad restaurants, before feeling compelled to return to Nigeria in 2016. Back in his homeland, Elégbèdé traveled widely to experience the diverse cultures and traditions that contribute to Nigerian Cuisine. He uses these lessons at Ìtàn to reimagine Nigerian classics through a tasting menu experience at a 16-seater chef's table.

TAKASHI ENDO

RESTAURANT SAN
78 Minamikyogokuchou
Shimogyo-ku
Kyoto 600-8117
Japan

After graduating from university Takashi Endo moved to Tokyo to pursue a career as a chef. He worked in various Japanese restaurants in Kyoto, Kanazawa, and Nagoya to master the techniques of Japanese cuisine and gain experience. Through his deep love for antique Japanese porcelain platters he met Shintaro Yabe, and together they opened Restaurant San in September 2018. At San, Endo uses both contemporary and antique Japanese ceramics to present his washoku tasting menu.

JAMES FERGUSON

THE KINNEUCHAR INN
9–11 Main Street
Kilconquhar, Fife KY9 1LF
Scotland, UK

James Ferguson is known for his particular take on modern British cooking with an eye on diverse global influences. An executive chef with 20 years of experience in the industry, he has worked with, amongst others, Angela Hartnett at the Connaught, and with Margot Henderson at Rochelle Canteen. Originally from Halifax with Scottish/Greek heritage, James grew up helping in the kitchen of his parents' acclaimed Yorkshire restaurant. He trained as a classical pianist before going back to his true first love: cooking.

MONIQUE FISO

HIAKAI
40 Wallace Street
Mount Cook, Wellington
New Zealand 6021

Monique Fiso is considered one of New Zealand's most important chefs. Monique owns and operates Hiakai which was named as one of *TIME* magazine's 100 Greatest Places of 2019. She also starred in Netflix's *The Final Table*, and alongside Chef Gordon Ramsay on National Geographic's *Uncharted*. Using traditional Māori cooking techniques and ingredients in combination with her Michelin training, Fiso has taken Māori cuisine to a new level of sophistication and pushed it into the next chapter in its story.

THOMAS FREBEL

INUA
2-13-12 Fujimi
Chiyoda-ku
Tokyo 102-8552
Japan

German-born Thomas Frebel, and the former Head of Research and Development at Copenhagen's Noma, opened the door to Inua, in Tokyo in the summer of 2018. Thomas had first visited Japan in 2014, in preparation for the Noma pop-up at the Mandarin Oriental. Seeing his time in Japan as 'unfinished business', he vowed one day to return. Inua dishes up Japanese seasonal ingredients with a Scandinavian approach all the whilst paying homage to their Nordic roots and humble beginnings. In July 2020, Frebel made the sad announcement that Inua would remain closed following the Covid-19 pandemic.

EVAN FUNKE

FELIX TRATTORIA
1023 Abbot Kinney Blvd.
Venice, CA 90291
USA

Evan Funke is a two-time James Beard-nominated chef, author and critically acclaimed master pasta maker. After many years with Wolfgang Puck at iconic Spago, Funke departed for Bologna where he apprenticed under master sfoglina Alessandra Spisni at La Vecchia Scuola Bolognese. In 2017, Funke opened Felix Trattoria in Venice, California, where he honors regional Italian tradition. His book *American Sfoglino* and docuseries *The Shape of Pasta* have both garnered rave reviews, furthering his dedication to the craft.

WILLIAM GLEAVE & GIUSEPPE BELVEDERE

BRIGHT RESTAURANT
1 Westgate Street
London E8 3RL
UK

Will Gleave was born in London and began cooking professionally after completing an MA at Manchester University. He trained at The Square and Arbutus in London and Garagistes in Tasmania, Australia. He founded Bright Restaurant in 2018 with the Noble Fine Liquor team following his success at P Franco in Hackney, London. Born in Sardinia, Giuseppe Belvedere takes a lot of influence from his homeland but, like the rest of today's avant-garde, takes cues from all food cultures. His soulful approach to cooking brought him to lead the kitchen at Brawn, where he was the head chef for two years. After a residency at P Franco, he opened Bright with Gleave and the Noble Fine Liquor team.

MATT HARPER

KENSINGTON QUARTERS
1310 Frankford Ave
Philadelphia, PA 19125
USA

Matt Harper was born and raised in a small town in Northeast Arkansas. Harper's style of cooking is based around hyper-local sourcing and sustainability with a focus on vegetables. Currently the executive chef at Orto in Baltimore, Harper was most recently executive chef at Kensington Quarters in Philadelphia, where his menu continually evolved with the changes of the seasons and the bounty of the farmers. Previously Harper worked as chef de cuisine at Zahav, in Philadelphia, and executive sous chef of Empire State South in Atlanta. Harper's talent has earned him a Zagat "30 Under 30" nod, as well as the title of Philly Star Chef 2019.

JAMES HENRY

LE DOYENNÉ
5 rue Saint-Antoine
91770 Saint-Vrain
France

James Henry was born in Australia and raised but raised in a variety of places including Canberra, Paris, Riyadh, and San Francisco. His connection to food was born in the family home. After flirting with different career choices, he took a plunge into professional kitchens in his early twenties, spending time in Sumatra, Byron Bay, Australia, and then Melbourne, where he worked for Andrew McConnell. Thereafter James opened Au Passage, in Paris, quickly putting it on the map; then his own restaurant, Bones. For the last five years he has been working on his new project, Le Doyenné, a restaurant set in the kitchen garden where he has been growing vegetables for the last few years.

JORDAN KAHN

VESPERTINE
3599 Hayden Avenue
Culver City, CA 90232
USA

Jordan Kahn is the chef/creator of Vespertine, a multi-sensory fine-dining restaurant project conceived to reimagine and explore the ritual of dining. The experience takes guests through a transportive journey of discovery in which the menu unfolds as they ascend and descend a four-level tower of twisted steel and glass. The convergence of food, art, architecture, music, and sculpture is woven throughout to create an immersive event.

MATTHEW KAMMERER

THE HARBOR HOUSE INN
5600 South Highway 1
Elk, CA 95432
USA

Matthew Kammerer's culinary journey has taken him around the globe, from Boston, Australia, Japan, Hong Kong, Belgium to San Francisco. He's the Chef of Harbor House Inn, the first and only Michelin-starred restaurant in Mendocino County in California. Matt is known for his hyperlocal and coastal focused cuisine celebrating products sourced from nearby waters and the restaurant's own gardens. Matthew is a 2019 *Food & Wine* Best New Chef and Best Chef of the West semi-finalist by the James Beard Foundation.

CHIHO KANZAKI & MARCELO DI GIACOMO

VIRTUS
29 rue de Cotte
75012 Paris
France

Chiho Kanzaki is a Japanese chef, head of the restaurant Virtus with her unwavering companion, the Argentinian Marcelo di Giacomo. They honed their skills with great chefs at Lucas Carton, Jean-Paul Jeunet for her and Jean-Paul Bondoux for him. They met working with Mauro Colagreco, and together absorbed a fundamental respect for product. Virtus obtained a first Michelin star in January 2019.

KUNIHIKO KATO

UBUKA
2–14 Arakicho
Shinjuku-ku
Tokyo 160-0007
Japan

Born in Sendai in the Miyagi prefecture, Kunihiko Kato's passion for shrimp and crab inspired him to become a chef. He learned the basic cooking techniques for crustaceans and then trained in traditional high-end Japanese restaurants (*ryotei*) in Kyoto for three and a half years. Later, he gained experience at a Japanese restaurant in New Zealand, and then returned to Japan where he worked in a Chinese restaurant in Tokyo. In 2012, he opened Ubuka, where he serves a variety of shrimps and crabs, creating dishes that make the most of each crustacean.

GAVIN KAYSEN

SPOON AND STABLE
211 North First Street
Minneapolis, MN 55401
USA

An award-winning chef and founder of Soigné Hospitality Group , Gavin Kaysen helms three Minneapolis-area restaurants: Spoon and Stable , a 2015 James Beard Award finalist for Best New Restaurant; Bellecour Bakery, a French-inspired daytime bakery and bistro; and Demi, an intimate 20-seat tasting menu experience. He is a founding member of the Ment'or BKB Foundation and currently serves as President of Team USA. Chef Kaysen is the proud winner of two James Beard Awards – 2008 Rising Star Chef and 2018 Best Chef: Midwest.

JAMES KENT

CROWN SHY
70 Pine Street
New York, NY 10005
USA

A Greenwich Village native, James Kent started his culinary career as a summer apprentice at Bouley when he was fifteen. He graduated from Johnson and Wales, and later became the sous chef and then chef de cuisine at Eleven Madison Park, where he led the restaurant to numerous accolades including three Michelin stars. Later, he was executive chef at the NoMad, earning a Michelin star there as well. In 2017, James left the NoMad to pursue his first solo project, a pair of restaurants in a landmark Art Deco building in Manhattan's financial district. The first, Crown Shy, was heralded as one of the best new restaurant opening of 2019 and earned its first Michelin star just six months after it opened.

IZUMI KIMURA

SUSHIJIN
3-5-7 Shinnezukamachi
Toyama 939-8205
Japan

Born in Tokyo, Izumi Kimura began his working life as a businessman. His passion for sushi saw him quit his black-suit life and move home to Toyama bay and its abundance of fresh fish. He opened the first Sushijin in 1999, however, he was undertrained and it soon closed. Sushijin 2.0 opened in 2005 with Kimura having a deeper understanding of the craft and the customer. Serving edomae-style sushi, Kimura has established himself as one of the leading, new wave sushi chefs in Japan.

KEITA KITAMURA

ERH
11 rue Tiquetonne
75002 Paris
France

Born in Shiga prefecture, Japan, Keita Kitamura graduated from Tsuji Culinary Institute in Osaka at the age of 19. He worked at La Napoule and Le Création Narisawa in the company of chef Yoshihiro Narisawa where he acquired the basics of classical French cuisine. He moved to France to perfect his technique alongside chefs such as Pierre Gagnaire and Ghislaine Arabian, and then became at chef Bon Accueil. In 2017, he opened restaurant ERH within La Maison du Saké, where he improvises daily, creating French cuisine without forgetting his Japanese roots.

ANTONIA KLUGMANN

L'ARGINE A VENCÒ
Località vencò 15
34070 Dolegna del Collio
Italy

Antonia Klugmann is the Italian chef of L'Argine a Vencò. She opened her restaurant in 2014 in the Collio, a rural area in the northeast of Italy close to the Slovenian border. L'Argine is a small countryside restaurant with the world as a horizon. She received her first Michelin Star in 2015.

ZACH KOLOMEIR

DREYFUS
96 Harbord Street
Toronto, Ontario M5S 1G6
Canada

Born and raised in Montreal in a Jewish household, Zach Kolomeir's food-focused family get-togethers were an automatic inspiration for the future. He always dreamed of opening a restaurant but never knew which direction to take. In the meantime, he spent many years working on both front- and back-of-house at Joe Beef and Liverpool House in Montreal, and then at restaurants in Philadelphia before moving to Toronto to open Dreyfus. He credits the foundation of his life in Montreal with helping him realize this dream.

BERNARD KORAK

KORAK FAMILY ESTATE
Plešivica 34
10450 Jastrebarsko
Croatia

The son of a renowned Croatian winemaker, self-taught chef Bernard Korak trained with Priska Thuring, Ana Roš and Massimo Bottura. He served as sous chef at Chef Roš' restaurant Hiša Franko, and in 2019 he returned to his family's estate in Plešivica to open a seasonally driven fine-dining restaurant at the winery.

LUKA KOŠIR

BRUNARICA GRIČ
Šentjošt nad Horjulom 24d
1354 Horjul
Slovenia

Luka Košir went to culinary school and then trained at JB restaurant before taking over his family's restaurant, open since 1993, in 2010. Wanting the business to be more self-sustaining, he led the family to replant the gardens and orchards on the estate, and started a free-range duck farm. They now produce 80 percent of the vegetables and 50 percent of the fruit served at the restaurant, in addition to making preserves and pickles, and foraging.

PATRICK KRISS

ALO/ALOETTE
163 Spadina Avenue
Toronto, Ontario M5V 2L6
Canada

ALOBAR YORKVILLE/
SALON
162 Cumberland Street
Toronto, Ontario M5R 1A8
Canada

Patrick's culinary career began in his hometown of Toronto before heading to New York to work for Daniel Boulud at his eponymous restaurant. In 2015, having since returned to Toronto, Patrick opened a tasting-menu restaurant, Alo, which was awarded a rare four stars in the *Globe & Mail* and has since been named Canada's best restaurant each year since 2017. Following Alo, he has opened two more casual restaurants, Aloette and Alobar, and a space for private dining, Salon.

MERLIN LABRON-JOHNSON

OSIP
1 High Street
Bruton
Somerset
BA10 0AB
UK

Merlin Labron-Johnson honed his skills throughout Europe, working at Michelin-starred restaurants including the Portland (where he earned his first Michelin star at 24), Clipstone, Albert 1er and In De Wulf. Osip is Labron-Johnson's first solo project, where he farms his own vegetables, herbs and fruit and he cooks a daily changing set menu based on whatever produce is good that day, supplemented with wild game and poultry. Passionate about the future of food, he also supports a number of charitable and altruistic initiatives.

THI LE

ANCHOVY
338 Bridge Road
Richmond VIC 3121
Australia

Thi Le fell into a career in cooking halfway through completing a degree in design (she wanted to design bars and restaurants for a living). Since completing her apprenticeship, she has traded Sydney for Melbourne, worked in kitchens that appreciate the simplicity of produce, and has just celebrated her award-winning restaurant's fifth birthday. As a chef-owner of Anchovy, Thi places equal importance on developing her menu as she does her team that works with her day in and day out.

PÍA LEÓN

KJOLLE RESTAURANTE
Av. Pedro de Osma 301
Barranco, 15063 Lima
Peru

Pía Léon was born and raised in Lima, Perú. She graduated from Le Cordon Bleu Lima and began her career in 2009 when she joined the kitchen staff at Central. Through her unique ability and determination, she became head chef and, alongside her husband Virgilio Martínez, Pía was a key in establishing Central as the gold star for both Peruvian and global gastronomic standards. Kjolle is Pía's first independent project. Although in line with the philosophy of Central, Pía highlights biodiversity in a unique way, marking a new beginning with a broader outlook and wider space to create.

YUVAL LESHEM

HASALON
735 10th Avenue
New York, NY 10019
USA

In 2019, Yuval Leshem opened the New York City HaSalon outpost of Eyal Shani's Tel Aviv restaurant. Featuring an open kitchen and Israeli cuisine inspired by international influences, the restaurant turns into a dance party in the late hours of the evening. Housed in New York City, near the theater district, the menu, which changes daily, features ingredients from local greenmarkets. Prior to his New York experience, Leshem worked with Shani for over a decade and was the restaurant group's culinary director in Tel Aviv.

MEI LIN

NIGHTSHADE RESTAURANT
923 E. 3rd Street #109
Los Angeles, CA 90013
USA

Born in China, chef Mei Lin grew up Michigan working alongside her mother and father at their family-owned and -operated Chinese restaurant; and where she learned the fundamentals of being a well-rounded cook and how to run a restaurant. At Nightshade, opened in 2019, the menu features a concise point of view, showcasing an elegant elevation of classic Asian dishes. Nightshade is the culmination of Lin's personal culinary history and has garnered rave reviews including *Food & Wine* and *GQ's* 2019 Best New Restaurants lists.

ROSETTA LIN

VOISIN ORGANIQUE
L2, S209 Upper Hills
5001 Huanggang Road
Futian District, Shenzhen
China

Rosetta Lin supports sustainable agricultural through her organic restaurant. During the 5 yearss Voisin Organique has been open, she has studied, explored, and experimented with traditional Chinese and western cooking techniques on her own, and developed a one-of-a-kind cuisine. Rosetta creates compositions that appeal to the five senses like a perfumer, and makes decorative and mouthwatering plating as a floral designer. She aims to present the idea of classic and fun with surprises to her patrons.

MAT LINDSAY

ESTER RESTAURANT AND BAR
46-52 Meagher Street
Chippendale, Sydney NSW2008
Australia

Mat Lindsay had his first restaurant kitchen experience at age fifteen. He then moved to Sydney and worked at Kylie Kwong's noodle bar Wockpool. His next career move was as head chef at her Chinese restaurant, Billy Kwong, and the Italian restaurant 121 BC Cantina & Enoteca. The first restaurant of his own was Ester, with a focus on wood-fired ingredients; then he opened the wine bar Ester and Shawarmama. His modern Australian cuisine, married with European, Southeast Asian, and indigenous influences, have garnered much acclaim.

NORMA LISTMAN & SAQIB KEVAL

MASALA Y MAÍZ
Calle Marsella 72
Colonia Juarez, CP. 06600
CDMX
Mexico

Chef-owners Norma and Saqib opened Masala y Maíz in 2017 to create a space that sat at the intersections of their artistic, gastronomic and political principles while serving food that felt and tasted like home. Masala y Maíz explores the migration of people, culinary techniques, ingredients, cultural food ways and political movements between South Asia, East Africa, and Mexico. The restaurant reflects the chefs' beliefs that food is a powerful tool for social justice and that chefs have the responsibility to advocate for better labor conditions for everyone in the food industry. In an effort to create more financial stability and food security for workers in the food chain, Masala y Maíz launched a cooperative grocery store in 2020 in which the staff of the restaurant can be co-owners.

LISA LOV

TIGERMOM RESTAURANT
Ryesgade 25
Copenhagen N 2200
Denmark

Born to Chinese-Cambodian refugee parents in New Zealand, Lisa Lov earned a dual degree in Law and Psychology before discovering her passion for cooking while working at a restaurant part time alongside a job in recruiting. She staged around the world ultimately landing at Relæ in Copenhagen where she started as an apprentice and ultimately held the sous chef position for five years. Love opened Tigermom in 2018 where she dishes out tastes from all corners of Asia, in a casual and relaxed environment.

JAMIE MALONE

GRAND CAFÉ
3804 Grand Ave South
Minneapolis, MN 55409
USA

EASTSIDE
305 South Washington Ave
Minneapolis, MN 55415
USA

In 2017 Jamie Malone opened her first restaurant, Grand Café, serving classical French cuisine in a romantic eighty year-old space. In 2018 it was a semi finalist for the the James Beard Best New Restaurant award, and also named one of *Food & Wine* magazine's Best New Restaurants. Malone is also the owner of Eastside, a fun, downtown shellfish and ham bar with great cocktails.

DIEUVEIL MALONGA

MEZA MALONGA RESTAURANT
KG 8 Avenue 18
Kigali
Rwanda

Dieuveil Malonga is an award-winning chef and entrepreneur hailing from Congo-Brazzaville. His signature "Afro fusion" cuisine is a subtle blend of tradition, modernity and cultures. Malonga honed his culinary skills in Germany at Michelin-starred restaurants Schote, La Vie and Aqua; and was a finalist of the prestigious Basque Culinary World Prize 2018. His restaurant MEZA Malonga has been acclaimed by *Travel + Leisure* and *Food & Wine* as one of the world's best restaurants.

JUAN JOSÉ MARQUÉS GARRIDO

RESTAURANT MARAN
Gran Via de Jaume I, 8
17001 Girona
Spain

Juan José Marqués Garrido was born in Teruel and he attended the Escuela Superior de Hostelería de Sevilla. He has worked in several top restaurants including El Celler de Can Roca, in Girona, Le Baratin, in Paris, and El Guggenheim, in Bilbao. His solid training and his experience has directed him toward his current way of cooking, based on high quality products and classic formulas, combined with innovative processes. At the end of 2016, together with his partner, the sommelier Ferran Ansesa Batallé, they began their own project with Restaurant Maran in Girona.

AMAIUR MARTÍNEZ ORTUZAR

GANBARA
Calle San Jeronimo 21
20003 San Sebastián
Spain

Amaiur Martínez Ortuzar is the third generation of his family in the restaurant business. He earned a degree in television production and then worked for a Spanish television channel for four years before deciding to return to his family's business. He has now been at Ganbara for ten years. He focuses on traditional, handmade, seasonal and inshore fishing products, and a wine list of small producers with personality that engage with Ganbara's philosophy.

DULCE MARTÍNEZ

EL MOLÍN DE MINGO
33540 Peruyes
Asturias
Spain

Dulce Martínez was born in the city of Mieres, almost 100 kilometers away from Peruyes. When her father lost her job her parents decided to make a change and move to her grandparents' house: El Molín de Mingo. The neighbors encouraged her parents to reopen the windmill as a bar gather together over some drinks. Having always loved the gastronomy world, Martínez decided to leave her studies and enroll at a hostelry school. Now, for twenty years she has been running her own business in her family home, dedicating her life to what she loves the most.

JUAN LUIS MARTÍNEZ & JOSE LUIS SAUME

MÉRITO
Calle 28 de Julio 206
Barranco, Lima
Peru

Venezuelan-born Juan Luis Martínez began his career working in Martín Berasategui in 2007, Bordeaux from 2011–13, and in Madrid for David Muñoz during 2013. In 2014 he settled in Lima where he joined the team at Central working for Virgilio Martínez and Pía León until 2016. Saume followed a similar path, working together with Carlos García in Caracas in 2006 and in 2007 he joined Martín Berasategui in the Basque Country where he met Juan Luis. The friends joined forces in Lima in 2018 to realize their dream of opening their own restaurant. As well as an accomplished craft, Martínez and Saume share an experimental yet deferential approach to ingredients, which they treat as a shared Latin American vernacular joining their native Venezuela with their current home in Peru.

FLYNN MCGARRY

GEM
116 Forsyth Street
New York NY 10002
USA

Flynn McGarry began cooking at the age of ten. He started a supper club operating out of his mother's home at twelve, and staged in top restaurants in Los Angeles, New York and Seattle before he was sixteen. In 2014, he was the cover story of the food and drink issue of the *New York Times Magazine*. In 2018, at the age of nineteen, he opened his first permanent restaurant, Gem, in New York City's Lower East Side, which received a glowing two-star review from the *New York Times*. In November that same year, he was the subject of a documentary called *Chef Flynn* that debuted in theaters nationwide.

VICTOR MORENO

MORENO
Hotel Altamira Village
Avenida Luis Roche, Caracas
Venezuela

Victor Moreno is the executive chef and partner in the eponymous Moreno restaurant in his hometown of Caracas, Venezuela, where he also attended the Center for Gastronomic Studies (CEGA). A renown ambassador for Venezuelan cuisine, Moreno has taught at CEGA, participated in culinary festivals and congresses worldwide, and been a host on numerous Venezuelan television programs. In addition to running his restaurant, he hosts a weekly radio program with his father, a culinary historian, and serves as the Venezuelan ambassador for World Central Kitchen, Chef José Andrés' NGO.

TAKAYUKI NAKATSUKA

NAKATSUKA
299 Kinoshitacho
Nakagyo-ku
Kyoto, 604-8104
Japan

Takayuki Nakatsuka was born in Kyoto and attended the Tsuji Culinary Institute before training with Yoshihiro Narisawa at La Napoule. In 2006 he moved to Europe where he worked at restaurants in France, Spain and Belgium, before returning to Japan to work for Narisawa again in 2013. He opened his eponymous restaurant, Nakatsuka, in Kyoto in 2017, and received a Bib Gourmand designation from the *Guide Michelin* in 2020.

TOYOMITSU NAKAYAMA

RESTAURANT TOYO
17 rue Jules Chaplain
75006 Paris
France

1-1-2, Yuurakutyou
Chiyoda-ku
Tokyo 100-0006
Japan

Toyomitsu Nakayama opened his Restaurant Toyo in Paris, France in 2009. Previously, he worked at Restaurant Issé in Paris, and was the private chef for fashion designer Kenzo Takada, founder of Kenzo, for many years. He is also the chef and partner of Restaurant Toyo in Tokyo, Japan.

JOSH NILAND

SAINT PETER
362 Oxford St
Paddington NSW 2021
Australia

FISH BUTCHERY
388 Oxford St
Paddington NSW 2021
Australia

Josh Niland's first forays into cooking were as a child inspired by television cooking shows, magazines and cookbooks. At fifteen, he started his apprenticeship and, once qualified, his career included prominent kitchens in Australia, as well as the Fat Duck Development Kitchen in the UK. Having cooked in many notable seafood restaurants, his respect for fish was matched by frustration at discarded product and waste. In 2016, Josh and wife Julie opened the multi-award-winning Saint Peter, an Australian fish eatery in Sydney, where he introduced 'whole fish' cookery. A few doors up from Saint Peter is Josh's Fish Butchery, which opened in 2018.

JESSICA NOËL

VIN MON LAPIN
150 rue Saint-Zotique Est
Montréal, Qc, H2S 1K8
Canada

Jessica Noël started her cooking career at the age of twenty-six. Deciding to go head first without turning back, she staged in restaurants in Montreal, in New York and in Europe. Her greatest influence came from working at Blue Hill at Stone Barns. Working alongside Dan Barber and his team built her mindset of letting the freshest ingredients shine. She returned to Montreal in 2017, and Marc-Olivier Frappier offered her the position of chef de cuisine at Mon Lapin where she serves seasonal small plates showcasing Quebec produce.

OSWALDO OLIVA

LOREA
Sinaloa 141
Roma Norte, Mexico City
Mexico

Oswaldo Oliva's decade-long journey from his homeland to Spain took him to two of the most iconic restaurants of the world. He returned to Mexico to open his first restaurant in 2017. At Lorea, Oliva creates a new tasting menu every day, highlighting Mexican produce and elegant vegetal flavors. Oliva's goal is to give his customers an extraordinary experience. He speaks passionately about Mexican cuisine, ethical suppliers and sustainable neighborhoods.

TOMOS PARRY

BRAT
4 Redchurch Street
Hackney, London E1 6JL
UK

Tomos Parry was born in Anglesey, an island on the coast of north Wales. He began his career at the River Café, followed by Michelin-starred Kitchen Table in Fitzrovia, before progressing to head chef at Climpson's Arch in Hackney. From there, he went on to open Kitty Fisher's in Mayfair, and was instrumental in its success. In March 2018, Tomos opened his first restaurant, Brat, in Shoreditch. Brat was awarded its first Michelin star in October 2018, just six months after opening.

NATALIE PAULL

BEATRIX BAKES
688 Queensberry Street
North Melbourne
VIC 3051
Australia

Natalie Paull's Beatrix Bakes started out as a tiny bakery that has attained 'cake cult' status in Melbourne. Despite her success, Natalie never loses sight of the love it takes to bake a cake. Nat believes we don't need cake to exist but the act of baking is undeniably a powerful elixir of small pleasure and handcrafted kindness. In her baking, simple tradition is emulsified with seasonal flavor. The Beatrix Bakes logo is two old-fashioned rotary beaters, representing the call to arms that small batch baking has been all her life.

CARLA PEREZ-GALLARDO & HANNAH BLACK

LIL' DEB'S OASIS
747 Columbia Street
Hudson, NY 12534
USA

Lil' Deb's Oasis is an ongoing restaurant/installation/performance project, created by artist-chefs Carla Perez-Gallardo and Hannah Black. Lil' Deb's Oasis is a community-centered space based in Hudson, NY, that frequently collaborates with artists, galleries and the like-minded. Lil' Deb's Oasis is proud to be continuing a legacy of women-powered business, intending to move forth with the spirit of matriarchy.

CAROLE PEYRICHOU

LA NAUTIQUE
12 rue des Nautiquards
11100 Narbonne
France

Carole Peyrichou came to the food industry by chance, while working as a server to help pay for her studies. Through this work she met several chefs—including Gilles Bernard, Raquel Carena, Philippe Pinoteau, Fabien Lefebvre, and David Moreno—who cooked with enthusiasm, sincerity and dedication, and who inspired her to start cooking herself. She trained with Carena and worked for several years with Lefebvre at Octopus, and opened La Natique in 2015.

JAKOB PINTAR

TABAR
Ribji trg 6
1000 Ljubljana
Slovenia

Jakob Pintar trained in Slovenia and then went abroad to meet new challenges, cooking for Gordon Ramsay and Joël Robuchon in London, in Denmark, and for Heinz Reitbauer in Vienna. In 2018 he returned to Ljubljana where he opened TaBar, where he serves "fun dining," supports the best local producers, and fosters new culinary talent in his kitchen team. In 2019 he was awarded Best Young Chef by the Gault Millau.

SEBASTIÁN PINZÓN GIRALDO & JAMIE RODRÍGUEZ CAMACHO

CELELE
Calle del Espíritu Santo (cra 10C) #29-200
Barrio Getsemani, Cartagena de Indias
Colombia

Sebastián Pinzón is chef of sustainable development and research of Celele restaurant (named as One To Watch Latin Americas 50 Best 2019) and co-founder of the "Proyecto Caribe Lab." Since his return to Colombia at the end of 2014 he has lived in Cartagena de Indias, where he serves food inspired by the local cuisine, traditions, and culture of the Colombian Caribbean. Jaime Rodríguez is the hef of creative development at Celele restaurant. He has been working for several years to promote Colombian gastronomy, traveling throughout the country collecting information on products, traditional, ancestral, and popular cuisine to inspire his creations.

ANNA & DAVID POSEY

ELSKE
1530 West Randolph Street
Chicago, IL 60607
USA

Elske, Danish for "love," is a modern American restaurant from chefs Anna and David Posey. The restaurant places a strong focus on an evolving philosophy, centering on simplistic fare, local and seasonal ingredients, and energetic hospitality. Their accolade highlights include hitting number two on the 2017 *Bon Appétit* Best New Restaurants list, *Eater* Best New Restaurants in America, one Michelin star since 2017, and two finalist nominations for Best Chefs Great Lakes by the James Beard Foundation in 2018 and 2019.

PHILIP RACHINGER

RESTAURANT MÜHLTALHOF
Unternberg 6
4120 Neufelden
Austria

Born and raised in Neufelden, Philip Rachinger attended tourism school in Bad Ischl. Before working at Steirereck for the Reitbauer family, for Pierre Gagnaire at Sketch, and later at the Clove Club for Isaac McHale. He then moved to Paris where he worked for Sven Chartier at Saturne. He returned to Austria in 2014, where he spent four years in the kitchen at Mühltalhof with his father before taking over.

ELENA REYGADAS

ROSETTA
Colima 166, Roma Norte
Cuauhtémoc, 06700
Ciudad de México
Mexico

PANADERÍA ROSETTA
Colima 179, Roma Norte
Cuauhtémoc, 06700
Ciudad de México
Mexico

LARDO
Agustín Melgar 6, Colonia Condesa
Cuauhtémoc, 06140
Ciudad de México
Mexico

CAFÉ NIN
Havre 73, Juárez
Ciudad de México, 06600
Mexico

Elena Reygadas is among the most important figures in the Mexican culinary scene. In 2014, she was named Latin America's Best Female Chef. She is the chef and owner of the acclaimed Rosetta, and a group of popular restaurants and bakeries: La Panadería Rosetta, Lardo, and Café Nin. As a cook, Elena Reygadas is committed to the defense of local Mexican products and involved with food-related social causes. She supports diverse initiatives that support small-scale producers and traditional sustainable agricultural systems.

JONATHAN "JONNY" RHODES

INDIGO
517 Berry Road
Houston, TX 77022
USA

For Jonathan Rhodes, cooking is about the culture. Following stints at Gramercy Tavern, The Inn at Dos Brisas, and Oxheart, Rhodes launched Indigo—an intimate dining experience that uses history and culture to guide its menu. Rhodes has since earned a semi-finalist nomination for James Beard's 2019 Rising Star Chef of the Year, while Indigo has earned top spots on *Food & Wine*, *GQ*, *Eater* and *Texas Monthly's* Best New Restaurants Lists as well as *TIME's* "World's 100 Greatest Places of 2019." In April 2020, Chef Rhodes also fulfilled a lifelong mission of opening a self-sustaining grocery store for his community: Broham Fine Soul Food & Groceries. To sustain the project, Chef Rhodes has also launched a farm initiative dubbed Food Fight Farms.

MELISSA RODRIGUEZ

DEL POSTO
85 10th Avenue
New York, NY 10011
USA

Melissa Rodriguez is executive chef at Del Posto. After graduating from the Culinary Institute of America, where she earned a degree in Culinary Arts, Melissa spent time cooking with Elaine Bell Catering and Oceana. In 2006, she was hired as a line cook at Daniel Boulud's flagship Restaurant Daniel, where she quickly rose the ranks to sous chef. After five years at Daniel, Melissa joined the team at Del Posto in 2011 where she was promoted to chef de cuisine in 2015. Two years later, she became executive chef and partner.

DIEGO ROSSI

TRATTORIA TRIPPA
Via Giorgio Vasari 1
20135 Milan
Italy

Diego Rossi was born in Verona. Before opening Trippa with his partner Pietro Caroli, he had earned a Michelin star at the restaurant "Delle Antiche Contrade" in Cuneo, together with co-chef Juri Chiotti. Since the day Trippa opened its doors in 2015, Diego Rossi has been rewriting the canon of the Italian trattoria. His guiding principles are the tradition of Italian gastronomy, the respect for seasonality, and above all an insistence in putting the ingredients front-and-center, so that they're always recognizable on the plate.

PRATEEK SADHU

MASQUE
Unit G3, Laxmi Woollen Mills
Shakti Mills Lane
Mumbai 400011
India

Growing up around family farms led Prateek to the kitchen by his tenth birthday, and later to work in restaurants at the Taj group. He graduated from the Culinary Institute of America with double gold medals, followed by stints at some of the world's finest kitchens including Alinea, Le Bernardin, the French Laundry, and Noma. Committed to spotlighting local Indian produce, Sadhu opened Masque in Mumbai in 2016 with entrepreneur Aditi Dugar. A keen exploration of his own roots through a new lens—in tandem with techniques both modern and traditional—have led Sadhu and his distinct style of cooking to the forefront of a new wave of modern Indian cuisine.

LENA SAREINI

SELDEN STANDARD
3921 2nd Avenue
Detroit, MI 48201
USA

Inspired by a family of food lovers and a passion for the arts, Lena Sareini combined her lifelong interests and became a pastry chef. She draws inspiration from Lebanese culinary traditions to create one-of-a-kind New American desserts. She was most recently the executive pastry chef at the seasonally driven restaurant Selden Standard, where she never repeated a dessert on her menu. Lena is a three-time James Beard Award nominee, was a 2018 Eater Young Gun winner, and a 2020 *Food & Wine* Best New Chef.

JASON SAXBY

RAES ON WATEGOS
6–8 Marine Parade
Byron Bay NSW 2481
Australia

In Byron Bay, Jason Saxby is surrounded and inspired by some of the best produce in Australia, and his reflections on the time he's spent in the kitchens of some of the world's great chefs shapes how he looks at these products and other ingredients native to the area. Cooking with a love of Italian food but with a local sensibility has allowed him to create food with a true sense of time and place. He cooks delicious, sustainable food with a purpose, a story, and a history told through new eyes.

RAMAEL SCULLY

SCULLY
4 St James's Market
St. James's, London SW1Y 4AH
UK

Scully is Ramael Scully's first solo venture. Born in Malaysia and brought up in Sydney, with a mother of Chinese/Indian descent and an Irish/Balinese father, he moved to Sydney as a child. He attended culinary school there and decided to pursue cooking, training in fine dining restaurants in Sydney, Moscow and in London. Having had the benefit of a diverse cultural upbringing in addition to vast experience traveling the world, Scully developed a cooking style influenced by Asia, the Middle East and Europe. At the restaurant, guests can expect an explosion of flavors using sustainable, locally sourced ingredients where possible, created and served in an informal yet refined setting.

ELDAD SHMUELI

ELCHANAN BREAD CULTURE
Kibbutz Misharmot
Pardes Hanna-Karkur 3784000
Israel

After his service in the Israeli military, Eldad Shmueli moved to Paris where he attended the Ferrandi school and staged at Alain Ducasse au Plaza Athénée. He later staged at the French Laundry and the Fat Duck. He then returned to Israel, where he was sous-chef at Shakuf, a pioneer of Israeli cuisine, and then head chef at Eyal Shani's North Abraxas and at Ran Shmueli's Claro. He opened the Elchanan bakery in 2016.

RYAN SMITH

STAPLEHOUSE
541 Edgewood Avenue SE
Atlanta, GA 30312
USA

Ryan Smith is chef/partner at the award-winning Staplehouse. Originally from State College, Pennsylvania, he moved to Atlanta in 2000 after graduating from the Culinary Institute of America. Ryan has worked in some of Atlanta's most prominent restaurants, including Bacchanalia, Canoe, Restaurant Eugene, Holeman & Finch, and Empire State South. Since opening in September 2015, Staplehouse has been named *Bon Appetit's* Best New Restaurant in America, *GQ's* Best New Restaurant, *Atlanta* magazine's #1 Restaurant in Atlanta. It was also a James Beard finalist for Best New Restaurant. Ryan has been a James Beard finalist for best chef Southeast in 2016, 2017, and 2019.

JOHNNY SPERO

REVERIE
3201 Cherry Hill Lane NW
Washington, DC 20007
USA

Chef Johnny Spero began his culinary career at sixteen in Baltimore County, Maryland, where he grew up. With a desire to learn more, Johnny moved to Washington, DC in 2007. Over the next decade he spent time working with Johnny Monis of Komi, his culinary mentor John Shields at Townhouse, José Andrés at Minibar, and also took time to stage abroad in Copenhagen at Noma in 2010 and spent a season at Mugaritz in 2015. After returning home from Spain, Johnny began working on his restaurant, Reverie, which opened in the Georgetown neighborhood of Washington DC in 2018.

JEREMIAH STONE & FABIÁN VON HAUSKE VALTIERRA

CONTRA
138 Orchard Street
New York, NY 10002
USA

WILDAIR
142 Orchard Street
New York, NY 10002
USA

Jeremiah Stone and Fabián von Hauske Valtierra are the chef-owners behind the internationally recognized Contra Group, which includes Contra, Wildair, Peoples wine shop and the Bar at Peoples. After meeting at the French Culinary Institute, the duo drew inspiration from their time spent training in critically-acclaimed restaurants throughout Europe to introduce a new way of dining to New York City's Lower East Side: ambitious yet accessible with a focus on local flavors and a dedication to natural wine.

JONATHAN TAM

RESTAURANT RELÆ
Jægersborggade 41
Copenhagen 2200
Denmark

Trained at a culinary school in his hometown of Edmonton, Alberta, Canada, Jonathan Tam landed a stage at Noma in 2007 which eventually turned into two years of cooking for René Redzepi. Noma is also where he first met Christian Puglisi, his eventual mentor. Relæ was the first restaurant opened by Christian, with Jonathan part of the opening team. His rise to head chef was a natural progression, as he's been creating dishes with Puglisi from the beginning in 2010.

OMAR TATE

HONEYSUCKLE PROJECTS
Philadelphia, PA
USA

Omar Tate is a Philadelphia-based artist and chef with over fifteen years' experience in some of New York and Philadelphia's best restaurants. In 2018 Omar launched Honeysuckle Pop-Up using food, art, and literature in tandem to explore the nuances of Black life and culture. Honeysuckle has received critical acclaim not only as a food concept but also as a leading philosophy of the future of food thought and discourse over equity. Currently, Omar is working to open Honeysuckle as a food-focused community center in West Philadelphia. His work has been featured in the *New York Times*, *Esquire* magazine, *Okayplayer*, *Eater*, and the *Philadelphia Inquirer*, among others.

PIM TECHAMUANVIVIT

KIN KHAO
55 Cyril Magnin Street
San Francisco, CA 94102
USA

NAHM
27 S Sathon Road
Sathon, Bangkok 10120
Thailand

NARI
1625 Post Street
San Francisco, CA 94115
USA

Trained not as a chef but as a cognitive scientist, Pim made a career change by opening Kin Khao in 2014 to serve the food she missed from her childhood in Thailand. Focusing on local, seasonal, and housemade ingredients, Kin Khao received its first Michelin star only a year later. In 2018, she took over the legendary Nahm in Bangkok, and has retained its Michelin star. In 2019 she opened Nari, named as a tribute to Thai women who taught her to cook.

KWANG UH

BAROO
5706 Santa Monica Blvd
Los Angeles, CA 90038
USA

Kwang Uh is the chef and co-owner of Baroo in Los Angeles. Born and raised in Seoul, South Korea, he graduated from the Culinary Institute of America and received his master's degree from the University of Gastronomic Sciences in Italy. Kwang's free-style, fermentation-focused approach at Baroo, which opened in 2015, earned him a James Beard award nomination, among other accolades. Baroo closed in 2018, and Kwang and his wife, Mina Park, plan to open Shiku in autumn 2021 and reopen Baroo in 2022.

COŞKUN UYSAL

TULUM
217 Carlisle Street
Balaclava VIC 3183
Melbourne
Australia

Humble beginnings, three years of hard work and boundless culinary creativity have culminated in a slew of success for Coşkun Uysal's Tulum restaurant. Growing up in Istanbul, Coşkun's fondest childhood memories stem from his mother's heartfelt cooking. Drawing inspiration from the classic dishes of his youth and the regions of Turkey, Coşkun rewrites the rulebook on modern Anatolian cuisine in Australia. Coşkun's ability to channel nostalgic memories and weave the story of his past into Tulum's contemporary menu has earned the praises of his diners, critics, and peers worldwide.

DAVE VERHEUL

EMBLA
LESA
122 Russell St
Melbourne, VIC 3000
Australia

In December 2015, Dave Verheul opened Embla with business partner Christian McCabe. The natural wine bar serves produce-driven small plates from a wood-fired oven and grill. Verheul and McCabe opened sister restaurant Lesa in the space above Embla in August 2018. Embracing a slower pace of dining, Lesa offers multi-course dining options from a regularly changing, produce-driven menu, executed in signature Verheul style. Firmly established as a leading chef in the Australian culinary world, Verheul's approach celebrates integrity of produce, with a distinctive style characterized by thought, detail, lightness, and balance.

AARON VERZOSA

ARCHIPELAGO
5607 Rainier Avenue South
Seattle, WA 98118
USA

Pacific Northwest native Aaron Verzosa graduated from the University of Washington, then attended the Seattle Culinary Academy. While working at the Basque focused restaurant the Harvest Vine, Aaron joined Modernist Cuisine, and in 2012 completed a stint in Paris with David Toutain. At Archipelago, Aaron is dedicated to showcasing how a region's identity is not defined solely by when and where, but by who—and how the Filipinos in the Pacfic Northwest have done so for over a hundred years.

SILVANA & MARIANA VILLEGAS

MASA
Calle 70 # 4 - 83
Calle 81 # 9 - 12
Calle 105 # 18ª- 68
Bogota
Colombia

Masa is an all-day bakery and café with four locations in Bogotá, Colombia. Founding sisters, Silvana and Mariana Villegas were born and raised in Bogota, Colombia, in a family where they were always surrounded by food. Silvana left at a young age to study at the Culinary Institute of America, and then worked with New York's most respected chefs including Jean Georges Vongerichten, Kurt Gutenbrunner, Gordon Ramsay, and Gray Kunz. Mariana's first studied Business Administration at CESA University and later on she decided to go to culinary school at the Institute of Culinary Education in New York City, and subsequently worked at Cosme mentored by Daniela Soto-Innes. Masa opened in 2011.

FRANCESCO VINCENZI

FRANCESCHETTA58
Via Vignolese 58
41124 Modena
Italy

Francesco Vincenzi was born not far from Modena and in 2010 he arrived at Osteria Francescana, right after attending the Scuola Alberghiera e di Ristorazione of Serramazzoni. Originally assigned to a front-of-house position, Vincenzi was encouraged by Massimo Bottura to explore his passion for hospitality, and he found his way into the kitchen. Vincenzi worked in the kitchen of the three-Michelin-starred restaurant for ten years, and in 2017 became the head chef of Franceschetta58, the group's Modenese bistrot. There, he creates seasonal menus by combining the Emilian culinary traditions with a modern approach, influenced by his travel experiences and memories. In 2019, Vincenzi was also honored by Identità Golose with Best Italian Chef Under 30 award for his accomplishments thus far.

TAKAYOSHI WATANABE

TERUZUSHI
3-1-7 Sugawara
Tobata-ku, Kitakyushu
Fukuoka 804-0044
Japan

Takayoshi Watanabe grew up in the countryside of Kitakyushu. He is the third-generation owner of his sushi restaurant, that has been open for 56 years and was founded by his grandmother in the 1960s. Because the town is so small, however, the restaurant always had few guests. Watanabe took it upon himself to revamp the business, and sought a new style of sushi implementing theatrics, entertainment, and of course top quality ingredients. Chef Watanabe has become world renowned for his signature pose and look. He now attracts an international crowd to his sushiya, Teruzushi, in Kitakyushu, Japan.

DYLAN WATSON-BRAWN

ERNST
Gerichtstraße 54
13347 Berlin
Germany

Dylan Watson-Brawn is the head chef and co-owner of Ernst, an intimate produce-driven restaurant that he set up with fellow Vancouver-native Spencer Christenson in the north Berlin neighborhood of Wedding in late 2017. Watson-Brawn is highly influenced by Japanese technique, dating from his visit to restaurant Ryugin at seventeen, where he ultimately was given the opportunity to apprentice in the Kaiseki kitchen. He was extremely inspired by Japanese sensibility, the approach and respect for produce and its preparation and presentation to the guest.

BRADY WILLIAMS

CANLIS
2576 Aurora Avenue North
Seattle, Washington 98119
USA

Brady Williams is the chef of Canlis in Seattle, WA, and the restaurant's sixth-ever chef in its storied sixty-nine-year history. Since joining in 2015, Brady has garnered numerous accolades, including a James Beard Foundation award for Best Chef: Northwest in 2019 and nomination for "Rising Star Chef" in 2017, as well as being named one of *Food & Wine* magazine's Best New Chefs in 2018. His cuisine thoughtfully melds his Japanese heritage with the abundant bounty of the Pacific Northwest.

JUSTIN WOODWARD

CASTAGNA RESTAURANT
1752 SE Hawthorne Boulevard
Portland, OR 97214
USA

OK OMENS
1758 SE Hawthorne Boulevard
Portland, OR 97214
USA

Justin grew up in Southern California, working walking distance from famed Chino Farms. His first professional working experience was with chefs from the kitchens of Thomas Keller, Alice Waters, and Alain Ducasse. These two things shaped his cooking most dramatically. In 2008, Justin took a position at WD~50 under Alex Stupak, where he honed his modern pastry skills. After staging around NYC, Justin went to Noma, then Mugaritz, before landing the chef position at Castagna in 2011. In 2018 he opened OK Omens, a cheery natural wine bar.

AITOR ZABALA

SOMNI
465 S. La Cienega Boulevard
Los Angeles, CA 90048
USA

Aitor Zabala leads two-Michelin-starred Somni, the lauded 10-seat chef's counter experience he conceptualized and opened alongside José Andrés in 2018. Zabala orchestrates the 20-plus-course tasting menu that highlights avant-garde techniques, Spanish fine dining sensibilities, and the highest quality local and seasonal ingredients. A native of Spain, Zabala held instrumental roles at several Michelin-rated restaurants including elBulli, Alkimia, AbAC, and Akelarre before moving to the United States to join José Andrés' ThinkFoodGroup as Creative Director in 2010.

EMERGING CHEF BIOGRAPHIES

LEADING CHEF BIOGRAPHIES

HUGH ACHESON

FIVE & TEN
1073 S Milledge Avenue
Athens, GA 30605, USA
www.fiveandten.com

EMPIRE STATE SOUTH
999 Peachtree Street NE
Atlanta, GA 30309, USA
www.empirestatesouth.com

BY GEORGE
127 Peachtree Street NE
Atlanta, GA 30303, USA
www.bygeorgeatl.com

Hugh Acheson is a world-renowned chef and food writer who lives in Athens, Georgia. He is the co-owner/partner of 5&10 Restaurant in Athens, as well as Empire State South, By George, and coffee shop Spiller Park Coffee, all located in Atlanta, Georgia. *Food & Wine* magazine named him Best New Chef in 2002 and the James Beard Foundation awarded him Best Chef Southeast in 2012. He has written 5 cookbooks, starred in various cooking shows, and has his very own podcast called *Hugh Acheson Stirs the Pot*.

PALISA ANDERSON

CHAT THAI
Multiple locations, Sydney, NSW, Australia
www.chatthai.com.au

BOON CAFE
425 Pitt Street
Haymarket, Sydney, NSW 2000, Australia
www.booncafe.com

BOON LUCK FARM
69 Foxs Lane
Tyagarah NSW 2481, Australia

Palisa Anderson, is a second-generation restaurateur and first generation farmer. The original Chat Thai restaurant in Sydney, Australia was established by her mother Amy Chanta in 1989, since then they have expanded the operation to include eleven eateries, a grocery store, a travel agency and a farm. As a director of the business Palisa's role is truly varied, from overseeing operations to creating menus for each venue, or selecting varieties of heirloom produce to grow on her organic certified farm Boon Luck Farm Organics for her own businesses as well as other outstanding restaurants in Australia.

JOSÉ ANDRÉS

MINIBAR
501 9th Street NW
Washington, DC 20004
USA
www.minibarbyjosenadreas.com

É
3708 Las Vegas Boulevard South
Las Vegas, NV 89109
USA
www.ebyjoseandreas.com

MERCADO LITTLE SPAIN
10 Hudson Yards
New York, NY 10001
www.littlespain.com

Twice named to *TIME*'s 100 Most Influential People list, and awarded Outstanding Chef and Humanitarian of the Year by the James Beard Foundation, José Andrés is an internationally recognized chef, culinary innovator, author, educator, and owner/director of ThinkFoodGroup. A pioneer of Spanish tapas in America, he is known for his avant-garde cuisine and award-winning group of nearly three dozen restaurants including two with two Michelin stars. He is the founder of the non-profit World Central Kitchen, which has earned global respect for its chef-driven humanitarian and disaster relief operations.

SELASSIE ATADIKA

MIDUNU
21 Sixth Road
Accra, Ghana
www.midunu.com

Selassie Atadika is chef/owner of Midunu restaurant in Accra, Ghana, and a founding member of Trio Toque, the first nomadic restaurant in Dakar, Senegal. Atadika is a remarkable powerhouse in the culinary world, and has been sought out as an advisor and speaker by numerous institutions and media channels worldwide. She was also a finalist in the 2019 Basque Culinary World Prize. Atadika worked for a over a decade in humanitarian efforts with the United Nations, as well as quietly teaching herself the art of food. She then studied at the Culinary Institute of America before opening Midunu, the embodiment of "New African Cuisine." Here, Atadika celebrates a culinary heritage where culture and cuisine intersect with environment and sustainability. She later launched the Midunu Institute which aims to document and preserve Africa's culinary heritage.

DANIEL BOULUD

DANIEL
60 East 65th Street
New York, NY 10065
USA
www.danielnyc.com

CAFÉ BOULUD
20 East 76th Stree
New York, NY 10021
www.cafeboulud.com

DB BISTRO MODERNE
55 West 44th Street
New York, NY 10036
www.dbbistro.com

Daniel Boulud was born in Lyon, France, but has made New York City his home since 1982. He is now thought of a leading culinary authority in America and one of the most admired chefs in New York. He is best known for the eponymous restaurant DANIEL on Manhattan's Upper East Side. He is also the author of ten cookbooks, and the recipient of multiple James Beard Foundation awards including Outstanding Chef and Outstanding Restaurateur. He was named as the Culinary Institute of America's Chef of the Year in 2011, and awarded the World's 50 Best Restaurants Lifetime Achievement prize in 2015. He has established numerous eateries, with outposts in London, Singapore, Toronto, Montreal, Miami, Palm Beach, Washington DC, and Boston. Boulud was presented with a Chevalier de la Légion d'Honneur by the French government in 2006 in recognition of his contributions to French culture and cuisine.

RAQUEL CARENA

LE BARATIN
3 rue Jouye-Rouve
75020 Paris, France

Raquel Carena has been at the helm of at Le Baratin in Paris for more than thirty years. After arriving from Argentina, she made a name for herself by drawing inspiration from Paul Bocuse's *La cuisine du marché*. A traditionalist who cooks in the Lyon style, she also found her style by cultivating friendships with the likes of Olivier Rœllinger and the Roca brothers. Whether presenting slow-cooked, translucent jus, impeccably cooked vegetables, fish cooked with precision, local meat or variety meat, Raquel has only one passion—cooking for other people. This is undoubtedly what makes her bistro a timeless place, with natural wines and nurturing cuisine as its trademarks.

MAY CHOW

LITTLE BAO
Multiple locations including:
G/F 66 Staunton Street
Central, Hong Kong
www.little-bao.com

HAPPY PARADISE
UG/F 52–56 Staunton Street
Central, Hong Kong
www.happyparadise.hk

Canadian-born May Chow was named Asia's
Best Female Chef 2017. She is chef/founder of
several iterations of her neighborhood bao diner
and Hong Kong institution, Little Bao, as well as
the neo-Chinese bistro Happy Paradise. Chow's
cuisine is reflective of her Chinese ethnicity
as well as her North American culture. Chow
prides herself on reinventing Cantonese classics
showcasing underappreciated ingredients while
remaining respectful of local traditions. Chow
has been selected as a guest judge for *MasterChef
Asia* and *Top Chef* in America, as well as speaking
at the Melbourne Food & Wine Festival.

DOMINIQUE CRENN

ATELIER CRENN
3127 Fillmore Street
San Francisco, CA 94123, USA
www.ateliercrenn.com

BAR CRENN
3131 Fillmore Street
San Francisco, CA 94123, USA
www.barcrenn.com

PETIT CRENN
609 Hayes Street
San Francisco, CA 94102, USA
www.petitcrenn.com

In 2011, Dominique Crenn opened Atelier Crenn
where her self-styled "poetic culinaria" earned its
first Michelin Star in 2011, and a second in the
following year. As of November 2018, Domnique
Crenn beat her own record and became the first
female chef in the US to receive three Michelin
Stars. Bar Crenn was also awarded one Michelin
star the same year. Crenn was awarded World's
Best Female Chef in 2016 by the World's 50 Best
and in 2018 earned James Beard Foundation's
title of Best Chef: West.

SKYE GYNGELL

SPRING
Somerset House, New Wing
Lancaster Place
London, WC2R 1LA
UK
www.springrestaurant.co.uk

Born in Australia, Skye Gyngell worked at a
number of Sydney's culinary institutions, before
moving to Paris to complete her formal training
under Anne Willan at La Varenne. After a stint
at the Dodin-Bouffant, she moved to London
to work at the French House and notably, the
Dorchester with Anton Mosimann. As head chef
of Petersham Nurseries Cafe, Skye worked with
seasonal produce, creating food inspired by what
she saw growing around her. Her work at Petersham received comparisons by restaurant critic
Terry Durack to the work of Alice Walters, and
led to her appointment as the *Independent on Sun-
day*'s food writer, a post she held for 5 years. In
October 2014, Skye opened her much-anticipated
London restaurant, Spring. Located in the New
Wing of Somerset House, Spring encompasses
Skye's signature style of cooking led by seasonal
ingredients. Alongside Spring, Skye is culinary
director for a luxury Hampshire hotel, Heckfield
Place, which opened in 2018. She is also the
author of multiple award-winning cookbooks.

MARGOT HENDERSON

ROCHELLE CANTEEN
16 Playground Gardens
London, E2 7FA, United Kingdom
www.rochelleschool.org/rochelle-canteen

Born and raised in New Zealand, Margot Hen-
derson moved to the UK at the age of 20. In 1992
Margot met Melanie Arnold when they ran the
restaurant at the iconic French House in Soho.
Three years later Arnold & Henderson was born
and the duo went on to open Rochelle Canteen in
Shoreditch in 2004 and then in 2017 brought Ro-
chelle Canteen to the Institute of Contemporary
Arts. In 2012 Margot released her own cookbook
You're All Invited: Margot's Recipes for Entertaining.

DAVID KINCH

MANRESA
320 Village Lane
Los Gatos, CA 95030, USA
www.manresarestaurant.com

David Kinch, chef/owner of Manresa, has forged
a distinctive culinary path, putting him at the
forefront of contemporary California cuisine.
Manresa has received three Michelin stars, a
Five Star Forbes Travel award, and membership
in Relais & Chateaux and Les Grande Tables du
Monde. He has been nominated four times for
Outstanding Chef by the James Beard Foundation, and his international peers voted him into
the Top 10 of the World's Best Chefs 2019 via *Le
Chef* magazine.

JESSICA KOSLOW

SQIRL
720 N Virgil Avenue #4
Los Angeles, CA 90029, USA
www.sqirlla.com

Jessica Koslow is the chef and owner of Sqirl, a
bearkfast/lunch cafe in Silverlake, Los Angeles,
and a three-time James Beard Award nominee.
Koslow started her career in pastry, at the celebrated Bacchanalia in Atlanta, Georgia. Then in
2011, after working in the television industry in
New York and a stint in Australia, she moved to
Los Angeles. Sqirl has been lauded by the *Times*
as The Restaurant of Los Angeles, appeared on
Eater's 38 Best Restaurants in America, and Jonathan Gold's 101 Best Restaurants list. In 2014,
Eater LA named Koslow Chef of the Year. Koslow is also the author of the cookbook *Everything
I Want to Eat*.

VIRGILIO MARTÍNEZ

CENTRAL
Avenida Pedro de Osma 301
Lima, Barranco 15063, Peru
www.centralrestaurante.com.pe

Virgilio Martínez is a Peruvian chef and restaurateur born in Lima in 1977. Chef at Central
restaurante in Lima, and Mil near Cusco, Peru,
he is a key mover in the organically formed movement of Peruvian chefs promoting their heritage
and cuisine on the global stage. Through his food
he showcases Peruvian agrobiodiversity and the
importance of social and ecological concerns by
creating very particular food concepts. Virgilio's
philosophy and cooking style are based on exploring everything there is "outside," as his research
center Mater also aims to do.

DAVID MCMILLAN

JOE BEEF
2491 Notre-Dame Street West
Montreal, QC H3J 1N6
Canada

LIVERPOOL HOUSE
2501 Notre-Dame Street West
Montreal, QC H3J 1N6
Canada

LE VIN PAPILLON
2519 Notre-Dame Street West
Montréal, QC H3J 1N4
Canada
www.joebeef.ca

David McMillan is the chef and co-owner of Joe
Beef restaurant in Montreal, along with Liverpool House, Le Vin Papillon, and McKiernan
luncheonette. Born and raised in Quebec City
and involved in Montreal restaurants since the
age of seventeen, David continues to explore,
teach, and be fascinated by unique traditional French country cooking. The James Beard
Award- nominated chef is also co-author of two
popular cookbooks.

YOSHIHIRO NARISAWA

NARISAWA
2-6-15 Minamiaoyama
Minato-ku
Tokyo 107-0062
Japan
www.narisawa-yoshihiro-en.com

BEES CAFE & BAR
B1, 2-14-15 Minami Aoyama
Minato-ku
Tokyo 107-0062
Japan
www.beesbar-narisawa-en.com

Yoshihiro Narisawa began his culinary training in 1988, first in Europe travelling though Switzerland, France, and Italy. After nearly a decade, he returned to Japan to open La Napoule in Odawara. He later moved to Tokyo to open a restaurant now known as Narisawa. His cuisine is acclaimed for his French technique married with fresh Japanese ingredients, for which he visits with every producer. His restaurant, of which he is the head chef and proprietor, is #22 on the World's 50 Best Restaurants list, which also awarded him the first ever Sustainable Restaurant Award. Narisawa is also #9 on the Asia's 50 Best Restaurants list.

YOTAM OTTOLENGHI

OTTOLENGHI
Multiple locations including:
63 Ledbury Road, Notting Hill
London W11 2AD
UK
www.ottolenghi.co.uk

ROVI
59 Wells Street
London W1A 3AE
UK

NOPI
21–22 Warwick Street
London W1B 5NE
UK

Yotam Ottolenghi is a food writer and chef/owner of the Ottolenghi delis, and the restaurants ROVI and NOPI. He writes a weekly column in *The Guardian*'s *Feast* magazine and a monthly column in the *New York Times* and has published seven bestselling cookbooks: *Plenty* and *Plenty More*; *Ottolenghi: The Cookbook* and *Jerusalem* co-authored with Sami Tamimi; and *NOPI: The Cookbook* with Ramael Scully. *Sweet*, with Helen Goh, is his baking and desserts cookbook. His latest award-winning book is *Ottolenghi Simple*, with Tara Wigley and Esme Howarth. Yotam has made two *Mediterranean Feasts* series for More 4, along with a BBC 4 documentary, *Jerusalem on a Plate*.

ANA ROŠ

HIŠA FRANKO
Staro selo 1
5222 Kobarid, Slovenia
www.hisafranko.com

Slovenian Ana Roš was a sports and travel enthusiast from a very young age, earning a place in the national youth alpine skiing team before heading to Italy to study international diplomacy, where she met her partner Valter Kramer. It was just as she finished her studies that Kramer's parents decided to retire from running the restaurant Hiša Franko and the pair returned to Slovenia to take it on. She has since been awarded the world's best female chef in 2017 by *Restaurant* magazine, and Hiša Franko is known as one of the leading restaurants in Europe, awarded 38th position in the 50 Best list of 2019. She is a self-taught cook and aims to express the seasons, the locality, her own character, her travels and femininity in her cuisine.

MARCUS SAMUELSSON

RED ROOSTER HARLEM
310 Lenox Avenue
Harlem, NY 10027
USA
www.redroosterharlem.com

MARCUS BP
56 Halsey Street
Newark, NJ 07102
USA
www.marcusbp.com

NORDA
Clarion Hotel The Hub
Biskop Gunnerusgate 3
0155 Oslo
Sweden
www.nordarestaurant.com

Marcus Samuelsson is the acclaimed chef behind many restaurants worldwide. He has won multiple James Beard Foundation awards for his work as a chef and as host of *No Passport Required*, his public television series with Vox/Eater. Samuelsson was crowned champion of *Top Chef Masters* and *Chopped All Stars*, and was the guest chef for President Obama's first state dinner. A committed philanthropist, Samuelsson is co-chair of Careers through Culinary Arts Program (C-CAP), which focuses on underserved youth. Author of several cookbooks in addition to the *New York Times* bestselling memoir *Yes, Chef*, Samuelsson also co-produces the annual Harlem EatUp! festival, which celebrates the food, art, and culture of Harlem. During the Covid-19 pandemic, Samuelsson converted his restaurants Red Rooster Harlem, Marcus B&P in Newark, and Red Rooster Overtown in Miami into community kitchens in partnership with World Central Kitchen, serving well over 100,000 meals to those in need. He also hosts the podcast *This Moment* with Swedish rapper Timbuktu.

EYAL SHANI

MIZNON
Multiple locations including:
King George Street 30
Tel Aviv-Yafo
Israel

435 W 15th Street
New York, NY 10011
USA
www.miznonnyc.com

HASALON
735 10th Avenue
New York, NY 10019
USA
www.hasalonnyc.com

Eyal Shani was born in Jerusalem in 1959. His culinary passion was first instilled in him by his grandfather, an agronomist and a dedicated vegan, whom he would accompany to local markets, fields and vineyards as a child. Shani first studied cinema at Beit Zvi School of Performing Arts, before turning to food as a career. In 1989 he went on to open his first restaurant, Oceanus, in his hometown of Jerusalem. There he developed a unique culinary language based on regional Mediterranean products: olive oil, fish, tahini, fresh seasonal vegetables and of course, the tomato. In 1999 a second branch of Oceanus was opened in the seaside town of Herzliya. In 2008, together with his partner Shahar Segal, Shani opened HaSalon in Tel Aviv. Since then, he is the executive chef of seven highly successful restaurants under the group named The Better Guys. Shani is considered to be one of the leading figures in the Israeli culinary scene, appearing on the panel of judges during the past six seasons of Israeli *Master Chef*.

DANIELA SOTO-INNES

COSME
35 East 21st Street
New York, NY 10010, USA
www.cosmenyc.com

ATLA
372 Lafayette Street
New York, NY 10012, USA
www.atlanyc.com

Daniela Soto-Innes is the creative visionary behind Cosme and Atla, the contemporary Mexican restaurants in New York City, as well as Elio in Las Vegas and a forthcoming restaurant in Los Angeles. A Mexico City native who comes from a line of women that love cooking, Soto-Innes (a 2016 James Beard Rising Star Chef, 2017 *Forbes* magazine 30 under 30) has led her restaurants as the chef/partner to much critical acclaim, including the number 23 spot on the 2019 World's 50 Best list. She continues to find joy in elevating simple ingredients while working actively to change traditional kitchen culture by seeking out new ways to empower her staff.

INDEX

ACKNOWLEDGMENTS

The publisher would like to thank the 20 leading curator chefs—Hugh Acheson, Palisa Anderson, José Andrés, Selassie Atadika, Daniel Boulud, Raquel Carena, May Chow, Dominique Crenn, Skye Gyngell, Margot Henderson, David Kinch, Jessica Koslow, Virgilio Martínez, David McMillan, Yoshihiro Narisawa, Yotam Ottlenghi, Ana Roš, Marcus Samuelsson, Eyal Shani, and Daniela Soto-Innes—and the 100 selected emerging chefs. We would also like to thank Céline Bossart, Sophie Dening, Drew Lazor, Grace Mitchel Tada, Tarajia Morrell, and Carole Saturno for their work on the texts. The following individuals and organizations provided translations into English: from the French, Cillero & De Motta and Jocelyn Miller; from the Japanese, Yuma Gartner; and from the Spanish, Steven McCutcheon Rubio. For their editorial work on the book, we would like to thank Jocelyn Miller, Kate Slate, Carrie Bradley Neves, Jane Ace, Linda Lee, and Ken DellaPenta.

RECIPE NOTES

The recipes in this book were edited in such a way as to preserve the voices of the chefs who submitted them, and are not designed to be uniform in tone or style. Unless otherwise stated, eggs are assumed to be large and individual vegetables and fruits, such as onions and apples, are assumed to be medium. Unless otherwise stated, pepper is freshly ground pepper. Cooking times are for guidance only, as individual ovens vary. If using a fan oven, follow the manufacturer's instructions concerning oven temperatures. Some words of caution Some recipes include raw or very lightly cooked eggs. These should be avoided particularly by the elderly, infants, pregnant women, convalescents, and anyone with an impaired immune system. A number of the recipes require advanced techniques, specialist equipment, and professional experience to achieve good results. Exercise a very high level of caution when carrying out recipes involving any potentially hazardous activity, including the use of high temperatures, open flames and when deep frying. In particular, when deep frying add food carefully to avoid splashing, wear long sleeves and never leave the pan unattended. Some of the recipes include the use of liquid nitrogen; this substance should not be handled without training in how to use it safely.

PICTURE CREDITS

PHAIDON PRESS LIMITED
2 COOPERAGE YARD
LONDON E15 2QR

PHAIDON PRESS INC.
65 BLEECKER STREET
NEW YORK, NY 10012

PHAIDON.COM

FIRST PUBLISHED 2021
© 2021 PHAIDON PRESS LIMITED

ISBN: 978 1 83866 135 9

A CIP CATALOGUE RECORD FOR THIS BOOK IS AVAILABLE FROM
THE BRITISH LIBRARY AND THE LIBRARY OF CONGRESS.

COMMISSIONING EDITOR: EMILY TAKOUDES
PROJECT EDITOR: ANNE GOLDBERG
PRODUCTION CONTROLLER: NERISSA DOMINGUEZ VALES
DESIGN: ARIANE SPANIER

PRINTED IN ITALY